COLLECTED WORKS OF JOHN STUART MILL

VOLUME III

Principles of Political Economy

with Some of Their Applications to Social Philosophy

by JOHN STUART MILL

BOOKS III–V AND APPENDICES

Introduction by
V. W. BLADEN

Dean of Arts and Professor of Political Economy,
University of Toronto

Textual Editor
J. M. ROBSON

Associate Professor of English,
Victoria College, University of Toronto

Liberty Fund
Indianapolis

This book is published by Liberty Fund, Inc., a foundation established to encourage study of the ideal of a society of free and responsible individuals.

The cuneiform inscription that serves as our logo and as the design motif for our endpapers is the earliest-known written appearance of the word "freedom" (*amagi*), or "liberty." It is taken from a clay document written about 2300 B.C. in the Sumerian city-state of Lagash.

This Liberty Fund paperback edition of 2006 is a reprint from the original edition published by The University of Toronto Press in 1965.
© 1965 The University of Toronto Press.

06   07   08   09   10   P   5   4   3   2   1

Library of Congress Cataloging-in-Publication Data
Mill, John Stuart, 1806–1873.
[Works.   2006]
The collected works / of John Stuart Mill
p.   cm.
Reprint. Originally published: Toronto, Ont.; Buffalo, N.Y.: University of Toronto Press, 1965–1981.
Includes bibliographical references and index.
ISBN-13: 978-0-86597-658-0   (set: alk. paper: pbk.)
ISBN-10: 0-86597-658-9   (set: alk. paper: pbk.)
ISBN-13: 978-0-86597-652-8   (v. 3: alk. paper: pbk.)
ISBN-10: 0-86597-652-X   (v. 3: alk. paper: pbk.)
1. Philosophy. 2. Political science. 3. Economics. I. Title.
B1602.A2   2006
192—dc22   2005044313

The text of this book was set in Times Roman, a typeface designed by Stanley Morison for the *Times* of London and introduced by that newspaper in 1932. Also used for book work throughout the world, Times Roman is among the most important type designs of the twentieth century.

Printed on paper that is acid-free and meets the requirements of the American National Standard for Permanence of Paper for Printed Library Materials, Z39.48-1992. ♾

Cover design by Erin Kirk New, Watkinsville, Georgia
Printed and bound by The University of Toronto Press Inc.

Liberty Fund, Inc.
8335 Allison Pointe Trail, Suite 300
Indianapolis, Indiana 46250-1684

Contents

VOLUME 3

BOOK III: EXCHANGE[1]

[1]In this Table of Contents the only variants indicated are those involving major alterations in sections.

º–º+52, 57, 62, 65, 71
ᵖ–ᵖ48, 49 § 6.

$^{q-q}$48, 49, 52, 57, 62   not really connected with the value of money, but often
confounded with it

$^{r-r}$48, 49 the labourers in the profits of industrial undertakings
$^{s-s}$48, 49 Probable future developement of this principle
$^{t-t}$+52, 57, 62, 65, 71

BOOK V: ON THE INFLUENCE OF GOVERNMENT

APPENDICES

ᵘ57 [*in addition*] APPENDIX Latest Information on the French Industrial Associations [*see* Appendix E]

FACSIMILES

PRINCIPLES OF POLITICAL ECONOMY

BOOK III

EXCHANGE

CHAPTER I

Of Value

§ 1. [*Preliminary remarks*] The subject on which we are now about to enter fills so important and conspicuous a position in political economy, that in the apprehension of some thinkers its boundaries confound themselves with those of the science itself. One eminent writer has proposed as a name for Political Economy, "Catallactics," or the science of exchanges: by others it has been called the Science of Values. If these denominations had appeared to me logically correct, I must have placed the discussion of the elementary laws of value at the commencement of our inquiry, instead of postponing it to the Third Part; and the possibility of so long deferring it is alone a sufficient proof that this view of the nature of Political Economy is too confined. It is true that in the preceding Books we have not escaped the necessity of anticipating some small portion of the theory of Value, especially as to the value of labour and of land. It is nevertheless evident, that of the two great departments of Political Economy, the production of wealth and its distribution, the consideration of Value has to do with the latter alone; and with that, only so far as competition, and not usage or custom, is the distributing agency. The conditions and laws of Production would be the same as they are, if the arrangements of society did not depend on Exchange, or did not admit of it. Even in the present system of industrial life, in which employments are minutely subdivided, and all concerned in production depend for their remuneration on the price of a particular commodity, exchange is not the fundamental law of the distribution of the produce, no more than roads and carriages are the essential laws of motion, but merely a part of the machinery for effecting it. To confound these ideas, seems to me, not only a logical, but a practical blunder. It is a case of the error too common in political economy, of not distinguishing between necessities arising from *the nature of things*[a], and those created by social arrangements: an error, which appears to me to be at all times producing two opposite mischiefs; on the one hand, causing political economists to class the merely temporary truths of their subject among its permanent and universal laws; and on the other, leading many persons to mistake the permanent laws of Production (such as those on

[a–a]MS, 48, 49   laws of nature

which the necessity is grounded of restraining population) for temporary accidents arising from the existing constitution of society—which those who would frame a new system of social arrangements, are at liberty to disregard.

In a state of society, however, in which the industrial system is entirely founded on purchase and sale, each individual[b], for the most part,[b] living not on things in the production of which he himself bears a part, but on things obtained by a double exchange, a sale followed by a purchase—the question of Value is fundamental. Almost every speculation respecting the economical interests of a society thus constituted, implies some theory of Value: the smallest error on that subject infects with corresponding error all our other conclusions; and anything vague or misty in our conception of it, creates confusion and uncertainty in everything else. Happily, there is nothing in the laws of Value which remains for the present or any future writer to clear up; the theory of the subject is complete: the only difficulty to be overcome is that of so stating it as to solve by anticipation the chief perplexities which occur in applying it: and to do this, some minuteness of exposition, and considerable demands on the patience of the reader, are unavoidable. He will be amply repaid, however (if a stranger to these inquiries), by the ease and rapidity with which a thorough understanding of this subject will enable him to fathom most of the remaining questions of political economy.

§ 2. [*Definitions of Value in Use, Exchange Value, and Price*] We must begin by settling our phraseology. Adam Smith, in a passage often quoted, has touched upon the most obvious ambiguity of the word value; which, in one of its senses, signifies usefulness, in another, power of purchasing; in his own language, value in use and value in exchange. But (as Mr. De Quincey has remarked) in illustrating this double meaning, Adam Smith has himself fallen into another ambiguity. Things (he says) which have the greatest value in use have often little or no value in exchange; which is true, since that which can be obtained without labour or sacrifice will command no price, however useful or needful it may be. But he proceeds to add, that things which have the greatest value in exchange, as a diamond for example, may have little or no value in use. This is employing the word use, not in the sense in which political economy is concerned with it, but in that other sense in which use is opposed to pleasure. Political economy has nothing to do with the comparative estimation of different uses in the judgment of a philosopher or a moralist. The use of a thing, in political economy, means its capacity to satisfy a desire, or serve a purpose. Diamonds have this capacity in a high degree, and unless they

b-b+48, 49, 52, 57, 62, 65, 71

had it, would not bear any price. Value in use, or as Mr. De Quincey calls it, *teleologic* value, is the extreme limit of value in exchange. The exchange value of a thing may fall short, to any amount, of its value in use; but that it can ever exceed the value in use, implies a contradiction; it supposes that persons will give, to possess a thing, more than the utmost value which they themselves put upon it as a means of gratifying their inclinations.

The word Value, when used without adjunct, always means, in political economy, value in exchange; or as it has been called by Adam Smith and his successors, exchangeable value, a phrase which no amount of authority that can be quoted for it can make other than bad English. Mr. De Quincey substitutes the term Exchange Value, which is unexceptionable.

Exchange value requires to be distinguished from Price. The words Value and Price were used as synonymous by the early political economists, and are not always discriminated even by Ricardo. But the most accurate modern writers, to avoid the wasteful expenditure of two good scientific terms on a single idea, have employed Price to express the value of a thing in relation to money; the quantity of money for which it will exchange. By the price of a thing, therefore, we shall henceforth understand its value in money; by the value, or exchange value of a thing, its general power of purchasing; the command which its possession gives over purchaseable commodities in general.

§ 3. [*What is meant by general purchasing power*] But here a fresh demand for explanation presents itself. What is meant by command over commodities in general? The same thing exchanges for a great quantity of some commodities, and for a very small quantity of others. A suit of clothes exchanges for a great quantity of bread, and for a very small quantity of precious stones. The value of a thing in exchange for some commodities may be rising, for others falling. A coat may exchange for less bread this year than last, if the harvest has been bad, but for more glass or iron, if a tax has been taken off those commodities, or an improvement made in their manufacture. Has the value of the coat, *ᵃunderᵃ* these circumstances, fallen or risen? It is impossible to say: all that can be said is, that it has fallen in relation to one thing, and risen in respect to another. But there is another case, in which no one would have any hesitation in saying what sort of change had taken place in the value of the coat: namely, if the cause in which the disturbance of exchange values originated, was something directly affecting the coat itself, and not the bread or the glass. Suppose, for example, that an invention had been made in machinery, by which broadcloth could be woven at half the former

ᵃ⁻ᵃMS, 48, 49, 52, 57 in

cost. The effect of this would be to lower the value of a coat, and if lowered by this cause, it would be lowered not in relation to bread only or to glass only, but to all purchaseable things, except such as happened to be affected at the very time by a similar depressing cause. We should therefore say, that there had been a fall in the exchange value or general purchasing power of a coat. The idea of general exchange value originates in the fact, that there really are causes which tend to alter the value of a thing in exchange for things generally, that is, for all things which are not themselves acted upon by causes of similar tendency.

In considering exchange value scientifically, it is expedient to abstract from *b*it*b* all causes except those which originate in the very commodity under consideration. Those which originate in the commodities with which we compare it, affect its value in relation to *c*those*c* commodities; but those which originate in itself, affect its value in relation to all commodities. In order the more completely to confine our attention to these last, it is convenient to assume that all commodities but the one in question remain invariable in their relative values. When we are considering the causes which raise or lower the value of corn, we suppose that woollens, silks, cutlery, sugar, timber, &c., while varying in their power of purchasing corn, remain constant in the proportions in which they exchange for one another. On this assumption, any one of them may be taken as a representative of all the rest; since in whatever manner corn varies in value with respect to any one commodity, it varies in the same manner and degree with respect to every other; and the upward or downward movement of its value estimated in some one thing, is all that *d*need*d* be considered. Its money value, therefore, or price, will represent as well as anything else its general exchange value, or purchasing power; and from an obvious convenience, will often be employed by us in that representative character; with the proviso that money itself do not vary in its general purchasing power, but that the prices of all things, other than that which we happen to be considering, remain unaltered.

§ 4. [*Value a relative term. A general rise or fall of values is a contradiction*] The distinction between Value and Price, as we have now refined them, is so obvious, as scarcely to seem in need of any illustration. But in political economy the greatest errors arise from overlooking the most obvious truths. Simple as this distinction is, it has consequences with which a reader unacquainted with the subject would do well to begin early by making himself thoroughly familiar. The following is one of the principal.

b–b+62, 65, 71
*c–c*MS, 48, 49, 52, 57   these
*d–d*MS, 48, 49, 52, 57, 62   needs

There is such a thing as a general rise of prices. All commodities may rise in their money price. But there cannot be a general rise of values. It is a contradiction in terms. A can only rise in value by exchanging for a greater quantity of B and C; in which case these must exchange for a smaller quantity of A. All things cannot rise relatively to one another. If one-half of the commodities in the market rise in exchange value, the very terms imply a fall of the other half; and reciprocally, the fall implies a rise. Things which are exchanged for one another can no more all fall, or all rise, than a dozen runners can each outrun all the rest, or a hundred trees all overtop one another. Simple as this truth is, we shall presently see that ^{a}it is lost sight of in some of the most accredited doctrines both of theorists and of what are called practical men^a. And as a first specimen, we may instance the great importance attached in the imagination of most people to a rise or fall of general prices. Because when the price of any one commodity rises, the circumstance usually indicates a rise of its value, people have an indistinct feeling when all prices rise, as if all things simultaneously had risen in value, and all the possessors had become enriched. That the money prices of all things should rise or fall, provided they all rise or fall equally, is in itself^b, and apart from existing contracts,^{b} of no consequence ^{c} . It affects nobody's wages, profits, or rent. Every one gets more money in the one case and less in the other; but of all that is to be bought with money they get neither more nor less than before. It makes no other difference than that of using more or fewer counters to reckon by. The only thing which in this case is really altered in value is money; and the only persons who either gain or lose are the holders of money, or those who have to receive or to pay fixed sums of it. There is a difference to annuitants and to creditors the one way, and to those who are burthened with annuities, or with debts, the contrary way. There is a disturbance, in short, of fixed money contracts; and this is an evil, whether it takes place in the debtor's favour or in the creditor's. But as to future transactions there is no difference to any one. Let it therefore be remembered (and occasions will often arise for calling it to mind) that a general rise or a general fall of values is a contradiction; and that a general rise or a general fall of prices is merely tantamount to an alteration in the value of money, and is a matter of complete indifference, save in so far as it affects existing contracts for receiving and paying fixed pecuniary amounts^d, and (it must be added) as it affects the interests of the producers of money^d.

$^{a-a}$MS some of the most accredited doctrines both of theorists & of what are called practical men are grounded on forgetfulness of it
$^{b-b}$+48, 49, 52, 57, 62, 65, 71
^{c}MS to any body
$^{d-d}$+65, 71

§ 5. [*How the laws of Value are modified in their application to retail transactions*] Before commencing the inquiry into the laws of value and price, I have one further observation to make. I must give warning, once for all, that the cases I contemplate are those in which values and prices are determined by competition alone. In so far only as they are thus determined, can they be reduced to any assignable law. The buyers must be supposed as studious to buy cheap, as the sellers to sell dear. The values and prices, therefore, to which our conclusions apply, are mercantile values and prices; such prices as are quoted in price-currents; prices in the wholesale markets, in which buying as well as selling is a matter of business; in which the buyers take pains to know, and generally do know, the lowest price at which an article of a given quality can be obtained; and in which, therefore, the axiom is true, that there cannot be for the same article, of the same quality, two prices in the same market. Our propositions will be true in a much more qualified sense, of retail prices; the prices paid in shops for articles of personal consumption. For such things there often are not merely two, but many prices, in different shops, or even in the same shop; habit and accident having as much to do in the matter as general causes. Purchases for private use, even by people in business, are not always made on business principles: the feelings which come into play in the operation of getting, and in that of spending their income, are often extremely different. Either from indolence, or ᵃcarelessnessᵃ, or because people think it fine to pay and ask no questions, three-fourths of those who can afford it give much higher prices than necessary for the things they consume; while the poor often do the same from ignorance and defect of judgment, want of time for searching and making inquiry, and not unfrequently from coercion, open or disguised. For these reasons, retail prices do not follow with all the regularity which might be expected, the action of the causes which determine wholesale prices. The influence of those causes is ultimately felt in the retail markets, and is the real source of such variations in retail prices as are of a general and permanent character. But there is no regular or exact correspondence. Shoes of equally good quality are sold in different shops at prices which differ considerably; and the price of leather may fall without causing the richer class of buyers to pay less for shoes. Nevertheless, shoes do sometimes fall in price; and when they do, the cause is always some such general circumstance as the cheapening of leather: and when leather is cheapened, even if no difference shows itself in ᵇshops frequented by rich peopleᵇ, the artizan and the labourer generally get their shoes cheaper, and there is a visible diminution in the contract prices at which shoes are delivered for the supply of a

ᵃ⁻ᵃMS, 48, 49   insouciance
ᵇ⁻ᵇMS   Piccadilly or Bond Street

workhouse or of a regiment. In all reasoning about prices, the proviso must be understood, "supposing all parties to take care of their own interest." Inattention to these distinctions has led to improper applications of the abstract principles of political economy, and still oftener to an undue discrediting of those principles, through their being compared with a different sort of facts from those which they contemplate, or which can fairly be expected to accord with them.

CHAPTER II

^aOf^a Demand and Supply, in Their Relation to Value

§ 1. [*Two conditions of Value: Utility, and Difficulty of Attainment*] That a thing may have any value in exchange, two conditions are necessary. It must be of some use; that is (as already explained) it must conduce to some purpose, satisfy some desire. No one will pay a price, or part with anything which serves some of his purposes, to obtain a thing which serves none of them. But, secondly, the thing must not only have some utility, there must also be some difficulty in its attainment. "Any article whatever," says Mr. De Quincey,* "to obtain that artificial sort of value which is meant by exchange value, must begin by offering itself as a means to some desirable purpose; and secondly, even though possessing incontestably this preliminary advantage, it will never ascend to an exchange value in cases where it can be obtained gratuitously and without effort; of which last terms both are necessary as limitations. For often it will happen that some desirable object may be obtained gratuitously; stoop, and you gather it at your feet; but still, because the continued iteration of this stooping exacts a laborious effort, very soon it is found, that to gather for yourself virtually is not gratuitous. In the vast forests of the Canadas, at intervals, wild strawberries may be gratuitously gathered by shiploads: yet such is the exhaustion of a stooping posture, and of a labour so monotonous, that everybody is soon glad to resign the service into mercenary hands."

As was pointed out in the last chapter, the utility of a thing in the estimation of the purchaser, is the extreme limit of its exchange value: higher the value cannot ascend; peculiar circumstances are required to raise it so high. This topic is happily illustrated by Mr. De Quincey. "Walk into almost any possible shop, buy the first article you see; what will determine its price? In ^bthe^b ninety-nine cases out of a hundred, simply the element D—difficulty of attainment. The other element U, or intrinsic utility, will be perfectly inoperative. Let the thing (measured by its uses) be, for your

Logic of Political Economy [Edinburgh: Blackwood and Sons, 1844], p. 13[–4].

^{a–a}52 On   ^{b–b}+62, 65, 71 [*not in* Source]

purposes, worth ten guineas, so that you would rather give ten guineas than lose it; yet, if the difficulty of producing it be only worth one guinea, one guinea is the price which it will bear. But still not the less, though U is inoperative, can U be supposed absent? By no possibility; for, if it *had* been absent, assuredly you would not have bought the article even at the lowest price. U acts upon *you*, though it does not act upon the price. On the other hand, in the hundredth case, we will suppose the circumstances reversed: you are on Lake Superior in a steam-boat, making your way to an unsettled region 800 miles a-head of civilization, and consciously with no chance at all of purchasing any luxury whatsoever, little luxury or big luxury, for the space of ten years to come *c*. One*c* fellow-passenger, whom you will part with before sunset, has a powerful musical snuff-box; knowing by experience the power of such a toy over your own feelings, the magic with which at times it lulls your agitations of mind, you are vehemently desirous to purchase it. In the hour of leaving London you had forgot to do so; here is a final chance. But the owner, aware of your situation not less than yourself, is determined to operate by a strain pushed to the very uttermost upon U, upon the intrinsic worth of the article in your individual estimate for your individual purposes. He will not hear of D as any controlling power or mitigating agency in the case; and finally, although at six guineas a-piece in London or Paris you might have loaded a waggon with such boxes, you pay sixty rather than lose it when the last knell of the clock has sounded, which summons you to buy now or to forfeit for ever. Here, as before, only one element is operative; before it was D, now it is U. But after all, D was not absent, though inoperative. The inertness of D allowed U to put forth its total effect. The practical compression of D being withdrawn, U springs up like water in a pump when released from the pressure of air. Yet still that D was present to your thoughts, though the price was otherwise regulated, is evident; both because U and D must coexist in order to found any case of exchange value whatever, and because undeniably you take into very particular consideration this D, the extreme difficulty of attainment (which here is the greatest possible, viz. an impossibility) before you consent to have the price racked up to U. The special D has vanished; but it is replaced in your thoughts by an unlimited D. Undoubtedly you have submitted to U in extremity as the regulating force of the price; but it was under a sense of D's latent presence. Yet D is so far from exerting any positive force, that the retirement of D from all agency whatever on the price—this it is which creates as it were a perfect vacuum, and through that vacuum U rushes up to its highest and ultimate gradation."[*]

[*De Quincey, pp. 24–8.]

*c–c*Source, MS   : one

This case, in which the value is wholly regulated by the necessities or desires of the purchaser, is the case of strict and absolute monopoly; in which, the article desired being only obtainable from one person, he can exact any equivalent, short of the point at which no purchaser could be found. But it is not a necessary consequence, even of complete monopoly, that the value should be forced up to this ultimate limit; as will be seen when we have considered the law of value in so far as depending on the other element, difficulty of attainment.

§ 2. [*Three kinds of Difficulty of Attainment*] The difficulty of attainment which determines value, is not always the same kind of difficulty. It sometimes consists in an absolute limitation of the supply. There are things of which it is physically impossible to increase the quantity beyond certain narrow limits. Such are those wines which can be grown only in peculiar circumstances of soil, climate, and exposure. Such also are ancient sculptures; pictures by *a* old masters; rare books or coins, or other articles of antiquarian curiosity. Among such may also be reckoned houses and building-ground, in a town of definite extent (such as Venice, or any fortified town where fortifications are necessary to security); the most desirable sites in any town whatever; houses and parks peculiarly favoured by natural beauty, in places where that advantage is uncommon. Potentially, all land whatever is a commodity of this class; and might be practically so, in countries fully occupied and cultivated.

But there is another category (embracing the majority of all things that are bought and sold), in which the obstacle to attainment consists only in the labour and expense requisite to produce the commodity. Without a certain labour and expense it cannot be had: but when any one is willing to incur *b*these*b*, there needs be no limit to the multiplication of the product. If there were labourers enough and machinery enough, cottons, woollens, or linens might be produced by thousands of yards for every single yard now manufactured. There would be a point, no doubt, where further increase would be stopped by the incapacity of the earth to afford more of the material. But there is no need, for any purpose of political economy, to contemplate a time when this ideal limit could become a practical one.

There is a third case, intermediate between the two preceding, and rather more complex, which I shall at present merely indicate, but the importance of which in political economy is extremely great. There are commodities which can be multiplied to an indefinite extent by labour and expenditure, but not by a fixed amount of labour and expenditure. Only a limited quantity can be produced at a given cost: if more is wanted, it must be produced at a greater cost. To this class, as has been often repeated, agricultural produce belongs; and generally all the rude produce

*a*MS, 48, 49, 52, 57, 62   the   *b-b*MS, 48, 49, 52, 57   this

of the earth; and this peculiarity is a source of very important consequences; one of which is the necessity of a limit to population; and another, the payment of rent.

§ 3. [*Commodities which are absolutely limited in quantity*] These being the three classes, in one or other of which all things that are bought and sold must take their place, we shall consider them in their order. And first, of things absolutely limited in quantity, such as ancient sculptures or pictures.

Of such things it is commonly said, that their value depends upon their scarcity: but the expression is not sufficiently definite to serve our purpose. Others say, with somewhat greater precision, that the value depends on the demand and the supply. But even this statement requires much explanation, to make it a clear exponent of the relation between the value of a thing, and the causes of which that value is an effect.

The supply of a commodity is an intelligible expression: it means the quantity offered for sale; the quantity that is to be had, at a given time and place, by those who wish to purchase it. But what is meant by the demand? Not the mere desire for the commodity. A beggar may desire a ᵃdiamondᵃ; but his desire, however great, will have no influence on the price. Writers have therefore given a more limited sense to demand, and have defined it, the wish to possess, combined with the power of purchasing. To distinguish demand in this technical sense, from the demand which is synonymous with desire, they call the former *effectual* demand.* After this explanation, it is usually supposed that there remains no further difficulty, and that the value depends upon the ratio between the effectual demand, as thus defined, and the supply.

These phrases, however, fail to satisfy any one who requires clear ideas, and a perfectly precise expression of them. Some confusion must always attach to a phrase so inappropriate as that of a *ratio* between two things not of the same denomination. What ratio can there be between a quantity and a desire, or even a desire combined with a power? A ratio between demand and supply is only intelligible if by demand we mean the quantity demanded, and if the ratio intended is that between the quantity demanded and the quantity supplied. But again, the quantity demanded is not a fixed quantity, even at the same time and place; it varies according to the value;

*Adam Smith, who introduced the expression "effectual demand," employed it to denote the demand of those who are willing and able to give for the commodity what he calls its natural price, that is, the price which will enable it to be permanently produced and brought to market.—See his chapter on Natural and Market Price [of Commodities] (book i. ch. 7 [Vol. I, pp. 142–56].)

ᵃ⁻ᵃMS, 48, 49   pine-apple

if the thing is cheap, there is usually a demand for more of it than when it is dear. The demand, therefore, partly depends on the value. But it was before laid down that the value depends on the demand. From this contradiction how shall we extricate ourselves? How solve the paradox, of two things, each depending upon the other?

Though the solution of these difficulties is obvious enough, the difficulties themselves are not fanciful; and I bring them forward thus prominently, because I am certain that they obscurely haunt every inquirer into the subject who has not openly faced and distinctly realized them. Undoubtedly the true solution must have been frequently given, though I cannot call to mind any one who had given it before myself, except the eminently clear thinker and skilful expositor, J. B. Say. I should have imagined, however, that it must be familiar to all political economists, if the writings of several did not give evidence of some want of clearness on the point, and if the *b*instance of Mr. De Quincey did not prove that the complete non-recognition and implied denial of it are compatible with great intellectual ingenuity, and close intimacy with the subject matter*b*.

§ 4. [*The Equation of Demand and Supply is the law of their value*] Meaning, by the word demand, the quantity demanded, and remembering that this is not a fixed quantity, but in general varies according to the value, let us suppose that the demand at some particular time exceeds the supply, that is, there are persons ready to buy, at the market value, a greater quantity than is offered for sale. Competition takes place on the side of the buyers, and the value rises: but how much? In the ratio (some may suppose) of the deficiency: if the demand exceeds the supply by one-third, the value rises one-third. By no means: for when the value has risen one-third, the demand may still exceed the supply; there may, even at that higher value, be a greater quantity wanted than is to be had; and the competition of buyers may still continue. If the article is a necessary of life, which, rather than resign, people are willing to pay for at any price, a deficiency of one-third may raise the price to double, triple, or quadruple.* Or, on the

---

*"The price of corn in this country has risen from 100 to 200 per cent and upwards, when the utmost computed deficiency of the crops has not been more than between one-sixth and one-third below an average, and when that deficiency has been relieved by foreign supplies. [MS *ellipsis indicated by* . .] If there should be a deficiency of the crops amounting to one-third, without any surplus from a former year, and without any chance of relief by importation, the price might rise five, six, or even tenfold."—Tooke's *History of Prices*, vol. i. pp. 13–5 [12–5].

*b-b*MS complete non-recognition & implied denial of it, by such a writer as Mr. De Quincey, did not prove that the greatest subtlety of intellect, & the closest intimacy with the subject matter, do not always ensure a perfection of what are apparently its most obvious principles

contrary, the competition may cease before the value has risen in even the proportion of the deficiency. A rise, short of one-third, may place the article beyond the means, or beyond the inclinations, of purchasers to the full amount. At what point, then, will the rise be arrested? At the point, whatever it be, which equalizes the demand and the supply: at the price which cuts off the extra third from the demand, or brings forward additional sellers sufficient to supply it. When, in either of these ways, or by a combination of both, the demand becomes equal and no more than equal to the supply, the rise of value will stop.

The converse case is equally simple. Instead of a demand beyond the supply, let us suppose a supply exceeding the demand. The competition will now be on the side of the sellers: the extra quantity can only find a market by calling forth an additional demand equal to itself. This is accomplished by means of cheapness; the value falls, and brings the article within *the* reach of more numerous *customers*, or induces those who were already consumers to make increased purchases. *The fall of value required to re-establish equality, is different in different cases.* The kinds of things in which *it* is commonly greatest are at the two extremities of the scale; absolute necessaries, or those peculiar luxuries, the taste for which is confined to a small class. In the case of food, as those who have already enough do not require more on account of its cheapness, but rather expend in other things what they save in food, the increased consumption occasioned by cheapness, carries off, as experience shows, *only a* small part of the extra supply caused by *an abundant* harvest;* and the fall is practically arrested only when the farmers withdraw their corn, and hold it back in hopes of a higher price; or by the operations of speculators who buy corn when it is cheap, and store it up to be brought *out* when more urgently wanted. Whether the demand and supply are equalized by an increased demand, the result of cheapness, or by withdrawing a part of the supply, equalized they are in either case.

Thus we see that the idea of a *ratio*, as between demand and supply, is out of place, and has no concern in the matter: the proper mathematical analogy is that of an *equation*. Demand and supply, the quantity demanded and the quantity supplied, will be made equal. If unequal at any moment, competition equalizes them, and the manner in which this is done is by an

*See Tooke [vol. I, pp. 17–8], and the Report of the Agricultural Committee of [MS, 48, 49, 52, 57   Committee in] 1821 [*Parliamentary Papers*, 1821, IV, pp. 8–9, 224–40, 287–98, 344–55].

a–a+48, 49, 52, 57, 62, 65, 71
*b–b*MS,48   consumers
*c–c*MS   It may require a great fall, or only a little fall, to reestablish equality.
*d–d*MS   the fall required   *e–e*MS, 48, 49   a very
*f–f*MS, 48, 49   a good   *g–g*MS, 48, 49, 52, 57   forth

adjustment of the value. If the demand increases, the value rises; if the demand diminishes, the value falls: again, if the supply falls off, the value rises; and falls if the supply is increased. The rise or the fall continues until the demand and supply are again equal to one another: and the value which a commodity will bring in any market, is no other than the value which, in that market, gives a demand just sufficient to carry off the existing or expected supply.

This, then, is the Law of Value, with respect to all commodities not susceptible of being multiplied at pleasure. Such commodities, no doubt, are exceptions. There is another law for that much larger class of things, which admit of *ʰindefiniteʰ* multiplication. But it is not the less necessary to conceive distinctly and grasp firmly the theory of this exceptional case. In the first place, it will be found to be of great assistance in rendering the more common case intelligible. And in the next place, the principle of the exception stretches wider, and embraces more cases, than might at first be supposed.

§ 5. [*Miscellaneous cases falling under this law*] There are but few commodities which are naturally and necessarily limited in supply. But any commodity whatever may be artificially so. Any commodity may be the subject of a monopoly: like tea, in this country, up to 1834; tobacco in France, *ᵃ* opium in British India, at present. The price of a monopolized commodity is commonly supposed to be arbitrary; depending on the will of the monopolist, and limited only (as in Mr. De Quincey's case of the musical box in the wilds of America) by the buyer's extreme estimate of its worth to himself. This is in one sense true, but forms no exception, nevertheless, to the dependence of the value on supply and demand. The monopolist can fix the value as high as he pleases, short of what the consumer either could not or would not pay; but he can only do so by limiting the supply. The Dutch East India Company obtained a monopoly price for the produce of the Spice Islands, but to do so they were obliged, in good seasons, to destroy a portion of the crop. Had they persisted in selling all that they produced, they must have forced a market by reducing the price, so low, perhaps, that they would have received for the larger quantity a less total return than for the smaller: at least they showed that such was their opinion by destroying the surplus. Even on Lake Superior, Mr. De Quincey's huckster could not have sold his box for sixty guineas, if he had possessed two musical boxes and desired to sell them both. Supposing the cost price of each to be six guineas, he would have taken seventy for the two in preference to sixty for one; that is, although his monopoly was the closest possible, he would have sold the boxes at thirty-five guineas

ʰ⁻ʰ49   definite [*printer's error?*]   *ᵃ*MS, 48, 49, 52   salt and

each, notwithstanding that sixty was not beyond the buyer's estimate of the article for his purposes. Monopoly value, therefore, does not depend on any peculiar principle, but is a mere variety of the ordinary case of demand and supply.

Again, though there are few commodities which are at all times and for ever unsusceptible of increase of supply, any commodity whatever may be temporarily so; and with some commodities this is habitually the case. Agricultural produce, for example, cannot be increased in quantity before the next harvest; the quantity of corn already existing in the world, is all that can be had for sometimes a year to come. During that interval, corn is practically assimilated to things *of which the quantity* cannot be increased. In the case of most commodities, it requires a certain time to increase their quantity; and if the demand increases, then until a corresponding supply can be brought forward, that is, until the supply can accommodate itself to the demand, the value will so rise as to accommodate the demand to the supply.

There is another case, the exact converse of this. There are some articles of which the supply may be indefinitely increased, but cannot be rapidly diminished. There are things so durable that the quantity in existence is at all times very great in comparison with the annual produce. Gold, and the more durable metals, are things of this sort; and also houses. The supply of such things might *c* be at once diminished by destroying them; but to do this could only be the interest of the possessor if he had a monopoly of the article, and could repay himself for the destruction of a part by the increased value of the remainder. The value, therefore, of such things may continue for a long time so low, either from excess of supply or falling off in the demand, as to put a complete stop to further production; the diminution of supply by wearing out being so slow a process, that a long time is requisite, even under a total suspension of production, to restore the original value. During that interval the value will be regulated solely by supply and demand, and will rise very gradually as the existing stock wears out, until there is again a remunerating value, and production resumes its course.

Finally, there are commodities of which, though capable of being increased or diminished to a great, and even an unlimited extent, the value never depends upon anything but demand and supply. This is the case, in particular, with the commodity Labour; of the value of which we have treated copiously in the preceding Book: and there are many cases besides, in which we shall find it necessary to call in this principle to solve difficult questions of exchange value. This will be particularly exemplified when we treat of International Values; that is, of the terms of interchange between things produced in different countries, or, to speak more generally, in distant places. But into these questions we cannot enter, until we shall have examined the case of commodities which can be increased in quantity indefinitely and at pleasure; and shall have determined by what law, other than that of Demand and Supply, the permanent or average values of such commodities are regulated. This we shall do in the next chapter.

CHAPTER III

Of Cost of Production, in Its Relation to Value

§ 1. [*Commodities which are susceptible of indefinite multiplication without increase of cost. Law of their Value, Cost of Production*] When the production of a commodity is the effect of labour and expenditure, whether the commodity is susceptible of unlimited multiplication or not, there is a minimum value which is the essential condition of its being permanently produced. The value at any particular time is the result of supply and demand; and is always that which is necessary to create a market for the existing supply. But unless that value is sufficient to repay the Cost of Production, and to afford, besides, the ordinary *a*expectation*a* of profit, the commodity will not continue to be produced. Capitalists will not go on permanently producing at a loss. They will not even go on producing at a profit less than they can live on. Persons whose capital is already embarked, and cannot *b*be easily*b* extricated, will persevere for a considerable time without profit, and have been known to persevere even at a loss, in *c*hope*c* of better times. But they will not do so indefinitely, or when there is nothing to indicate that times are likely to improve. No new capital will be invested in an employment, unless there be an expectation not only of some profit, but of a profit as great (regard being had to the degree of eligibility of the employment in other respects) as can be hoped for in any other occupation at that time and place. When such profit is evidently not to be had, if people do not actually withdraw their capital, they at least abstain from replacing it when consumed. The cost of production, together with the ordinary profit, may therefore be called the *necessary* price, or value, of all things made by labour and capital. Nobody willingly produces in the prospect of loss. Whoever does so, does it under a miscalculation, which he corrects as fast as he is able.

When a commodity is not only made by labour and capital, but can be made by them in indefinite quantity, this Necessary Value, the minimum

*a–a*MS, 48, 49, 52, 57   expectations
*b–b*MS, 48, 49, 52   easily be
*c–c*MS, 48, 49, 52, 57, 62   hopes

with which the producers will be content, is also, if competition is free [d]and active[d], the maximum which they can expect. If the value of a commodity is such that it repays the cost of production not only with the customary, but with a higher rate of profit, capital rushes to share in this extra gain, and by increasing the supply of the article, reduces its value. This is not a mere supposition or surmise, but a fact familiar to those conversant with commercial operations. Whenever a new line of business presents itself, offering a hope of unusual profits, and whenever any established trade or manufacture is believed to be yielding a greater profit than customary, there is sure to be in a short time so large a production or importation of the commodity, as not only destroys the extra profit, but generally goes beyond the mark, and sinks the value as much too low as it had before been raised too high; until the oversupply is corrected by a total or partial suspension of further production. As [e] already intimated,* these variations in the quantity produced do not presuppose or require that any person should change his employment. Those whose business is thriving, increase their produce by availing themselves more largely of their credit, while those who are not making the ordinary profit, restrict their operations, and (in manufacturing phrase) work short time. In this mode is surely and speedily effected the equalization, not of profits perhaps, but of the expectations of profit, in different occupations.

As a general rule, then, things tend to exchange for one another at such values as will enable each producer to be repaid the cost of production with the ordinary profit; in other words, such as will give to all producers the same rate of profit on their outlay. But in order that the profit may be equal where the outlay, that is, the cost of production, is equal, things must on the average exchange for one another in the ratio of their cost of production: things of which the cost of production is the same, must be of the same value. For only thus will an equal outlay yield an equal return. If a farmer with a capital equal to 1000 quarters of corn, can produce 1200 quarters, yielding him a profit of 20 per cent; whatever else can be produced in the same time by a capital of 1000 quarters, must be worth, that is, must exchange for, 1200 quarters, otherwise the producer would gain either more or less than 20 per cent.

Adam Smith and Ricardo have called that value of a thing which is proportional to its cost of production, its Natural Value (or its Natural Price). They meant by this, the point about which the value oscillates, and to which it always tends to return; the [f]centre[f] value, towards which, as

*Supra, p. 407.

[d–d]+52, 57, 62, 65, 71
[e]MS, 48, 49   I have
[f–f]MS, 48, 49, 52   central

Adam Smith expresses it, the market value of a thing is constantly gravitating; and any deviation from which is but a temporary irregularity, which, the moment it exists, sets forces in motion tending to correct it. On an average of years sufficient to enable the oscillations on one side of the central line to be compensated by those on the other, the market value agrees with the natural value; but it very seldom coincides exactly with it at any particular time. The sea everywhere tends to a level; but it never *is* at an exact level; its surface is always ruffled by waves, and often agitated by storms. It is enough that no point, at least in the open sea, is permanently higher than another. Each place is alternately elevated and depressed; but the ocean preserves its level.

§ 2. [*Law of their Value, Cost of Production operating through potential, but not actual, alterations of supply*] The latent influence by which the values of things are made to conform in the long run to the cost of production, is the variation that would otherwise take place in the supply of the commodity. *The* supply would be increased if the thing continued to sell above the ratio of its cost of production, and *would be* diminished if it fell below that ratio. But we must not therefore suppose it to be necessary that the supply should *actually* be either diminished or increased. Suppose that the cost of production of a thing is cheapened by some mechanical invention, or increased by a tax. The value of the thing would in a little time, if not immediately, fall in the one case, and rise in the other; and it would do so, *c* because if it did not, the supply would in the one case be increased, until the price fell, in the other diminished, until it rose. For this reason, and from the erroneous notion that value depends on the *proportion* between the demand and the supply, many persons suppose that this proportion must be altered whenever there is any change in the value of the commodity; that the value cannot fall through a diminution of the cost of production, unless the supply is permanently increased; nor rise, unless the supply is permanently diminished. But this is not the fact: there is no need that there should be any actual alteration of supply; and when there is, the alteration, if permanent, is not the cause, but the consequence of the alteration in value. If, indeed, the supply *could* not be increased, no diminution in the cost of production would lower the value: but there is by no means any necessity that it *should*. The* mere possibility often suffices; the dealers are aware of what *would* happen, and their mutual competition makes them anticipate the result by lowering the price. Whether *f* there

*g–g*MS *is*
*a–a*49, 52 That
*c*MS, 48, 49, 52 *simply*
*e–e*MS, 48, 49 *would*

b–b+48, 49, 52, 57, 62, 65, 71
*d–d*MS : the
*f*MS or not

will be a greater permanent supply of the commodity after its production has been cheapened, depends on quite another question, namely, on whether a greater quantity is wanted at the reduced value. Most commonly a greater quantity is wanted, but not necessarily. "A man," says Mr. De Quincey,* "buys an article of instant applicability to his own purposes the more readily and the more largely as it happens to be cheaper^g. Silk^g handkerchiefs having fallen to half-price, he will buy, perhaps, in threefold quantity; but he does not buy more steam-engines because the price is lowered. His demand for steam-engines is almost always predetermined by the circumstances of his situation. So far as he considers the cost at all, it is much more the cost of working this engine than the cost upon its purchase. But there are many articles for which the market is absolutely and merely limited by a pre-existing *system*, to which those articles are attached as subordinate parts or members. How could we force the dials or faces of timepieces by artificial cheapness to sell more plentifully than the inner works or movements of such timepieces? Could the sale of wine-vaults be increased without increasing the sale of wine? Or the tools of shipwrights find an enlarged market whilst shipbuilding was stationary? . . . . Offer to a town of 3000 inhabitants a stock of hearses, no cheapness will tempt that town into buying more than one. Offer a stock of yachts, the chief cost lies in manning, victualling, repairing; no diminution upon the mere price to a purchaser will tempt into the market any man whose habits and propensities had not already disposed him to such a purchase. So of professional costume for bishops, lawyers, students at Oxford." Nobody doubts, however, that the price and value of all these things would be eventually lowered by any diminution of their cost of production; and lowered through the apprehension entertained of new competitors, and an increased supply; though the great hazard to which a new competitor would expose himself, in ^{h}an^h article not susceptible of any considerable ^{i}extension^i of its market, would enable the established dealers to maintain their original prices much longer than they could do in an article offering more encouragement to competition.

Again, reverse the case, and suppose the cost of production increased, as for example by laying a tax on the commodity. The value would rise; and that, probably, immediately. Would the supply be diminished? Only if the increase of value diminished the demand. Whether this effect followed, would soon appear, and if it did, the value would recede somewhat, from excess of supply, until the production was reduced, and ^{j}would^j then rise again. There are many articles for which it requires a very considerable

Logic of Political Economy, pp. 230–1.

$^{g-g}$Source, MS : silk $^{h-h}$52, 57, 62   any
$^{i-i}$MS   increase $^{j-j}$+48, 49, 52, 57, 62, 65, 71

rise of price, materially to reduce the demand; in particular, articles of necessity, such as the habitual food of the people; in England, wheaten bread: of which there is probably *almost* as much *consumed*, at *the present* cost price, as there would be *with the present population* at a price considerably lower. Yet it is especially in such things that dearness or high price is popularly confounded with scarcity. Food may be dear from scarcity, as after a bad harvest; but the dearness (for example) which is the effect of taxation, or of corn laws, has nothing whatever to do with insufficient supply: such causes do not much diminish the quantity of food in a country: it is other things rather than food that are diminished in quantity by them, since, those who pay more for food not having so much to expend otherwise, the production of other things contracts itself to the limits of a smaller demand.

It is, therefore, strictly correct to say, that the value of things which can be increased in quantity at pleasure, does not depend (except accidentally, and during the time necessary for production to adjust itself,) upon demand and supply; on the contrary, demand and supply depend upon it. There is a demand for a certain quantity of the commodity at its *natural or cost* value, and to that the supply in the long run endeavours to conform. When *at any time* it fails of so conforming, it is either from miscalculation, or from a change in some of the elements of the problem: either in the natural value, that is, in the cost of production; or in the demand, from an alteration in public taste or in the number or wealth of the consumers. These causes of disturbance are very liable to occur, and when any one of them does occur, the market value of the article ceases to agree with the natural value. The real law of demand and supply, the equation between them, *still* holds good *r* : if a value different from the natural value be necessary to make the demand equal to the supply, the market value will deviate from the natural value; but only for a time; for the permanent tendency of supply is to conform itself to the demand which is found by experience to exist for the commodity when selling at its natural value. If the supply is either more or less than this, it is so accidentally, and affords either more or less than the ordinary rate of profit; which, under free *and active* competition, cannot long continue to be the case.

To recapitulate: demand and supply govern the value of all things which cannot be indefinitely increased; except that even for them, when produced by industry, there is a minimum value, determined by the cost of production. But in all things which admit of indefinite multiplication, demand and

---

k–k+62, 65, 71
*l–l*MS, 48, 49, 52   produced
n–n+62, 65, 71
p–p+49, 52, 57, 62, 65, 71
*r*MS, 48, 49, 52, 57, 62, 65   in all cases

*m–m*MS, 48, 49   a high
*o–o*MS, 48, 49   *natural*
q–q+71
s–s+52, 57, 62, 65, 71

supply only determine the perturbations of value, during a period which cannot exceed the length of time necessary for altering the supply. While thus ruling the oscillations of value, they themselves obey a superior force, which makes value gravitate towards Cost of Production, and which would settle it and keep it there, if fresh disturbing influences were not continually arising to make it again deviate. To pursue the same strain of metaphor, demand and supply always rush to an equilibrium, but the condition of *stable* equilibrium is when things exchange for each other according to their cost of production, or, in the expression we have used, when things are at their Natural Value.

CHAPTER IV

Ultimate Analysis of Cost
of Production

§ 1. [*Principal element in Cost of Production—Quantity of Labour*]
The component elements of Cost of Production have been set forth in the
First Part of this enquiry.* The principal of them, and so much the principal as to be nearly the sole, we found to be Labour. What the production
of a thing costs to its producer, or its series of producers, is the labour
expended in producing it. If we consider as the producer the capitalist who
makes the advances, the word Labour may be replaced by the word Wages:
what the produce costs to him, is the wages which he has had to pay. At
the first glance indeed this seems to be only a part of his outlay, since he
has not only paid wages to labourers, but has likewise provided them with
tools, materials, and perhaps buildings. These tools, materials, and buildings, however, were produced by labour and capital; and their value, like
that of the article to the production of which they are subservient, depends
on cost of production, which again is resolvable into labour. The cost of
production of broadcloth does not wholly consist in the wages of weavers;
which alone are directly paid by the cloth manufacturer. It consists also
of the wages of spinners and woolcombers, and, it may be added, of
shepherds, all of which the clothier has paid for in the price of yarn. It
consists too of the wages of builders and brickmakers, which he has
reimbursed in the contract price of erecting his factory. It partly consists
of the wages of machine-makers, iron-founders, and miners. And to these
must be added the wages of the carriers who transported any of the means
and appliances of the production to the place where they were to be used,
and the product itself to the place where it is to be sold.

The value of commodities, therefore, depends principally (we shall
presently see whether it depends solely) on the quantity of labour required
for their production; including in the idea of production, that of conveyance
to the market. "In estimating," says Ricardo,† "the exchangeable value of

*Supra, pp. 31–2.
†*Principles of Political Economy and Taxation*, ch. i. sect. 3. [3rd ed.
London: Murray, 1821, p. 18–20.]

stockings, for example, we shall find that their value, comparatively with other things, depends on the total quantity of labour necessary to manufacture them and bring them to market. First, there is the labour necessary to cultivate the land on which the raw cotton is grown; secondly, the labour of conveying the cotton to the country where the stockings are to be manufactured, which includes a portion of the labour bestowed in building the ship in which it is conveyed, and which is charged in the freight of the goods; thirdly, the labour of the spinner and weaver; fourthly, a portion of the labour of the engineer, smith, and carpenter, who erected the buildings and machinery by the help of which they are made; fifthly, the labour of the retail dealer and of many others, whom it is unnecessary further to particularize. The aggregate sum of these various kinds of labour, determines the quantity of other things for which these stockings will exchange, while the same consideration of the various quantities of labour which have been bestowed on those other things, will equally govern the portion of them which will be given for the stockings.

"To convince ourselves that this is the real foundation of exchangeable value, let us suppose any improvement to be made in the means of abridging labour in any one of the various processes through which the raw cotton must pass before the manufactured stockings come to the market to be exchanged for other things; and observe the effects which will follow. If fewer men were required to cultivate the raw cotton, or if fewer sailors were employed in navigating, or shipwrights in constructing, the ship in which it was conveyed to us; if fewer hands were employed in raising the buildings and machinery, or if these, when raised, were rendered more efficient; the stockings would inevitably fall in value, and command less of other things. They would fall, because a less quantity of labour was necessary to their production, and would therefore exchange for a smaller quantity of those things in which no such abridgement of labour had been made.

"Economy in the use of labour never fails to reduce the relative value of a commodity, whether the saving be in the labour necessary to the manufacture of the commodity itself, or in that necessary to the formation of the capital, by the aid of which it is produced. In either case the price of stockings would fall, whether there were fewer men employed as bleachers, spinners, and weavers, persons immediately necessary to their manufacture; or as sailors, carriers, engineers, and smiths, persons more indirectly concerned. In the one case, the whole saving of labour would fall on the stockings, because that portion of labour was wholly confined to the stockings; in the other, a portion only would fall on the stockings, the remainder being applied to all those other commodities, to the production of which the buildings, machinery, and carriage, were subservient."

§ 2. [*Wages not an element in Cost of Production*] It will have been observed that Ricardo expresses himself as if the *quantity* of labour which it costs to produce a commodity and bring it to market, were the only thing on which its value depended. But since the cost of production to the capitalist is not labour but wages, and since wages may be either greater or less, the quantity of labour being the same; it would seem that the value of the product cannot be determined solely by the quantity of labour, but by the quantity together with the remuneration; and that values must partly depend on wages.

In order to decide this point, it must be considered, that value is a relative term: that the value of a commodity is not a name for an inherent and substantive quality of the thing itself, but means the quantity of other things which can be obtained in exchange for it. The value of one thing, must always be understood relatively to some other thing, or to things in general. Now the relation of one thing to another cannot be altered by any cause which affects them both alike. A rise or fall of general wages is a fact which affects all commodities in the same manner, and therefore affords no reason why they should exchange for each other in one rather than in another proportion. To suppose that high wages make high values, is to suppose that there can be such a thing as general high values. But this is a contradiction in terms: the high value of some things is synonymous with the low value of others. The mistake arises from not attending to values, but only to prices. Though there is no such thing as a general rise of values, there is such a thing as a general rise of prices. As soon as we form distinctly the idea of values, we see that high or low wages can have nothing to do with them; but that high wages make high prices, is a popular and widely-spread opinion. The whole amount of error involved in this proposition can only be seen thoroughly when we come to the theory of money; at present we need only say that if it be true, there can be no such thing as a real rise of wages; for if wages could not rise without a proportional rise of the price of everything, they could not, for any substantial purpose, rise at all. This surely is a sufficient *reductio ad absurdum*, and shows the amazing folly of the propositions which may and do become, and long remain, accredited doctrines of popular political economy. It must be remembered too that general high prices, even supposing them to exist, can be of no use to a producer or dealer, considered as such; for if they increase his money returns, they increase in the same degree all his expenses. There is no mode in which capitalists can compensate themselves for a high cost of labour, through any action on values or prices. It cannot be prevented from taking its effect *on* low profits. If the labourers really

*a–a*MS, 48, 49, 52, 57, 62   in

get more, that is, get the produce of more labour, a smaller percentage must remain for profit. From this Law of Distribution, resting as it does on a law of arithmetic, there is no escape. The mechanism of Exchange and Price may hide it from us, but is quite powerless to alter it.

§ 3. [*Wages not an element in Cost of Production except in so far as they vary from employment to employment*] Although, however, *general* wages, whether high or low, do not affect values, yet if wages are higher in one employment than *ᵃ* another, or if they rise *ᵇ*and*ᵇ* fall permanently in one employment without doing so in others, these inequalities do really operate upon values. The causes which make wages vary from one employment to another, have been considered in a former chapter. When the wages of an employment permanently exceed the average rate, the value of the thing produced will, in the same degree, exceed the standard determined by mere quantity of labour. Things, for example, which are made by skilled labour, exchange for the produce of a much greater quantity of unskilled labour; for no reason but because the labour is more highly paid. If, through the extension of education, the labourers competent to skilled employments were so increased in number as to diminish the difference between their wages and those of common labour, all things produced by labour of the superior kind would fall in value, compared with things produced by common labour, and these might be said therefore to rise in value. We have before remarked that the difficulty of passing from one class of employments to a class greatly superior, has hitherto caused the wages of all those classes of labourers who are separated from one another by any very marked barrier, to depend more than might be supposed upon the increase of the population of each class considered separately; and that the inequalities in the remuneration of labour *ᶜ* are much greater than could exist if the competition of the labouring people generally could be brought practically to bear on each particular employment. It follows from this that wages in different employments do not rise or fall simultaneously, but are, for short and sometimes even for long periods, nearly independent of one another. All such disparities evidently alter the *relative* costs of production of different commodities, and will therefore be completely represented in their natural or average value.

It thus appears that the maxim laid down by some of the best political economists, that wages do not enter into value, is expressed with greater latitude than the truth warrants, or than accords with their own meaning.

ᵃMS, 48, 49, 52, 57   in
ᵇ⁻ᵇMS, 48, 49, 52, 57, 62   or
ᶜMS, 48, 49   which cannot be accounted for by differences of hardness or disagreeableness,

Wages do enter into value. The relative *wages* of the labour necessary for producing different commodities, *ᵈaffectᵈ* their value just as much as the relative *quantities* of labour. It is true, the absolute wages paid have no effect upon values; but neither has the absolute quantity of labour. If that were to vary simultaneously and equally in all commodities, values would not be affected. If, for instance, the general efficiency of all labour were increased, so that all things without exception could be produced in the same quantity as before with a smaller amount of labour, no trace of this general diminution of cost of production would show itself in the values of commodities*ᵉ*. Any*ᵉ* change which might take place in them would only represent the unequal degrees in which the improvement affected different things; and would consist in cheapening those in which the saving of labour had been the greatest, while those in which there had been some, but a less saving of labour, would actually rise in value. In strictness, therefore, wages of labour have as much to do with value as quantity of labour: and neither Ricardo nor any one else has denied the fact. In considering, however, the causes of *variations* in value, quantity of labour is the thing of chief importance; for when that varies, it is generally in one or a few commodities at a time, but the variations of wages (except passing fluctuations) are usually general, and have no considerable effect on *ᶠvalueᶠ*.

§ 4. [*Profits an element in Cost of Production, in so far as they vary from employment to employment*] Thus far of labour, or wages, as an element in cost of production. But in our analysis, in the First Book, of the requisites of production, we found that there is another necessary element in it besides labour. There is also capital; and this being the result of abstinence, the produce, or its value, must be sufficient to remunerate, not only all the labour required, but the abstinence of all the persons by whom the remuneration of the different classes of labourers was advanced. The return for abstinence is Profit. And profit, we have also seen, is not exclusively the surplus remaining to the capitalist after he has been compensated for his outlay, but forms, in most cases, no unimportant part of the outlay itself. The flax-spinner, part of whose expenses consists of the purchase of flax and of machinery, has had to pay, in their price, not only the wages of the labour by which the flax was grown and the machinery made, but the profits of the grower, the flax-dresser, the miner, the iron-founder, and the machine-maker. All these profits, together with those of the spinner himself, were again advanced by the weaver, in the price of his material, linen yarn: and along with them the profits of a fresh set of

ᵈ⁻ᵈMS   affects
ᵉ⁻ᵉMS   : any
ᶠ⁻ᶠMS   values

machine-makers, and ^{a}of^a the miners and iron-workers who supplied them with their metallic material. All these advances form part of the cost of production of linen. Profits, therefore, as well as wages, enter into the cost of production which determines the value of the produce.

Value, however, being purely relative, cannot depend upon absolute profits, no more than upon absolute wages, but upon relative profits only. High general profits cannot, any more than high general wages, be a cause of high values, because high general values are an absurdity and a contradiction. In so far as profits enter into the cost of production of all things, they cannot affect the value of any. It is only by entering in a greater degree into the cost of production of some things than of others, that they can have any influence on value.

For example, we have seen that there are causes which necessitate a permanently higher rate of profit in certain employments than in others. There must be a compensation for superior risk, trouble, and disagreeableness. This can only be obtained by selling the commodity at a value above that which is due to the quantity of labour necessary for its production. If gunpowder exchanged for other things in no higher ratio than that of the labour required from first to last for producing it, no one would set up a powder-mill. Butchers are certainly a more prosperous class than bakers, and do not seem to be exposed to greater risks, since it is not remarked that they are oftener bankrupts. They seem, therefore, to obtain higher profits, which can only arise from the more limited competition caused by the unpleasantness, and to a certain degree, the unpopularity, of their trade. But this higher profit implies that they sell ^{b}their commodity^b at a higher value than that due to their labour and outlay. All inequalities of profit which are necessary and permanent, are represented in the relative values of the commodities.

§ 5. [*Profits an element in Cost of Production, in so far as they are spread over unequal lengths of time*] Profits, however, may enter more largely into the conditions of production of one commodity than of another, even though there be no difference in the *rate* of profit between the two employments. The one commodity may be called upon to yield profit during a longer period of time than the other. The example by which this case is usually illustrated is that of wine. Suppose a quantity of wine, and a quantity of cloth, made by equal amounts of labour, and that labour paid at the same rate. The cloth does not improve by keeping; the wine does. Suppose that, to attain the desired quality, the wine requires to be kept five years. The producer or dealer will not keep it, unless at the end of five years he

$^{a-a}$+48, 49, 52, 57, 62, 65, 71
$^{b-b}$MS   meat

can sell it for as much more than the cloth, as amounts to five years' profit, accumulated at compound interest. The wine and the cloth were made by the same original outlay. Here then is a case in which the natural values, relatively to one another, of two commodities, do not conform to their cost of production alone, but to their cost of production *plus* something else. Unless, indeed, for the sake of generality in the expression, we include the profit which the wine-merchant foregoes during the five years, in the cost of production of the wine: looking upon it as a kind of additional outlay, over and above his other advances, for which outlay he must be indemnified at last.

All commodities made by machinery are assimilated, at least approximately, to the wine in the preceding example. *^aIn comparison^a* with things made wholly by immediate labour, profits enter more largely into their cost of production. Suppose two commodities, A and B, each requiring a year for its production, by means of a capital which we will on this occasion denote by money, and suppose to be 1000*l.* A is made wholly by immediate labour, the whole 1000*l.* being expended directly in wages. B is made by means of labour which ^bcosts^b 500*l.* and a machine which cost 500*l.*, and the machine is worn out by one year's use. The two commodities will be exactly of the same value; which, if computed in money, and if profits are 20 per cent per annum, will be 1200*l.* But of this 1200*l.*, in the case of A, only 200*l.*, or one-sixth, is profit: while in the case of B there is not only the 200*l.*, but as much of 500*l.* (the price of the machine) as consisted of the profits of the machine-maker; which, if we suppose the machine also to have taken a year for its production, is again one-sixth. So that in the case of A only one-sixth of the entire return is profit, whilst in B the element of profit comprises not only a sixth of the whole, but an additional sixth of a large part.

The greater the proportion of the whole capital which consists of machinery, or buildings, or material, or anything else which must be provided before the immediate labour can commence, the more largely will profits enter into the cost of production. It is equally true, though not so obvious at first sight, that greater durability in the portion of capital which consists of machinery or buildings, has precisely the same effect as a greater amount of it. As we just supposed one extreme case, ^c of a machine entirely worn out by a year's use, let us now suppose the opposite and still more extreme case of a machine which lasts for ever, and requires no repairs. In this case, which is as well suited for ^dthe purpose^d of illustration as if it were a possible one, it will be unnecessary that the manufacturer should ever be repaid the 500*l.* which he gave for the machine, since he has always the machine itself, worth 500*l*.; but he must be paid, as before, a profit on it. The commodity B, therefore, which in the case previously supposed was sold for 1200*l*. of which *ᵉ*sum*ᵉ* 1000*l*. were to replace the capital and 200*l*. were profit, can now be sold for 700*l*., being 500*l*. to replace wages, and 200*l*. profit on the entire capital. Profit, therefore, enters into the value of B in the ratio of 200*l*. out of 700*l*., being two-sevenths of the whole, or 28⁴⁄₇ per cent, while in the case of A, as before, it enters only in the ratio of one-sixth, or 16⅔ per cent. The case is of course purely ideal, since no machinery or other fixed capital lasts for ever; but the more durable it is, the nearer it approaches to this ideal case, and the more largely does profit enter into the return. If, for instance, a machine worth 500*l*. loses one-fifth of its value by each year's use, 100*l*. must be added to the return to make up this loss, and the price of the commodity will be 800*l*. Profit therefore will enter into it in the ratio of 200*l*. to 800*l*., or one-fourth, which is still a much higher proportion than one-sixth, or 200*l*. in 1200*l*., as in case A.

From the unequal proportion in which, in different employments, profits enter into the advances of the capitalist, and therefore into the returns required by him, two consequences follow in regard to value. One is, that commodities do not exchange in the ratio simply of the quantities of labour required to produce them; not even if we allow for the unequal rates at which *ᶠ* different kinds of labour are permanently remunerated. We have already illustrated this *ᵍ* by the example of wine: we shall now further exemplify it by the case of commodities made by machinery. Suppose, as before, an article A made by a thousand pounds' worth of immediate labour. But instead of B, made by 500*l*. worth of immediate labour and a machine worth 500*l*., let us suppose C, made by 500*l*. worth of immediate labour with the aid of a machine which has been produced by another 500*l*. worth of immediate labour: the machine requiring a year for making, and worn out by a year's use; profits being as before 20 per cent. A and C are made by equal quantities of labour, paid at the same rate: A costs 1000*l*. worth of direct labour; C, only 500*l*. worth, which however is made up to 1000*l*. by the labour expended in the construction of the machine. If labour, or its remuneration, were the sole ingredient of cost of production, these two things would exchange for one another. But will they do so? Certainly not. The machine having been made in a year by an outlay of 500*l*., and profits being 20 per cent, the natural price of the machine is 600*l*.: making an additional 100*l*. which must be advanced, over and above his other expenses, by the manufacturer of C, and repaid to him with a profit of 20 per cent. While, therefore, the commodity A is sold for 1200*l*., C cannot be permanently sold for less than 1320*l*.

ᵉ⁻ᵉ+48, 49, 52, 57, 62, 65, 71
*ᶠ*MS some   *ᵍ*MS truth

A second consequence is, that every rise or fall of general profits will have an effect on values. Not indeed by raising or lowering them generally, (which, as we have so often said, is a contradiction and an impossibility): but by altering the proportion in which the values of things are affected by the unequal lengths of time for which profit is due. When two things, though made by equal labour, are of unequal value because the one is called upon to yield profit for a greater number of years or months than the other; this difference of value will be greater when profits are greater, and less when they are less. The wine which has to yield five years' profit more than the cloth, will surpass it in value much more if profits are 40 per cent, than if they are only 20. The commodities A and C, which, though made by equal quantities of labour, were sold for 1200*l.* and 1320*l.*, a difference of 10 per cent, would, if profits had been only half as much, have been sold for 1100*l.* and 1155*l.*, a difference of only 5 per cent.

It follows from this, that even a general rise of wages, when it involves a real increase in the cost of labour, does in some degree influence values. It does not affect them in the manner vulgarly supposed, by raising them universally. But an increase *h*in*h* the cost of labour, lowers profits; and therefore lowers in natural value the things into which profits enter in a greater proportion than the average, and raises those into which they enter in a less proportion than the average. All commodities in the production of which machinery bears a large part, especially if the machinery is very durable, are lowered in their relative value when profits fall; or, what is equivalent, other things are raised in value relatively to them. This truth is sometimes expressed in a phraseology more plausible than sound, by saying that a rise of wages raises the *i*value*i* of things made by labour, in comparison with those made by machinery. But things made by machinery, just as much as any other things, are made by labour, namely, the labour which made the machinery itself: the only difference being that profits enter somewhat more largely into the production of things for which machinery is used, though the principal item of the outlay is still labour. It is better, therefore, to associate the effect with fall of profits than with rise of wages; especially as this last expression is extremely ambiguous, suggesting the idea of an increase of the labourer's real remuneration, rather than of what is alone to the purpose here, namely, the cost of labour to its employer.

§ 6. [*Occasional elements in Cost of Production: taxes, and scarcity value of materials*] Besides the natural and necessary elements in cost of production—labour and profits—there are others which are artificial and

*h–h*MS, 48, 49, 52, 57   of
*i–i*MS, 48, 49, 52   values

casual, as for instance a tax. The ªtax on malt isª as much a part of the cost of production of ᵇthat articleᵇ as the wages of the labourers. The expenses which the law imposes, as well as those which the nature of things imposes, must be reimbursed with the ordinary profit from the value of the produce, or the things will not continue to be produced. But the influence of taxation on ᶜvalueᶜ is subject to the same conditions as the influence of wages and of profits. It is not general taxation, but differential taxation, that produces the effect. If all productions were taxed ᵈso as to take an equal percentage from all profitsᵈ, relative values would be in no way disturbed. If only a few commodities were taxed, their value would rise: and if only a few were left untaxed, their value would fall. If half were taxed and the remainder untaxed, the first half would rise and the last would fall relatively to each other. This would be necessary ᵉin orderᵉ to equalize the expectation of profit in all employments, without which the taxed employments would ultimately, if not immediately, be abandoned. But general taxation, when equally imposed, and not disturbing the ᶠrelationsᶠ of different productions to one another, cannot produce any effect on values.

We have thus far supposed that all the means and appliances which enter into the cost of production of commodities, are things whose own value depends on their cost of production. Some of them, however, may belong to the class of things which cannot be increased *ad libitum* in quantity, and which therefore, if the demand goes beyond a certain amount, command a scarcity value. The materials of many of the ornamental articles manufactured in Italy are the substances called rosso, giallo, and verde antico, which, whether truly or falsely I know not, are asserted to be solely derived from the destruction of ancient columns and other ornamental structures; the quarries from which the stone was originally cut being exhausted, or their locality forgotten.* A material of such a nature, if in much demand, must be at a scarcity value; and this value enters into the cost of production, and consequently into the value, of the finished article. The time seems to be approaching when the more valuable furs will come under the influence of a scarcity value of the material. Hitherto the diminishing number of the animals which produce them, in the wildernesses of Siberia, and on the coasts of the Esquimaux Sea, has operated on the value only through the greater labour which has become necessary for securing any given quantity of the article, since, without doubt, by employ-

*[62] Some of these quarries, I believe, have been rediscovered, and are again worked.

ª⁻ªMS, 48, 49 taxes on bricks and malt are] 52, 57 taxes on paper and malt are] 62 taxes on hops and malt are
ᵇ⁻ᵇMS, 48, 49, 52, 57, 62 those articles
ᶜ⁻ᶜMS values   ᵈ⁻ᵈMS, 48 by a fixed percentage on their value
ᵉ⁻ᵉ+48, 49, 52, 57, 62, 65, 71   ᶠ⁻ᶠMS, 48, 49, 52, 57 relation

ing labour enough, it might still be obtained in much greater abundance for some time longer.

But the case in which scarcity value chiefly operates in adding to cost of production, is the case of natural agents. These, when unappropriated, and to be had for the taking, do not enter into cost of production, save to the extent of the labour which may be necessary to fit them for use. Even when appropriated, they do not (as we have already seen) bear a value from the mere fact of the appropriation, but only from scarcity, that is, from limitation of supply. But it is equally certain that they often do bear a scarcity value. Suppose a fall of water, in a place where there are more mills wanted than there is water-power to supply *them*, the use of the fall of water will have a scarcity value, sufficient either to bring the demand down to the supply, or to pay for the creation of an artificial power, by steam or otherwise, equal in efficiency to the water-power.

A natural agent being a possession in perpetuity, and being only serviceable by the products resulting from its continued employment, the ordinary mode of deriving benefit from its ownership is by an annual equivalent, paid by the person who uses it, from the proceeds of its use. This equivalent always might be, and generally is, termed rent. The question, therefore, respecting the influence which the appropriation of natural agents produces on values, is often stated in this form: Does Rent enter into Cost of Production? and the answer of the best political economists is in the negative. The temptation is strong to the adoption of these sweeping expressions, even by those who are aware of the restrictions with which they must be taken; for there is no denying that they stamp a *general* principle more firmly *on* the mind, than if it were hedged round in theory with all its practical limitations. But they also puzzle and mislead, and create an impression unfavourable to political economy, as if it disregarded the evidence of facts. *No one* can deny that rent sometimes enters into cost of *production.* If I buy or rent a piece of ground, and build a cloth manufactory on it, *the ground-rent forms* legitimately a part of my expenses of production, which must be repaid by the *product.* And since all factories are built on ground, and most of them in places where ground is peculiarly valuable, the rent paid for it must, on the average, be compensated in the values of all things made in factories. In what sense it is true that rent does not enter into the cost of production or affect the value of agricultural produce, will be shown in the succeeding chapter.

ᵍ-ᵍ+MS, 65, 71
*ʰ-ʰ*MS great
*ʲ-ʲ*MS, 48, 49 Who
*ˡ-ˡ*MS, 48, 49 does not the ground-rent form

*ⁱ-ⁱ*MS, 48, 49, 52, 57 in
*ᵏ-ᵏ*MS, 48, 49 production?
*ᵐ-ᵐ*MS, 48, 49 product?

CHAPTER V

Of Rent, in Its Relation to Value

§ 1. [*Commodities which are susceptible of indefinite multiplication, but not without increase of cost. Law of their Value is Cost of Production in the most unfavourable existing circumstances*] We have investigated the laws which determine the value of two classes of commodities: the small class which, being limited to a definite quantity, have their value entirely determined by demand and supply, save that their cost of production (if they have any) constitutes a minimum below which they cannot permanently fall; and the large class, which can be multiplied *ad libitum* by labour and capital, and of which the cost of production fixes the maximum as well as the minimum at which they can permanently exchange. But there is still a third kind of commodities *ªto be considered:ª* those which have, not one, but several costs of production: which can always be increased in quantity by labour and capital, but not by the same amount of labour and capital; of which so much may be produced at a given cost, but a further quantity not without a greater cost. These commodities form an intermediate class, partaking of the character of both the others. The principal of them is agricultural produce. We have already made abundant reference to the fundamental truth, that in agriculture, the state of the art being given, doubling the labour does not double the produce; that if an increased quantity of produce is required, the additional supply is obtained at a greater cost than the first. Where a hundred quarters of corn are all that is at present required from the lands of a given village, if the growth of population made it necessary to raise a hundred more, either by breaking up worse land now uncultivated, or by a more elaborate cultivation of the land already under the plough, the additional hundred, or some part of them at least, might cost double or treble as much per quarter as the former supply.

If the first hundred quarters were all raised at the same expense (only the best land being cultivated); and *ᵇifᵇ* that expense would be remunerated

ª⁻ªMS   , which we have not yet particularly considered; being
ᵇ⁻ᵇ+48, 49, 52, 57, 62, 65, 71

with the ordinary profit by a price of 20s. the quarter; the natural price of wheat, so long as no more than that quantity was required, would be 20s.; and it could only rise above, or fall below that price, from vicissitudes of seasons, or other casual variations in supply. But if the population of the district advanced, a time would arrive when more than a hundred quarters would be necessary to feed it. We must suppose that there is no access to any foreign supply. By the hypothesis, no more than a hundred quarters can be produced in the district, unless by either bringing worse land into cultivation, or altering the system of culture to a more expensive one. Neither of these things will be done without a rise ^cin^c price. ^dThis^d rise of price will gradually be brought about by the increasing demand. So long as the price has risen, but not risen enough to repay with the ordinary profit the cost of producing an additional quantity, the increased value of the limited supply partakes of the nature of a scarcity value. Suppose that it will not answer to cultivate the second best land, or land of the second degree of remoteness, for a less return than 25s. the quarter; and that this price is also necessary to remunerate the expensive operations by which an increased produce might be raised from land of the first quality. If so, the price will rise, through the increased demand, until it reaches 25s. That will now be the natural price; being the price without which the quantity, for which society has a demand at that price, will not be produced. At that price, however, society can go on for some time longer; could go on perhaps for ever, if population did not increase. The price, having attained that point, will not again permanently recede (though it may fall temporarily from accidental abundance); nor will it advance further, so long as society can obtain the supply it requires without a second increase of the cost of production.

I have made use of Price in this reasoning, as a convenient symbol of Value, from the greater familiarity of the idea; and I shall continue to do so as far ^eas may appear^e to be necessary.

In the case supposed, different portions of the supply of corn have different costs of production. Though the 20, or 50, or 150 quarters additional have been produced at a cost proportional to 25s., the original hundred quarters per annum are still produced at a cost only proportional to 20s. This is self-evident, if the original and the additional supply are produced on different qualities of land. It is equally true if they are produced on the same land. Suppose that land of the best quality, which produced 100 quarters at 20s., has been made to produce 150 by an expensive process, which it would not answer to undertake without a price of 25s. The cost which requires 25s. is incurred for the sake of 50 quarters alone: the first hundred might have continued for ever to be produced at

^{c–c}MS, 48   of   ^{d–d}MS The   ^{e–e}MS   , as I may find

the original cost, and with the benefit, on that quantity, of the whole rise of price caused by the ʲincreasedʲ demand: no one, therefore, will incur the additional expense for the sake of the additional fifty, unless they alone will pay for the whole of it. The fifty, therefore, will be produced at their natural price, proportioned to the cost of their production; while the other hundred will now bring in 5s. a quarter more than their natural price—than the price corresponding to, and sufficing to remunerate, their lower cost of production.

If the production of any, even the smallest, portion of the supply, requires as a necessary condition a certain price, that price will be obtained for all the rest. We are not able to buy one loaf cheaper than another because the corn from which it was made, being grown on a richer soil, has cost less to the grower. The value, therefore, of an article (meaning its natural, which is the same with its average value) is determined by the cost of that portion of the supply which is produced and brought to market at the greatest expense. This is the Law of Value of the third of the three classes into which all commodities are divided.

§ 2. [*Such commodities, when produced in circumstances more favourable, yield a rent equal to the difference of cost*] If the portion of produce raised in the most unfavourable circumstances, obtains a value proportioned to its cost of production; all the portions raised in more favourable circumstances, selling as they must do at the same value, obtain a value more than proportioned to their cost of production. Their value is not, correctly speaking, a scarcity value, for it is determined by the circumstances of the production of the commodity, and not by the degree of dearness necessary for keeping down the demand to the level of a limited supply. The owners, however, of those portions of the produce enjoy a privilege; they obtain a value which yields them more than the ordinary profit. If this advantage depends upon any special exemption, such as being free from a tax, or upon any personal advantages, physical or mental, or any peculiar process only known to themselves, or upon the possession of a greater capital than other people, or upon various other things which might be enumerated, they retain it to themselves as an extra gain, over and above the general profits of capital, of the nature, in some sort, of a monopoly profit. But when, as in the case which we are more particularly considering, the advantage depends on the possession of a natural agent of peculiar quality, as for instance of more fertile land than that which determines the general value of the commodity; and when this natural agent is not owned by themselves; the person who does own it, is able to exact from them, in the form of rent, the whole extra gain derived from its use. We are thus brought by another

ʲ-ʲMS, 48   increase of

road to the Law of Rent, investigated in the concluding chapter of the Second Book. Rent, we again see, is the difference between the unequal returns to different parts of the capital employed on the soil. Whatever surplus any portion of agricultural capital produces, beyond what is produced by the same amount of capital on the worst soil, or under the most expensive mode of cultivation, which the existing demands of society compel a recourse to; that surplus will naturally be paid as rent from that capital, to the owner of the land on which it is employed.

It was long thought by political economists, among the rest even by Adam Smith, that the produce of land is always at a monopoly value, because (they said) in addition to the ordinary rate of profit, it always yields something *further* for rent. This we now see to be erroneous. A thing cannot be at a monopoly value, *when its supply* can be increased to an indefinite extent if we are only willing to incur the cost. If no more corn than the existing quantity is grown, it is because the value has not risen high enough to remunerate any one for growing it. Any land *(not reserved for other uses, or for pleasure)* which at the existing price, and by the existing processes, will yield the ordinary profit, is tolerably certain, unless some artificial hindrance intervenes, to be cultivated, although nothing may be left for rent. As long as there is any land fit for cultivation, which at the existing price cannot be profitably cultivated at all, there must be some land a little better, which will yield the ordinary profit, but allow nothing for rent: and that land, if within the boundary of a farm, will be cultivated by the farmer; if not so, probably by the proprietor, or by some other person on sufferance. Some such land at least, under cultivation, there can scarcely fail to be.

Rent, therefore, forms no part of the cost of production which determines the value of agricultural produce. Circumstances no doubt may be conceived in which it might do so, and very largely too. We can imagine a country so fully peopled, and with all its cultivable soil so completely occupied, that to produce any additional quantity would require more labour than the produce would feed: and if we suppose this to be the condition of the whole world, or of a country debarred from foreign supply, then, if population continued increasing, both the land and its produce would really rise to a monopoly or scarcity price. But this state of things never can have really existed anywhere, unless possibly in some small island cut off from the rest of the world; nor is there any danger whatever that it should exist. It certainly exists in no known region at present. Monopoly, we have seen, can take effect on value, only through limitation of supply. In all countries of any extent there is more cultivable land than is yet cultivated; and while there is any such surplus, it is the same thing, so far as that quality of land is concerned, as if there were an infinite quantity. What is practically limited in supply is only the better qualities; and even for those, so much rent cannot be demanded as would bring in the competition of the lands not yet in cultivation; the rent of a piece of land must be somewhat less than the whole excess of its productiveness over that of the best land which it is not yet profitable to cultivate; that is, it must be about equal to the excess above the worst land which it ^{d}is^d profitable to cultivate. The land or the capital most unfavourably circumstanced among those actually employed, pays no rent; and that land or capital determines the cost of production which regulates the value of the whole produce. ^{e}Thus^e rent is, as we have already seen, no cause of value, but the price of the privilege which the inequality of the returns to different portions of agricultural produce confers on all except the least favoured ^{f}portions^f.

Rent, in short, merely equalizes the profits of different farming capitals, by enabling the landlord to appropriate all extra gains occasioned by superiority of natural advantages. If all landlords were unanimously to forego their rent, they would but transfer it to the farmers, without benefiting the consumer; for the existing price of corn would still be an indispensable condition of the production of part of the existing supply, and ^{g}if a part obtained that price the whole would obtain^g it. Rent, therefore, unless artificially increased by restrictive laws, is no burthen on the consumer: it does not raise the price of corn, and is no otherwise a detriment to the public, than inasmuch as if the state had retained it, or imposed an equivalent in the shape of a land-tax, it would then have been a fund applicable to general instead of private advantage.

§ 3. [*Rent of mines and fisheries, and ground-rent of buildings*] Agricultural productions are not the only commodities which have several different costs of production at once, and which, in consequence of that difference, and in proportion to it, afford a rent. Mines are also an instance. Almost all kinds of raw material extracted from the interior of the earth— ^{a}metal^a, coals, precious stones, &c., are obtained from mines differing considerably in fertility, that is, yielding very different quantities of the product to the same quantity of labour and capital. This being the case, it is an obvious question, why ^{b}are not the most fertile mines^b so worked as to supply the whole ^{c}market?^{c} No such question can arise as to land;

$^{d-d}$MS, 48, 49, 52, 57 *is*
$^{e-e}$MS And
$^{f-f}$MS, 48, 49, 52, 57, 62 portion
$^{g-g}$MS, 48, 49, 52, 57 a part could not obtain that price unless the whole obtained
$^{a-a}$MS, 48, 49, 52, 57, 62 metals
$^{b-b}$MS the most fertile mines are not $^{c-c}$MS market.

it being self-evident, that the most fertile lands could not possibly be made to supply the whole demand of a fully-peopled country; and even of what they do yield, a part is extorted from them by a labour and outlay as great as that required to grow the same amount on worse land. But it is not so with mines; at least, not universally. There are, perhaps, cases in which it is impossible to extract from a particular vein, in a given time, more than a certain quantity of ore, because there is only a limited surface of the vein exposed, on which more than a certain number of labourers cannot be simultaneously employed. But this is not true of all mines. In collieries, for example, some other cause of limitation must be sought for. In some instances the owners limit the quantity raised, in order not too rapidly to exhaust the mine: in others there are said to be combinations of owners, to keep up a monopoly price by limiting the production. Whatever be the causes, it is a fact that ^dmines of different degrees of richness are in opera-tion^d, and since the value of the produce must be proportional to the cost of production at the worst mine (fertility and situation taken together), it is more than proportional to that of the best. All mines superior in produce to the worst actually worked, will yield, therefore, a rent equal to the excess. They may yield more; and the worst mine may itself yield a rent. Mines being comparatively few, their qualities do not graduate gently into one another, as the qualities of land do; and the demand may be such as to keep the value of the produce considerably above the cost of produc-tion at the worst mine now worked, without being sufficient to bring into operation a still worse. During the interval, the produce is really at a scarcity value.

Fisheries are another example. Fisheries in the open sea are not appro-priated, but fisheries in lakes or rivers almost always are so, and likewise oyster-beds or other particular fishing grounds on coasts. We may take salmon fisheries as an example of the whole class. Some rivers are far more productive in salmon than others. None, however, without being exhausted, can supply more than a very limited demand. The demand of a country like England can only be supplied by taking salmon from many different rivers of unequal productiveness, and the value must be sufficient to repay the cost of obtaining the fish from the least productive of these. All others, therefore, will if appropriated afford a rent equal to the value of their superiority. Much higher than this it cannot be, if there are salmon rivers accessible which from distance or inferior produc-tiveness have not yet contributed to supply the market. If there are not, the value, doubtless, may rise to a scarcity rate, and the worst fisheries in use may then yield a considerable rent.

Both in the case of mines and of fisheries, the natural order of events is

^{d-d}MS   the mines in operation are of different degrees of richness

liable to be interrupted by the opening of a new mine, or a new fishery, of superior quality to some of those already in use. The first effect of such an incident is an increase of the supply; which of course lowers the value to call forth an increased demand. This reduced value may be no longer sufficient to remunerate the worst of the existing mines or fisheries, and these may consequently be abandoned. If the superior mines or fisheries, with the addition of the one newly opened, produce as much of the commodity as is required *e* at the lower value corresponding to their lower cost of production, the fall of value will be permanent, and there will be a corresponding fall in the rents of those mines or fisheries which are not abandoned. In this case, when things have permanently adjusted themselves, the result will be, that the scale of qualities which supply the market will have been cut short at the lower end, while a new insertion will have been made in the scale at some point higher up; and the worst mine or fishery in use—the one which regulates the rents of the superior qualities and the value of the commodity—will be a mine or fishery of better quality than that by which they were previously regulated.

Land is used for other purposes than agriculture, especially for residence; and when so used, yields a rent, determined by principles similar to those already laid down. The ground rent of a building, and the rent of a garden or park attached to it, *f*will not*f* be less than the rent which the same land would afford in agriculture: but *g* may be greater than this to an indefinite amount; the surplus being either in consideration of beauty or of convenience, the convenience often consisting in superior facilities for pecuniary gain. Sites of remarkable beauty are generally limited in supply, and therefore, if in great demand, are at a scarcity *h* value. Sites superior only in convenience are governed as to their value by the ordinary principles of rent. The ground rent of a house in a small village is but little higher than the rent of a similar patch of ground in the open fields: but that of a shop in Cheapside will exceed these, by the whole amount at which people estimate the superior facilities of money-making in the more crowded place. The rents of wharfage, dock and harbour room, water-power, and many other privileges, may be analysed on similar principles.

§ 4. [*Cases of extra profit analogous to rent*] Cases of extra profit analogous to rent, are more frequent in the transactions of industry than is sometimes supposed. Take the case, for example, of a patent, or exclusive privilege for the use of a process by which cost of production is lessened. If the value of the product continues to be regulated by what it costs to those who are obliged to persist in the old process, the patentee will make an

*e*MS even
*g*MS, 48, 49, 52, 57 it

*f-f*MS cannot
*h*MS , or as it is sometimes termed a *fancy*,

extra profit equal to the advantage which his process possesses over theirs. This extra profit is essentially similar to rent, and sometimes even assumes the form of it; the patentee allowing to other producers the use of his privilege, in consideration of an annual payment. So long as he, and those whom he associates in the privilege, do not produce enough to supply the whole market, so long the original cost of production, being the necessary condition of producing a part, will regulate the value of the whole; and the patentee will be enabled to keep up his rent to a full equivalent for the advantage which his process gives him. In the commencement indeed he will probably forego a part of this advantage for the sake of underselling others: the increased supply which he brings forward will lower the value, and make the trade a bad one for those who do not share in the privilege: many of whom therefore will gradually retire, or restrict their operations, or enter into arrangements with the patentee: as his supply increases theirs will diminish, the value meanwhile continuing slightly depressed. But if he stops short in his operations before the market is wholly supplied by the new process, things will again adjust themselves to what was the natural value before the invention was made, and the benefit of the improvement will accrue solely to the patentee.

The extra gains which any producer or dealer obtains through superior talents for business, or superior business arrangements, are very much of a similar kind. If all his competitors had the same advantages, and used them, the benefit would be transferred to their customers, through the diminished value of the article: he only retains it for himself because he is able to bring his commodity to market at a lower cost, while its value is determined by a higher. All advantages, in fact, which one competitor has over another, whether natural or acquired, whether personal or the result of social arrangements, bring the commodity, so far, into ^athe^a Third Class, and assimilate the possessor of the advantage to a receiver of rent. Wages and profits represent the universal elements in production, while rent may be taken to represent the differential and peculiar: any difference in favour of certain producers, or ^bin favour of production in^b certain circumstances, being the source of a gain, which, though not called rent unless paid periodically by one person to another, is governed by laws entirely the same with it. The price paid for a differential advantage in producing a commodity, cannot enter into the general cost of production of the commodity.

A commodity may no doubt, in some contingencies, yield a rent even under the most disadvantageous circumstances of its production: but only when it is, for the time, in the condition of those commodities which are absolutely limited in supply, and is therefore selling at a scarcity value;

which never is, nor has been, nor can be, a permanent condition of any of the great rent-yielding commodities: unless through their approaching exhaustion, if they are mineral products (coal for example), or through an increase of population, continuing after a further increase of production becomes impossible: ^{c}a contingency,^{c} which the almost inevitable progress of human culture and improvement in the long interval which has first to elapse, forbids us to consider as probable.

$^{c-c}$+48, 49, 52, 57, 62, 65, 71

CHAPTER VI

Summary of the Theory
of Value

§ 1. [*The theory of Value recapitulated in a series of propositions*] We have now attained a favourable point for looking back, and taking a simultaneous view of the space which we have traversed since the commencement of the present Book. The following are the principles of the theory of Value, so far as we have yet ascertained them.

I. Value is a relative term. The value of a thing means the quantity of some other thing, or of things in general, which it exchanges for. The values of all things can never, therefore, rise or fall simultaneously. There is no such thing as a general rise or a general fall of values. Every rise of value supposes a fall, and every fall a rise.

II. The temporary or market value of a thing, depends on the demand and supply; rising as the demand rises, and falling as the supply rises. The demand, however, varies with the value, being generally greater when the thing is cheap than when it is dear; and the value always adjusts itself in such a manner, that the demand is equal to the supply.

III. Besides their temporary value, things have also a permanent, or as it may be called, a Natural Value, to which the market value, after every variation, always tends to return; and the oscillations compensate for one another, so that, on the average, commodities exchange at about their natural value.

IV. The natural value of some things is a scarcity value; but most things naturally exchange for one another in the ratio of their cost of production, or at what may be termed their Cost Value.

V. The things which are naturally and permanently at a scarcity value, are those of which the supply cannot be increased at all, or not sufficiently to satisfy the whole of the demand which would exist for them at their cost value.

VI. A monopoly value means a scarcity value. Monopoly cannot give a value to anything except through a limitation of the supply.

VII. Every commodity of which the supply can be indefinitely increased by labour and capital, exchanges for other things proportionally to the

cost necessary for producing and bringing to market the most costly portion of the supply required. The natural value is synonymous with the
Cost Value, and the cost value of a thing, means the cost value of the most
costly portion of it.

VIII. Cost of Production consists of several elements, some of which
are constant and universal, others occasional. The universal elements of cost
of production are, the wages of the labour, and the profits of the capital.
The occasional elements are taxes, and *any* extra cost occasioned by a
scarcity value of some of the requisites.

IX. Rent is not an element in the cost of production of the commodity
which yields it; except in the cases (rather conceivable than actually existing) in which it results from, and represents, a scarcity value. But when
land capable of yielding rent in agriculture is applied to some other purpose, the rent which it would have yielded is an element in the cost of
production of the commodity which it is employed to produce.

X. Omitting the occasional elements; things which admit of indefinite
increase, naturally and permanently exchange for each other according
to the comparative amount of wages which must be paid for producing
them, and the comparative amount of profits which must be obtained by
the capitalists who pay those wages.

XI. The *comparative* amount of wages does not depend on what wages
are in themselves. High wages do not make high values, nor low wages
low values. The comparative amount of wages depends partly on the
comparative quantities of labour required, and partly on the comparative
rates of its remuneration.

XII. So, the comparative rate of profits does not depend on what
profits are in themselves; nor do high or low profits make high or low
values. It depends partly on the comparative lengths of time during which
the capital is employed, and partly on the comparative rate of profits in
different employments.

XIII. If two things are made by the same quantity of labour, and that
labour paid at the same rate, and if the wages of the *labourer* have to be
advanced for the same space of time, and the nature of the *employment*
does not require that there be a permanent difference in their rate of profit;
then, whether wages and profits be high or low, and whether the quantity
of labour expended be much or little, these two things will, on the average,
exchange for one another.

XIV. If one of two things commands, on the average, a greater value
than the other, the cause must be that it requires for its production either
a greater quantity of labour, or a kind of labour permanently paid at a
higher rate; or that the capital, or part of the capital, which supports that

*a–a*MS the   *b–b*MS labour   *c–c*MS employments

labour, must be advanced for a longer period; or lastly, that the production is attended with some circumstance which requires to be compensated by a permanently higher rate of profit.

XV. Of these elements, the quantity of labour required for the production is the most important: the effect of the others is smaller, though none of them are insignificant.

XVI. The lower profits are, the less important become the minor elements of cost of production, and the less do commodities deviate from a value proportioned to the quantity and quality of the labour required for their production.

XVII. But every fall of profits lowers, in some degree, the cost value of things made with much or durable machinery, and raises that of things made by hand; and every rise of profits does the reverse.

§ 2. [*How the theory of Value is modified by the case of labourers cultivating for subsistence*] Such is the general theory of Exchange Value. It is necessary, however, to remark that this theory contemplates a system of production carried on by capitalists for profit, and not by labourers for subsistence. In proportion as we *admit* this last supposition—and in most countries we must admit it, at least in respect of agricultural produce, to a very *great* extent—such of the preceding theorems as relate to the dependence of value on cost of production will require modification. Those theorems are all grounded on the supposition, that the producer's object and aim is to derive a profit from his capital. This granted, it follows that he must sell his commodity at the price which will afford the ordinary rate of profit, that is to say, it must exchange for other commodities at its cost value. But the peasant proprietor, the metayer, and even the peasant-farmer or allotment-holder—the labourer, under whatever name, producing on his own account—is seeking, not an investment for his little capital, but an advantageous employment for his time and labour. His disbursements, beyond his own maintenance and that of his family, are so small, that nearly the whole proceeds of the sale of *the produce are* wages of *d* labour. When he and his family have been fed from the produce of *the* farm (and perhaps clothed with materials grown thereon, and manufactured in the family) he may, in respect of the supplementary remuneration derived from the sale of *the* surplus produce, be compared to those labourers who, deriving their subsistence from an independent source, can afford to sell their labour at any price which is to their minds worth the exertion. A

*a–a*MS let in
*b–b*MS large
*c–c*MS, 48, 49 his produce are the
*d*MS his
*e–e*MS, 48, 49 his   *f–f*MS, 48, 49 his

peasant, who supports himself and his family with one portion of his produce, will often sell the remainder very much below what would be its
cost value to *the* capitalist.

There is, however, even in this case, a minimum, or inferior limit, of
value. The *h* produce which he carries to market, must bring in to him
the value of all necessaries which he is compelled to purchase; and it must
enable him to pay his rent. Rent, under peasant cultivation, is not governed
by the principles set forth in the chapters immediately preceding, but is
either determined by custom, as in the case of metayers, or, if fixed by
competition, depends on the ratio of population to land. Rent, therefore,
in this case, is an element of cost of production. The peasant must work
until he has cleared his rent and the price of all purchased necessaries.
After this, he will go on working only if he can sell the produce for such
a price as will overcome his aversion to labour.

The minimum just mentioned is what the peasant must obtain in exchange for the whole of his surplus produce. But inasmuch as this surplus
is not a fixed quantity, but may be either greater or less according to the
degree of his industry, a minimum value for the whole of it does not
give any minimum value for a definite quantity of the commodity. In this
state of things, therefore, it can hardly be said, that the value depends at
all on cost of production. It depends entirely on demand and supply, that is,
on the proportion between the quantity of surplus food which the peasants
choose to produce, and the numbers of the non-agricultural, or rather of
the non-peasant population. If the buying class *were* numerous and the
growing class lazy, food *might* be permanently at a scarcity price. I am
not aware that this case has anywhere a real existence. If the growing class
is energetic and industrious, and the buyers few, food will be extremely
cheap. This also is a rare case, though some parts of France perhaps
approximate to it. The common cases are, either that, as in Ireland *until
lately*, the peasant class is indolent and the buyers few, or the peasants
industrious and the town population numerous and opulent, as in Belgium,
the north of Italy, and parts of Germany. The price of the produce will
adjust itself to these varieties of *circumstances*, unless modified, as in
many cases it is, by the competition of producers who are not peasants,
or by the prices of foreign markets.

§ 3. [*How the theory of Value is modified by the case of slave labour*]
Another anomalous case is that of slave-grown produce: which presents,
however, by no means the same degree of complication. The slave-owner

*ᵍ–ᵍ*MS, 48, 49, 52, 57 a   *ʰ*MS, 48, 49 part of his
*ⁱ–ⁱ*MS, 48 is   *ʲ–ʲ*MS, 48 may
ᵏ–ᵏ+62, 65, 71   *ˡ–ˡ*MS circumstance

is a capitalist, and his inducement to *production* consists in a profit on his capital. This profit must amount to the ordinary rate. In respect to his expenses, he is in the same position as if his slaves were free labourers working with their present efficiency, and *were* hired with wages equal to their present cost. If the cost is less in proportion to the work done, than the wages of free labour would be, so much the greater are his profits: but if all other producers in the country possess the same advantage, the values of commodities will not be at all affected by it. The only case in which they can be affected, is when the privilege of cheap labour is confined to particular branches of production, free labourers at *proportionally* higher wages being employed in the remainder. In this *case,* as in all cases of permanent inequality between the wages of different employments, prices and values receive the impress of the inequality. Slave-grown will exchange for non-slave-grown commodities in a less ratio than that of the *quantity* of labour required for their production; the value of the former will be less, *f* of the latter greater, than if slavery did not exist.

The further adaptation of the theory of value to the varieties of existing or possible industrial systems may be left with great advantage to the intelligent reader. It is well said by Montesquieu, "Il ne faut pas toujours tellement épuiser un sujet, qu'on ne laisse rien à faire au lecteur. Il ne s'agit pas de faire lire, mais de faire penser." *

Esprit des Lois, liv. xi. *ad finem*. [Geneva: Barillot, [1748], Book XI, Chap. xx; JSM quotes from p. 294.]

*a–a*MS   produce
b–b+48, 49, 52, 57, 62, 65, 71
*c–c*48, 49   proportionably [*printer's error?*]
d–d+48, 49, 52, 57, 62, 65, 71
*e–e*MS   quantities
*f*MS, 48   and

CHAPTER VII

Of Money

§ 1. [*Purposes of a Circulating Medium*] Having proceeded thus far in ascertaining the general laws of Value, without introducing the idea of Money (except occasionally for illustration,) it is time that we should now superadd that idea, and consider in what manner the principles of the mutual interchange of commodities are affected by the use of what is termed a Medium of Exchange.

In order to understand the manifold functions of a Circulating Medium, there is no better way than to consider what are the principal inconveniences which we should experience if we had not such a medium. The first and most obvious would be the want of a common measure for values of different sorts. If a tailor had only coats, and wanted to buy bread or a horse, it would be very troublesome to ascertain how much bread he ought to obtain for a coat, or how many coats he should give for a horse. The calculation must be recommenced on different data, every time he bartered his coats for a different kind of article; and there could be no current price, or regular quotations of value. Whereas now each thing has a current price in money, and he gets over all difficulties by reckoning his coat at 4*l.* or 5*l.*, and a four-pound loaf at 6*d.* or 7*d.* As it is much easier to compare different lengths by expressing them in a common language *ᵃof*ᵃ feet and inches, so it is much easier to compare values by means of a common language *ᵇof*ᵇ pounds, shillings, and pence. In no other way can values be arranged one above another in a scale; in no other can a person conveniently calculate the sum of his possessions; and it is easier to ascertain and remember the relations of many things to one thing, than their innumerable cross relations with one another. This advantage of having a common language in which values may be expressed, is, even by itself, so important, that some such mode of expressing and computing them would probably be used even if a pound or a shilling did not express any real thing, but a mere unit of calculation. It is said that there are African tribes in which this somewhat artificial contrivance actually prevails. They calculate the value of things in a sort of money of account, called macutes.

ᵃ⁻ᵃ48, 49   called
ᵇ⁻ᵇ48, 49   called

They say, one thing is worth ten macutes, another fifteen, another twenty.* There is no real thing called a macute: it is a conventional unit, for the more convenient comparison of things with one another.

This advantage, however, forms but an inconsiderable part of the economical benefits derived from the use of money. The inconveniences of barter are so great, that without some more commodious means of effecting exchanges, the division of employments could hardly have been carried to any considerable extent. A tailor, who had nothing but coats, might starve before he could find any person having bread to sell who wanted a coat: besides, he would not want as much bread at a time as would be worth a coat, and the coat could not be divided. Every person, therefore, would at all times hasten to dispose of his commodity in exchange for anything which, though it might not be fitted to his own immediate wants, was in great and general demand, and easily divisible, so that he might be sure of being able to purchase with it whatever was offered for sale. The primary necessaries of life possess these properties in a high degree. Bread is extremely divisible, and an object of universal desire. Still, this is not the sort of thing required: for, of food, unless in expectation of a scarcity, no one wishes to possess more at once, than is wanted for immediate consumption; so that a person is never sure of finding an immediate purchaser for articles of food; and unless soon disposed of, most of them perish. The thing which people would select to keep by them for making purchases, must be one which, besides being divisible and generally desired, does not deteriorate by keeping. This reduces the choice to a small number of articles.

§ 2. [*Why Gold and Silver are fitted for the purposes of a Circulating Medium*] By a tacit concurrence, almost all nations, at a very early period, fixed upon certain metals, and especially gold and silver, to serve this purpose. No other substances unite the necessary qualities in so great a degree, with so many subordinate advantages. Next to food and clothing, and in some climates even before clothing, the strongest inclination in a rude state of society is for personal ornament, and for the kind of distinction which is obtained by rarity or costliness in such ornaments. After the immediate necessities of life were satisfied, every one was eager to accumulate as great a store as possible of things at once costly and ornamental; which were chiefly gold, silver, and jewels. These were the things which it most pleased every one to possess, and which there was most certainty of finding others willing to receive in exchange for any kind of produce. They were among the most imperishable of all substances. They were also portable, and containing great value in small bulk, were easily hid; a consideration of

*Montesquieu, *Esprit des Lois*, liv. xxii, ch. 8. [Vol. II, pp. 92–3.]

much importance in an age of insecurity. Jewels are inferior to gold and silver in the quality of divisibility; and are of very various qualities, not to be accurately discriminated without great trouble. Gold and silver are eminently divisible, and when pure, always of the same quality; and their purity may be ascertained and certified by a public authority.

Accordingly, though furs have been employed as money in some countries, cattle in others, in Chinese Tartary cubes of tea closely pressed together, the shell called cowries on the coast of Western Africa, and in Abyssinia at this day blocks of rock salt; though even of metals, the less costly have sometimes been chosen, as iron in Lacedæmon from an ascetic policy, copper in the early Roman republic from the poverty of the people; gold and silver have been ᵃgenerallyᵃ preferred by nations which were able to obtain them, either by industry, commerce, or conquest. To the qualities which originally recommended them, another came to be added, the importance of which only unfolded itself by degrees. Of all commodities, they are among the least influenced by any of the causes which produce fluctuations of value. No commodity is quite free from such fluctuations. Gold and silver have sustained, since the beginning of history, one great permanent alteration of value, from the discovery of the American mines; and some temporary variations, such as that which, in the last great war, was produced by the absorption of the metals in hoards, and in the military chests of the immense armies constantly in the field. In the present age the opening of ᵇnew sources of supply, so abundant as the Ural mountains, California, and Australiaᵇ, may be the commencement of another period of decline, on the limits of which it would be useless at present to speculate. But on the whole, no commodities are so little exposed to causes of variation. They ᶜfluctuate lessᶜ than almost any other things in their cost of production. And from their durability, the total quantity in existence is at all times so great in proportion to the annual supply, that the effect on value even of a change in the cost of production is not sudden: a very long time being required to diminish materially the quantity in existence, and even to increase it very greatly ᵈnot being aᵈ rapid process. Gold and silver, therefore, are more fit than any other commodity to be the subject of engagements for receiving or paying a given quantity at some distant period. If the engagement were made in corn, a failure of crops might increase the burthen of the payment in one year to fourfold what was intended, or an exuberant harvest sink it in another to one-fourth. If stipulated in cloth, some manufacturing invention might permanently reduce the

ᵃ⁻ᵃ48   everywhere
ᵇ⁻ᵇ48   a new source of supply, so abundant as the mines of the Ural mountains and of Siberia] 49   *as* 48 . . . Siberia, to which may now be added California
ᶜ⁻ᶜ48, 49   are more constant
ᵈ⁻ᵈ48, 49, 52, 57   being no

payment to a tenth of its original value. Such things have *occurred* even in the case of payments stipulated in gold and silver; but the great fall of their value after the discovery of America, is, *as yet,* the only authenticated instance; and in this case the change was extremely gradual, being spread over a period of many years.

When gold and silver had become virtually a medium of exchange, by becoming the things for which people generally sold, and with which they generally bought, whatever they had to sell or to buy; the contrivance of coining obviously suggested itself. By this process the metal was divided into convenient portions, of any degree of smallness, and bearing a recognised proportion to one another; and the trouble was saved of weighing and assaying at every change of possessors, an inconvenience which on the occasion of small purchases would soon have become insupportable. Governments found it their interest to take the operation into their own hands, and to interdict all coining by private persons; indeed, their guarantee was often the only one which would have been relied on, a reliance however which very often it ill deserved; profligate governments having until a very modern period *seldom* scrupled, for the sake of robbing their creditors, to confer on all other debtors a licence to rob theirs, by the shallow and impudent artifice of lowering the standard; that least covert of all modes of knavery, which consists in calling a shilling a pound, that a debt of *one* hundred pounds may be cancelled by the payment of a hundred shillings. It would have been as simple a plan, and would have answered the purpose as well, to have enacted that "a hundred" should always be interpreted to mean five, which would have affected the same reduction in all pecuniary contracts, and would not have been at all more shameless. Such strokes of policy have not wholly ceased to be recommended, but they have ceased to be practised; except occasionally through the medium of paper money, in which case the character of the transaction, from the greater obscurity of the subject, is a little less barefaced.

§ 3. [*Money is a mere contrivance for facilitating exchanges, which does not affect the laws of Value*] Money, when its use has grown habitual, is the medium through which the incomes of the different members of the community are distributed to them, and the measure by which they estimate their possessions. As it is always by means of money that people provide for their different necessities, there grows up in their minds a powerful association leading them to regard money as wealth in a more peculiar sense than any other article; and even those who pass their lives in the

---

*e-e*48, 49   been known to occur
f-f+49, 52, 57, 62, 65, 71
*g-g*48   never   *h-h*48, 49, 52, 57, 62   a

production of the most useful objects, acquire the habit of regarding those objects as chiefly important by their capacity of being exchanged for money. A person who parts with money to obtain commodities, unless he intends to sell them, appears to the imagination to be making a worse bargain than a person who parts with commodities to get money; the one seems to be spending his means, the other adding to them. Illusions which, though now in some measure dispelled, were long powerful enough to overmaster the mind of every politician, both speculative and practical, in Europe.

It must be evident, however, that the mere introduction of a particular mode of exchanging things for one another, by first exchanging a thing for money, and then exchanging the money for something else, makes no difference in the essential character of transactions. It is not with money that things are really purchased. Nobody's income (except that of the gold or silver miner) is derived from the precious metals. The pounds or shillings which a person receives weekly or yearly, are not what constitutes his income; they are a sort of tickets or orders which he can present for payment at any shop he pleases, and which entitle him to receive a certain value of any commodity that he makes choice of. The farmer pays his labourers and his landlord in these tickets, as the most convenient plan for himself and them; but their real income is their share of his corn, cattle, and hay, and it makes no essential difference whether he distributes it to them ᵃdirectlyᵃ, or sells it for them and gives them the price; but as they would have to sell it for money if he did not, and as he is a seller at any rate, it best suits the purposes of all, that he should sell their share along with his own, and leave the labourers more leisure for work and the landlord for being idle. The capitalists, except those who are producers of the precious metals, derive no part of their income from those metals, since they only get them by buying them with their own produce: while all other persons have their incomes paid to them by the capitalists, or by those who have received payment from the capitalists, and as the capitalists have nothing, from the first, except their produce, it is that and nothing else which supplies all incomes furnished by them. There cannot, in short, be intrinsically a more insignificant thing, in the economy of society, than money; except in the character of a contrivance for sparing time and labour. It is a ᵇmachineᵇ for doing quickly and commodiously, what would be done, though less quickly and commodiously, without it: and like many other kinds of machinery, it only exerts a distinct and independent influence of its own when it gets out of order.

The introduction of money does not interfere with the operation of any of the Laws of Value laid down in the preceding chapters. The reasons which make the temporary or market value of things depend on the

ᵃ⁻ᵃ48, 49, 52, 57   direct   ᵇ⁻ᵇ48, 49   machinery

demand and supply, and their average and permanent values upon their cost of production, are as applicable to a money system as to a system of barter. Things which by barter would exchange for one another, will, if sold for money, sell for an equal amount of it, and so will exchange for one another still, though the process of exchanging them will consist of two operations instead of only one. The relations of commodities to one another remain unaltered by money: the only new relation introduced, is their relation to money itself; how much or how little money they will exchange for; in other words, how the Exchange Value of money itself is determined. And this is not a question of any difficulty, when the illusion is dispelled, which caused money to be looked upon as a peculiar ^cthing^c, not governed by the same laws as other things. Money is a commodity, and its value is determined like that of other commodities, temporarily by demand and supply, permanently and on the average by cost of production. The illustration of these principles, considered in their application to money, must be given in some detail, on account of the confusion which, in minds not ^dscientifically^d instructed on the subject, envelopes the whole matter; partly from a lingering remnant of the old misleading associations, and partly from the mass of vapoury and baseless speculation with which this, more than any other topic of political economy, has in latter times become surrounded. I shall therefore treat of the Value of Money in a chapter apart.

^{c–c}48, 49, 52, 57   something
^{d–d}48, 49   systematically

CHAPTER VIII

Of the Value of Money, as Dependent on Demand and Supply

§ 1. [*The value of money is an ambiguous expression*] It is unfortunate that in the very outset of the subject we have to clear from our path a formidable ambiguity of language. The Value of Money is to appearance an expression as precise, as free from possibility of misunderstanding, as any in science. The value of a thing, is what it will exchange for: the value of money, is what money will exchange for; the purchasing power of money. If prices are low, money will buy much of other things, and is of high value; if prices are high, it will buy little of other things, and is of low value. The value of money is inversely as general prices: falling as they rise, and rising as they fall.

But unhappily the same phrase is also employed, in the current language of commerce, in a very different sense. Money, which is so commonly understood as the synonyme of wealth, is more especially the term in use to denote it when *it is the subject of borrowing*. When one person lends to another, as well as when he pays wages or rent to another, what he transfers is not the mere money, but a right to a certain value of the produce of the country, to be selected at pleasure; the lender having first bought this right, by giving for it a portion of his capital. What he really lends is so much capital; the money is the mere instrument of transfer. But the capital usually passes from the lender to the receiver through the means either of money, or of an order to receive money, and at any rate it is in money that the capital is computed and estimated. Hence, borrowing capital is universally called borrowing money; the loan market is called the money market: those who have their capital disposable for investment on loan are called the monied class: and the equivalent given for the use of capital, or in other words, interest, is not only called the interest of money, but, by a grosser perversion of terms, the value of money. This misapplication of language, assisted by some fallacious appearances which

*a–a*48, 49, 52, 57 borrowing is spoken of

we shall notice and clear up hereafter,* has created a general notion among persons in business, that the Value of Money, meaning the rate of interest, has an intimate connexion with the Value of Money in its proper sense, the value or purchasing power of the circulating medium. We shall ^{b}return^b to this subject before long: at present it is enough to say, that by Value I shall always mean Exchange Value, and by money the medium of exchange, not the capital which is passed from hand to hand through that medium.

§ 2. [*The value of money depends,* cæteris paribus, *on its quantity*] The value or purchasing power of money depends, in the first instance, on demand and supply. But demand and supply, in relation to money, present themselves in a somewhat different shape from the demand and supply of other things.

The supply of a commodity means the quantity offered for sale. But it is not usual to speak of offering money for sale. People are not usually said to buy or sell money. This, however, is merely an accident of language. In point of fact, money is bought and sold like other things, whenever other things are bought and sold *for* money. Whoever sells corn, or tallow, or cotton, buys money. Whoever buys bread, or wine, or clothes, sells money to the dealer in those articles. The money with which people are offering to buy, is money offered for sale. The supply of money, then, is the quantity of it which people are wanting to lay out; that is, all the money they have in their possession, except what they are hoarding, or at least keeping by them as a reserve for future contingencies. The supply of money, in short, is all the money in *circulation* at the time.

The demand for money, again, consists of all the goods offered for sale. Every seller of goods is a buyer of money, and the goods he brings with him constitute his demand. The demand for money differs from the demand for other things in this, that it is limited only by the means of the purchaser. The demand for other things is for so much and no more; but there is always a demand for as much money as can be got. Persons may indeed refuse to sell, and withdraw their goods from the market, if they cannot get for them what they consider a sufficient price. But this is only when they think that the price will rise, and that they shall get more money by waiting. If they thought the low price likely to be permanent, they would take what they could get. It is always a *sine quâ non* with a dealer to dispose of his goods.

As the whole of the goods in the market compose the demand for

*Infra, chap. xxiii [pp. 647–59].

$^{b-b}$48, 49, 52, 57   come

money, so the whole of the money constitutes the demand for goods. The money and the goods are seeking each other for the purpose of being exchanged. They are reciprocally supply and demand to one another. It is indifferent whether, in characterizing the phenomena, we speak of the demand and ^a supply of goods, or the supply and the demand of money. They are equivalent expressions.

We shall proceed to illustrate this proposition more fully. And in doing this, the reader will remark a great difference between the class of questions which now occupy us, and those which we previously had under discussion respecting Values. In considering Value, we were only concerned with causes which acted upon particular commodities apart from the rest. Causes which affect all commodities alike, do not act upon values. But in considering the relation between goods and money, it is with the causes that operate upon all goods whatever, that we are ^bspecially^b concerned. We are comparing goods of all sorts on one side, with money on the other side, as things to be exchanged against each other.

Suppose, everything else being the same, that there is an increase ^cin^c the quantity of money, say by the arrival of a foreigner in a place, with a treasure of gold and silver. When he commences expending it (for this question it matters not whether productively or unproductively), he adds to the supply of money, and by the same act, to the demand for goods. Doubtless he adds, in the first instance, to the demand only for certain kinds of goods, namely, those which he selects for purchase; he will immediately raise the price of those, and so far as he is individually concerned, of those only. If he spends his funds in giving entertainments, he will raise the prices of food and wine. If he expends them in establishing a manufactory, he will raise the prices of labour and materials. But at the higher prices, more money will pass into the hands of the sellers of these different articles; and they, whether labourers or dealers, having more money to lay out, will create an increased demand for all the things which they are accustomed to purchase: these accordingly will rise in price, and so on until the rise has reached everything. I say everything, though it is of course possible that the influx of money might take place through the medium of some new class of consumers, or in such a manner as to alter the proportions of different classes of consumers to one another, so that a greater share of the national income than before would thenceforth be expended in some articles, and a smaller in others; exactly as if a change had taken place in the tastes and wants of the community. If this were the case, then until production had accommodated itself to this change in the comparative demand for different things, there would be a real alteration

^a48, 49, 52, 57   the
^{b–b}48, 49, 52, 57, 62, 65   especially   ^{c–c}48, 49, 52   of

in values, and some things would rise in price more than others, while some perhaps would not rise at all. These effects, however, would evidently proceed, not from the mere increase of money, but from accessory circumstances attending it. We are now only called upon to consider what would be the effect of an increase of money, considered by itself. Supposing the money in the hands of individuals to be increased, the wants and inclinations of the community collectively in respect to consumption remaining exactly the same; the increase of demand would reach all things equally, and there would be an universal rise of prices. We might suppose, with Hume, that some morning, every person in the nation should wake and find a gold coin in his pocket: this example, however, would involve an alteration of the proportions in the demand for different commodities; the luxuries of the poor would, in the first instance be raised in price, in a much greater degree than other things. Let us rather suppose, therefore, that to every pound, or shilling, or penny, in the possession of any one, another pound, shilling, or penny, were suddenly added. There would be an increased money demand, and consequently an increased money value, or price, for things of all sorts. This increased value would do no good to any one; would make no difference, except that of having to reckon pounds, shillings, and pence, in higher numbers. It would be an increase of values only as estimated in money, a thing only wanted to buy other things with; and would not enable any one to buy more of them than before. Prices would have risen in a certain ratio, and the value of money would have fallen in the same ratio.

It is to be remarked that this ratio would be precisely that in which the quantity of money had been increased. If the whole money in circulation was doubled, prices would be doubled. If it was only increased one-fourth, prices would rise one-fourth. There would be one-fourth more money, all of which would be used to purchase goods of some description. When there had been time for the increased supply of money to reach all markets, or (according to the conventional metaphor) to permeate all the channels of circulation, all prices would have risen one-fourth. But the general rise of price is independent of this diffusing and equalizing process. Even if some prices were raised more, and others less, the average rise would be one-fourth. This is a necessary consequence of the fact, that a fourth more money would have been given for only the same quantity of goods. *General* prices, therefore, would in any case be a fourth higher.

The very same effect would be produced on prices if we suppose the goods diminished, instead of the money increased: and the contrary effect if the goods were increased or the money diminished. If there were less money in the hands of the community, and the same amount of goods to be sold, less money altogether would be given for them, and they would be sold at lower prices; lower, too, in the precise ratio in which the money was diminished. So that the value of money, other things being the same, varies inversely as its quantity; every increase of quantity lowering the value, and every diminution raising it, in a ratio exactly equivalent.

This, it must be observed, is a property peculiar to money. We did not find it to be true of commodities generally, that every diminution of supply raised the value exactly in proportion to the deficiency, or that every increase lowered it in the precise ratio of the excess. Some things are usually affected in a greater ratio than that of the excess or deficiency, others usually in a less: because, in ordinary cases of demand, the desire, being for the thing itself, may be stronger or weaker: and the amount of what people are willing to expend on it, being in any case a limited quantity, may be affected in very unequal degrees by difficulty or facility of attainment. But in the case of money, which is desired as the means of universal purchase, the demand consists of everything which people have to sell; and the only limit to what they are willing to give, is the limit set by their having nothing more to offer. The whole of the goods being in any case exchanged for the whole of the money which comes into the market to be laid out, they will sell for less or more of it, exactly according as less or more is brought.

§ 3. [*The value of money depends also on the rapidity of circulation*] From what precedes, it might for a moment be supposed, that all the goods on sale in a country at any one time, are exchanged for all the money existing and in circulation at that same time: or in other words, that there is always in circulation in a country, a quantity of money equal in value to the whole of the goods then and there on sale. But this would be a complete misapprehension. The money laid out is equal in value to the goods it purchases; but the quantity of money laid out is not the same thing with the quantity in circulation. As the money passes from hand to hand, the same piece of money is laid out many times, before all the things on sale at one time are purchased and finally removed from the market: and each pound or dollar must be counted for as many pounds or dollars, as the number of times it changes hands in order to effect this object. The greater part of the goods must also be counted more than once, not only because most things pass through the hands of several sets of manufacturers and dealers before they assume the form in which they are finally consumed, but because in times of speculation (and all times are so, more or less) the same goods are often bought repeatedly, to be resold for a profit, before they are bought for the purpose of consumption at all.

If we assume the quantity of goods on sale, and the number of times those goods are resold, to be fixed quantities, the value of money will depend upon its quantity, together with the average number of times that each piece changes hands in the process. The whole of the goods sold (counting each resale of the same goods as so much added to the goods) have been exchanged for the whole of the money, multiplied by the number of purchases made on the average by each piece. Consequently, the amount of goods and of transactions being the same, the value of money is inversely as its quantity multiplied by what is called the rapidity of circulation. And the quantity of money in circulation, is equal to the money value of all the goods sold, divided by the number which expresses the rapidity of circulation.

The phrase, rapidity of circulation, requires some comment. It must not be understood to mean, the number of purchases made by each piece of money in a given time. Time is not the thing to be considered. The state of society may be such, that each piece of money hardly performs more than one purchase in a year; but if this arises from the small number of transactions—from the small amount of business done, the want of activity in traffic, or because what traffic there is, mostly takes place by barter— it constitutes no reason why prices should be lower, or the value of money higher. The essential point is, not how often the same money changes hands in a given time, but how often it changes hands in order to perform a given amount of traffic. We must compare the number of purchases made by the money in a given time, not with the time itself, but with the goods sold in that same time. If each piece of money changes hands on an average ten times while goods are sold to the value of a million sterling, it is evident that the money required to circulate those goods is 100,000*l.* And conversely, if the money in circulation is 100,000*l.*, and each piece changes hands by the purchase of goods ten times in a month, the sales of goods for money which take place every month must amount on the average to 1,000,000*l.*

Rapidity of circulation being a phrase so ill adapted to express the only thing which it is of any importance to express by it, and having a tendency to confuse the subject by suggesting a meaning extremely different from the one intended, it would be a good thing if the phrase could be got rid of, and another substituted, more directly significant of the idea meant to be conveyed. Some such expression as "the efficiency of money," though not unexceptionable, would do better; as it would point attention to the quantity of work done, without suggesting the idea of estimating it by time. Until an appropriate term can be devised, we must be content *ᵃwhen ambiguity is to be apprehended,ᵃ* to express the idea by the circumlocution

ᵃ⁻ᵃ+52, 57, 62, 65, 71

which alone conveys it adequately, namely, the average number of purchases made by each piece in order to effect a given pecuniary amount of
transactions.

§ 4. [*Explanations and limitations of this principle*] The proposition
which we have laid down respecting the dependence of general prices upon
the quantity of money in circulation, must *ᵃ* be understood as applying only
to a state of things in which money, that is, gold or silver, is the exclusive
instrument of exchange, and actually passes from hand to hand at every
purchase, credit in any of its shapes being unknown. When credit comes
into play as a means of purchasing, distinct from money in hand, we shall
hereafter find that the connexion between prices and the amount of the
circulating medium is much less direct and intimate, and that such connexion as does exist, no longer admits of so simple a mode of expression.
But on a subject so full of complexity as that of currency and prices, it is
necessary to lay the foundation of our theory in a thorough understanding
of the most simple cases, which we shall always find lying as a groundwork or substratum under those which arise in practice. That an increase
of the quantity of money raises prices, and a diminution lowers them, is
the most elementary proposition in the theory of currency, and without
it we should have no key to any of the others. In any state of things, however, except the simple and primitive one which we have supposed, the
proposition is only true other things being the same: and what those other
things are, which must be the same, we are not yet ready to pronounce. We
can, however, point out, even now, one or two of the cautions with which
the principle must be guarded in attempting to make use of it for the
practical explanation of phenomena; cautions the more indispensable, as
the doctrine, though a scientific truth, has of late years been the foundation of a greater mass of false theory, and erroneous interpretation of
facts, than any other proposition relating to interchange. From the time
of the resumption of cash payments by the Act of 1819, and especially
since the commercial crisis of 1825, the favourite explanation of every rise
or fall of prices has been "the currency;" and like most popular theories,
the doctrine has been applied with little regard to the conditions necessary
for making it *ᵇ*correct*ᵇ*.

For example, it is habitually assumed that whenever there is a greater
amount of money in the country, or in existence, a rise of prices must
necessarily follow. But this is by no means an inevitable consequence.
In no commodity is it the quantity in existence, but the quantity offered
for sale, that determines the value. Whatever may be the quantity of
money in the country, only that part of it will affect prices, which goes into

*ᵃ*48, 49, 52 for the present   *ᵇ⁻ᵇ*48 true the ᶜmarket ofᶜ commodities, and is there actually exchanged against goods. Whatever increases the amount of this portion of the money in the country, ᵈ tends to raise prices. But money hoarded does not act on prices. Money kept in reserve by individuals to meet contingencies which do not occur, does not act on prices. The money in the coffers of the Bank, or retained as a reserve by private bankers, does not act on prices until drawn out, nor even then unless drawn out to be expended in commodities.

It frequently happens that money, to a considerable amount, is brought into the country, is there actually ᵉinvestedᵉ as capital, and again flows out, without having ever once acted upon the markets of commodities, but only upon the market of securities, or, as it is commonly though improperly called, the money market. Let us return to the case already put for illustration, that of a foreigner landing in the country with a treasure. We supposed him to employ his treasure in the purchase of goods for his own use, or in setting up a manufactory and employing labourers; and in either case he would, *cæteris paribus*, raise prices. But instead of doing either of these things, he might very probably prefer to invest his fortune at interest; which we shall suppose him to do in the most obvious way, by becoming a competitor for a portion of the stock, exchequer bills, railway debentures, mercantile bills, mortgages, &c., which are at all times in the hands of the public. By doing this he would raise the prices of those different securities, or in other words would lower the rate of interest; and since this would disturb the relation previously existing between the rate of interest on capital in the country itself, and that in foreign countries, it would probably induce some of those who had floating capital seeking employment, to send it abroad for foreign investment rather than buy securities at home at the ᶠadvancedᶠ price. As much money might thus go out as had previously come in, while the prices of commodities would have shown no trace of its temporary presence. This is a case highly deserving of attention: and it is a fact now beginning to be recognised, that the passage of the precious metals from country to country is determined much more than was formerly supposed, by the state of the loan market in different countries, and much less by the state of prices.

Another point must be adverted to, in order to avoid serious error in the interpretation of mercantile phenomena. If there be, at any time, an increase in the number of money transactions, a thing continually liable to happen from differences in the activity of speculation, and even in the time of year (since certain kinds of business are transacted only at particular seasons); an increase of the currency which is only proportional to this increase of transactions, and is of no longer duration, has no tendency to raise prices.

ᶜ⁻ᶜ48   markets for] 49, 52   market for   ᵈ48, 49   certainly
ᵉ⁻ᵉ48, 49   employed   ᶠ⁻ᶠ48, 49, 52, 57   advance of

At the quarterly periods when the public dividends are paid at the Bank, a sudden increase takes place of the money in the hands of the public; an increase estimated at from a fifth to two-fifths of the whole issues of the Bank of England. Yet this never has any effect on prices; and in a very few weeks, the currency has again shrunk into its usual dimensions, by a mere reduction in the demands of the public (after so copious a supply of ready money) for accommodation from the Bank in the way of discount or loan. In like manner the currency of the agricultural districts fluctuates in amount at different seasons of the year. It is always lowest in August: "it rises generally towards Christmas, and obtains its greatest elevation about Lady-day, when the farmer commonly lays in his stock, and has to pay his rent and summer taxes," and when he therefore makes his principal applications to country bankers for loans. "Those variations occur with the same regularity as the season, and with just as little disturbance of the markets as the quarterly fluctuations of the notes of the Bank of England. As soon as the extra payments have been completed, the superfluous" currency, which is estimated at half a million, "as certainly and immediately is reabsorbed and disappears."*

If extra currency were not forthcoming to make these extra payments, one of three things must happen. Either the payments must be made without money, by a resort to some of those contrivances by which its use is dispensed with; or there must be an increase in the rapidity of circulation, the same sum of money being made to perform more payments; or if neither of these things took place, money to make the extra payments must be withdrawn from the market for commodities, and prices, consequently, must fall. An increase of the circulating medium, conformable in extent and duration to the temporary stress of business, does not raise prices, but merely prevents this fall.

The sequel of our investigation will point out many other ᵍ qualifications with which the proposition must be received, that the value of the circulating medium depends on the demand and supply, and is in the inverse ratio of the quantityʰ; qualifications which, under a complex system of credit like that existing in England, render the proposition ⁱan extremelyⁱ incorrect expression of the factʰ.

*[John] Fullarton on the *Regulation of Currencies*, 2nd edit. [London: Murray, 1845,] pp. 87–9 [88–9].

ᵍ48, 49, 52   explanations and
ʰ⁻ʰ+57, 62, 65, 71
ⁱ⁻ⁱ57   a totally

CHAPTER IX

Of the Value of Money,
as Dependent on Cost of Production

§ 1. [*The value of money, in a state of freedom, conforms to the value of the bullion contained in it*] But money, no more than commodities in general, has its value definitively determined by demand and supply. The ultimate regulator of its value is Cost of Production.

We are supposing, of course, that things are left to themselves. Governments have not always left things to themselves. They have undertaken to prevent the quantity of money from adjusting itself according to spontaneous laws, and have endeavoured to regulate it at their pleasure; generally with a view of keeping a greater quantity of money in the country, than would otherwise have remained there. It was, until lately, the policy of all governments to interdict the exportation and the melting of money; while, by encouraging the exportation and impeding the importation of other things, they endeavoured to have a stream of money constantly flowing in. By this course they gratified two prejudices; they drew, or thought that they drew, more money into the country, which they believed to be tantamount to more wealth; and they gave, or thought that they gave, to all producers and dealers, high prices, which, though no real advantage, people are always inclined to suppose to be one.

In this attempt to regulate the value of money artificially by means of the supply, governments have never succeeded in the degree, or even in the manner, which they intended. Their prohibitions against exporting or melting the coin have never been effectual. A commodity of such small bulk in proportion to its value is so easily smuggled, and still more easily melted, that it has been impossible by the most stringent measures to prevent these operations. All the risk which it was in the power of governments to attach to them, was outweighed by a very moderate profit.* In

*The effect of the prohibition cannot, however, have been so entirely insignificant as it has been supposed to be by writers on the subject. The facts adduced by Mr. Fullarton, in the note to page 7 of his work on the Regulation of Currencies, show that it required a greater percentage of difference in value between coin and bullion than has commonly been imagined, to bring the coin to the melting-pot.

the more indirect mode of aiming at the same purpose, by throwing difficulties in the way of making the returns for exported goods in any other commodity than money, they have not been quite so unsuccessful. They have not, indeed, succeeded in making money flow continuously into the country; but they have to a certain extent been able to keep it at a higher than its natural level; and have, thus far, removed the value of money from exclusive dependence on the causes which fix the ᵃvalueᵃ of things not artificially interfered with.

We are, however, to suppose a state, not of artificial regulation, but of freedom. In that state, and assuming no charge to be made for coinage, the value of money will conform to the value of the bullion of which it is made. A pound weight of gold or silver in coin, and the same weight in an ingot, will precisely exchange for one another. On the supposition of freedom, the metal cannot be worth more in the state of bullion than of coin; for as it can be melted without any loss of time, and with hardly any expense, this would of course be done until the quantity in circulation was so much diminished as to equalize its value with that of the same weight in bullion. It may be thought however that the coin, though it cannot be of less, may be, and being a manufactured article will naturally be, of greater value than the bullion contained in it, on the same principle on which linen cloth is of more value than an equal weight of linen yarn. This would be true, were it not that Government, in this country, and in some others, coins money gratis for any one who furnishes the metal. The labour and expense of coinage, when not charged to the possessor, do not raise the value of the article. If Government opened an office where, on delivery of a given weight of yarn, it returned the same weight of cloth to any one who asked for it, cloth would be worth no more in the market than the yarn it contained. As soon as coin is worth a fraction more than the value of the bullion, it becomes the interest of the holders of bullion to send it to be coined. If Government, however, throws the expense of coinage, as is reasonable, upon the holder, by making a charge to cover the expense (which is done by giving back rather less in coin than has been received in bullion, and is called levying a seignorage), the coin will rise, to the extent of the seignorage, above the value of the bullion. If the Mint kept back one per cent, to pay the expense of coinage, it would be against the interest of the holders of bullion to have it coined, until the coin was more valuable than the bullion by at least that fraction. The coin, therefore, would be kept one per cent higher in value, which could only be by keeping it one per cent less in quantity, than if its coinage were gratuitous.

The Government might attempt to obtain a profit by the transaction, and might lay on a seignorage calculated for that purpose; but whatever

ᵃ⁻ᵃ48, 49, 52, 57, 62, 65   values

they took for coinage beyond its expenses, would be so much profit on private coining. Coining, though not so easy an operation as melting, is far from a difficult one, and, when the coin produced is of full weight and standard fineness, is very difficult to detect. If, therefore, a profit could be made by coining good money, it would certainly be done: and the attempt to make seignorage a source of revenue would be defeated. Any attempt to keep the value of the coin at an artificial elevation, not by a seignorage, but by refusing to coin, would be frustrated in the same manner.*

§ 2. [*The value of bullion is determined by the cost of production*] The value of money, then, conforms, permanently, and, in a state of freedom, almost immediately, to the value of the metal of which it is made; with the addition, or not, of the expenses of coinage, according as those expenses are borne by the individual or by the state. This simplifies extremely the question which we have here to consider: since gold and silver bullion are commodities like any others, and their value depends, like that of other things, on their cost of production.

To the majority of civilized countries, gold and silver are foreign products: and the circumstances which govern the values of foreign products, present some questions which we are not yet ready to examine. For the present, therefore, we must suppose the country which is the subject of our inquiries, to be supplied with gold and silver by its own mines, reserving for future consideration how far our conclusions require modification to adapt them to the more usual case.

Of the three classes into which commodities are divided—those absolutely limited in supply, those which may be had in unlimited quantity at a given cost of production, and those which may be had in unlimited quantity, but at an increasing cost of production—the precious metals, being the produce of mines, belong to the third class. Their natural value, therefore, is *in the long run* proportional to their cost of production in the most unfavourable existing circumstances, that is, at the worst mine which it is necessary to work in order to obtain the required supply. A

*In England, though there is no seignorage on gold coin, (the Mint returning in coin the same weight of pure metal which it receives in bullion) there is a delay of a few weeks after the bullion is deposited, before the coin can be obtained, occasioning a loss of interest, which, to the holder, is equivalent to a trifling seignorage. From this cause, the value of coin is in general slightly above that of the bullion it contains. An ounce of gold, according to the quantity of metal in a sovereign, should be worth 3*l*. 17*s*. 10½*d*.; but it was usually quoted at 3*l*. 17*s*. 6*d*., until the Bank Charter Act of 1844 made it imperative on the Bank to give its notes for all bullion offered to it at the rate of 3*l*. 17*s*. 9*d*.

a-a+52, 57, 62, 65, 71

pound weight of gold will, in the ^{b}gold-producing countries, ultimately tend to exchange^b for as much of every other commodity, as is produced at a cost equal to its own; meaning by its own cost the cost ^{c}in labour and expense, at the least productive sources of supply which the then^c existing demand makes it necessary to work. The average value of gold is made to conform to its natural value, in the same manner as the values of other things are made to conform to their natural value. Suppose that it were selling above its natural value; that is, above the value which is an equivalent for the labour and expense of mining, and for the risks attending a branch of industry in which nine out of ten experiments ^{d}have usually been^d failures. A part of the mass of floating capital which is on the look out for investment, would take the direction of mining enterprise; the supply would thus be increased, and the value would fall. If, on the contrary, it were selling below its natural value, miners would not be obtaining the ordinary profit; they would slacken their works; if the depreciation was great, some of the inferior mines would perhaps stop working altogether: and a falling off in the annual supply, preventing the annual wear and tear from being completely compensated, would by degrees reduce the quantity, and restore the value.

When examined more closely, the following are the details of the process. If gold is above its natural or cost value—the coin, as we have seen, conforming in its value to the bullion—money will be of high value, and the prices of all things, labour included, will be low. These low prices will lower the expenses of all producers; but as their returns will also be lowered, no advantage will be obtained by any producer, except the producer of gold: whose returns from his mine, not depending on price, will be the same as before, and his expenses being less, he will obtain extra profits, and will be stimulated to increase his production. *E converso* if the metal is below its natural value: since this is as much as to say that prices are high, and the money expenses of all producers unusually great: for this, however, all other producers will be compensated by increased money returns: the miner alone will extract from his mine no more metal than before, while his expenses will be greater: his profits therefore being diminished or annihilated, he will diminish his production, if not abandon his employment.

In this manner it is that the value of money is made to conform to the cost of production of the metal of which it is made. It may be well, however, to repeat (what has been said before) that the adjustment takes a long time to effect, in the case of a commodity so generally desired and at the same time so durable as the precious metals. Being so largely used not only as money but for plate and ornament, there is at all times a very large quantity of these metals in existence: while they are so slowly worn out, that a comparatively small annual production is sufficient to keep up the supply, and to make any addition to it which may be required by the increase of goods to be circulated, or by the increased demand for gold and silver articles by wealthy consumers. Even if this small annual supply were stopt entirely, *e* it would require many years to reduce the quantity so much as to make any very material difference in prices. The quantity may be increased, much more rapidly than it can be diminished; but the increase must be very great before it can make itself much felt over such a mass of the precious metals as exists in the whole commercial world. And hence the effects of all changes in the conditions of production of the precious metals are at first, and continue to be for many years, questions of quantity only, with little reference to cost of production. *f*More especially is this the case when, as at the present time, many new sources of supply have been simultaneously opened, most of them practicable by labour alone, without any capital in advance beyond a pickaxe and a week's food; and when the operations are as yet wholly experimental, the comparative permanent productiveness of the different sources being entirely unascertained.*f*

§ 3. [*How this law is related to the principle laid down in the preceding chapter*] Since, however, the value of money really conforms, like that of other things, though more slowly, to its cost of production, some political economists have objected altogether to the statement that the value of money depends on its quantity combined with the rapidity of circulation; which, they think, is assuming a law for money that does not exist for any other commodity, when the truth is that it is governed by the very same laws. To this we may answer, in the first place, that the statement in question assumes no peculiar law. It is simply the law of demand and supply, which is acknowledged to be applicable to all commodities, and which, in the case of money as of most other things, is controlled, but not set aside, by the law of cost of production, since cost of production would have no effect on value if it could have none on supply. But, secondly, there really is, in one respect, a closer connexion between the value of money and its quantity, than between the values of other things and their quantity. The value of other things conforms to the changes in the cost of production, without requiring, as a condition, that there should be any actual alteration of the supply: the potential alteration is sufficient; and if there even be an actual alteration, it is but a temporary one, except in so far as the altered

*e*48, 49, 52   (which it never is, the richer mines continuing to be worked, though at some diminution of rent)   *f-f*+52, 57, 62, 65, 71

value may make a difference in the demand, and so require an increase or diminution of supply, as a consequence, not a cause, of the alteration in value. Now this is also true of gold and silver, considered as articles of expenditure for ornament and luxury; but it is not true of money. If the *a*permanent*a* cost of production of gold were reduced one-fourth, *b* it might happen that there would not be more of it bought for plate, gilding, or jewellery, than before; and if so, though the value would fall, the quantity extracted from the mines for these purposes would be no greater than previously. Not so with the portion used as money; that portion could not fall in value one-fourth, unless actually increased one-fourth; for, at prices one-fourth higher, one-fourth more money would be required to make the accustomed purchases; and if this were not forthcoming, some of the commodities would be without purchasers, and prices could not be kept up. Alterations, therefore, in the cost of production of the precious metals, do not act upon the value of money except just in proportion as they increase or diminish its quantity; which cannot be said of any other commodity. It would therefore, I conceive, be an error both scientifically and practically, to discard the proposition which asserts a connexion between the value of money and its quantity.

It is evident, however, that the cost of production, in the long run, regulates the quantity; and that every country (temporary fluctuations excepted) will possess, and have in circulation, just that quantity of money, which will perform all the exchanges required of it, consistently with maintaining a value conformable to its cost of production. The prices of things will, on the average, be such that money will exchange for its own cost in all other goods: and, precisely because the quantity cannot be prevented from affecting the value, the quantity itself will *c*(by a sort of self-acting machinery)*c* be kept at the amount consistent with that standard of prices—at the amount necessary for performing, at those prices, all the business required of it.

"The quantity wanted will depend partly on the cost of producing gold, and partly on the rapidity of its circulation. The rapidity of circulation being given, it would depend on the cost of production: and the cost of production being given, the quantity of money would depend on the rapidity of its circulation."* After what has been already said, I hope that neither of these propositions stands in need of any further illustration.

*From some printed, but not published, Lectures of Mr. Senior: in which the great differences in the business done by money, as well as in the rapidity of its circulation, in different states of society and civilization, are interestingly illustrated. [*Three Lectures on the Value of Money, delivered before the University of Oxford, in 1829.* London: Fellowes, 1840, p. 21.]

a-a+52, 57, 62, 65, 71
*b*48, 49   by the discovery of more fertile mines,
c-c+49, 52, 57, 62, 65, 71

Money, then, like commodities in general, having a value dependent on, and proportional to, its cost of production; the theory of money is, by the admission of this principle, stript of a great part of the mystery which apparently surrounded it. We must not forget, however, that this doctrine only applies to the places in which the precious metals are actually produced; and that we have yet to enquire whether the law of the dependence of value on cost of production applies to the exchange of things produced at distant places. But however this may be, our propositions with respect to value will require no other alteration, where money is an imported commodity, than that of substituting for the cost of its production, the cost of obtaining it in the country. Every foreign commodity is bought by giving for it some domestic production; and the labour and capital which a foreign commodity costs to us, is the labour and capital expended in producing the quantity of our own goods which we give in exchange for it. What this quantity depends upon,—what determines the proportions of interchange between the productions of one country and those of another, —is indeed a question of somewhat greater complexity than those we have hitherto considered. But this at least is indisputable, that within the country itself the value of imported commodities is determined by the value, and consequently by the cost of production, of the equivalent given for them; and money, where it is an imported commodity, is subject to the same law.

CHAPTER X

Of a Double Standard, and Subsidiary Coins

§ 1. [*Objections to a double standard*] Though the qualities necessary to fit any commodity for being used as money are rarely united in any considerable perfection, there are two commodities which possess them in an eminent, and nearly an equal degree; the two precious metals, as they are called; gold and silver. Some nations have accordingly attempted to compose their circulating medium of these two metals indiscriminately.

There is an obvious convenience in making use of the more costly metal for larger payments, and the cheaper one for smaller; and the only question relates to the mode in which this can best be done. The mode most frequently adopted has been to establish between the two metals a fixed proportion; to decide, for example, that a gold coin called a sovereign should be equivalent to twenty of the silver coins called shillings: both the one and the other being called, in the ordinary money of account of the country, by the same denomination, a pound: and it being left free to every one who has a pound to pay, either to pay it in the one metal or in the other.

At the time when the valuation of the two metals relatively to each other, say twenty shillings to the sovereign, or twenty-one shillings to the guinea, was first made, the proportion probably corresponded, as nearly as it could be made to do, with the ordinary relative values of the two metals grounded on their cost of production: and if those natural or cost values always continued to bear the same ratio to one another, the arrangement would be unobjectionable. This, however, is far from being the fact. Gold and silver, though the least variable in value of all commodities, are not invariable, and do not always vary simultaneously. Silver, for example, was lowered in permanent value more than gold, by the discovery of the American mines; and those small variations of value which take place occasionally, do not affect both metals alike. Suppose such a variation to take place: the value of the two metals relatively to one another no longer agreeing with their rated proportion, one or other of them will now be rated below its bullion value, and there will be a profit to be made by melting it.

Suppose, for example, that gold rises in value relatively to silver, so that the quantity of gold in a sovereign is now worth more than the quantity of silver in twenty shillings. Two consequences will ensue. No debtor will any longer find it his interest to pay in gold. He will always pay in silver, because twenty shillings are a legal tender for a debt of one pound, and he can procure silver convertible into twenty shillings for less gold than that contained in a sovereign. The other consequence will be, that unless a sovereign can be sold for more than twenty shillings, all the sovereigns will be melted, since as bullion they will purchase a greater number of shillings than they exchange for as coin. The converse of all this would happen if silver, instead of gold, were the metal which had risen in comparative value. A sovereign would not now be worth so much as twenty shillings, and whoever had a pound to pay would prefer paying it by a sovereign; while the silver coins would be collected for the purpose of being melted, and sold as bullion for gold at their real value, that is, above the legal valuation. The money of the community, therefore, would never really consist of both metals, but of the one only which, at the particular time, best suited the interest of debtors; and the standard of the currency would be constantly liable to change from the one metal to the other, at a loss *a* , on each change, of the expense of coinage on the metal which fell out of use.

It appears, therefore, that the value of money is liable to more frequent fluctuations when both metals are a legal tender at a fixed valuation, than when the exclusive standard of the currency is either gold or silver. Instead of being only affected by variations in the cost of production of one metal, it is subject to derangement from those of two. The particular kind of variation to which a currency is rendered more liable by having two legal standards, is a fall of value, or what is commonly called a depreciation; since practically that one of the two metals will always be the standard, of which the real has fallen below the rated value. If the tendency of the metals be to rise in value, all payments will be made in the one which has risen least; and if to fall, then in that which has fallen most.

§ 2. [*How the use of the two metals as money is obtained without making both of them legal tender*] The plan of a double standard is still occasionally brought forward by here and there a writer or orator as a great improvement in currency. It is probable that, with most of its adherents, its chief merit is its tendency to a sort of depreciation, there being at all times abundance of supporters for any mode, either open or covert, of lowering the standard. Some, however, are influenced by an exaggerated estimate of an advantage which to a certain extent is real, that of being able to have recourse, for replenishing the circulation, to the united stock of gold

*a*48, 49   to the public

and silver in the commercial world, instead of being confined to one of them, which, from accidental absorption, may not be obtainable with sufficient rapidity. The advantage without the disadvantages of a double standard, seems to be best obtained by those nations with whom one only of the two metals is a legal tender, but the other also is coined, and allowed to pass for whatever value the market assigns to it. *a*

When this plan is adopted, it is naturally the more costly metal which is left to be bought and sold as an article of commerce. But nations which, like England, adopt the more costly of the two as their standard, resort to a different expedient for retaining them both in circulation, namely, to make silver a legal tender, but only for small payments. In England, no one can be compelled to receive silver in payment for a larger amount than forty shillings. With this regulation there is necessarily combined another, namely, that silver coin should be rated, in comparison with gold, somewhat above its intrinsic value; that there should not be, in twenty shillings, as much silver as is worth a sovereign: for if there were, a very slight turn of the market in its favour would make it worth more than a sovereign, and it would be profitable to melt the silver coin. The over-valuation of the silver coin creates an inducement to buy silver and send it to the Mint to be coined, since it is *b*given*b* back at a higher value than properly belongs to it: this, however, has been guarded against, by limiting the quantity of the silver coinage, which is not left, like that of gold, to the discretion of individuals, but is determined by the government, and restricted to the amount supposed to be required for small payments. The only precaution necessary is, not to put so high a valuation upon the silver, as to hold out a strong temptation to private coining.

*a*48   This is the case in France. Silver alone is (I believe) a legal tender, and all sums are expressed and accounts kept in francs, a silver coin. Gold is also coined, for convenience, but does not pass at a fixed valuation: the twenty francs marked on a napoleon are merely nominal, napoleons being never to be bought for that sum, but always bearing a small premium, or agio, as it is called; though, as the agio is very trifling, (the bullion value differing very little from twenty francs) it is seldom possible to pass a napoleon for more than that sum in ordinary retail transactions. Silver, then, is the real money of the country, and gold coin only a merchandize; but though not a legal tender, it answers all the real purposes of one, since no creditor is at all likely to refuse receiving it at the market price, in payment of his debt.]
49   [*paragraph*] In France, silver alone . . . *as* 48
    *b–b*48, 49   received

CHAPTER XI

Of Credit, as a Substitute
for Money

§ 1. [*Credit is not a creation but a transfer of the means of production*]
The functions of credit have been a subject of as much misunderstanding
and as much confusion of ideas, as any single topic in Political Economy.
This is not owing to any peculiar difficulty in the theory of the subject, but
to the complex nature of some of the mercantile phenomena arising from
the forms in which credit clothes itself; by which attention is diverted from
the properties of credit in general, to the peculiarities of its particular
forms.

As a specimen of the confused notions entertained respecting the nature
of credit, we may advert to the exaggerated language so often used respecting its national importance. Credit has a great, but not, as many people
seem to suppose, a magical power; it cannot make something out of
nothing. How often is an extension of credit talked of as equivalent to
a creation of capital, or as if credit actually were capital. It seems strange
that there should be any need to point out, that credit being only permission to use the capital of another person, the means of production cannot be increased by it, but only transferred. If the borrower's means of
production and of employing labour are increased by the credit given
him, the lender's are as much diminished. The same sum cannot be used
as capital both by the owner and also by the person to whom it is lent: it
cannot supply its *entire* value in wages, tools, and materials, to two sets
of labourers at once. It is true that the capital which A has borrowed from
B, and makes use of in his business, still forms part of the wealth of B
for other purposes: he can enter into *arrangements* in reliance on it, and
can *c* borrow, when needful, an equivalent sum on the security of it; so
that to a superficial eye it might seem as if both B and A had the use of it
at once. But the smallest consideration will show that when B has parted
with his capital to A, the use of it as capital rests with A alone, and that B

*a–a*48, 49, 52, 57   full
*b–b*48, 49, 52, 57   engagements
*c*48, 49, 52   even

has no other service from it than in so far as his ultimate claim upon it serves him to obtain the use of another capital from a third person C. All capital (not his own) of which any person has really the use, is, and must be, so much subtracted from the capital of some one else.*

§ 2. [*In what manner credit assists production*] But though credit is ^abut^a a transfer of capital from hand to hand, it is generally, and naturally, a transfer to hands more competent to employ the capital efficiently in production. If there were no such thing as credit, or if, from general insecurity and want of confidence, it were scantily practised, many persons who possess more or less of capital, but who, from their occupations, or for want of the necessary skill and knowledge, cannot personally superintend its employment, would derive no benefit from it: their funds would either lie idle, or would be, perhaps, wasted and annihilated in unskilful attempts to make them yield a profit. All this capital is now lent at interest, and made available for production. Capital thus circumstanced forms a large portion of the productive resources of any commercial country; and is naturally attracted to those producers or traders who, being in the greatest business, have the means of employing it to most advantage; because such are both the most desirous to obtain it, and able to give the best security. Although, therefore, the productive funds of the country

*[65] To make the proposition in the text strictly true, a corrective, though a very slight one, requires to be made. The circulating medium existing in a country at a given time, is partly employed in purchases for productive, and partly for unproductive consumption. According as a larger proportion of it is employed in the one way or in the other, the real capital of the country is greater or less. If, then, an addition were made to the circulating medium in the hands of unproductive consumers exclusively, a larger portion of the existing stock of commodities would be bought for unproductive consumption, and a smaller for productive, which state of things, while it lasted, would be equivalent to a diminution of capital; and on the contrary, if the addition made be to the portion of the circulating medium which is in the hands of producers, and destined for their business, a greater portion of the commodities in the country will for the present be employed as capital, and a less portion unproductively. Now an effect of this latter character naturally attends some extensions of credit, especially when taking place in the form of bank notes, or other instruments of exchange. The additional bank notes are, in ordinary course, first issued to producers or dealers, to be employed as capital: and though the stock of commodities in the country is no greater than before, yet as a greater share of that stock now comes by purchase into the hands of producers and dealers, to that extent what would have been unproductively consumed is applied to production, and there is a real increase of capital. The effect ceases, and a counter-process takes place, when the additional credit is stopped, and the notes called in.

^{a–a}48, 49, 52, 57, 62   never anything more than

are not increased by credit, they are called into a more complete state of productive activity. As the confidence on which credit is grounded extends itself, means are developed by which even the smallest portions of capital, the sums which each person keeps by him to meet contingencies, are made available for productive uses. The principal instruments for this purpose are banks of deposit. Where these do not exist, a prudent person must keep a sufficient sum unemployed in his own possession, to meet every demand which he has even a slight reason for thinking himself liable to. When the practice, however, has grown up of keeping this reserve not in his own custody but with a banker, many small sums, previously lying idle, become aggregated in the banker's hands; and the banker, being taught by experience what proportion of the amount is likely to be wanted in a given time, and knowing that if one depositor happens to require more than the average, another will require less, is able to lend the remainder, that is, the far greater part, to producers and dealers: thereby adding the amount, not indeed to the capital in existence, but to that in employment, and making a corresponding addition to the aggregate production of the community.

While credit is thus indispensable for rendering the whole capital of the country productive, it is also ^{b}a^b means by which the industrial talent of the country is turned to ^{c}better^c account for purposes of production. Many a person who has either no capital of his own, or very little, but who has qualifications for business which are known and appreciated by some ^{d}possessors^d of capital, is enabled to obtain either advances in money, or more frequently goods on credit, by which his industrial capacities are made instrumental to the increase of the public wealth; and this benefit will be reaped far more largely, whenever, through better laws and better education, the community shall have made such progress in integrity, that personal character can be accepted as a sufficient guarantee not only against dishonestly appropriating, but against dishonestly risking, what belongs to another.

Such are, in the most general point of view, the uses of credit to the productive resources of the world. But these considerations only apply to the credit given to the industrious classes—to producers and dealers. Credit given ^{e}by^e dealers to unproductive consumers is never an addition, but always a detriment, to the sources of public wealth. It makes over in temporary use, not the capital of the unproductive classes to the productive, but that of the productive to the unproductive. If A, a dealer, supplies goods to B, a landowner or annuitant, to be paid for at the end of five years, as much of the capital of A as is equal to the value of these

$^{b-b}$48, 49   the
$^{c-c}$48, 49   most
$^{d-d}$48, 49   persons $^{e-e}$48   by

goods, remains for five years unproductive. During such a period, if payment had been made at once, the sum might have been several times expended and replaced, and goods to the amount might have been several
times produced, consumed, and reproduced: consequently B's withholding
100*l.* for five years, even if he pays at last, has cost to the labouring classes
of the community during that period an absolute loss of probably several
times that amount. A, individually, is compensated, by putting a higher
price upon his goods, which is ultimately paid by B: but there is no compensation made to the labouring classes, the chief sufferers by every
diversion of capital, whether permanently or temporarily, to unproductive
uses. The country has had 100*l.* less of capital during those five years, B
having taken that amount from A's capital, and spent it unproductively, in
anticipation of his own means, and having only after five years set apart
a sum from his income and converted it into capital for the purpose of
indemnifying A.

§ 3. [*Function of credit in economizing the use of money*] Thus far of the
general functions of Credit in production. It is not a productive power in
itself, though, without it, the productive powers already existing could not
be brought into complete employment. But a more intricate portion of the
theory of Credit is its influence on prices; the chief cause of most of the
mercantile phenomena which perplex observers. In a state of commerce
in which much credit is habitually given, general prices at any moment
depend much more upon the state of credit than upon the quantity of
money. For credit, though it is not productive power, is purchasing power;
and a person who, having credit, avails himself of it in the purchase of
goods, creates just as much demand for the goods, and tends quite as
much to raise their price, as if he made an equal amount of purchases
with ready money.

The credit which we are now called upon to consider, as a distinct
purchasing power, independent of money, is of course not credit in its
simplest form, that of money lent by one person to another, and paid
directly into his hands; for when the borrower expends this in purchases,
he makes the purchases with money, not credit, and exerts no purchasing
power over and above that conferred by the money. The forms of credit
which create purchasing power, are those in which no money passes at the
time, and very often *none passes* at all, the transaction being included
with a mass of other transactions in an account, and nothing paid but a
balance. This takes place in a variety of ways, which we shall proceed to
examine, beginning, as is our custom, with the simplest.

First: Suppose A and B to be two dealers, who have transactions with

*ᵃ⁻ᵃ*48, 49, 52, 57   does not pass

each other both as buyers and as sellers. A buys from B on credit. B does the like with respect to A. At the end of the year, the sum of A's debts to B is set against the sum of B's debts to A, and it is ascertained to which side a balance is due. This balance, which may be less than the amount of many of the transactions singly, and is necessarily less than the sum of the transactions, is all that is paid in money; and perhaps even this is not paid, but carried over in an account current to the next year. A single payment of a hundred pounds may in this manner suffice to liquidate a long series of transactions, some of them to the value of thousands.

But secondly: The debts of A to B may be paid without the intervention of money, even though there be no reciprocal debts of B to A. A may satisfy B by making over to him a debt due to himself from a third person, C. This is conveniently done by means of a written instrument, called a bill of exchange, which is, in fact, a transferable order by a creditor upon his debtor, and when *accepted* by the debtor, that is authenticated by his signature, becomes an acknowledgment of debt.

§ 4. [*Bills of exchange*] Bills of exchange were first introduced to save the expense and risk of transporting the precious metals from place to place. "Let it be supposed," says Mr. Henry Thornton,* "that there are in London ten manufacturers who sell their article to ten shopkeepers in York, by whom it is retailed; and that there are in York ten manufacturers of another commodity, who sell it to ten shopkeepers in London. There would be no occasion for the ten shopkeepers in London to send yearly to York guineas for the payment of the York manufacturers, and for the ten York shopkeepers to send yearly as many guineas to London. It would only be necessary for the York manufacturers to receive from each of the shopkeepers at their own door the money in question, giving in return letters which should acknowledge the receipt of it; and which should also direct the money, lying ready in the hands of their debtors in London, to be paid to the London manufacturers, so as to cancel the debt in London in the same manner as that at York. The expense and the risk of all transmission of money would thus be saved. Letters ordering the transfer of the debt are termed, in the language of the present day, bills of exchange. They are bills by which the debt of one person is exchanged for the debt of another; and the debt, perhaps, which is due in one place, for the debt due in another."

*Enquiry into the Nature and Effects of the Paper Credit of Great Britain [London: Hatchard, 1802], p. 24 [–5]. This work, published in 1802, is even now the clearest exposition that I am acquainted with, in the English language, of the modes in which credit is given and taken in a mercantile community.

b–b48, 49, 52, 57, 62 *accepted*

Bills of exchange having been found convenient as means of paying debts at distant places without the expense of transporting the precious metals, their use was afterwards greatly extended from another motive. It is usual in every trade to give a certain length of credit for goods bought: three months, six months, a year, even two years, according to the convenience or custom of the particular trade. A dealer who has sold goods, for which he is to be paid in six months, but who desires to receive *a*payment*a* sooner, draws a bill on his debtor payable in six months, and gets the bill discounted by a banker or other money-lender, that is, transfers the bill to him, receiving the amount, minus interest for the time it has still to run. It has become one of the chief functions of bills of exchange to serve as a means by which a debt due from one person can thus be made available for obtaining credit from another. The convenience of the expedient has led to the frequent creation of bills of exchange not grounded on any debt previously due to the drawer of the bill by the person on whom it is drawn. These are called *accommodation* bills; and sometimes, with a tinge of disapprobation, *fictitious* bills. Their nature is so clearly stated, and with such judicious remarks, by the author whom I have just quoted, that I shall transcribe the entire passage.*

"A, being in want of 100*l.*, requests B to accept a note or bill drawn at two months, which B, therefore, on the face of it, is bound to pay; it is understood, however, that A will take care either to discharge the bill himself, or to furnish B with the means of paying it. A obtains ready money for the bill on the joint credit of the two parties. A fulfils his promise of paying it when due, and thus concludes the transaction. This service rendered by B to A is, however, not unlikely to be requited, at a more or less distant period, by a similar acceptance of a bill on A, drawn and discounted for B's convenience.

"Let us now compare such a bill with a real bill. Let us consider in what points they differ, or seem to differ; and in what they agree.

"They agree, inasmuch as each is a discountable article; each has also been created for the purpose of being discounted; and each is, perhaps, discounted in fact. Each, therefore, serves equally to supply means of speculation to the merchant. So far, moreover, as bills and notes constitute what is called the circulating medium, or paper currency of the country, and prevent the use of guineas, the fictitious and the real bill are upon an equality; and if the price of commodities be raised in proportion to the quantity of paper currency, the one contributes to that rise exactly in the same manner as the other.

"Before we come to the points in which they differ, let us advert to

*Pp. 29–33.

*a–a*48, 49 the amount

one point in which they are commonly supposed to be unlike; but in which they cannot be said always or necessarily to differ.

"Real notes (it is sometimes said) represent actual property. There are actual goods in existence, which are the counterpart to every real note. Notes which are not drawn in consequence of a sale of goods, are a species of false wealth, by which a nation is deceived. These supply only an imaginary capital; the others indicate one that is real.

"In answer to this statement it may be observed, first, that the notes given in consequence of a real sale of goods cannot be considered as on that account *certainly* representing any actual property. Suppose that A sells 100*l*. worth of goods to B at six months' credit, and takes a bill at six months for it; and that B, within a month after, sells the same goods, at a like credit, to C, taking a like bill; and again, that C, after another month, sells them to D, taking a like bill, and so on. There may then, at the end of six months, be six bills of 100*l*. each, existing at the same time; and every one of these may possibly have been discounted. Of all these bills, then, only one represents any actual property.

"In order to justify the supposition that a real bill (as it is called) represents actual property, there ought to be some power in the bill-holder to prevent the property which the bill represents, from being turned to other purposes than that of paying the bill in question. No such power exists; neither the man who holds the real bill, nor the man who discounts it, has any property in the specific goods for which it was given: he as much trusts to the general ability to pay of the giver of the bill, as the holder of any fictitious bill does. The fictitious bill may, in many cases, be a bill given by a person having a large and known capital, a part of which the fictitious bill may be said in that case to represent. The supposition that real bills represent property, and that fictitious bills do not, seems, therefore, to be one by which more than justice is done to one of these species of bills, and something less than justice to the other.

"We come next to some point in which they differ.

"First, the fictitious note, or note of accommodation, is liable to the objection that it professes to be what it is not. This objection, however, lies only against those fictitious bills which are passed as real. In many cases it is sufficiently obvious what they are. Secondly, the fictitious bill is, in general, less likely to be punctually paid than the real one. There is a general presumption, that the dealer in fictitious bills is a man who is a more adventurous speculator than he who carefully abstains from them. It follows, thirdly, that fictitious bills, besides being less safe, are less subject to limitation as to their quantity. The extent of a man's actual sales forms some limit to the amount of his real notes; and as it is highly desirable in commerce that credit should be dealt out to all persons in some sort of regular and due proportion, the measure of a man's actual sales, certified by the appearance of his bills drawn in virtue of those sales, is some rule in the case, though a very imperfect one in many respects.

"A fictitious bill, or bill of accommodation, is evidently in substance the same as any common promissory note; and even better in this respect, that there is but one security to the promissory note, whereas in the case of the bill of accommodation, there are two. So much jealousy subsists lest traders should push their means of raising money too far, that paper, the same in its general nature with that which is given, being the only paper which can be given, by men out of business, is deemed somewhat discreditable when coming from a merchant. And because such paper, when in the merchant's hand, necessarily imitates the paper, which passes on the occasion of a sale of goods, the epithet fictitious has been cast upon it; an epithet which has seemed to countenance the confused and mistaken notion, that there is something altogether false and delusive in the nature of a certain part both of the paper and of the apparent wealth of the country."

A bill of exchange, when merely discounted, and kept in the portfolio of the discounter until it falls due, does not perform the functions or supply the place of money, but is itself bought and sold for money. It is no more currency than the public funds, or any other securities. But when a bill drawn upon one person is paid to another (or even to the same person) in discharge of a debt or a pecuniary claim, it does something for which, if the bill did not exist, money would be required: it performs the functions of currency. This is a use to which bills of exchange are often applied. "They not only," continues Mr. Thornton,* "spare the use of ready money; they also occupy its place in many cases. Let us imagine a farmer in the country to discharge a debt of 10*l.* to his neighbouring grocer, by giving him a bill for that sum, drawn on his cornfactor in London for grain sold in the metropolis; and the grocer to transmit the bill, he having previously indorsed it to a neighbouring sugar-baker, in discharge of a like debt; and the sugar-baker to send it, when again indorsed, to a West India merchant in an outport, and the West India merchant to deliver it to his country banker, who also indorses it, and sends it into further circulation. The bill in this case will have effected five payments, exactly as if it were a 10*l.* note payable to *ᵇ*a*ᵇ* bearer on demand. A multitude of bills pass between trader and trader in the country, in the manner which has been described; and they evidently form, in the strictest sense, a part of the circulating medium of the kingdom."

*P. 40.

ᵇ⁻ᵇ+71 [*not in* Source]

Many bills, both domestic and foreign, are at last presented for payment quite covered with indorsements, each of which represents either a fresh discounting, or a pecuniary transaction in which the bill has performed the functions of money. *Within the present generation*, the circulating medium of Lancashire for sums above five pounds, was almost entirely composed of such bills.

§ 5. [*Promissory notes*] A third form in which credit is employed as a substitute for currency, is that of promissory notes. A bill drawn upon any one and accepted by him, and a note of hand by him promising to pay the same sum, are, as far as he is concerned, exactly equivalent, except that the former commonly bears interest and the latter generally does not[a]; and that the former is commonly payable only after a certain lapse of time, and the latter payable at sight[a]. But it is chiefly in the latter form that it has become in commercial countries, an express occupation to issue such substitutes for money. Dealers in money (as lenders by profession are improperly called) desire, like other dealers, to stretch their operations beyond what can be carried on by their own means: they wish to lend, not their capital merely, but their credit, and not only such portion of their credit as consists of funds actually deposited with them, but their power of obtaining credit from the public generally, so far as they think they can safely employ it. This is done in a very convenient manner by lending their own promissory notes payable to bearer on demand: the borrower being willing to accept these as so much money, because the credit of the lender makes other people willingly receive them on the same footing, in purchases or other payments. These notes, therefore, perform all the functions of currency, and render an equivalent amount of money which was previously in circulation, unnecessary. As, however, being payable on demand, they may be at any time returned on the issuer, and money demanded for them, he must, on pain of bankruptcy, keep by him as much money as will enable him to meet any claims of that sort which can be expected to occur within the time necessary for providing himself with more: and prudence also requires that he should not attempt to issue notes beyond the amount which experience shows can remain in circulation without being presented for payment.

The convenience of this mode of (as it were) coining credit, having once been discovered, governments have availed themselves of the same expedient, and have issued their own promissory notes in payment of their expenses; a resource the more useful, because it is the only mode in which they are able to borrow money without paying interest, their promises to

[c-c]48, 49, 52 Up to twenty years ago
[a-a]+57, 62, 65, 71

pay on demand being, in the estimation of the holders, equivalent to money in hand. The practical differences between such government notes and the issues of private bankers, and the further diversities of which this class of substitutes for money are susceptible, will be considered presently.

§ 6. [*Deposits and cheques*] A fourth mode of making credit answer the purposes of money, by which, when carried far enough, money may be very completely superseded, consists in making payments by cheques. The custom of keeping the spare cash reserved for immediate use or against contingent demands, in the hands of a banker, and making all payments, except small ones, by orders on bankers, is in this country spreading to a continually larger portion of the public. If the person making the payment, and the person receiving it, ^akeep^a their money with the same banker, the payment ^btakes^b place without any intervention of money, by the mere transfer of its amount in the banker's books from the credit of the payer to that of the receiver. If all persons in London kept their cash at the same banker's and made all their payments by means of cheques, no money would be required or used for any transactions beginning and terminating in London. This ideal limit is almost attained in fact, so far as regards transactions between dealers. It is chiefly in the retail transactions between dealers and consumers, and in the payment of wages, that money or bank notes now pass, and then only when the amounts are small. In London, even shopkeepers of any amount of capital or extent of business have generally an account with a banker; which, besides the safety and convenience of the practice, is to their advantage in another respect, by giving them an understood claim to have their bills discounted in cases when they could not otherwise expect it. As for the merchants and larger dealers, they habitually make all payments in the course of their business by cheques. They do not, however, all deal with the same banker, and when A gives a cheque to B, B usually pays it not into the same but into some other bank. But the convenience of business has given birth to an arrangement which makes all the banking houses of the City of London, for certain purposes, virtually one establishment. A banker does not send the cheques which are paid into his banking house, to the banks on which they are drawn, and demand money for them. There is a building called the Clearing-house, to which every City banker sends, each afternoon, all the cheques on other bankers which he has received during the day, and they are there exchanged for the cheques on him which have come into the hands of other bankers, the balances only being paid in money^c; or even these not in money, but in cheques on the Bank of England^c. By this contrivance, all the business

a–a48, 49   kept
b–b48, 49   would take   c–c+57, 62, 65, 71

transactions of the City of London during that day, amounting often to millions of pounds, and a vast amount besides of country transactions, represented by bills which country bankers have drawn upon their London correspondents, are liquidated by payments not exceeding on the average 200,000*l.**

By means of the various instruments of credit which have now been explained, the immense business of a country like Great Britain is transacted with an amount of the precious metals surprisingly small; many times smaller, in proportion to the pecuniary value of the commodities bought and sold, than is found necessary in France, or any other country in which, the habit and the disposition to give credit not being so generally diffused, these "economizing expedients," as they have been called, are not practised to the same extent. What becomes of the money thus superseded in its functions, and by what process it is made to disappear from circulation, are questions the discussion of which must be for a short time postponed.

*According to Mr. [Thomas] Tooke (Inquiry into the Currency Principle [*The Connection of the Currency with Prices, and the Expediency of a Separation of Issue from Banking.* London: Longman, Brown, Green, and Longmans, 1844], p. 27) the adjustments at the clearing-house "in the year 1839 amounted to 954,401,600*l.*, making an average amount of payments of upwards of 3,000,000*l.* of bills of exchange and cheques daily effected through the medium of little more than 200,000*l.* of bank notes." [62] At present a very much greater amount of transactions is daily liquidated, without bank notes at all, cheques on the Bank of England supplying their place.

CHAPTER XII

Influence of Credit on Prices

§ 1. [*The influence of bank notes, bills, and cheques, on price is a part of the influence of Credit*] Having now formed a general idea of the modes in which credit is made available as a substitute for money, we have to consider in what manner the use of these substitutes affects the value of money, or, what is equivalent, the prices of commodities. It is hardly necessary to say that the permanent value of money—the natural and average prices of commodities—are not in question here. These are determined by the cost of producing or of obtaining the precious metals. An ounce of gold or silver will in the long run exchange for as much of every other commodity, as can be produced or imported at the same cost with itself. And an order, or note of hand, or bill payable at sight, for an ounce of gold, while the credit of the giver is unimpaired, is worth neither more nor less than the gold itself.

It is not, however, with ultimate or average, but with immediate and temporary prices, that we are now concerned. These, as we have seen, may deviate very widely from the standard of cost of production. Among other causes of fluctuation, one we have found to be, the quantity of money in circulation. Other things being the same, an increase of the money in circulation raises prices, a diminution lowers them. If more money is thrown into circulation than the quantity which can circulate at a value conformable to its cost of production, the value of money, so long as the excess lasts, will remain below the standard of cost of production, and general prices will be sustained above the natural rate.

But we have now found that there are other things, such as bank notes, bills of exchange, and cheques, which circulate as money, and perform all the functions of it: and the question arises, Do these various substitutes operate on prices in the same manner as money itself? Does an increase in the quantity of transferable paper tend to raise prices, in the same manner and degree as an increase in the quantity of money? There has been no small amount of discussion on this point among writers on currency, without any result so conclusive as to have yet obtained general assent.

I apprehend that bank notes, bills, or cheques, as such, do not act on prices at all. What does act on prices is Credit, in whatever shape given, and whether it gives rise to any transferable instruments capable of passing into circulation, or not.

I proceed to explain and substantiate this opinion.

§ 2. [*Credit is a purchasing power similar to money*] Money acts upon prices in no other way than by being tendered in exchange for commodities. The demand which influences the prices of commodities consists of the money offered for them. But the money offered, is not the same thing with the money possessed. It is sometimes less, sometimes very much more. In the long run indeed, the money which people lay out will be neither more nor less than the money which they have to lay out: but this is far from being the case at any given time. Sometimes they keep money by them for fear of an emergency, or in expectation of a more advantageous opportunity for expending it. In that case the money is said not to be in circulation: in plainer language, it is not offered, nor about to be offered, for commodities. Money not in circulation has no effect on prices. The converse, however, is a much commoner case; people make purchases with money not in their possession. An article, for instance, which is paid for by a cheque on a banker, is bought with money which not only is not in the payer's possession, but generally not even in the banker's, having been lent by him (all but the usual reserve) to other persons. We just now made the imaginary supposition that all persons dealt with a bank, and all with the same bank, payments being universally made by cheques. In this ideal case, there would be no money anywhere except in the hands of the banker: who might then safely part with all of it, by selling it as bullion, or lending it, to be sent out of the country in exchange for goods or foreign securities. But though there would then be no money in possession, or ultimately perhaps even in existence, money would be offered, and commodities bought with it, just as at present. People would continue to reckon their incomes and their capitals in money, and to make their usual purchases with orders for the receipt of a thing which would have literally ceased to exist. There would be in all this nothing to complain of, so long as the money, in disappearing, left *a* an equivalent value in other things, applicable when required to the reimbursement of those to whom the money originally belonged.

In the case however of payment by cheques, the purchases are at any rate made, though not with money in the buyer's possession, yet with money to which he has a right. But he may make purchases with money which he only expects to have, or even only pretends to expect. He may obtain goods in return for his acceptances payable at a future time; or on his note of hand; or on a simple book credit, that is, on a mere promise

a 48, 49   behind it

to pay. All these purchases have exactly the same effect on price, as if they were made with ready money. The amount of purchasing power which a person can exercise is composed of all the money in his possession or due to him, and of all his credit. For exercising the whole of this power he finds a sufficient motive only under peculiar circumstances; but he always possesses it; and the portion of it which he at any time does exercise, is the measure of the effect which he produces on price.

Suppose that, in the expectation that some commodity will rise in price, he determines, not only to invest in it all his ready money, but to take up on credit, from the producers or importers, as much of it as their opinion of his resources will enable him to obtain. Every one must see that by thus acting he produces a greater effect on price, than if he limited his purchases to the money he has actually in hand. He creates a demand for the article to the full amount of his money and credit taken together, and raises the price proportionally to both. And this effect is produced, though none of the written instruments called substitutes for currency may be called into existence; though the transaction may give rise to no bill of exchange, nor to the issue of a single bank note. The buyer, instead of taking a mere book credit, might have given a bill for the amount; or might have paid for the goods with bank notes borrowed for that purpose from a banker, thus making the purchase not on his own credit with the seller, but on the banker's credit with the seller, and his own with the banker. Had he done so, he would have produced as great an effect on price as by a simple purchase to the same amount on a book credit, but no greater effect. The credit itself, not the form and mode in which it is given, is the operating cause.

§ 3. [*Effects of great extensions and contractions of credit. Phenomena of a commercial crisis analyzed*] The inclination of the mercantile public to increase their demand for commodities by making use of all or much of their credit as a purchasing power, depends on their expectation of profit. When there is a general impression that the price of some commodity is likely to rise, from an extra demand, a short crop, obstructions to importation, or any other cause, there is a disposition among dealers to increase their stocks, in order to profit by the expected rise. This disposition tends in itself to produce the effect which it looks forward to, a rise of price: and if the rise is considerable and progressive, other speculators are attracted, who, so long as the price has not begun to fall, are willing to believe that it will continue rising. These, by further purchases, produce a further advance: and thus a rise of price for which there were originally some rational grounds, is often heightened by merely speculative purchases, until it greatly exceeds what the original grounds will justify.

After a time this begins to be perceived; the price ceases to rise, and the holders, thinking it *a* time to realize their gains, are anxious to sell. Then the price begins to decline: the holders rush into the market to avoid a still greater loss, and, few being willing to buy in a falling market, the price falls much more suddenly than it rose. Those who have bought at a higher price than reasonable calculation justified, and who have been overtaken by the revulsion before they had realized, are losers in proportion to the greatness of the fall, and to the quantity of the commodity which they hold, or have bound themselves to pay for.

Now all these effects might take place in a community to which credit was unknown: the prices of some commodities might rise from speculation, to an extravagant height, and then fall rapidly back. But if there were no such thing as credit, this could hardly happen with respect to commodities generally. If all purchases were made with ready money, the payment of increased prices for some articles would draw an unusual proportion of the money of the community into the markets for those articles, and must therefore draw it away from some other class of commodities, and thus lower their prices. The vacuum might, it is true, be partly filled up by increased rapidity of circulation; and in *b*this manner*b* the money of the community *c*is*c* virtually increased in a time of speculative activity, because people keep little of it by them, but hasten to lay it out in some tempting adventure as soon as possible after they receive it. This resource, however, is limited: on the whole, people cannot, while the quantity of money remains the same, lay out much more of it in some things, without laying out less in others. But what they cannot do by ready money, they can do by an extension of credit. When people go into the market and purchase with money which they hope to receive hereafter, they are drawing upon an unlimited, not a limited fund. Speculation, thus supported, may be going on in any number of commodities, without disturbing the regular course of business in others. It might even be going on in all commodities at once. We could imagine that in an epidemic fit of the passion of gambling, all dealers, instead of giving only their accustomed orders to the manufacturers or growers of their commodity, commenced buying up all of it which they could procure, as far as their capital and credit would go. All prices would rise enormously, even if there *d*were*d* no increase of money, and no paper credit, but a mere extension of purchases on book credits. After a time those who had bought would wish to sell, and prices would collapse.

This is the ideal extreme case of what is called a commercial crisis. There is said to be a commercial crisis, when a great number of merchants

*a*48, 49, 52 is   *b-b*48 fact
*c-c*48 *is*   *d-d*49, 52 was

and traders at once, either have, or apprehend that they shall have, a difficulty in meeting their engagements. The most usual cause of this general embarrassment, is the recoil of prices after they have been raised by a spirit of speculation, intense in degree, and extending to many commodities. Some accident which excites expectations of rising prices, such as the opening of a new foreign market, or simultaneous indications of a short supply of several great articles of commerce, sets speculation at work in several leading departments at once. The prices rise, and the holders realize, or appear to have the power of realizing, great gains. In certain states of the public mind, such examples of rapid increase of fortune call forth numerous imitators, and speculation not only goes much beyond what is justified by the original grounds for expecting rise of price, but extends itself to articles in which there never was any such ground: these, however, rise like the rest as soon as speculation sets in. At periods of this kind, a great extension of credit takes place. Not only do all whom the contagion reaches, employ their credit much more freely than usual; but they really have more credit, because they seem to be making unusual gains, and because a generally reckless and adventurous feeling prevails, which disposes people to give as well as take credit more largely than at other times, and give it to persons not entitled to it. In this manner, in the celebrated speculative year 1825, and at various other periods during the present century, the prices of many of the principal articles of commerce rose greatly, without any fall in others, so that general prices might, without incorrectness, be said to have risen. When, after such a rise, the reaction comes, and prices begin to fall, though at first perhaps only through the desire of the holders to realize, speculative purchases cease: but were this all, prices would only fall to the level from which they rose, or to that which is justified by the state of the consumption and of the supply. They fall, however, much lower; for as, when prices were rising, and everybody apparently making a fortune, it was easy to obtain almost any amount of credit, so now, when everybody seems to be losing, and many fail entirely, it is with difficulty that firms of known solidity can obtain even the credit to which they are accustomed, and which it is the greatest inconvenience to them to be without; because all dealers have engagements to fulfil, and nobody feeling sure that the portion of his means which he has entrusted to others will be available in time, no one likes to part with ready money, or to postpone his claim to it. To these rational considerations there is superadded, in extreme cases, a panic as unreasoning as the previous overconfidence; money is borrowed for short periods at almost any rate of interest, and sales of goods for immediate payment are made at almost any sacrifice. Thus general prices, during a commercial revulsion, fall as much below the usual level, as during the previous period of speculation they *have* risen above it: the fall, as well as the rise, originating not in anything affecting money, but in the state of credit; an unusually extended employment of credit during the earlier period, followed by a great diminution, never amounting however to an entire cessation of it, in the later.

It is not, however, universally true that the contraction of credit, characteristic of a commercial crisis, must have been preceded by an extraordinary and irrational extension of it. There are other causes; and *one of the more* recent *crises*, that of 1847, is an instance, having been preceded by no particular extension of credit, and by no speculations; except those in railway shares, which, though in many cases extravagant enough, yet being carried on mostly with that portion of means which the speculators could afford to lose, were not calculated to produce the widespread ruin which arises from vicissitudes of price in the commodities in which men habitually deal, and in which the bulk of their capital is invested. The crisis of 1847 belonged to another class of mercantile phenomena. There occasionally happens a concurrence of circumstances tending to withdraw from the loan market a considerable portion of the capital which usually supplies it. These circumstances, in the present case, were great foreign payments, (occasioned by *a* high price of cotton and *an* unprecedented importation of food,) together with the continual demands on the circulating capital of the country by railway calls and the loan transactions of railway companies, for the purpose of being converted into fixed capital and made unavailable for future lending. These various demands fell principally, as such demands always do, on the loan market. A great, though not the greatest part of the imported food, was actually paid for by the proceeds of a government loan. The extra payments which purchasers of corn and cotton, and railway shareholders, found themselves obliged to make, were either made with their own spare cash, or with money raised for the occasion. On the first supposition, they were made by withdrawing deposits from bankers, and thus cutting off a part of the streams which fed the loan market; on the second supposition, they were made by actual drafts on the loan market, either by the sale of securities, or by taking up money at interest. This combination of a fresh demand for loans, with a curtailment of the capital disposable for them, raised the rate of interest, and made it impossible to borrow except on the very best security. Some firms, therefore, which by an improvident and unmercantile mode of conducting business had allowed their capital to become either temporarily or permanently unavailable, became unable

*e-e*48, 49, 52, 57   had
*f-f*48, 49, 52, 57   the most] 62, 65   one of the most
*g-g*48, 49, 52, 57   crisis
*h-h*48, 49, 52, 57   the   *i-i*48, 49, 52, 57   the

to command that perpetual renewal of credit which had previously
enabled them to struggle on. These firms stopped payment: their failure
involved more or less deeply many other firms which had trusted them;
and, as usual in such cases, the general distrust, commonly called a panic,
began to set in, and might have produced a destruction of credit equal to
that of 1825, had not circumstances which may almost be called accidental,
given to a very simple measure of the government ʲ(the suspension of the
Bank Charter Act of 1844)ʲ a fortunate power of allaying panic, to which,
when considered in itself, it had no sort of claim.*

§ 4. [*Bills are a more powerful instrument for acting on prices than
book credits, and bank notes than bills*] The general operation of credit
upon prices being such as we have described, it is evident that if any
particular mode or form of credit is calculated to have a greater operation
on prices than others, it can only be by giving greater facility, or greater
encouragement, to the multiplication of credit transactions generally. If
bank notes, for instance, or bills, have a greater effect on prices than book
credits, it is not by any difference in the transactions themselves, which
are essentially the same, whether taking place in the one way or in the
other: it must be that there are likely to be more of them. If credit is likely
to be more extensively used as a purchasing power when bank notes or
bills are the instruments used, than when the credit is given by mere entries
in an account, to that extent and no more there is ground for ascribing to
the former a greater power over the markets than belongs to the latter.

Now it appears that there is some such distinction. As far as respects
the particular ᵃtransactionsᵃ, it makes no difference in the effect on price
whether A buys goods of B on simple credit, or gives a bill for them, or
pays for them with bank notes lent to him by a banker C. The difference
is in a subsequent stage. If A has bought the goods on a book credit, there
is no obvious or convenient mode by which B can make A's debt to him
a means of extending his own credit. Whatever credit he has, will be due
to the general opinion entertained of his solvency; he cannot specifically
pledge A's debt to a third person, as a security for money lent or goods
bought. But if A has given him a bill for the amount, he can get this
discounted, which is the same thing as borrowing money on the joint credit

*[65] The commercial difficulties, not however amounting to a commercial
crisis, of 1864, had essentially the same origin. Heavy payments for cotton
imported at high prices, and large investments in banking and other joint stock
projects, combined with the loan operations of foreign governments, made such
large drafts upon the loan market as to raise the rate of discount on mercantile
bills as high as nine per cent.

ʲ⁻ʲ+52, 57, 62, 65, 71   ᵃ⁻ᵃ48, 49, 52, 57, 62, 65   transaction of A and himself: or he may pay away the bill in exchange for goods, which is obtaining goods on the same joint credit. In either case, here is a second credit transaction, grounded on the first, and which would not have taken place if the first had been transacted without the intervention of a bill. Nor need the transactions end here. The bill may be again discounted, or again paid away for goods, several times before it is itself presented for payment. Nor would it be correct to say that these successive holders, if they had not had the bill, might have attained their purpose by purchasing goods on their own credit with the dealers. They may not all of them be persons of credit, or they may already have stretched their credit as far as it will go. And at all events, either money or goods are more readily obtained on the credit of two persons than of one. Nobody will pretend that it is as easy a thing for a merchant to borrow a thousand pounds on his own credit, as to get a bill discounted to the same amount, when the drawee is of known solvency *b* .

If we now suppose that A, instead of giving a bill, obtains a loan of bank notes from a banker C, and with them pays B for his goods, we shall find the difference to be still greater. B is now independent even of a discounter: A's bill would have been taken in payment only by those who were acquainted with his reputation for solvency, but a banker is a person who has credit with the public generally, and whose notes are taken in payment by every one, at least in his own neighbourhood: insomuch that, by a custom which has grown into law, payment in bank notes is a complete acquittance to the payer, whereas if he has paid by a bill, he still remains liable to the debt, if the person on whom the bill is drawn fails to pay it when due. B therefore can expend the whole of the bank notes without at all involving his own credit; and whatever power he had before of obtaining goods on book credit, remains to him unimpaired, in addition to the purchasing power he derives from the possession of the notes. The same remark applies to every person in succession, into whose hands the notes may come. It is only A, the first holder, (who used his credit to obtain the notes as a loan from the issuer,) who can possibly find the credit he possesses in other quarters abated by it; and even in his case that result is not probable; for though, in reason, and if all his circumstances were known, every draft already made upon his credit ought to diminish by so much his power of obtaining more, yet in practice the reverse more frequently happens, and his having been trusted by one person is supposed to be *c*evidence that*c* he may safely be trusted by others also.

It appears, therefore, that bank notes are a more powerful instrument

*b*48, 49, 52   ; or that he can as easily obtain goods on a book credit, as by paying for them with such a bill

*c–c*48, 49, 52   a reason why

for raising prices than bills, and bills than book credits. It does not, indeed, follow that credit *will* be more used because it *can* be. When the state of trade holds out no particular temptation to make large purchases on credit, dealers will use only a small portion of the credit power, and it will depend only on convenience whether the portion which they use will be taken in one form or in another. It is not until the circumstances of the markets, and the state of the mercantile mind, render many persons desirous of stretching their credit to an unusual extent, that the distinctive properties of the different forms of credit display themselves. Credit already stretched to the utmost in the form of book debts, would be susceptible of ^{d}a^d great additional extension by means of bills, and of ^{e}a^e still greater by means of bank notes. The first, because each dealer, in addition to his own credit, would be enabled to create a further purchasing power out of the credit which he had himself given to others: the second, because the banker's credit with the public at large, coined into notes, as bullion is coined into pieces of money to make it portable and divisible, is so much purchasing power superadded, in the hands of every successive holder, to that which he may derive from his own credit. To state the matter otherwise; one single exertion of the credit-power in the form of book credit, is only the foundation of a single purchase: but if a bill is drawn, that same portion of credit may serve for as many purchases as the number of times the bill changes hands: while every bank note issued, renders the credit of the banker a purchasing power to that amount in the hands of all the successive holders, without impairing any power they may possess of effecting purchases on their own credit. Credit, in short, has exactly the same purchasing power with money; and as money tells upon prices not simply in proportion to its amount, but to its amount multiplied by the number of times it changes hands, so also does credit; and credit transferable from hand to hand is in that proportion more potent, than credit which only performs one purchase.

§ 5. [*The distinction between bills, book credits, and bank notes is of little practical importance*] All this purchasing power, however, is operative upon prices, only according to the proportion of it which is used; and the effect, therefore, is only felt in a state of circumstances calculated to lead to an unusually extended use of credit. In such a state of circumstances, that is, in speculative times, it cannot, I think, be denied, that prices are likely to rise higher if the speculative purchases are made with bank notes, than when they are made with bills, and when made by bills than when made by book credits. This, however, is of far less practical importance than might at first be imagined; because, in point of fact, speculative

$^{d\text{-}d}$+49, 52, 57, 62, 65, 71
$^{e\text{-}e}$+62, 65, 71

purchases are not, in the great majority of cases, made either with bank notes or with bills, but are made almost exclusively on book credits. "Applications to the Bank for extended discount," says the highest authority on such subjects,* (and the same thing must be true of applications to other banks) "occur rarely if ever in the origin or progress of extensive speculations in commodities. These are entered into, for the most part if not entirely, in the first instance, on credit, for the length of term usual in the several trades; thus entailing on the parties no immediate necessity for borrowing so much as may be wanted for the purpose beyond their own available capital. This applies particularly to speculative purchases of commodities on the spot, with a view to resale. But these generally form the smaller proportion of engagements on credit. By far the largest of those entered into on the prospect of a rise of prices, are such as have in view importations from abroad. The same remark, too, is applicable to the export of commodities, when a large proportion is on the credit of the shippers or their consignees. As long as circumstances hold out the prospect of a favourable result, the credit of the parties is generally sustained. If some of them wish to realize, there are others with capital and credit ready to replace them; and if the events fully justify the grounds on which the speculative transactions were entered into (thus admitting of sales for consumption in time to replace the capital embarked) there is no unusual demand for borrowed capital to sustain them. It is only when by the vicissitudes of political events, or of the seasons, or other adventitious circumstances, the forthcoming supplies are found to exceed the computed rate of consumption, and a fall of prices ensues, that an increased demand for capital takes place; the market rate of interest then rises, and increased applications are made to the Bank of England for discount." So that the multiplication of bank notes and other transferable paper does not, for the most part, accompany and facilitate the speculation; but comes into play chiefly when the tide is turning, and difficulties begin to be felt.

Of the extraordinary height to which speculative transactions can be carried upon mere book credits, without the smallest addition to what is commonly called the currency, very few persons are at all aware. "The power of purchase," says Mr. Tooke,† "by persons having capital and credit, is much beyond anything that those who are unacquainted practically with speculative markets have any idea of. . . . A person having the reputation of capital enough for his regular business, and enjoying good credit in his trade, if he takes a sanguine view of the prospect of a rise of price

---

*Tooke's *History of Prices* [London: Longman, Brown, Green, and Longmans, 1848], vol. iv. pp. 125–6. [48   *From the fourth volume, just published, of Mr. Tooke's *History of Prices*, pp. 125–6.]

†Inquiry into the Currency Principle, pp. 79 and 136–8.

of the article in which he deals, and is favoured by circumstances in the
outset and progress of his speculation, may effect purchases to an extent
perfectly enormous, compared with his capital." Mr. Tooke confirms this
statement by some remarkable instances, exemplifying the immense
purchasing power which may be exercised, and rise of price which may
be produced, by credit not represented by either bank notes or bills of
exchange.

"Amongst the *earlier* speculators for an advance in the price of tea, in
consequence of our dispute with China in 1839, were several retail grocers
and tea-dealers. There was a general disposition among the trade to get
into stock: that is, to lay in at once a quantity which would meet the
probable demand from their customers for several months to come. Some,
however, among them, more sanguine and adventurous than the rest,
availed themselves of their credit with the importers and wholesale dealers,
for purchasing quantities much beyond the estimated demand in their own
business. As the purchases were made in the first instance ostensibly, and
perhaps really, for the legitimate purposes and within the limits of their
regular business, the parties were enabled to buy without the condition of
any deposit; whereas speculators, known to be such, are required to pay
2*l.* per chest, to cover any probable difference of price which might arise
before the expiration of the prompt, which, for this article, is three months.
Without, therefore, the outlay of a single farthing of actual capital or
currency in any shape, they made purchases to a considerable extent; and
with the profit realized on the resale of a part of these purchases, they were
enabled to pay the deposit on further quantities when required, as was
the case when the extent of the purchases attracted attention. In this way,
the speculation went on at advancing prices (100 per cent and upwards)
till nearly the expiration of the prompt, and if at that time circumstances
had been such as to justify the apprehension which at one time prevailed,
that all future supplies would be cut off, the prices might have still further
advanced, and at any rate not have retrograded. In this case, the speculators
might have realized, if not all the profit they had anticipated, a very
handsome sum, upon which they might have been enabled to extend their
business greatly, or to retire from it altogether, with a reputation for great
sagacity in thus making their fortune. But instead of this favourable result,
it so happened that two or three cargoes of tea which had been transhipped
were admitted, contrary to expectation, to entry on their arrival here, and
it was found that further indirect shipments were in progress. Thus the
supply was increased beyond the calculation of the speculators: and at the
same time, the consumption had been diminished by the high price. There
was, consequently, a violent reaction on the market; the speculators were

*a–a*Source, 48   earliest

unable to sell without such a sacrifice as disabled them from fulfilling their engagements, and several of them consequently failed. Among these, one was mentioned, who having a capital not exceeding 1200*l*. which was locked up in his business, had contrived to buy 4000 chests, value above 80,000*l*., the loss upon which was about 16,000*l*.

"The other example which I have to give, is that of the operation on the corn market between 1838 and 1842. There was an instance of a person who, when he entered on his extensive speculations, was, as it appeared by the subsequent examination of his affairs, possessed of a capital not exceeding 5000*l*., but being successful in the outset, and favoured by circumstances in the progress of his operations, he contrived to make purchases to such an extent, that when he stopped payment his engagements were found to amount to between 500,000*l*. and 600,000*l*. Other instances might be cited of parties without any capital at all, who, by dint of mere credit, were enabled, while the aspect of the market favoured their views, to make purchases to a very great extent.

"And be it observed, that these speculations, involving enormous purchases on little or no capital, were carried on in 1839 and 1840, when the money market was in its most contracted state; or when, according to modern phraseology, there was the greatest scarcity of money."

But though the great instrument of speculative purchases is book credits, it cannot be contested that in speculative periods an increase does take place in the quantity both of bills of exchange and of bank notes. This increase, indeed, so far as bank notes are concerned, hardly ever takes place in the earliest stage of the speculations: advances from bankers (as Mr. Tooke observes) not being applied for in order to purchase, but in order to hold on without selling when the usual term of credit has expired, and the high price which was calculated on has not arrived. But the tea speculators mentioned by Mr. Tooke could not have carried their speculations beyond the three months which are the usual term of credit in their trade, unless they had been able to obtain advances from bankers, which, if the expectation of a rise of price had still continued, they probably could have done.

Since, then, credit in the form of bank notes is a more potent instrument for raising prices than book credits, an unrestrained power of resorting to this instrument may contribute to prolong and heighten the speculative rise of prices, and hence to aggravate the subsequent recoil. But in what degree? and what importance ought we to ascribe to this possibility? It may help us to form some judgment on this point, if we consider the proportion which the utmost increase of bank notes in a period of speculation, bears, I do not say to the whole mass of credit in the country, but to the bills of exchange alone. The average amount of bills in existence at any one time is supposed *greatly* to exceed a hundred millions sterling.* The bank note circulation of Great Britain and Ireland *seldom exceeds forty* millions, and the increase in speculative periods at most two or three. And even this, as we have seen, hardly ever comes into play until that advanced period of the speculation at which the tide shows signs of turning, and the dealers generally are rather thinking of the means of fulfilling their existing engagements, than meditating an extension of them: while the quantity of bills in existence is largely increased from the very commencement of the speculations.

§ 6. [*Cheques are an instrument for acting on prices, equally powerful with bank notes*] It is well known that of late years, an artificial limitation of the issue of bank notes has been regarded by many political economists, and by a great portion of the public, as an expedient of supreme efficacy for preventing, and when it cannot prevent, for moderating, the fever of speculation; and this opinion received the recognition and sanction of the legislature by the Currency Act of 1844. At the point, however, which our

*The most approved estimate is that of Mr. Leatham, grounded on the official returns of bill stamps issued. The following are the results:—

Year	Bills created in Great Britain and Ireland, founded on returns of Bill Stamps issued from the Stamp Office	Average amount in circulation at one time in each year
1832	£ 356,153,409	£ 89,038,352
1833	383,659,585	95,914,896
1834	379,155,052	94,788,763
1835	405,403,051	101,350,762
1836	485,943,473	121,485,868
1837	455,084,445	113,771,111
1838	465,504,041	116,376,010
1839	528,493,842	132,123,460

"Mr. Leatham," says Mr. Tooke, "gives the process by which, upon the data furnished by the returns of stamps, he arrives at these results; and I am disposed to think that they are as near an approximation to the truth as the nature of the materials admits of arriving at."—*Inquiry into the Currency Principle*, p. 26. [62] Mr. Newmarch (Appendix No. 39 *to Report of the Committee on the Bank Acts in* 1857 [*Parliamentary Papers*, 1857 (Sess. 2), X. ii, 326], and *History of Prices* [*and of the State of the Circulation, during the Nine Years 1848–1856*. London: Longman, Brown, Green, Longmans, and Roberts, 1857], vol. vi. p. 587) shows grounds for the opinion that the total bill circulation in 1857 was not much less than 180 millions sterling, and that it sometimes rises to 200 millions.

*b–b*48, 49, 52, 57   considerably
*c–c*48, 49, 52, 57   is less than thirty-five

inquiries have reached, though we have conceded to bank notes a greater power over prices than is possessed by bills or book credits, we have not found reason to think that this superior efficacy has much share in producing the rise of prices which accompanies a period of speculation, nor consequently that any restraint applied to this one instrument can be efficacious to the degree which is often supposed, in moderating either that rise, or the recoil which follows it. We shall be still less inclined to think so, when we consider that there is a fourth form of credit transactions, by cheques on bankers, and transfers in a banker's books, which is exactly parallel in every respect to bank notes, giving equal facilities to an extension of credit, and capable of acting on prices quite as powerfully. In the words of Mr. Fullarton,* "there is not a single object at present attained through the agency of Bank of England notes, which might not be as effectually accomplished by each individual keeping an account with the bank, and transacting all his payments of five pounds and upwards by cheque." A bank, instead of lending its notes to a merchant or dealer, might open an account with him, and credit the account with the sum it had agreed to advance: on an understanding that he should not draw out that sum in any other mode than by drawing cheques against it in favour of those to whom he had occasion to make payments. These cheques might possibly even pass from hand to hand like bank notes; more commonly however the receiver would pay them into the hands of his own banker, and when he wanted the money, would draw a fresh cheque against it: and hence an objector may *urge* that as the original cheque would very soon be presented for payment, when it must be paid either in notes or in coin, notes or coin to an equal amount must be provided as the ultimate means of liquidation. It is not so, however. The person to whom the cheque is transferred, may perhaps deal with the same banker, and the cheque may return to the very bank on which it was drawn: this is very often the case in country districts; if so, no payment will be called for, but a simple transfer in the banker's books will settle the transaction. If the cheque is paid into a different bank, it will not be presented for payment, but liquidated by set-off against other cheques; and in a state of circumstances favourable to a general extension of banking credits, a banker who has granted more credit, and has therefore more cheques drawn on him, will also have more cheques on other bankers paid to him, and will only have to provide notes or cash for the payment of balances; for which purpose the ordinary reserve of prudent bankers, one-third of their liabilities, will abundantly suffice. Now, if he had granted the extension of credit by means of an issue of his own notes, he must equally have retained, in coin *or Bank of England notes,* the usual

*On the Regulation of Currencies, p. 41.

*ᵃ⁻ᵃ*48, 49 suggest,   *ᵇ⁻ᵇ*+52, 57, 62, 65, 71

reserve: so that he can, as Mr. Fullarton says, give every facility of credit by what may be termed a cheque circulation, which he could give by a note circulation.

This extension of credit by entries in a banker's books, has all that superior efficiency in acting on prices, which we ascribed to an extension by means of bank notes. As a bank note of 20*l*., paid to any one, gives him 20*l*. of purchasing-power based on credit, over and above whatever credit he had of his own, so does a cheque paid to him do the same: for, although he may make no purchase with the cheque itself, he deposits it with his banker, and can draw against it. As this act of drawing a cheque against another which has been exchanged and cancelled, can be repeated as often as a purchase with a bank note, it effects the same increase of purchasing power. The original loan, or credit, given by the banker to his customer, is potentially multiplied as a means of purchase, in the hands of the successive persons to whom portions of the credit are paid away, just as the purchasing power of a bank note is multiplied by the number of persons through whose hands it passes before it is returned to the issuer.

These considerations abate very much from the importance of any effect which can be produced in allaying the vicissitudes of commerce, by so superficial a contrivance as the one so much relied on of late, the restriction of the issue of bank notes by an artificial rule. An examination of all the consequences of that restriction, and *c*an*c* estimate of the reasons for and against it, must be deferred until we have treated of the foreign exchanges, and the international movements of bullion. At present we are only concerned with the general theory of prices, of which the different influence of different kinds of credit is an essential part.

a§ 7. [*Are bank notes money?*] There has been a great amount of discussion and argument on the question whether several of these forms of credit, and in particular whether bank notes, ought to be considered as money. The question is so purely verbal as to be *b*scarcely worth raising*b*, and one would have some difficulty in comprehending why so much importance is attached to it, if there were not some *c*authorities*c* who, still adhering to the doctrine of the infancy of society and of political economy, that the quantity of money compared with that of commodities, determines general prices, think it important to prove that bank notes and no other forms of credit are money, in order to support the inference that bank notes and no other forms of credit influence prices. It is obvious, however, that prices do not depend on money, but on purchases. Money left with a banker, and not drawn against, or drawn against for other purposes than buying commodities, has no effect on prices, any more than credit which

*c–c*48, 49, 52   a full   *a–a*553+57, 62, 65, 71
*b–b*57   almost frivolous   *c–c*57   writers

is not used. Credit which ^{d}is^d used to purchase commodities, affects prices in the same manner as money. Money and credit are thus exactly on a par, in their effect on prices; and whether we choose to class bank notes with the one or the other, is in this respect entirely immaterial.

Since, however, this question of nomenclature has been raised, it seems desirable that it should be answered. The reason given for considering bank notes as money, is, that by law and usage they have the property, in common with metallic money, of finally closing the transactions in which they are employed; while no other mode of paying one debt by transferring another, has that privilege. The first remark which here suggests itself is, that on this showing, the notes at least of private banks are not money; for a creditor cannot be forced to accept them in payment of a debt. They certainly close the transaction if he does accept them; but so, on the same supposition, would a bale of cloth, or a pipe of wine; which are not for that reason regarded as money. It seems to be an essential part of the idea of money, that it be legal tender. An inconvertible paper which is legal tender is universally admitted to be money; in the French language the phrase *papier-monnaie* actually *means* inconvertibility, convertible notes being merely *billets à porteur*. It is only in the case of Bank of England notes under the law of convertibility, that any difficulty arises; those notes not being a legal tender from the Bank itself, though a legal tender from all other persons. Bank of England notes undoubtedly do close transactions, so far as respects the buyer. When he has once paid in Bank of England notes, he can in no case be required to pay over again. But I confess I cannot see how the transaction can be deemed complete as regards the seller, when he will only be found to have received the price of his commodity provided the Bank keeps its promise to pay. An instrument which would be deprived of all value by the insolvency of a corporation, cannot be money in any sense in which money is opposed to credit. It either is not money, or it is money and credit too. It may be most suitably described as coined credit. The other forms of credit may be distinguished from it as credit in ingots.^{a}

^{a}§ 8.^{a} [*There is no generic distinction between bank notes and other forms of credit*] Some high authorities have claimed for bank notes, as compared with other modes of credit, a greater distinction in respect to influence on price, than we have seen reason to allow; a difference, not in degree, but in kind. They ground this distinction on the fact, that ^{b} all bills and cheques, as well as all book-debts, are from the first intended to be,

$^{d-d}$57, 62 *is*
$^{a-a}$48, 49, 52 §7.
^{b}48, 49, 52 bank notes have the property, in common with metallic money, of finally closing the transactions in which they are employed; while no other mode of paying one debt by transferring another, has that privilege, but, on the contrary,

and actually are, ultimately liquidated either in coin or in notes. The bank notes in circulation, jointly with the coin, are therefore, according to these authorities, the basis on which all the other expedients of credit rest; and in proportion to the basis will be the superstructure; insomuch that the quantity of bank notes determines that of all the other forms of credit. If bank notes are multiplied, there will, they seem to think, be more bills, more payments by cheque, and I presume, more book credits; and by regulating and limiting the issue of bank notes, they think that all other forms of credit are, by an indirect consequence, brought under a similar limitation. I believe I have stated the opinion of these authorities correctly, though I have nowhere seen the grounds of it set forth with such distinctness as to make me feel quite certain that I understand them. ᶜIt may be true, that according as there are more or fewer bank notes, there is also in general (though not invariably,), more or less of other descriptions of credit; for the same state of affairs which leads to an increase of credit in one shape, leads to an increase of it in other shapes. But I see no reason for believing that the one is the cause of the other.ᶜ If indeed we begin by assuming, as I suspect is tacitly done, that prices are regulated by coin and bank notes, the proposition maintained will certainly follow; for, according as prices are higher or lower, the same purchases will give rise to bills, cheques, and book credits of a larger or ᵈaᵈ smaller amount. But the premise in this reasoning is the very proposition to be proved. Setting this assumption aside, I know not how the conclusion can be substantiated. The credit given to any one by those with whom he deals, does not depend on the quantity of bank notes or coin in circulation at the time, but on their opinion of his solvency: if any consideration of a more general character enters into their calculation, it is only in a time of pressure on the loan market, when they are not certain of being themselves able to obtain the credit on which they have been accustomed to rely; and even then, what they look to is the general state of the loan market, and not (preconceived theory apart) the amount of bank notes. So far, as to the willingness to *give* credit. And the willingness of ᵉa dealerᵉ to *use* his credit, depends on his expectations of gain, that is, on his opinion of the probable future price of his commodity; an opinion grounded either on the rise or fall already going on, or on his prospective judgment respecting the supply and the rate of consumption. When a dealer extends his purchases beyond his immediate means of payment, engaging to pay at a specified time, he does so in the expectation either that the transaction will have terminated favourably before that time arrives, or that he shall then be in possession of sufficient funds from the

ᶜ⁻ᶜ48, 49, 52 I can see no reason for the doctrine, that according as there are more or fewer bank notes, there will be more or less of other descriptions of credit.
ᵈ⁻ᵈ+49, 52, 57, 62, 65, 71   ᵉ⁻ᵉ48 any one

proceeds of his other transactions. The fufilment of these expectations depends upon prices, but not *especially* upon the amount of bank notes. He may, doubtless, also ask himself, in case he should be disappointed in these expectations, to what quarter he can look for a temporary advance, to enable him, at the worst, to keep his engagements. But in the first place, this prospective reflection on the somewhat more or less of difficulty which he may have in tiding over his embarrassments, seems too slender an inducement to be much of a restraint in a period supposed to be one of rash adventure, and upon persons so confident of success as to involve themselves beyond their certain means of extrication. And further, I apprehend that their confidence of being helped out in the event of ill-fortune, will mainly depend on their opinion of their own individual credit, with, perhaps, some consideration, not of the quantity of the currency, but of the general state of the loan market. They are aware that, in case of a commercial crisis, they shall have difficulty in obtaining advances. But if they thought it likely that a commercial crisis would occur before they had realized, they would not speculate. If no great contraction of general credit occurs, they will feel no doubt of obtaining any advances which they absolutely require, provided the state of their own affairs at the time affords in the estimation of lenders a sufficient prospect that those advances will be repaid.

*1-1*48, 49, 52, 57, 62, 65   **specially**

CHAPTER XIII

Of an Inconvertible Paper Currency

§ 1. [*The value of an inconvertible paper, depending on its quantity, is a matter of arbitrary regulation*] After experience had shown that pieces of paper, of no intrinsic value, by merely bearing upon them the written profession of being equivalent to a certain number of francs, dollars, or pounds, could be made to circulate as such, and to produce all the benefit to the issuers which could have been produced by the coins which they purported to represent; governments began to think that it would be a happy device if they could appropriate to themselves this benefit, free from the condition to which individuals issuing such paper substitutes for money were subject, of giving, when required, for the sign, the thing signified. They determined to try whether they could not emancipate themselves from this unpleasant obligation, and make a piece of paper issued by them pass for a pound, by merely calling it a pound, and consenting to receive it in payment of the taxes. And such is the influence of almost all established governments, that they have generally succeeded in attaining this object: I believe I might say they have always succeeded for a time, and the power has only been lost to them after they had compromised it by the most flagrant abuse.

In the case supposed, the functions of money are performed by a thing which derives its power ªforª performing them solely from convention; but convention is quite sufficient to confer the power; since nothing more is needful to make a person accept anything as money, and even at any arbitrary value, than the persuasion that it will be taken from him on the same terms by others. The only question is, what determines the value of such a ᵇcurrency;ᵇ since it cannot be, as in the case of gold and silver (or paper exchangeable for them at pleasure), the cost of production.

We have seen, however, that even in the case of a metallic currency, the immediate agency in determining its value is its quantity. If the quantity, instead of depending on the ordinary mercantile motives of profit and loss, could be arbitrarily fixed by authority, the value would depend on the fiat of that authority, not on cost of production. The quantity of a paper

ª⁻ª48, 49, 52, 57, 62   of
ᵇ⁻ᵇ48, 49   currency?

currency not convertible into the metals at the option of the holder, ^{c}can^c be arbitrarily fixed; especially if the issuer is the sovereign power of the state. The value, therefore, of such a currency, is entirely arbitrary.

Suppose that, in a country of which the currency is wholly metallic, a paper currency is suddenly issued, to the amount of half the metallic circulation; not by a banking establishment, or in the form of loans, but by the government, in payment of salaries and purchase of commodities. The currency being suddenly increased by one-half, all prices will rise, and among the rest, the prices of all things made of gold and silver. An ounce of manufactured gold will become more valuable than an ounce of gold coin, by more than that customary difference which compensates for the value of the workmanship; and it will be profitable to melt the coin for the purpose of being manufactured, until as much has been taken from the currency by the subtraction of gold, as had been added to it by the issue of paper. Then prices will relapse to what they were at first, and there will be nothing changed except that a paper currency has been substituted for half of the metallic currency which existed before. Suppose, now, a second emission of paper; the same series of effects will be renewed; and so on, until the whole of the metallic money has disappeared: that is, if paper be issued of as low a denomination as the lowest coin; if not, as much will remain, as convenience requires for the smaller payments. The addition made to the quantity of gold and silver disposable for ornamental purposes, will somewhat reduce, for a time, the value of the article; and as long as this is the case, even though paper has been issued to the original amount of the metallic circulation, as much coin will remain in circulation along with it, as will keep the value of the currency down to the reduced value of the metallic material; but the value having fallen below the cost of production, a stoppage or diminution of the supply from the mines will enable the surplus to be carried off by the ordinary agents of destruction, after which, the metals and the currency will recover their natural value. We are here supposing, as we have supposed throughout, that the country has mines of its own, and no commercial intercourse with other countries; for, in a country having foreign trade, the coin which is rendered superfluous by an issue of paper is carried off by a much prompter method.

Up to this point, the effects of a paper currency are substantially the same, whether it is convertible into specie or not. It is when the metals have been completely superseded and driven from circulation, that the difference between convertible and inconvertible paper begins to be operative. When the gold or silver has all gone from circulation, and an equal quantity of paper has taken its place, suppose that a still further issue is superadded. The same series of phenomena recommences: prices rise, among the rest

$^{c-c}$48, 49, 52, 57, 62   can

the prices of gold and silver articles, and it becomes an object as before to procure coin in order to convert it into bullion. There is no longer any coin in circulation; but if the paper currency is convertible, coin may still be obtained from the issuers, in exchange for notes. All additional notes, therefore, which are attempted to be forced into circulation after the metals have been completely superseded, will return upon the issuers in exchange for coin; and they will not be able to maintain in circulation such a quantity of convertible paper, as to sink its value below the metal which it represents. It is not so, however, with an inconvertible currency. To the increase of that (if permitted by law) there is no check. The issuers may add to it indefinitely, lowering its value and raising prices in proportion; they may, in other words, depreciate the currency without limit.

Such a power, in whomsoever vested, is an intolerable evil. All variations in the value of the circulating medium are mischievous: they disturb existing contracts and expectations, and the liability to such changes renders every pecuniary engagement of long date entirely precarious. The person who buys for himself, or ^{d}gives^d to another, an annuity of 100*l.*, does not know whether it will be equivalent to 200*l.* or to 50*l.* a few years hence. Great as this evil would be if it depended only on accident, it is still greater when placed at the arbitrary disposal of ^{e}an individual^e or a body of ^{f}individuals^f; who may have any kind or degree of interest to be served by an artificial fluctuation in fortunes; and who have at any rate a strong interest in issuing as much as possible, each issue being in itself a source of profit. Not to add, that the issuers may have, and in the case of a government paper, always have, a direct interest in lowering the value of the currency, because it is the medium in which their own debts are computed.

§ 2. [*If regulated by the price of bullion, an inconvertible currency might be safe, but not expedient*] In order that the value of the currency may be secure from being altered by design, and may be as little as possible liable to fluctuation from accident, the articles least liable of all known commodities to vary in their value, the precious metals, have been made in all civilized countries the standard of value for the circulating medium; and no paper currency ought to exist of which the value cannot be made to conform to theirs. Nor has this fundamental maxim ever been entirely lost sight of, even by the governments which have most abused the power of creating inconvertible paper. If they have not (as they generally have) professed an intention of paying in specie at some indefinite future time, they have at least, by giving to their paper issues the names of their coins, made a virtual, though generally a false, profession of intending to keep them at a value corresponding to that of the coins. This is not impracticable,

$^{d\text{-}d}$48, 49   grants $^{e\text{-}e}$48, 49   a man $^{f\text{-}f}$48, 49   men

even with an inconvertible paper. There is not indeed the self-acting check which convertibility brings with it. But there is a clear and unequivocal indication by which to judge whether the currency is depreciated, and to what extent. That indication is, the price of the precious metals. When holders of paper cannot demand coin to be converted into bullion, and when there is none left in circulation, bullion rises and falls in price like other things; and if it is above the Mint price, if an ounce of gold, which would be coined into the equivalent of 3*l.* 17*s.* 10½*d.*, is sold for 4*l.* or 5*l.* in paper, the value of the currency has sunk just that much below what the value of a metallic currency would be. If, therefore, the issue of inconvertible paper were subjected to strict rules, one rule being that whenever bullion rose above the Mint price, the issues should be contracted until the market price of bullion and the Mint price were again in accordance, such a currency would not be subject to any of the evils usually deemed inherent in an inconvertible paper.

But also such a system of currency would have no advantages sufficient to recommend it to adoption. An inconvertible currency, regulated by the price of bullion, would conform exactly, in all its variations, to a convertible one; and the only advantage gained, would be that of exemption from the necessity of keeping any reserve of the precious metals; which is not a very important consideration, especially as a government, so long as its good faith is not suspected, needs not keep so large a reserve as private issuers, being not so liable to great and sudden demands, since there never can be any real doubt of its solvency. Against this small advantage is to be set, in the first place, the possibility of fraudulent tampering with the price of bullion for the sake of acting on the currency; in the manner of the fictitious sales of corn, to influence the averages, so much and so justly complained of while the corn laws were in force. But a still stronger consideration is the importance of adhering to a simple principle, intelligible to the most untaught capacity. Everybody can understand convertibility; every one sees that what can be at any moment exchanged for five pounds, is worth five pounds. Regulation by the price of bullion is a more complex idea, and does not recommend itself through the same familiar associations. There would be nothing like the same confidence, by the public generally, in an inconvertible currency so regulated, as in a convertible one: and the most instructed person might reasonably doubt whether such a rule would be as likely to be inflexibly adhered to. The grounds of the rule not being so well understood by the public, opinion would probably not enforce it with as much rigidity, and, in any circumstances of difficulty, would be likely to turn against it; while to the government itself a suspension of convertibility would appear a much stronger and more extreme measure, than a relaxation of what might possibly be considered a somewhat artificial rule.

There is therefore a great preponderance of reasons in favour of a convertible, in preference to even the best regulated inconvertible currency.
The temptation to over-issue, in certain financial emergencies, is so strong,
that nothing is admissible which can tend, in however slight a degree, to
weaken the barriers that restrain it.

§ 3. [*Examination of the doctrine that an inconvertible currency is safe
if representing actual property*] Although no doctrine in political economy
rests on more obvious grounds than the mischief of a paper currency not
maintained at the same value with a metallic, either by convertibility, or by
some principle of limitation equivalent to it; and although, accordingly,
this doctrine has, though not till after the discussions of many years, been
tolerably effectually drummed into the public mind; yet dissentients are
still numerous, and projectors every now and then start up, with plans for
curing all the economical evils of society by means of an unlimited issue
of inconvertible paper. There is, in truth, a great charm in the idea. To be
able to pay off the national debt, defray the expenses of government without taxation, and in fine, to make the fortunes of the whole community,
is a brilliant prospect, when once a man is capable of believing that printing
a few characters on bits of paper will do it. The philosopher's stone could
not be expected to do more.

As these projects, however often slain, always resuscitate, it is not
superfluous to examine one or two of the fallacies by which the schemers
impose upon themselves. One of the commonest is, that a paper currency
cannot be issued in excess so long as every note issued *represents* property,
or has a *foundation* of actual property to rest on. These phrases, of representing and resting, seldom convey any distinct or well-defined idea: when
they do, their meaning is no more than this–that the issuers of the paper
must *have* property, either of their own, or entrusted to them, to the value
of all the notes they issue: though for what purpose does not very clearly
appear; for if the property cannot be claimed in exchange for the notes,
it is difficult to divine in what manner its mere existence can serve to uphold
their value. I presume, however, it is intended as a guarantee that the
holders would be finally reimbursed, in case any untoward event should
cause the whole concern to be wound up. On this theory there have been
many schemes for "coining the whole land of the country into money"
and the like.

In so far as this notion has any connexion at all with reason, it
seems to originate in confounding two entirely distinct evils, to which a
paper currency is liable. One is, the insolvency of the issuers; which, if the
paper is grounded on their credit—if it makes any promise of payment in
cash, either on demand or at any future time—of course deprives the paper

of any value which it derives from *the* promise. To this evil paper credit is equally liable, however moderately used; and against it, a proviso that all issues should be "founded on property," as for instance that notes should only be issued on the security of some valuable thing expressly pledged for their redemption, would really be efficacious as a precaution. But the theory takes no account of another evil, which is incident to the notes of the most solvent firm, company, or government; that of being depreciated in value from being issued in excessive quantity. The assignats, during the French Revolution were *an example* of a currency grounded on these principles. The assignats "represented" an immense amount of highly valuable property, namely the lands of the crown, the church, the monasteries, and the emigrants; amounting *possibly* to half the territory of France. They were, in fact, orders or assignments on this mass of land. The revolutionary government had the idea of "coining" these lands into money; but, to do them justice, they did not originally contemplate the immense multiplication of issues to which they were eventually driven by the failure of all other financial resources. They imagined that the assignats would come rapidly back to the issuers in exchange for land, and that they should be able to reissue them continually until the lands were all disposed of, without having at any time more than a very moderate quantity in circulation. Their hope was frustrated: the land did not sell so quickly as they expected; buyers were not inclined to invest their money in possessions which were likely to be resumed without compensation if the Revolution succumbed: the bits of paper which represented land, becoming prodigiously multiplied, could no more keep up their value than the land itself would have done if it had all been brought to market at once; and the result was that it at last required an assignat of *six* hundred francs to pay for a *pound of butter*.

The example of the assignats has been said not to be conclusive, because an assignat only represented land in general, but not a definite quantity of land. To have prevented their depreciation, the proper course, it is affirmed, would have been to have made a valuation of all the confiscated property at its metallic value, and to have issued assignats up to, but not beyond, that limit; giving to the holders a right to demand any piece of land, at its registered valuation, in exchange for assignats to the same amount. There can be no question about the superiority of this plan over the one actually adopted. Had this course been followed, the assignats could never have been depreciated to the inordinate degree they were; for—as they would have retained all their purchasing power in relation to land, however much

*–*48, 49   that
*–*48, 49   a model   *–*48, 49, 52, 57   perhaps
*–*48, 49, 52, 57, 62   five   *–*48, 49, 52, 57, 62   cup of coffee

they might have fallen in respect to other things—before they had lost very much of their market value, they would probably have been brought in to be exchanged for land. It must be remembered, however, that their not being depreciated would presuppose that no greater number of them continued in circulation than would have circulated if they had been convertible into cash. However convenient, therefore, in a time of revolution, this currency convertible into land on demand might have been, as a contrivance for selling rapidly a great quantity of land with the least possible sacrifice; it is difficult to see what advantage it would have, as the permanent system of a country, over a currency convertible into coin: while it is not at all difficult to see what would be its disadvantages; since land is far more variable in value than gold and silver; and besides, land, to most persons, being rather an encumbrance than a desirable possession, except to be converted into money, people would submit to a much greater depreciation before demanding land, than they will before demanding gold or silver.*

ᵃ§ 4.ᵃ [ᵇExamination of the doctrine that an increase of the currency promotes industryᵇ] ᶜ Another of the fallacies from which the advocates

*Among the schemes of currency to which, strange to say, intelligent writers [48, 49   men] have been found to give their sanction, one is as follows: that the state should receive in pledge or mortgage, any kind or amount of property, such as land, stock, &c., and should advance to the owners inconvertible paper money to the estimated value. Such a currency would not even have the recommendations of the imaginary assignats supposed in the text: since those into whose hands the notes were paid by the persons who received them, could not return them to the Government, and demand in exchange land or stock which was only pledged, not alienated. There would be no reflux of such assignats as these, and their depreciation would be indefinite.

ᵃ⁻ᵃ49, 52, 57   §5. [for §4. in 49, 52, 57 see ᵇ⁻ᵇ and ᶜ below]

ᵇ⁻ᵇ49, 52, 57   Examination of the doctrine that a convertible currency does not expand with the increase of wealth

ᶜ49   One of the most transparent of the fallacies by which the principle of the convertibility of paper money has been assailed, is that which pervades a recent work by Mr. John Gray:* the author of the most ingenious, and least exceptionable plan of an inconvertible currency which I have happened to meet with. This writer has seized several of the leading doctrines of political economy with no ordinary grasp, and among others, the important one, that commodities are the real market for commodities, and that Production is essentially the cause and measure of Demand. But this proposition, true in a state of barter, he affirms to be false under a monetary system regulated by the precious metals, because if the aggregate of goods is increased faster than the aggregate of money, prices must fall, and all producers must be losers; now neither gold nor silver, nor any other valuable thing "can by any possibility be increased ad libitum, as fast as all other valuable things put together:" a limit, therefore, is arbitrarily set to the amount of production which can take place without loss to the producers: and on this foundation Mr. Gray accuses the existing system of rendering the produce of this country less by at least one hundred million

of an inconvertible currency derive support, is the notion that an increase of the currency quickens industry. This idea was set afloat by Hume, in his Essay on Money, and has had many devoted adherents since; witness the Birmingham currency school *d* , of whom Mr. Attwood was *e*at one*e* time the most conspicuous representative. Mr. Attwood maintained that a rise of prices produced by an increase of paper currency, stimulates every producer to his utmost *f*exertions*f*, and brings all the capital and labour of the country into complete employment; and that this has invariably happened in all periods of rising prices, when the rise was on a sufficiently great scale. I presume, however, that the inducement which, according to Mr. Attwood, excited this unusual ardour in all persons engaged in production, must have been the expectation of getting more *g* commodities generally, more real wealth, in exchange for the produce of their labour, and not merely more pieces of paper. This expectation, however, must have been, by the very terms of the supposition, disappointed, since, all prices being supposed to rise equally, no one was really better paid for his goods than before. Those who agree with Mr. Attwood could only succeed

---

pounds annually, than it would be under a currency which admitted of expansion in exact proportion to the increase of commodities.

But, in the first place, what hinders gold, or any other commodity whatever, from being "increased as fast as all other valuable things put together?" If the produce of the world, in all commodities taken together, should come to be doubled, what is to prevent the annual produce of gold from being doubled likewise? for that is all that would be necessary, and not, (as might be inferred from Mr. Gray's language) that it should be doubled as many times over as there are other "valuable things" to compare it with. Unless it can be proved that the production of bullion cannot be increased by the application of increased labour and capital, it is evident that the stimulus of an increased value of the commodity will have the same effect in extending the mining operations, as it is admitted to have in all other branches of production.

But, secondly, even if the currency could not be increased at all, and if every addition to the aggregate produce of the country must necessarily be accompanied by a proportional diminution of general prices; it is incomprehensible how any person who has attended to the subject can fail to see that a fall of price, thus produced, is no loss to producers: they receive less money; but the smaller amount goes exactly as far, in all expenditure, whether productive or personal, as the larger quantity did before. The only difference would be in the increased burthen of fixed money payments; and of that (coming, as it would, very gradually) a very small portion would fall on the productive classes, who have rarely any debts of old standing, and who would suffer almost solely in the increased onerousness of their contribution to the taxes which pay the interest of the National Debt. I should not have thought it necessary to be thus particular in pointing out so obvious a blunder, if the work of Mr. Gray had not been very widely circulated, and if the writer were not apparently capable of better things than he has in this instance exhibited. [*footnote:*] *"Lectures on the Nature and Use of Money. By John Gray." [Edinburgh: Black, 1848. *JSM quotes from* p. 250.]] 52, 57 *as* 49 . . . National Debt.

*d*48, 49 of the present day

*e-e*48, 49 for a

*f-f*48, 49 exertion   *g*48, 49, 52, 57, 62 of

in winning people on to these unwonted exertions, by a prolongation of what would in fact be a delusion; contriving matters so, that by a progressive rise of money prices, every producer shall always seem to be in the very act of obtaining an increased remuneration which he never, in reality, does obtain. It is unnecessary to advert to any other of the objections to this plan, than that of its total impracticability. It calculates on finding the whole world persisting for ever in the belief that more pieces of paper are more riches, and never discovering that, with all their paper, they cannot buy more of anything than they could before. No such mistake was made during any of the periods of high prices, on the experience of which this school lays so much stress. At the periods which Mr. Attwood mistook for times of prosperity, and which were simply (as all periods of high prices, under a convertible currency, must be) times of speculation, the speculators did not think they were growing rich because the high prices would last, but because they would not last, and because whoever contrived to realize while they did last, would find himself, after the recoil, in possession of a greater number of pounds sterling, without their having become of less value. If, at the close of the speculation, an issue of paper had been made, sufficient to keep prices up to the point which they attained when at the highest, no one would have been more disappointed than the speculators; since the gain which they thought to have reaped by realizing in time (at the expense of their competitors, who bought when they sold, and had to sell after the revulsion) would have faded away in their hands, and instead of it they would have got nothing except a few more paper tickets to count by.

Hume's version of the doctrine differed in a slight degree from Mr. Attwood's. He thought that all commodities would not rise in price simultaneously, and that some persons therefore would obtain a real gain, by getting more money for what they had to sell, while the things which they wished to buy might not yet have risen. And those who would reap this gain would always be (he seems to think) the first comers. It seems obvious, however, that for every person who thus gains more than usual, there is necessarily some other person who gains less. The loser, if things took place as Hume supposes, would be the seller of the commodities which are slowest to rise; who, by the supposition, parts with his goods at the old prices, to purchasers who have already benefited by the new. This seller has obtained for his commodity only the accustomed quantity of money, while there are already some things of which that money will no longer purchase as much as before. If, therefore, he knows what is going on, he will raise his price, and then the buyer will not have the gain, which is supposed to stimulate his industry. But if, on the contrary, the seller does not know the state of the case, and only discovers it when he finds, in laying his money out, that it does not go so far, he then obtains less than the ordinary remuneration for his labour and capital; and if the other dealer's industry is encouraged, it should seem that his must, from the opposite cause, be impaired.

§ 5. [*Depreciation of currency is a tax on the community, and a fraud on creditors*] There is no way in which a general and permanent rise of prices, or in other words, depreciation of money, can benefit anybody, except at the expense of somebody else. The substitution of paper for [b] metallic currency is a national gain: any further increase of paper beyond this is but a form of robbery.

An issue of notes is a manifest gain to the issuers, who, until the notes are returned for payment, obtain the use of them as if they were a real capital: and so long as the notes are no permanent addition to the currency, but merely supersede gold or silver to the same amount, the gain of the issuer is a loss to no one; it is obtained by saving to the community the expense of the more costly material. But if there is no gold or silver to be superseded—if the notes are added to the currency, instead of being substituted for the metallic part of it—all holders of currency lose, by the depreciation of its value, the exact equivalent of what the issuer gains. A tax is virtually levied on them for his benefit. It will be objected by some, that gains are also made by the producers and dealers who, by means of the increased issue, are accommodated with loans. Theirs, however, is not an additional gain, but a portion of that which is reaped by the issuer at the expense of all possessors of money. The profits arising from the contribution levied upon the public, he does not keep to himself, but divides with his customers.

But besides the benefit reaped by the issuers, or by others through them, at the expense of the public generally, there is another unjust gain obtained by a larger class, namely by those who are under fixed pecuniary obligations. All such persons are freed, by a depreciation of the currency, from a portion of the burthen of their debts or other engagements: in other words, part of the property of their creditors is gratuitously transferred to them. On a superficial view it may be imagined that this is an advantage to industry; since the productive classes are great borrowers, and generally owe larger debts to the unproductive (if we include among the latter all persons not actually in business) than the unproductive classes owe to them; especially if the national debt be included. It is only thus that a general rise of prices can be a source of benefit to producers and dealers; by diminishing the pressure of their fixed burthens. And this might be accounted an advantage, if integrity and good faith were of no importance

*a–a*49, 52, 57 §6.   *b*48 a

to the world, and to industry and commerce in particular. Not many, however, have been found to say that the currency ought to be depreciated
on the simple ground of its being desirable to rob the national creditor and
private creditors of a part of what is in their bond. The schemes which
have tended that way have almost always had some appearance of special
and circumstantial justification, such as the necessity of compensating for
a prior injustice committed in the contrary direction.

   [a]§ 6.[a] [*Examination of some pleas for committing this fraud*] Thus in
England, [b]for many years subsequent to 1819, it was[b] pertinaciously contended, that a large portion of the national debt, and a multitude of private
debts still in existence, were contracted between 1797 and 1819, when
the Bank of England was exempted from giving cash for its notes; and that
it is grossly unjust to borrowers, (that is, in the case of the national debt,
to all tax-payers) that they should [c] be paying interest on the same nominal
sums in a currency of full value, which were borrowed in a depreciated one.
The depreciation, according to the views and objects of the particular
writer, [d]was[d] represented to have averaged thirty, fifty, or even more than
fifty per cent: and the conclusion [e]was[e], that either we ought to return to
this depreciated currency, or to strike off from [f]the national debt, and
from mortgages or other private debts of old standing[f], a percentage
corresponding to the estimated amount of the depreciation.
   To this doctrine, the following [g]was[g] the answer usually made. Granting
that, by returning to cash payments without lowering the standard, an
injustice was done to debtors, in holding them liable for the same amount
of a currency enhanced in value, which they had borrowed while it was
depreciated; it is now too late to make reparation for this injury. The
debtors and creditors of to-day are not the debtors and creditors of 1819:
the lapse of years has entirely altered the pecuniary relations of the
community; and it being impossible now to ascertain the particular persons
who were either benefited or injured, to attempt to retrace our steps would
[h]not be[h] redressing a wrong, but superadding a second act of wide-spread
injustice to the one already committed. This argument is certainly conclusive on the practical question; but it places the honest conclusion on too
narrow and too low a ground. It concedes that the measure of 1819, called

   [a-a]49, 52, 57   §7.
   [b-b]48, 49, 52, 57   from 1819 to the present time, it has been
   [c]48, 49, 52, 57   now
   [d-d]48, 49, 52, 57   is
   [e-e]48, 49, 52, 57   is
   [f-f]48, 49   private debts of old standing (such as mortgages)
   [g-g]48, 49, 52, 57   is
   [h-h]48, 49, 52, 57, 62, 65   be not

Peel's Bill, by which cash payments were resumed at the original standard of 3*l*. 17*s*. 10½*d.*, was really the injustice it *'*was*'* said to be. This is an admission wholly opposed to the truth. Parliament had no alternative; it was absolutely bound to adhere to the acknowledged standard; as may be shown on three distinct grounds, two of fact, and one of principle.

The reasons of fact are these. In the first place it is not true that the debts, private or public, incurred during the Bank restriction, were contracted in a currency of lower value than that in which the interest is now paid. It is indeed true that the suspension of the obligation to pay in specie, did put it in the power of the Bank to depreciate the currency. It is true also that the Bank really exercised that power, though to a far less extent than is often pretended; since the difference between the market price of gold and the Mint valuation, during the greater part of the interval, was very trifling, and when it was greatest, during the last five years of the war, did not much exceed thirty per cent. To the extent of that difference, the currency was depreciated, that is, its value was below that of the standard to which it professed to adhere. But the state of Europe at that time was such—there was so unusual an absorption of the precious metals, by hoarding, and *ʲ*in*ʲ* the military chests of the vast armies which then desolated the Continent, that the value of the standard itself was very considerably raised: and the best authorities, among whom it is sufficient to name Mr. Tooke, have, after an elaborate investigation, satisfied themselves that the difference between paper and bullion was not greater than the enhancement in value of gold itself, and that the paper, though depreciated relatively to the then value of gold, did not sink below the ordinary value, at other times, either of gold or of a convertible paper. If this be true (and the evidences of the fact are conclusively stated in Mr. Tooke's *History of Prices*) the foundation of the whole case against the fundholder and other creditors on the ground of depreciation is subverted.

But, secondly, even if the currency had really been lowered in value at each period of the Bank restriction, in the same degree in which it was depreciated in relation to its standard, we must remember that a part only of the national debt, or of other permanent engagements, *ᵏ*was*ᵏ* incurred during the Bank restriction. A large part had been contracted before 1797; a still larger during the early years of the restriction, when the difference between paper and gold was yet small. To the holders of the former part, an injury was done, by paying the interest for twenty-two years in a depreciated currency: those of the second, suffered an injury during the years in which the interest was paid in a currency more depreciated than that in which the loans were contracted. To have resumed cash payments at a lower standard would have been to perpetuate the injury to these two

*ⁱ⁻ⁱ*48, 49, 52, 57 is   *ʲ⁻ʲ*48, 49, 52, 57 by   *ᵏ⁻ᵏ*48, 49, 52 were classes of creditors, in order to avoid giving an undue benefit to a third class, who had lent their money during the few years of greatest depreciation. As it is, there was an underpayment to one set of persons, and an overpayment to another. The late Mr. Mushet took the trouble to make an arithmetical comparison between the two amounts. He ascertained by calculation, that if an account had been made out in 1819, of what the fundholders had gained and lost by the variation of the paper currency from its standard, they would have been found as a body to have been losers; so that if any compensation was due on the ground of depreciation, it would not be *from* the fundholders collectively, but *to* them.

Thus it is with the facts of the case. But these reasons of fact are not the strongest. There is a reason of principle, still more powerful. Suppose that, not a part of the debt merely, but the whole, had been contracted in a depreciated currency, depreciated not only in comparison with its standard, but with its own value before and after; and that we *were* now paying the interest of this debt in a currency fifty or even a hundred per cent more valuable than that in which it was contracted. What difference would this make in the obligation of paying it, if the condition that it should be so paid was part of the original compact? Now this is not only truth, but less than the truth. The compact stipulated better terms for the fundholder than he has received. During the whole continuance of the Bank restriction, there was a parliamentary pledge, by which the legislature was as much bound as any legislature is capable of binding itself, that cash payments should be resumed on the original footing, at farthest in six months after the conclusion of a general peace. This was therefore an actual condition of every loan; and the terms of the *loan* were more favourable in consideration of it. Without some such stipulation, the Government could not have expected to borrow, unless on the terms on which *loans are made* to the native princes of India. If it had been understood and avowed that, after borrowing the money, the standard at which it was *commuted* might be permanently lowered, to any extent which to the "collective wisdom" of a legislature of borrowers might seem fit—who can say what rate of interest would have been a sufficient inducement to *persons* of common sense to risk *their* savings in such an adventure? However much the fundholders had gained by the resumption of cash pay-

<hr>

*l-l*48, 49, 52, 57, 62, 65   *from*
*m-m*48, 49, 52, 57, 62   *to*
*n-n*48, 49, 52, 57   are
*o-o*48, 49, 52   loans
*p-p*48, 49   men lend
*q-q*48, 49, 52, 57, 62, 65   computed [*printer's error?*]
*r-r*48, 49   a person
*s-s*48, 49   his

ments, the terms of the contract insured their giving ample value for it. They gave value for more than they received; since cash payments were not resumed in six months, but in as many years, after the peace. So that waving all our arguments except the last, and conceding all the facts asserted on the other side of the question, the fundholders, instead of being unduly benefited, are the injured party; and would have a claim to compensation, if such claims were not very properly barred by the impossibility of adjudication, and by the salutary general maxim of law and policy, "quod interest reipublicæ ut sit finis litium."

CHAPTER XIV

Of Excess of Supply

§ 1. [*Can there be an oversupply of commodities generally?*] After the elementary exposition of the theory of money contained in the last few chapters, we shall return to a question in the general theory of Value, which could not be satisfactorily discussed until the nature and operations of Money were in some measure understood, because the errors against which we have to contend mainly originate in a misunderstanding of those operations.

We have seen that the value of everything gravitates towards a certain medium point (which has been called the Natural Value), namely, that at which it exchanges for every other thing in the ratio of their cost of production. We have seen, too, that the actual or market value coincides, or nearly so, with the natural value, only on an average of years; and is continually either rising above, or falling below it, from alterations in the demand, or casual fluctuations in the supply: but that these variations correct themselves, through the tendency of the supply to accommodate itself to the demand which exists for the commodity at its natural value. A general convergence thus results from the balance of opposite divergences. Dearth, or scarcity, on· the one hand, and over-supply, or in mercantile language, glut, on the other, are incident to all commodities. In the first case, the commodity affords to the producers or sellers, while the deficiency lasts, an unusually high rate of profit: in the second, the supply being in excess of that for which a demand exists at such a value as will afford the ordinary profit, the sellers must be content with less, and must ^a , in extreme cases, submit to a loss.

Because this phenomenon of over-supply, and consequent inconvenience or loss to the producer or dealer, may exist in the case of any one commodity whatever, many persons, including some distinguished political economists, have thought that it may exist with regard to all commodities; that there may be a general over-production of wealth; a supply of commodities in the aggregate, surpassing the demand; and a consequent depressed condition of all classes of producers. Against this doctrine, of which Mr. Malthus and Dr. Chalmers in this country, and M. de Sismondi

^a48, 49 even

on the Continent, were the chief apostles, I have already contended in the First Book;* but it was not possible, in that stage of our inquiry, to enter into a complete examination of an error (as I conceive) essentially grounded on a misunderstanding of the phenomena of Value and Price.

The doctrine appears to me to involve so much inconsistency in its very conception, that I feel considerable difficulty in giving any statement of it which shall be at once clear, and satisfactory to its supporters. They agree in maintaining that there may be, and sometimes is, an excess of productions in general beyond the demand for them; that when this happens, purchasers cannot be found at prices which will repay the cost of production with a profit; that there ensues a general depression of prices or values (they are seldom accurate in discriminating between the two), so that producers, the more they produce, find themselves the poorer, instead of richer; and Dr. Chalmers accordingly inculcates on capitalists the practice of a moral restraint in reference to the pursuit of gain; while Sismondi deprecates machinery, and the various inventions which increase productive power. They both maintain that accumulation of capital may proceed too fast, not merely for the moral, but for the material interests of those who produce and accumulate; and they enjoin the rich to guard against this evil by an ample unproductive consumption.

§ 2. [*The supply of commodities in general cannot exceed the power of purchase*] When these writers speak of the supply of commodities as outrunning the demand, it is not clear which of the two elements of demand they have in view—the desire to possess, or the means of purchase; whether their meaning is that there are, in such cases, more consumable products in existence than the public desires to consume, or merely more than it is able to pay for. In this uncertainty, it is necessary to examine both suppositions.

First, let us suppose that the quantity of commodities produced is not greater than the community would be glad to consume: is it, in that case, possible that there should be a deficiency of demand for all commodities, for want of the means of payment? Those who think so cannot have considered what it is which constitutes the means of payment for commodities. It is simply commodities. Each person's means of paying for the productions of other people consists of those which he himself possesses. All sellers are inevitably and *ex vi termini* buyers. Could we suddenly double the productive powers of the country, we should double the supply of commodities in every market; but we should, by the same stroke, double the purchasing power. Everybody would bring a double demand as well as supply: everybody would be able to buy twice as much, because every one

*Supra, vol. i. pp. 66–8.

would have twice as much to offer in exchange. It is probable, indeed, that there would now be a superfluity of certain things. Although the community would willingly double its aggregate consumption, it may already have as much as it desires of some commodities, and it may prefer to do more than double its consumption of others, or to exercise its increased purchasing power on some new thing. If so, the supply will adapt itself accordingly, and the values of things will continue to conform to their cost of production. At any rate, it is a sheer absurdity that all things should fall in value, and that all producers should, in consequence, be insufficiently remunerated. If values remain the same, what becomes of prices is immaterial, since the remuneration of producers does not depend on how much money, but on how much of consumable articles, they obtain for their goods. Besides, money is a commodity; and if all commodities are supposed to be doubled in quantity, we must suppose money to be doubled too, and then prices would no more fall than values would.

§ 3. [*The supply of commodities in general never does exceed the inclination to consume*] A general over-supply, or excess of all commodities above the demand, so far as demand consists in means of payment, is thus shown to be an impossibility. But it may perhaps be supposed that it is not the ability to purchase, but the desire to possess, that falls short, and that the general produce of industry may be greater than the community desires to consume—the part, at least, of the community which has an equivalent to give. It is evident enough, that produce makes a market for produce, and that there is wealth in the country with which to purchase all the wealth in the country; but those who have the means, may not have the wants, and those who have the wants may be without the means. A portion, therefore, of the commodities produced may be unable to find a market, from the absence of means in those who have the desire to consume, and the want of desire in those who have the means.

This is much the most plausible form of the doctrine, and does not, like that which we first examined, involve a contradiction. There may easily be a greater quantity of any particular commodity than is desired by those who have the ability to purchase, and it is abstractedly conceivable that this might be the case with all commodities. The error is in not perceiving that though all who have an equivalent to give, *might* be fully provided with every consumable article which they desire, the fact that they go on adding to the production proves that this is not *actually* the case. Assume the most favourable hypothesis for the purpose, that of a limited community, every member of which possesses as much of necessaries and of all known luxuries as he desires: and since it is not conceivable that persons whose wants were completely satisfied would labour and economize to obtain what they did not desire, suppose that a foreigner arrives and produces an additional quantity of something of which there was already enough. Here, it will be said, is over-production: true, I reply; over-production of that particular article: the community wanted no more of that, but it wanted something. The old inhabitants, indeed, wanted nothing; but did not the foreigner himself want something? When he produced the superfluous article, was he labouring without a motive? He has produced, but the wrong thing instead of the right. He wanted, perhaps, food, and has produced watches, with which everybody was sufficiently supplied. The new comer brought with him into the country a demand for commodities, equal to all that he could produce by his industry, and it was his business to see that the supply he brought should be suitable to that demand. If he could not produce something capable of exciting a new want or desire in the community, for the satisfaction of which some one would grow more food and give it to him in exchange, he had the alternative of growing food for himself; either on fresh land, if there was any unoccupied, or as a tenant, or partner, or servant, of some former occupier, willing to be partially relieved from labour. He has produced a thing not wanted, instead of what was wanted; and he himself, perhaps, is not the kind of producer who is wanted; but there is no over-production; production is not excessive, but merely ill assorted. We saw before, that whoever brings additional commodities to the market, brings an additional power of purchase; we now see that he brings also an additional desire to consume; since if he had not that desire, he would not have troubled himself to produce. Neither of the elements of demand, therefore, can be wanting, when there is an additional supply; though it is perfectly possible that the demand may be for one thing, and the supply may unfortunately consist of another.

Driven to his last retreat, an opponent may perhaps allege, that there are persons who produce and accumulate from mere habit; not because they have any object in growing richer, or desire to add in any respect to their consumption, but from *vis inertiæ*. They continue producing because the machine is ready mounted, and save and re-invest their savings because they have nothing on which they care to expend them. I grant that this is possible, and in some few instances probably happens; but these do not in the smallest degree affect our conclusion. For, what do these persons do with their savings? They invest them productively; that is, expend them in employing labour. In other words, having a purchasing power belonging to them, more than they know what to do with, they make over the surplus of it for the general benefit of the labouring class. Now, will that class also not know what to do with it? Are we to suppose that they too have their wants perfectly satisfied, and go on labouring from mere habit? Until this is the case; until the working classes have also reached the point of satiety—there will be no want of demand for the produce of capital, however rapidly it may accumulate: since, if there is nothing else for it to do, it can always find employment in producing the necessaries or luxuries of the labouring class. And when they too had no further desire for necessaries or luxuries, they would take the benefit of any further increase of wages by diminishing their work; so that the over-production which then for the first time would be possible in idea, could not even then take place in fact, for want of labourers. Thus, in whatever manner the question is looked at, even though we go to the extreme verge of possibility to invent a supposition favourable to it, the theory of general over-production implies an absurdity.

§ 4. [*Origin and explanation of the notion of general oversupply*] What then is it by which men who have reflected much on economical phenomena, and have even contributed to throw new light upon them by original speculations, have been led to embrace so irrational a doctrine? I conceive them to have been deceived by a mistaken interpretation of certain mercantile facts. They imagined that the possibility of a general over-supply of commodities was proved by experience. They believed that they saw this phenomenon in certain conditions of the markets, the true explanation of which is totally different.

I have already described the state of the markets for commodities which accompanies what is termed a commercial crisis. At such times there is really an excess of all commodities above the money demand: in other words, there is an under-supply of money. From the sudden annihilation of a great mass of credit, every one dislikes to part with ready money, and many are anxious to procure it at any sacrifice. Almost everybody therefore is a seller, and there are scarcely any buyers; so that there may really be, though only while the crisis lasts, an extreme depression of general prices, from what may be indiscriminately called a glut of commodities or a dearth of money. But it is a great error to suppose, with Sismondi, that a commercial crisis is the effect of a general excess of production. It is simply the consequence of an excess of speculative purchases. It is not a gradual advent of low prices, but a sudden recoil from prices extravagantly high: its immediate cause is a contraction of credit, and the remedy is, not a diminution of supply, but the restoration of confidence. It is also evident that this temporary derangement of markets is an evil only because it is temporary. The fall being solely of money prices, if prices did not rise again no dealer would lose, since the smaller price would be worth as much to him as the larger price was before. In no *manner* does this phenomenon answer to the description which these celebrated economists have given of the evil of over-production. *bThe*b permanent decline in the circumstances of producers, for want of markets, which those writers contemplate, is a conception to which the nature of a commercial crisis gives no support.

The other phenomenon from which the notion of a general excess of wealth and superfluity of accumulation seems to derive countenance, is one of a more permanent nature, namely, the fall of profits and interest which naturally takes place with the progress of population and production. The cause of this decline of profit is the increased cost of maintaining labour, which results from an increase of population and of the demand for food, outstripping the advance of agricultural improvement. This important feature in the economical progress of nations will receive full consideration and discussion in the succeeding Book.* It is obviously a totally different thing from a want of market for commodities, though often confounded with it in the complaints of the producing and trading classes. The true interpretation of the modern or present state of industrial economy, is, that there is hardly any amount of business which may not be done, if people will be content to do it on small profits; and this, all active and intelligent persons in business perfectly well know: but even those who comply with the necessities of their time, grumble at what they comply with, and wish that there were less capital, or as they express it, less competition, in order that there might be greater profits. Low profits, however, are a different thing from deficiency of demand; and the production and accumulation which merely reduce profits, cannot be called excess of supply or of production. What the phenomenon really is, and its effects and necessary limits, will be seen when we treat of that express subject.

I know not of any economical facts, except the two I have specified, which can have given occasion to the opinion that a general over-production of commodities ever presented itself in actual experience. I am convinced that there is no fact in commercial affairs, which, in order to its explanation, stands in need of that chimerical supposition.

The point is fundamental; any difference of opinion on it involves radically different conceptions of Political Economy, especially in its practical aspect. On the one view, we have only to consider how a sufficient production may be combined with the best possible distribution; but on the other there is a third thing to be considered—how a market can be created for produce, or how production can be limited to the capabilities of the market. Besides; a theory so essentially self-contradictory cannot intrude itself without carrying confusion into the very heart of the subject, and making it impossible even to conceive with any distinctness many of the

*Infra, book iv. chap. 4 [pp. 733–46].

*b-b*48, 49, 52, 57, 62, 65   That

more complicated economical workings of society. This error has been, I conceive, fatal to the systems, as systems, of the three distinguished economists to whom I before referred, Malthus, Chalmers, and Sismondi; all of whom have admirably conceived and explained several of the elementary theorems of political economy, but this fatal misconception has spread itself like a veil between them and the more difficult portions of the subject, not suffering one ray of light to penetrate. Still more is ᶜthisᶜ same confused idea constantly crossing and bewildering the speculations of minds inferior to theirs. It is but justice to two eminent names, to call attention to the fact, that the merit of having placed this most important point in its true light, belongs principally, on the Continent, to the judicious J. B. Say, and in this country to Mr. Mill; who (besides the conclusive exposition which he gave of the subject in his Elements of Political Economy) had set forth the correct doctrine with great force and clearness in an early pamphlet, called forth by a temporary controversy, and entitled, "Commerce Defended;"[*] the first of his writings which attained any celebrity, and which he prized more as having been his first introduction to the friendship of David Ricardo, the most valued and most intimate friendship of his life.

[*Mill, James. *Commerce Defended. An Answer to the Arguments by which Mr. Spence, Mr. Cobbett, and others, have attempted to prove that Commerce is not a Source of National Wealth.* London: Baldwin, 1808.]

ᶜ⁻ᶜ48, 49, 52   the

CHAPTER XV

Of a Measure of Value

§ 1. [*In what sense a Measure of Exchange Value is possible*] There has been much discussion among political economists respecting a Measure of Value. An importance has been attached to the subject, greater than it deserved, and what has been written respecting it has contributed not a little to the reproach of logomachy, which is brought, with much exaggeration, but not altogether without ground, against the speculations of political economists. It is necessary however to touch upon the subject, if only to show how little there is to be said on it.

A Measure of Value, in the ordinary sense of the word measure, would mean, something, by comparison with which we may ascertain what is the value of any other thing. When we consider farther, that value itself is relative, and that two things are necessary to constitute it, independently of the third thing which is to measure it; we may define a Measure of Value to be something, by comparing with which any two other things, we may infer their value in relation to one another.

In this sense, any commodity will serve as a measure of value at a given time and place; since we can always infer the proportion in which things exchange for one another, when we know the proportion in which each exchanges for any third thing. To serve as a convenient measure of value is one of the functions of the commodity selected as a medium of exchange. It is in that commodity that the values of all other things are habitually estimated. We say that one thing is worth 2*l.*, another 3*l.*; and it is then known without express statement, that one is worth two-thirds of the other, or that the things exchange for one another in the proportion of 2 to 3. Money is a complete measure of their value.

But the desideratum sought by political economists is not a measure of the value of things at the same time and place, but a measure of the value of the same thing at different times and places: something by comparison with which it may be known whether any given thing is of greater or less value now than a century ago, or in this country than in America or China. And for this also, money, or any other commodity, will serve quite as well as at the same time and place, provided we can obtain the same data; provided we are able to compare with the measure not one commodity only, but the two or more which are necessary to the idea of value. If wheat is now *40s.* the quarter, and a fat sheep the same, and if in the time of Henry the Second wheat was 20s., and a sheep 10s., we know that a quarter of wheat was then worth two sheep, and is now only worth one, and that the value therefore of a sheep, estimated in wheat, is twice as great as it was then; quite independently of the value of money at the two periods, either in relation to those two articles (in respect to both of which we suppose it to have fallen), or to other commodities, in respect to which we need not make any supposition.

What seems to be desired, however, by writers on the subject, is some means of ascertaining the value of a commodity by merely comparing it with the measure, without referring it specially to any other given commodity. They would wish to be able, from the mere fact that wheat is now *40s.* the quarter, and was formerly 20s., to decide whether wheat has varied in its value, and in what degree, without selecting a second commodity, such as a sheep, to compare it with; because they are *desirous of knowing, not* how much wheat has varied in value relatively to sheep, but how much it has varied relatively to things in general.

The first obstacle arises from the necessary indefiniteness of the idea of general exchange value—value in relation not to some one commodity, but to commodities at large. Even if we knew exactly how much a quarter of wheat would have purchased at the earlier period, of every marketable article considered separately, and that it will now purchase more of some things and less of others, we should often find it impossible to say whether it had risen or fallen in relation to things in general. How much more impossible, when we only know how it has varied in relation to the measure. To enable the money price of a thing at two different periods to measure the quantity of things in general which it will exchange for, the same sum of money must correspond at both periods to the same quantity of things in general, that is, money must always have the same exchange value, the same general purchasing power. Now, not only is this not true of money, or of any other commodity, but we cannot *even* suppose any state of circumstances in which it would be true.

§ 2. [*A Measure of Cost of Production*] A measure of exchange value, therefore, being impossible, writers have formed a notion of something, under the name of a measure of value, which would be more properly

---

*a–a*48, 49   50s.
*b–b*48, 49   50s.
*c–c*48, 49, 52, 57, 62   not desirous of knowing
*d–d*48, 49   , even in mere hypothesis,

termed a measure of cost of production. They have imagined a commodity invariably produced by the same quantity of labour; to which supposition it is necessary to add, that the fixed capital employed in the production must bear always the same proportion to the wages of the immediate labour, and must be always of the same durability: in short, the same capital must be advanced for the same length of time, so that the element of value which consists of profits, as well as that which consists of wages, may be unchangeable. We should then have a commodity always produced under one and the same combination of all the circumstances which affect permanent value. Such a commodity would be by no means constant in its exchange value; for (even without reckoning the *temporary* fluctuations arising from supply and demand) its exchange value would be altered by every change in the circumstances of production of the things against which it was exchanged. But if there existed such a commodity, we should derive this advantage from it, that whenever any other thing varied *permanently* in relation to it, we should know that the cause of variation was not in it, but in the other thing. It would thus be *suited* to serve as a measure, not indeed of the value of other things, but of their cost of production. If a commodity acquired a greater permanent purchasing power in relation to the invariable commodity, its cost of production must have become greater; and in the contrary case, less. This measure of cost, is what political economists have generally meant by a measure of value.

But a measure of cost, though perfectly conceivable, can no more exist in fact, than a measure of exchange value. There is no commodity which is invariable in its cost of production. Gold *and silver are the least variable, but even these are liable to changes in their* cost of production, from the exhaustion of old *sources of supply*, the discovery of new, and improvements in the mode of working. If we attempt to ascertain the changes in the cost of production of any commodity from the changes in its money price, the conclusion will require to be corrected by the best allowance we can make for the intermediate changes in the cost of the production of money itself.

Adam Smith fancied that there were two commodities peculiarly fitted to serve as a measure of value: corn, and labour. Of corn, he said that although its value fluctuates much from year to year, it does not vary greatly from century to century. This we now know to be an error: corn tends to

^{a–a}+52, 57, 62, 65, 71
^{b–b}+62, 65, 71
^{c–c}48, 49, 52, 57, 62   fitted
^{d–d}48, 49   comes nearest to the idea; but gold is liable to vary in
^{e–e}48, 49   mines

rise in cost of production with every increase of population, and to fall with every improvement in agriculture, either in the country itself, or in any foreign country from which it draws a portion of its supplies. The supposed constancy of the cost of ʲtheʲ production of corn depends on the maintenance of a complete equipoise between these antagonizing forces, an equipoise which, if ever realized, can only be accidental. With respect to labour as a measure of value, the language of Adam Smith is not uniform. He sometimes speaks of it as a good measure only for short periods, saying that the value of labour (or wages) does not vary much from year to year, though it does from generation to generation. On other occasions he speaks as if labour were intrinsically the most proper measure of value, on the ground that one day's ordinary muscular exertion of one man, may be looked upon as always, to him, the same amount of effort or sacrifice. But this proposition, whether in itself admissible or not, discards the idea of exchange value altogether, substituting a totally different idea, more analogous to value in use. If a day's labour will purchase in America twice as much of ordinary consumable articles as in England, it seems a vain subtlety to insist on saying that labour is of the same value in both countries, and that it is the value of the other things which is different. Labour, in this case, may be correctly said to be twice as valuable, both in the market and to the labourer himself, in America as in England.

If the object were to obtain an approximate measure by which to estimate value in use, perhaps nothing better could be chosen than one day's subsistence of an average man, reckoned in the ordinary food consumed by the class of unskilled labourers. If in ᵍany countryᵍ a pound of maize flour will support a labouring man for a day, a thing might be deemed more or less valuable in proportion to the number of pounds of maize flour it exchanged for. If one thing, either by itself or by what it would purchase, could maintain a labouring man for a day, and another could maintain him for a week, there would be some reason in saying that the one was worth, for ordinary human uses, seven times as much as the other. But this would not measure the worth of the thing to its possessor for his own purposes, which might be greater to any amount, though it could not be less, than the worth of the food which the thing would purchase.

The idea of a Measure of Value must not be confounded with the idea of the regulator, or determining principle, of value. When it is said by Ricardo and others, that the value of a thing is regulated by quantity of labour, they do not mean the quantity of labour for which the thing will exchange, but the quantity required for producing it. This, they mean to

ʲ⁻ʲ+49, 52, 57, 62, 65, 71
ᵍ⁻ᵍ48, 49, 52, 57, 62   America

affirm, determines its value; causes it to be of the value it is, and of no other. But when Adam Smith and Malthus say that labour is a measure of value, they do not mean the labour by which the thing was or can be made, but the quantity of labour which it will exchange for, or purchase; in other words the value of the thing, estimated in labour. And they do not mean that this *regulates* the general exchange value of the thing, or has any effect in determining what that value shall be, but only ascertains what it is, and whether and how much it varies from time to time and from place to place. To confound these two ideas, would be much the same thing as to overlook the distinction between the thermometer and the fire.

CHAPTER XVI

Of Some Peculiar Cases of Value

§ 1. [*Values of Commodities which have a joint cost of production*]
The general laws of value, in all the more important cases of the interchange
of commodities in the same country, have now been investigated. We
examined, first, the case of monopoly, in which the value is determined by
either a natural or an artificial limitation of quantity, that is, by demand
and supply; secondly, the case of free competition, when the article can be
produced in indefinite quantity at the same cost; in which case the permanent value is determined by the cost of production, and only the fluctuations by supply and demand; thirdly, a mixed case, that of the articles
which can be produced in indefinite quantity, but not at the same cost; in
which case the permanent value is determined by the greatest cost which
it is necessary to incur in order to obtain the required supply. And lastly,
we have found that money itself is a commodity of the third class; that its
value, in a state of freedom, is governed by the same laws as the values of
other commodities of its class; and that prices, therefore, follow the same
laws as values.

From this it appears that demand and supply govern the fluctuations
of values and prices in all cases, and the permanent values and prices of
all things of which the supply is determined by any agency other than that
of free competition: but that, under the régime of competition, things are,
on the average, exchanged for each other at such values, and sold at such
prices, as afford equal expectation of advantage to all classes of producers;
which can only be when things exchange for one another in the ratio of
their cost of production.

It is now, however, necessary to take notice of certain cases, to which,
from their peculiar nature, this law of exchange value is inapplicable.

It sometimes happens that two different commodities have what may be
termed a joint cost of production. They are both products of the same
operation, or set of operations, and the outlay is incurred for the sake of
both together, not part for one and part for the other. The same outlay
would have to be incurred for either of the two, if the other were not
wanted or used at all. There are not a few instances of commodities thus
associated in their production. For example, coke and coal-gas are both

produced from the same material, and by the same operation. In a more partial sense, mutton and wool are an example: beef, hides, and tallow: calves and dairy produce: chickens and eggs. Cost of production can have nothing to do with deciding the value of the associated commodities relatively to each other. It only decides their joint value. The gas and the coke together have to repay the expenses of their production, with the ordinary profit. To do this, a given quantity of gas, together with the coke which is the residuum of its manufacture, must exchange for other things in the ratio of their joint cost of production. But how much of the remuneration of the producer shall be derived from the coke, and how much from the gas, remains to be decided. Cost of production does not determine their prices, but the sum of their prices. A principle is wanting to apportion the expenses of production between the two.

Since cost of production here fails us, we must revert to a law of value anterior to cost of production, and more fundamental, the law of demand and supply. *The* law is, that the demand for a commodity varies with its value, and that the value adjusts itself so that the demand shall be equal to the supply. This supplies the principle of repartition which we are in quest of.

Suppose that a certain quantity of gas is produced and sold at a certain price, and that the residuum of coke is offered at a price which, together with that of the gas, repays the expenses with the ordinary rate of profit. Suppose, too, that at the price put upon the gas and coke respectively, the whole of the gas finds an easy market, without either surplus or deficiency, but that purchasers cannot be found for all the coke corresponding to it. The coke will be offered at a lower price in order to force a market. But this lower price, together with the price of the gas, will not be remunerating: the manufacture, as a whole, will not pay its expenses with the ordinary profit, and will not, on these terms, continue to be carried on. The gas, therefore, must be sold at a higher price, to make up for the deficiency on the coke. The demand consequently contracting, the production will be somewhat reduced; and prices will become stationary when, by the joint effect of the rise of gas and the fall of coke, so much less of the first is sold, and so much more of the second, that there is now a market for all the coke which results from the existing extent of the gas manufacture.

Or suppose the reverse case; that more coke is wanted at the present prices, than can be supplied by the operations required by the existing demand for gas. Coke, being now in deficiency, will rise in price. The whole operation will yield more than the usual rate of profit, and additional capital will be attracted to the manufacture. The unsatisfied demand for coke will be supplied; but this cannot be done without increasing the supply of gas

*a–a*48 That

too; and as the existing demand was fully supplied already, an increased quantity can only find a market by lowering the price. The result will be that the two together will yield the return required by their joint cost of production, but that more of this return than before will be furnished by the coke, and less by the gas. Equilibrium will be attained when the demand for each article fits so well with the demand for the other, that the quantity required of each is exactly as much as is generated in producing the quantity required of the other. If there is any surplus or deficiency on either side; if there is a demand for coke, and not a demand for all the gas produced along with it, or *vice versâ;* the values and prices of the two things will so readjust themselves that both shall find a market.

When, therefore, two or more commodities have a joint cost of production, their natural values relatively to each other are those which will create a demand for each, in the ratio of the quantities in which they are sent forth by the productive process. This theorem is not in itself of any great importance: but the illustration it affords of the law of demand, and of the mode in which, when cost of production fails to be applicable, *ᵇtheᵇ* other principle steps in to supply the vacancy, is worthy of particular attention, as we shall find in the next chapter but one that something very similar takes place in cases of much greater moment.

§ 2. [*Values of the different kinds of agricultural produce*] Another case of values which merits attention, is that of the different kinds of agricultural produce. This is rather a more complex question than the last, and requires that attention should be paid to a greater number of influencing circumstances.

The case would present nothing peculiar, if different agricultural products were either grown indiscriminately and with equal advantage on the same soils, or wholly on different soils. The difficulty arises from two things: first, that most soils are fitter for one kind of produce than another, without being absolutely unfit for any; and secondly, the rotation of crops.

For simplicity, we will confine our supposition to two kinds of agricultural produce; for instance, wheat and oats. If all soils were equally adapted for wheat and for oats, both would be grown indiscriminately on all soils, and their relative cost of production, being the same everywhere, would govern their relative value. If the same labour which grows three quarters of wheat on any given soil, would always grow on that soil five quarters of oats, the three and the five quarters would be of the same value. If again, wheat and oats could not be grown on the same soil at all, the value of each would be determined by its peculiar cost of production on the least favourable of the soils adapted for it which the existing demand

ᵇ⁻ᵇ48, 49 that

required a recourse to. The fact, however, is that both wheat and oats can be grown on almost any soil which is capable of producing either: but some soils, such as the stiff clays, are better adapted for wheat, while others (the light sandy soils) are more suitable for oats. There *might* be some soils which *would* yield, to the same quantity of labour, only four quarters of oats to three of wheat; others perhaps less than three of wheat to five quarters of oats. Among these diversities, what determines the relative value of the two things?

It is evident that each grain will be cultivated in preference, on the soils which are better adapted for it than for the other; and if the demand is supplied from these alone, the values of the two grains will have no reference to one another. But when the demand for both is such as to require that each should be grown not only on the soils peculiarly fitted for it, but on the medium soils which, without being specifically adapted to either, are about equally suited for both, the cost of production on those medium soils will determine the relative value of the two grains; while the rent of the soils specifically adapted to each, will be regulated by their productive power, considered with reference to that one alone to which they are peculiarly applicable. Thus far the question presents no difficulty, to any one to whom the general principles of value are familiar.

It may happen, however, that the demand for one of the two, as for example wheat, may so outstrip the demand for the other, as not only to occupy the soils specially suited for wheat, but to engross entirely those equally suitable to both, and even encroach upon those which are better adapted to oats. To create an inducement for this unequal apportionment of the cultivation, wheat must be relatively dearer, and oats cheaper, than according to the cost of their production on the medium land. Their relative value must be in proportion to the cost on that quality of land, whatever it may be, on which the comparative demand for the two grains requires that both of them should be grown. If, from the state of the demand, the two cultivations meet on land more favourable to one than to the other, that one will be cheaper and the other dearer, in relation to each other and to things in general, than if the proportional demand were as we at first supposed.

Here, then, we obtain a fresh illustration, in a somewhat different manner, of the operation of demand, not as an occasional disturber of value, but as a permanent regulator of it, conjoined with, or supplementary to, cost of production.

The case of rotation of crops does not require separate analysis, being a case of joint cost of production, like that of gas and coke. If it were the

*a–a*48, 49   may
*b–b*48, 49   will

practice to grow white and green crops on all ᶜlandsᶜ in alternate years, the one being necessary as much for the sake of the other as for its own sake; the farmer would derive his remuneration for two years' expenses from one white and one green crop, and the prices of the two would so adjust themselves as to create a demand which would carry off an equal ᵈbreadthᵈ of white and of green crops.

There would be little difficulty in finding other anomalous cases of value, which it might be a useful exercise to resolve: but it is neither desirable nor possible, in a work like the present, to enter more into details than is necessary for the elucidation of principles. I now therefore proceed to the only part of the general theory of exchange which has not yet been touched upon, that of International Exchanges, or to speak more generally, exchanges between distant places.

ᶜ⁻ᶜ48, 49, 52, 57   land
ᵈ⁻ᵈ48, 49   number

CHAPTER XVII

Of International Trade

§ 1. [*Cost of production is not the regulator of international values*] The causes which occasion a commodity to be brought from a distance, instead of being produced, as convenience would seem to dictate, as near as possible to the market where it is to be sold for consumption, are usually conceived in a rather superficial manner. Some things it is physically impossible to produce, except in particular circumstances of heat, soil, water, or atmosphere. But there are many things which, though they could be produced at home without difficulty, and in any quantity, are yet imported from a distance. The explanation which would be popularly given of this would be, that it is cheaper to import than to produce them: and this is the true reason. But this reason itself requires that a reason be given for it. Of two things produced in the same place, if one is cheaper than the other, the reason is that it can be produced with less labour and capital, or, in a word, at less cost. Is this also the reason as between things produced in different places? Are things never imported but from places where they can be produced with less labour (or less of the other element of cost, time) than in the place to which they are brought? Does the law, that permanent value is proportioned to cost of production, hold good between commodities produced in distant places, as it does between those produced in adjacent places?

We shall find that it does not. A thing may sometimes be sold cheapest, by being produced in some other place than that at which it can be produced with the smallest amount of labour and abstinence. England might import corn from Poland and pay for it in cloth, even though *England* had a decided advantage over Poland in the production of both the one and the other. England might send cottons to Portugal in exchange for wine, although Portugal might be able to produce cottons with a less amount of labour and capital than England could.

This could not happen between adjacent places. If the north bank of the Thames possessed an advantage over the south bank in the production of shoes, no shoes would be produced on the south side; the shoemakers would remove themselves and their capitals to the north bank, or would have established themselves there originally; for being competitors in the

*a–a*48, 49 she

same market with those on the north side, they could not compensate themselves for their disadvantage at the expense of the consumer: the amount of it would fall entirely on their profits; and they would not long content themselves with a smaller profit, when, by simply crossing a river, they could increase it. But between distant places, and especially between different countries, profits may continue different; because persons do not usually remove themselves or their capitals to a distant place, without a very strong motive. If capital ^{b}removed^b to remote parts of the world as readily, and for as small an inducement, as it moves to another quarter of the same town; if people would transport their manufactories to America or China whenever they could save a small percentage in their expenses by it; profits would be alike ^{c}(or equivalent)^c all over the world, and all things would be produced in the places where the same labour and capital would produce them in greatest quantity and of best quality. A tendency may, even now, be observed towards such a state of things; capital is becoming more and more cosmopolitan; there is so much greater similarity of manners and institutions than formerly, and so much less alienation of feeling, among the more civilized countries, that both population and capital ^{d} now move from one of those countries to another on much less temptation than heretofore. But there are still extraordinary differences, both of wages and of profits, between different parts of the world. It needs but a small motive to transplant capital, or even persons, from Warwick-shire to Yorkshire; but a much greater to make them remove to India, the colonies, or Ireland. To France, Germany, or Switzerland, capital moves perhaps almost as readily as to the colonies; the difference of language and government being scarcely so great a hindrance as climate and distance. To countries still barbarous, or, like Russia or Turkey, only beginning to be civilized, capital will not migrate, unless under the inducement of a very great extra profit.

Between all distant places therefore in some degree, but especially between different countries (whether under the same supreme government or not,) there may exist great inequalities in the return to labour and capital, without causing them to move from one place to the other in such quantity as to level those inequalities. The capital belonging to a country will, to a great extent, remain in the country, even if there be no mode of employing it in which it would not be more productive elsewhere. Yet even a country thus circumstanced might, and probably would, carry on trade with other countries. It would export articles of some sort, even to places which could make them with less labour than itself; because those countries, supposing them to have an advantage over it in all productions, would have a greater advantage in some things than in others, and would find it their interest to import the articles in which their advantage was smallest, that

$^{b-b}$48, 49, 52, 57 moved $^{c-c}$+52, 57, 62, 65, 71 ^{d}48 will

they might employ more of their labour and capital on those in which it was greatest.

§ 2. [*Interchange of commodities between distant places is determined by differences not in their absolute, but in their comparative, cost of production*] As I have said elsewhere* after Ricardo (the *ᵃthinker who has done mostᵃ* towards clearing up this subject)† "it is not a difference in the *absolute* cost of production, which determines the interchange, but a difference in the *comparative* cost. It may be to our advantage to procure iron from Sweden in exchange for cottons, even although the mines of England as well as her manufactories should be more productive than those of Sweden; for if we have an advantage of one-half in cottons, and only an advantage of a quarter in iron, and could sell our cottons to Sweden at the price which Sweden must pay for them if she produced them herself, we should obtain our iron with an advantage of one-half as well as our cottons. We may often, by trading with foreigners, obtain their commodities at a smaller expense of labour and capital than they cost to the foreigners themselves. The bargain is still advantageous to the foreigner, because the commodity which he receives in exchange, though it has cost us less, would have cost him more."[*]

To illustrate the cases in which interchange of commodities will not, and those in which it will, take place between two countries, Mr. Mill, in his Elements of Political Economy,‡ makes the supposition that Poland has an advantage over England in the production *ᵇboth ofᵇ* cloth and of corn. He first supposes the advantage to be of equal amount in both commodities; the cloth and the corn, each of which required 100 days' labour in Poland, requiring each 150 days' labour in England. "It would

*Essays on some Unsettled Questions of Political Economy, Essay I. ["Of the Laws of Interchange between Nations; and the Distribution of the Gains of Commerce among the Countries of the Commercial World."]

†[62] I at one time believed Mr. Ricardo to have been the sole author of the doctrine now universally received by political economists, on the nature and measure of the benefit which a country derives from foreign trade. But Colonel Torrens, by the republication of one of his early writings, "The Economists Refuted," has established at least a joint claim with Mr. Ricardo to the origination of the doctrine, and an exclusive one to its earliest publication. [Torrens, Robert. *The Economists Refuted; or, an Inquiry into the Nature and Extent of the Advantages derived from Trade.* London: S. A. Oddy, 1808. Reprinted in *The Principles and Practical Operation of Sir Robert Peel's Act of 1844 Explained and Defended.* 2nd ed. London: Longman, Brown, Green, Longmans, and Roberts, 1857. On p. xvi of the latter work Torrens puts forward the claim here recognized by JSM.]

[*Pp. 2–3.]

‡Third ed. p. 120 [–1].

ᵃ⁻ᵃ48, 49, 52   first who made any great step   ᵇ⁻ᵇ48   of both

follow, that the cloth of 150 days' labour in England, if sent to Poland, would be equal to the cloth of 100 days' labour in Poland; if exchanged for corn, therefore, it would exchange for the corn of only 100 days' labour. But the corn of 100 days' labour in Poland, was supposed to be the same quantity with that of 150 days' labour in England. With 150 days' labour in cloth, therefore, England would only get as much corn in Poland, as she could raise with 150 days' labour at home; and she would, in importing it, have the cost of carriage besides. In these circumstances no exchange would take place." In this case the comparative costs of the two articles in England and in Poland were supposed to be the same, though the absolute costs were different; on which supposition we see that there would be no labour saved to either country, by confining its industry to one of the two productions, and importing the other.

It is otherwise when the comparative, and not merely the absolute costs of the two articles are different in the two countries. "If," continues the same author, "while the cloth produced with 100 days' labour in Poland was produced with 150 days' labour in England, the corn which was produced in Poland with 100 days' labour could not be produced in England with less than 200 days' labour; an adequate motive to exchange would immediately arise. With a quantity of cloth which England produced with 150 days' labour, she would be able to purchase as much corn in Poland as was there produced with 100 days' labour; but the quantity which was there produced with 100 days' labour, would be as great as the quantity produced in England with 200 days' labour." By importing corn, therefore, from Poland, and paying for it with cloth, England would obtain for 150 days' labour what would otherwise cost her 200; being a saving of 50 days' labour on each repetition of the transaction: and not merely a saving to England, but a saving absolutely; for it is not obtained at the expense of Poland, who, with corn that costs her 100 days' labour, has purchased cloth which, if produced at home, would have cost her the same. Poland, therefore, on this supposition, loses nothing; but also she derives no advantage from the trade, the imported cloth costing her as much as if it were made at home. To enable Poland to gain anything by the interchange, something must be abated from the gain of England: the corn produced in Poland by 100 days' labour, must be able to purchase from England more cloth than Poland could produce by that amount of labour; more therefore than England could produce by 150 days' labour, England thus obtaining the corn which would have cost her 200 days, at a cost exceeding 150, though short of 200. England therefore no longer gains the whole of the labour which is saved to the two jointly by trading with one another.

§ 3. [*The direct benefits of commerce consist in increased efficiency of the productive powers of the world*] From this exposition we perceive in what consists the benefit of international exchange, or in other words, foreign commerce. Setting aside its enabling countries to obtain commodities which they could not themselves produce at all; its advantage consists in a more efficient employment of the productive forces of the world. If two countries which trade together attempted, as far as was physically possible, to produce for themselves what they now import from one another, the labour and capital of the two countries would not be so productive, the two together would not obtain from their industry so great a quantity of commodities, as when each employs itself in producing, both for itself and for the other, the things in which its labour is relatively most efficient. The addition thus made to the produce of the two combined, constitutes the advantage of the trade. It is possible that one of the two countries may be altogether inferior to the other in productive capacities, and that its labour and capital could be employed to greatest advantage by being removed bodily to the other. The labour and capital which have been sunk in rendering Holland habitable, would have produced a much greater return if transported to America or Ireland. The produce of the whole world would be greater[a], or the labour less,[a] than it is, if everything were produced where there is the greatest absolute facility for its production. But nations do not, at least in modern times, emigrate *en masse*; and while the labour and capital of a country remain in the country, they are most beneficially employed in producing, for foreign markets as well as for its own, the things in which it lies under the least disadvantage, if there be none in which it possesses an advantage.

§ 4. [*The direct benefits of commerce do not consist in a vent for exports, or in the gains of merchants*] Before proceeding further, let us contrast this view of the benefits of international commerce with other theories which have prevailed, and which to a certain extent still prevail, on the same subject.

According to the doctrine now stated, the only direct advantage of foreign commerce consists in the imports. A country obtains things which it either could not have produced at all, or which it must have produced at a greater expense of capital and labour than the cost of the things which it exports to pay for them. It thus obtains a more ample supply of the commodities it wants, for the same labour and capital; or the same supply, for less labour and capital, leaving the surplus disposable to produce other things. The vulgar theory disregards this benefit, and deems the advantage of commerce to reside in the exports: as if not what a country obtains, but what it parts with, by its foreign trade, was supposed to constitute the gain to it. An extended market for its produce—an abundant consumption for its goods—a vent for its surplus—are the phrases by which it has been

a-a+52, 57, 62, 65, 71

customary to designate the uses and recommendations of commerce with foreign countries. This notion is intelligible, when we consider that the authors and leaders of opinion on mercantile questions have always hitherto been the selling class. It is in truth a surviving relic of the Mercantile Theory, according to which, money being the only wealth, selling, or in other words, exchanging goods for money, was (to countries without mines of their own) the only way of growing rich—and importation of goods, that is to say, parting with money, was so much subtracted from the benefit.

The notion that money alone is wealth, has been long defunct, but it has left many of its progeny behind it; and even its destroyer, Adam Smith, retained some opinions which it is impossible to trace to any other origin. Adam Smith's theory of the benefit of foreign trade, was that it afforded an outlet for the surplus produce of a country, and enabled a portion of the capital of the country to replace itself with a profit. These expressions suggest ideas inconsistent with a clear conception of the phenomena. The expression, surplus produce, seems to imply that a country is under some kind of necessity of producing the corn or cloth which it exports; so that the portion which it does not itself consume, if not wanted and consumed elsewhere, would either be produced in sheer waste, or if it were not produced, the corresponding portion of capital would remain idle, and the mass of productions in the country would be diminished by so much. Either of these suppositions would be entirely erroneous. The country produces an exportable article in excess of its own wants, from no inherent necessity, but as the cheapest mode of supplying itself with other things. If prevented from exporting this surplus, it would cease to produce it, and would no longer import anything, being unable to give an equivalent; but the labour and capital which had been employed in producing with a view to exportation, would find [a] employment in producing those desirable objects which were previously brought from abroad: or, if some of them could not be produced, in producing substitutes for them. These articles would of course be produced at a greater cost than that of the things with which they had previously been purchased from foreign countries. But the value and price of the articles would rise in proportion; and the capital would just as much be replaced, with the ordinary profit from the returns, as it was when employed in producing for the foreign market. The only losers (after the temporary inconvenience of the change) would be the consumers of the heretofore imported articles; who would be obliged either to do without them, consuming in lieu of them something which they did not like [b]as[b] well, or to pay a higher price for them than before.

There is much misconception in the common notion of what commerce does for a country. When commerce is spoken of as a source of national wealth, the imagination fixes itself upon the large fortunes acquired by

[a]48, 49   immediate   [b-b]48, 49, 52, 57   so

merchants, rather than upon the saving of price to consumers. But the gains of merchants, when they enjoy no exclusive privilege, are no greater than the profits obtained by the employment of capital in the country itself. If it be said that the capital now employed in foreign trade could not find employment in supplying the home market, I might reply, that this is the fallacy of general over-production, discussed in a former chapter: but the thing is in this particular case too evident, to require an appeal to any general theory. We not only see that the capital of the merchant would find employment, but we see what employment. There would be employment created, equal to that which would be taken away. Exportation ceasing, importation to an equal value would cease also, and all that part of the income of the country which had been expended in imported commodities, would be ready to expend itself on the same things produced at home, or on others instead of them. Commerce is virtually a mode of cheapening production; and in all such cases the consumer is the person ultimately benefited; the dealer, in the end, is sure to get his profit, whether the buyer obtains much or little for his money. This is said without prejudice to the effect (already touched upon, and to be hereafter fully discussed) which the cheapening of commodities may have in raising profits; in the case when the commodity cheapened, being one of those consumed by labourers, enters into the cost of labour, by which the rate of profits is determined.

§ 5. [*Indirect benefits of commerce, economical and moral, are still greater than the direct*] Such, then, is the direct economical advantage of foreign trade. But there are, besides, indirect effects, which must be counted as benefits of a high order. One is, the tendency of every extension of the market to improve the processes of production. A country which produces for a larger market than its own, can introduce a more extended division of labour, can make greater use of machinery, and is more likely to make inventions and improvements in the processes of production. Whatever causes a greater quantity of anything to be produced in the same place, tends to the general increase of the productive powers of the world.* There is another consideration, principally applicable to an early stage of industrial advancement. A people may be in a quiescent, indolent, unculti-vated state, with *a* all their tastes *b* either fully satisfied or entirely unde-veloped, and they may fail to put forth the whole of their productive ener-gies for want of any sufficient object of desire. The opening of a foreign trade, by making them acquainted with new objects, or tempting them by the easier acquisition of things which they had not previously thought attainable, sometimes works a *c*sort of*c* industrial revolution in a country

*Vide supra, book i. chap. ix. § 1 [pp. 131–5].

*a*48, 49   few wants and wishes,
*b*48, 49   being   *c-c*48, 49   complete

whose resources were previously undeveloped for want of energy and ambition in the people: inducing those who were satisfied with scanty comforts and little work, to work harder for the gratification of their new tastes, and even to save, and accumulate capital, for the still more complete satisfaction of those tastes at a future time.

But the economical advantages of commerce are surpassed in importance by those of its effects which are intellectual and moral. It is hardly possible to overrate the value, *d*in the present low state of human improvement, of placing human beings in*d* contact with persons dissimilar to themselves, and with modes of thought and action unlike those with which they are familiar. Commerce is now what war once was, the principal source of this contact. Commercial adventurers from more advanced countries have generally been the first civilizers of barbarians. And commerce is the purpose of the far greater part of the communication which takes place between civilized nations. Such communication has always been, and is peculiarly in the present age, one of the primary sources of progress. To *e*human beings*e*, who, as hitherto educated, can scarcely cultivate even a good quality without running it into a fault, it is indispensable to be perpetually comparing *f*their*f* own notions and customs with the experience and example of persons in different circumstances from *g*themselves*g*: and there is no nation which does not need to borrow from others, not merely particular arts or practices, but essential points of character in which its own type is inferior. Finally, commerce first taught nations to see with good will the wealth and prosperity of one another. Before, the patriot*h*, unless sufficiently advanced in culture to feel the world his country,*h* wished all countries weak, poor, and ill-governed, but his own: he now sees in their wealth and progress a direct source of wealth and progress to his own country. *i* It is commerce which is rapidly rendering war obsolete, by strengthening and multiplying the personal interests which are in natural opposition to it. And *j* it may be said without exaggeration that the great extent and rapid increase of international trade, in being the principal guarantee of the peace of the world, is the great permanent security for the uninterrupted progress of the ideas, the institutions, and the character of the human race.

*d-d*48, 49   for the improvement of human beings, of things which bring them into
*e-e*48, 49   a being like man
*f-f*48, 49   his
*g-g*48, 49   himself
h-h+52, 57, 62, 65, 71
*i*48, 49   It was in vain to inculcate feelings of brotherhood among mankind by moral influences alone, unless a sense of community of interest could also be established; and that sense we owe to commerce.
*j*48, 49   since war is now almost the only event, not highly improbable, which could throw back for any length of time the progress of human improvement,

CHAPTER XVIII

Of International Values

§ 1. [*The values of imported commodities depend on the terms of international interchange*] The values of commodities produced at the same place, or in places sufficiently adjacent for capital to move freely between them—let us say, for simplicity, of commodities produced in the same country—depend (temporary fluctuations apart) upon their cost of production. But the value of a commodity brought from a distant place, especially from a foreign country, does not depend on its cost of production in the place from whence it comes. On what, then, does it depend? The value of a thing in any place, depends on the cost of its acquisition in that place; which in the case of an imported article, means the cost of production of the thing which is exported to pay for it.

Since all trade is in reality barter, money being a mere instrument for exchanging things against one another, we will, for simplicity, begin by supposing the international trade to be in form, what it always is in reality, an actual trucking of one commodity against another. As far as we have hitherto proceeded, we have found all the laws of interchange to be essentially the same, whether money is used or not; money never governing, but always obeying, those general laws.

If, then, England imports wine from Spain, giving for every pipe of wine a bale of cloth, the exchange value of a pipe of wine in England will not depend upon what the production of the wine may have cost in ᵃSpainᵃ, but upon what the production of the cloth has cost in England. Though the wine may have cost in ᵇSpainᵇ the equivalent of only ten days' labour, yet, if the cloth costs in England twenty days' labour, the wine, when brought to England, will exchange for the produce of twenty days' English labour, *plus* the cost of carriage; including the usual profit on the importer's capital, during the time it is locked up, and withheld from other employment.

The value, then, in any country, of a foreign commodity, depends on the quantity of home produce which must be given to the foreign country in exchange for it. In other words, the values of foreign commodities depend on the terms of international exchange. What, then, do these depend

ᵃ⁻ᵃ48, 49, 52   Portugal
ᵇ⁻ᵇ48, 49, 52   Portugal

upon? What is it, which, in the case supposed, causes a pipe of wine from Spain to be exchanged with England for exactly that quantity of cloth? We have seen that it is not their cost of production. If the cloth and the wine were both made in Spain, they would exchange at their cost of production in Spain; if they were both made in England, they would exchange at their cost of production in England: but all the cloth being made in England, and all the wine in Spain, they are in circumstances to which we have already determined that the law of cost of production is not applicable. We must accordingly, as we have done before in a similar embarrassment, fall back upon an antecedent law, that of supply and demand: and in this we shall again find the solution of our difficulty.

I have ^{c}discussed this question^c in a separate Essay, already once referred to;[*] and a ^{d}quotation^d of part of the exposition then given, will ^{e}be the best introduction to my present view of the subject^e. I must give notice that we are now in the region of the most complicated questions which political economy affords; that the subject is one which cannot possibly be made elementary; and that a more continuous effort of attention than has yet been required, will be necessary to follow the series of deductions. The thread, however, which we are about to take in hand, is in itself very simple and manageable; the only difficulty is in following it through the windings and entanglements of complex international transactions.

§ 2. [*The terms of international interchange depend on the Equation of International Demand*] "When the trade is established between the two countries, the two commodities will exchange for each other at the same rate of interchange in both countries—bating the cost of carriage, of which, for the present, it will be more convenient to omit the consideration. Supposing, therefore, for the sake of argument, that the carriage of the commodities from one country to the other could be effected without labour and without cost, no sooner would the trade be opened than the value of the two commodities, estimated in each other, would come to a level in both countries.

"Suppose that 10 yards of broadcloth cost in England as much labour as 15 yards of linen, and in Germany as much as 20." In common with most of my predecessors, I find it advisable, in these intricate investigations, to give distinctness and fixity to the conception by numerical examples. These examples must sometimes, as in the present case, be purely supposititious.

[*See p. 589n *above*.]

$^{c-c}$48, 49   entered into this question very fully
$^{d-d}$48, 49   repetition
$^{e-e}$48   answer our purpose better than an alteration made merely for alteration's sake] 49   *as* 48 . . . merely made . . . *as* 48

I should have *a* preferred real ones; but all that is essential is, that the numbers should be such as admit of being easily followed through the subsequent combinations into which they enter.

This supposition then being made, it would be the interest of England to import linen from Germany, and of Germany to import cloth from England. "When each country produced both commodities for itself, 10 yards of cloth exchanged for 15 yards of linen in England, and for 20 in Germany. They will now exchange for the same number of yards of linen in both. For what number? If for 15 yards, England will be just as she was, and Germany will gain all. If for 20 yards, Germany will be as before, and England will derive the whole of the benefit. If for any number intermediate between 15 and 20, the advantage will be shared between the two countries. If, for example, 10 yards of cloth exchange for 18 of linen, England will gain an advantage of 3 yards on every 15, Germany will save 2 out of every 20. The problem is, what are the causes which determine the proportion in which the cloth of England and the linen of Germany will exchange for each other.

"As exchange value, in this case as in every other, is proverbially fluctuating, it does not matter what we suppose it to be when we begin: we shall soon see whether there be any fixed point about which it oscillates, which it has a tendency always to approach to, and to remain at. Let us suppose, then, that by the effect of what Adam Smith calls the higgling of the market, 10 yards of cloth in both countries, exchange for 17 yards of linen.

"The demand for a commodity, that is, the quantity of it which can find a purchaser, varies as we have before remarked, according to the price. In Germany the price of 10 yards of cloth is now 17 yards of linen, or whatever quantity of money is equivalent in Germany to 17 yards of linen. Now, that being the price, there is some particular number of yards of cloth, which will be in demand, or will find purchasers, at that price. There is some given quantity of cloth, more than which could not be disposed of at that price; less than which, at that price, would not fully satisfy the demand. Let us suppose this quantity to be 1000 times 10 yards.

"Let us now turn our attention to England. There, the price of 17 yards of linen is 10 yards of cloth, or whatever quantity of money is equivalent in England to 10 yards of cloth. There is some particular number of yards of linen which, at that price, will exactly satisfy the demand, and no more. Let us suppose that this number is 1000 times 17 yards.

"As 17 yards of linen are to 10 yards of cloth, so are 1000 times 17 yards to 1000 times 10 yards. At the existing exchange value, the linen which England requires will exactly pay for the quantity of cloth which,

*a*48, 49 greatly

on the same terms of interchange, Germany requires. The demand on each side is precisely sufficient to carry off the supply on the other. The conditions required by the principle of demand and supply are fulfilled, and the two commodities will continue to be interchanged, as we supposed them to be, in the ratio of 17 yards of linen for 10 yards of cloth.

"But our suppositions might have been different. Suppose that, at the assumed rate of interchange, England ᵇhasᵇ been disposed to consume no greater quantity of linen than 800 times 17 yards: it is evident that, at the rate supposed, this would not have sufficed to pay for the 1000 times 10 yards of cloth which we have supposed Germany to require at the assumed value. Germany would be able to procure no more than 800 times 10 yards at that price. To procure the remaining 200, which she would have no means of doing but by bidding higher for them, she would offer more than 17 yards of linen in exchange for 10 yards of cloth: let us suppose her to offer 18. At ᶜthisᶜ price, perhaps, England would be inclined to purchase a greater quantity of linen. She would consume, possibly, at that price, 900 times 18 yards. On the other hand, cloth having risen in price, the demand of Germany for it would probably have diminished. If, instead of 1000 times 10 yards, she is now contented with 900 times 10 yards, these will exactly pay for the 900 times 18 yards of linen which England is willing to take at the altered price: the demand on each side will again exactly suffice to take off the corresponding supply; and 10 yards for 18 will be the rate at which, in both countries, cloth will exchange for linen.

"The converse of all this would have happened, if, instead of 800 times 17 yards, we had supposed that England, at the rate of 10 for 17, would have taken 1200 times 17 yards of linen. In this case, it is England whose demand is not fully supplied; it is England who, by bidding for more linen, will alter the rate of interchange to her own disadvantage; and 10 yards of cloth will fall, in both countries, below the value of 17 yards of linen. By this fall of cloth, or what is the same thing, this rise of linen, the demand of Germany for cloth will increase, and the demand of England for linen will diminish, till the rate of interchange has so adjusted itself that the cloth and the linen will exactly pay for one another; and when once this point is attained, values will remain without further alteration.

"It may be considered, therefore, as established, that when two countries trade together in two commodities, the exchange value of these commodities relatively to each other will adjust itself to the inclinations and circumstances of the consumers on both sides, in such manner that the quantities required by each country, of the articles which it imports from its neigh-

ᵇ⁻ᵇSource, 48, 49, 52, 57, 62, 65   had   ᶜ⁻ᶜSource, 48, 49, 52, 57   that

bour, shall be exactly sufficient to pay for one another. As the inclinations and circumstances of consumers cannot be reduced to any rule, so neither can the proportions in which the two commodities will be interchanged. We know that the limits within which the variation is confined, are the ratio between their costs of production in the one country, and the ratio between their costs of production in the other. Ten yards of cloth cannot exchange for more than 20 yards of linen, nor for less than 15. But they may exchange for any intermediate number. The ratios, therefore, in which the advantage of the trade may be divided between the two nations, are various. The circumstances on which the proportionate share of each country more remotely depends, admit only of a very general indication.

"It is even possible to conceive an extreme case, in which the whole of the advantage resulting from the interchange would be reaped by one party, the other country gaining nothing at all. There is no absurdity in the hypothesis that, of some given commodity, a certain quantity is all that is wanted at any price; and that, when that quantity is obtained, no fall in the exchange value would induce other consumers to come forward, or those who are already supplied, to take more. Let us suppose that this is the case in Germany with cloth. Before her trade with England commenced, when 10 yards of cloth cost her as much labour as 20 yards of linen, she nevertheless consumed as much cloth as she wanted under any circumstances, and, if she could obtain it at the rate of 10 yards of cloth for 15 of linen, she would not consume more. Let this fixed quantity be 1000 times 10 yards. At the rate, however, of 10 for 20, England would want more linen than would be equivalent to this quantity of cloth. She would consequently, offer a higher value for linen; or, what is the same thing, she would offer her cloth at a cheaper rate. But, as by no lowering of the value could she prevail on Germany to take a greater quantity of cloth, there would be no limit to the rise of linen or fall of cloth, until the demand of England for linen was reduced by the rise of its value, to the quantity which 1000 times 10 yards of cloth would purchase. It might be, that to produce this diminution of the demand a less fall would not suffice than that which would make 10 yards of cloth exchange for 15 of linen. Germany would then gain the whole of the advantage, and England would be exactly as she was before the trade commenced. It would be for the interest, however, of Germany herself to keep her linen a little below the value at which it could be produced in England, in order to keep herself from being supplanted by the home producer. England, therefore, would always benefit in some degree by the existence of the trade, though it might be *d* a very trifling one."[*]

[*Mill, J. S. *Essays on Some Unsettled Questions*, pp. 6–14.]

*d*Source, 48, 49, 52, 57 in

In this statement, I conceive, is contained the *first elementary* principle of International Values *1* . I have, as is indispensable in such abstract and hypothetical cases, supposed the circumstances to be much less complex than they really are: in the first place, by suppressing the cost of carriage; next, by supposing that there are only two countries trading together; and lastly, that they trade only in two commodities. To *render the exposition of the principle complete*, it is necessary to restore the various circumstances thus temporarily left out to simplify the argument. Those who are accustomed to any kind of scientific investigation will probably see, without formal proof, that the introduction of these circumstances cannot alter the theory of the subject. Trade among any number of countries, and in any number of commodities, must take place on the same essential principles as trade between two countries and in two commodities. Introducing a greater number of agents precisely similar, cannot change the law of their action, no more than putting additional weights into the two scales of a balance alters the law of gravitation. It alters nothing but the numerical results. For more complete satisfaction, however, we will enter into the complex cases with the same particularity with which we have stated the simpler one.

§ 3. [*Influence of cost of carriage on international values*] First, let us introduce the element of cost of carriage. The chief difference will then be, that the cloth and the linen will no longer exchange for each other at precisely the same rate in both countries. Linen, having to be carried to England, will be dearer there by its cost of carriage; and cloth will be dearer in Germany by the cost of carrying it from England. Linen, estimated in cloth, will be dearer in England than in Germany, by the cost of carriage of both articles: and so will cloth in Germany, estimated in linen. Suppose that the cost of carriage of each is equivalent to one yard of linen; and suppose that, if they could have been carried without cost, the terms of interchange would have been 10 yards of cloth for 17 of linen. It *may seem* at first that each country will pay its own cost of carriage; that is, the carriage of the article it imports; that in Germany 10 yards of cloth will exchange for 18 of linen, namely, the original 17, and 1 to cover the cost of carriage of the cloth; while in England, 10 yards of cloth will only purchase 16 of linen, 1 yard being deducted for the cost of carriage of the linen. This, however, cannot be affirmed with certainty; it will only be true, if the linen which the English consumers would take at the price of 10 for 16, exactly pays for the cloth which the German consumers

e-e+52, 57, 62, 65, 71
*f*48, 49   ; which it only remains to follow into its applications
*g-g*48, 49   complete the exposition   *a-a*48, 49   seems

would take at 10 for 18. The values*b*, whatever they are, must*b* establish this equilibrium. No absolute rule, therefore, can be laid down for the division of the cost, no more than for the division of the advantage: and it does not follow that in whatever ratio the one is divided, the other will be divided in the same. It is impossible to say, if the cost of carriage could be annihilated, whether the producing or the importing country would be most benefited. *c*This*c* would depend on the play of international demand.

Cost of carriage has one effect more. But for it, every commodity would *d*(if trade be supposed free)*d* be either regularly imported or regularly exported. A country would make nothing for itself which it did not also make for other countries. But in consequence of cost of carriage there are many things, especially bulky articles, which every, or almost every country produces within itself. After exporting the things in which it can employ itself most advantageously, and importing those in which it is under the greatest disadvantage, there are many lying between, of which the relative cost of production in that and in other countries differs so little, that the cost of carriage would absorb more than the whole saving in cost of production which would be obtained by importing one and exporting another. This is the case with numerous commodities of common consumption; including the coarser qualities of many articles of food and manufacture, of which the finer kinds are the subject of extensive international traffic.

§ 4. [*The law of values which holds between two countries and two commodities, holds of any greater number*] Let us now introduce a greater number of commodities than the two we have hitherto supposed. Let cloth and linen, however, be still the articles of which the comparative cost of production in England and in Germany differs the most; so that if they were confined to two commodities, these would be the two which it would be most their interest to exchange. We will now again omit cost of carriage, which, having been shown not to affect the essentials of the question, does but embarrass unnecessarily the statement of it. Let us suppose, then, that the demand of England for linen is either so much greater than that of Germany for cloth, or so much more extensible by cheapness, that if England had no commodity but cloth which Germany would take, the demand of England would force up the terms of interchange to 10 yards of cloth for only 16 of linen, so that England would gain only the difference between 15 and 16, Germany the difference between 16 and 20. But let us now suppose that England has also another commodity, say iron, which is in demand in Germany, and that the quantity of iron which is of equal

---

*b–b*48, 49   must be those, whatever they are, which will
*c–c*48, 49   All   *d–d*+49, 52, 57, 62, 65, 71

value in England with 10 yards of cloth, (let us call this quantity a hundredweight) will, if produced in Germany, cost as much labour as 18 yards of linen, so that if offered by England for 17, it will undersell the German producer. In these circumstances, linen will not be forced up to the rate of 16 yards for 10 of cloth, but will stop[a], suppose[a] at 17; for although, at that rate of interchange, Germany will not take enough cloth to pay for all the linen required by England, she will take iron for the remainder, and it is the same thing to England whether she gives a hundredweight of iron or 10 yards of cloth, both being made at the same cost. If we now superadd coals or cottons on the side of England, and wine, or corn, or timber, on the side of Germany, it will make no difference in the principle. The exports of each country must exactly pay for the imports; meaning now the aggregate exports and imports, not those of particular commodities taken singly. The produce of fifty days' English labour, whether in cloth, coals, iron, or any other exports, will exchange for the produce of forty, or fifty, or sixty days' German labour, in linen, wine, corn, or timber, according to the international demand. There is some proportion at which the demand of the two countries for each other's products will exactly correspond: so that the things supplied by England to Germany will be completely paid for, and no more, by those supplied by Germany to England. This accordingly will be the ratio in which the produce of English and the produce of German labour will exchange for one another.

If, therefore, it be asked what country draws to itself the greatest share of the advantage of any trade it carries on, the answer is, the country for whose productions there is in other countries the greatest demand, and a demand the most susceptible of increase from additional cheapness. In so far as the productions of any country possess this property, the country obtains all foreign commodities at less cost. It gets its imports cheaper, the greater the intensity of the demand in foreign countries for its exports. It also gets its imports cheaper, the less the extent and intensity of its own demand for them. The market is cheapest to those whose demand is small. A country which desires few foreign productions, and only a limited quantity of them, while its own commodities are in great request in foreign countries, will obtain its limited imports at extremely small cost, that is, in exchange for the produce of a very small quantity of its labour and capital.

Lastly, having introduced more than the original two commodities into the hypothesis, let us also introduce more than the original two countries. After the demand of England for the linen of Germany has raised the rate of interchange to 10 yards of cloth for 16 of linen, suppose a trade opened between England and some other country which also exports linen. And let us suppose that if England had no trade but with this third country, the play of international demand would enable her to obtain from it, for 10 yards of cloth or its equivalent, 17 yards of linen. She evidently would not go on buying linen from Germany at the former rate: Germany would be undersold, and must consent to give 17 yards, like the other country. In this case, the circumstances of production and of demand in the third country are supposed to be in themselves more advantageous to England than the circumstances of Germany; but this supposition is not necessary: we might suppose that if the trade with Germany did not exist, England would be obliged to give to the other country the same advantageous terms which she gives to Germany; 10 yards of cloth for 16, or even less than 16, of linen. Even so, the opening of the third country makes a great difference in favour of England. There is now a double market for English exports, while the demand of England for linen is only what it was before. This necessarily obtains for England more advantageous terms of interchange. The two countries, requiring much more of her produce than was required by either alone, must, in order to obtain it, force an increased demand for their exports, by offering them at a lower value.

It deserves notice, that this effect in favour of England from the opening of another market for her exports, will equally be produced even though the country from which the demand comes should have nothing to sell which England is willing to take. Suppose that the third country, though ᵇrequiringᵇ cloth or iron from England, produces no linen, nor any other article which is in demand there. She however produces exportable articles, or she would have no means of paying for imports: her exports, though not suitable to the English consumer, can find a market somewhere. As we are only supposing three countries, we must assume her to find this market in Germany, and to pay for what she imports from England by orders on her German customers. Germany, therefore, besides having to pay for her own imports, now owes a debt to England on account of the third country, and the means for both purposes must be derived from her exportable produce. She must therefore tender that produce to England on terms sufficiently favourable to force a demand equivalent to this double debt. Everything will take place precisely as if the third country had bought German produce with her own goods, and offered that produce to England in exchange for hers. There is an increased demand for English goods, for which German goods have to furnish the payment; and this can only be done by forcing an increased demand for them in England, that is, by lowering their value. Thus an increase of demand for a country's

ᵇ⁻ᵇ48, 49   she requires

exports in any foreign country, enables her to obtain more cheaply even those imports which she procures from other quarters. And conversely, an increase of her own demand for any foreign commodity compels her, *cæteris paribus,* to pay dearer for all foreign commodities.

c The law which we have now illustrated, may be appropriately named, the Equation of International Demand. It may be concisely stated as follows. The produce of a country exchanges for the produce of other countries, at such values as are required in order that the whole of her exports may exactly pay for the whole of her imports. This law of International Values is but an extension of the more general law of Value, which we called the Equation of Supply and Demand.* We have seen that the value of a commodity always so adjusts itself as to bring the demand to the exact level of the supply. But all trade, either between nations or individuals, is an interchange of commodities, in which the things that they respectively have to sell, constitute also their means of purchase: the supply brought by the one constitutes his demand for what is brought by the other. So that supply and demand are but another expression for reciprocal demand: and to say that value will adjust itself so as to equalize demand with supply, is in fact to say that it will adjust itself so as to equalize the demand on one side with the demand on the other.

a§ 5.*a* [*Effect of improvements in production on international values*] To trace the consequences of *b*this*b* law of International Values through their wide ramifications, would occupy more space than can be *c*here*c* devoted to such a purpose *d*. But there is one of its applications which I will notice, as being in itself not unimportant,*d* as bearing on the question which will occupy us in the next chapter, *e*and*e* especially as conducing to the more full and clear understanding of the law itself.

We have seen that the value at which a country purchases a foreign commodity, does not conform to the cost of production in the country

*Supra, book iii, chap. ii. § 4 [pp. 466–8].

*c*48, 49   §5.
a–a+52, 57, 62, 65, 71
*b–b*48, 49   the
c–c+52, 57, 62, 65, 71
*d–d*48, 49   in the present treatise. Several of those consequences were indicated in the Essay already quoted; and others have been pointed out in the writings of Colonel Torrens, who appears to me substantially correct in his general view of the subject, and who has supported it with great closeness and consecutiveness of reasoning, though his conclusions are occasionally pushed much beyond what appear to me the proper limits of the principle on which they are grounded.
There is one special application of the law, which I think it advisable to notice, both as being in itself not unimportant, and
*e–e*48, 49   but

from which the commodity comes. Suppose now a change in that cost of production; an improvement, for example, in the process of manufacture. Will the benefit of the improvement be fully participated in by other countries? Will the commodity be sold as much cheaper to foreigners, as it is produced cheaper at home? This question, and the considerations which must be entered into in order to resolve it, are well adapted to try the worth of the theory.

Let us first suppose, that the improvement is of a nature to create a new branch of export: to make foreigners resort to the country for a commodity which they had previously produced at home. On this supposition, the foreign demand for the productions of the country is increased; which necessarily alters the international values to its advantage, and to the disadvantage of foreign countries, who, therefore, though they participate in the benefit of the new product, must purchase that benefit by paying for all the other productions of the country at a dearer rate than before. How much dearer, will depend on the degree necessary for re-establishing, under these new conditions, the Equation of International Demand. These consequences follow in a very obvious manner from the law of international values, and I shall not occupy space in illustrating them, but shall pass to the more frequent case, of an improvement which does not create a new article of export, but lowers the cost of production of something which the country already exported.

It being advantageous, in discussions of this complicated nature, to employ definite numerical amounts, we shall return to our original example. Ten yards of cloth, if produced in Germany, would require the same amount of labour and capital as twenty yards of linen; but by the play of international demand, they can be obtained from England for seventeen. Suppose now, that by a mechanical improvement made in Germany, and not capable of being transferred to England, the same quantity of labour and capital which produced twenty yards of linen, is enabled to produce thirty. Linen falls one-third in value in the German market, as compared with other commodities produced in Germany. Will it also fall one-third as compared with English cloth, thus giving to England, in common with Germany, the full benefit of the improvement? Or (ought we not rather to say), since the cost to England of *obtaining* linen was not regulated by the cost to Germany of *producing* it, and since England, accordingly, did not get the entire benefit even of the twenty yards which Germany *could* have given for ten yards of cloth, but only obtained seventeen—why should she now obtain more, merely because this theoretical limit is removed ten degrees further off?

f–f48   obtaining
g–g48   producing   h–h48   could

It is evident that in the outset, the improvement will lower the value of linen in Germany, in relation to all other commodities in the German market, including, among the rest, even the imported commodity, cloth. If 10 yards of cloth previously exchanged for 17 yards of linen, they will now exchange for half as much more, or 25½ yards. But whether they will continue to do so, will [i] depend on the effect which this increased cheapness of linen produces on the international demand. The demand for linen in England could scarcely fail to be increased. But it might be increased either in proportion to the cheapness, or in a greater proportion than the cheapness, or in a less proportion.

If the demand was increased in the same proportion with the cheapness, England would take as many times 25½ yards of linen, as the number of times 17 yards which she took previously. She would expend in linen exactly as much of cloth, or of the equivalents of cloth, as much in short of the collective income of her people, as she did before. Germany on her part, would probably require, at that rate of interchange, the same quantity of cloth as before, because it would in reality cost her exactly as much; 25½ yards of linen being now of the same value in her market, as 17 yards were before. In this case, therefore, 10 yards of cloth for 25½ of linen is the rate of interchange which under these new conditions would restore the equation of international demand; and England would obtain linen one-third cheaper than before, being the same advantage as was obtained by Germany.

It might happen, however, that this great cheapening of linen would increase the demand for it in England in a greater ratio than the increase of cheapness; and that if she before wanted 1000 times 17 yards, she would now require more than 1000 times 25½ yards to satisfy her demand. If so, the equation of international demand cannot establish itself at that rate of interchange; to pay for the linen England must offer cloth on more advantageous terms; say, for example, 10 yards for 21 of linen; so that England will not have the full benefit of the improvement in the production of linen, while Germany, in addition to that benefit, will also pay less for cloth. But again, it is possible that England might not desire to increase her consumption of linen in even so great a proportion as that of the increased cheapness; she might not desire so great a quantity as 1000 times 25½ yards: and in that case Germany must force a demand, by offering more than 25½ yards of linen for 10 of cloth: linen will be cheapened in England in a still greater degree than in Germany; while Germany will obtain cloth on more unfavourable terms; and at a higher exchange value than before.

[i]48, 49   wholly

After what has already been said, it is not necessary to particularize the manner in which these results might be modified by introducing into the hypothesis other countries and other commodities. There is a further circumstance by which they may also be modified. In the case supposed the consumers of Germany have had a part of their incomes set at liberty by the increased cheapness of linen, which they may indeed expend in increasing their consumption of that article, but which they may likewise expend in other articles, and among others, in cloth or other imported commodities. This would be an additional element in the international demand, and would modify more or less the terms of interchange.

Of the three possible varieties in the influence of cheapness on demand, which is the more *probable—that* the demand would be increased more than the cheapness, as much as the cheapness, or less than the cheapness? This depends on the nature of the particular commodity, and on the tastes of purchasers. When the commodity is one in general request, and the fall of its price brings it within *k* reach of a much larger class of incomes than before, the demand is often increased in a greater ratio than the fall of price, and a larger sum of money is on the whole expended in the article. Such was the case with coffee, when its price was lowered by successive reductions of taxation; and such would probably be the case with sugar, wine, and a large class of commodities which, though not necessaries, are largely consumed, and in which many consumers indulge when the articles are cheap and economize when they are dear. But it more frequently happens that when a commodity falls in price, less money is spent in it than before: a greater quantity is consumed, but not so great a value. The consumer who saves money by the cheapness of the article, will be likely to expend part of *the* saving in increasing his consumption of other things: and unless the low price attracts a large class of new purchasers who were either not consumers of the article at all, or only in small quantity and occasionally, a less aggregate sum will be expended on it. Speaking generally, therefore, the third of our three cases is the most probable: and an improvement in an exportable article is likely to be as beneficial *(if not more beneficial)* to foreign countries, *as* to the country where the article is produced.

*§ 6. [*The preceding theory not complete*] Thus far had the theory of international values been carried in the first and second editions of this

---

*ʲ-ʲ*48, 49   probable? that
*k*48, 49, 52, 57, 62, 65   the
*m-m*48, 49   , if not more beneficial,
*a-a*615+52, 57, 62, 65, 71

*l-l*48, 49   his
*n-n*48, 49   than

work. But intelligent criticisms *b*(chiefly those of my friend Mr. William Thornton)*b*, and subsequent further investigation, have shown that the doctrine stated in the preceding pages, though correct as far as it goes, is not yet the complete theory of the subject matter.

It has been shown that the exports and imports between the two countries (or, if we suppose more than two, between each country and the world) must in the aggregate pay for each other, and must therefore be exchanged for one another at such values as will be compatible with the equation of international demand. That this, however, does not furnish the complete law of the phenomenon, appears from the following consideration: that several different rates of international value may all equally fulfil the conditions of this law.

The supposition was, that England could produce 10 yards of cloth with the same labour as 15 of linen, and Germany with the same labour as 20 of linen; that a trade was opened between the two countries; that England thenceforth confined her production to cloth, and Germany to linen; and, that if 10 yards of cloth should thenceforth exchange for 17 of linen, England and Germany would exactly supply each other's demand: that, for instance, if England wanted at that price 17,000 yards of linen, Germany would want exactly the 10,000 yards of cloth, which, at that price, England would be required to give for the linen. Under these suppositions it appeared, that 10 cloth for 17 linen, would be, in point of fact, the international values.

But it is quite possible that some other rate, such as 10 cloth for 18 linen, might also fulfil the conditions of the equation of international demand. Suppose that at this last rate, England would want more linen than at the rate of 10 for 17, but not in the ratio of the cheapness; that she would not want the 18,000 which she could now buy with 10,000 yards of cloth, but would be content with 17,500, for which she would pay (at the new rate of 10 for 18) 9722 yards of cloth. Germany, again, having to pay dearer for cloth than when it could be bought at 10 for 17, would probably reduce her consumption to an amount below 10,000 yards, perhaps to the very same number, 9722. Under these conditions the Equation of International Demand would still exist. Thus, the rate of 10 for 17, and that of 10 for 18, would equally satisfy the Equation of Demand: and many other rates of interchange might satisfy it in like manner. It is conceivable that the conditions might be equally satisfied by every numerical rate which could be supposed. There is still therefore a portion of indeterminateness in the rate at which the international values

b-b+65, 71

would adjust themselves; showing that the whole of the influencing circumstances cannot yet have been taken into *c* account.

§ 7. [*International values depend not solely on the quantities demanded, but also on the means of production available in each country for the supply of foreign markets*] It will be found that to supply this deficiency, we must take into consideration not only, as we have already done, the quantities demanded in each country, of the imported commodities; but also the extent of the means of supplying that demand, which are set at liberty in each country by the change in the direction of its industry.

To illustrate this point it will be necessary to choose more convenient numbers than those which we have hitherto employed. Let it be supposed that in England 100 yards of cloth, previously to the trade, exchanged for 100 of linen, but that in Germany 100 of cloth exchanged for 200 of linen. When the trade was opened, England would supply cloth to Germany, Germany linen to England, at an exchange value which would depend partly on the element already discussed, viz. the comparative degree in which, in the two countries, increased cheapness operates in increasing the demand; and partly on some other element not yet taken into account. In order to isolate this unknown element, it will be necessary to make some definite and invariable supposition in regard to the known element. Let us therefore assume, that the influence of cheapness on demand conforms to some simple law, common to both countries and to both commodities. As the simplest and most convenient, let us suppose that in both countries any given increase of cheapness produces an exactly proportional increase of consumption: or, in other words, that the value expended in the commodity, the cost incurred for the sake of obtaining it, is always the same, whether that cost affords a greater or a smaller quantity of the commodity.

Let us now suppose that England, previously to the trade, required a million of yards of linen, which were worth at the English cost of production, a million yards of cloth. By turning all the labour and capital with which that linen was produced, to the production of cloth, she would produce for exportation a million yards of cloth. Suppose that this is the exact quantity which Germany is accustomed to consume. England can dispose of all this cloth in Germany at the German price; she must consent indeed to take a little less until she has driven the German producer from the market, but as soon as this is effected, she can sell her million of cloth for two millions of linen; being the quantity that the German clothiers are enabled to make, by transferring their whole labour and capital from

*c*52, 57, 62, 65 the

cloth to linen. Thus England would gain the whole benefit of the trade, and Germany nothing. This would be perfectly consistent with the equation of international demand: since England (according to the hypothesis in the preceding paragraph) now requires two millions of linen (being able to get them at the same cost at which she previously obtained only one), while the prices in Germany not being altered, Germany requires as before exactly a million of cloth, and can obtain it by employing the labour and capital set at liberty from the production of cloth, in producing the two millions of linen required by England.

Thus far we have supposed that the additional cloth which England could make, by transferring to cloth the whole of the capital previously employed in making linen, was exactly sufficient to supply the whole of Germany's existing demand. But suppose next that it is more than sufficient. Suppose that while England could make with her liberated capital a million yards of cloth for exportation, the cloth which Germany had heretofore required was 800,000 yards only, equivalent at the German cost of production to 1,600,000 yards of linen. England therefore could not dispose of a whole million of cloth in Germany at the German prices. Yet she wants, whether cheap or dear (by our supposition), as much linen as can be bought for a million of cloth: and since this can only be obtained from Germany, or by the more expensive process of production at home, the holders of the million of cloth will be forced by each other's competition to offer it to Germany on any terms (short of the English cost of production) which will induce Germany to take the whole. What terms these would be, the supposition we have made enables us exactly to define. The 800,000 yards of cloth which Germany consumed, cost her the equivalent of 1,600,000 linen, and that invariable cost is what she is willing to expend in cloth, whether the quantity it obtains for her be more or less. England therefore, to induce Germany to take a million of cloth, must offer it for 1,600,000 of linen. The international values will thus be 100 cloth for 160 linen, intermediate between the ratio of the costs of production in England and that of the costs of production in Germany: and the two countries will divide the benefit of the trade, England gaining in the aggregate 600,000 yards of linen, and Germany being richer by 200,000 additional yards of cloth.

Let us now stretch the last supposition still farther, and suppose that the cloth previously consumed by Germany was not only less than the million yards which England is enabled to furnish by discontinuing her production of linen, but less in the full proportion of England's advantage in the production, that is, that Germany only required half a million. In this case, by ceasing altogether to produce cloth, Germany can add a million, but a million only, to her production of linen, and this million, being the equivalent of what the half million previously cost her, is all that she can be induced by any degree of cheapness to expend in cloth. England will be forced by her own competition to give a whole million of cloth for this million of linen, just as she was forced in the preceding case to give it for 1,600,000. But England could have produced at the same cost a million yards of linen for herself. England therefore derives, in this case, no advantage from the international trade. Germany gains the whole; obtaining a million of cloth instead of half a million, at what the half million previously cost her. Germany, in short, is in this third case, exactly in the same situation as England was in the first case; which may easily be verified by reversing the figures.

As the general result of the three cases, it may be laid down as a theorem, that under the supposition we have made of a demand exactly in proportion to the cheapness, the law of international value will be as follows:—

The whole of the cloth which England can make with the capital previously devoted to linen, will exchange for the whole of the linen which Germany can make with the capital previously devoted to cloth.

Or, still more generally,

The whole of the commodities which the two countries can respectively make for exportation, with the labour and capital thrown out of employment by importation, will exchange against one another.

This law, and the three different possibilities arising from it in respect to the division of the advantage, may be conveniently generalized by means of algebraical symbols, as follows:—

Let the quantity of cloth which England can make with the labour and capital withdrawn from the production of linen, be $= n$.

Let the cloth previously required by Germany (at the German cost of production) be $= m$.

Then n of cloth will always exchange for exactly $2m$ of linen.

Consequently if $n = m$, the whole advantage will be on the side of England.

If $n = 2m$, the whole advantage will be on the side of Germany.

If n be greater than m, but less than $2m$, the two countries will share the advantage; England getting $2m$ of linen where she before got only n; Germany getting n of cloth where she before got only m.

It is almost superfluous to observe that the figure 2 stands where it does, only because it is the figure which expresses the advantage of Germany over England in linen as estimated in cloth, and (what is the same thing) of England over Germany in cloth as estimated in linen. If we had supposed that in Germany, before the trade, 100 of cloth exchanged for 1000 instead of 200 of linen, then n (after the trade commenced) would have exchanged for $10m$ instead of $2m$. If instead of 1000 or 200 we had supposed only 150, n would have exchanged for only $\frac{3}{2}$ m. If (in fine) the cost value of cloth (as estimated in linen) in Germany, exceeds the cost value similarly estimated in England, in the ratio of p to q, then will n, after the opening of the trade, exchange for p/q m.*

§ 8. [*The practical result is little affected by this additional element*] We have now arrived at what seems a law of International Values, of great simplicity and generality. But we have done so by setting out from a purely arbitrary hypothesis respecting the relation between demand and cheapness. We have assumed their relation to be fixed, though it is essentially variable. We have supposed that every increase of cheapness produces an exactly proportional extension of demand; in other words, that the same invariable

*[52] It may be asked, why we have supposed the number n to have as its extreme limits, m and $2m$ (or p/q m)? why may not n be less than m, or greater than $2m$; and if so, what will be the result?

This we shall now examine, and when we do so it will appear that n is always, practically speaking, confined within these limits.

Suppose, for example, that n is less than m; or, reverting to our former figures, that the million yards of cloth, which England can make, will not satisfy the whole of Germany's pre-existing demand; that demand being (let us suppose) for 1,200,000 yards. It would then, at first sight, appear that England would supply Germany with cloth up to the extent of a million; that Germany would continue to supply herself with the remaining 200,000 by home production: that this portion of the supply would regulate the price of the whole; that England therefore would be able permanently to sell her million of cloth at the German cost of production (viz. for two millions of linen) and would gain the whole advantage of the trade, Germany being no better off than before.

That such, however, would not be the practical result, will soon be evident. The residuary demand of Germany for 200,000 yards of cloth furnishes a resource to England for purposes of foreign trade of which it is still her interest to avail herself; and though she has no more labour and capital which she can withdraw from linen for the production of this extra quantity of cloth, there must be some other commodities in which Germany has a relative advantage over her (though perhaps not so great as in linen): these she will now import, instead of producing, and the labour and capital formerly employed in producing them will be transferred to cloth, until the required amount is made up. If this transfer just makes up the 200,000 and no more, this augmented n will now be equal to m; England will sell the whole 1,200,000 at the German values; and will still gain the whole advantage of the trade. But if the transfer makes up more than the 200,000, England will have more cloth than 1,200,000 yards to offer; n will become greater than m, and England must part with enough of the advantage to induce Germany to take the surplus. Thus the case which seemed at first sight to be beyond the limits, is transformed practically into a case either coinciding with one of the limits or between them. And so with every other case which can be supposed.

value is laid out in a commodity whether it be cheap or dear; and the law which we have investigated holds good only on this hypothesis, or some other practically equivalent to it. Let us now, therefore, combine the two variable elements of the question, the variations of each of which we have considered separately. Let us suppose the relation between demand and cheapness to vary, and to become such as would prevent the rule of interchange laid down in the last theorem from satisfying the conditions of the Equation of International Demand. Let it be supposed, for instance, that the demand of England for linen is exactly proportional to the cheapness, but that of Germany for cloth, not proportional. To revert to the second of our three cases, the case in which England by discontinuing the production of linen could produce for exportation a million yards of cloth, and Germany by ceasing to produce cloth could produce an additional 1,600,000 yards of linen. If the one of these quantities exactly exchanged for the other, the demand of England would on our present supposition be exactly satisfied, for she requires all the linen which can be got for a million yards of cloth: but Germany perhaps, though she required 800,000 cloth at a cost equivalent to 1,600,000 linen, yet when she can get a million of cloth at the same cost, may not require the whole million; or may require more than a million. First, let her not require so much; but only as much as she can now buy for 1,500,000 linen. England will still offer a million for these 1,500,000; but even this may not induce Germany to take so much as a million; and if England continues to expend exactly the same aggregate cost on linen whatever be the price, she will have to submit to take for her million of cloth any quantity of linen (not less than a million) which may be requisite to induce Germany to take a million of cloth. Suppose this to be 1,400,000 yards. England has now reaped from the trade a gain not of 600,000 but only of 400,000 yards; while Germany, besides having obtained an extra 200,000 yards of cloth, has obtained it with only seven-eighths of the labour and capital which she previously expended in supplying herself with cloth, and may expend the remainder in increasing her own consumption of linen, or of any other commodity.

Suppose on the contrary that Germany, at the rate of a million cloth for 1,600,000 linen, requires more than a million yards of cloth. England having only a million which she can give without *trenching* upon the quantity she previously reserved for herself, Germany must bid for the extra cloth at a higher rate than 160 for 100, until she reaches a rate (say 170 for 100) which will either bring down her own demand for cloth to the limit of a million, or else tempt England to part with some of the cloth she previously consumed at home.

*a–a*52   entrenching

Let us next suppose that the proportionality of demand to cheapness, instead of holding good in one country but not in the other, does not hold good in either country, and that the deviation is of the same kind in both; that, for instance, neither of the two increases its demand in a degree equivalent to the increase of cheapness. On this supposition, at the rate of one million cloth for 1,600,000 linen, England will not want so much as 1,600,000 linen, nor Germany so much as a million cloth: and if they fall short of that amount in exactly the same degree: if England only wants linen to the amount of nine-tenths of 1,600,000 (1,440,000), and Germany only nine hundred thousand of cloth, the interchange will continue to take place at the same rate. And so if England wants a tenth more than 1,600,000, and Germany a tenth more than a million. This coincidence (which, it is to be observed, supposes demand to extend cheapness in a corresponding, but not in an equal degree*) evidently could not exist unless by mere accident: and in any other case, the equation of international demand would require a different adjustment of international values.

The only general law, then, which can be laid down, is this. The values at which a country exchanges its produce with foreign countries depend on two things: first, on the amount and extensibility of their demand for its commodities, compared with its demand for theirs; and secondly, on the capital which it has to spare, from the production of domestic commodities for its own consumption. The more the foreign demand for its commodities exceeds its demand for foreign commodities, and the less capital it can spare to produce for foreign markets, compared with what foreigners spare to produce for its markets, the more favourable to it will be the terms of interchange: that is, the more it will obtain of foreign commodities in return for a given quantity of its own.

But these two influencing circumstances are in reality reducible to one: for the capital which a country has to spare from the production of domestic commodities for its own use, is in proportion to its own demand for foreign commodities: whatever proportion of its collective income it expends in purchases from abroad, that same proportion of its capital is left without a home market for its productions. The new element, therefore, which for the sake of scientific correctness we have introduced into the theory of international values, does not seem to make any very material

---

*[52] The increase of demand from 800,000 to 900,000, and that from a million to 1,440,000, are neither equal in themselves, nor bear an equal proportion to the increase of cheapness. Germany's demand for cloth has [52 is] increased one-eighth, while the cheapness is increased one-fourth. England's demand for linen is increased 44 per cent, while the cheapness is increased 60 per cent.

difference in the practical result. It still appears [b] , that the countries which carry on their foreign trade on the most advantageous terms, are those whose commodities are most in demand by foreign countries, and which have themselves the least demand for foreign commodities. From which, among other consequences, it follows, that the richest countries, *cæteris paribus*, gain the least by a given amount of foreign commerce: since, having a greater demand for commodities generally, they are likely to have a greater demand for foreign commodities, and thus modify the terms of interchange to their own disadvantage. Their aggregate gains by foreign trade, doubtless, are generally greater than those of poorer countries, since they carry on a greater amount of such trade, and gain the benefit of cheapness on a larger consumption: but their gain is less on each individual article consumed.[a]

[a]§ 9.[a] [*On what circumstances the cost to a country of its imports depends*] We now pass to another essential part of the theory of the subject. There are two senses in which a country obtains commodities cheaper by foreign trade; in the sense of Value, and in the sense of Cost. It gets them cheaper in the first sense, by their falling in value relatively to other things: the same quantity of them exchanging, in the country, for a smaller quantity than before of the other produce of the country. [b]To revert to our original figures; in England, all consumers of linen obtained, after the trade was opened,[b] 17 or some greater number of yards for the same quantity of all other things for which they before obtained only 15. The degree of cheapness, in this sense of the term, depends on the [c]laws of International Demand, so copiously illustrated in the preceding sections[c]. But in the other sense, that of Cost, a country gets a commodity cheaper when it obtains a greater quantity of the commodity with the same expenditure of labour and capital. In this sense of the term, cheapness in a great measure depends upon a cause of a different nature: a country gets its imports cheaper, in proportion to the general productiveness of its domestic industry; to the general efficiency of its labour. The labour of one country may be, as a whole, much more efficient than that of another: all or most of the commodities capable of being produced in both, may be produced in one at less absolute cost than in the other; which, as we have seen, will not necessarily prevent the two countries from exchanging commodities. The things which the more favoured country will import

---

[b]52, 57   to me

[a-a]48, 49   §6.
[b-b]48, 49   In England, after the trade was opened, all consumers of linen obtained
[c-c]48   law which has now been so copiously illustrated, that of the Equation of International Demand] 49   *as* 48 . . . of Equation . . . *as* 48

from others, are of course those in which it is least superior; but by importing them it acquires, even in those commodities, the same advantage which it possesses in the articles it gives in exchange for them. Thus the countries which obtain their own productions at least cost, also get their imports at least cost.

This *d* will be made *e*still*e* more obvious if we suppose two competing countries. England sends cloth to Germany, and gives 10 yards of it for 17 yards of linen, or for something else which in Germany is the equivalent of those 17 yards. Another country, as for example France, does the same. The one giving 10 yards of cloth for a certain quantity of German commodities, so must the other: if, therefore, in England, these 10 yards are produced by only half as much labour as that by which they are produced in France, the linen or other commodities of Germany will cost to England only half the amount of labour which they will cost to France. England would thus obtain her imports at less cost than France, in the ratio of the greater efficiency of her labour in the production of cloth: which might be taken*f*, in the case supposed,*f* as an *g*approximate*g* estimate of the efficiency of her labour generally; since France, as well as England, by selecting cloth as her article of export, would have shown that *h*with her also it was the commodity in which*h* labour was relatively the most efficient. It follows, therefore, that every country gets its imports at less cost, in proportion to the general efficiency of its labour.

This proposition was first clearly seen and expounded by Mr. Senior,* but only as applicable to the importation of the precious metals. I think it important to point out that the proposition holds equally true of all other imported commodities; and further, that it is only a portion of the truth. For, in the case supposed, the cost to England of the linen which she pays for with ten yards of cloth, does not depend solely upon the cost to herself of ten yards of cloth, but partly also upon how many yards of linen she obtains in exchange for them. What her imports cost to her is a function of two variables; the quantity of her own commodities which she gives for them, and the cost of those commodities. Of these, the last *i*alone*i* depends on the efficiency of her labour: the first depends on the law of international values; that is, on the intensity and extensibility of the foreign demand for her commodities, compared with her demand for foreign commodities.

*Three Lectures on the Cost of Obtaining Money. [London: Murray, 1830.]

*d*48, 49   truth
e-e+52, 57, 62, 65, 71
f-f+52, 57, 62, 65, 71
*g-g*52   approximative [*printer's error?*]
*h-h*48, 49   (notwithstanding her absolute inferiority) it was still the commodity in which her
*i-i*48, 49, 52, 57   only

In the case just now supposed, of a competition between England and France, the state of international values affected both competitors alike, since they were supposed to trade with the same country, and to export and import the same commodities. The difference, therefore, in what their imports cost them, depended solely on the other cause, the unequal efficiency of their labour. They gave the same quantities; the difference could only be in the cost of production. But if England traded to Germany with cloth, and France with iron, the comparative demand in Germany for those two commodities would bear a share in determining the comparative cost, in labour and capital, with which England and France would obtain German products. If iron were more in demand in Germany than cloth, France would recover, through that channel, part of her disadvantage; if less, her disadvantage would be increased. The efficiency, therefore, of a country's labour, is not the only thing which determines even the *cost* at which that country obtains imported commodities—while it has no share whatever in determining either their exchange *value*, or, as we shall presently see, their *price*.

CHAPTER XIX

Of Money, Considered
as an Imported Commodity

§ 1. [*Money imported in two modes; as a commodity, and as a medium of exchange*] The degree of progress which we have now made in the theory of Foreign Trade, puts it in our power to supply what was previously deficient in our view of the theory of Money; and this, when completed, will in its turn enable us to conclude the subject of Foreign Trade.

Money, or the material of which it is composed, is, in Great Britain, and in most other countries, a foreign commodity. Its value and distribution must therefore be regulated, not by the law of value which obtains in adjacent places, but by that which is applicable to imported commodities—the law of International Values.

In the discussion into which we are now about to enter, I shall use the terms Money and the Precious Metals indiscriminately. This may be done without leading to any error; it having been shown that the value of money, when it consists of the precious metals, or ^{a} of a paper currency convertible into them on demand, is entirely governed by the value of the metals themselves: from which it never ^{b}permanently^b differs, except by the expense of coinage when this is paid by the individual and not by the state.

Money is brought into a country in two different ways. It is imported (chiefly in the form of bullion) like any other merchandize, as being an advantageous article of commerce. It is also imported in its other character of a medium of exchange, to pay some debt due to the country, either for goods exported or on any other account. There are other ways in which it may be introduced casually; these are the two in which it is received in the ordinary course of business, and which determine its value. The existence of these two distinct modes in which money flows into a country, while other commodities are habitually introduced only in the first of these modes, occasions somewhat more of complexity and obscurity than exists

^{a}48, 49   even
$^{b-b}$+57, 62, 65, 71

in the case of other commodities, and for this reason only is any special and minute exposition necessary.

§ 2. [*As a commodity, it obeys the same laws of value as other imported commodities*] In so far as the precious metals are imported in the ordinary way of commerce, their value must depend on the same causes, and conform to the same laws, as the value of any other foreign production. It is in this mode chiefly that gold and silver diffuse themselves from the mining countries into all other parts of the commercial world. They are the staple commodities of those countries, or at least are among their great articles of regular export; and are shipped on speculation, in the same manner as other exportable commodities. The quantity, therefore, which a country (say England) will give of its own produce, for a certain quantity of bullion, will depend, if we suppose only two countries and two commodities, upon the demand in England for bullion, compared with the demand in the mining country (which we will call Brazil) for what England has to give. They must exchange in such proportions as will leave no unsatisfied demand on either side, to alter values by its competition. The bullion required by England must exactly pay for the cottons or other English commodities required by Brazil. If, however, we substitute for this simplicity the degree of complication which really exists, the equation of international demand must be established not between the bullion wanted in England and the cottons or broadcloth wanted in Brazil, but between the whole of the imports of England and the whole of her exports. The demand in foreign countries for English products, must be brought into equilibrium with the demand in England for the products of foreign countries; and all foreign commodities, bullion among the rest, must be exchanged against English products in such proportions, as will, by the effect they produce on the demand, establish this equilibrium.

There is nothing in the peculiar nature or uses of the precious metals, which should make them an exception to the general principles of demand. So far as they are wanted for purposes of luxury or the arts, the demand increases with the cheapness, in the same irregular way as the demand for any other commodity. So far as they are required for money, the demand increases with the cheapness in a perfectly regular way, the quantity needed being always in inverse proportion to the value. This is the only real difference, in respect to demand, between money and other things; and for the present purpose it is a difference altogether immaterial.

Money, then, if imported solely as a merchandize, will, like other imported commodities, be of lowest value in the countries for whose exports there is the greatest foreign demand, and which have themselves the least demand for foreign commodities. To these two circumstances it is however necessary to add two others, which produce their effect through cost of carriage. The cost of obtaining bullion is compounded of two elements; the goods given to purchase it, and the expense of transport: of which last, the bullion countries will bear a part, (though an uncertain part,) in the adjustment of international values. The expense of transport is partly that of carrying the goods to the bullion countries, and partly that of bringing back the bullion; both these items are influenced by the distance from the mines; and the former is also much affected by the bulkiness of the goods. Countries whose exportable produce consists of the finer manufactures, obtain bullion, as well as all other foreign articles, *cæteris paribus*, at less expense than countries which export nothing but bulky raw produce.

To be quite accurate, therefore, we must say—The countries whose exportable productions are most in demand abroad, and contain greatest value in smallest bulk, which are nearest to the mines, and which have least demand for foreign productions, are those in which money will be of lowest value, or in other words, in which prices will habitually range the highest. If we are speaking not of the value of money, but of its cost, (that is, the quantity of the country's labour which must be expended to obtain it,) we must add to these four conditions of cheapness a fifth condition, namely, "whose productive industry is the most efficient." This *ᵃlastᵃ*, however, does not at all affect the value of money, estimated in commodities: it affects the general abundance and facility with which all things, money and commodities together, can be obtained.

Although, therefore, Mr. Senior is right in pointing out the great efficiency of English labour as the chief cause why the precious metals are obtained at less *cost* by England than by most other countries, I cannot admit that it at all accounts for their being of less *value*; for their going less far in the purchase of commodities. This, in so far as it is a fact, and not an illusion, must be occasioned by the great demand in foreign countries for the staple commodities of England, and the generally unbulky character of those commodities, compared with the corn, wine, timber, sugar, wool, hides, tallow, hemp, flax, tobacco, raw cotton, &c., which form the exports of other commercial countries. These two causes will account for a somewhat higher range of general prices in England than elsewhere, notwithstanding the counteracting influence of her own great demand for foreign commodities. I am, however, strongly of opinion that the high prices of commodities, and low purchasing power of money in England, are more apparent than real. Food, indeed, is somewhat dearer; and food composes so large a portion of the expenditure when the income is small and the family large, that to such families England is a dear country. Services, also, of most

ᵃ⁻ᵃ+57, 62, 65, 71

descriptions, are dearer than [b]in the other countries of Europe, from the less costly mode of living of the poorer classes on the Continent. But manufactured commodities (except most of those in which good taste is required)[b] are decidedly cheaper; or would be so, if buyers would be content with the same quality of material and of workmanship. What is called the dearness of living in England, is mainly an affair not of necessity but of foolish custom; it being thought imperative by all classes in England above the condition of a day-labourer, that the things they consume should either be of the same quality with those used by much richer people, or at least should be as nearly as possible undistinguishable from them in outward appearance.

§ 3. [*Its value does not depend exclusively on its cost of production at the mines*] From the preceding considerations, it appears that those are greatly in error who contend [a] that the value of money, in countries where it is an imported commodity, must be entirely regulated by its value in the countries which produce it; and cannot be raised or lowered in any permanent manner unless some change has taken place in the cost of production at the mines. On the contrary, any circumstance which disturbs the equation of international demand with respect to a particular country, not only may, but must, affect the value of money in that country—its value at the mines remaining the same. The opening of a new branch of export trade from England; an increase in the foreign demand for English products, either by the natural course of events, or by the abrogation of duties; a check to the demand in England for foreign commodities, by the laying on of import duties in England or of export duties elsewhere; these and all other events of similar tendency, would make the imports of England (bullion and other things taken together) no longer an equivalent for [b]the[b] exports; and the countries which take her exports would be obliged to offer their commodities, and bullion among the rest, on cheaper terms, in order to re-establish the equation of demand: and thus England would obtain money cheaper, and would acquire a generally higher range of prices. Incidents the reverse of these would produce effects the reverse— would reduce prices; or, in other words, raise the value of the precious metals. It must be observed, however, that money would be thus raised in value only with respect to home commodities: in relation to all imported articles it would remain as before, since their values would be affected in

[b-b]48, 49   on the Continent, from the less costly manner in which the poorer classes on the Continent are contented to live. But almost all sorts of manufactured commodities

[a]48, 49   (as has been done in the controversies called forth by the recent publications of Colonel Torrens)

[b-b]48, 49   her

the same way and in the same degree with its own. A country which, from any of the causes mentioned, gets money cheaper, obtains all its other imports cheaper likewise.

It is by no means necessary that the increased demand for English commodities, which enables England to supply herself with bullion at a cheaper rate, should be a demand in the mining countries. England might export nothing whatever to those countries, and yet might be the country which obtained bullion from them on the lowest terms, provided there were a sufficient intensity of demand in other foreign countries for English goods, which would be paid for circuitously, with gold and silver from the mining countries. The whole of its exports are what a country exchanges against the whole of its imports, and not its exports and imports to and from any one country; and the general foreign demand for its productions will determine what equivalent it must give for imported goods, in order to establish an equilibrium between its sales and purchases generally; without regard to the maintenance of a similar equilibrium between it and any country singly.

CHAPTER XX

Of the Foreign Exchanges

§ 1. [*Purposes for which money passes from country to country as a medium of exchange*] We have thus far considered the precious metals as a commodity, imported like other commodities in the common course of trade, and have examined what are the circumstances which would in that case determine their value. But those metals are also imported in another character, that which belongs to them as a medium of exchange; not as an article of commerce, to be sold for money, but as themselves money, to pay a debt, or effect a transfer of property. It remains to consider whether the liability of gold and silver to be transported from country to country for such purposes, in any way modifies the conclusions we have already arrived at, or places those metals under a different law of value from that to which, in common with all other imported commodities, they would be subject if international trade were an affair of direct barter.

Money is sent from one country to another for various purposes: such as the payment of tributes or subsidies; remittances of revenue to or from dependencies, or of rents or other incomes to their absent owners; emigration of capital, or transmission of it for foreign investment. The most usual purpose, however, is that of payment for goods. To show in what circumstances money actually passes from country to country for this or any of the other purposes mentioned, it is necessary briefly to state the nature of the mechanism by which international trade is carried on, when it takes place not by barter but through the medium of money.

§ 2. [*Mode of adjusting international payments through the exchanges*] In practice, the exports and imports of a country not only are not exchanged directly against each other, but often do not even pass through the same hands. Each is separately bought and paid for with money. We have seen, however, that, even in the same country, money does not actually pass from hand to hand each time that purchases are made with it, and still less does this happen between different countries. The habitual mode of paying and receiving payment for commodities, between country and country, is by bills of exchange.

A merchant in England, A, has exported English commodities, consigning them to his correspondent B in France. Another merchant in France, C, has exported French commodities, suppose of equivalent value, to a merchant D in England. It is evidently unnecessary that B in France should send money to A in England, and that D in England should send an equal sum of money to C in France. The one debt may be applied to the payment of the other, and the double cost *and risk* of carriage be thus saved. A draws a bill on B for the amount which B owes to him: D, having an equal amount to pay in France, buys this bill from A, and sends it to C, who, at the expiration of the number of days which the bill has to run, presents it to B for payment. Thus the debt due from France to England, and the debt due from England to France, are both paid without sending an ounce of gold or silver from one country to the other.

In this statement, however, it is supposed, that the sum of the debts due from France to England, and the sum of those due from England to France, are equal; that each country has exactly the same number of ounces of gold or silver to pay and to receive. This implies (if we exclude for the present any other international payments than those occurring in the course of commerce), that the exports and imports exactly pay for one another, or in other words, that the equation of international demand is established. When such is the fact, the international transactions are liquidated without the passage of any money from one country to the other. But if there is a greater sum due from England to France, than is due from France to England, or *vice versâ*, the debts cannot be simply written off against one another. After the one has been applied, as far as it will go, towards covering the other, the balance must be transmitted in the precious metals. In point of fact, the merchant who has the amount to pay, will even then pay for it by a bill. When a person has a remittance to make to a foreign country, he does not himself search for some one who has money to receive from that country, and ask him for a bill of exchange. In this as in other branches of business, there is a class of middlemen or brokers, who bring buyers and sellers together, or stand between them, buying bills from those who have money to receive, and selling bills to those who have money to pay. When a customer comes to a broker for a bill on Paris or Amsterdam, the broker sells to him, perhaps the bill he may himself have bought that morning from a merchant, perhaps a bill on his own correspondent in the foreign city: and to enable his correspondent to pay, when due, all the bills he has granted, he remits to him all those which he has bought and has not resold. In this manner these *brokers* take upon themselves the whole settlement of the pecuniary transactions between distant places, being

a-a+52, 57, 62, 65, 71
*b-b*48   bill-brokers, or exchange-brokers,

remunerated by a small commission or percentage on the amount of each bill which they either sell or buy. Now, if the brokers find that they are asked for bills on the one part, to a greater amount than bills are offered to them on the other, they do not on this account refuse to give them; but since, in that case, they have no means of enabling the correspondents on whom their bills are drawn, to pay them when due, except by transmitting part of the amount in gold or silver, they require from those to whom they sell bills an additional price, sufficient to cover the freight and insurance of the gold and silver, with a profit sufficient to compensate them for their trouble and for the temporary occupation of a portion of their capital. This premium (as it is called) the buyers are willing to pay, because they must otherwise go to the expense of remitting the precious metals themselves, and it is done cheaper by those who make doing it a part of their especial business. But though only some of those who have a debt to pay would have actually to remit money, all will be obliged, by each other's competition, to pay the premium; and the brokers are for the same reason obliged to pay it to those whose bills they buy. The reverse of all this happens, if on the comparison of exports and imports, the country, instead of having a balance to pay, has a balance to receive. The brokers find more bills offered to them, than are sufficient to cover those which they are required to grant. Bills on foreign countries consequently fall to a discount; and the competition among the brokers, which is exceedingly active, prevents them from retaining this discount as a profit for themselves, and obliges them to give the benefit of it to those who buy the bills for purposes of remittance.

Let us suppose that all countries had the same currency, as in the progress of political improvement they one day will have: and, as ᶜtheᶜ most familiar to the reader, ᵈthough not the best,ᵈ let us suppose this currency to be the English. When England had the same number of pounds sterling to pay to France, which France had to pay to her, one set of merchants in England would want bills, and another set would have bills to dispose of, for the very same number of pounds sterling; and consequently a bill on France for 100*l.* would sell for exactly 100*l.*, or, in the phraseology of merchants, the exchange would be at par. As France also, on this supposition, would have an equal number of pounds sterling to pay and to receive, bills on England would be at par in France, whenever bills on France were at par in England.

If, however, England had a larger sum to pay to France than to receive from her, there would be persons requiring bills on France for a greater number of pounds sterling than there were bills drawn by persons to whom money was due. A bill on France for 100*l.* would then sell for more than

ᶜ⁻ᶜ+52, 57, 62, 65, 71
ᵈ⁻ᵈ+52, 57, 62, 65, 71

100*l*., and bills would be said to be at a premium. The premium, however, could not exceed the cost and risk of making the remittance in gold, together with a trifling profit; because if it did, the debtor would send the gold itself, in preference to buying the bill.

If, on the contrary, England had more money to receive from France than to pay, there would be bills offered for a greater number of pounds than were wanted for remittance, and the price of bills would fall below par: a bill for 100*l*. might be bought for somewhat less than 100*l*., and bills would be said to be at a discount.

When England has more to pay than to receive, France has more to receive than to pay, and *vice versâ*. When, therefore, in England, bills on France bear a premium, then, in France, bills on England are at a discount: and when bills on France are at a discount in England, bills on England are at a premium in France. If they are at par in either country, they are so, as we have already seen, in both.

Thus do matters stand between countries, or places, which have the same currency. So much of barbarism, however, still remains in the transactions of the most civilized nations, that almost all independent countries choose to assert their nationality by having, to their own inconvenience and that of their neighbours, a peculiar currency of their own. To our present purpose this makes no other difference, than that instead of speaking of *equal* sums of money, we have to speak of *equivalent* sums. By equivalent sums, when both currencies are composed of the same metal, are meant sums which contain exactly the same quantity of the metal, in weight and fineness; but when, as in the case of France and England, the metals are different, what is meant is that the quantity of gold in the one sum, and the quantity of silver in the other, are of the same value in the general market of the world: there being no material difference between one place and another in the relative value of these metals. Suppose 25 francs to be (as within a trifling fraction it is) the equivalent of a pound sterling. The debts and credits of the two countries would be equal, when the one owed as many times 25 francs, as the other owed pounds. When this was the case, a bill on France for 2500 francs would be worth in England 100*l*., and a bill on England for 100*l*. would be worth in France 2500 francs. The exchange is then said to be at par: and 25 francs (in reality 25 francs and a trifle more)* is called the par of exchange with France. When England owed to France more than the equivalent of what France owed to her, a bill for 2500 francs would be at a premium, that is, would

*[62] Written before the change in the relative value of the two metals produced by the gold discoveries. The par of exchange between gold and silver currencies is now variable, and no one can foresee at what point it will ultimately rest.

be worth more than 100*l.* When France owed to England more than the equivalent of what England owed to France, a bill for 2500 francs would be worth less than 100*l.*, or would be at a discount.

When bills on foreign countries are at a premium, it is customary to say that the exchanges are against the country, or unfavourable to it. In order to understand these phrases, we must take notice of what "the exchange," in the language of merchants, really means. It means the power which the money of the country has of purchasing the money of other countries. Supposing 25 francs to be the exact par of exchange, then when it requires more than 100*l.* to buy a bill for 2500 francs, 100*l.* of English money are worth less than their real equivalent of French money: and this is called an exchange unfavourable to England. The only persons in England, however, to whom it is really unfavourable, are those who have money to pay in France; for they come into the bill market as buyers, and have to pay a premium: but to those who have money to receive in France, the same state of things is favourable; for they come as sellers, and receive the premium. The premium, however, indicates that a balance is due by England, which *e*might have to*e* be eventually liquidated in the precious metals: and since, according to the old theory, the benefit of a trade consisted in bringing money into the country, this prejudice introduced the practice of calling the exchange favourable when it indicated a balance to receive, and unfavourable when it indicated one to pay: and the phrases in turn tended to maintain the prejudice.

§ 3. [*Distinction between variations in the exchanges which are self-adjusting, and those which can only be rectified through prices*] It might be supposed at first sight that when the exchange is unfavourable, or in other words, when bills are at a premium, the premium must always amount to a full equivalent for the cost of transmitting money: since, as there is really a balance to pay, and as the full cost must therefore be incurred by some of those who have remittances to make, their competition will compel all to submit to an equivalent sacrifice. And such would certainly be the case, if it were always necessary that whatever is destined to be paid should be paid immediately. The expectation of great and immediate foreign payments sometimes produces a most startling effect on the exchanges.* But

---

*On the news of Bonaparte's landing from Elba, the price of bills advanced in one day as much as ten per cent. Of course this premium was not a mere equivalent for cost of carriage, since the freight of such an article as gold, even with the addition of war insurance, could never have amounted to so much. This great price was an equivalent not for the difficulty of sending gold, but for the anticipated difficulty of procuring it to send; the expectation being that

*e-e*48, 49, 52, 57, 62   must

a small excess of imports above exports, or any other small amount of debt to be paid to foreign countries, does not usually affect the exchanges to the full extent of the cost and risk of transporting bullion. The length of credit allowed, generally permits, on the part of some of the debtors, a postponement of payment, and in the mean time the balance may turn the other way, and restore the equality of debts and credits without any actual transmission of the metals. And this is the more likely to happen, as there is a self-adjusting power in the variations of the exchange itself. Bills are at a premium because a greater money value has been imported than exported. But the premium is itself an extra profit to those who export. Besides the price they obtain for their goods, they draw for the amount and gain the premium. It is, on the other hand, a diminution of profit to those who import. Besides the price of the goods, they have to pay a premium for remittance. So that what is called an unfavourable exchange is an encouragement to export, and a discouragement to import. And if the balance due is of small amount, and is the consequence of some merely casual disturbance in the ordinary course of trade, it is soon liquidated in commodities, and the account adjusted by means of bills, without the transmission of any bullion. Not so, however, when the excess of imports above exports, which has made the exchange unfavourable, arises from a permanent cause. In that case, what disturbed the equilibrium must have been the state of prices, and it can only be restored by acting on prices. It is impossible that prices should be such as to invite to an excess of imports, and yet that the exports should be kept permanently up to the imports by the extra profit on exportation derived from the premium on bills; for if the exports *were* kept up to the imports, bills would not be at a premium, and the extra profit would not exist. It is through the prices of commodities that the correction must be administered.

Disturbances, therefore, of the equilibrium of imports and exports, and consequent disturbances of the exchange, may be considered as of two classes; the one casual or accidental, which, if not on too large a scale, correct themselves through the premium on bills, without any transmission of the precious metals; the other arising from the general state of prices, which cannot be corrected without the subtraction of actual money from the

---

there would be such immense remittances to the Continent in subsidies and for the support of armies, as would press hard on the stock of bullion in the country (which was then entirely denuded of specie), and this, too, in a shorter time than would allow of its being replenished. Accordingly the price of bullion rose likewise, with the same suddenness. It is hardly necessary to say that this took place during the Bank restriction. In a convertible state of the currency, no such thing could have occurred until the Bank stopped payment.

*a–a*48, 49, 52 *were*

circulation of one of the countries, or an annihilation of credit equivalent to it; since the mere transmission of bullion (as distinguished from money), not having any effect on prices, is of no avail to abate the cause from which the disturbance proceeded.

It remains to observe, that the exchanges do not depend on the balance of debts and credits with each country separately, but with all countries taken together. England may owe a balance of payments to France; but it does not follow that the exchange with France will be against England, and that bills on France will be at a premium; because a balance may be due to England from Holland or Hamburg, and she may pay her *debts* to France with bills on those places; which is technically called arbitration of exchange. There is some little additional expense, partly commission and partly loss of interest, in settling debts in this circuitous manner, and to the extent of that small difference the exchange with one country may vary apart from that with others; but in the main, the exchanges with all foreign countries vary together, according as the country has a balance to receive or to pay on the general result of its foreign transactions.

*-*48, 49, 52, 57   debt

CHAPTER XXI

Of the Distribution
of the Precious Metals Through
the Commercial World

§ 1. [*The substitution of money for barter makes no difference in exports and imports, nor in the law of international values*] Having now examined the mechanism by which the commercial transactions between nations are actually conducted, we have next to inquire whether this mode of conducting them makes any difference in the conclusions respecting international values, which we previously arrived at on the hypothesis of barter.

The nearest analogy would lead us to presume the negative. We did not find that the intervention of money and its substitutes made any difference in the law of value as applied to adjacent places. Things which would have been equal in value if the mode of exchange had been by barter, are worth equal sums of money. The introduction of money is a mere addition of one more commodity, of which the value is regulated by the same laws as that of all other commodities. We shall not be surprised, therefore, if we find that international values also are determined by the same causes under a money and bill system, as they would be under a system of barter; and that money has little to do in the matter, except to furnish a convenient mode of comparing values.

All interchange is, in substance and effect, barter: ªwheeverª sells ᵇcommoditiesᵇ for money, and with that money buys other goods, really buys those goods with his own ᶜcommoditiesᶜ. And so of nations: their trade is a mere exchange of exports for imports: and whether money is employed or not, things are only in their permanent state when the exports and imports exactly pay for each other. When this is the case, equal sums of money are due from each country to the other, the debts are settled by bills, and there is no balance to be paid in the precious metals. The trade is in a state like that which is called in mechanics a condition of stable equilibrium.

ª⁻ª48, 49   he who   ᵇ⁻ᵇ48, 49   his productions   ᶜ⁻ᶜ48, 49   produce

But the process by which things are brought back to this state when they happen to deviate from it, is, at least outwardly, not the same in a barter system and in a money system. Under the first, the country which wants more imports than its exports will pay for, must offer its exports at a cheaper rate, as the sole means of creating a demand for them sufficient to re-establish the equilibrium. When money is used, the country seems to do a thing totally different. She takes the additional imports at the same price as before, and as she exports no equivalent, the balance of payments turns against her; the exchange becomes unfavourable, and the difference has to be paid in money. This is in appearance a very distinct operation from the former. Let us see if it differs in its essence, or only in its mechanism.

Let the country which has the balance to pay be England, and the country which receives it, France. By this transmission of the precious metals, the quantity of the currency is diminished in England, and increased in France. This I am at liberty to assume. As we shall see hereafter, it would be a very erroneous assumption if made in regard to *all* payments of international balances. A balance which has only to be paid once, such as the payment made for an extra importation of corn in a season of dearth, may be paid from hoards, or from the reserves of bankers, without acting on the circulation. But we are now supposing that there is an excess of imports over exports, arising from the fact that the equation of international demand is not yet established: that there is at the ordinary prices a permanent demand in England for more French goods than the English goods required in France at the ordinary prices will pay for. When this is the case, if a change were not made in the prices, there would be a perpetually renewed balance to be paid in money. The imports require to be permanently diminished, or the exports to be increased; which can only be accomplished through prices; and hence, even if the balances are at first paid from hoards, or by the exportation of bullion, they will reach the circulation at last, for until they do, nothing can stop the drain.

When, therefore, the state of prices is such that the equation of international demand cannot establish itself, the country requiring more imports than can be paid for by ᵈtheᵈ exports; it is a sign that the country has more of the precious metals or their substitutes, in circulation, than can permanently circulate, and must necessarily part with some of them before the balance can be restored. ᵉTheᵉ currency is accordingly contracted: prices fall, and among the rest, the prices of exportable articles; for which, accordingly, there arises, in foreign countries, a greater demand: while imported commodities have possibly risen in price, from the influx of money into foreign countries, and at all events have not participated in the general

ᵈ⁻ᵈ48, 49   her   ᵉ⁻ᵉ48, 49   Her

fall. But until the increased cheapness of English goods induces foreign countries to take a greater pecuniary value, or until the increased dearness (positive or comparative) of foreign goods makes England take a less pecuniary value, the exports of England will be no nearer to paying for *the* imports than before, and the stream of the precious metals which had begun to flow out of England, will still flow on. This efflux will continue, until the fall of prices in England brings within reach of the foreign market some commodity which England did not previously send thither; or until the reduced price of the things which she did send, has forced a demand abroad for a sufficient quantity to pay for the imports, aided, perhaps, by a reduction of the English demand for foreign goods, *through* their enhanced price, either positive or comparative.

Now this is the very process which took place on our original supposition of barter. Not only, therefore, does the trade between nations tend to the same equilibrium between exports and imports, whether money is employed or not, but the means by which this equilibrium is established are essentially the same. The country whose exports are not sufficient to pay for her imports, offers them on cheaper terms, until she succeeds in forcing the necessary demand: in other words, the Equation of International Demand, under a money system as well as under a barter system, is *the* law of international trade. Every country exports and imports the very same things, and in the very same quantity, under the one system as under the other. In a barter system, the trade gravitates to the point at which the sum of the imports exactly exchanges for the sum of the exports: in a money system, it gravitates to the point at which the sum of the imports and the sum of the exports exchange for the same quantity of money. And since things which are equal to the same thing are equal to one another, the exports and imports which are equal in money price, would, if money were not used, precisely exchange for one another.*

*The subjoined extract from the separate Essay previously referred to, will give some assistance in following the course of the phenomena. It is adapted to the imaginary case used for illustration throughout that Essay, the case of a trade between England and Germany in cloth and linen.

"We may, at first, make whatever supposition we will with respect to the value of money. Let us suppose, therefore, that before the opening of the trade, the price of cloth is the same in both countries, namely, six shillings per yard. As ten yards of cloth were supposed to exchange in England for 15 yards of linen, in Germany for 20, we must suppose that linen is sold in England at four shillings per yard, in Germany at three. Cost of carriage and importer's profit are left, as before, out of consideration.

"In this state of prices, cloth, it is evident, cannot yet be exported from England into Germany: but linen can be imported from Germany into England. It will be so; and, in the first instance, the linen will be paid for in money.

*-f*48, 49 her   *g-g*48, 49, 52 from   *h-h*52, 57 a

§ 2. [*The preceding theorem further illustrated*] It thus appears that the law of international values, and, consequently, the division of the advantages of trade among the nations which carry it on, are the same, on the supposition of money, as they would be in a state of barter. In international, as in ordinary domestic interchanges, money is to commerce only what oil is to machinery, or railways to locomotion—a contrivance to diminish friction. In order still further to test these conclusions, let us

---

"The efflux of money from England, and its influx into Germany, will raise money prices in the latter country, and lower them in the former. Linen will rise in Germany above three shillings per yard, and cloth above six shillings. Linen in England, being imported from Germany, will (since cost of carriage is not reckoned) sink to the same price as in that country, while cloth will fall below six shillings. As soon as the price of cloth is lower in England than in Germany, it will begin to be exported, and the price of cloth in Germany will fall to what it is in England. As long as the cloth exported does not suffice to pay for the linen imported, money will continue to flow from England into Germany, and prices generally will continue to fall in England and rise in Germany. By the fall, however, of cloth in England, cloth will fall in Germany also, and the demand for it will increase. By the rise of linen in Germany, linen must rise in England also, and the demand for it will diminish. As cloth fell in price and linen rose, there would be some particular price of both articles at which the cloth exported and the linen imported would exactly pay for each other. At this point prices would remain, because money would then cease to move out of England into Germany. What this point might be, would entirely depend upon the circumstances and inclinations of the purchasers on both sides. If the fall of cloth did not much increase the demand for it in Germany, and the rise of linen did not diminish very rapidly the demand for it in England, much money must pass before the equilibrium is restored; cloth would fall very much, and linen would rise, until England, perhaps, had to pay nearly as much for it as when she produced it for herself. But if, on the contrary, the fall of cloth caused a very rapid increase of the demand for it in Germany, and the rise of linen in Germany reduced very rapidly the demand in England from what it was under the influence of the first cheapness produced by the opening of the trade; the cloth would very soon suffice to pay for the linen, little money would pass between the two countries, and England would derive a large portion of the benefit of the trade. We have thus arrived at precisely the same conclusion, in supposing the employment of money, which we found to hold under the supposition of barter.

"In what shape the benefit accrues to the two nations from the trade is clear enough. Germany, before the commencement of the trade, paid six shillings per yard for broadcloth: she now obtains it at a lower price. This, however, is not the whole of her advantage. As the money-prices of all her other commodities have risen, the money-incomes of all her producers have increased. This is no advantage to them in buying from each other, because the price of what they buy has risen in the same ratio with their means of paying for it: but it is an advantage to them in buying anything which has not risen, and, still more, anything which has fallen. They, therefore, benefit as consumers of

proceed to re-examine, on the supposition of money, a question which we have already investigated on the hypothesis of barter, namely, to what extent the benefit of an improvement in the production of an exportable article, is participated in by the countries importing it.

The improvement may either consist in the cheapening of some article which was already a staple production of the country, or in the establishment of some new branch of industry, or of some process rendering an article exportable which had not till then been exported at all. It will be convenient to begin with the case of a new export, as being somewhat the simpler of the two.

---

cloth, not merely to the extent to which cloth has fallen, but also to the extent to which other prices have risen. Suppose that this is one-tenth. The same proportion of their [48   these] money-incomes as before, will suffice to supply their other wants; and the remainder, being increased one-tenth in amount, will enable them to purchase one-tenth more cloth than before, even though cloth had not fallen: but it has fallen; so that they are doubly gainers. They purchase the same quantity with less money, and have more to expend upon their other wants.

"In England, on the contrary, general money-prices have fallen. Linen, however, has fallen more than the rest, having been lowered in price by importation from a country where it was cheaper; whereas the others have fallen only from the consequent efflux of money. Notwithstanding, therefore, the general fall of money-prices, the English producers will be exactly as they were in all other respects, while they will gain as purchasers of linen.

"The greater the efflux of money required to restore the equilibrium, the greater will be the gain of Germany, both by the fall of cloth and by the rise of her general prices. The less the efflux of money requisite, the greater will be the gain of England; because the price of linen will continue lower, and her general prices will not be reduced so much. It must not, however, be imagined that high money-prices are a good, and low money-prices an evil, in themselves. But the higher the general money-prices in any country, the greater will be that country's means of purchasing those commodities which, being imported from abroad, are independent of the causes which keep prices high at home." [Mill, J. S. *Essays on Some Unsettled Questions*, pp. 14–7.]

In practice, the cloth and the linen would not, as here supposed, be at the same price in England and in Germany: each would be dearer in money-price in the country which imported than in that which produced it, by the amount of the cost of carriage, together with the ordinary profit on the importer's capital for the average length of time which elapsed before the commodity could be disposed of. But it does not follow that each country pays the cost of carriage of the commodity it imports; for the addition of this item to the price may operate as a greater check to demand on one side than on the other; and the equation of international demand, and consequent equilibrium of payments, may not be maintained. Money would then flow out of one country into the other, until, in the manner already illustrated, the equilibrium was restored: and, when this was effected, one country would be paying more than its own cost of carriage, and the other less.

The first effect is that the article falls in price, and a demand arises for it abroad. This new exportation disturbs the balance, turns the exchanges, money flows into the country (which we shall suppose to be England), and continues to flow until prices rise. This higher range of prices will somewhat check the demand *in* foreign countries for the new article of export; and diminish the demand which existed abroad for the other things which England was in the habit of exporting. The exports will thus be diminished; while at the same time the English public, having more money, will have a greater power of purchasing foreign commodities. If they make use of this increased power of purchase, there will be an increase of imports: and by this, and the check to exportation, the equilibrium of imports and *exports* will be restored. The result to foreign countries will be, that they have to pay dearer than before for their other imports, and obtain the new commodity cheaper than before, but not so much cheaper as England herself does. I say this, being well aware that the article would be actually at the very same price (cost of carriage excepted) in England and in other countries. The cheapness, however, of the article is not measured solely by the money-price, but by that price compared with the money incomes of the consumers. The price is the same to the English and to the foreign consumers; but the former pay that price from money incomes which have been increased by the new distribution of the precious metals; while the latter have had their money incomes probably diminished by the same cause. The trade, therefore, has not imparted to the foreign consumer the whole, but only a portion, of the benefit which the English consumer has derived from the improvement; while England has also benefited in the prices of foreign commodities. Thus, then, any industrial improvement which leads to the opening of a new branch of export trade, benefits a country not only by the cheapness of the article in which the improvement has taken place, but by a general cheapening of all imported products.

Let us now change the hypothesis, and suppose that the improvement, instead of creating a new export from England, cheapens an existing one. When we examined this case on the supposition of barter, it appeared to us that the foreign consumers might either obtain the same benefit from the improvement as England herself, or a less benefit, or even a greater benefit, according to the degree in which the consumption of the cheapened article is calculated to extend itself as the article diminishes in price. The same conclusions will be found true on the supposition of money.

Let the commodity in which there is an improvement, be cloth. The first effect of the improvement is that its price falls, and there is an increased demand for it in the foreign market. But this demand is of uncertain amount. Suppose the foreign consumers to increase their purchases in the

---

*a–a*48   on [*printer's error?*]   *b–b*49   export, [*printer's error?*]

exact ratio of the cheapness, or in other words, to lay out in cloth the same sum of money as before; the same aggregate payment as before will be due from foreign countries to England; the equilibrium of exports and imports will remain undisturbed, and foreigners will obtain the full advantage of the increased cheapness of cloth. But if the foreign demand for cloth is of such a character as to increase in a greater ratio than the cheapness, a larger sum than formerly will be due to England for cloth, and when paid will raise English prices, the price of cloth included; this rise, however, will affect only the foreign purchaser, English incomes being raised in a corresponding proportion; and the foreign consumer will thus derive a less advantage than England from the improvement. If, on the contrary, the cheapening of cloth does not extend the foreign demand for it in a proportional degree, a less sum of debts than before will be due to England for cloth, while there will be the usual sum of debts due from England to foreign countries; the balance of trade will turn against England, money will be exported, prices (that of cloth included) will fall, and cloth will eventually be cheapened to the foreign purchaser in a still greater ratio, than the improvement has cheapened it to England. These are the very conclusions which we deduced on the hypothesis of barter.

The result of the preceding discussion cannot be better summed up than in the words of Ricardo.* "Gold and silver having been chosen for the general medium of circulation, they are, by the competition of commerce, distributed in such proportions amongst the different countries of the world as to accommodate themselves to the natural traffic which would take place if no such metals existed, and the trade between countries were purely a trade of barter." Of this principle, so fertile in consequences, previous to which the theory of foreign trade was an unintelligible chaos, Mr. Ricardo, though he did not pursue it into its ramifications, was the real originator. No writer who preceded him appears to have had a glimpse of it: and few are those who even since his time have had an adequate conception of its scientific value.

§ 3. [*The precious metals, as money, are of the same value, and distribute themselves according to the same law, with the precious metals as a commodity*] It is now necessary to inquire, in what manner this law of the distribution of the precious metals by means of the exchanges, affects the exchange value of money itself; and how it tallies with the law by which we found that the value of money is regulated when imported as a mere article of merchandize. For there is here a semblance of contradiction, which has, I think, contributed more than anything else to make some distinguished political economists resist the evidence of the preceding

*Principles of Political Economy and Taxation, 3rd ed. p. 143.

doctrines. Money, they justly think, is no exception to the general laws of value; it is a commodity like any other, and its average or natural value must depend on the cost of producing, or at least of obtaining it. That its distribution through the world, therefore, and its different value in different places, should be liable to be altered, not by causes affecting itself, but by a hundred causes unconnected with it; by everything which affects the trade in other commodities, so as to derange the equilibrium of exports and imports; appears to these thinkers a doctrine altogether inadmissible.

But the supposed anomaly exists only in semblance. The causes which bring money into or carry it out of a country through the exchanges, to restore the equilibrium of trade, and which thereby raise its value in some countries and lower it in others, are the very same causes on which the local value of money would depend, if it were never imported except as a merchandize, and never except directly from the mines. When the value of money in a country is permanently lowered by an influx of it through the balance of trade, the cause, if it is not diminished cost of production, must be one of those causes which compel a new adjustment, more favourable to the country, of the equation of international demand: namely, either an increased demand abroad for her commodities, or a diminished demand on her part for those of foreign countries. Now an increased foreign demand for the commodities of a country, or a diminished demand in the country for imported commodities, are the very causes which, on the general principles of trade, enable a country to purchase all imports, and consequently the precious metals, at a lower value. There is therefore no contradiction, but the most perfect accordance in the results of the two different modes in which the precious metals may be obtained. When money flows from country to country in consequence of changes in the international demand for commodities, and by so doing alters its own local value, it merely realizes, by a more rapid process, the effect which would otherwise take place more slowly, by an alteration in the relative breadth of the streams by which the precious metals flow into different regions of the earth from the mining countries. As therefore we before saw that the use of money as a medium of exchange does not in the least alter the law on which the values of other things, either in the same country or internationally, depend, so neither does it alter the law of the value of the precious metal itself: and there is in the whole doctrine of international values as now laid down, a unity and harmony which is a strong collateral presumption of truth.

§ 4. [*International payments* *ᵃof a non-commercialᵃ character*] Before closing this discussion, it is fitting to point out in what manner and degree

ᵃ⁻ᵃ48, 49   *not of a commercial*

the preceding conclusions are affected by the existence of international payments not originating in commerce, and for which no equivalent in either money or commodities is expected or received; such as a tribute, or remittances of rent to absentee landlords, or of interest to foreign creditors, or a government expenditure abroad, such as England incurs in the management of some of her colonial dependencies.

To begin with the case of barter. The supposed annual remittances being made in commodities, and being exports for which there is to be no return, it is no longer requisite that the imports and exports should pay for one another: on the contrary, there must be an annual excess of exports over imports, equal to the value of the remittance. If, before the country became liable to the annual payment, foreign commerce was in its natural state of equilibrium, it will now be necessary for the purpose of effecting the *b*remittance*b*, that foreign countries should be induced to take a greater quantity of exports than before: which can only be done by offering those exports on cheaper terms, or in other words, by paying dearer for foreign commodities. The international values will so adjust themselves that either by greater exports, or smaller imports, or both, the requisite excess on the side of exports will be brought about; and this excess will become the permanent state. The result is that a country which makes regular payments to foreign countries, besides losing what it pays, loses also something more, by the less advantageous terms on which it is forced to exchange its productions for foreign commodities.

The same results follow on the supposition of money. Commerce being supposed to be in a state of equilibrium when the obligatory remittances begin, the first remittance is necessarily made in money. This lowers prices in the remitting country, and raises them in the receiving. The natural effect is that more commodities are exported than before, and fewer imported, and that, on the score of commerce alone, a balance of money will be constantly due from the receiving to the paying country. When the debt thus annually due to the tributary country becomes equal to the annual tribute or other regular payment due from it, no further transmission of money takes place; the equilibrium of exports and imports will no longer exist, but that of payments will; the exchange will be at par, the two debts will be set off against one another, and the tribute or remittance will be virtually paid in goods. The result to the *c*interest*c* of the two countries will be as already pointed out: the paying country will give a higher price for all that it buys from the receiving country, while the latter, besides receiving the tribute, obtains the exportable produce of the tributary country at a lower price.

*b–b*48, 49, 52, 57, 62   remittances
*c–c*48, 49, 52, 57, 62, 65   interests

CHAPTER XXII

Influence of the Currency on ᵃtheᵃ Exchanges and on Foreign Trade

§ 1. [*Variations in the exchange which originate in the currency*] In our inquiry into the laws of international trade, we commenced with the principles which determine international exchanges and international values on the hypothesis of barter. We next showed that the introduction of money as a medium of exchange, makes no difference in the laws of exchanges and of values between country and country, no more than between individual and individual: since the precious metals, under the influence of those same laws, distribute themselves in such proportions among the different countries of the world, as to allow the very same exchanges to go on, and at the same values, as would be the case under a system of barter. We lastly considered how the value of money itself is affected, by those alterations in the state of trade which arise from alterations either in the demand and supply of commodities, or in their cost of production. It remains to consider the alterations in the state of trade which originate not in commodities but in money.

Gold and silver may vary like other things, though they are not ᵇso likely to varyᵇ as other things, in their cost of production. The demand for them in foreign countries may also vary. It may increase, by augmented employment of the metals for purposes of art and ornament, or because the increase of production and of transactions has created a greater amount of business to be done by the circulating medium. It may diminish, for the opposite reasons; or from the extension of the economizing expedients by which the use of metallic money is partially dispensed with. These changes act upon the trade between other countries and the mining countries, and upon the value of the precious metals, according to the general laws of the value of imported commodities: which have been set forth in the previous chapters with sufficient fulness.

ᵃ⁻ᵃ+48, 49, 57, 62, 65, 71
ᵇ⁻ᵇ48, 49   liable to vary so much] 52   so liable to vary

What I propose to examine in the present chapter, is not those circumstances affecting money, which alter the permanent conditions of its value; but the effects produced on international trade by casual or temporary variations in the value of money, which have no connexion with any causes affecting its permanent value. This is a subject of importance, on account of its bearing upon the practical problem which has excited so much discussion for ᶜsixtyᶜ years past, the regulation of the currency.

§ 2. [*Effect of a sudden increase of a metallic currency, or of the sudden creation of bank notes or other substitutes for money*] Let us suppose in any country a circulating medium purely metallic, and a sudden casual increase made to it; for example, by bringing ᵃ into circulation hoards of treasure, which had been concealed in a previous period of foreign invasion or internal disorder. The natural effect would be a rise of prices. This would check exports, and encourage imports; the imports would exceed the exports, the exchanges would become unfavourable, and the newly acquired stock of money would diffuse itself over all countries with which the supposed country carried on trade, and from them, progressively, through all parts of the commercial world. The money which thus overflowed would spread itself to an equal depth over all commercial countries. For it would go on flowing until the exports and imports again balanced one another: and this (as no change is supposed in the permanent circumstances of international demand) could only be, when the money had diffused itself so equally that prices had risen in the same ratio in all countries, so that the alteration of price would be for all practical purposes ineffective, and the exports and imports, though at a higher money valuation, would be exactly the same as they were originally. This diminished value of money throughout the world, ᵇ(at least if the diminution was considerable)ᵇ would cause a suspension, or at least a diminution, of the annual supply from the mines: since the metal would no longer command a value equivalent to its highest cost of production. The annual waste would, therefore, not be fully made up, and the usual causes of destruction would gradually reduce the aggregate quantity of the precious metals to its former amount; after which their production would recommence on its former scale. The discovery of the treasure would thus produce only temporary effects; namely, a brief disturbance of international trade until the treasure had disseminated itself through the world, and then a temporary depression in the value of the metal, below that which corresponds to the cost of producing or of obtaining it; which depression would gradually be corrected, by a temporarily diminished production in the producing countries, and importation in the importing countries.

ᶜ⁻ᶜ48, 49, 52, 57   fifty   ᵃ48, 49   again   ᵇ⁻ᵇ+52, 57, 62, 65, 71

The same effects which would thus arise from the discovery of a treasure, accompany the process by which bank notes, or any of the other substitutes for money, take the place of the precious metals. Suppose that England possessed a currency wholly metallic, of twenty millions sterling, and that suddenly twenty millions of bank notes were sent into circulation. If these were issued by bankers, they would be employed in loans, or in the purchase of securities, and would therefore create a sudden fall in the rate of interest, which would probably send a great part of the twenty millions of gold out of the country as capital, to seek a higher rate of interest elsewhere, before there had been time for any action on prices. But we will suppose that the notes are not issued by bankers, or money-lenders of any kind, but by manufacturers, in the payment of wages and purchase of materials, or by the government in its ordinary expenses, so that the whole amount would be rapidly carried into the markets for commodities. The following would be the natural order of consequences. All prices would rise greatly. Exportation would almost cease; importation would be prodigiously stimulated. A great balance of payments would become due; the exchanges would turn against England, to the full extent of the cost of exporting money; and the surplus coin would pour itself rapidly forth, over the various countries of the world, in the order of their proximity, geographically and commercially, to England. The efflux would continue until the currencies of all countries had come to a level; by which I do not mean, until money became of the same value everywhere, but until the differences were only those which existed before, and which corresponded to permanent differences in the cost of obtaining it. When the rise of prices had extended itself in an equal degree to all countries, exports and imports would everywhere revert to what they were at first, would balance one another, and the exchanges would return to par. ᶜIf such a sum of money as twenty millions, when spread over the whole surface of the commercial world, were sufficient to raise the general level in a perceptible degree, the effect would be of no long duration.ᶜ No alteration having occurred in the general conditions under which the metals were procured, either in the world at large or in any part of it, the reduced value would no longer be remunerating, and the supply from the mines would cease partially or wholly, until the twenty millions were absorbed;* after which absorption, the currencies

---

*[62] I am here supposing a state of things in which gold and silver mining are a permanent branch of industry, carried on under known conditions; and not the present state of uncertainty, in which gold-gathering is a game of chance, prosecuted (for the present) in the spirit of an adventure, not in that of a regular industrial pursuit.

ᶜ⁻ᶜ48, 49 So large a sum of money as twenty millions, even when spread over the whole surface of the commercial world, would probably raise the general level in a perceptible degree; but for no very long period.

of all countries would be, in quantity and in value, nearly at their original level. I say nearly, for in strict accuracy there would be a slight difference. A somewhat smaller annual supply of the precious metals would now be required, there being in the world twenty millions less of metallic money undergoing waste. The equilibrium of payments, consequently, between the mining countries and the rest of the world, would thenceforth require that the mining countries should either export rather more of something else, or import rather less of foreign commodities; which implies a somewhat lower range of prices than previously in the mining countries, and a somewhat higher in all others; a scantier currency in the former, and rather fuller currencies in the latter. This effect, which would be too trifling to require notice except for the illustration of a principle, is the only permanent change which would be produced on international trade, or on the value or quantity of the currency of any country.

Effects of another kind, however, will have been produced. Twenty millions which formerly existed in the unproductive form of metallic money, have been converted into what is, or is capable of becoming, productive capital. This gain is at first made by England at the expense of other countries, who have taken her superfluity of this costly and unproductive article off her hands, giving for it an equivalent value in other commodities. By degree the loss is made up to those countries by diminished influx from the mines, and finally the world has gained a virtual addition of twenty millions to its productive resources. Adam Smith's illustration, though so well known, deserves for its extreme aptness to be once more repeated. He compares the substitution of paper in the room of the precious metals, to the construction of a highway through the air, by which the ground now occupied by roads would become available for agriculture. As in that case a portion of the soil, so in this a part of the accumulated wealth of the country, would be relieved from a function in which it was only employed in rendering other soils and capitals productive, and would itself become applicable to production; the office it previously fulfilled being equally well discharged by a medium which costs nothing.

The value saved to the community by thus dispensing with metallic money, is a clear gain to those who provide the substitute. They have the use of twenty millions of circulating medium which have cost them only the expense of an engraver's plate. If they employ this accession to their fortunes as productive capital, the produce of the country is increased, and the community benefited, as much as by any other capital of equal amount. Whether it is so employed or not, depends, in some degree, upon the mode of issuing it. If issued by the government, and employed in paying off debt, it would probably become productive capital. The government, however, may prefer employing this extraordinary resource in its ordinary expenses; may squander it uselessly, or make it a mere temporary substitute for taxation to an equivalent amount; in which last case the amount is saved by the taxpayers at large, who either add it to their capital or spend it as income. When paper currency is supplied, as in our own country, by bankers and banking companies, the amount is almost wholly turned into productive capital: for the issuers, being at all times liable to be called upon to refund the value, are under the strongest inducements not to squander it, and the only cases in which it is not forthcoming are cases of fraud or mismanagement. A banker's profession being that of a money-lender, his issue of notes is a simple extension of his ordinary occupation. He lends the amount to farmers, manufacturers, or dealers, who employ it in their several businesses. So employed, it yields, like any other capital, wages of labour and profits of stock. The profit is shared between the banker, who receives interest, and a succession of borrowers, mostly for short periods, who after paying the interest, gain a profit in addition, or a convenience equivalent to profit. The capital itself in the long run becomes entirely wages, and when replaced by the sale of the produce, becomes wages again; thus affording a perpetual fund, of the value of twenty millions, for the maintenance of productive labour, and increasing the annual produce of the country by all that can be produced through the means of a capital of that value. To this gain must be added a further saving to the country, of the annual supply of the precious metals necessary for repairing the wear and tear, and other waste, of a metallic currency.

The substitution, therefore, of paper for the precious metals, should always be carried as far as is consistent with safety; no greater amount of metallic currency being retained than is necessary to maintain, both in fact and in public belief, the convertibility of the paper. A country with the extensive commercial relations of England is liable to be suddenly called upon for large foreign payments, sometimes in loans, or other investments of capital abroad, sometimes as the price of some unusual importation of goods, the most frequent case being that of large importations of food consequent on a bad harvest. To meet such demands it is necessary that there should be, either in circulation or in the coffers of the banks, coin or bullion to a very considerable amount, and that this, when drawn out by any emergency, should be allowed to return after the emergency is past. But since gold wanted for exportation is almost invariably drawn from the reserves of the banks, and is never likely to be taken directly from the circulation while the banks remain solvent, the only advantage which can be obtained from retaining partially a metallic currency for daily purposes is, that the banks may occasionally replenish their reserves from it.

§ 3. [*Effect of the increase of an inconvertible paper currency. Real and nominal exchange*] When metallic money had been entirely superseded and expelled from circulation, by the substitution of an equal amount of bank notes, any attempt to keep a still further quantity of paper in circulation must, if the notes are convertible, be a complete failure. The new issue would again set in motion the same train of consequences by which the gold coin had already been expelled. The metals would, as before, be required for exportation, and would be for that purpose demanded from the banks, to the full extent of the superfluous notes; which thus could not possibly be retained in circulation. If, indeed, the notes were inconvertible, there would be no such obstacle to the increase of their quantity. An inconvertible paper acts in the same way as a convertible, while there remains any coin for it to supersede: the difference begins to manifest itself when all the coin is driven from circulation (except what may be retained for the convenience of small change), and the issues still go on increasing. When the paper begins to exceed in quantity the metallic currency which it superseded, prices of course rise; things which were worth 5*l.* in metallic money, become worth 6*l.* in inconvertible paper, or more, as the case may be. But this rise of price will not, as in the cases before examined, stimulate import, and discourage export. The imports and exports are determined by the metallic prices of things, not by the paper prices: and it is only when the paper is exchangeable at pleasure for the metals, that *ᵃpaperᵃ* prices and metallic prices must correspond.

Let us suppose that England is the country which has the depreciated paper. Suppose that some English production could be bought, while the currency was still metallic, for 5*l.*, and sold in France for 5*l.* 10*s.*, the difference covering the expense and risk, and affording a profit to the merchant. On account of the depreciation this commodity will now cost in England 6*l.*, and cannot be sold in France for more than 5*l.* 10*s.*, and yet it will be exported as before. Why? Because the 5*l.* 10*s.* which the exporter can get for it in France, is not depreciated paper, but gold or silver: and since in England bullion has risen, in the same proportion with other things—if the merchant brings the gold or silver to England, he can sell his 5*l.* 10*s.* for 6*l.* 12*s.*, and obtain as before 10 per cent for profit and expenses.

It thus appears, that a depreciation of the currency does not affect the foreign trade of the country: this is carried on precisely as if the currency maintained its value. But though the trade is not affected, the exchanges are. When the imports and exports are in equilibrium, the exchange, in a metallic currency, would be at par; a bill on France for the equivalent of five sovereigns, would be worth five sovereigns. But five sovereigns, or the

ᵃ⁻ᵃ49   metal [*printer's error?*]

quantity of gold contained in them, having come to be worth in England
6*l*., it follows that a bill on France for 5*l*. will be worth 6*l*. When, therefore,
the *real* exchange is at par, there will be a *nominal* exchange against the
country, of as much per cent as the amount of the depreciation. If the
currency is depreciated 10, 15, or 20 per cent, then in whatever way the
real exchange, arising from the variations of international debts and credits,
may vary, the *b*quoted*b* exchange will always differ 10, 15, or 20 per cent
from it. However high this nominal premium may be, it has no tendency
to send gold out of the country, for the purpose of drawing a bill against it
and profiting by the premium; because the gold so sent must be procured,
not from the banks and at par, as in the case of a convertible currency,
but in the market at an advance of price equal to the premium. In such
cases, instead of saying that the exchange is unfavourable, it would be
a more correct representation to say that the par has altered, since there is
now required a larger quantity of English currency to be equivalent to the
same quantity of foreign. The exchanges, however, continue to be computed
according to the metallic par. The quoted exchanges, therefore, when there
is a depreciated currency, are compounded of two elements or factors; the
real exchange, which follows the variations of international payments, and
the nominal exchange, which varies with the depreciation of the currency,
but which, while there is any depreciation at all, must always be unfavourable. Since the amount of depreciation is exactly measured by the degree in
which the market price of bullion exceeds the Mint valuation, we have a
sure criterion to determine what portion of the quoted exchange, being
referable to depreciation, may be struck off as nominal; the result so
corrected expressing the real exchange.

The same disturbance of the exchanges and of international trade, which
is produced by an increased issue of convertible bank notes, is in like
manner produced by those extensions of credit, which, as was so fully
shown in a preceding chapter, have the same effect on prices as an increase
of the currency. Whenever circumstances have given such an impulse to
the spirit of speculation as to occasion a great increase of purchases on
credit, money prices rise, just as much as they would have risen if each
person who so buys on credit had bought with money. All the effects,
therefore, must be similar. As a consequence of high prices, exportation is
checked and importation stimulated; though in fact the increase of importation seldom waits for the rise of prices which is the consequence of
speculation, inasmuch as some of the great articles of import are usually
among the things in which speculative overtrading first shows itself. There
is, therefore, in such periods, usually a great excess of imports over exports;
and when the time comes at which these must be paid for, the exchanges

*b-b*48, 49, 52   *quoted*

become unfavourable, and gold flows out of the country. In what precise manner this efflux of gold takes effect on prices, depends on circumstances of which we shall presently speak more fully; but that its effect is to make them recoil downwards, is certain and evident. The recoil, once begun, generally becomes a total rout, and the unusual extension of credit is rapidly exchanged for an unusual contraction of it. Accordingly, when credit has been imprudently stretched, and the speculative spirit carried to excess, the turn of the exchanges, and consequent pressure on the banks to obtain gold for exportation, are generally the proximate cause of the catastrophe. But these phenomena, though a conspicuous accompaniment, are no essential part, of the collapse of credit called a commercial crisis; which, as we formerly showed,* might happen to as great an extent, and is quite as likely to happen, in a country, if any such there were, altogether destitute of foreign trade.

*Supra, pp. 540–1.

CHAPTER XXIII

Of the Rate of Interest

§ 1. [*The rate of interest depends on the demand and supply of loans*]
The present seems the most proper place for discussing the circumstances
which determine the rate of interest. The interest of loans, being really a
question of exchange value, falls naturally into the present division of our
subject: and the two topics of Currency and Loans, though in themselves
distinct, are so intimately blended in the phenomena of what is called the
money market, that it is impossible to understand the one without the
other, and in many minds the two subjects are mixed up in the most
inextricable confusion.

In the preceding Book* we defined the relation in which interest stands
to profit. We found that the gross profit of capital might be distinguished
into three parts, which are respectively the remuneration for risk, for
trouble, and for the capital itself, and may be termed insurance, wages of
superintendence, and interest. After making compensation for risk, that is,
after covering the average losses to which capital is exposed either by the
general circumstances of society or by the hazards of the particular employment, there remains a surplus, which partly goes to repay the owner of the
capital for his abstinence, and partly the employer of it for his time and
trouble. How much goes to the one and how much to the other, is shown
by the amount of the remuneration which, when the two functions are
separated, the owner of capital can obtain from the employer for its use.
This is evidently a question of demand and supply. Nor have demand and
supply any different meaning or effect in this case from what they have in
all others. The rate of interest will be such as to equalize the demand for
loans with the supply of them. It will be such, that exactly as much as some
people are desirous to borrow at that rate, others shall be willing to lend.
If there is more offered than demanded, interest will fall; if more is
demanded than offered, it will rise; and in both cases, to the point at which
the equation of supply and demand is re-established.

Both the demand and supply of loans fluctuate more incessantly than
any other demand or supply whatsoever. The fluctuations in other things

*Supra, book ii. ch. xv, § 1. [pp. 400–2].

depend on a limited number of influencing circumstances; but the desire to borrow, and the willingness to lend, are more or less influenced by every circumstance which affects the state or prospects of industry or commerce, either generally or in any of their branches. The rate of interest, therefore, on good security, which alone we have here to consider (for interest in which considerations of risk bear a part may swell to any amount) is seldom, in the great centres of money transactions, precisely the same for two days together; as is shown by the never-ceasing variations in the quoted prices of the funds and other negotiable securities. Nevertheless, there must be, as in other cases of value, some rate which (in the language of Adam Smith and Ricardo) may be called the natural rate; some rate about which the market rate oscillates, and to which it always tends to return. This rate partly depends on the amount of accumulation going on in the hands of persons who cannot themselves attend to the employment of their savings, and partly on the comparative taste existing in the community for the active pursuits of industry, or for the leisure, ease, and independence of an annuitant.

§ 2. [*Circumstances which determine the permanent demand and supply of loans*] To exclude casual fluctuations, we will suppose commerce to be in a quiescent condition, no employment being unusually prosperous, and none particularly distressed. In these circumstances, the more thriving producers and traders have their capital fully employed, and many are able to transact business to a considerably greater extent than they have capital for. These are naturally borrowers: and the amount which they desire to borrow, and can *obtain credit* for, constitutes the demand for loans on account of productive employment. To these must be added the loans required by Government, and by landowners, or other unproductive consumers who have good security to give. This constitutes the mass of loans for which there is an habitual demand.

Now it is conceivable that there might exist, in the hands of persons disinclined or disqualified for engaging personally in business, a mass of capital equal to, and even exceeding, this demand. In that case there would be an habitual excess of competition on the part of lenders, and the rate of interest would bear a low proportion to the rate of profit. Interest would be forced down to the point which would either tempt borrowers to take a greater amount of loans than they had a reasonable expectation of being able to employ in their business, or would so discourage a portion of the lenders, as to make them either forbear to accumulate, or endeavour to increase their income by engaging in business on their own account, and incurring the risks, if not the labours, of industrial employment.

a-a48, 49, 52, 57, 62, 65   give security

On the other hand, the capital owned by persons who prefer lending it at interest, or whose avocations prevent them from personally superintending its employment, may be short of the habitual demand for loans. It may be in great part absorbed by the investments afforded by the public debt and by mortgages, and the remainder may not be sufficient to supply the wants of commerce. If so, the rate of interest will be raised so high as in some way to re-establish the equilibrium. When there is only a small difference between interest and profit, many borrowers may no longer be willing to increase their responsibilities and involve their credit for so small a remuneration: or some who would otherwise have engaged in business, may prefer leisure, and become lenders instead of borrowers: or others, under the inducement of high interest and easy investment for their capital, may retire from business earlier, and with smaller fortunes, than they otherwise would have done. Or, lastly, there is another process by which, in England and other commercial countries, a large portion of the requisite supply of loans is obtained. Instead of its being afforded by persons not in business, the affording it may itself become a business. A portion of the capital employed in trade may be supplied by a class of professional money lenders. These money lenders, however, must have more than a mere interest; they must have the ordinary rate of profit on their capital, risk and all other circumstances being allowed for. But it can never answer to any one who borrows for the purposes of his business, to pay a full profit for capital from which he will only derive a full profit: and money-lending, as an employment, for the regular supply of trade, cannot, therefore, be carried on except by persons who, in addition to their own capital, can lend their credit, or, in other words, the capital of other people: that is, bankers, and persons (such as bill-brokers) who are virtually bankers, since they receive money in deposit. A bank which lends its notes, lends capital which it borrows from the community, and for which it pays no interest. A bank of deposit lends capital which it collects from the community in small parcels; sometimes without paying any interest, as is the case with the London private bankers; and if, like the Scotch, the joint stock, and most of the country banks, it does pay interest, it still pays much less than it receives; for the depositors, who in any other way could mostly obtain for such small balances no interest worth taking any trouble for, are glad to receive even a little. Having this subsidiary resource, bankers are enabled to obtain, by lending at interest, the ordinary rate of profit on their own capital. In any other manner, money-lending could not be carried on as a regular mode of business, except upon terms on which none would consent to borrow but persons either counting on extraordinary profits, or in urgent need: unproductive consumers who have exceeded their means, or merchants in fear of bankruptcy. The disposable capital deposited in banks ^{b}; that^b represented by bank notes ^{c}; the capital of bankers themselves, and that which their credit in any way in which they use it, enables them to dispose of; these^c, together with the funds belonging to those who, either from necessity or preference, live upon the interest of their property, constitute the general loan fund of the country: and the amount of this aggregate fund, when set against the habitual demands of producers and dealers, and those of the Government and of unproductive consumers, ^{d}determines^d the permanent or average rate of interest; which must always be such as to adjust these two amounts to one another.* But while the whole of this mass of lent capital takes effect upon the *permanent* rate of interest, the *fluctuations* depend almost entirely upon the portion which is in the hands of bankers; for it is that portion almost exclusively, which, being lent for short times only, is continually in the market seeking an investment. The capital of those who live on the interest of their own fortunes, has generally sought and found some fixed investment, such as the public funds, mortgages, or the bonds of public companies, which investment, except under peculiar temptations or necessities, is not changed.

§ 3. [*Circumstances which determine the fluctuations*] Fluctuations in the rate of interest arise from variations either in the demand for loans, or in the supply. The supply is liable to variation, though less so than the demand. The willingness to lend is greater than usual at the commencement of a period of speculation, and much less than usual during the revulsion which follows. In speculative times, money-lenders as well as other people are inclined to extend their business by stretching their credit; they lend more than usual (just as other classes of dealers and producers employ more than usual) of capital which does not belong to them. Accordingly, these are the times when the rate of interest is low; though for this too (as

*I do not include in the general loan fund of the country the capitals, large as they sometimes are, which are habitually employed in speculatively buying and selling the public funds and other securities. It is true that all who buy securities add, for the time, to the general amount of money on loan, and lower *pro tanto* the rate of interest. But as the persons I speak of buy only to sell again at a higher price, they are alternately in the position of lenders and of borrowers: their operations raise the rate of interest at one time, exactly as much as they lower it at another. Like all persons who buy and sell on speculation, their function is to equalize, not to raise or lower, the value of the commodity. When they speculate prudently, they temper the fluctuations of price; when imprudently, they often aggravate them.

$^{b-b}$48, 49, 52, 57, 62   , or
$^{c-c}$+65, 71
$^{d-d}$48, 49, 52, 57, 62, 65   determine

we shall *hereafter* see) there are other causes. During the revulsion, on the contrary, interest always rises inordinately, because, while there is a most pressing need on the part of many persons to borrow, there is a general disinclination to lend. This disinclination, when at its extreme point, is called a panic. It occurs when a succession of unexpected failures has created in the mercantile, and sometimes also in the non-mercantile public, a general distrust in each other's solvency; disposing every one not only to refuse fresh credit, except on very onerous terms, but to call in, if possible, all credit which he has already given. Deposits are withdrawn from banks; notes are returned on the issuers in exchange for specie; bankers raise their rate of discount, and withhold their customary advances; merchants refuse to renew mercantile bills. At such times the most calamitous consequences were formerly experienced from the attempt of the law to prevent more than a certain limited rate of interest from being given or taken. Persons who could not borrow at five per cent, had to pay, not six or seven, but ten or fifteen per cent, to compensate the lender for risking the penalties of the law: or had to sell securities or goods for ready money at a still greater sacrifice. *b*

*c*In the intervals between commercial crises, there is usually a tendency in the rate of interest to a progressive decline,*c* from the gradual process of accumulation: which process, *d* in the great commercial countries, is sufficiently rapid to account for the almost periodical recurrence of these fits of speculation; since, when a few years have elapsed without a crisis, and no new and tempting channel for investment has been opened in the meantime, there is always found to have occurred in those few years so large an increase of capital seeking investment, as to have lowered considerably the rate of interest, whether indicated by the prices of securities or by the rate of discount on bills; and this diminution of interest tempts the *e*possessor*e* to incur hazards in hopes of a more considerable return.

*f*The rate of interest is, at times, affected more or less permanently by circumstances, though not of frequent, yet of occasional occurrence, which tend to alter the proportion between the class of interest-receiving and that of profit-receiving capitalists. Two causes of this description, operating in contrary ways, have manifested themselves of late years, and are now producing considerable effects in England. One is, the gold discoveries. The masses of the precious metals which are constantly arriving from the

*a-a*48, 49, 52, 57, 62   immediately
*b*48, 49, 52   These evils have been less felt, since mercantile bills have been exempted by statute from the operation of the usury laws.
*c-c*48, 49, 52, 57, 62   Except at such periods, the amount of capital disposable on loan is subject to little other variation than that which arises
*d*48, 49, 52, 57, 62   however,
*e-e*48, 49, 52, 57, 62, 65   possessors   *f-f*1652+65, 71

gold countries, are, it may safely be said, wholly added to the funds that supply the loan market. So great an additional capital, not divided between the two classes of capitalists, but aggregated bodily to the capital of the interest-receiving class, disturbs the pre-existing ratio between the two, and tends to depress interest relatively to profit. Another circumstance of still more recent date, but tending to the contrary effect, is the legalization of joint-stock associations with limited liability. The shareholders in these associations, now so rapidly multiplying, are drawn almost exclusively from the lending class; from those who either left their disposable funds in deposit, to be lent out by bankers, or invested them in public or private securities, and received the interest. To the extent of their shares in any of these companies (with the single exception of banking companies) they have become traders on their own capital; they have ceased to be lenders, and have even, in most cases, passed over to the class of borrowers. Their subscriptions have been abstracted from the funds which feed the loan market, and they themselves have become competitors for a share of the remainder of those funds: of all which, the natural effect is a rise of interest. And it would not be surprising if, for a considerable time to come, the ordinary rate of interest in England should bear a higher proportion to the common rate of mercantile profit, than it has borne at any time since the influx of new gold set in.*[f]

The demand for loans varies much more largely than the supply, and embraces longer cycles of years in its aberrations. A time of war, for example, is a period of unusual drafts on the loan [g]market[g]. The Government, at such times, generally incurs new loans, and as these usually succeed each other rapidly as long as the war lasts, the general rate of interest is kept higher in war than in peace, without reference to the rate of profit, and productive industry is stinted of its usual supplies. During [h] part of the last [i]war with France[i], the Government could not

*[65] To the cause of augmentation in the rate of interest, mentioned in the text, must be added another, forcibly insisted on by the author of an able article in the Edinburgh Review for January, 1865 [Göschen, George. "Seven Per Cent.," *Edinburgh Review,* 121 (Jan., 1865), 223–51]; the increased and increasing willingness to send capital abroad for investment. Owing to the vastly augmented facilities of access to foreign countries, and the abundant information incessantly received from them, foreign investments have ceased to inspire the terror that belongs to the unknown; capital flows, without misgiving, to any place which affords an expectation of high profit; and the loan market of the whole commercial world is rapidly becoming one. The rate of interest, therefore, in the part of the world out of which capital most freely flows, cannot any longer remain so much inferior to the rate elsewhere, as it has hitherto been.

[g-g]48, 49, 52, 57   markets
[h]48, 49 a
[i-i]48, 49, 52   war] 57, 62, 65   French war

borrow under six per cent, and of course all other borrowers had to pay at least as much. Nor does the influence of these loans altogether cease when the Government ceases to contract others; for those already contracted continue to afford an investment for a greatly increased amount of the disposable capital of the country, which if the national debt were paid off, would be added to the mass of capital seeking investment, and (independently of temporary disturbance) could not but, to some extent, permanently lower the rate of interest.

The same effect on interest which is produced by Government loans for war expenditure, is produced by the sudden opening of any new and generally attractive mode of permanent investment. The only instance of the kind in recent history on a scale comparable to that of the war loans, is the absorption of capital in the construction of railways. This capital must have been principally drawn from the deposits in banks, or from savings which would have gone into deposit, and which were destined to be ultimately employed in buying securities from persons who would have employed the purchase money in discounts or other loans at interest: in either case, it was a draft on the general loan fund. It is, in fact, evident, that unless savings were made expressly to be employed in railway adventure, the amount thus employed must have been derived either from the actual capital of persons in business, or from capital which would have been lent to persons in business. In the first case, the subtraction, by crippling their means, obliges them to be larger borrowers; in the second, it leaves less for them to borrow; in either case it equally tends to raise the rate of interest.

§ 4. [*The rate of interest *a*, how far, and in what sense connected with the value of money*a] *b*I have, thus far, considered loans, and the rate of interest, as a matter which concerns capital in general, in direct opposition to the popular notion, according to which it only concerns money. In loans, as in all other money transactions, I have regarded the money which

*a–a*48, 49, 52, 57, 62 *not really connected with the value of money, but often confounded with it*
*b–b*65748 From the preceding considerations it would be seen, even it [*sic*] were not otherwise evident, how great an error it is to imagine that the rate of interest bears any necessary relation to the quantity or value of the money in circulation. An increase of the currency has in itself no effect, and is incapable of having any effect, on the rate of interest. A paper currency issued by government in the payment of its ordinary expenses, in however great excess it may be issued, affects the rate of interest in no manner whatever. It diminishes indeed the power of money to purchase commodities, but not the power of money to purchase money. If a hundred pounds will buy a perpetual annuity of four pounds a year, a depreciation which makes the hundred pounds worth only half as much as before, has precisely the same effect on the four pounds, and therefore cannot alter the relation between the two. Unless, indeed, it is known and reckoned upon that the depreciation will only be temporary;

passes, only as the medium, and commodities as the thing really transferred —the real subject of the transaction. And this is, in the main, correct: because the purpose for which, in the ordinary course of affairs, money is borrowed, is to acquire a purchasing power over commodities. In an industrious and commercial country, the ulterior intention commonly is, to employ the commodities as capital: but even in the case of loans for unproductive consumption, as those of spendthrifts, or of the Government, the amount borrowed is taken from a previous accumulation, which would otherwise have been lent to carry on productive industry; it is, therefore, so much subtracted from what may correctly be called the amount of loanable capital.

There is, however, a not unfrequent case, in which the purpose of the borrower is different from what I have here supposed. He may borrow money, neither to employ it as capital nor to spend it unproductively, but to pay a previous debt. In this case, what he wants is not purchasing power, but legal tender, or something which a creditor will accept as equivalent to it. His need is specifically for money, not for commodities or capital. It is the demand arising from this cause, which produces almost all the great and sudden variations of the rate of interest. Such a demand forms one of the earliest features of a commercial crisis. At such a period, many persons in business who have contracted engagements, have been prevented by a change of circumstances from obtaining in time the means on which they calculated for fulfilling them. These means they must obtain at any sacrifice, or submit to bankruptcy; and what they must have is money. Other capital, however much of it they may possess, cannot answer the purpose unless money can first be obtained for it; while, on the

---

for people certainly might be willing to lend the depreciated currency on cheaper terms if they expected to be repaid in money of full value.

It is perfectly true that in England, and most other commercial countries, an addition to the currency almost always *seems* to have the effect of lowering the rate of interest; because it is almost always accompanied by something which really has that tendency. The currency in common use, being a currency provided by bankers, is all issued in the way of loans, except such part as happens to be employed in the purchase of gold or silver. The same operation, therefore, which adds to the currency, also adds to the loans, or to the capital seeking investment on loan; properly, indeed, the currency is only increased in order that the loans may be increased. Now, though as currency these issues have not an effect on interest, as loans they have. Inasmuch therefore as an expansion or contraction of paper currency, when that currency consists of bank notes, is always also an expansion or contraction of credit; the distinction is seldom properly drawn between the effects which belong to it in the former and in the latter character. The confusion is thickened by the unfortunate misapplication of language, which designates the rate of interest by a phrase ("the value of money") which properly expresses the purchasing power of the circulating medium.] 49   *as* 48 . . . seen, even if it . . . England, and in most . . . *as* 48] 52   *as* 49 . . . money to buy commodities . . . money to buy money . . . *as* 49] 57, 62   *as* 52 . . . purchase of gold and silver . . . *as* 48

contrary, without any increase of the capital of the country, a mere increase of circulating instruments of credit (be they of as little worth for any other purpose as the box of one pound notes discovered in the vaults of the Bank of England during the panic of 1825) will effectually serve their turn if only they are allowed to make use of it. An increased issue of notes, in the form of loans, is all that is required to satisfy the demand, and put an end to the accompanying panic. But although, in this case, it is not capital, or purchasing power, that the borrower needs, but money as money, it is not only money that is transferred to him. The money carries its purchasing power, with it wherever it goes; and money thrown into the loan market really does, through its purchasing power, turn over an increased portion of the capital of the country into the direction of loans. Though money alone was wanted, capital passes; and it may still be said with truth that it is by an addition to loanable capital that the rise of the rate of interest is met and corrected.

Independently of this, however, there is a real relation, which it is indispensable to recognise, between loans and money. Loanable capital is all of it in the form of money. Capital destined directly for production exists in many forms; but capital destined for lending exists normally in that form alone. Owing to this circumstance, we should naturally expect that among the causes which affect more or less the rate of interest, would be found not only causes which act through capital, but some causes which act, directly at least, only through money.

The rate of interest bears no necessary relation to the quantity or value of the money in circulation. The permanent amount of the circulating medium, whether great or small, affects only prices; not the rate of interest. A depreciation of the currency, when it has become an accomplished fact, affects the rate of interest in no manner whatever. It diminishes indeed the power of money to buy commodities, but not the power of money to buy money. If a hundred pounds will buy a perpetual annuity of four pounds a year, a depreciation which makes the hundred pounds worth only half as much as before, has precisely the same effect on the four pounds, and cannot therefore alter the relation between the two. The greater or smaller number of counters which must be used to express a given amount of real wealth, makes no difference in the position or interests of lenders or borrowers, and therefore makes no difference in the demand and supply of loans. There is the same amount of real capital lent and borrowed; and if the capital in the hands of lenders is represented by a greater number of pounds sterling, the same greater number of pounds sterling will, in consequence of the rise of prices, be now required for the purposes to which the borrowers intend to apply them.

But though the greater or less quantity of money makes in itself no difference in the rate of interest, a change from a less quantity to a greater, or from a greater to a less, may and does make a difference in it.

Suppose money to be in process of depreciation by means of an inconvertible currency, issued by a government in payment of its expenses. This fact will in no way diminish the demand for real capital on loan; but it will diminish the real capital loanable, because, this existing only in the form of money, the increase of quantity depreciates it. Estimated in capital, the amount offered is less, while the amount required is the same as before. Estimated in currency, the amount offered is only the same as before, while the amount required, owing to the rise of prices, is greater. Either way, the rate of interest must rise. So that in this case increase of currency really affects the rate of interest, but in the contrary way to that which is generally supposed; by raising, not by lowering it.

The reverse will happen as the effect of calling in, or diminishing in quantity, a depreciated currency. The money in the hands of lenders, in common with all other money, will be enhanced in value, that is, there will be a greater amount of real capital seeking borrowers; while the real capital wanted by borrowers will be only the same as before, and the money amount less: the rate of interest, therefore, will tend to fall.

We thus see that depreciation, merely as such, while in process of taking place, tends to raise the rate of interest: and the expectation of further depreciation adds to this effect; because lenders who expect that their interest will be paid and the principal perhaps redeemed, in a less valuable currency than they lent, of course require a rate of interest sufficient to cover this contingent loss.

But this effect is more than counteracted by a contrary one, when the additional money is thrown into circulation not by purchases but by loans. In England, and in most other commercial countries, the paper currency in common use, being a currency provided by bankers, is all issued in the way of loans, except the part employed in the purchase of gold and silver. The same operation, therefore, which adds to the currency also adds to the loans: the whole increase of currency in the first instance swells the loan market. Considered as an addition to loans it tends to lower interest, more than in its character of depreciation it tends to raise it; for the former effect depends on the ratio which the new money bears to the money lent, while the latter depends on its ratio to all the money in circulation. An increase, therefore, of currency issued by banks, tends, while the process continues, to bring down or to keep down the rate of interest. A similar effect is produced by the increase of money arising from the gold discoveries; almost the whole of which, as already noticed, is, when brought to Europe, added to the deposits in banks, and consequently to the amount of loans; and when drawn out and invested in securities, liberates an equivalent amount of other loanable capital. The newly-arrived gold can only get itself invested, in any given state of business, by lowering the rate of interest; and as long as the influx continues, it cannot fail to keep interest lower than, all other circumstances being supposed the same, would otherwise have been the case.

As the introduction of additional gold and silver, which goes into the loan market, tends to keep down the rate of interest, so any considerable abstraction of them from the country invariably raises it; even when occurring in the course of trade, as in paying for the extra importations caused by a bad harvest, or for the high-priced cotton which ^{c}, under the influence of the American civil war, was^c imported from so many parts of the world. The money required for these payments is taken in the first instance from the deposits in the hands of bankers, and to that extent starves the fund that supplies the loan market.

The rate of interest, then, depends essentially and permanently on the comparative amount of real capital offered and demanded in the way of loan; but is subject to temporary disturbances of various sorts, from increase and diminution of the circulating medium; which derangements are somewhat intricate, and sometimes in direct opposition to first appearances. All these distinctions are veiled over and confounded, by the unfortunate misapplication of language which designates the rate of interest by a phrase ("the value of money") which properly expresses the purchasing power of the circulating medium. The public, even mercantile, habitually fancies that ease in the money market, that is, facility of borrowing at low interest, is proportional to the quantity of money in circulation.^{b} Not only, therefore, are bank notes supposed to produce effects as currency, which they only produce as loans, but attention is habitually diverted from effects similar in kind and much greater in degree, when produced by an action on loans which does not happen to be accompanied by any action on the currency.

For example, in considering the effect produced by the proceedings of banks in encouraging the excesses of speculation, an immense effect is usually attributed to their issues of notes, but until of late hardly any attention was paid to the management of their deposits; though nothing is more certain than that their imprudent extensions of credit take place more frequently by means of their deposits than of their issues. "There is no doubt," says Mr. Tooke,* "that banks, whether private or joint stock, may, if imprudently conducted, minister to an undue extension of credit for the purpose of speculations, whether in commodities, or in overtrading in exports or imports, or in building or mining operations, and that they have

*Inquiry into the Currency Principle, ch. xiv [pp. 88, 91].

$^{c-c}$65 is, just now,

so ministered not unfrequently, and in some cases to an extent ruinous to themselves, and without ultimate benefit to the parties to whose views their resources were made subservient." But, "supposing all the deposits received by a banker to be in coin, is he not, just as much as the issuing banker, exposed to the importunity of customers, whom it may be impolitic to refuse, for loans or discounts, or to be tempted by a high interest? and may he not be induced to encroach so much upon his deposits as to leave him, under not improbable circumstances, unable to meet the demands of his depositors? In what respect, indeed, would the case of a banker in a perfectly metallic circulation, differ from that of a London banker at the present day? He is not a creator of money, he cannot avail himself of his privilege as an issuer in aid of his other business, and yet there have been lamentable instances of London bankers issuing money in excess."

In the discussions, too, which have been for so many years carried on respecting the operations of the Bank of England, and the effects produced by those operations on the state of credit, though for nearly half a century there never has been a commercial crisis which the Bank has not been strenuously accused either of producing or of aggravating, it has been almost universally assumed that the influence of its acts was felt only through the amount of its notes in circulation, and that if it could be prevented from exercising any discretion as to that one feature in its position, it would no longer have any power liable to abuse. This at least is an error which, after the experience of the year 1847, we may hope has been committed for the last time. During that year the hands of the bank were absolutely tied, in its character of a bank of issue; but through its operations as a bank of deposit it exercised as great an influence, or apparent influence, on the rate of interest and the state of credit, as at any former period; it was exposed to as vehement accusations of abusing that influence; and a crisis occurred, such as few that preceded it had equalled, and none perhaps surpassed, in intensity.

§ 5. [*The rate of interest determines the price of land and of securities*]
Before quitting the general subject of this chapter, I will make the obvious remark, that the rate of interest determines the value and price of all those saleable articles which are desired and bought, not for themselves, but for the income which they are capable of yielding. The public funds, shares in joint-stock companies, and all descriptions of securities, are at a high price in proportion as the rate of interest is low. They are sold at the price which will give the market rate of interest on the purchase money, with allowance for all differences in the risk incurred, or in any circumstance of convenience. Exchequer bills, for example, usually sell at a higher price than consols, proportionally to the interest which they yield; because,

though the security is the same, yet the former being annually paid off at par ᵃunless renewed by the holderᵃ, the purchaser (unless obliged to sell in a moment of general emergency), is in no danger of losing anything by the resale, except the premium he may have paid.

The price of land, mines, and all other fixed sources of income, depends in like manner on the rate of interest. Land usually sells at a higher price, in proportion to the income afforded by it, than the public funds, not only because it is thought, even in this country, to be somewhat more secure, but because ideas of power and dignity are associated with its possession. But these differences are constant, or nearly so; and in the variations of price, land follows, *cæteris paribus*, the permanent (though of course not the daily) variations of the rate of interest. When interest is low, land will naturally be dear; when interest is high, land will be cheap. The last ᵇlongᵇ war presented a striking exception to this rule, since the price of land as well as the rate of interest was then remarkably high. For this, however, there was a special cause. The continuance of a very high average price of corn for many years, had raised the rent of land even more than in propor- tion to the rise of interest and fall of the selling price of fixed incomes. Had it not been for this accident, chiefly dependent on the seasons, land must have sustained as great a depreciation in value as the public funds: which it probably would do, were a ᶜsimilarᶜ war to break out hereafter; to the signal disappointment of those landlords and farmers who, generalizing from the casual circumstances of a remarkable period, so long persuaded themselves that a state of war was peculiarly advantageous, and a state of peace disadvantageous, to what they chose to call the interests of agriculture.

ᵃ⁻ᵃ+49, 52, 57, 62, 65, 71
ᵇ⁻ᵇ+57, 62, 65, 71
ᶜ⁻ᶜ+57, 62, 65, 71

CHAPTER XXIV

Of the Regulation of a Convertible Paper Currency

§ 1. [*Two contrary theories respecting the influence of bank issues*] The frequent recurrence during the last half century of the painful series of phenomena called a commercial crisis, has directed much of the attention both of economists and of practical politicians to the contriving of expedients for averting, or at the least, mitigating its evils. And the habit which grew up during the era of the Bank restriction, of ascribing all alternations of high and low *ª*prices*ª* to the issues of banks, has caused inquirers in general to fix their hopes of success in moderating those vicissitudes, upon schemes for the regulation of bank notes. A scheme of this nature, after having obtained the sanction of high authorities, so far established itself in the public mind, as to be, with general approbation, converted into a law, at the *ᵇ* renewal of the Charter of the Bank of England *ᶜ*in 1844*ᶜ*: and the regulation is still in force, though with a great abatement of its popularity, and with its *prestige* impaired by *ᵈ*three temporary suspensions*ᵈ*, on the responsibility of the executive, *ᵉ*the earliest little*ᵉ* more than three years after its enactment. It is proper that the merits of this plan for the regulation of a convertible bank note currency should be here considered. Before touching upon the practical provisions of Sir Robert Peel's Act of 1844, I shall briefly state the nature, and examine the grounds, of the theory on which it is founded.

It is believed by many, that banks of issue universally, or the Bank of England in particular, have a power of throwing their notes into circulation, and thereby raising prices, arbitrarily; that this power is only limited by the degree of moderation with which they think fit to exercise it; that when they increase their issues beyond the usual amount, the rise of prices, thus produced, generates a spirit of speculation in commodities, which

*ª–ª*48, 49   price
*ᵇ*48, 49, 52, 57   last
ᶜ–ᶜ+62, 65, 71
*ᵈ–ᵈ*48, 49, 52, 57   a temporary suspension] 62, 65   two temporary suspensions
*ᵉ–ᵉ*48, 49, 52, 57   little] 62, 65   the earlier of the two, little

carries prices still higher, and ultimately causes a reaction and recoil, amounting in extreme cases to a commercial crisis; and that every such crisis which has occurred in this country within mercantile memory, has been either originally produced by this cause, or greatly aggravated by it. To this extreme length the currency theory has not been carried by the eminent political economists who have given to a more moderate form of the same theory the sanction of their names. But I have not overstated the extravagance of the popular version; which is a remarkable instance to what lengths a favourite theory will hurry, not the closet students whose competency in such questions is often treated with so much contempt, but men of the world and of business, who pique themselves on the practical knowledge which they have at least had ample opportunities of acquiring. Not only has this fixed idea of the currency as the prime agent in the fluctuations of price, made them shut their eyes to the multitude of circumstances which, by influencing the expectation of supply, are the true causes of almost all speculations, and of almost all fluctuations of price; but in order to bring about the chronological agreement required by their theory, between the variations of bank issues and those of prices, they have played such fantastic tricks with facts and dates as would be thought incredible, if an eminent practical authority had not taken the trouble of meeting them, on the ground of mere history, with an elaborate *ᶠ* exposure. I refer, as all conversant with the subject must be aware, to Mr. Tooke's History of Prices. The result of Mr. Tooke's investigations was thus stated by himself, in his examination before the Commons' Committee on the Bank Charter question in 1832; and the evidences of it stand recorded in his book: "In point of fact, and historically, as far as my researches have gone, in every signal instance of a rise or fall of prices, the rise or fall has preceded, and therefore could not be the effect of, an enlargement or contraction of the bank circulation."[*]

The extravagance of the currency theorists, in attributing almost every rise or fall of prices to an enlargement or contraction of the issues of bank notes, has raised up, by reaction, a theory the extreme opposite of the former, of which, in scientific discussion, the most prominent representatives are Mr. Tooke and Mr. Fullarton. This counter-theory denies to bank notes, so long as their convertibility is maintained, any power whatever of raising prices, and to banks any power of increasing their circulation, except as a consequence of, and in proportion to, an increase of the business to be done. This last statement is supported by the unanimous assurances of all the country bankers who have been examined before successive Parliamentary Committees on the subject. They all bear testi-

[*Parliamentary Papers, 1831–32, VI, 441.]

ᶠ48, 49   and systematic

mony that (in the words of Mr. Fullarton*) "the amount of their issues is exclusively regulated by the extent of local dealings and expenditure in their respective districts, fluctuating with the fluctuations of production and price, and that they neither can increase their issues beyond the limits which the range of such dealings and expenditure prescribes, without the certainty of having their notes immediately returned to them, nor diminish them, but at an almost equal certainty of the vacancy being filled up from some other source." From these premises it is argued by Mr. Tooke and Mr. Fullarton, that bank issues, since they cannot be increased in amount unless there be an increased demand, cannot possibly raise prices; cannot encourage speculation, nor occasion a commercial crisis; and that the attempt to guard against that evil by an artificial management of the issue of notes, is of no effect for the intended purpose, and liable to produce other consequences extremely calamitous.

§ 2. [*Examination of each theory*] As much of this doctrine as rests upon testimony, and not upon inference, appears to me incontrovertible. I give complete credence to the assertion of the country bankers, very clearly and correctly condensed into a small compass in the sentence just quoted from Mr. Fullarton. I am convinced that they cannot possibly increase their issue of notes in any other circumstances than those which are there stated. I believe, also, that the theory, grounded by Mr. Fullarton upon this fact, contains a large portion of truth, and is far nearer to being the expression of the whole truth than any form whatever of the currency theory.

There are two states of the markets: one which may be termed the quiescent state, the other the expectant, or speculative state. The first is that in which there is nothing tending to engender in any considerable portion of the mercantile public a desire to extend their operations. The producers produce and the dealers purchase only their usual stocks, having no expectation of a more than usually rapid vent for them. Each person transacts his ordinary amount of business, and no more; or increases it only in correspondence with the increase of his capital or ^aconnexion^a, or with the gradual growth of the demand for his commodity, occasioned by the public prosperity. Not meditating any unusual extension of their own operations, producers and dealers do not need more than the usual accommodation from bankers and other money lenders; and as it is only by extending their loans that bankers increase their issues, none but a momentary augmentation of issues is in these circumstances possible. If at a certain time of the year a portion of the public have larger payments to make than at other times, or if an individual, under some peculiar exigency, requires an extra advance, they may apply for more bank notes,

_____

**Regulation of Currencies*, p. 85 [–6].

^{a–a}48, 49, 52   connexions

and obtain them; but the notes will no more remain in circulation, than the extra quantity of Bank of England notes which are issued once in every three months in payment of the dividends. The person to whom, after being borrowed, the notes are paid away, has no extra payments to make, and no peculiar exigency, and he keeps them by him unused, or sends them into deposit, or repays with them a previous advance made to him by some banker: in any case he does not buy commodities with them, since by the supposition there is nothing to induce him to lay in a larger stock of commodities than before. *Even if we suppose, as we may do, that bankers create an artificial increase of the demand for loans by offering them below the market rate of interest, the notes they issue will not remain in circulation; for when the borrower, having completed the transaction for which he availed himself of them, has paid them away, the creditor or dealer who receives them, having no demand for the immediate use of an extra quantity of notes, sends them into deposit.* In this case, therefore, there can be no addition, at the discretion of bankers, to the general circulating medium: any increase of their issues either comes back to them, or remains idle in the hands of the public, and no rise takes place in prices.

But there is another state of the markets, strikingly contrasted with the preceding, and to this state it is not so obvious that the theory of Mr. Tooke and Mr. Fullarton is applicable; namely, when an impression prevails, whether well founded or groundless, that the supply of one or more great articles of commerce is likely to fall short of the ordinary consumption. In such circumstances all persons connected with those commodities desire to extend their operations. The producers or importers desire to produce or import a larger quantity, speculators desire to lay in a stock in order to profit by the expected rise of price, and holders of the commodity desire additional advances to enable them to continue holding. All these classes are disposed to make a more than ordinary use of their credit, and to this desire it is not denied that bankers very often unduly administer. Effects of the same kind may be produced by anything which, exciting more than usual hopes of profit, gives increased briskness to business: for example, a sudden foreign demand for commodities on a large scale, or the expectation of it; such as occurred on the opening of Spanish America to English trade, and has occurred on various occasions in the trade with the United States. Such occurrences produce a tendency to a rise of price in exportable articles, and generate speculations, sometimes of a reasonable, and (as long as a large proportion of men in business prefer excitement to safety) frequently of an irrational or immoderate character. In such cases there is a desire in the mercantile classes, or in some portion of them, to employ their credit, in a more than usual degree, as a power of purchasing. This is a state of business which, when pushed to an extreme length, brings

–+62, 65, 71

on the revulsion called a commercial crisis; and it is a known fact that such periods of speculation hardly ever pass off without having been attended, during some part of their progress, by a considerable increase of bank notes.

To this, however, it is replied by Mr. Tooke and Mr. Fullarton, that the increase of the circulation always follows instead of preceding the rise of prices, and is not its cause, but its effect. That in the first place, the speculative purchases by which prices are raised, are not effected by bank notes but by cheques, or still more commonly on a simple book credit: and secondly, even if they were made with bank notes borrowed for that express purpose from bankers, the notes, after being used for that purpose, would, if not wanted for current transactions, be returned into deposit by the persons receiving them. In this I fully concur, and I regard it as proved, both scientifically and historically, that during the ascending period of speculation, and as long as it is confined to transactions between dealers, the issues of bank notes are seldom materially increased, nor contribute anything to the speculative rise of prices. It seems to me, however, that this can no longer be affirmed when speculation has proceeded so far as to reach the producers. Speculative orders given by merchants to manufacturers induce them to extend their operations, and to become applicants to bankers for increased advances, which if made in notes, are not paid away to persons who return them into deposit, but are partially expended in paying wages, and pass into the various channels of retail trade, where they become directly effective in producing a further rise of prices. I cannot but think that this employment of bank notes must have been powerfully operative on prices at the time when notes of one and two pounds value were permitted by law. Admitting, however, that the prohibition of notes below five pounds has now rendered this part of their operation comparatively insignificant by greatly limiting their applicability to the payment of wages, there is another form of their instrumentality which comes into play in the ᶜlatterᶜ stages of speculation, and which forms the principal argument of the more moderate supporters of the currency theory. Though advances by bankers are seldom demanded for the purpose of buying on speculation, they are largely demanded by unsuccessful speculators for the purpose of holding on; and the competition of these speculators for a share of the loanable capital, makes even those who have not speculated, more dependent than before on bankers for the advances they require. Between the ascending period of speculation and the revulsion, there is an interval extending to weeks and sometimes months, of struggling against a fall. The tide having shown signs of turning, the speculative holders are unwilling to sell in a falling market, and in the meantime they require funds to

ᶜ⁻ᶜ48, 49, 52, 57, 62, 65   later [*printer's error?*]

enable them to fulfil even their ordinary engagements. It is this stage that is ordinarily marked by a considerable increase in the amount of the bank-note circulation. That such an increase does usually take place, is denied by no one. And I think it must be admitted that this increase tends to pro-long the duration of the speculations; that it enables the speculative prices to be kept up for some time after they would otherwise have collapsed; and therefore prolongs and increases the drain of the precious metals for exportation, which is a leading feature of this stage in the progress of a commercial crisis: the continuance of which drain at last endangering the power of the banks to fulfil their engagement of paying their notes on demand, they are compelled to contract their credit more suddenly and severely than would have been necessary if they had been prevented from propping up speculation by increased advances, after the time when the recoil had become inevitable.

§ 3. [*Reasons for thinking that the Currency Act of 1844 produces a part of the beneficial effect intended by it*] To prevent this retardation of the recoil, and ultimate aggravation of its severity, is the object of the scheme for regulating the currency, of which *a*Lord Overstone*a*, Mr. Norman, and Colonel Torrens, were the first promulgators, and which has, in a slightly modified form, been enacted into law.*

According to the scheme in its original purity, the issue of promissory

*[57] I think myself justified in affirming that the mitigation of commercial revulsions is the real, and only serious, purpose of the Act of 1844. I am quite aware that its supporters insist (especially since 1847) on its supreme efficacy in "maintaining the convertibility of the Bank note." But I must be excused for not attaching any serious importance to this one among its alleged merits. The convertibility of the Bank note was maintained, and would have continued to be maintained, at whatever cost, under the old system. As was well said by Lord Overstone in his Evidence, the Bank can always, by a sufficiently violent action on credit, save itself at the expense of the mercantile public. That the Act of 1844 mitigates the violence of that process, is a sufficient claim to prefer in its behalf. Besides, if we suppose such a degree of mismanagement, on the part of the Bank, as, were it not for the Act, would endanger the continuance of convertibility, the same (or a less) degree of mismanagement, practised under the Act, would suffice to produce a suspension of payments by the Bank-ing Department; an event which the compulsory separation of the two depart-ments brings much nearer to possibility than it was before, and which, in-volving as it would the probable stoppage of every private banking establishment in London, and perhaps also the non-payment of the dividends to the national creditor, would be a far greater immediate calamity than a brief interruption of the convertibility of the note; insomuch that, to enable the Bank to resume payment of its deposits, no Government would hesitate a moment to suspend payment of the notes, if suspension of the Act of 1844 proved insufficient.

*a-a*48, 49, 52   Mr. Loyd

notes for circulation was to be confined to one body. In the form adopted by Parliament, all existing issuers [b]were[b] permitted to retain this privilege, but none [c]were[c] to be [d]hereafter[d] admitted to it, even in the place of those who [e]might[e] discontinue their issues: and, for all except the Bank of England, a maximum of issues [f]was[f] prescribed, on a scale intentionally low. To the Bank of England no maximum [g]was[g] fixed for the aggregate amount of its notes, but only for the portion [h] issued on securities, or in other words, on loan. These [i]were[i] never to exceed a certain limit, fixed [j]in the first instance[j] at fourteen millions.* All issues beyond that amount must be in exchange for bullion; of which the Bank is bound to purchase, at a trifle below the Mint valuation, any quantity which is offered to it, giving its notes in exchange. In regard, therefore, to any issue of notes beyond the limit of fourteen millions, the Bank is purely passive, having no function but the compulsory one of giving its notes for gold at $3l.$ $17s.$ $9d.$, and gold for its notes at $3l.$ $17s.$ $10\frac{1}{2}d.$, whenever and by whomsoever it is called upon to do so.

The object for which this mechanism is intended is, that the bank-note currency may vary in its amount at the exact times, and in the exact degree, in which a purely metallic currency would vary. [k]And the[k] precious metals being [l] the commodity [m]that has hitherto approached[m] nearest to that invariability in all the circumstances influencing value, which fits a commodity for being adopted as a medium of exchange, it [n]seems to be thought that the excellence of the Act of 1844 is fully made out, if under its operation the issues conform in all their variations of quantity, and therefore, as is inferred, of value, to the variations which would take place in a currency wholly metallic.

Now, all reasonable opponents of the Act, in common with its sup-

---

*A conditional increase of this maximum is permitted, but only when by arrangement with any country bank the issues of that bank are discontinued, and Bank of England notes substituted; and even then the increase is [48, 49   capriciously] limited to two-thirds of the amount of the country notes to be thereby superseded. [62] Under this provision the amount of notes which the Bank of England is now at liberty to issue against securities, is about fifteen millions [62, 65   rather under fourteen and a half millions].

[b-b]48, 49   are   [c-c]48, 49   are
[d-d]52, 57, 62   thereafter   [e-e]48, 49   may
[f-f]48, 49   is   [g-g]48, 49   is
[h]48, 49   which are   [i-i]48, 49   are
[j-j]48, 49, 52   for the present   [k-k]48, 49, 52   The
[l]48, 49   by universal experience [m-m]48, 49   approaching
[n-n]667 48, 49, 52   is an essential requisite of any substitute for those metals that it should conform exactly in its value to a metallic currency, and for that purpose it is very plausibly considered necessary that it should conform in its quantity likewise.
How far this purpose is really fulfilled by the means adopted, we shall presently examine. First, however, let us consider whether the measure

porters, acknowledge as an essential requisite of any substitute for the precious metals, that it should conform exactly in its permanent value to a metallic standard. And they say, that so long as it is convertible into specie on demand, it does and must so conform. But when the value of a metallic or of any other currency is spoken of, there are two points to be considered; the permanent or average value, and the fluctuations. It is to the permanent value of a metallic currency, that the value of a paper currency ought to conform. But there is no obvious reason why it should be required to conform to the fluctuations too. The only object of its conforming at all, is steadiness of value; and with respect to fluctuations the sole thing desirable is that they should be the smallest possible. Now the fluctuations in the value of the currency are determined, not by its quantity, whether it consist of gold or of paper, but by the expansions and contractions of credit. To discover, therefore, what currency will conform the most nearly to the °permanent° value of the precious metals, we must find under what currency the variations in credit are least frequent and least extreme. Now, whether this object is best attained by a metallic currency (and therefore by a paper currency exactly conforming in quantity to it) is precisely the question to be decided. If it should prove that a paper currency which follows all the fluctuations in quantity of a metallic, leads to more violent revulsions of credit than one which is not held to this rigid conformity, it will follow that the currency which agrees most exactly in quantity with a metallic currency is not that which adheres closest to its value; that is to say, its permanent value, with which alone agreement is desirable.

Whether this is really the case or not we will now inquire. And first, let us consider whether the Act[n] effects the practical object chiefly relied on in its defence by the more sober of its advocates, that of arresting speculative extensions of credit at an earlier period, with a less drain of gold, and consequently by a milder and more gradual process. I think it must be admitted that to a certain degree it is successful in this object.

I am aware of what may be urged, and reasonably urged, in opposition to this opinion. It ᵖmayᵖ be said, that when the time arrives at which the banks are pressed for increased advances to enable speculators to fulfil their engagements, a limitation of the issue of notes will not prevent the banks, if otherwise willing, from making these advances; that they have still their deposits as a source from which loans may be made beyond the point which is consistent with prudence as bankers; and that even if they refused to do so, the only effect would be, that the deposits themselves would be drawn out to supply the wants of the depositors; which would be just as much an addition to the bank notes and coin in the hands of the public, as if the notes themselves were increased. This is true, and is a sufficient anwer to those who think that the advances of banks to prop up failing speculations are objectionable chiefly as an increase of the currency. But the mode in which they are really objectionable, is as an extension of credit. If, instead of ^qincreasing their discounts, the banks allow their deposits to be drawn out^q, there is the same increase of currency (for a short time at least), but there is not an increase of loans ^r, at the time when there ought to be a diminution. If they do increase their discounts, not by means of notes, but at the expense of the deposits alone, their deposits (properly so called) are definite and exhaustible, while notes may be increased to any amount, or, after being returned, may be re-issued without limit. It is true that a bank, if willing to add indefinitely to its liabilities, has the power of making its nominal deposits as unlimited a fund as its issues could be; it has only to make its advances in a book credit, which is creating deposits out of its own liabilities, the money for which it has made itself responsible becoming a deposit in its hands, to be drawn against by cheques; and the cheques when drawn may be liquidated (either at the same bank or at the clearing house) without the aid of notes, by a mere transfer of credit from one account to another. I apprehend it is chiefly in this way that undue extensions of credit, in periods of speculation, are commonly made. But the banks are not likely to persist in this course when the tide begins to turn. It is not when their deposits have already begun to flow out, that they are likely to create deposit accounts which represent, instead of funds placed in their hands, fresh liabilities of their own. But experience proves that extension of credit, when in the form of notes, goes on long after the recoil from over-speculation has commenced. When this mode of resisting the revulsion is made impossible, and deposits and book credits are left as the only sources from which undue advances can be made, the rate of interest is not so often, or so long, prevented from rising, after^r the difficulties consequent on excess of speculation begin to be felt. ^sOn the contrary, the necessity which the banks feel of diminishing their advances to maintain their solvency, when they find their deposits flowing out, and cannot supply the vacant place by their own notes, accelerates the rise of the rate of interest.^s Speculative holders are ^ttherefore^t obliged to submit earlier to that loss by resale, which could not have been prevented from coming on them at last: the recoil of prices and collapse of general credit take place sooner.

^{q-q}48, 49, 52, 57, 62 lending their notes, the banks allow the demand of their customers for disposable capital to act on the deposits

^{r-r}48, 49, 52, 57, 62 . The rate of interest, therefore, is not prevented from rising at the first moment when

^{s-s}+57, 62, 65, 71

^{t-t}+57, 62, 65, 71

To appreciate the *"effects"* which this acceleration of the crisis has in mitigating its intensity, let us advert more particularly to the nature and effects of that leading feature in the period just preceding the collapse, the drain of gold. A rise of prices produced by a speculative extension of credit, even when bank notes have not been the instrument, is not the less effectual (if it lasts long enough) in turning the exchanges: and when the exchanges have turned from this cause, they can only be turned back, and the drain of gold stopped, either by a fall of prices or by a rise of the rate of interest. A fall of prices will stop it by removing the cause which produced it, and by rendering goods a more advantageous remittance than gold, even for paying debts already due. A rise of the rate of interest, and *"consequent fall"* of the prices of securities, will accomplish the purpose still more rapidly, by inducing foreigners, instead of taking away the gold which is due to them, to leave it for investment within the country, and even send gold into the country to take advantage of the increased rate of interest. Of this last mode of stopping a drain of gold, the year 1847 afforded signal examples. But until one of these two things takes place— until either prices fall, or the rate of interest rises—nothing can possibly arrest, or even moderate, the efflux of gold. Now, neither will prices fall nor interest rise, so long as the unduly expanded credit is upheld by the continued advances of bankers. It is well known that when a drain of gold has set in, even if bank notes have not increased in quantity, it is upon them that the contraction first falls, the gold wanted for exportation being always obtained from the Bank of England in exchange for its notes. But under the system which preceded 1844, the Bank of England, being subjected, in common with other banks, to the importunities for fresh advances which are characteristic of such a time, could, and often did, immediately re-issue the notes which had been returned to it in exchange for bullion. It is a great error, certainly, to suppose that the mischief of this re-issue chiefly consisted in preventing a contraction of the currency. It was, however, quite as mischievous as it has ever been supposed to be. As long as it lasted, the efflux of gold could not cease, since neither would prices fall nor interest rise while these advances continued. Prices, having risen without any increase of bank notes, could well have fallen without a diminution of them; but having risen in consequence of an extension of credit, they could not fall without a contraction of it. As long, therefore, as the Bank of England and the other banks persevered in this course, so long gold continued to flow out, until so little was left that the Bank of England, being in danger of suspension of payments, was compelled at last to contract its discounts *"* so greatly and suddenly as to produce a

*u–u*48, 49, 52, 57, 62, 65   effect
*v–v*48, 49   fall, consequently,   *w*48, 49   and other loans

much more extreme variation in the rate of interest, inflict much greater loss and distress on individuals, and destroy a much greater amount of the ordinary credit of the country, than any real necessity required.

I acknowledge, (and the experience of 1847 has proved *ᵃ* to those who overlooked it before,) that the mischief now described, may be wrought, and in large measure, by the Bank of England, through its deposits alone. It may continue or even increase its discounts and advances, when it ought to contract them: with the ultimate effect of making the contraction much more severe and sudden than necessary. I cannot but think, however, that banks which commit this error with their deposits, would commit it still more if they were at liberty to make increased loans with their issues as well as their deposits. I am compelled to think that the being restricted from increasing their issues, is a real impediment to their making those advances which arrest the tide at its turn, and make it rush like a torrent afterwards*ᵞ*: and*ᵞ* when the Act is blamed for interposing obstacles at a time when not obstacles but facilities are needed, it must in justice receive credit for interposing them when they are an acknowledged benefit. In this particular, therefore, I think it cannot be denied, that the new system is a real improvement upon the old.

§ 4. [*But the Currency Act produces mischiefs more than equivalent*] But *ᵃ*however this may be, it seems to me certain*ᵃ* that these advantages, whatever value may be put on them, are purchased by still greater disadvantages.

In the first place, a large extension of credit by bankers, though most hurtful when, credit being already in an inflated state, it can only serve to

---

*ᵃ*48, 49   even

*ᵞ–ᵞ*48, 49   . If the restrictions of the Act of 1844 were no obstacle to the advances of banks in the interval preceding the crisis, why were they found an insuperable obstacle during the crisis? an obstacle which nothing less would overcome than a suspension of the law, through the assumption by Government of a temporary dictatorship? Evidently they are an obstacle;* and [*footnote:*] *It would not be to the purpose to say, by way of objection, that the obstacle may be evaded by granting the increased advance in book credits, to be drawn against by cheques, without the aid of bank notes. This is indeed possible, as Mr. Fullarton has remarked, and as I have myself said in a former chapter. But this substitute for bank-note currency certainly has not yet been organized; and the law having clearly manifested its intention that, in the case supposed, increased credits should not be granted, it is yet a problem whether the law would not reach what might be regarded as an evasion of its prohibitions, or whether deference to the law would not produce (as it has hitherto done) on the part of banking establishments, conformity to its spirit and purpose, as well as to its mere letter.] 52   *as* 48 . . . currency has not . . . *as* 48] 57, 62   *as* 48 . . . currency has never . . . granted, it is a . . . *as* 48

*ᵃ–ᵃ*48, 49, 52, 57, 62   though I am compelled to differ thus far from the opinion of Mr. Tooke and of Mr. Fullarton, I concur with them in thinking

retard and aggravate the collapse, is most salutary when the collapse has come, and when credit instead of being in excess is in distressing deficiency, and increased advances by bankers, instead of being an addition to the ordinary amount of floating credit, serve to replace a mass of other credit which has been suddenly destroyed. Antecedently to 1844, if the Bank of England occasionally aggravated the severity of a commercial revulsion by rendering the collapse of credit more tardy and *hence* more violent than necessary, it in return rendered invaluable services during the revulsion itself, by coming forward with advances to support solvent firms, at a time when all other paper and almost all mercantile credit had become comparatively valueless. This service was eminently conspicuous in the crisis of 1825-6, the severest probably ever experienced; during which the Bank increased what is called its circulation by many millions, in advances to those mercantile firms of whose ultimate solvency it felt no doubt; advances which if it had been obliged to withhold, the severity of the crisis would have been *still* greater than it was. If the Bank, it is justly remarked by Mr. Fullarton,* complies with such applications, "it must comply with them by an issue of notes, for notes constitute the only instrumentality through which the Bank is in the practice of lending its credit. But those notes are not intended to circulate, nor do they circulate. There is no more demand for circulation than there was before. On the contrary, the rapid decline of prices which the case in supposition presumes, would necessarily contract the demand for circulation. The notes would either be returned to the Bank of England, as fast as they were issued, in the shape of deposits, or would be locked up in the drawers of the private London bankers, or distributed by them to their correspondents in the country, or intercepted by other capitalists, who, during the fervour of the previous excitement, had contracted liabilities which they might be imperfectly prepared on the sudden to encounter. In such emergencies, every man connected with business, who has been trading on other means than his own, is placed on the defensive, and his whole object is to make himself as strong as possible, an object which cannot be more effectually answered than by keeping by him as large a reserve as possible in paper which the law has made a legal tender. The notes themselves never find their way into the produce market; and if they at all contribute to retard" (or, as I should rather say, to moderate) "the fall of prices, it is not by promoting in the slightest degree the effective demand for commodities, not by enabling consumers to buy more largely for consumption, and so giving briskness to commerce, but by a process *exactly* the reverse, by

*P. 106 [-7].

b-b48, 49, 52, 57, 62, 65   thence
c-c48, 49, 52   even   d-dSource, 48, 49, 52, 57, 62, 65   precisely

enabling the holders of commodities to hold on, by obstructing traffic and repressing consumption."

The opportune relief thus afforded to credit, during the excessive contraction which succeeds to an undue expansion, is consistent with the principle of the new system; for an extraordinary contraction of credit, and fall of prices, inevitably draw gold into the country, and the principle of the system is that the bank-note currency shall be permitted, and even compelled, to enlarge itself, in all cases in which a metallic currency would do the same. But, what the principle of the law would encourage, its provisions in this instance preclude, by not suffering the increased issues to take place until the gold has actually arrived: which is never until the worst part of the crisis *has passed*, and almost all the losses and failures attendant on it are consummated. The machinery of the system withholds, until for many purposes it comes too late, the very medicine which the theory of the system prescribes as the *appropriate* remedy.*

This function of banks in filling up the gap made in mercantile credit by the consequences of undue speculation and its revulsion, is so entirely indispensable, that if the Act of 1844 continues unrepealed, there can be no difficulty in foreseeing that its provisions must be suspended, as they were in 1847, in every period of great commercial difficulty, as soon as the crisis has really and completely set in.† Were this all, there would be no absolute inconsistency in maintaining the restriction as a means of preventing a crisis, and relaxing it for the purpose of relieving one. But there is another objection, of a still more radical and comprehensive character, to the new system.

Professing, in theory, to require that a paper currency shall vary in its amount in exact conformity to the variations of a metallic currency, it provides, in fact, that in every case of an efflux of gold, a corresponding diminution shall take place in the quantity of bank notes; in other words, that every exportation of the precious metals shall be virtually drawn from the circulation; it being assumed that this would be the case if the currency were wholly metallic. This theory, and these practical arrangements, are

*[57] True, the Bank is not precluded from making increased advances from its deposits, which are likely to be of unusually large amount, since, at these periods, every one leaves his money in deposit in order to have it within call. But, that the deposits are not always sufficient, was conclusively proved in 1847, when the Bank stretched to the very utmost the means of relieving commerce which its deposits afforded, without allaying the panic, which however ceased at once when the Government decided on suspending the Act.

†[62] This prediction was verified on the very next occurrence of a commercial crisis, in 1857; when Government were again under the necessity of suspending, on their own responsibility, the provisions of the Act.

e–e48, 49, 52, 57, 62   is past   f–f48, 49   sovereign

adapted to the case in which the drain of gold originates in a rise of prices produced by an undue expansion of currency or credit; but they are adapted to no case beside.

When the efflux of gold is the last stage of a series of effects arising from an increase of the currency, or from an expansion of credit tantamount in its effect on prices to an increase of currency, it is in that case a fair assumption that in a purely metallic system the gold exported would be drawn from the currency itself; because such a drain, being in its nature unlimited, will necessarily continue as long as currency and credit are undiminished. But an exportation of the precious metals often arises from no causes affecting currency or credit, but simply from an unusual extension of foreign payments, arising either from the state of the markets for commodities, or from some circumstance not commercial. In this class of causes, four, of powerful operation, are included, of each of which the last fifty years of English history afford repeated instances. The first is that of an extraordinary foreign expenditure by government, either political or military; as in the *g*revolutionary war, and, as long as it lasted, during the *h*Crimean war*hg*. The second is the case of a large exportation of capital for foreign investment; such as the loans and mining operations which partly contributed to the crisis of 1825, and the American speculations which were the principal cause of the crisis of 1839. The third is a failure of crops in the countries which supply *i* the raw material of important manufactures; such as the cotton failure in America, which compelled England, in 1847, to incur unusual liabilities for the purchase of that commodity at an advanced price. The fourth is a bad harvest, and a great consequent importation of food; of which the years 1846 and 1847 *j*presented*j* an example surpassing all antecedent experience.

In none of these cases, if the currency were metallic, would the gold or silver exported for the purposes in question be necessarily, or even probably, drawn *k*wholly*k* from the circulation. It would be drawn from the hoards, which under a metallic currency always exist to a very large amount; in uncivilized countries, in the hands of all who can afford it; in civilized countries chiefly in the form of bankers' reserves. Mr. Tooke, in his "Inquiry into the Currency Principle," bears testimony to this fact; but it is to Mr. Fullarton that the public are indebted for the clearest and most satisfactory elucidation of it. As I am not aware that this part of the theory of currency has been set forth by any other writer with anything like the same degree of completeness, I shall quote somewhat largely from this able production.

"No person who has ever resided in an Asiatic country, where hoarding is carried on to a far larger extent in proportion to the existing stock of wealth, and where the practice has become much more deeply engrafted in the habits of the people, by traditionary apprehensions of insecurity and the difficulty of finding safe and remunerative investments, than in any European community—no person who has had personal experience of this state of society, can be at a loss to recollect innumerable instances of large metallic treasures extracted in times of pecuniary difficulty from the coffers of individuals by the temptation of a high rate of interest, and brought in aid of the public necessities, nor, on the other hand, of the facility with which those treasures have been absorbed again, when the inducements which had drawn them into light were no longer in operation. In countries more advanced in civilization and wealth than the Asiatic principalities, and where no man is in fear of attracting the cupidity of power by an external display of riches, but where the interchange of commodities is still almost universally conducted through the medium of a metallic circulation, as is the case with most of the commercial countries on the Continent of Europe, the motives for amassing the precious metals may be less powerful than in the majority of Asiatic principalities; but the ability to accumulate being more widely extended, the absolute quantity amassed will be found probably to bear a considerably larger proportion to the population.* In those states which lie exposed to hostile invasion, or whose social condition is unsettled and menacing, the motive indeed must still be very strong; and in a nation carrying on an extensive commerce, both foreign and internal, without any considerable aid from any of the banking substitutes for money, the reserves of gold and silver indispensably required to secure the regularity of payments, must of themselves engross a share of the circulating coin which it would not be easy to estimate.

"In this country, where the banking system has been carried to an extent and perfection unknown in any other part of Europe, and may be said to have entirely superseded the use of coin, except for retail dealings and the purposes of foreign commerce, the incentives to private hoarding exist no longer, and the hoards have all been transferred to the banks, or rather, I should say, to the Bank of England. But in France, where the bank-note circulation is still comparatively limited, the quantity of gold

*It is known, from unquestionable facts, that the hoards of money at all times existing in the hands of the French peasantry, often from a remote date, surpass any amount which could have been imagined possible; and even in so poor a country as Ireland, it has of late been ascertained, that the small farmers sometimes possess hoards quite disproportioned to their visible means of subsistence. [*JSM's footnote*]

and silver coin in existence I find now currently estimated, on what are described as the latest authorities, at the enormous sum of 120 millions sterling; nor is the estimate at all at variance with the reasonable probabilities of the case. Of this vast treasure there is every reason to presume that a very large proportion, probably by much the greater part, is absorbed in the hoards. If you present for payment a bill for a thousand francs to a French banker, he brings you the silver in a sealed bag from his strong room. And not the banker only, but every merchant and trader, according to his means, is under the necessity of keeping by him a stock of cash sufficient not only for his ordinary disbursements, but to meet any unexpected demands. That the quantity of specie accumulated in these innumerable depôts, not in France only, but all over the Continent, where banking institutions are still either entirely wanting or very imperfectly organized, is not merely immense in itself, but admits of being largely drawn upon, and transferred even in vast masses from one country to another, with very little, if any, effect on prices, or other material derangements, we have had some remarkable proofs:" among others, "the signal success which attended the simultaneous efforts of some of the principal European powers (Russia, Austria, Prussia, Sweden, and Denmark) to replenish their treasuries, and to replace with coin a considerable portion of the depreciated paper which the necessities of the war had forced upon them, and this at the very time when the available stock of the precious metals over the world had been reduced by the exertions of England to recover her metallic currency. . . . . There can be no doubt that these combined operations were on a scale of very extraordinary magnitude, that they were accomplished without any sensible injury to commerce or public prosperity, or any other effect than some temporary derangement of the exchanges, and that the private hoards of treasure accumulated throughout Europe during the war must have been the principal source from which all this gold and silver was collected. And no person, I think, can fairly contemplate the vast superflux of metallic wealth thus proved to be at all times in existence, and, though in a dormant and inert state, always ready to spring into activity on the first indication of a sufficiently intense demand, without feeling themselves compelled to admit the possibility of the mines being even shut up for years together, and the production of the metals altogether suspended, while there might be scarcely a perceptible alteration in the exchangeable value of the metal."*

Applying this to the currency doctrine and its advocates, "one might imagine," says Mr. Fullarton,† "that they supposed the gold which is

*Fullarton on the *Regulation of Currencies*, pp. 71–4.
†Ib. pp. 139–42.

drained off for exportation from a country using a currency exclusively metallic, to be collected by driblets at the fairs and markets, or from the tills of the grocers and mercers. They never even allude to the existence of such a thing as a great hoard of the metals, though upon the action of the hoards depends the whole economy of international payments between specie-circulating communities, while any operation of the money collected in hoards upon prices must, even according to the currency hypothesis, be wholly impossible. We know from experience what enormous payments in gold and silver specie-circulating countries are capable, at times, of making, without the least disturbance of their internal prosperity; and whence is it supposed that these payments come, but from their hoards? Let us think how the money market of a country transacting all its exchanges through the medium of the precious metals only, would be likely to be affected by the necessity of making a foreign payment of several millions. Of course the necessity could only be satisfied by a transmission of capital; and would not the competition for the possession of capital for transmission which the occasion would call forth, necessarily raise the market rate of interest? If the payment was to be made by the government, would not the government, in all probability, have to open a new loan on terms more than usually favourable to the lender?" If made by merchants, would it not be drawn either from the deposits in banks, or from the reserves which merchants keep by them in default of banks, or would it not oblige them to obtain the necessary amount of specie by going into the money market as borrowers? "And would not all this inevitably act upon the hoards, and draw forth into activity a portion of the gold and silver which the money-dealers had been accumulating, and some of them with the express view of watching such opportunities for turning their treasures to advantage? [1] . . . .

"To[1] come to the present time [1844], the balance of payments with nearly all Europe has for about four years past been in favour of this country, and gold has been pouring in till the influx amounts to the unheard-of sum of about fourteen millions sterling. Yet in all this time, has any one heard a complaint of any serious suffering inflicted on the people of the Continent? Have prices there been greatly depressed beyond their

---

[1-1]Source, 48, 49, 52 [*paragraph*] "I would desire, indeed, no more convincing evidence of the competency of the machinery of the hoards in specie-paying countries to perform every necessary office of international adjustment, without any sensible aid from the general circulation, than the facility with which France, when but just recovering from the shock of a destructive foreign invasion, completed within the space of twenty-seven months the payment of her forced contribution of nearly twenty millions to the allied powers, and a considerable proportion of that sum in specie, without any perceptible contraction or derangement of her domestic currency, or even any alarming fluctuation of her exchanges.
"Or, to

range in this country? Have wages fallen, or have merchants been extensively ruined by the universal depreciation of their stock? There has occurred nothing of the kind. The tenor of commercial and monetary affairs has been everywhere even and tranquil; and in France more particularly, an improving revenue and extended commerce bear testimony to the continued progress of internal prosperity. It may be doubted, indeed, if this great efflux of gold has withdrawn from that portion of the metallic wealth of the nation which really circulates, a single napoleon. And it has been equally obvious, from the undisturbed state of credit, that not only has the supply of specie indispensable for the conduct of business in the retail market been all the while uninterrupted, but that the hoards have continued to furnish every facility requisite for the regularity of mercantile payments. It is of the very essence of the metallic system, that the hoards, in all cases of probable occurrence, should be equal to both objects; that they should, in the first place, supply the bullion demanded for exportation, and in the next place, should keep up the home circulation to its legitimate complement. Every man trading under that system, who, in the course of his business, may have frequent occasion to remit large sums in specie to foreign countries, must either keep by him a sufficient treasure of his own or must have the means of borrowing enough from his neighbours, not only to make up when wanted the amount of his remittances, but to enable him, moreover, to carry on his ordinary transactions at home without interruption."

In a country in which credit is carried to so great an extent as in England, one great reserve, in a single establishment, the Bank of England, supplies the place, as far as the precious metals are concerned, of the multitudinous reserves of other countries. The theoretical principle, therefore, of the currency doctrine would require, that all those drains of the metal, which, if the currency were purely metallic, would be taken from the hoards, should be allowed to operate freely upon the reserve in the coffers of the Bank of England, without any attempt to stop it either by a diminution of the currency or by a contraction of credit. Nor to this would there be any well-grounded objection, unless the drain were so great as to threaten the exhaustion of the reserve, and a consequent stoppage of payments; a danger against which it is ^{m}possible^m to take adequate precautions, because in the cases which we are considering, the drain is for foreign payments of definite amount, and stops of itself as soon as these are effected. And in all systems it is admitted that the habitual reserve of the Bank should exceed the utmost amount to which experience warrants the belief that such a drain may extend; which extreme limit Mr. Fullarton affirms to be seven

$^{m-m}$48, 49, 52   easy

millions, but Mr. Tooke recommends an average reserve of ten[n], and in his last publication, of twelve millions[n]. [o]Under these circumstances, the habitual reserve, which would never be employed in discounts, but kept to be paid out exclusively in exchange for cheques or bank notes, would be sufficient for a crisis of this description; which therefore would pass off without having its difficulties increased by a contraction either of credit or of the circulation. But this, the most advantageous *dénouement* that the case admits of, and not only consistent with but required by the professed principle of the system, the panegyrists of the system claim for it as a great merit that it prevents. They boast, that on the first appearance of a drain for exportation—whatever may be its cause, and whether, under a metallic currency, it would involve a contraction of credit or not—the Bank is at once obliged to curtail its advances.[o] And this, be it remembered, when there has been no speculative rise of prices which it is indispensable to correct, no unusual extension of credit requiring contraction; but the demand for gold is solely occasioned by foreign payments on account of government, or large corn importations consequent on a bad harvest.[p]

[n-n]+57, 62, 65, 71

[o-o]48, 49, 52 [*paragraph*] The machinery, however, of the new system insists upon bringing about by force, what its principle not only does not require, but positively condemns. Every drain for exportation, whatever may be its cause, and whether under a metallic currency it would affect the circulation or not, is now compulsorily drawn from that source alone. The bank-note circulation, and the discounts or other advances of the Bank, must be diminished by an amount equal to that of the metal exported, though it be to the full extent of seven or ten millions.] 57, 62 *as* 48 . . . bank-note circulation must . . . or twelve millions.

[p-p]68048, 49, 52 "There is at least one object, therefore," says Mr. Fullarton,* "which would be effectually accomplished by acting on this system. It would be perfectly calculated, I think, to ensure, that no derangement of the exchange, or none at least subsisting in coincidence with anything like pressure on the money market, should ever be permitted to pass off, without one of those crises hitherto fortunately of rare occurrence, but of which the results, when they have occurred, have been so extensive and deplorable."

Are not the events of 1847 a fulfilment of this prediction? The crisis of that year was preceded by no inflation of credit, no speculative rise of prices. The only speculations (the corn market excepted) were those in railway shares, which had no tendency to derange the imports and exports of commodities, or to send any gold out of the country, except the small amounts paid in instalments by shareholders in this country to foreign railways. The drain of gold, great as it was, originated solely in the bad harvest of 1846 and the potato failure of that and the following year, and in the increased price of raw cotton in America. There was nothing in these circumstances which could require either a fall of general prices or a contraction of credit. An unusual demand for credit existed at the time, in consequence of the pressure of railway calls, and this necessitated a rise of the rate of interest. If the bullion in the Bank of England was sufficient to bear the drain without exhaustion, where was the necessity for adding to the distress and difficulty of the time, by requiring all who wanted gold for exportation, either to draw it from the deposits, that is, to subtract it from the already insufficient loanable capital of the country, or to become themselves competitors for a portion of that inadequate

*q*Even supposing that the reserve is insufficient to meet the foreign payments, and that*q* the means wherewith to make them *r*have to be taken*r* from the loanable capital of the country, the consequence of which is a rise of the rate of interest*s*; in*s* such circumstances some pressure on the money market is unavoidable, but that pressure is much increased in severity by the *t*separation of the banking from the issue department*t*. The case is generally stated as if the Act only operated in one way, namely, by preventing the Bank, when it has parted with (say) three millions of bullion in exchange for three millions of its notes, from again lending those notes, in discounts or other advances. But the Act really does much more than this. It is well known, that the first operation of a drain is always on the banking department. The bank deposits constitute the bulk of the unemployed and disposable capital of the country; and capital wanted for foreign payments is almost always obtained mainly by drawing out deposits. Supposing three millions to be the amount wanted, three millions of notes are drawn from the banking department (either directly or through the private bankers, who keep the bulk of their reserves with the Bank of England), and the three millions of notes, thus obtained, are presented at the Issue Department, and exchanged against gold for exportation. Thus a drain upon the country at large of only three millions, is a drain upon the Bank virtually of six millions. The deposits have lost three millions, and the reserve of the Issue Department has lost an equal amount. As the two departments, so long as the Act remains in operation, cannot even in the utmost extremity help one another, each must take its separate precautions for its own safety. Whatever measures, therefore, on the part of the Bank, would have been required under the old system by a drain of six millions, are now rendered necessary by a drain only of three. The Issue Department protects itself in the manner prescribed by the Act, by not re-issuing the three millions of notes which have been returned to it. But the Banking Department must take measures to replenish its reserve, which has been reduced by three millions. Its liabilities having also decreased three millions, by the loss of that amount of deposits, the reserve, on the ordinary banking principle of a third of the liabilities, will bear a reduction of one million. But the other two millions it must procure by letting that amount of

fund, thus still further raising the rate of interest? The only necessity was created by the Act of 1844, which would not suffer the Bank to meet this extra demand of credit by lending its notes, not even the notes returned to it in exchange for gold. The crisis of 1847 was of that sort which the provisions of the Act had not the smallest tendency to avert; and when the crisis came, the mercantile difficulties were probably doubled by its existence. [*footnote:*] *P. 137.

*q-q*57, 62   I grant that when large foreign payments require to be made,
*r-r*57, 62   must in general be drawn
*s-s*57, 62   interest. In
*t-t*57, 62   operation of the Act of 1844

advances "out, and not renewing" them. Not only v must it raise its rate of interest, but it must effect, by whatever means, a diminution of two millions in the total amount of its discounts^w: or it must sell securities to an equal amount^w. This violent action on the money market for the purpose of replenishing the Banking reserve, is wholly occasioned by the Act of 1844. If the restrictions of that Act did not exist, the Bank, instead of contracting its discounts, would simply transfer two millions, either in gold or in notes, from the Issue to the Banking Department; not in order to lend them to the public, but to secure the solvency of the Banking Department in the event of further unexpected demands by the depositors. And unless the drain continued, and reached so great an amount as to seem likely to exceed the whole of the gold in the reserves of both departments, the Bank would be under no necessity, while the pressure lasted, of withholding from commerce its accustomed amount of accommodation, at a rate of interest corresponding to the increased demand.*^{p}

I am aware it will be said that by allowing drains of this character to operate freely upon the Bank reserve until they cease of themselves, a contraction of the currency and of credit would not be prevented, but only postponed; since if a limitation of issues were not resorted to for the purpose of checking the drain in its commencement, the same or a still

*[62] This, which I have called "the double action of drains," has been strangely [62 enough,] understood as if I had asserted that the Bank is compelled to part with six millions' worth of property by a drain of three millions. Such an assertion would be too absurd to require any refutation. Drains have a double action, not upon the pecuniary position of the Bank itself, but upon the measures it is forced to take in order to stop the drain. Though the Bank itself is no poorer, its two reserves, the reserve in the banking department and the reserve in the issue department, have each [62 each] been reduced three millions by a drain of only three. And as the separation of the departments renders it necessary that each of them separately should be kept as strong as the two together need be if they could help one another, the Bank's action on the money market must be as violent on a drain of three millions, as would have been required on the old system for one of six. The reserve in the banking department being less than it otherwise would be by the entire amount of the bullion in the issue department, and the whole amount of the drain falling in the first instance on that diminished reserve, the pressure of the whole drain on the half reserve is as much felt, and requires as strong measures to stop it, as a pressure of twice the amount on the entire reserve. As I have said elsewhere,† "it is as if a man having to lift a weight were restricted from using both hands to do it, and were only allowed to use one hand at a time: in which case it would be necessary that each of his hands should be as strong as the two together." [*footnote*:]† Evidence before the Committee of the House of Commons on the Bank Acts, in 1857. [*Parliamentary Papers*, 1857 (Sess. 2), X. i, 179, 204.]

$^{u-u}$57, 62   run out, and refusing to renew
^{v}57, 62   therefore $^{w-w}$+62, 65, 71

greater limitation must take place afterwards, in order, by acting on prices, to bring back *this large* quantity of gold, for the indispensable purpose of replenishing the Bank reserve. But in this argument several things are overlooked. In the first place, the gold might be brought back, not by a fall of prices, but by the much more rapid and convenient medium of a rise of the rate of interest, involving no fall of any prices except the *price* of securities. Either English securities would be bought on account of foreigners, or foreign securities held in England would be sent abroad for sale, both which operations took place largely during the mercantile difficulties of 1847, and not only checked the efflux of gold, but turned the tide and brought the metal back. It was not, therefore, brought back by a contraction of the currency, though in this case it certainly was so by a contraction of loans. But *even this is not* always *indispensable.* For in the second place, it is not necessary that the gold should return with the same suddenness with which it went out. A great portion would probably return in the ordinary way of commerce, in payment for exported commodities. The extra gains made by dealers and producers in foreign countries through the extra payments they receive from this country, are very likely to be partly expended in increased purchases of English commodities, either for consumption or on speculation, though the effect may not manifest itself with sufficient rapidity to enable the transmission of gold to be dispensed with in the first instance. These extra purchases would turn the balance of payments in favour of the country, and gradually restore a portion of the exported gold; and the remainder would probably be brought back, *without any considerable* rise of the rate of interest in England, *c* by the fall of it in foreign countries, occasioned by the addition of some millions of gold to the loanable capital of those countries. *Indeed, in the state of things consequent on the gold discoveries, when the enormous quantity of

---

*x–x*48, 49 so large a	*v–v*48, 49, 52, 57, 62 prices
*z–z*48, 49 is even this	*a–a*48, 49 indispensable?
*b–b*48, 49, 52 not by a	*c*48, 49, 52 but

*d–d*68248, 49, 52   If it were necessary to accelerate the process by an artificial action on the rate of interest in England, a very moderate rise would be sufficient, instead of the very great one which is the consequence of allowing the whole demand for gold for exportation to act suddenly and at once on the existing resources of the loan market.

Thus stand, according to the best judgment I am able to form, the advantages and disadvantages of the currency system established by the Act of 1844: of which, as it seems to me, the disadvantages greatly preponderate. I am, however, far from thinking that on a subject at once so intricate and so new, a subject which has only begun to be understood through the controversies of the last few years, experience and discussion have nothing further to disclose. I give the foregoing opinions as the results to which I have been guided by the lights that have hitherto fallen on the subject; conscious that additional lights are almost sure to be struck out when the knowledge of principles and of facts necessary for the elucidation of the question becomes united in a greater number of individuals.

gold annually produced in Australia, and much of that from California, is distributed to other countries through England, and a month seldom passes without a large arrival, the Bank reserves can replenish themselves without any re-importation of the gold previously carried off by a drain. All that is needful is an intermission, and a very brief intermission is sufficient, of the exportation.

For these reasons it appears to me, that notwithstanding the beneficial operation of the Act of 1844 in the first stages of one kind of commercial crisis (that produced by over-speculation), it on the whole materially aggravates the severity of commercial revulsions. And not only are contractions of credit made more severe by the Act, they are also made greatly more frequent. "Suppose," says Mr. George Walker, in a clear, impartial, and conclusive series of papers in the *Aberdeen Herald*, forming one of the best existing discussions of the present question—"suppose that, of eighteen millions of gold, ten are in the issue department and eight are in the banking department. The result is the same as under a metallic currency with only eight millions in reserve, instead of eighteen. . . . . . The effect of the Bank Act is, that the proceedings of the Bank under a drain are not determined by the amount of gold within its vaults, but are, or ought to be, determined by the portion of it belonging to the banking department. With the whole of the gold at its disposal, it may find it unnecessary to interfere with credit, or force down prices, if a drain leave a fair reserve behind. With only the banking reserve at its disposal, it must, from the narrow margin it has to operate on, meet all drains by counteractives more or less strong, to the injury of the commercial world; and if it fail to do so, as it may fail, the consequence is destruction. Hence the extraordinary and frequent variations of the rate of interest under the Bank Act. Since 1847, when the eyes of the Bank were opened to its true position, it has felt it necessary, as a precautionary measure, that every variation in the reserve should be accompanied by an alteration in the rate of interest."[*] To make the Act innocuous, therefore, it would be necessary that the Bank, in addition to the whole of the gold in the Issue Department, should retain as great a reserve in gold or notes in the Banking Department alone, as would suffice under the old system for the security both of the issues and of the deposits.[d]

§ 5. [*Should the issue of bank notes be confined to a single establishment?*] There remain two questions respecting a bank-note currency, which have also been a subject of considerable discussion of late years: whether the privilege of providing it should be confined to a single establishment,

[*Aberdeen Herald*, 26 April, 1856, p. 6. *The series, entitled* "The Bank Charter Act," *appears in the numbers for* 15, 22, 29 March; 12, 26 April; 3 May.]

such as the Bank of England, or a plurality of issuers should be allowed; and in the latter case, whether any peculiar precautions are requisite or advisable, to protect the holders of notes against losses occasioned by the insolvency of the issuers.

The course of the preceding speculations has led us to attach so much less of peculiar importance to bank notes, as compared with other forms of credit, than accords with the notions generally current, that questions respecting the regulation of so very small a part of the general mass of credit, cannot appear to us of such momentous import as they are sometimes considered. Bank notes, however, have so far a real peculiarity, that they are the only form of credit sufficiently convenient for all the purposes of circulation, to be able entirely to supersede the use of metallic money for internal purposes. Though the extension of the use of cheques has a tendency more and more to diminish the number of bank notes, as it would that of the sovereigns or other coins which would take their place if they were abolished; there is sure, for a long time to come, to be a considerable supply of them, wherever the necessary degree of commercial confidence exists, and their free use is permitted. The exclusive privilege, therefore, of issuing them, if reserved to the Government or to some one body, is a source of great pecuniary gain. That this gain should be obtained for the nation at large is both practicable and desirable: and if the management of a bank-note currency ought to be so completely mechanical, so entirely a thing of fixed rule, as it is made by the Act of 1844, there seems no reason why this mechanism should be worked for the profit of any private issuer, rather than for the public treasury. If, however, a plan be preferred which leaves the variations in the amount of issues in any degree whatever to the discretion of the issuers, it is not desirable that to the ever-growing attributions of the Government, so delicate a function should be superadded; and that the attention of the heads of the state should be diverted from larger objects, by their being besieged with the applications, and made a mark for all the attacks, which are never spared to those deemed to be responsible for any acts, however minute, connected with the regulation of the currency. It would be better that treasury notes, exchangeable for gold on demand, should be issued to a fixed amount, not exceeding the minimum of a bank-note currency; the remainder of the notes which may be required being left to be supplied either by one or by a number of private banking establishments. Or an establishment like the Bank of England might supply the whole country, on condition of lending fifteen or twenty millions of its notes to the government without interest; which would give the same pecuniary advantage to the state as if it issued that number of its own notes.

The reason ordinarily alleged in condemnation of the system of plurality of issuers which existed in England before the Act of 1844, and under certain limitations still subsists, is that the competition of these different issuers induces them to increase the amount of their notes to an injurious extent. But we have seen that the power which bankers have of augmenting their issues, and the degree of mischief which they can produce by it, are quite trifling compared with the current over-estimate. As remarked by Mr. Fullarton,* the extraordinary increase of banking competition occasioned by the establishment of the joint-stock banks, a competition often of the most reckless kind, has proved utterly powerless to enlarge the aggregate mass of the bank-note circulation; that aggregate circulation having, on the contrary, actually decreased. In *a*the absence of any special case for an exception to freedom of industry, the general rule ought to prevail. It appears desirable, however,*a* to maintain one great establishment like the Bank of England, distinguished from other banks of issue in this, that it alone is required to pay in gold, the others being at liberty to pay their notes with notes of the central establishment. The object of this is that there may be one body, responsible for maintaining a reserve of the precious metals sufficient to meet any drain that can reasonably be expected to take place. By disseminating this responsibility among a number of banks, it is prevented from operating efficaciously upon any: or if it be still enforced against one, the reserves of the metals retained by all the others are capital kept idle in pure waste, which may be dispensed with by allowing them at their option to pay in Bank of England notes.

§ 6. [*Should the holders of notes be protected in any peculiar manner against failure of payment?*] The question remains whether, in case of a plurality of issuers, any peculiar precautions are needed to protect the holders of notes from the consequences of failure of payment. Before 1826, the insolvency of banks of issue was a frequent and very serious evil, often spreading distress through a whole neighbourhood, and at one blow depriving provident industry of the results of long and painful saving. This was one of the chief reasons which induced Parliament, in that year, to prohibit the issue of bank notes of a denomination below five pounds, that the labouring classes at least might be as little as possible exposed to participate in this suffering. As an additional safeguard, it has been suggested to give the holders of notes a priority over other creditors, or to require bankers to deposit stock or other public securities as a pledge for the whole amount of their issues. The insecurity *a* of the former bank-

*Pp. 89–92.

*a–a*48, 49, 52, 57, 62   any case it appears desirable
*a*48, 49, 52   , however,

note currency of England was ᵇpartlyᵇ the work of the law, which, in order to give a qualified monopoly of banking business to the Bank of England, had actually made the formation of safe banking establishments a punishable offence, by prohibiting the existence of any banks, in town or country, whether of issue or deposit, with a number of partners exceeding six. This truly characteristic specimen of the old system of monopoly and restriction was done away with in 1826, both as to issues and deposits, everywhere but in a district of sixty-five miles radius round London, and in 1833 in that district also, as far as relates to deposits. ᶜIt was hoped that the numerous joint-stock banks since established would have furnished a more trustworthy currency, and that under their influence the banking system of England would have been almost as secure to the public as that of Scotland (where banking was always free) has been for two centuries past. But the almost incredible instances of reckless and fraudulent mismanagement which these institutions have of late afforded (though in some of the most notorious cases the delinquent establishments have not been banks of issue), have shown only too clearly that, south of the Tweed at least, the joint-stock principle applied to banking is not the adequate safeguard it was so confidently supposed to be: and it is difficult now to resist the conviction, that if plurality of issuers is allowed to exist ᵈ , some kind of special security in favour of the holders of notes should be exacted as an imperative condition.ᶜ

ᵇ⁻ᵇ48, 49, 52   altogether
ᶜ⁻ᶜ48, 49   The numerous joint-stock banks since established, have, by furnishing a more trustworthy currency, made it almost impossible for any private banker to maintain his circulation, unless his capital and character inspire the most complete confidence, And although there has been in some instances very gross mis management by joint-stock banks (less, however, in the department of issues than in that of deposits) the failure of these banks is extremely rare, and the cases still rarer in which loss has ultimately been sustained by any one except the shareholders. The banking system of England is now almost as secure to the public, as that of Scotland (where banking was always free) has been for two centuries past; and the legislature might without any bad consequences, at least of this kind, revoke its interdict (which was never extended to Scotland) against one and two pound notes. I cannot therefore think it at all necessary, or that it would be anything but vexatious meddling, to enforce any kind of special security in favour of the holders of notes. The true protection to creditors of all kinds is a good law of insolvency (a part of the law at present shamefully deficient), and, in the case of joint-stock companies at least, complete publicity of their accounts: the publicity now very properly given to their issues, being a very small portion of what the state has a right to require in return for their being allowed to constitute themselves, and be recognized by the law, as a collective body.] 52   as 48 . . . insolvency, and . . . as 48
ᵈ57, 62   at all

CHAPTER XXV

Of the Competition of Different Countries in the Same Market

§ 1. [*Causes which enable one country to undersell another*] In the phraseology of the Mercantile System, the language and doctrines of which are still the basis of what may be called the political economy of the selling classes, as distinguished from the buyers or consumers, there is no word of more frequent recurrence or more perilous import than the word *underselling*. To undersell other countries—not to be undersold by other countries—were spoken of, and are still very often spoken of, almost as if they were the sole purposes for which production and commodities exist. The feelings of rival tradesmen, prevailing among nations, overruled for centuries all sense of the general community of advantage which commercial countries derive from the prosperity of one another: and that commercial spirit which is now one of the strongest obstacles to wars, was during a certain period of European history their principal cause.

Even in the more enlightened view now attainable of the nature and consequences of international commerce, some, though a comparatively small, space must still be made for the fact of commercial rivalry. Nations may, like individual dealers, be competitors, with opposite interests, in the markets of some commodities, while in others they are in the more fortunate relation of reciprocal customers. The benefit of commerce does not consist, as it was once thought to do, in the commodities sold; but, since the commodities sold are the means of obtaining those which are bought, a nation would be cut off from the real advantage of commerce, the imports, if it could not induce other nations to take any of its commodities in exchange; and in proportion as the competition of other countries compels it to offer its commodities on cheaper terms, on pain of not selling them at all, the imports which it obtains by its foreign trade are procured at greater cost.

These points have been adequately, though incidentally, illustrated in some of the preceding chapters. But the great space which the topic has filled, and continues to fill, in economical speculations, and in the practical anxieties both of politicians and of dealers and manufacturers, makes it desirable, before quitting the subject of international exchange, to subjoin a few observations on the things which do, and on those which do not, enable countries to undersell one another.

One country can only undersell another in a given market, to the extent of entirely expelling her from it, on two conditions. In the first place, she must have a greater advantage than the second country in the production of the article exported by both; meaning by a greater advantage (as has been already so fully explained) not absolutely, but in comparison with other commodities; and in the second place, such must be her relation with the customer country in respect to the demand for each other's products, and such the consequent state of international values, as to give away to the customer country more than the whole advantage possessed by the rival country; otherwise the rival will still be able to hold her ground in the market.

Let us revert to the imaginary hypothesis [a] of a trade between England and Germany in cloth and linen: England being capable of producing 10 yards of cloth at the same cost with 15 yards of linen, Germany at the same cost with 20, and the two commodities being exchanged between the two countries (cost of carriage apart) at some intermediate rate, say 10 for 17. Germany could not be permanently undersold in the English market, and expelled from it, unless by a country which offered not merely more than 17, but more than 20 yards of linen for 10 of cloth. Short of that, the competition would only oblige Germany to pay dearer for cloth, but would not disable her from exporting linen. The country, therefore, which could undersell Germany, must, in the first place, be able to produce linen at less cost, compared with cloth, than Germany herself; and in the next place, must have such a demand for cloth, or other English commodities, as would compel her, even when she became sole occupant of the market, to give a greater advantage to England than Germany could give by resigning the whole of hers; to give, for example, 21 yards for 10. For if not—if, for example, the equation of international demand, after Germany was excluded, gave a ratio of 18 for 10, Germany could again enter into the competition; Germany would be now the underselling nation; and there would be a point, perhaps 19 for 10, at which both countries would be able to maintain their ground, and to sell in England enough linen to pay for the cloth, or other English commodities, for which, on these newly-adjusted terms of interchange, they had a demand. In like manner, England, as an exporter of cloth, could only be driven from the German market by some rival whose superior advantages in the production of cloth enabled her, and the intensity of whose demand for German produce compelled her,

[a]48, 49   which we have found so convenient, that

to offer 10 yards of cloth, not merely for less than 17 yards of linen, but for less than 15. In that case, England could no longer carry on the trade without loss; but in any case short of this, she would merely be obliged to give to Germany more cloth for less linen than she had previously given.

It thus appears that the alarm of being permanently undersold may be taken much too easily; may be taken when the thing really to be anticipated is not the loss of the trade, but the minor inconvenience of carrying it on at a diminished advantage; an inconvenience chiefly falling on the consumers of foreign commodities, and not on the producers or sellers of the exported article. It is no sufficient ground of apprehension to the English producers, to find that some other country can sell cloth in foreign markets at some particular time, a trifle cheaper than they can themselves afford to do in the existing state of prices in England. Suppose them to be temporarily undersold, and their exports diminished; the imports will exceed the exports, there will be a new distribution of the precious metals, prices will fall, and as all the money expenses of the English producers will be diminished, they will be able (if the case falls short of that stated in the preceding paragraph) again to compete with their rivals. The loss which England will incur, will not fall upon the exporters, but upon those who consume imported commodities; who, with money incomes reduced in amount, will have to pay the same or even an increased price for all things produced in foreign countries.

§ 2. [*Low wages is one of the causes which enable one country to undersell another*] Such, I conceive, is the true theory, or rationale, of underselling. It will be observed that it takes no account of some things which we hear spoken of, oftener perhaps than any others, in the character of causes exposing a country to be undersold.

According to the preceding doctrine, a country cannot be undersold in any commodity, unless the rival country has a stronger inducement than itself for devoting its labour and capital to the production of the commodity; arising from the fact that by doing so it occasions a greater saving of labour and capital, to be shared between itself and its customers—a greater increase of the aggregate produce of the world. The underselling, therefore, though a loss to the undersold country, is an advantage to the world at large; the substituted commerce being one which economizes more of the labour and capital of mankind, and adds more to their collective wealth, than the commerce superseded by it. The advantage, of course, consists in being able to produce the commodity of better quality, or with less labour (compared with other things); or perhaps not with less labour, but in less time; with a less prolonged detention of the capital employed. This may arise from greater natural advantages (such as soil, climate, richness of mines); superior capability, either natural or acquired, in the labourers; better division of labour, and better tools, or machinery. But there is no place left in this theory for the case of lower wages. This, however, in the theories commonly current, is a favourite cause of underselling. We continually hear of the disadvantage under which the British producer labours, both in foreign markets and even in his own, through the lower wages paid by his foreign rivals. These lower wages, we are told, enable, or are always on the point of enabling them to sell at lower prices, and to dislodge the English manufacturer from all markets in which he is not artificially protected.

Before examining this opinion on grounds of principle, it is worth while to bestow a moment's consideration upon it as a question of fact. Is it true, that the wages of manufacturing labour are lower in foreign countries than in England, in any sense in which low wages are an advantage to the capitalist? The artisan of Ghent or Lyons may earn less wages in a day, but does he not do less work? Degrees of efficiency considered, does his labour cost less to his employer? Though wages may be lower on the Continent, is not the Cost of Labour, which is the real element in the competition, very nearly the same? That it is so seems the opinion of competent judges, and is confirmed by the very little difference in the rate of profit between England and the Continental countries. But if so, the opinion is absurd that English producers can be undersold by their Continental rivals from this cause. It is only in America that the supposition is *primâ facie* admissible. In America, wages are much higher than in England, if we mean by wages the daily earnings of a labourer: but the productive power of American labour is so great—its efficiency, combined with the favourable circumstances in which it is exerted, makes it worth so much to the purchaser, that the Cost of Labour is lower in America than in England; as is *a*indicated*a* by the fact that the general rate of profits and of interest is *b* higher.

§ 3. [*Low wages is one of those causes when peculiar to certain branches of industry*] But is it true that low wages, even in the sense of low Cost of Labour, enable a country to sell cheaper in the foreign market? I *a*mean, of course*a*, low wages which are common to the whole productive industry of the country.

If wages, in any of the departments of industry which supply exports, are kept, artificially, or by some accidental cause, below the general rate of wages in the country, this is a real advantage in the foreign market. It lessens the *comparative* cost of production of those articles, in relation to

*a-a*48, 49, 52, 57, 62   proved   *b*48, 49, 52, 57, 62   very much
*a-a*48, 49   of course mean

others; and has the same effect as if their production required so much less labour. Take, for instance, the case of the United States in respect to certain commodities[b], prior to the civil war. Tobacco[b] and cotton, two great articles of export, [c]were[c] produced by slave labour, while food and manufactures generally [d]were[d] produced by free labourers, [e]either working[e] on their own account or [f] paid by wages. In spite of the inferior efficiency of slave labour, there can be no reasonable doubt that in a country where the wages of free labour [g]were[g] so high, the work executed by slaves [h]was[h] a better bargain to the capitalist. To whatever extent it [i]was[i] so, this smaller cost of labour, being not general, but limited to those employments, [j]was[j] just as much a cause of cheapness in the products, both in the home and in the foreign market, as if they had been made by a less quantity of labour. If[k], when[k] the slaves in the Southern States were [l] emancipated, [m] their wages rose to the general level of the earnings of free labour in America, [n]that country[n] might [o]have been[o] obliged to erase some of the slave-grown articles from the catalogue of [p]its[p] exports, and would certainly be unable to sell any of them in the foreign market at the [q]accustomed[q] price. [r]Accordingly, American cotton is now habitually at a much higher price than before the war. Its previous cheapness was[r] partly an artificial cheapness, which may be compared to that produced by a bounty on production or on exportation: or, considering the means by which it [s]was[s] obtained, an apter comparison would be with the cheapness of stolen goods.

An advantage of a similar economical, though of a very different moral character, is that possessed by domestic manufactures; fabrics produced in the leisure hours of families partially occupied in other pursuits, who, not depending for subsistence on the produce of the manufacture, can afford to sell it at any price, however low, for which they think it worth while to take the trouble of producing. In an account of the Canton of Zurich, to which I have had occasion to refer on another subject, it is observed,* "The workman of Zurich is to-day a manufacturer, to-morrow again an agriculturist, and changes his [t]occupations[t] with the seasons, in a continual

_____

*_Historisch- geographisch- statistisches Gemälde der Schweiz._ Erstes Heft, 1834, p. 105.

[b-b]48, 49, 52, 57, 62, 65   . In that country, tobacco
[c-c]48, 49, 52, 57, 62, 65   are   [d-d]48, 49, 52, 57, 62, 65   are
[e-e]48, 49, 52, 57, 62, 65   who either work   [f]48, 49, 52, 57, 62, 65   are
[g-g]48, 49, 52, 57, 62, 65   are   [h-h]48, 49, 52, 57, 62, 65   is
[i-i]48, 49, 52, 57, 62, 65   is   [j-j]48, 49, 52, 57, 62, 65   is
[k-k]+71   [l]65   all
[m]48, 49, 52, 57, 62, 65   and   [n-n]48   she
[o-o]48, 49, 52, 57, 62, 65   be   [p-p]48   her
[q-q]48, 49, 52, 57, 62   present
[r-r]48, 49, 52, 57, 62, 65   . Their cheapness is
[s-s]48, 49, 52, 57, 62, 65   is   [t-t]48, 49, 52, 57   occupation

round. Manufacturing industry and tillage advance hand in hand, in inseparable alliance, and in this union of the two occupations the secret may be found, why the simple and unlearned Swiss manufacturer can always go on competing, and increasing in prosperity, in the face of those extensive establishments fitted out with great economic, and (what is still more important) intellectual, resources. Even in those parts of the Canton where manufactures have extended themselves the most widely, only one-seventh of all the families belong to manufactures alone; four-sevenths combine that employment with agriculture. The advantage of this domestic or family manufacture consists chiefly in the fact, that it is compatible with all other avocations, or rather that it may in part be regarded as only a supplementary employment. In winter in the dwellings of the operatives, the whole family employ themselves in it: but as soon as spring appears, those on whom the early field labours devolve, abandon the in-door work; many a shuttle stands still; by degrees, as the field-work increases, one member of the family follows another, till at last, at the harvest, and during the so-called 'great works,' all hands seize the implements of husbandry; but in unfavourable weather, and in all otherwise vacant hours, the work in the cottage is resumed, and when the ungenial season again recurs, the people return in the same gradual order to their home occupation, until they have all resumed it."

In the case of these domestic manufactures, the comparative cost of production, on which the interchange between countries depends, is much lower than in proportion to the quantity of labour employed. The work-people, looking to the earnings of their loom for a part only, if for any part, of their actual maintenance, can afford to work for a less remuneration than the lowest rate of wages which can "permanently" exist in the employments by which the labourer has to support the whole expense of a family. Working, as they do, not for an employer but for themselves, they may be said to carry on the manufacture at no cost at all, except the small expense of a loom and of the material; and the limit of possible cheapness is not the necessity of living by their trade but that of earning enough by the work to make that social employment of their leisure hours not disagreeable.

§ 4. [*Low wages is not one of those causes when common to all branches of industry*] These two cases, of slave labour and of domestic manufactures, exemplify the conditions under which low wages enable a country to sell its commodities cheaper in foreign markets, and consequently to undersell its rivals, or to avoid being undersold by them. But no such advantage is conferred by low wages when common to all branches

$^{u-u}$+52, 57, 62, 65, 71

of industry. General low wages never caused any country to undersell its rivals, nor did general high wages ever hinder it from doing so.

To demonstrate this, we must return to an elementary principle which was discussed in a former chapter.* General low wages do not cause low prices, nor high wages high prices, within the country itself. General prices are not raised by a rise of wages, any more than they would be raised by an increase of the quantity of labour required in all production. Expenses which affect all commodities equally, have no influence on prices. If the maker of broadcloth or cutlery, and nobody else, had to pay higher wages, the price of his commodity would rise, just as it would if he had to employ more labour; because otherwise he would gain less profit than other producers, and nobody would engage in the employment. But if everybody has to pay higher wages, or everybody to employ more labour, the loss must be submitted to; as it affects everybody alike, no one can hope to get rid of it by a change of employment, each therefore resigns himself to a diminution of profits, and prices remain as they were. In like manner, general low wages, or a general increase in the productiveness of labour, does not make prices low, but profits high. If wages fall, (meaning here by wages the cost of labour,) why, on that account, should the producer lower his price? He will be forced, it may be said, by the competition of other capitalists who will crowd into his employment. But other capitalists are also paying lower wages, and by entering into competition with him they would gain nothing but what they are gaining already. The rate then at which labour is paid, as well as the quantity of it which is employed, affects neither the value nor the price of the commodity produced, except in so far as it is peculiar to that commodity, and not common to commodities generally.

Since low wages are not a cause of low prices in the country itself, so neither do they cause it to offer its commodities in foreign markets at a lower price. It is quite true that if the cost of labour is lower in America than in England, America could sell her cottons to Cuba at a lower price than England, and still gain as high a profit as the English manufacturer. But it is not with the profit of the English manufacturer that the American cotton spinner will make his comparison; it is with the profits of other American capitalists. These enjoy, in common with himself, the benefit of a low cost of labour, and have accordingly a high rate of profit. This high profit the cotton spinner must also have: he will not content himself with the English profit. It is true he may go on for a time at that lower rate, rather than change his employment; and a trade may be carried on, sometimes for a long period, at a much lower profit than that for which it would have been originally engaged in. Countries which have a low

*Supra, book iii. ch. iv [pp. 477–81].

cost of labour, and high profits, do not for that reason undersell others, but they do oppose a more obstinate resistance to being undersold, because the producers can often submit to a diminution of profit without being unable to live, and even to thrive, by their business. But *this* is all which their advantage does for them: and in this resistance they will not long persevere, when a change of times which may give them equal profits with the rest of their countrymen has become manifestly hopeless.

§ 5. [*Some anomalous cases of trading communities examined*] There is a class of trading and exporting communities, on which a few words of explanation seem to be required. These are hardly to be looked upon as countries, carrying on an exchange of commodities with other countries, but more properly as outlying agricultural or manufacturing establishments belonging to a larger community. Our West India colonies, for example, cannot be regarded as countries, with a productive capital of their own. If Manchester, instead of being where it is, were on a rock in the North Sea, (its present industry nevertheless continuing,) it would still be but a town of England, not a country trading with England; it would be merely, as now, *a* place where England finds it convenient to carry on her cotton manufacture. The West Indies, in like manner, are the place where England finds it convenient to carry on the production of sugar, coffee, and a few other tropical commodities. All the capital employed is English capital; almost all the industry is carried on for English uses; there is little production of anything except the staple commodities, and these are sent to England, not to be exchanged for things exported to the colony and consumed by its inhabitants, but to be sold in England for the benefit of the proprietors there. The trade with the West Indies is therefore hardly to be considered as external trade, but more resembles the traffic between town and country, and is amenable to the principles of the home trade. The rate of profit in the colonies will be regulated by English profits; the expectation of profit must be about the same as in England, with the addition of compensation for the disadvantages attending the more distant and hazardous employment: and after allowance is made for those disadvantages, the value and price of West India produce in the English market must be regulated, (or rather must have been regulated formerly,) like that of any English commodity, by the cost of production. For the last *twelve or fifteen* years this principle has been in abeyance: the price was first kept up beyond the ratio of the cost of production by deficient supplies, which could not, owing to *the* deficiency of labour, be increased; and more recently the admission of foreign competition has introduced

---

*a–a*48, 49   that

*a–a*48, 49, 52   the   *b–b*48, 49, 52, 57, 62   ten or twelve   *c–c*+62, 65, 71

another element, and ^{d}some of the West India Islands^d are undersold, not so much because wages are higher than in Cuba and Brazil, as because they are higher than in England: for were they not so, Jamaica could sell her sugars at Cuban prices, and still obtain, though not a Cuban, an English rate of profit.

It is worth while also to notice another class of small, but in this case mostly independent communities, which have supported and enriched themselves almost without any productions of their own, (except ships and marine equipments,) by a mere carrying trade, and commerce of *entrepôt*; by buying the produce of one country, to sell it at a profit in another. Such were Venice and the Hanse Towns. The case of these communities is very simple. They made themselves and their capital the instruments, not of production, but of accomplishing exchanges between the productions of other countries. These exchanges ^{e}are^e attended with an advantage to those countries—an increase of the aggregate returns to industry—part of which went to indemnify the agents for the necessary expenses of transport, and another part to remunerate the use of their capital and mercantile skill. The countries themselves had not capital disposable for the operation. When the Venetians became the agents of the general commerce of Southern Europe, they had scarcely any competitors: the thing would not have been done at all without them, and there was really no limit to their profits except the limit to what the ignorant feudal nobility ^{f}could and^f would give for the unknown luxuries then first presented to their sight. At a later period competition arose, and the profit of this operation, like that of others, became amenable to natural laws. The carrying trade was taken up by Holland, a country with productions of its own and a large accumulated capital. The other nations of Europe also had now capital to spare, and were capable of conducting their foreign trade for themselves: but Holland, having, from a variety of circumstances, a lower rate of profit at home, could afford to carry for other countries at a smaller advance on the original cost of the goods, than would have been required by their own capitalists; and Holland, therefore, engrossed the greatest part of the carrying trade of all those countries which did not keep it to themselves by Navigation Laws, constructed, like those of England, for ^{g}that^g express purpose.

$^{d-d}$48, 49, 52, 57   the West Indies
$^{e-e}$48, 49, 52, 57   were
$^{f-f}$+62, 65, 71
$^{g-g}$48, 49, 52, 57, 62   the

CHAPTER XXVI

Of Distribution, as Affected by Exchange

§ 1. [*Exchange and Money make no difference in the law of wages*] We have now completed, as far as is compatible with *ᵃour purposes and limitsᵃ*, the exposition of the machinery through which the produce of a country is apportioned among the different classes of its inhabitants; which is no other than the machinery of Exchange, and has for the exponents of its operation, the laws of Value and of Price. We shall now avail ourselves of the light thus acquired, to cast a retrospective glance at the subject of Distribution. The division of the produce among the three classes, Labourers, Capitalists, and Landlords, when considered without any reference to Exchange, appeared to depend on certain general laws. It is fit that we should now consider whether these same laws still operate, when the distribution takes place through the complex mechanism of exchange and money; or whether the properties of the mechanism interfere with and modify the presiding principles.

The primary division of the produce of human exertion and frugality is, as we have seen, into three shares, wages, profits, and rent; and these shares are portioned out to the persons entitled to them, in the form of money, and by a process of exchange; or rather, the capitalist, with whom in the usual arrangements of society the produce remains, pays in money, to the other two sharers, the market value of their labour and land. If we examine, on what the pecuniary value of labour, and the pecuniary value of the use of land, depend, we shall find that it is on the very same causes by which we found that wages and rent would be regulated if there were no money and no exchange of commodities.

It is evident, in the first place, that the law of Wages is not affected by the existence or non-existence of Exchange or Money. Wages depend on the ratio between population and capital; and would do so if all the capital in the world were the property of one association, or if the capitalists among whom it is shared maintained each an establishment for the pro-

ᵃ⁻ᵃ48, 49   the purposes and limits of this treatise

duction of every article consumed in the community, exchange of commodities having no existence. As the ratio between capital and population,
*b*in all old countries*b*, depends on the strength of the checks by which the
too rapid increase of population is restrained, it may be said, popularly
speaking, that wages depend on the checks to population; that when the
check is not death, by starvation or disease, wages depend on the prudence
of the labouring people; and that wages in any country are habitually at
the lowest rate, to which in that country the *c*labourer*c* will suffer them to
be depressed rather than put a restraint upon multiplication.

What is here meant, however, by wages, is the labourer's real scale of
comfort; the quantity he obtains of the things which nature or habit has
made necessary or agreeable to him: wages in the sense in which they
are of importance to the receiver. In the sense in which they are of importance to the payer, they do not depend exclusively on such simple
principles. Wages in the first sense, the wages on which the labourer's comfort depends, we *d*will*d* call real wages, or wages in kind. Wages in the
second sense, we may be permitted to call, for the present, money wages;
assuming, as it is allowable to do, that money remains for the time an
invariable standard, no alteration taking place in the conditions under
which the circulating medium itself is produced or obtained. If money
itself undergoes no variation in cost, the money price of labour is an exact
measure of the Cost of Labour, and may be made use of as a convenient
symbol to express it.

The money wages of labour are a compound result of two elements:
first, real wages, or wages in kind, or in other words, the quantity which
the labourer obtains of the ordinary articles of consumption; and secondly,
the money prices of those articles. In all old countries—all countries in
which the increase of population is in any degree checked by the difficulty
of obtaining subsistence—the habitual money price of labour is that which
will just enable the labourers, one with another, to purchase the commodities without which they *e*either cannot or will not keep up the population at its customary rate of increase*e*. Their standard of comfort being
given, (and by the standard of comfort in a labouring class, is meant that,
rather than forego which, they will abstain from multiplication,) money
wages depend on the money price, and therefore on the cost of production,
of the various articles which the labourers habitually consume: because
if their wages cannot procure them a given quantity of these, their increase
will slacken, and their wages rise. Of these articles, food and other

---

*b-b*48, 49, 52, 57, 62   everywhere but in new colonies
*c-c*48, 49, 52   labourers
*d-d*48, 49   shall
*e-e*48, 49   will not consent to continue the race

agricultural produce are so much the principal, as to leave little influence to anything else.

It is at this point that we are enabled to invoke the aid of the principles which have been laid down in this Third Part. The cost of production of food and agricultural produce has been analyzed in a preceding chapter. It depends on the productiveness of the least fertile land, or of the least productively employed portion of capital, which the necessities of society have as yet put in requisition for agricultural purposes. The cost of production of the food grown in these least advantageous circumstances, determines, as we have seen, the exchange value and money price of the whole. In any given state, therefore, of the *labourers' habits, their* money wages depend on the productiveness of the least fertile land, or least productive agricultural capital; on the point which cultivation has reached in its downward progress—in its encroachments on the barren lands, and its gradually increased strain upon the powers of the more fertile. Now, the force which urges *g* cultivation in this downward course, is the increase of people; while the counter-force which checks the descent, is the improvement of agricultural science and practice, enabling the same soil to yield to the same labour more ample returns. The costliness of the most costly part of the produce of cultivation, is an exact expression of the state, at any given moment, of the race which population and agricultural skill are always running against each other.

§ 2. [*Exchange and Money make no difference in the law of rent*] It is well said by Dr. Chalmers, that many of the most important lessons in political economy are to be learnt at the extreme margin of cultivation, the last point which the culture of the soil has reached in its contest with the spontaneous agencies of nature. The degree of productiveness of this extreme margin, is an index to the existing state of the distribution of the produce among the three classes, of labourers, capitalists, and landlords.

When the demand of an increasing population for more food cannot be satisfied without extending cultivation to less fertile land or incurring additional outlay, with a less proportional return, on land already in cultivation, it is a necessary condition of this increase of agricultural produce, that the value and price of that produce must first rise. But as soon as the price has risen sufficiently to give to the additional outlay of capital the ordinary profit, the rise will not go on still further for the purpose of enabling the new land, or the new expenditure on old land, to yield rent as well as profit. The land or capital last put in requisition, and occupying what Dr. Chalmers calls the margin of cultivation, will yield, and

*f-f*48, 49   labourer's habits, his
*g*48, 49   on

continue to yield, no rent. But if this yields no rent, the rent afforded by all other land or agricultural capital will be exactly so much as it produces more than this. The price of food will always on the average be such, that the worst land, and the least productive instalment of the capital employed on the better lands, shall just replace the expenses with the ordinary profit. If the least favoured land and capital just do thus much, all other land and capital will yield an extra profit, equal to the proceeds of the extra produce due to their superior productiveness; and this extra profit becomes, by competition, the prize of the landlords. Exchange, and money, therefore, make no difference in the law of rent: it is the same as we originally found it. Rent is the extra return made to agricultural capital when employed with peculiar advantages; the exact equivalent of what those advantages enable the producers to economize in the cost of production: the value and price of the produce being regulated by the cost of production to those producers who have no advantages; by the return to that portion of agricultural capital, the circumstances of which are the least favourable.

§ 3. [*Exchange and Money make no difference in the law of profits*] Wages and Rent being thus regulated by the same principles when paid in money, as they would be if apportioned in kind, it follows that Profits are so likewise. For the surplus, after replacing wages and paying rent, constitutes Profits.

We found in the last chapter of the Second Book, that the advances of the capitalist, when analyzed to their ultimate elements, consist either in the purchase or maintenance of labour, or in the profits of former capitalists; and that therefore profits, in the last resort, depend upon the Cost of Labour, falling as that rises, and rising as it falls. Let us endeavour to trace more minutely the operation of this law.

There are two modes in which the Cost of Labour, which is correctly represented (money being supposed invariable) by the money wages of the labourer, may be increased. The labourer may obtain greater comforts; wages in kind—real wages—may rise. Or the progress of population may force down cultivation to inferior soils, and more costly processes; thus raising the cost of production, the value, and the price, of the chief articles of the labourer's consumption. On either of these suppositions, the rate of profit will fall.

If the labourer obtains more abundant commodities, only by reason of their greater cheapness; if he obtains a greater quantity, but not on the whole a greater cost; [a] real wages will be increased, but not [b] money wages, and there will be nothing to affect the rate of profit. But if he obtains a greater quantity of commodities of which the cost of production is not

[a]48, 49 his   [b]48, 49 his

lowered, he obtains a greater cost; his money wages are higher. The expense of these increased money wages falls wholly on the capitalist. There are no conceivable means by which he can shake it off. It may be said—it ^cis, not unfrequently,^c said—that he will get rid of it by raising his price. But this opinion we have already, and more than once, fully refuted.*

The doctrine, indeed, that a rise of wages causes an equivalent rise of prices, is, as we formerly observed, self-contradictory: for if it did so, it would not be a rise of wages; the labourer would get no more of any commodity than he had before, let his money wages rise ever so much; a rise of real wages would be an impossibility. This being equally contrary to reason and to fact, it is evident that a rise of money wages does not raise prices; that high wages are not a cause of high prices. A rise of general wages falls on profits. There is no possible alternative.

Having disposed of the case in which the increase of money wages, and of the Cost of Labour, arises from the labourer's obtaining more ample wages in kind, let us now suppose it to arise from the increased cost of production of the things which he consumes; owing to an increase of population, unaccompanied by an equivalent increase of agricultural skill. The augmented supply required by the population would not be obtained, unless the price of food rose sufficiently to remunerate the farmer for the increased cost of production. The farmer, however, in this case sustains a twofold disadvantage. He has to carry on his cultivation under less favourable conditions of productiveness than before. For this, as it is a disadvantage belonging to him only as a farmer, and not shared by other employers, he will, on the general principles of value, be compensated by a rise of the price of his commodity: indeed, until this rise has taken place, he will not bring to market the required increase of produce. But this very rise of price involves him in another necessity, for which he is not compensated. ^dAs the real wages of labour are by supposition unaltered, he^d must pay higher money wages to his labourers. This necessity, being common to him with all other capitalists, forms no ground for a rise of price. The price will rise, until it has placed him in as good a situation in respect of profits, as other employers of labour: it will rise so as to in-demnify him for the increased labour which he must now employ in order to produce a given quantity of food: but the increased wages of that labour are a burthen common to all, and for which no one can be indemnified. It will be paid wholly from profits.

Thus we see that increased wages, when common to all descriptions of productive labourers, and when really representing a greater Cost of

*Supra, book iii. ch. iv. § 2, and ch. xxv. § 4. [Pp. 479–80, 691–3.]

^{c-c}48, 49, 52, 62, 65   used formerly to be
^{d-d}48, 49, 52, 57, 62, 65   He

Labour, are always and necessarily at the expense of profits. And by reversing the cases, we should find in like manner that diminished wages, when representing a really diminished Cost of Labour, are equivalent to a rise of profits. But the opposition of pecuniary interest thus indicated between the class of capitalists and that of labourers, is to a great extent only apparent. Real wages are a very different thing from the Cost of Labour, and are generally highest at the times and places where, from the easy terms on which the land yields all the produce as yet required from it, the value and price of food being low, the cost of labour to the employer, notwithstanding its ample remuneration, is comparatively cheap, and the rate of profit consequently high *e* . We thus obtain a full confirmation of our original theorem that Profits depend on the Cost of Labour: or, to express the meaning with still greater accuracy, the rate of profit and the cost of labour vary inversely as one another, and are joint effects of the same agencies or causes.

But does not this proposition require to be slightly modified, by making allowance for that portion (though comparatively small) of the expenses of the capitalist, which does not consist in wages paid by himself or reimbursed to previous capitalists, but in the profits of those previous capitalists? Suppose, for example, an invention in the manufacture of leather, the advantage of which should consist in rendering it unnecessary that the hides should remain for so great a length of time in the tan-pit. Shoemakers, saddlers, and other workers in leather, would save a part of that portion of the cost of their material which consists of the tanner's profits during the time his capital is locked up; and this saving, it may be said, is a source from which they might derive an increase of profit, though wages and the Cost of Labour remained exactly the same. In the case here supposed, however, the consumer alone would benefit, since the prices of shoes, harness, and all other articles into which leather enters, would fall, until the profits of the producers were reduced to the general level. To obviate this objection, let us suppose that a similar saving of *ƒexpenseƒ* takes place in all departments of production at once. In that case, since values and prices would not be affected, profits would probably be raised; but if we look more closely into the case we shall find, that it is because the cost of labour would be lowered. In this as in any other case of increase in the general productiveness of labour, if the labourer obtained only the same real wages, profits would be raised: but the same real wages would imply a smaller Cost of Labour; the cost of production of all things having been, by the supposition, diminished. If, on the other hand, the real wages of labour rose proportionally, and the Cost of Labour to the

*e*48, 49, 52, 57, 62   ; as at present in the United States
*ƒ-ƒ*48, 49, 52, 57, 62, 65   expenses

employer remained the same, the advances of the capitalist would bear the same ratio to his returns as before, and the rate of profit would be unaltered. The reader who may wish for a more minute examination of this point, will find it in the volume of separate Essays to which reference has before been made.* The question is too intricate in comparison with its importance, to be further entered into in a work like the present; and I will merely say, that it seems to result from the considerations adduced in the Essay, that there is nothing in the case in question to affect the integrity of the theory which affirms an exact correspondence, in an inverse direction, between the rate of profit and the Cost of Labour.

*[Mill, J. S. *Essays on Some Unsettled Questions,*] Essay IV. on *Profits and Interest.*

BOOK IV

INFLUENCE OF THE PROGRESS OF SOCIETY
ON PRODUCTION AND DISTRIBUTION

CHAPTER I

General Characteristics
of a Progressive State of Wealth

§ 1. [*Introductory remarks*] The three preceding Parts include as detailed a view as ^aour limits^a permit, of what, by a happy generalization of a mathematical phrase, has been called the Statics of the subject. We have surveyed the field of economical facts, and have examined how they stand related to one another as causes and effects; what circumstances determine the amount of production, of employment for labour, of capital and population; what laws regulate rent, profits, and wages; under what conditions and in what proportions commodities are interchanged between individuals and between countries. We have thus obtained a collective view of the economical phenomena of society, considered as existing simultaneously. We have ascertained, to a certain extent, the principles of their interdependence; and when the state of some of the elements is known, we should now be able to infer, in a general way, the contemporaneous state of most of the others. All this, however, has only put us in possession of the economical laws of a stationary and unchanging society. We have still to consider the economical condition of mankind as liable to change, and indeed (in the more advanced portions of the race, and in all regions to which their influence reaches) as at all times undergoing progressive changes. We have to consider what these changes are, what are their laws, and what their ultimate tendencies; thereby adding a theory of motion to our theory of equilibrium—the Dynamics of political economy to the Statics.

In this inquiry, it is natural to commence by tracing the operation of known and acknowledged agencies. Whatever may be the other changes which the economy of society is destined to undergo, there is one actually in progress, concerning which there can be no dispute. In the leading countries of the world, and in all others as they come within the influence of those leading countries, there is at least one progressive movement which continues with little interruption from year to year and from generation to generation; a progress in wealth; an advancement ^bof^b what is called

---

^{a–a}48, 49   the limits of this Treatise
^{b–b}48, 49, 52, 57, 62   in

material prosperity. All the nations which we are accustomed to call civilized, increase gradually in production and in population: and there is no reason to doubt, that not only these nations will for some time continue so to increase, but that most of the other nations of the world, including some not yet founded, will successively enter upon the same career. It will, therefore, be our first object to examine the nature and consequences of this progressive change; the elements which constitute it, and the effects it produces on the various economical facts of which we have been tracing the laws, and especially on wages, profits, rents, values, and prices.

§ 2. [*Tendency of the progress of society towards increased command over the powers of nature; increased security; and increased capacity of co-operation*] Of the features which characterize this progressive economical movement of civilized nations, that which first excites attention, through its intimate connexion with the phenomena of Production, is the perpetual, and so far as human foresight can extend, the unlimited, growth of man's power over nature. Our knowledge of the properties and laws of physical objects shows no sign of approaching its ultimate boundaries: it is advancing more rapidly, and in a greater number of directions at once, than in any previous age or generation, and affording such frequent glimpses of unexplored fields beyond, as to justify the belief that our acquaintance with nature is still almost in its infancy. This increasing physical knowledge is now, too, more rapidly than at any former period, converted, by practical ingenuity, into physical power. The most marvellous of modern inventions, one which realizes the imaginary feats of the magician, not metaphorically but literally—the electro-magnetic telegraph— *a*sprang*a* into existence but a few years after the establishment of the scientific theory which it realizes and exemplifies. Lastly, the manual part of these great scientific operations is now never wanting to the intellectual: there is no difficulty in finding or forming, in a sufficient number of the working hands of the community, the *b*skill requisite*b* for executing the most delicate processes of the application of science to practical uses. From this union of conditions, it is impossible not to look forward to a vast multiplication and long succession of contrivances for economizing labour and increasing its produce; and to an ever wider diffusion of the use and benefit of those contrivances.

Another change, which has always hitherto characterized, and will assuredly continue to characterize, the progress of civilized society, is a continual increase of the security of person and property. The people of every country in Europe, the most backward as well as the most advanced,

*a–a*48, 49   sprung
*b–b*48, 49   requisite skill, combined with the requisite intelligence,

are, in each generation, better protected against the violence and rapacity of one another, both by a more efficient judicature and police for the suppression of private crime, and by the decay and destruction of those mischievous privileges which enabled certain classes of the community to prey with impunity upon the rest. They are also, in every generation, better protected, either by institutions or by manners and opinion, against *c* arbitrary exercise of the power of government. Even in semi-barbarous Russia, acts of spoliation directed against individuals, who have not made themselves politically obnoxious, are not *d*supposed to be*d* now so frequent as much to affect any person's feelings of security. Taxation, in all European countries, grows less arbitrary and oppressive, both in itself and in the manner of levying it. Wars, and the destruction they cause, are now *e*usually*e* confined, in almost every country, to those distant and outlying possessions at which it comes into contact with savages. Even the vicissitudes of fortune which arise from inevitable natural calamities, are more and more softened to those on whom they fall, by the continual extension of the salutary practice of insurance.

Of this increased security, one of the most unfailing effects is a great increase both of production and of accumulation. Industry and frugality cannot exist, where there is not a preponderant probability that those who labour and spare will be permitted to enjoy. And the nearer this probability approaches to *f* certainty, the more do industry and frugality become pervading qualities in a people. Experience has shown that a large proportion of the results of labour and abstinence may be taken away by fixed taxation, without impairing, and sometimes even with the effect of stimulating, the qualities from which a great production and an abundant capital take their rise. But those qualities are not proof against a high degree of uncertainty. *g*The Government*g* may carry off a part; but there must be assurance that *h*it*h* will not interfere, nor suffer any one to interfere, with the remainder.

One of the changes which most infallibly attend the progress of modern society, is an improvement in the business capacities of the general mass of mankind. I do not mean that the practical sagacity of an individual human being is greater than formerly. I am inclined to believe that economical progress has hitherto had even a contrary effect. A person of good natural endowments, in a rude state of society, can do a *i*great*i* number of things *j*tolerably*j* well, has a greater power of adapting means to ends, is more capable of extricating himself and others from an unforeseen em-

*c*48, 49   the
e-e+57, 62, 65, 71
*g-g*48, 49   You
*i-i*48, 49, 52, 57, 62   greater

d-d+52, 57, 62, 65, 71
*f*48, 49, 52, 57, 62   a
*h-h*48, 49   you
j-j+57, 62, 65, 71

barrassment, than ninety-nine in a hundred of those who have known only
[k]what is called[k] the civilized form of life. How far these points of inferiority
of faculties are compensated, and by what means they might be compensated still more completely, to the civilized man as an individual being,
is a question belonging to a different inquiry from the present. But to
civilized human beings collectively considered, the compensation is ample.
What is lost in the separate [l] efficiency of each, is far more than made up
by [m]the[m] greater capacity of united action. In [n] proportion as they put off
the qualities of the savage, they become amenable to discipline; capable
of adhering to plans concerted beforehand, and about which they may not
have been consulted; of subordinating their individual caprice to a preconceived determination, and performing severally the parts allotted to
them in a combined undertaking. Works of all sorts, impracticable to the
savage or the half-civilized, are daily accomplished by civilized nations,
not by any greatness of faculties in the actual agents, but through the
[o] fact that each is able to rely with certainty on the others for the portion
of the work which they respectively undertake. The peculiar characteristic,
in short, of civilized beings, is the capacity of co-operation; and this, like
other faculties, tends to improve by practice, and becomes capable of
assuming a constantly wider sphere of action.

   Accordingly there is no more certain incident of the progressive change
taking place in society, than the continual growth of the principle and
practice of co-operation. Associations of individuals voluntarily combining
their small contributions, now perform works, both of an industrial and
of many other characters, which no one person or small number of persons
are rich enough to accomplish, or for the performance of which the few
persons capable of accomplishing them were formerly enabled to exact
the most inordinate remuneration. As wealth increases and business
capacity improves, we may look forward to a great extension of establishments, both for industrial and other purposes, formed by the collective
contributions of large numbers; establishments like those [p]called[p] by the
technical name of joint-stock companies, or the associations less formally
constituted, which are so numerous in England, to raise funds for public
or philanthropic objects [q], or, lastly, those associations of workpeople
either for production, or to buy goods for their common consumption,
which are now specially known by the name of co-operative societies[q].

   The progress which is to be expected in the physical sciences and arts,
combined with the greater security of property, and greater freedom in

[k]-[k]+52, 57, 62, 65, 71
[l]48, 49   bodily and mental
[n]48, 49   exact
[p]-[p]48, 49, 52, 57, 62   known

[m]-[m]48, 49, 52   their
[o]48, 49, 52   simple
[q]-[q]+65, 71

disposing of it, which are obvious features in the civilization of modern nations, and with the more extensive and more skilful employment of the joint-stock principle, afford space and scope for an indefinite increase of capital and production, and for the increase of population which is its ordinary accompaniment. That the growth of population will overpass the increase of production, there is not much reason to apprehend; and that it should even keep pace with it, is inconsistent with the supposition of any real improvement in the poorest classes of the people. It is, however, quite possible that there might be a great progress in industrial improvement, and in the signs of what is commonly called national prosperity; a great increase of aggregate wealth, and even, in some respects, a better distribution of it; that not only the rich might grow richer, but many of the poor might grow rich, that the intermediate classes might become more numerous and powerful, and the means of enjoyable existence be more and more largely diffused, while yet the great class at the base of the whole might increase in numbers only, and not in comfort nor in cultivation. We must, therefore, in considering the effects of the progress of industry, admit as a supposition, however greatly we deprecate as a fact, an increase of population as long-continued, as indefinite, and possibly even as rapid, as the increase of production and accumulation.

With these preliminary observations on the causes of change at work in a society which is in a state of economical progress, I proceed to a more detailed examination of the changes themselves.

CHAPTER II

Influence of the Progress
of Industry and Population
on Values and Prices

§ 1. [*Tendency to a decline of the value and cost of production of all commodities*] The changes which the progress of industry causes or pre-supposes in the circumstances of production, are necessarily attended with changes in the values of commodities.

The permanent values of all things which are neither under a natural, nor under an artificial monopoly, depend, as we have seen, on their cost of production. But the increasing power which mankind are constantly acquiring over nature, increases more and more the efficiency of human exertion, or in other words, diminishes cost of production. All inventions by which a greater quantity of any commodity can be produced with the same labour, or the same quantity with less labour, or which abridge the process, so that the capital employed needs not be advanced for so long a time, lessen the cost of production of the commodity. As, however, value is relative; if inventions and improvements in production were made in all commodities, and all in the same degree, there would be no altera-tion in values. Things would continue to exchange for each other at the same rates as before; and mankind would obtain a greater quantity of all things in return for their labour and abstinence, without having that greater abundance measured and declared (as it is when it affects only one thing) by the diminished exchange value of the commodity.

As for prices, in these circumstances they would be affected or not, according as the improvements in production did or did not extend to the precious metals. If the materials of money were an exception to the general diminution of cost of production, the values of all other things would fall in relation to money, that is there would be a fall of general prices throughout the world. But if money, like other things, and in the same degree as other things, were obtained in greater abundance and cheapness, prices would be no more affected than values would: and there would be no visible sign in the state of the markets, of any of the changes which had taken place; except that there would be (if people continued to labour as much as before) a greater quantity of all sorts of commodities, circulated at the same prices by a greater quantity of money.

Improvements in production are not the only circumstance accompanying the progress of industry, which tends to diminish the cost of producing, or at least of obtaining, commodities. Another circumstance is the increase of intercourse between different parts of the world. As commerce extends, and the ignorant attempts to restrain it by tariffs become obsolete, commodities tend more and more to be produced in the places in which their production can be carried on at the least expense of labour and capital to mankind. As civilization spreads, and security of person and property becomes established, in parts of the world which have not hitherto had that advantage, the productive capabilities of those places are called into fuller activity, for the benefit both of their own inhabitants and of foreigners. The ignorance and misgovernment in which many of the regions most favoured by nature are still grovelling, afford work, probably, for many generations before those countries *will* be raised even to the present level of the most civilized parts of Europe. Much will also depend on the increasing migration of labour and capital to unoccupied parts of the earth, of which the soil, climate, and situation are found, by the ample means of exploration now possessed, to promise not only a large return to industry, but great facilities of producing commodities suited to the markets of old countries. Much as the collective industry of the earth is likely to be increased in efficiency by the extension of science and of the industrial arts, a still more active source of increased cheapness of production will be found, probably, for some time to come, in the gradually unfolding consequences of Free Trade, and in the increasing scale on which Emigration and Colonization will be carried on.

From the causes now enumerated, unless counteracted by others, the progress of things enables a country to obtain at less and less of real cost, not only its own productions but those of foreign countries. Indeed, whatever diminishes the cost of its own productions, when of an exportable character, enables it, as we have already seen, to obtain its imports at less real cost.

§ 2. [*Tendency to a decline of the value and cost of production of all commodities except the products of agriculture and mining, which have a tendency to rise*] But is it the fact, that these tendencies are not counteracted? Has the progress of wealth and industry no effect in regard to cost of production, but to diminish it? Are no causes of an opposite character

*a–a*48   can

brought into operation by the same progress, sufficient in some cases not only to neutralize, but to overcome the former, and convert the descending movement of cost of production into an ascending movement? We are already aware that there are such causes, and that, in the case of the most important classes of commodities, food and materials, there is a tendency diametrically opposite to that of which we have been speaking. The cost of production of these commodities tends to increase.

This is not a property inherent in the commodities themselves. If population were stationary, and the produce of the earth never needed to be augmented in quantity, there would be no cause for greater cost of production. Mankind would, on the contrary, have the full benefit of all improvements in agriculture, or in the arts subsidiary to it, and there would be no difference, in this respect, between the products of agriculture and those of manufactures. *a* The only products of industry, which, if population did not increase, would be liable to a real increase of cost of production, are those which, depending on a material which is not renewed, are either wholly or partially exhaustible; such as coal, and most if not all metals; for even iron, the most abundant as well as most useful of metallic products, which forms an ingredient of most minerals and of almost all rocks, is susceptible of exhaustion so far as regards its richest and most tractable ores.

When, however, population increases, as it has never yet failed to do when the increase of industry and of the means of subsistence *b*made*b* room for it, the demand for most of the productions of the earth, and particularly for food, increases in a corresponding proportion. And then comes into effect that fundamental law of production from the soil, on which we have so frequently had occasion to expatiate; the law, that increased labour, in any given state of agricultural skill, is attended with a less than proportional increase of produce. The cost of production of the fruits of the earth increases, *cæteris paribus*, with every increase of the demand.

No tendency of a like kind exists with respect to manufactured articles. The tendency is in the contrary direction. The larger the scale on which manufacturing operations are carried on, the more cheaply they can in general be performed. Mr. Senior has gone the length of enunciating as an inherent law of manufacturing industry, that in it increased production takes place at a smaller cost, while in agricultural industry increased production takes place at a greater cost. I cannot think, however, that even

---

*a*48   The former, indeed, so far as present foresight can extend, does not seem to be susceptible of improved processes to so great a degree as some branches of manufacture; but inventions may be in reserve for the future, which may invert this relation.] 49   *as* 48 . . . degree by . . . *as* 48] 52   *as* 48 . . . present experience extends, has not seemed . . . *as* 49] 57   *as* 52 . . . degree as . . . *as* 48
    *b–b*48, 49   makes

in manufactures, increased cheapness follows increased production by anything amounting to a law. It is a probable and usual, but not a necessary, consequence.

As manufactures, however, depend for their materials either upon agriculture, or mining, or the spontaneous produce of the earth, manufacturing industry is subject, in respect of one of its essentials, to the same law as agriculture. But the crude material generally forms so small a portion of the total cost, that any tendency which may exist to a progressive increase in that single item, is much over-balanced by the diminution continually taking place in all the other elements; to which diminution it is impossible at present to assign any limit.

The tendency, then, being to a perpetual increase of the productive power of labour in manufactures, while in agriculture and mining there is a conflict between two tendencies, the one towards an increase of productive power, the other towards a diminution of it, the cost of production being lessened by every improvement in the *c*processes*c*, and augmented by every addition to population; it follows that the exchange values of manufactured articles, compared with the products of agriculture and of mines, have, as population and industry advance, a certain and decided tendency to fall. Money being a product of mines, it may also be laid down as a rule, that manufactured articles tend, as society advances, to fall in money price. The industrial history of modern nations, especially during the last hundred years, fully bears out this assertion.

§ 3. [*That tendency from time to time is counteracted by improvements in production*] Whether agricultural produce increases in absolute as well as comparative cost of production, depends on the conflict of the two antagonist agencies, increase of population, and improvement in agricultural skill. In some, perhaps in most, states of society, (looking at the whole surface of the earth,) both agricultural skill and population are either stationary, or increase very slowly, and the cost of production of food, therefore, is nearly stationary. In a society which is advancing in wealth, population generally increases faster than agricultural skill, and food consequently tends to become more costly; but there are times when a strong impulse sets in towards agricultural improvement. Such an impulse has shown itself in Great Britain during the last *a*twenty or thirty*a* years. In England and Scotland agricultural skill has of late increased considerably faster than population, insomuch that food and other agricultural produce, notwithstanding the increase of people, can be grown at less cost than they were thirty years ago: and the abolition of the Corn Laws has given

*c-c*48, 49   process
*a-a*48, 49, 52, 57, 62   fifteen or twenty] 65   twenty or five-and-twenty

an additional stimulus to the spirit of improvement. In some other countries, and particularly in France, the improvement of agriculture gains ground still more decidedly upon population, because though agriculture, except in a few provinces, advances slowly, population advances still more slowly, and even with increasing slowness; its growth being kept down, not by poverty, which is diminishing, but by prudence.

Which of the two conflicting agencies is gaining upon the other at any particular time, might be conjectured with tolerable accuracy from the money price of agricultural produce (supposing bullion not to vary materially in value), provided a sufficient number of years could be taken, to form an average independent of the fluctuations of seasons. This, however, is hardly practicable, since Mr. Tooke has shown that even so long a period as half a century may include a much greater proportion of abundant and a smaller of deficient seasons than is properly due to it. A mere average, therefore, might lead to conclusions only the more misleading, for their deceptive semblance of accuracy. There would be less danger of error in taking the average of only a small number of years, and correcting it by a conjectural allowance for the character of the seasons, than in trusting to a longer average without any such correction. It is hardly necessary to add, that in founding conclusions on quoted prices, allowance must also be made as far as possible for any changes in the general exchange value of the precious metals.*

§ 4. [*Effect of the progress of society in moderating fluctuations of value*] Thus far, of the effect of the progress of society on the permanent or average values and prices of commodities. It remains to be considered, in what manner the same progress affects their fluctuations. Concerning the answer to this question there can be no doubt. It tends in a very high degree to diminish them.

In poor and backward societies, as in the East, and in Europe during the Middle Ages, extraordinary differences in the price of the same commodity might exist in places not very distant from each other, because the want of roads and canals, the imperfection of marine navigation, and the insecurity of communications generally, prevented things from being transported from the places where they were cheap to those where they were dear. The things most liable to fluctuations in value, those directly influenced by the seasons, and especially food, were seldom carried to any great distances. Each locality depended, as a general rule, on its own produce and that of its immediate neighbourhood. In most years,

*[52] A still better criterion, perhaps, than that suggested in the text, would be the increase or diminution of the amount of the labourer's wages estimated in agricultural produce.

accordingly, there was, in some part or other of any large country, a real dearth. Almost every season must be unpropitious to some among the many soils and climates to be found in an extensive tract of country; but as the same season is also in general more than ordinarily favourable to others, it is only occasionally that the aggregate produce of the whole country is deficient, and even then in a less degree than that of many separate portions; while a deficiency at all considerable, extending to the whole world, is a thing almost unknown. In modern times, therefore, there is only dearth, where there formerly would have been famine, and sufficiency everywhere when anciently there would have been scarcity in some places and superfluity in others.

The same change has taken place with respect to all other articles of commerce. The safety and cheapness of communications, which enable a deficiency in one place to be supplied from the surplus of another, at a moderate or even a small advance on the ordinary price, render the fluctuations of prices much less extreme than formerly. This effect is much promoted by the existence of large capitals, belonging to what are called speculative merchants, whose business it is to buy goods in order to *resell* them at a profit. These dealers naturally buying things when they are cheapest, and storing them up to be brought again into the market when the price has become unusually high; the tendency of their operations is to equalize price, or at least to moderate its inequalities. The prices of things are neither so much depressed at one time, nor so much raised at another, as they would be if speculative dealers did not exist.

Speculators, therefore, have a highly useful office in the economy of society; and (contrary to common opinion) the most useful portion of the class are those who speculate in commodities affected by the vicissitudes of seasons. If there were no corn-dealers, not only would the price of corn be liable to variations much more extreme than at present, but in a deficient season the necessary supplies might not be forthcoming at all. Unless there were speculators in corn, or unless, in default of dealers, the farmers became speculators, the price in a season of abundance would fall without any limit or check, except the wasteful consumption that would invariably follow. That any part of the surplus of one year remains to supply the deficiency of another, is owing either to farmers who withhold corn from the market, or to dealers who buy it when at the cheapest and lay it up in store.

§ 5. [*Examination of the influence of speculators, and in particular of corn-dealers*] Among persons who have not much considered the subject, there is a notion that the gains of speculators are often made by causing

*a-a*57   sell

an artificial scarcity; that they create a high price by their own purchases, and then profit by it. This may easily be shown to be fallacious. If a corndealer makes purchases on speculation, and produces a rise, when there is neither at the time nor afterwards any cause for a rise of price except his own proceedings; he no doubt appears to grow richer as long as his purchases continue, because he is a holder of an article which is quoted at a higher and higher price: but this apparent gain only seems within his reach so long as he does not attempt to realize it. If he has bought, for instance, a million of quarters, and by withholding them from the market, has raised the price ten shillings a quarter; just so much as the price has been raised by withdrawing a million quarters, will it be lowered by bringing them back, and the best that he can hope is that he will lose nothing except interest and his expenses. If by a gradual and cautious sale he is able to realize, on some portion of his stores, a part of the increased price, so also he will undoubtedly have had to pay *a part of* that price on some portion of his purchases. He runs considerable risk of incurring a still greater loss; for the temporary high price is very likely to have tempted others, who had no share in causing it, and who might otherwise not have found their way to *his* market at all, to bring their corn there, and intercept a part of the advantage. So that instead of profiting by a scarcity caused by himself, he is by no means unlikely, after buying in an average market, to be forced to sell in a superabundant one.

As an individual speculator cannot gain by a rise of price solely of his own creating, so neither can a number of speculators gain collectively by a rise which their operations have artificially produced. Some among a number of speculators may gain, by superior judgment *or good fortune* in selecting the time for realizing, but they make this gain at the expense, not of the consumer, but of the other speculators who are less judicious. They, in fact, convert to their own benefit the high price produced by the speculations of the others, leaving to these the loss resulting from the recoil. It is not to be denied, therefore, that speculators may enrich themselves by other people's loss. But it is by the losses of other speculators. As much must have been lost by one set of dealers as is gained by another set.

When a speculation in a commodity proves profitable to the speculators as a body, it is because, in the interval between their buying and reselling, the price rises from some cause independent of them, their only connexion with it consisting in having foreseen it. In this case, their purchases make the price begin to rise sooner than it otherwise would do, thus spreading the privation of the consumers over a longer period, but mitigating it at the time of its greatest height: evidently to the general advantage. In this,

a–a+49, 52, 57, 62, 65, 71
b–b48, 49, 52, 57, 62   this   c–c+52, 57, 62, 65, 71

however, it is assumed that they have not overrated the rise which they looked forward to. For it often happens that speculative purchases are made in the expectation of some increase of demand, or deficiency of supply, which after all does not occur, or not to the extent which the speculator expected. In that case the speculation, instead of moderating *d*fluctuation*d*, has caused a fluctuation of price which otherwise would not have happened, or aggravated one which would. But in that case, the speculation is a losing one, to the speculators collectively, however much some individuals may gain by it. All that part of the rise of price by which it exceeds what there are independent grounds for, cannot give to the speculators as a body any benefit, since the price is as much depressed by their sales as it was raised by their purchases; and while they gain nothing by it, they lose, not only their trouble and expenses, but almost always much more, through the effects incident to the artificial rise of price, in checking consumption, and bringing forward supplies from unforeseen quarters. The operations, therefore, of speculative dealers, are useful to the public whenever profitable to themselves; and though they are sometimes injurious to the public, by heightening the fluctuations which their more usual office is to alleviate, yet whenever this happens the speculators are the greatest losers. The interest, in short, of the speculators as a body, coincides with the interest of the public; and as they can only fail to serve the public interest in proportion as they miss their own, the best way to promote the one is to leave them to pursue the other in perfect freedom.

I do not deny that speculators may aggravate a *local* scarcity. In collecting corn from the villages to supply the towns, they make the dearth penetrate into nooks and corners which might otherwise have escaped from bearing their share of it. To buy and resell in the same place, tends to alleviate scarcity; to buy in one place and resell in another, may increase it in the former of the two places, but relieves it in the latter, where the price is higher, and which, therefore, by the very supposition, is likely to be suffering more. And these sufferings always fall hardest on the poorest consumers, since the rich, by outbidding, can obtain their accustomed *e*supply*e* undiminished if they choose. To no persons, therefore, are the operations of corn-dealers on the whole so beneficial as to the poor. Accidentally and exceptionally, the poor may suffer from them: it might sometimes be more advantageous to the rural poor to have corn cheap in winter, when they are entirely dependent on it, even if the consequence were a dearth in spring, when they can perhaps obtain partial substitutes. But there are no substitutes, procurable at that season, which serve in any great degree to replace bread-corn as the chief article of food: if there

*d–d*48, 49, 52, 57, 62, 65   fluctuations
*e–e*48, 49   ration

were, its price would fall in the spring, instead of continuing, as it always does, to rise till the approach of harvest.

There is an opposition of immediate interest, at the moment of sale, between the dealer in corn and the consumer, as there always is between the seller and the buyer: and a time of dearth being that in which the speculator makes his largest profits, he is an object of dislike and jealousy at that time, to those who are suffering while he is gaining. It is an error, however, to suppose that the corn-dealer's business affords him any extraordinary profit: he makes his gains not constantly, but at particular times, and they must therefore occasionally be great, but the chances of profit in a business in which there is so much competition, cannot on the whole be greater than in other employments. A year of scarcity, in which great gains are made by corn-dealers, rarely comes to an end without a recoil which places many of them in the list of bankrupts. There have been few more promising seasons for corn-dealers than the year 1847, and seldom was there a greater break-up among the speculators than in the autumn of that year. The chances of failure, in this most precarious trade, are a set off against great occasional profits. If the corn-dealer were to sell his stores, during a dearth, at a lower price than that which the competition of the consumers assigns to him, he would make a sacrifice, to charity or philanthropy, of the fair profits of his employment, which may be quite as reasonably required from any other person of equal means. His business being a useful one, it is the interest of the public that the ordinary motives should exist for carrying it on, and that neither law nor opinion should prevent an operation beneficial to the public from being attended with as much private advantage as is compatible with full and free competition.

It appears, then, that the fluctuations of values and prices arising from variations of supply, or from alterations in real (as distinguished from speculative) demand, may be expected to become more moderate as society advances. With regard to those which arise from miscalculation, and especially from the alternations of undue expansion and excessive contraction of credit, which occupy so conspicuous a place among commercial phenomena, the same thing cannot be affirmed with equal confidence. Such vicissitudes, beginning with irrational speculation and ending with a commercial crisis, have not hitherto become either less frequent or less violent with the growth of capital and extension of industry. Rather they may be said to have become more so: in consequence, as is often said, of increased competition; but, as I prefer to say, of a low rate of profits and interest, which ʰmakesʰ capitalists dissatisfied with the ordinary course of safe mercantile gains. The connexion of this low rate of profit with the advance of population and accumulation, is one of the points to be illustrated in the ensuing chapters.

*1-1*52, 57   make

CHAPTER III

Influence of the Progress
of Industry and Population, on
Rents, Profits, and Wages

§ 1. [*First case; population increasing, capital stationary*] Continuing the inquiry into the nature of the economical changes taking place in a society which is in a state of industrial progress, we shall next consider what is the effect of that progress on the distribution of the produce among the various classes *ᵃwhoᵃ* share in it. We may confine our attention to the system of distribution which is the most complex, and which virtually includes all others—that in which the produce of manufactures is shared between two classes, labourers and capitalists, and the produce of agriculture among three, labourers, capitalists, and landlords.

The characteristic features of what is commonly meant by industrial progress, resolve themselves mainly into three, increase of capital, increase of population, and improvements in production; understanding the last expression in its widest sense, to include the process of procuring commodities from a distance, as well as that of producing them. The other changes which take place are chiefly consequences of these; as, for example, the tendency to a progressive increase of the cost of production of food; *ᵇarisingᵇ* from an increased demand, *ᶜwhich may beᶜ* occasioned either by increased population, or by an increase of capital and wages, enabling the poorer classes to increase their consumption. It will be convenient to set out by considering each of the three causes, as operating separately; after which we can suppose them combined in any manner we think fit.

Let us first suppose that population increases, capital and the arts of production remaining stationary. One of the effects of this change of circumstances is sufficiently obvious: wages will fall; the labouring class will be reduced to an inferior condition. The state of the capitalist, on the contrary, will be improved. With the same capital, he can purchase more labour, and obtain more produce. His rate of profit is increased. The

ᵃ⁻ᵃ48, 49 which   ᵇ⁻ᵇ48, 49 which arises   ᶜ⁻ᶜ+52, 57, 62, 65, 71

dependence of the rate of profits on the cost of labour is here verified; for the labourer obtaining a diminished quantity of commodities, and no alteration being supposed in the circumstances of their production, the diminished quantity represents a diminished cost. The labourer obtains not only a smaller real reward, but the product of a smaller quantity of labour. The first circumstance is the important one to himself, the last to his employer.

Nothing has occurred, thus far, to affect in any way the value of any commodity; and no reason, therefore, has yet shown itself, why rent should be either raised or lowered. But if we look forward another stage in the series of effects, we may see our way to such a consequence. The labourers have increased in numbers: their condition is reduced in the same proportion; the increased numbers divide among them only the produce of the same amount of labour as before. But they may economize in their other comforts, and not in their food: each may consume as much food, and of as costly a quality as previously; or they may submit to a reduction, but not in proportion to the increase of numbers. On this supposition, notwithstanding the diminution of real wages, the increased population will require an increased quantity of food. But since industrial skill and knowledge are supposed to be stationary, more food can only be obtained by resorting to worse land, or to methods of cultivation which are less productive in proportion to the outlay. Capital for this extension of agriculture will not be wanting; for though, by hypothesis, no addition takes place to the capital in existence, a sufficient amount can be spared from the industry which previously supplied the other and less pressing wants which the labourers have been obliged to curtail. The additional supply of food, therefore, will be produced, but produced at a greater cost; and the exchange value of agricultural produce must rise. It may be objected, that profits having risen, the extra cost of producing food can be defrayed from profits, without any increase of price. It could, undoubtedly, but it will not ^{d}; because^{d} if it did, the agriculturist would be placed in an inferior position to other capitalists. The increase of profits, being the effect of diminished wages, is common to all employers of labour. The increased expenses arising from the necessity of a more costly cultivation, affect the agriculturist alone. For this peculiar burthen he must be peculiarly compensated, whether the general rate of profit be high or low. He will not submit indefinitely to a deduction from his profits, to which other capitalists are not subject. He will not extend his cultivation by laying out fresh capital, unless for a return sufficient to yield him as high a profit as could be obtained by the same capital in other investments. The value, therefore, of his commodity will rise, and rise in proportion to the increased cost. The farmer will thus be indemnified for the burthen which is peculiar to

$^{d-d}$48, 49   . Why? Because

himself, and will also enjoy the augmented rate of profit which is common to all capitalists.

It follows, from principles with which we are already familiar, that in these circumstances rent will rise. Any land can afford to pay, and under free competition will pay, a rent equal to the excess of its produce above the return to an equal capital on the worst land, or under the least favourable conditions. Whenever, therefore, agriculture is driven to descend to worse land, or more onerous processes, rent rises. Its rise will be two-fold, for, in the first place, rent in kind, or corn rent, will rise; and in the second, since the value of agricultural produce has also risen, rent, estimated in manufactured or foreign commodities (which is represented, *cæteris paribus*, by money rent) will rise still more.

The steps of the process (if, after what has been formerly said, it is necessary to retrace them) are as follows. Corn rises in price, to repay with the ordinary profit the capital required for producing additional corn on worse land or by more costly processes. So far as regards this additional corn, the increased price is but an equivalent for the additional expense; but the rise, extending to all corn, affords on all, except the last produced, an extra profit. If the farmer was accustomed to produce 100 quarters of wheat at 40*s*., and 120 quarters are now required, of which the last twenty cannot be produced under 45*s*., he obtains the extra five shillings on the entire 120 quarters, and not on the last twenty alone. He has thus an extra 25*l*. beyond the ordinary profits, and this, in a state of free competition, he will not be able to retain. He cannot however be compelled to give it up to the consumer, since a less price than 45*s*. would be inconsistent with the production of the last twenty quarters. The price, then, will remain at 45*s*., and the 25*l*. will be transferred by competition not to the consumer but to the landlord. A rise of *e*rents*e* is therefore inevitably consequent on an increased demand for agricultural produce, when unaccompanied by increased facilities for its production. A truth which, after this final illustration, *f*we may henceforth*f* take for granted.

The new element now introduced—an increased demand for food—besides occasioning an increase of rent, still further disturbs the distribution of the produce between capitalists and labourers. The increase of population will have diminished the reward of labour: and if its cost *g*is*g* diminished as greatly as its real remuneration, profits will be increased by the full amount. If, however, the increase of population leads to an increased production of food, which cannot be supplied but at an enhanced cost of production, the cost of labour will not be so much diminished as the real reward of it, and profits, therefore, will not be so much raised. It

---

*e–e*48, 49, 52, 57, 62, 65   rent
*f–f*48, 49   I may be permitted henceforth to
*g–g*48, 49   was

is even possible that they might not be raised at all. The labourers may previously have been so well provided for, that the whole of what they now lose may be struck off from their other indulgences, and they may not, either by necessity or choice, undergo any reduction in the quantity or quality of their food. To produce the food for the increased number may be attended with such an increase of expense, that wages, though reduced in quantity, may represent as great a cost, may be the product of as much labour, as before, and the capitalist may not be at all benefited. On this supposition the loss to the labourer is partly absorbed in the additional labour required for producing the last instalment of agricultural produce; and the remainder is gained by the landlord, the only sharer who always benefits by an increase of population.

§ 2. [*Second case; capital increasing, population stationary*] Let us now reverse our hypothesis, and instead of supposing capital stationary and population advancing, let us suppose capital advancing and population stationary; the facilities of production, both natural and acquired, being, as before, unaltered. The real wages of labour, instead of falling, will now rise; and since the cost of production of the things consumed by the labourer is not diminished, this rise of wages implies an equivalent increase of the cost of labour, and diminution of profits. To state the same deduction in other terms; the labourers not being more numerous, and the productive power of their labour being only the same as before, there is no increase of the produce; the increase of wages, therefore, must be at the charge of the capitalist. It is not impossible that the cost of labour might be increased in even a greater ratio than its real remuneration. The improved condition of the labourers may increase the demand for food. The labourers may have been so ill off before, as not to have food enough; and may now consume more: or they may choose to expend their increased means partly or wholly in a more costly quality of food, requiring more labour and more land; wheat, for example, instead of oats, or potatoes. This extension of agriculture implies, as usual, a greater cost of production and a higher price, so that besides the increase of the cost of labour arising from the increase of its reward, there will be a further increase (and an additional fall of profits) from the increased costliness of the commodities of which that reward consists. The same causes will produce a rise of rent. What the capitalists lose, above what the labourers gain, is partly transferred to the landlord, and partly swallowed up in the cost of growing food on worse land or by a less productive process.

§ 3. [*Third case; population and capital increasing equally, the arts of production stationary*] Having disposed of the two simple cases, an increasing population and stationary capital, and an increasing capital and stationary population, we are prepared to take into consideration the mixed case, in which the two elements of expansion are combined, both population and capital increasing. If either element increases faster than the other, the case is so far assimilated with one or other of the two preceding: we shall suppose them, therefore, to increase with equal rapidity; the test of equality being, that each labourer obtains the same commodities as before, and the same quantity of those commodities. Let us examine what will be the effect, on rent and profits, of this double progress.

Population having increased, without any falling off in the *a*labourer's*a* condition, there is of course a demand for more food. The arts of production being supposed stationary, this food must be produced at an increased cost. To compensate for this greater cost of the additional food, the price of agricultural produce must rise. The rise extending over the whole amount of food produced, though the increased expenses only apply to a part, there is a greatly increased extra profit, which, by competition, is transferred to the landlord. Rent will rise both in quantity of produce and in cost; while wages, being supposed to be the same in quantity, will be greater in cost. The labourer obtaining the same amount of necessaries, money wages have risen; and as the rise is common to all branches of production, the capitalist cannot indemnify himself by changing his employment, and the loss must be borne by profits.

It appears, then, that the tendency of an increase of capital and population is to add to rent at the expense of profits: though rent does not gain all that profits lose, a part being absorbed in increased expenses of production, that is, in hiring or feeding a greater number of labourers to obtain a given amount of agricultural produce. By profits, must of course be understood the *rate* of profit; for a lower rate of profit on a larger capital may yield a larger pross profit, considered absolutely, though a smaller in proportion to the entire produce.

This tendency of profits to fall, is from time to time counteracted by improvements in production: whether arising from increase of knowledge, or from an increased use of the knowledge already possessed. This is the third of the three elements, the effects of which on the distribution of the produce we undertook to investigate; and the investigation will be facilitated by supposing, as in the case of the other two elements, that it operates, in the first instance, alone.

§ 4. [*Fourth case; the arts of production progressive, capital and population stationary*] Let us then suppose capital and population stationary, and a sudden improvement made in the arts of production; by the in-

*a–a*48, 49   labourers'

vention of more efficient machines, or less costly processes, or by obtaining access to cheaper commodities through foreign trade.

The improvement may either be in some of the necessaries or indulgences which enter into the habitual consumption of the labouring class; or it may be applicable only to luxuries consumed exclusively by richer people. Very few, however, of the great industrial improvements are altogether of this last description. Agricultural improvements, except such as specially relate to some of the rarer and more peculiar products, act directly upon the principal objects of the labourer's expenditure. The steam-engine, and every other invention which affords a manageable power, are applicable to all things, and of course to those consumed by the labourer. Even the power-loom and the spinning-jenny, though applied to the most delicate fabrics, are available no less for the coarse cottons and woollens worn by the labouring class. All improvements in locomotion cheapen the transport of necessaries as well as of luxuries. Seldom is a new branch of trade opened, without, either directly or in some indirect way, causing some of the articles which the mass of the people consume to be either produced or imported at smaller cost. It may safely be affirmed, therefore, that improvements in production generally tend to cheapen the commodities on which the wages of the labouring class are expended.

In so far as the commodities affected by an improvement are those which the labourers generally do not consume, the improvement has no effect in altering the distribution of the produce. Those particular commodities, indeed, are cheapened; being produced at less cost, they fall in value and in price, and all who consume them, whether landlords, capitalists, or skilled and privileged labourers, obtain increased means of enjoyment. The rate of profits, however, is not raised. There is a larger gross profit, reckoned in quantity of commodities. But the capital also, if estimated in those commodities, has risen in value. The profit is the same percentage on the capital that it was before. The capitalists are not benefited as capitalists, but as consumers. The landlords and the privileged *classes* of labourers, if they are consumers of the same commodities, share the same benefit.

The case is different with improvements which diminish the cost of production of the necessaries of life, or of commodities which enter habitually into the consumption of the great mass of labourers. The play of the different forces being here rather complex, it is necessary to analyse it with some minuteness.

As formerly observed,* there are two kinds of agricultural improvements. Some consist in a mere saving of labour, and enable a given

*Supra, vol. i. p. 180.

*a–a*48   class

quantity of food to be produced at less cost, but not on a smaller surface of land than before. Others enable a given extent of land to yield not only the same produce with less labour, but a greater produce; so that if no greater produce is required, a part of the land already under culture may be dispensed with. As the part rejected will be the least productive portion, the market will thenceforth be regulated by a better description of land than what was previously the worst under cultivation.

To place the effect of the improvement in a clear light, we must suppose it to take place suddenly, so as to leave no time during its introduction, for any increase of capital or of population. Its first effect will be a fall of the value and price of agricultural produce. This is a necessary consequence of either kind of improvement, but especially of the last.

An improvement of the first kind, not increasing the produce, does not dispense with any portion of the land; the margin of cultivation (as Dr. Chalmers terms it) remains where it was; agriculture does not recede, either in extent of cultivated land, or in elaborateness of ᵇmethodᵇ: and the price continues to be regulated by the same land, and by the same capital, as before. But since that land or capital, and all other land or capital which produces food, now yields its produce at smaller cost, the price of food will fall proportionally. If one-tenth of the expense of production has been saved, the price of produce will fall one-tenth.

But suppose the improvement to be of the second kind; enabling the land to produce, not only the same corn with one-tenth less labour, but a tenth more corn with the same labour. Here the effect is still more decided. Cultivation can now be contracted, and the market supplied from a smaller quantity of land. Even if this smaller surface of land were of the same average quality as the larger surface, the price would fall one-tenth, because the same produce would be obtained with a tenth less labour. But since the portion of land abandoned will be the least fertile portion, the price of produce will thenceforth be regulated by a better quality of land than before. In addition, therefore, to the original diminution of one-tenth in the cost of production, there will be a further diminution, corresponding with the recession of the "margin" of agriculture to land of greater fertility. There will thus be a twofold fall of price.

Let us now examine the effect of the improvements, thus suddenly made, on the division of the produce; and in the first place, on rent. By the former of the two kinds of improvement, rent would be diminished. By the second, it would be diminished still more.

Suppose that the demand for food requires the cultivation of three qualities of land, yielding, on an equal surface, and at an equal expense, 100, 80, and 60 bushels of wheat. The price of wheat will, on the average,

ᵇ⁻ᵇ48, 49, 52, 57, 62   methods

be just sufficient to enable the third quality to be cultivated with the ordinary profit. The first quality therefore will yield forty and the second twenty bushels of extra profit, constituting the rent of the landlord. And first, let an improvement be made, which, without enabling more corn to be grown, enables the same corn to be grown with one-fourth less labour. The price of wheat will fall one-fourth, and 80 bushels will be sold for the price for which 60 were sold before. But the produce of the land which produces 60 bushels is still required, and the expenses being as much reduced as the price, that land can still be cultivated with the ordinary profit. The first and second qualities will therefore continue to yield a surplus of 40 and 20 bushels, and corn rent will remain the same as before. But corn having fallen in price one-fourth, the same corn rent is equivalent to a fourth less of money and of all other commodities. So far, therefore, as the landlord expends his income in manufactured or foreign products, he is one-fourth worse off than before. His income as landlord is reduced to three-quarters of its amount: it is only as a consumer of corn that he is as well off.

If the improvement is of the other kind, rent will fall in a still greater ratio. Suppose that the amount of produce which the market requires, can be grown not only with a fourth less labour, but on a fourth less ^{c} land. If all the land already in cultivation continued to be cultivated, it would yield a produce much larger than necessary. Land, equivalent to a fourth of the produce, must now be abandoned: and as the third quality yielded exactly one-fourth, (being 60 out of 240,) that quality will go out of cultivation. The 240 bushels can now be grown on land of the first and second qualities only; being, on the first, 100 bushels plus one-third, or 133⅓ bushels; on the second, 80 bushels plus one-third, or 106⅔ bushels; together 240. The second quality of land, instead of the third, is now the lowest, and regulates the price. Instead of 60, it is sufficient if 106⅔ bushels repay the capital with the ordinary profit. The price of wheat will consequently fall, not in the ratio of 60 to 80, as in the other case, but in the ratio of 60 to 106⅔. Even this gives an insufficient idea of the degree in which rent will be affected. The whole produce of the second quality of land will now be required to repay the expenses of production. That land, being the worst in cultivation, will pay no rent. And the first quality will only yield the difference between 133⅓ bushels and 106⅔, being 26⅔ bushels instead of 40. The landlords collectively will have lost 33⅓ out of 60 bushels in corn rent alone, while the value and price of what is left will have been diminished in the ratio of 60 to 106⅔.

It thus appears, that the interest of the landlord is decidedly hostile to the sudden and general introduction of agricultural improvements. This assertion has been called a paradox, and made a ground for accusing its

^{c}48, 49, 52, 57   of

first promulgator, Ricardo, of great intellectual perverseness, to say nothing worse. I cannot discern in what the paradox consists; and the obliquity of vision seems to me to be on the side of his assailants. The opinion is only made to appear absurd by stating it unfairly. If the assertion were that a landlord is injured by the improvement of his estate, it would certainly be indefensible; but what is asserted is, that he is injured by the improvement of the estates of other people, although his own is included. Nobody doubts that he would gain greatly by the improvement if he could keep it to himself, and unite the ^{d}two^d benefits, ^{e} an increased produce from his ^{f} land, and a price as high as before. But if the increase of produce took place simultaneously on all lands, the price would not be as high as before; and there is nothing unreasonable in supposing that the landlords would be, not benefited, but injured. It is admitted that whatever permanently reduces the price of produce diminishes rent: and it is quite in accordance with common notions to suppose that if, by the increased productiveness of land, less land were required for cultivation, its value, like that of ^{g}other articles^g for which the demand had diminished, would fall.

I am quite willing to admit that rents have not really been lowered by the progress of agricultural improvement; but why? Because improvement has never in reality been sudden, but always slow; at no time much outstripping, and often falling far short of, the growth of capital and population, which tends as much to raise rent, as the other to lower it, and which is enabled, as we shall presently see, to raise it much higher, by means of the additional margin afforded by improvements in agriculture. First, however, we must examine in what manner the sudden cheapening of agricultural produce would affect profits and wages.

In the beginning, money wages would probably remain the same as before, and the labourers would have the full benefit of the cheapness. They would be enabled to increase their consumption either of food or of other articles, and would receive the same cost, and a greater quantity. So ^{h}far^h, profits would be unaffected. But the permanent remuneration of the labourers essentially depends on what we have called their habitual standard; the extent of the requirements which, as a class, they insist on satisfying before they choose to have children. If their tastes and requirements receive a durable impress from the sudden improvement in their condition, the benefit to the class will be permanent. But the same cause which enables them to purchase greater comforts and indulgences with the same wages, would enable them to purchase the same amount of comforts

$^{d-d}$+65, 71
^{e}48, 49, 52, 57, 62   of
^{f}48   own
$^{g-g}$48, 49, 52, 57, 62   any other article
$^{h-h}$48, 49, 52, 57, 62   long as this was the case

and indulgences with lower wages; and a greater population may now exist, without reducing the labourers below the condition to which they are accustomed. Hitherto this and no other has been the use which the labourers have commonly made of any increase of their means of living; they have treated it simply as convertible into food for a greater number of children. It is probable, therefore, that population would be stimulated, and that after the lapse of a generation the real wages of labour would be no higher than before the improvement: the reduction being partly brought about by a fall of money wages, and partly through the price of food, the cost of which, from the demand occasioned by the increase of population, would be ^{i} increased. To the extent to which money wages fell, profits would rise; the capitalist obtaining a greater quantity of equally efficient labour by the same outlay of capital. We thus see that a diminution of the cost of living, whether arising from agricultural improvements or from the importation of foreign produce, if the habits and requirements of the labourers are not raised, ^{j}usually^j lowers money wages and rent, and raises the general rate of profit.

What is true of improvements which cheapen the production of food, is true also of the substitution of a cheaper for a more costly variety of it. The same land yields to the same labour a much greater quantity of human nutriment in the form of maize or potatoes, than in the form of wheat. If the labourers were to give up bread, and feed only on those cheaper products, taking as their compensation not a greater quantity of other consumable commodities, but earlier marriages and larger families, the cost of labour would be much diminished, and if labour continued equally efficient, profits would rise; while rent would be much lowered, since food for the whole population could be raised on half or a third part of the land now sown with corn. At the same time, it being evident that land too barren to be cultivated for wheat might be made in case of necessity to yield potatoes sufficient to support the little labour necessary for producing them, cultivation might ultimately descend lower, and rent eventually rise higher, on a potato or maize system, than on a corn system; because the land would be capable of feeding a much larger population before reaching the limit of its powers.

If the improvement, which we suppose to take place, is not in the production of food, but of some manufactured article consumed by the labouring class, the effect on wages and profits will ^{k}at first^k be the same; but the effect on rent very different. ^{l}It will not be lowered; it will even^l, if the ultimate effect of the improvement is an increase of population, be

^{i}48, 49, 52, 57, 62   again
$^{j-j}$+52, 57, 62, 65, 71
$^{k-k}$+62, 65, 71 $^{l-l}$48, 49, 52 57   Instead of being lowered, it will

raised ^{m}: in which last case profits will be lowered^m. The reasons are too evident to require statement.

§ 5. [*Fifth case; all the three elements progressive*] We have considered, on the one hand, the manner in which the distribution of the produce into rent, profits, and wages, is affected by the ordinary increase of population and capital, and on the other, how it is affected by improvements in production, and more especially in agriculture. We have found that the former cause lowers profits, and raises rent and the cost of labour: while the tendency of agricultural improvements is to diminish rent; and all improvements which cheapen any article of the labourer's consumption, tend to diminish the cost of labour and to raise profits. The tendency of each cause in its separate state being thus ascertained, it is easy to determine the tendency of the actual course of things, in which the two movements are going on simultaneously, capital and population increasing with tolerable steadiness, while improvements in agriculture are made from time to time, and the knowledge and practice of improved methods ^{a}become diffused^a gradually through the community.

The habits and requirements of the labouring classes being given (which determine their real wages), ^{b}rents^b, profits, and money wages at any given time, are the result of the composition of these rival forces. If during any period agricultural improvement advances faster than population, rent and money wages during that period will tend downward, and profits upward. If population advances more rapidly than agricultural improvement, either the labourers will submit to a reduction in the quantity or quality of their food, or if not, rent and money wages will progressively rise, and profits will fall.

Agricultural skill and knowledge are of slow growth, and still slower diffusion. Inventions and discoveries, too, occur only occasionally, while the increase of population and capital are continuous agencies. It therefore seldom happens that improvement, even during a short time, has so much the start of population and capital as actually to lower rent, or raise the rate of profits. There are many countries in which the growth of population and capital ^{c}is^c not rapid, but in these agricultural improvement is less active still. Population ^{d}almost^d everywhere treads close on the heels of agricultural improvement, and effaces its effects as fast as they are produced.

The reason why agricultural improvement seldom lowers rent, is that it seldom cheapens food, but only prevents it from growing dearer; and seldom, if ever, throws land out of cultivation, but only enables worse and

$^{m-m}$+62, 65, 71
$^{a-a}$48   diffuses itself $^{b-b}$48, 49, 52, 57, 62, 65 rent
$^{c-c}$48, 49, 52, 57, 62, 65   are $^{d-d}$+57, 62, 65, 71

worse land to be taken in *for the supply of an increasing demand*. What is sometimes called the natural state of a country which is but half cultivated, namely, that the land is highly productive, and food obtained in great abundance by little labour, is only true of unoccupied countries colonized by a civilized people. In the United States the worst land in cultivation is of a high quality *(except sometimes in the immediate vicinity of *markets or means of conveyance*, where a bad quality is compensated by a good situation)*; and even if no further improvements were made in agriculture or locomotion, cultivation would have many steps yet to descend, before the increase of population and capital would be brought to a stand; but in Europe five hundred years ago, though so thinly peopled in comparison to the present population, it is probable that the worst land under the plough was, from the rude state of agriculture, quite as unproductive as the worst land now cultivated; and that cultivation had approached as near to the ultimate limit of profitable tillage, in those times as in the present. What the agricultural improvements since made have really done is, by increasing the capacity of production of land in general, to enable tillage to extend downwards to a much worse natural quality of land than the worst which at that time would have admitted of *cultivation by a capitalist for profit*; thus rendering a much greater increase of capital and population possible, and removing always a little and a little further off, the barrier which restrains them; population meanwhile always pressing so hard against the barrier, that there is never any visible margin left for it to seize, every inch of ground made vacant for it by improvement being at once filled up by its advancing columns. Agricultural improvement may thus be considered to be not so much a counterforce conflicting with increase of population, as a partial relaxation of the bonds which confine that increase.

The effects produced on the division of the produce by an increase of production, under the joint influence of increase of population and capital and improvements of agriculture, are very different from those deduced from the hypothetical cases previously discussed. In particular, the effect on rent is most materially different. We remarked that—while a great agricultural improvement made suddenly and universally would in the first instance inevitably lower rent—such improvements enable rent, in the progress of society, to rise gradually to a much higher limit than it could otherwise attain, since they enable a much lower quality of land to be ultimately cultivated. But in the case we are now supposing, which nearly corresponds to the usual course of things, this ultimate effect becomes the immediate effect. Suppose cultivation to have reached, or almost reached, the utmost limit permitted by the state of the industrial arts, and rent,

e-e+52, 57, 62, 65, 71   f-f+49, 52, 57, 62, 65, 71
g-g49   towns   h-h48   profitable cultivation

therefore, to have attained nearly the highest point to which it can be carried by the progress of population and capital, with the existing amount of skill and knowledge. If a great agricultural improvement were suddenly introduced, it might throw back rent for a considerable space, leaving it to regain its lost ground by the progress of population and capital, and afterwards to go on further. But, taking place, as such improvement always does, very gradually, it causes no retrograde movement of either rent or cultivation; it merely enables the one to go on rising, and the other extending, long after they must otherwise have stopped. It would do this even without the necessity of resorting to a worse quality of land; simply by enabling the lands already in cultivation to yield a greater produce, with no increase of the proportional cost. If by improvements of agriculture all the lands in cultivation could be made, even with double labour and capital, to yield a double produce, (supposing that in the meantime population increased so as to require this double quantity) all rents would be doubled.

To illustrate the point, let us revert to the numerical example in a former page. Three qualities of land yield respectively 100, 80, and 60 bushels to the same outlay on the same extent of surface. If No. 1 could be made to yield 200, No. 2, 160, and No. 3, 120 bushels, at only double the expense, and therefore without any increase of the cost of production, and if the population, having doubled, required all this increased quantity, the rent of No. 1 would be 80 bushels instead of 40, and of No. 2, 40 instead of 20, while the price and value per bushel would be the same as before: so that corn rent and money rent would both be doubled. I need not point out the difference between this result, and what we have shown would take place if there were an improvement in production without the accompaniment of an increased demand for food.

Agricultural improvement, then, is always ultimately, and in the manner in which it generally takes place also immediately, beneficial to the landlord. We may add, that when it takes place in that manner, it is beneficial to no one else. When the demand for produce fully keeps pace with the increased capacity of production, food is not cheapened; the labourers are not, even temporarily, benefited; the cost of labour is not diminished, nor profits raised. There is a greater aggregate production, a greater produce divided among the labourers, and a larger gross profit; but the wages being shared among a larger population, and the profits spread over a larger capital, no labourer is better off, nor does any capitalist derive from the same amount of capital a larger income.

The result of this long investigation may be summed up as follows. The economical progress of a society constituted of landlords, capitalists, and labourers, tends to the progressive enrichment of the landlord class; while the cost of the labourer's subsistence tends on the whole to increase, and profits to fall. Agricultural improvements are a counteracting force to *the two* last effects; but the first, though a case is conceivable in which it would be temporarily checked, is ultimately in a high degree promoted by those improvements; and the increase of population tends to transfer all the benefits derived from agricultural improvement to the landlords alone. What other consequences, in addition to these, or in modification of them, arise from the industrial progress of a society thus constituted, I shall endeavour to show in the succeeding chapter.

^{i–i}48, 49, 52   these

CHAPTER IV

Of the Tendency of Profits
to a Minimum

§ 1. [*Doctrine of Adam Smith on the competition of capital*] The tendency of profits to fall as society advances, which has been brought to notice in the preceding chapter, was early recognised by writers on industry and commerce; but the laws which govern profits not being then understood, the phenomenon was ascribed to a wrong cause. Adam Smith considered profits to be determined by what he called the competition of capital; and concluded that when capital increased, this competition must likewise increase, and profits must fall. It is not quite certain what sort of competition Adam Smith had here in view. His words in the chapter on Profits of Stock* are, "When the stocks of many rich merchants are turned into the same trade, their mutual competition naturally tends to lower its profits; and when there is a like increase of stock in all the different trades carried on in the same society, the same competition must produce the same effect in them all." This passage would lead us to infer that, in Adam Smith's opinion, the manner in which the competition of capital lowers profits is by lowering prices; that being *usually* the mode in which an increased investment of capital in any particular trade, *b* lowers the profits of that trade. But if this was his meaning, he overlooked the circumstance, that the fall of price, which if confined to one commodity really does lower the profits of the producer, ceases to have that effect as soon as it extends to all commodities; because, when all things have fallen, nothing has really fallen, except nominally; and even computed in money, the expenses of every producer have diminished as much as his returns. Unless indeed labour be the one commodity which has not fallen in money price, when all other things have: if so, what has really taken place is a rise of wages; and it is that, and not the fall of prices, which has lowered the profits of capital. There is another thing which escaped the notice of Adam Smith; that the supposed universal fall of prices, through increased competition of

*Wealth of Nations, book i. ch. 9 [p. 210].

a–a+52, 57, 62, 65, 71   b48, 49   usually

capitals, is a thing which cannot take place. Prices are not determined by the competition of the sellers only, but also by that of the buyers; by demand as well as supply. The demand which affects money prices consists of all the money in the hands of the community, destined to be laid out in commodities; and as long as the proportion of this to the commodities is not diminished, there is no fall of general prices. Now, howsoever capital may increase, and give rise to an increased production of commodities, a full share of the capital will be drawn to the business of producing or importing money, and the quantity of money will be augmented in an equal ratio with the quantity of commodities. For if this were not the case, and if money, therefore, were, as the theory supposes, perpetually acquiring increased purchasing power, those who produced or imported it would obtain constantly increasing profits; and this could not happen without attracting *c*labour and*c* capital to that occupation from *d* other employments. If a general fall of prices, and increased value of money, were really to occur, it could only be as *e*a*e* consequence of increased cost of production, from the gradual exhaustion of the mines.

It is not tenable, therefore, in theory, that the increase of capital produces, or tends to produce, a general decline of money prices. Neither is it true, that any *f* general decline of prices, as capital increased, has manifested itself in fact. The only things observed to fall in price with the progress of society, are those in which there have been improvements in production, greater than have taken place in the production of the precious metals; as for example, all spun and woven fabrics. Other things, again, instead of falling, have risen in price, because their cost of production, compared with that of gold and silver, has increased. Among these are all kinds of food, comparison being made with a much earlier period of history. The doctrine, therefore, that competition of capital lowers profits by lowering prices, is incorrect in fact, as well as unsound in principle.

But it is not certain that Adam Smith really held that doctrine; for his language on the subject is wavering and unsteady, denoting the absence of a definite and well-digested opinion. Occasionally he seems to think that the mode in which the competition of capital lowers profits, is by raising wages. And when speaking of the rate of profit in new colonies, he seems on the very verge of grasping the complete theory of the subject. "As the colony increases, the profits of stock gradually diminish. When the most fertile and best situated lands have been all occupied, less profit can be made by the *g*cultivators*g* of what is inferior both in soil and situation."[*]

[*Smith, *Wealth of Nations*, Vol. I, p. 217.]

c-c+52, 57, 62, 65, 71
*d*48   all
*f*48, 49, 52   such

*e-e*48, 49   the
*g-g*Source, 48, 49, 52, 57, 62, 65   cultivation

Had Adam Smith meditated longer on the subject, and systematized his view of it by harmonizing with each other the various glimpses which he caught of it from different points, he would have perceived that this last is the true cause of the fall of profits usually consequent upon increase of capital.

§ 2. [*Doctrine of Mr. Wakefield respecting the field of employment*] Mr. Wakefield, in his *a* Commentary on Adam Smith, *b*and his important writings on Colonization,*b* takes a much clearer view of the subject, and arrives, through a substantially correct series of deductions, at practical conclusions which appear to me just and important; but he is not equally happy in incorporating his valuable speculations with the results of previous thought, and reconciling them with other truths. Some of the theories of Dr. Chalmers, in his chapter "On the Increase and *c*Limits*c* of Capital,"[*] and the two chapters which follow it, coincide in their tendency and spirit with those of Mr. Wakefield; but Dr. Chalmers' ideas, though delivered, as is his *d*custom*d*, with a most attractive semblance of clearness, are really on this subject much more confused than even those of Adam Smith, and more decidedly infected with the often refuted notion that the competition of capital lowers general prices; the subject of Money apparently not *e*having been*e* included among the parts of Political Economy which this acute and vigorous writer had carefully studied.

Mr. Wakefield's explanation of the fall of profits is briefly this. Production is limited not solely by the quantity of capital and of labour, but also by the extent of the "field of employment." The field of employment for capital is two-fold; the land of the country, and the capacity of foreign markets to take its manufactured commodities. On a limited extent of land, only a limited quantity of capital can find employment at a profit. As the quantity of capital approaches this limit, profit falls; when the limit is attained, profit is annihilated; and can only be restored through an extension of the field of employment, either by the acquisition of fertile land, or by opening new markets in foreign countries, from which food and materials can be purchased with the products of domestic capital. These propositions are, in my opinion, substantially true; and, even to the phraseology in which they are expressed, considered as adapted to popular and practical rather than scientific uses, I have nothing to object. The error which seems to me imputable to Mr. Wakefield is that of supposing his doctrines to be

[*Chalmers, Thomas. *On Political Economy in connexion with the Moral State and Moral Prospects of Society*. 2nd ed. Glasgow: Collins, 1832, Chap. iii.]

*a*48   "England and America" and his
b-b+49, 52, 57, 62, 65, 71   *c-c*Source, 48   Limit
*d-d*48   wont   *e-e*48, 49, 52   being

in contradiction to the principles of the best school of preceding political economists, instead of being, as they really are, corollaries from those principles; though corollaries which, perhaps, would not always have been admitted by those political economists themselves.

The most scientific treatment of the subject which I have met with, is in an essay on the effects of Machinery, *published in the *Westminster Review* for January 1826,* by Mr. William Ellis;* which was doubtless unknown to Mr. Wakefield, but which had preceded him, though by a different path, in several of his leading conclusions. This essay excited little notice, partly from being published anonymously in a periodical, and partly because it was much in advance of the state of political economy at the time. In Mr. Ellis's view of the subject, the questions and difficulties raised by Mr. Wakefield's speculations and by those of Dr. Chalmers, find a solution consistent with the principles of political economy laid down in the present treatise.

§ 3. [*What determines the minimum rate of profit*] There is at every time and place some particular rate of profit, which is the lowest that will induce the people of that country and time to accumulate savings, and to employ those savings productively. This minimum rate of profit varies according to circumstances. It depends on two elements. One is, the strength of the effective desire of accumulation; the comparative estimate made by the people of that place and era, of future interests when weighed against present. This element chiefly affects the inclination to save. The other element, which affects not so much the willingness to save as the disposition to employ savings productively, is the degree of security of capital engaged in industrial operations. A state of general insecurity, no doubt affects also the disposition to save. A hoard may be a source of additional danger to its reputed possessor. But as it may also be a powerful means of averting dangers, the effects in this respect may perhaps be looked upon as balanced. But in employing any funds which a person may possess as capital on his own account, or in lending it to others to be so employed, there is always some additional risk, over and above that incurred by keeping it idle in his own custody. This extra risk is great in proportion as the general state of society is insecure: it may be equivalent to twenty, thirty, or fifty per cent, or to no more than one or two; something, however, it must

*[62] Now so much better known through [62 known by] his apostolic exertions, by [62 apostolic exertions, in] pen, purse, and person, for the improvement of popular education, and especially for the introduction into it of the elements of practical Political Economy. [*JSM refers to* "Employment of Machinery," *Westminster Review*, V (Jan., 1826), 101–30.]

*ƒ-ƒ*48, 49, 52, 57 [*in footnote to* Ellis *replaced in* 62 *by the note above*]

always be: and for this, the expectation of profit must be sufficient to compensate.

There would be adequate motives for a certain amount of saving, even if capital yielded no profit. There would be an inducement to lay by in good times a provision for bad; to reserve something for sickness and infirmity, or as a means of leisure and independence in the latter part of life, or a help to children in the outset of it. Savings, however, which have only these ends in view, have not much tendency to increase the amount of capital permanently in existence. These motives only prompt *persons* to save at one period of life what *they purpose* to consume at another, or what will be consumed by *their* children before they can completely provide for themselves. The savings by which an addition is made to the national capital, usually emanate from the desire of persons to improve what is termed their condition in life, or to make a provision for children or others, independent of their exertions. Now, to the strength of these inclinations it makes a very material difference how much of the desired object can be effected by a given amount and duration of self-denial; which again depends on the rate of profit. And there is in every country some rate of profit, below which persons in general will not find sufficient motive to save for the mere purpose of growing richer, or of leaving others better off than themselves. Any accumulation, therefore, by which the general capital is increased, requires as its necessary condition a certain rate of profit; a rate which an average person will deem to be an equivalent for abstinence, with the addition of a sufficient insurance against risk. There are always some persons in whom the effective desire of accumulation is above the average, and to whom less than this rate of profit is a sufficient inducement to save; but these merely step into the place of others whose taste for expense and indulgence is beyond the average, and who, instead of saving, perhaps even dissipate what they have received.

I have already observed that this minimum rate of profit, less than which is not consistent with the further increase of capital, is lower in some states of society than in others; and I may add, that the kind of social progress characteristic of our present civilization tends to diminish it. In the first place, one of the acknowledged effects of that progress is an increase of general security. Destruction by wars, and spoliation by private or public violence, are less and less to be apprehended: and the improvements which may be looked for in education and in the administration of justice, or, in their default, increased regard for opinion, afford a growing protection against fraud and reckless mismanagement. The risks attending the investment of savings in productive employment require, therefore, a smaller rate of profit to compensate for them than was required a century ago, and

^{a–a}48, 49   each person   ^{b–b}48, 49   he purposes   ^{c–c}48, 49   his

will hereafter require less than at present. In the second place, it is also one of the consequences of civilization that mankind become less the slaves of the moment, and more habituated to carry their desires and purposes forward into a distant future. This increase of providence is a natural result of the increased assurance with which futurity can be looked forward to; and is, besides, favoured by most of the influences which an industrial life exercises over the passions and inclinations of human nature. In proportion as life has fewer vicissitudes, as habits become more fixed, and great prizes are less and less to be hoped for by any other means than long perseverance, mankind become more willing to sacrifice present indulgence for future objects. This increased capacity of forethought and self-control may assuredly find other things to exercise itself upon than increase of riches, and some considerations connected with this topic will shortly be touched upon. The present kind of social progress, however, decidedly tends, though not perhaps to increase the desire of accumulation, yet to weaken the obstacles to it, and to diminish the amount of profit which people absolutely require as an inducement to save and accumulate. For these two reasons, diminution of risk and increase of providence, a profit or interest of three or four per cent is as sufficient a motive to the increase of capital in England at the present day, as thirty or forty per cent in the Burmese Empire, or in England at the time of King John. In Holland during the last century a return of two per cent, on government security, was consistent with an undiminished, if not with an increasing capital. But though the minimum rate of profit is thus liable to vary, and though to specify exactly what it is would at any given time be impossible, such a minimum always exists; and whether it be high or low, when once it is reached, no further increase of capital can for the present take place. The country has then attained what is known to political economists under the name of the stationary state.

§ 4. [*In opulent countries, profits are habitually near to the minimum*] We now *ᵃ* arrive at the fundamental proposition which this chapter is intended to inculcate. When a country has long possessed a large production, and a large net income to make savings from, and when, therefore, the means have long existed of making a great annual addition to capital; (the country not having, like America, a large reserve of fertile land still unused;) it is one of the characteristics of such a country, that the rate of profit is habitually within, as it were, a hand's breadth of the minimum, and the country therefore on the very verge of the stationary state. By this I do not mean that this state is likely, in any of the great countries of Europe, to be soon actually reached, or that capital does not still yield a

ᵃ48, 49, 52, 57   , therefore,

profit considerably greater than what is barely sufficient to induce the people of those countries to save and accumulate. My meaning is, that it would require but a short time to reduce profits to the minimum, if capital continued to increase at its present rate, and no circumstances having a tendency to raise the rate of profit occurred in the meantime. The expansion of capital would soon reach its ultimate boundary, if the boundary itself did not continually open and leave more space.

In England, the ordinary rate of interest on government securities, in which the risk is next to nothing, may be estimated at a little more than three per cent: in all other investments, therefore, the interest or profit calculated upon (exclusively of what is properly a remuneration for talent or exertion) must be as much more than this amount, as is equivalent to the degree of risk to which the capital is thought to be exposed. Let us suppose that in England even so small a net profit as one per cent, exclusive of insurance against risk, would constitute a sufficient inducement to save, but that less than this would not be a sufficient inducement. I now say, that the mere continuance of the present annual increase of capital, if no circumstance occurred to counteract its effect, would suffice in a small number of years to reduce the rate of net profit to one per cent.

To fulfil the conditions of the hypothesis, we must suppose an entire cessation of the exportation of capital for foreign investment. No more capital sent abroad for railways or loans; no more emigrants taking capital with them, to the colonies, or to other countries; no fresh advances made, or credits given, by bankers or merchants to their foreign correspondents. We must also assume that there are no fresh loans for unproductive expenditure, by the government, or on mortgage, or otherwise; and none of the waste of capital which now takes place by the failure of undertakings which people are tempted to engage in by the hope of a better income than can be obtained in safe paths at the present *habitually* low rate of profit. We must suppose the entire savings of the community to be annually invested in really productive employment within the country itself; and no new channels opened by industrial inventions, or by a more extensive substitution of the best known processes for inferior ones.

Few persons would hesitate to say, that there would be great difficulty in finding remunerative employment every year for so much new capital, and most would conclude that there would be what used to be termed a general glut; that commodities would be produced, and remain unsold, or be sold only at a loss. But the full examination which we have already given to this question,* has shown that this is not the mode in which the inconvenience would be experienced. The difficulty would not consist in any want

*Book iii. ch. 14 [pp. 570–6].

b–b48, 49   habitual

of a market. If the new capital were duly shared among many varieties of employment, it would raise up a demand for its own produce, and there would be no cause why any part of that produce should remain longer on hand than formerly. What would really be, not merely difficult, but impossible, would be to employ this capital without submitting to a rapid reduction of the rate of profit.

As capital increased, population either would also increase, or it would not. If it did not, wages would rise, and a greater capital would be distributed in wages among the same number of labourers. There being no more labour than before, and no improvements to render the labour more efficient, there would not be any increase of the produce; and as the capital, however largely increased, would only obtain the same gross return, the whole savings of each year would be exactly so much subtracted from the profits of the next and of every following year. It is hardly necessary to say that in such circumstances profits would very soon fall to the point at which further increase of capital would cease. An augmentation of capital, much more rapid than that of population, must soon reach its extreme limit, unless accompanied by increased efficiency of labour (through inventions and discoveries, or improved mental and physical education), or unless some of the idle people, or of the unproductive labourers, became productive.

If population did increase with the increase of capital, and in proportion to it, the fall of profits would still be inevitable. Increased population implies increased demand for agricultural produce. In the absence of industrial improvements, this demand can only be supplied at an increased cost of production, either by cultivating worse land, or by a more elaborate and costly cultivation of the land already under tillage. The cost of the labourer's subsistence is therefore increased; and unless the labourer submits to a deterioration of his condition, profits must fall. In an old country like England, if, in addition to supposing all improvement in domestic agriculture suspended, we suppose that there is no increased production in foreign countries for the English market, the fall of profits would be very rapid. If both these avenues to an increased supply of food were closed, and population continued to increase, as it is said to do, at the rate of a thousand a day, all waste land which admits of cultivation in the existing state of knowledge would soon be cultivated, and the cost of production and price of food would be so increased, that, if the ᶜlabourersᶜ received the increased money wages necessary to compensate for ᵈtheirᵈ increased expenses, profits would very soon reach the minimum. The fall of profits would be retarded if money wages did not rise, or rose in a less degree; but the margin which can be gained by a deterioration of the

ᶜ⁻ᶜ48, 49   labourer   ᵈ⁻ᵈ48, 49   his

[^e]labourers'[^e] condition is a very narrow one: in general [^f]they[^f] [^g]cannot[^g] bear much reduction; when [^h]they[^h] can, [^i]they have[^i] also a higher standard of necessary requirements, and *will* not. On the whole, therefore, we may assume that in such a country as England, if the present annual amount of savings were to continue, without any of the counteracting circumstances which now keep in check the natural influence of those savings in reducing profit, the rate of profit would speedily attain the minimum, and all further accumulation of capital would for the present cease.

§ 5. [*Profits are prevented from reaching the minimum by commercial revulsions*] What, then, are these counteracting circumstances, which, in the existing state of things, maintain a tolerably equal struggle against the downward tendency of profits, and prevent the great annual savings which take place in this country, from depressing the rate of profit much nearer to that lowest point to which it is always tending, and which, left to itself, it would so promptly attain? The resisting agencies are of several kinds.

First among them, we may notice one which is so simple and so conspicuous, that some political economists, especially M. de Sismondi and Dr. Chalmers, have attended to it almost to the exclusion of all others. This is, the waste of capital in periods of over-trading and rash speculation, and in the commercial revulsions by which such times are always followed. It is true that a great part of what is lost at such periods is not destroyed, but merely transferred, like a gambler's losses, to more successful speculators. But even of these mere transfers, a large portion is always to foreigners, by the hasty purchase of unusual quantities of foreign goods at advanced prices. And much also is absolutely wasted. Mines are opened, railways or bridges made, and many other works of uncertain profit commenced, and in these enterprises much capital is sunk which yields either no return, or none adequate to the outlay. Factories are built and machinery erected beyond what the market requires, or can keep in employment. Even if they are kept in employment, the capital is no less sunk; it has been converted from circulating into fixed capital, and has ceased to have any influence on wages or profits. Besides this, there is a great unproductive consumption of capital, during the stagnation which follows a period of general over-trading. Establishments are shut up, or kept working without any profit, hands are discharged, and numbers of persons in all ranks, being deprived of their income, and thrown for support on their savings, find themselves, after the crisis has passed away, in a condition of more or less impoverishment. Such are the effects of a commercial revulsion: and

[^e-e]48, 49   labourer's
[^f-f]48, 49   he
[^h-h]48, 49   he

[^g-g]48, 49, 52, 57, 62   *cannot*
[^i-i]48, 49   he has

that such revulsions are almost periodical, is a consequence of the very tendency of profits which we are considering. By the time a few years have passed over without a crisis, so much additional capital has been accumulated, that it is no longer possible to invest it at the accustomed profit: all public securities rise to a high price, the rate of interest on the best mercantile security falls very low, and the complaint is general among persons in business that no money is to be made. Does not this demonstrate how speedily profit would be at the minimum, and the stationary condition of capital would be attained, if these accumulations went on without any counteracting principle? But the diminished scale of all safe gains, inclines persons to give a ready ear to any projects which hold out, though at the risk of loss, the hope of a higher rate of profit; and speculations ensue, which, with the subsequent revulsions, destroy, or transfer to foreigners, a considerable amount of capital, produce a temporary rise of interest and profit, make room for fresh accumulations, and the same round is recommenced.

This, doubtless, is one considerable cause which arrests profits in their descent to the minimum, by sweeping away from time to time a part of the accumulated mass by which they are forced down. But this is not, as might be inferred from the language of some writers, the principal cause. If it were, the capital of the country would not increase; but in England it does increase greatly and rapidly. This is shown by the increasing productiveness of almost all taxes, by the continual growth of all the signs of national wealth, and by the rapid increase of population, while the condition of the labourers ᵃis certainly not declining, but on the whole improvingᵃ. These things prove that each commercial revulsion, however disastrous, is very far from destroying all the capital which has been added to the accumulations of the country since the last revulsion preceding it, and that, invariably, room is either found or made for the profitable employment of a perpetually increasing capital, consistently with not forcing down profits to a lower rate.

§ 6. [*Profits are prevented from reaching the minimum by improvements in production*] This brings us to the second of the counter-agencies, namely, improvements in production. ᵃThese evidently have the effect of extending what Mr. Wakefield terms the field of employmentᵃ, that is, they enable a greater amount of capital to be accumulated and employed without depressing the rate of profit: provided always that they do not raise, to a proportional extent, the habits and requirements of the labourer. If the

---

ᵃ⁻ᵃ48, 49, 52, 57, 62   certainly is not on the whole declining

---

ᵃ⁻ᵃ48   I am not sure whether these have been formally included by Mr. Wakefield among the modes of extending what he terms the field of employment. But they evidently have that effect

labouring class gain the full advantage of the increased cheapness, in other words, if money wages do not fall, profits are not raised, nor their fall retarded. But if the *b*labourers*b* people up to the improvement in their condition, and so relapse to their previous state, profits will rise. All inventions which cheapen any of the things consumed by the *c*labourers*c*, unless *d*their*d* requirements are raised in an equivalent degree, in time lower money wages: and by doing so, enable a greater capital to be accumulated and employed, before profits fall back to what they were previously.

Improvements which only affect things consumed exclusively by the richer classes, do not operate precisely in the same manner. The cheapening of lace or velvet has no effect in diminishing the cost of labour; and no mode can be pointed out in which it can raise the rate of profit, so as to make room for a larger capital before the minimum is attained. It, however, produces an effect which is virtually equivalent; it lowers, or tends to lower, the minimum itself. In the first place, *e*increased*e* cheapness of articles of consumption promotes the inclination to save, by affording to all consumers a surplus which they may lay by, consistently with their accustomed manner of living; and unless they were *f*previously*f* suffering actual hardships, it will require little self-denial to save some part at least of this surplus. In the next place, whatever enables people to live equally well on a smaller income, inclines them to lay by capital for a lower rate of profit. If people can live on an independence of 500*l.* a year in the same manner as they formerly could on one of 1000*l.*, some persons will be induced to save in hopes of the one, who would have been deterred by the more remote prospect of the other. All improvements, therefore, in the production of almost any commodity, tend in some degree to widen the interval which has to be passed before arriving at the stationary state: but this effect belongs in a much greater degree to the improvements which affect the articles consumed by the labourer, since these conduce to it in two ways; they induce people to accumulate for a lower profit, and they also raise the rate of profit itself.

§ 7. [*Profits are prevented from reaching the minimum by the importation of cheap necessaries and instruments*] Equivalent in effect to improvements in production, is the acquisition of any new power of obtaining cheap commodities from foreign countries. If necessaries are cheapened, whether they are so by improvements at home or importation from abroad, is exactly the same thing to wages and profits. Unless the labourer obtains, and by an improvement of his habitual standard, keeps, the whole benefit,

*b-b*48, 49   class
*c-c*48, 49   labourer
*e-e*48, 49, 52, 57   the

*d-d*48, 49   his
*f-f*48, 49, 52, 57   before

the cost of labour is lowered, and the rate of profit raised. As long as food can continue to be imported for an increasing population without any diminution of cheapness, so long the declension of profits through the increase of population and capital is arrested, and accumulation may go on without making the rate of profit draw nearer to the minimum. And on this ground it is believed by some, that the repeal of the corn laws has opened to this country a long era of rapid increase of capital with an undiminished rate of profit.

Before inquiring whether this expectation is reasonable, one remark must be made, which is much at variance with commonly received notions. Foreign trade does not necessarily increase the field of employment for capital. It is not the mere opening of a market for *a country's* productions, that tends to raise the rate of profits. If nothing were obtained in exchange for those productions but the luxuries of the rich, the expenses of no capitalist would be diminished; profits would not be at all raised, nor room made for the accumulation of more capital without submitting to a reduction of profits: and if the attainment of the stationary state were at all retarded, it would only be because the diminished cost at which a certain degree of luxury could be enjoyed, might induce people, in that prospect, to *make fresh savings* for a lower profit than they formerly were willing to do. When foreign trade makes room for more capital at the same profit, it is by enabling the necessaries of life, or the habitual articles of the labourer's consumption, to be obtained at smaller cost. It may do this in two ways; *by the importation either* of those commodities themselves, or of the means and appliances for producing them. Cheap iron has, in a certain measure, the same effect on profits and the cost of labour as cheap corn, because cheap iron makes cheap tools for agriculture and cheap machinery for clothing. But a foreign trade which neither directly, nor by any indirect consequence, increases the cheapness of anything consumed by the labourers, does not, any more than an invention or discovery in the like case, tend to raise profits or retard their fall; it merely substitutes the production of goods for foreign markets, in the room of the home production of luxuries, leaving the employment for capital neither greater nor less than before. It is true, that there is scarcely any export trade which, in a country that already imports necessaries or materials, comes within these conditions: for every increase of exports enables the country to obtain all its imports on cheaper terms than before.

A country which *, as is now the case with England,* admits food of all kinds, and all necessaries and the materials of necessaries, to be freely

*a–a*48, 49   British
*b–b*48, 49   continue saving
*c–c*48, 49, 52, 57   either by the importation   *d–d*+62, 65, 71

imported from all parts of the world, *e* no longer depends on the fertility of her own soil to keep up her rate of profits, but on the soil of the whole world. It remains to consider how far this resource can be counted upon, for making head during a very long period against the tendency of profits to decline as capital increases.

It must, of course, be supposed that with the increase of capital, population also increases; for if it did not, the consequent rise of wages would bring down profits, in spite of any cheapness of *f*food*f*. Suppose then that the population of Great Britain goes on increasing at its present rate, and demands every year a supply of imported food considerably beyond that of the year preceding. This annual increase in the food demanded from the exporting countries, can only be obtained either by great improvements in their agriculture, or by the application of a great additional capital to the growth of food. The former is likely to be a very slow process, from the rudeness and ignorance of the agricultural classes in the food-exporting countries of Europe, while the British colonies and the United States are already in possession of most of the improvements yet made, so far as suitable to their circumstances. There remains as a resource, the extension of cultivation. And on this it is to be remarked, that the capital by which any such extension can take place, is mostly still to be created. In Poland, *g* Russia, Hungary, Spain, the increase of capital is extremely slow. In America it is rapid, but not more rapid than the population. The principal fund at present available for supplying this country with a yearly increasing importation of food, is that portion of the annual savings of America which has *h*heretofore*h* been applied to increasing the manufacturing establishments of the United States, and which *i*free trade in corn may possibly divert*i* from that purpose to growing food for our market. This limited source of supply, unless great improvements take place in agriculture, cannot be expected to keep pace with the growing demand of so rapidly increasing a population as that of Great Britain; and if our population and capital continue to increase with their present rapidity, the only mode in which food can continue to be supplied cheaply to the one, is by sending the other abroad to produce it.

§ 8. [*Profits are prevented from reaching the minimum by the emigration of capital*] This brings us to the last of the counter-forces which check the downward tendency of profits, in a country whose capital increases faster than that of its neighbours, and whose profits are therefore nearer to the

----

*e*48, 49   (which is now very nearly, and will soon be entirely, our own case)] 52, 57   *as* 48 . . . entirely, the case of England)

*f-f*48, 49, 52   corn   *g*48   Southern
*h-h*48, 49, 52   hitherto   *i-i*48, 49, 52   may now possibly be diverted

minimum. This is, the perpetual overflow of capital into colonies or foreign countries, to seek higher profits than can be obtained at home. I believe this to have been for many years one of the principal causes by which the decline of profits in England has been arrested. It has a twofold operation. In the first place, it does what a fire, or an inundation, or a commercial crisis would have done: it carries off a part of the increase of capital from which the reduction of profits proceeds. Secondly, the capital so carried off is not lost, but is chiefly employed either in founding colonies, which become large exporters of cheap agricultural produce, or in extending and perhaps improving the agriculture of older communities. It is to the emigration of English capital, that we have chiefly to look for keeping up a supply of cheap food and cheap materials of clothing, proportional to the increase of our population; thus enabling an increasing capital to find employment in the country, without reduction of profit, in producing manufactured articles with which to pay for this supply of raw produce. Thus, the exportation of capital is an agent of great efficacy in extending the field of employment for that which remains: and it may be said truly that, up to a certain point, the more capital we send away, the more we shall possess and be able to retain at home.

In countries which are further advanced in industry and population, and have therefore a lower rate of profit, than others, there is always, long before the actual minimum is reached, a practical minimum, viz. when profits have fallen so much below what they are elsewhere, that, were they to fall lower, all further accumulations would go abroad. In the present state of the industry of the world, when *there is occasion*, in any rich and improving country, to take the minimum of profits at all into consideration for practical purposes, it is only this practical minimum that needs be considered. As long as there are old countries where capital increases very rapidly, and new countries where profit is still high, profits in the old countries will not sink to the rate which would put a stop to accumulation; the fall is stopped at the point which sends capital abroad. It is only, however, by improvements in production, and even in the production of things consumed by labourers, that the capital of a country like England is prevented from speedily reaching that degree of lowness of profit, which would cause all further savings to be sent to find employment in the colonies, or in foreign countries.

a-a48, 49, 52, 57   it is necessary

CHAPTER V

Consequences of the Tendency
of Profits to a Minimum

§ 1. [*Abstraction of capital is not necessarily a national loss*] The theory of the effect of accumulation on profits, laid down in the preceding chapter, materially alters many of the practical conclusions which might otherwise be supposed to follow from the general principles of Political Economy, and which were, indeed, long admitted as true by the highest authorities on the subject.

It must greatly abate, or rather, altogether destroy, in countries where profits are low, the immense importance which used to be attached by political economists to the effects which an event or a measure of government might have in adding to or subtracting from the capital of the country. We have now seen that the lowness of profits is a proof that the spirit of accumulation is so active, and that the increase of capital has proceeded at so rapid a rate, as to outstrip the two counter-agencies, improvements in production, and increased supply of cheap necessaries from abroad: and that unless a considerable portion of the annual increase of capital were either periodically destroyed, or exported for foreign investment, the country would speedily attain the point at which further accumulation would cease, or at least spontaneously slacken, so as no longer to overpass the march of invention in the arts which produce the necessaries of life. In such a state of things as this, a sudden addition to the capital of the country, unaccompanied by any increase of productive power, would be but of transitory duration; since by depressing profits and interest, it would either diminish by a corresponding amount the savings which would be made from income in the year or two following, or it would cause an equivalent amount to be sent abroad, or to be wasted in rash speculations. Neither, on the other hand, would a sudden abstraction of capital, unless of inordinate amount, have any real effect in impoverishing the country. After a few months or years, there would exist in the country just as much capital as if none had been taken away. The abstraction, by raising profits and interest, would give a fresh stimulus to the accumulative principle, which would speedily fill up the vacuum. Probably, indeed, the only effect that would ensue, would be that for some time afterwards less capital would be exported, and less thrown away in hazardous speculation.

In the first place, then, this view of things greatly weakens, in a wealthy and industrious country, the force of the economical argument against the expenditure of public money for really valuable, even though *industriously* unproductive, purposes. If for any great object of justice or philanthropic policy, such as the industrial regeneration of Ireland, or a comprehensive measure of colonization or of public education, it were proposed to raise a large sum by way of loan, politicians need not demur to the abstraction of so much capital, as tending to dry up the permanent sources of the country's wealth, and diminish the fund which supplies the subsistence of the labouring population. The utmost expense which could be requisite for any of these purposes, would not in all probability deprive one labourer of employment, or diminish the next year's production by one ell of cloth or one bushel of grain. In poor countries, the capital of the country requires the legislator's sedulous care; he is bound to be most cautious of encroaching upon it, and should favour to the utmost its accumulation at home, and its introduction from abroad. But in rich, populous, and highly cultivated countries, it is not capital which is the deficient element, but fertile land; and what the legislator should desire and promote, is not a greater aggregate saving, but a greater return to savings, either by improved cultivation, or by access to the produce of more fertile lands in other parts of the globe. In such countries, the government may take any moderate portion of the capital of the country and *expend it as* revenue, without affecting the national wealth: the whole being either drawn from that portion of the annual savings which would otherwise be sent abroad, or being subtracted from the unproductive expenditure of individuals for the next year or two, since every million spent makes room for another million to be saved before reaching the overflowing point. When the object in view is worth the sacrifice of such an amount of the expenditure that furnishes the daily enjoyments of the people, the only well-grounded economical objection against taking the necessary funds directly from capital, consists of the inconveniences attending the process of raising a revenue by taxation, to pay the interest of a debt.

The same considerations enable us to throw aside as unworthy of regard, one of the common arguments against emigration as a means of relief for the labouring class. Emigration, it is said, can do no good to the labourers, if, in order to defray the cost, as much must be taken away from the capital of the country as from its population. That anything like this proportion could require to be abstracted from capital for the purpose even of the

*a–a*48, 49, 52, 57   industrially   *b–b*48   convert it into

most extensive colonization, few, I should think, would now assert: but even on that untenable supposition, it is an error to suppose that no benefit would be conferred on the labouring class. If one-tenth of the labouring people of England were transferred to the colonies, and along with them one-tenth of the circulating capital of the country, either wages, or profits, or both, would be greatly benefited, by the diminished pressure of capital and population upon the fertility of the land. There would be a reduced demand for food: the inferior arable lands would be thrown out of cultivation, and would become pasture; the superior would be cultivated less highly, but with a greater proportional return; food would be lowered in price, and though money wages would not rise, every labourer would be considerably improved in circumstances, an improvement which, if no increased stimulus to population and fall of wages ensued, would be permanent; while if there did, profits would rise, and accumulation start forward so as to repair the loss of capital. The landlords alone would sustain some loss of income; and even they, only if colonization went to the length of actually diminishing capital and population, but not if it merely carried off the annual increase.

§ 2. [*In opulent countries, the extension of machinery is not detrimental but beneficial to labourers*] From the same principles we are now able to arrive at a final conclusion respecting the effects which machinery, and generally the sinking of capital for a productive purpose, produce upon the immediate and ultimate interests of the labouring class. The characteristic property of this class of industrial improvements is the conversion of circulating capital into fixed: and it was shown in the ^afirst^a Book,* that in a country where capital accumulates slowly, the introduction of machinery, permanent improvements of land, and the like, ^bmight^b be, for the time, extremely injurious; since the capital so employed ^cmight^c be directly taken from the wages fund, the subsistence of the people and the employment for labour curtailed, and the gross annual produce of the country actually diminished. But in a country of great annual savings and low profits, no such effects need be apprehended. Since even the emigration of capital, or its unproductive expenditure, or its absolute waste, do not in such a country, if confined within any moderate bounds, at all diminish the aggregate amount of the wages fund—still less can the mere conversion of a like sum into fixed capital, which continues to be productive, have that effect. It merely draws off at one orifice what was already flowing out at another; or if not, the greater vacant space left in the reservoir does but

*Supra, vol. i. pp. 93–4.

^{a–a}48, 49, 52, 57   First   ^{b–b}48   may   ^{c–c}48   may

cause a greater quantity to flow in. Accordingly, in spite of the mischievous derangements of the money-market which *were at one time* occasioned by the *sinking of great sums in railways, I was never able to* agree with those who *apprehended* mischief, from this source, to the productive resources of the country. *Not* on the absurd ground (which to any one acquainted with the elements of the subject needs no confutation) that railway expenditure is a mere transfer of capital from hand to hand, by which nothing is lost or destroyed. This is true of what is spent in the purchase of the land; a portion too of what is paid to parliamentary agents, counsel, engineers, and surveyors, is saved by those who receive it, and becomes capital again: but what is laid out in the *bonâ fide* construction of the railway itself, is lost and gone; when once expended, it is incapable of ever being paid in wages or applied to the maintenance of labourers again; as a matter of account, the result is that so much food and clothing and tools have been consumed, and the country has got a railway instead. But what I would urge is, that sums so applied are mostly a mere appropriation of the annual overflowing which would otherwise have gone abroad, or been thrown away unprofitably, leaving neither a railway nor any other tangible result. The railway gambling of 1844 and 1845 probably saved the country from a depression of profits and interest, and a rise of all public and private securities, which would have engendered still wilder speculations, and when the effects came afterwards to be complicated by the scarcity of food, would have ended in a still more formidable crisis than *was experienced in the years immediately following*. In the poorer countries of Europe, the rage for railway construction might have had worse consequences than in England, were it not that in those countries such enterprises are in a great measure carried on by foreign capital. The railway operations of the various nations of the world may be looked upon as a sort of competition for the overflowing capital of the countries where profit is low and capital abundant, as England and Holland. The English railway speculations are a struggle to keep our annual increase of capital at home; those of foreign countries are an effort to obtain it.*

It already appears from these considerations, that the conversion of

*[52] It is hardly needful to point out how fully the remarks in the text [52, 57, 62 (which I have left as they originally stood)] have been verified by subsequent facts. The capital of the country, far from having been in any degree impaired by the large amount sunk in railway construction, was soon [52 construction, is] again overflowing.

   *d–d*48, 49, 52, 57, 62, 65   have been
   *e–e*48, 49, 52, 57, 62   great sums in process of being sunk in railways, I cannot
   *f–f*48, 49, 52, 57, 62   apprehend any
   *g–g*48, 49, 52   My dissent does not rest
   *h–h*48, 49, 52   has recently been experienced

circulating capital into fixed, whether by railways, or ⁱmanufactoriesⁱ, or ships, or machinery, or canals, or mines, or works of drainage and irrigation, is not likely, in any rich country, to diminish the gross produce or the amount of employment for labour. How much then is the case strengthened, when we consider that these transformations of capital are of the nature of improvements in production, which, instead of ultimately diminishing circulating capital, are the necessary conditions of its increase, since they alone enable a country to possess a constantly augmenting capital without reducing profits to the rate which would cause accumulation to stop. There is hardly any increase of fixed capital which does not enable the country to contain eventually a larger circulating capital, than it otherwise could possess and employ within its own limits; for there is hardly any creation of fixed capital which, when it proves successful, does not cheapen the articles on which wages are habitually expended. All capital sunk in the permanent improvement of land, lessens the cost of food and materials; almost all improvements in machinery cheapen the labourer's clothing or lodging, or the tools with which these are made; improvements in locomotion, such as railways, cheapen to the consumer all things which are brought from a distance. All these improvements make the labourers better off with the same money wages, better off if they do not increase their rate of multiplication. But if they do, and wages consequently fall, at least profits rise, and, while accumulation receives an immediate stimulus, room is made for a greater amount of capital before a sufficient motive arises for sending it abroad. Even the improvements which do not cheapen the things consumed by the labourer, and which, therefore, do not raise profits nor retain capital in the country, nevertheless, as we have seen, by lowering the minimum of profit for which people will ultimately consent to save, leave an ampler margin than previously for eventual accumulation, before arriving at the stationary state.

We may conclude, then, that improvements in production, and emigration of capital to the more fertile soils and unworked mines of the uninhabited or thinly peopled parts of the globe, do not, as ʲ appears to a superficial view, diminish the gross produce and the demand for labour at home; but, on the contrary, are what we have chiefly to depend on for increasing both, and are even the necessary conditions of any great or prolonged augmentation of either. Nor is it any exaggeration to say, that within certain, and not very narrow, limits, the more capital a country like England expends in these two ways, the more she will have left.

ⁱ⁻ⁱ48, 49   factories
ʲ48, 49   it

CHAPTER VI

Of the Stationary State

§ 1. [*Stationary state of wealth and population is dreaded and deprecated by writers*] The preceding chapters comprise the general theory of the economical progress of society, in the sense in which those terms are commonly understood; the progress of capital, of population, and of the productive arts. But in contemplating any progressive movement, not in its nature unlimited, the mind is not satisfied with merely tracing the laws of the movement; it cannot but ask the further question, to what goal? Towards what ultimate point is society tending by its industrial progress? When the progress ceases, in what condition are we to expect that it will leave mankind?

It must always have been seen, more or less distinctly, by political economists, that the increase of wealth is not boundless: that at the end of what they term the progressive state lies the stationary state, that all progress in wealth is but a postponement of this, and that each step in advance is an approach to it. We have now been led to recognise that this ultimate goal is at all times near enough to be fully in view; that we are always on the verge of it, and that if we have not reached it long ago, it is because the goal itself flies before us. The richest and most prosperous countries would very soon attain the stationary state, if no further improvements were made in the productive arts, and if there were a suspension of the overflow of capital from those countries into the uncultivated or ill-cultivated regions of the earth.

This impossibility of ultimately avoiding the stationary state—this irresistible necessity that the stream of human industry should finally spread itself out into an apparently stagnant sea—must have been, to the political economists of the last two generations, an unpleasing and discouraging prospect; for the tone and tendency of their speculations goes completely to identify all that is economically desirable with the progressive state, and with that alone. With Mr. M'Culloch, for example, prosperity does not mean a large production and a good distribution of wealth, but a rapid increase of it; his test of prosperity is high profits; and as the tendency of that very increase of wealth, which he calls prosperity, is towards low profits, economical progress, according to him, must tend to the extinction of prosperity. Adam Smith always assumes that the condition of the mass of the people, though it may not be positively distressed, must be pinched and stinted in a stationary condition of wealth, and can only be satisfactory in a progressive state. The doctrine that, to however distant a time incessant struggling may put off our doom, the progress of society must "end in shallows and in miseries," far from being, as many people still believe, a wicked invention of Mr. Malthus, was either expressly or tacitly affirmed by his most distinguished predecessors, and can only be successfully combated on his principles. Before attention had been directed to the principle of population as the active force in determining the remuneration of labour, the increase of mankind was virtually treated as a constant quantity; it was, at all events, assumed that in the natural and normal state of human affairs population must constantly increase, from which it followed that a constant increase of the means of support was essential to the physical comfort of the mass of mankind. The publication of Mr. Malthus' Essay is the era from which better views of this subject must be dated; and notwithstanding the acknowledged errors of his first edition, few writers have done more than himself, in the subsequent editions, to promote these juster and more hopeful anticipations.

Even in a progressive state of capital, in old countries, a conscientious or prudential restraint on population is indispensable, to prevent the increase of numbers from outstripping the increase of capital, and the condition of the classes who are at the bottom of society from being deteriorated. Where there is not, in the people, or in some very large proportion of them, a resolute resistance to this deterioration—a determination to preserve an established standard of comfort—the condition of the poorest class sinks, even in a progressive state, to the lowest point which they will consent to endure. The same determination would be equally effectual to keep up their condition in the stationary state, and would be quite as likely to exist. Indeed, even now, the countries in which the greatest prudence is manifested in the regulating of population, are often those in which capital increases least rapidly. Where there is an indefinite prospect of employment for increased numbers, there is apt to appear less necessity for prudential restraint. If it were evident that a new hand could not obtain employment but by displacing, or succeeding to, one already employed, the combined influences of prudence and public opinion might ᵃin some measureᵃ be relied on for restricting the coming generation within the numbers necessary for replacing the present.

§ 2. [*But the stationary state is not in itself undesirable*] I cannot, therefore, regard the stationary state of capital and wealth with the unaffected

ᵃ⁻ᵃ48, 49   generally

aversion so generally manifested towards it by political economists of the old school. I am inclined to believe that it would be, on the whole, a very considerable improvement on our present condition. I confess I am not charmed with the ideal of life held out by those who think that the normal state of human beings is that of struggling to get on; that the trampling, crushing, elbowing, and treading on each other's heels, which form the existing type of social life, are the most desirable lot of human kind, or anything but the disagreeable symptoms of one of the phases of industrial progress. *It may be a necessary stage in the progress of civilization, and those European nations which have hitherto been so fortunate as to be preserved from it, may have it yet to undergo. It is an incident of growth, not a mark of decline, for it is not necessarily destructive of the higher aspirations and the heroic virtues; as America, in her great civil war, *has proved* to the world, both by her conduct as a people and by numerous splendid individual examples, and as England, it is to be hoped, would also prove, on an equally trying and exciting occasion. But it* is not a kind of social perfection which philanthropists to come will feel any very eager desire to assist in realizing. Most fitting, indeed, is it, that while riches are power, and to grow as rich as possible the universal object of ambition, the path to its attainment should be open to all, without favour or partiality. But the best state for human nature is that in which, while no one is poor, no one desires to be richer, nor has any reason to fear being thrust back, by the efforts of others to push themselves forward.

That the energies of mankind should be kept in employment by the struggle for riches, as they were formerly by the struggle of war, until the better minds succeed in educating the others into better things, is undoubtedly more desirable than that they should rust and stagnate. While minds are coarse they require coarse stimuli, and let them have them. In the meantime, those who do not accept the present very early stage of human improvement as its ultimate type, may be excused for being comparatively indifferent to the kind of economical progress which ᶜ excites

---

ᵃ⁻ᵃ48 The northern and middle states of America are a specimen of this stage of civilization in very favourable circumstances; having, apparently, got rid of all social injustices and inequalities that affect persons of Caucasian race and of the male sex, while the proportion of population to capital and land is such as to ensure abundance to every able-bodied member of the community who does not forfeit it by misconduct. They have the six points of Chartism, and they have no poverty: and all that these advantages do for them is that the life of the whole of one sex is devoted to dollar-hunting, and of the other to breeding dollar-hunters. This] 49 *as* 48 . . . advantages seem to have done for them (notwithstanding some incipient signs of a better tendency) is . . . *as* 48] 52, 57, 62 *as* 49 . . . to have yet done . . . *as* 49
ᵇ⁻ᵇ65 is proving
ᶜ48, 49 usually

the congratulations of ^{d}ordinary^d politicians; the mere increase of production and accumulation. For the safety of national independence it is essential that a country should not fall much behind its neighbours in these things. But in themselves they are of little importance, so long as either the increase of population or anything else prevents the mass of the people from reaping any part of the benefit of them. I know not why it should be matter of congratulation that persons who are already richer than any one needs to be, should have doubled their means of consuming things which give little or no pleasure except as representative of wealth; or that numbers of individuals should pass over, every year, from the middle classes into a richer class, or from the class of the occupied rich to that of the unoccupied. It is only in the backward countries of the world that increased production is still an important object: in those most advanced, what is economically needed is a better distribution, of which ^{e}one^e indispensable means is a stricter restraint on population. Levelling institutions, either of a just or of an unjust kind, cannot alone accomplish it; they may lower the heights of society, but they ^{f}cannot, of themselves, permanently raise^f the depths.

On the other hand, we may suppose this better distribution of property attained, by the joint effect of the prudence and frugality of individuals, and of a system of legislation favouring equality of fortunes, so far as is consistent with the just claim of the individual to the fruits, whether great or small, of his or her own industry. We may suppose, for instance (according to the suggestion thrown out in a former chapter*), a limitation of the sum which any one person may acquire by gift or inheritance, to the amount sufficient to constitute a moderate independence. Under this twofold influence, society would exhibit these leading features: a well-paid and affluent body of labourers; no enormous fortunes, except what were earned and accumulated during a single lifetime; but a much larger body of persons than at present, not only exempt from the coarser toils, but with sufficient leisure, both physical and mental, from mechanical details, to cultivate freely the graces of life, and afford examples of them to the classes less favourably circumstanced for their growth. This ^{g}condition of society, so greatly preferable to the present,^{g} is not only perfectly compatible with the stationary state, but, it would seem, more naturally allied with that state than with any other.

*Supra, vol. i. pp. 224–6.

$^{d-d}$+52, 57, 62, 65, 71
$^{e-e}$48   an
$^{f-f}$48   cannot raise] 49   cannot permanently raise
$^{g-g}$48   state of things, which seems, economically considered, to be the most desirable condition of society,] 49   most desirable condition of society

There is room in the world, no doubt, and even in old countries, for *a great* increase of population, supposing the arts of life to go on improving, and capital to increase. But *even if* innocuous, I confess I see very little reason for desiring it. The density of population necessary to enable mankind to obtain, in the greatest degree, all the advantages both of co-operation and of social intercourse, has, in all the *most* populous countries, been attained. A population may be too crowded, though all be amply supplied with food and raiment. It is not good for man to be kept perforce at all times in the presence of his species. A world from which solitude is extirpated, is a very poor ideal. Solitude, in the sense of being often alone, is essential to any depth of meditation or of character; and solitude in the presence of natural beauty and grandeur, is the cradle of thoughts and aspirations which are not only good for the individual, but which society could ill do without. Nor is there much satisfaction in contemplating the world with nothing left to the spontaneous activity of nature; with every rood of land brought into cultivation, which is capable of growing food for human beings; every flowery waste or natural pasture ploughed up, all quadrupeds or birds which are not domesticated for man's use exterminated as his rivals for food, every hedgerow or superfluous tree rooted out, and scarcely a place left where a wild shrub or flower could grow without being eradicated as a weed in the name of improved agriculture. If the earth must lose that great portion of its pleasantness which it owes to things that the unlimited increase of wealth and population would extirpate from it, for the mere purpose of enabling it to support a larger, but not a better or a happier population, I sincerely hope, for the sake of posterity, that they will be content to be stationary, long before necessity compels them to it.

It is scarcely necessary to remark that a stationary condition of capital and population implies no stationary state of human improvement. There would be as much scope as ever for all kinds of mental culture, and moral and social progress; as much room for improving the Art of Living, and much more likelihood of its being improved, when minds ceased to be engrossed by the art of getting on. Even the industrial arts might be as earnestly and as successfully cultivated, with this sole difference, that instead of serving no purpose but the increase of wealth, industrial improvements would produce their legitimate effect, that of abridging labour. Hitherto it is questionable if all the mechanical inventions yet made have lightened the day's toil of any human being. They have enabled a greater population to live the same life of drudgery and imprisonment, and an

h–h48, 49   an immense
i–i48, 49   , although it may be
j–j48, 49, 52   more

increased number of manufacturers and others to make [k] fortunes. They have increased the comforts of the middle classes. But they have not yet begun to effect those great changes in human destiny, which it is in their nature and in their futurity to accomplish. Only when, in addition to just institutions, the increase of mankind shall be under the deliberate guidance of [l] judicious foresight, can the conquests made from the powers of nature by the intellect and energy of scientific discoverers, become the common property of the species, and the means of improving and elevating the universal lot.

[k]48, 49, 52   large
[l]48, 49, 52   a

CHAPTER VII

On the Probable Futurity
of the Labouring Classes

§ 1. [*The theory of dependence and protection is no longer applicable to the condition of modern society*] The observations in the preceding chapter had for their principal object to deprecate a false ideal of human society. Their applicability to the practical purposes of present times, consists in moderating the inordinate importance attached to the mere increase of production, and fixing attention upon improved distribution, and a large remuneration of labour, as the *a*two*a* desiderata. Whether the aggregate produce increases absolutely or not, is a thing in which, after a certain amount has been obtained, neither the legislator nor the philanthropist need feel any strong interest: but, that it should increase relatively to the number of those who share in it, is of the utmost possible importance; and this, (whether the wealth of mankind be stationary, or increasing at the most rapid rate ever known in an old country,) must depend on the opinions and habits of the most numerous class, the class of manual labourers.

*b*When I speak, either in this place or elsewhere, of "the labouring classes," or of labourers as a "class," I use those phrases in compliance with custom, and as descriptive of an existing, but by no means a necessary or permanent, state of social relations. I do not recognise as either just or salutary, a state of society in which there is any "class" which is not labouring; any human beings, exempt from bearing their share of the necessary labours of human life, except those unable to labour, or who have fairly earned rest by previous toil. So long, however, as the great social evil exists of a non-labouring class, labourers also constitute a class, and may be spoken of, though only provisionally, in that character.*b*

*a–a*48, 49, 52   true
*b–b*48, 49   The economic condition of that class, and along with it of all society, depends therefore essentially on its moral and intellectual, and that again on its social, condition. In the details of political economy, general views of society and politics are out of place; but in the more comprehensive inquiries it is impossible to exclude them; since the various leading departments of human life do not develope themselves separately, but each depends on all, or is profoundly modified

Considered in its moral and social aspect, the state of the labouring people has latterly been a subject of much more speculation and discussion than formerly; and the opinion that it is not now what it ought to be, has become very general. The suggestions which have been promulgated, and the controversies which have been excited, on detached points rather than on the foundations of the subject, have put in evidence the existence of two conflicting theories, respecting the social position desirable for manual labourers. The one may be called the theory of dependence and protection, the other that of self-dependence.

According to the former theory, the lot of the poor, in all things which affect them collectively, should be regulated *for* them, not *by* them. They should not be required or encouraged to think for themselves, or give to their own reflection or forecast an influential voice in the determination of their destiny. It is *c*supposed to be*c* the duty of the higher classes to think for them, and to take the responsibility of their lot, as the commander and officers of an army take that of the soldiers composing it. This function *d*, it is contended,*d* the higher classes should prepare themselves to perform conscientiously, and their whole demeanour should impress the poor with a reliance on it, in order that, while yielding passive and active obedience to the rules prescribed for them, they may resign themselves in all other respects to a trustful *insouciance*, and repose under the shadow of their protectors. The relation between rich and poor*e*, according to this theory (a theory also applied to the relation between men and women)*e* should be only *f*partly*f* authoritative; it should be amiable, moral, and sentimental: affectionate tutelage on the one side, respectful and grateful deference on the other. The rich should be *in loco parentis* to the poor, guiding and restraining them like children. Of spontaneous action on their part there should be no need. They should be called on for nothing but to do their day's work, and to be moral and religious. Their morality and religion should be provided for them by their superiors, who should see them properly taught it, and should do all that is necessary to ensure their being, in return for labour and attachment, properly fed, clothed, housed, spiritually edified, and innocently amused.

This is the ideal of the future, in the minds of those whose dissatisfaction with the *g*present*g* assumes the form of affection and regret towards the *h*past*h*. Like other ideals, it exercises an unconscious influence on the

---

by them. To obtain any light on the great economic question of the future, which gives the chief interest to the phenomena of the present—the physical condition of the labouring classes—we must consider it, not separately, but in conjunction with all other points of their condition.

c-c+52, 57, 62, 65, 71   *d-d*+52, 57, 62, 65, 71
e-e+52, 57, 62, 65, 71   *f-f*48, 49, 52   partially
*g-g*48, 49, 52, 57, 62   Present   *h-h*48, 52, 57, 62   Past

opinions and sentiments of numbers who never consciously guide themselves by any ideal. It has also this in common with other ideals, that it
has never been historically realized. It makes its appeal to our imaginative
sympathies in the character of a restoration of the good times of our fore-
fathers. But no times can be pointed out in which the higher classes of this
or any other country performed a part even distantly resembling the one
assigned to them in this theory. It is an idealization, grounded on the conduct and character of here and there an individual. All privileged and
powerful classes, as such, have used their power in the interest of their
own selfishness, and have indulged their self-importance in despising, and
not in lovingly caring for, those who were, in their estimation, degraded*,
by being under the necessity of working for their benefit. I do not affirm
that* what has always been must always be, or that human improvement
has no tendency to correct the intensely selfish feelings engendered by
power *; but though the evil may be lessened, it cannot be eradicated, until
the power itself is withdrawn*. This, *at least*, seems to me undeniable,
that long before the superior classes could be sufficiently improved to
govern in the tutelary manner supposed, the inferior classes would be too
much improved to be so governed.

I am quite sensible of all that is seductive in the picture of society which
this theory presents. Though the facts of it have no prototype in the past,
the feelings have. In them lies all that there is of reality in the conception.
As the idea is essentially repulsive of a society only held together by *m* the
relations and feelings arising out of pecuniary interests, so there is something naturally attractive in a form of society abounding in strong
personal attachments and disinterested self-devotion. Of such feelings it
must be admitted that the relation of protector and protected has hitherto
been the richest source. The strongest attachments of human beings in
general, are towards the things or the persons that stand between them and
some dreaded evil. Hence, in an age of lawless violence and insecurity,
and general hardness and roughness of manners, in which life is beset
with dangers and sufferings at every step, to those who have neither a
commanding position of their own, nor a claim on the protection of some
one who has—a generous giving of protection, and a grateful receiving of
it, are the strongest ties which connect human beings; the feelings arising
from that relation are their warmest feelings; all the enthusiasm and tenderness of the most sensitive natures gather round it; loyalty on the one
part and chivalry on the other are principles exalted into passions. I do

i–i48, 49   by inferiority. That
j–j48, 49   does not tend more and more
k–k48, 49   , I should be sorry to affirm
l–l48, 49   however   m48, 49   bought services, and by

not desire to depreciate these [n]qualitics.[n] The error [o] lies in not perceiving, that these virtues and sentiments, like the clanship and the hospitality of the wandering Arab, belong emphatically to a rude and imperfect state of the social union; and that the feelings between protector and protected [p], whether between kings and subjects, rich and poor, or men and women,[p] can no longer have this beautiful and endearing character, where there are no longer any serious dangers from which to protect. What is there in the present state of society to make it natural that human beings, of ordinary strength and courage, should glow with the warmest gratitude and devotion in return for protection? The laws protect them[q], wherever the laws do not criminally fail in their duty[q]. To be under the power of some one, instead of being as formerly the sole condition of safety, is now, speaking generally, the only situation which exposes to grievous wrong [r]. The so-called protectors are now the only persons against whom, in any ordinary circumstances, protection is needed. The brutality and tyranny with which every police report is filled, are those of husbands to wives, of parents to children. That the law does not prevent these atrocities, that it [s]is only now making a first timid attempt[s] to repress and punish them, is no matter of necessity, but the deep disgrace of those by whom the laws are made and administered. No[r] man or woman who either possesses or is able to earn [t]an independent[t] livelihood, requires any other protection than that [u]which the law could and ought to give[u]. This being the case, it argues great ignorance of human nature to continue taking for granted that relations founded on protection must always subsist, and not to see that the assumption of the part of protector, and of the power which belongs to it, without any of the necessities which justify it, must engender feelings opposite to loyalty.

Of the working [v]men, at least in the more advanced countries of Europe,[v]

[n-n]48, 49   virtues. That the most beautiful developments of feeling and character often grow out of the most painful, and in many other respects the most hardening and corrupting circumstances of our condition, is now, and probably will long be, one of the chief stumbling-blocks both in the theory and in the practice of morals and education.
   [o]48, 49   in the present case
   [p-p]+52, 57, 62, 65, 71
   [q-q]48, 49   : where laws do not reach, manners and opinion shield them
   [r-r]48   ; and wrong against which laws and opinion are neither able, nor very seriously attempt, to afford effectual protection. We have entered into a state of civilization in which the bond that attaches human beings to one another, must be disinterested admiration and sympathy for personal qualities, or gratitude for unselfish services, and not the emotions of protectors towards dependents, or of dependents towards protectors. The arrangements of society are now such that no]
   49   as 48 . . . the emotion of . . . as 48
   [s-s]52   scarcely attempts, except nominally,
   [t-t]48, 49   a
   [u-u]48, 49   of the law   [v-v]48, 49   classes of Western Europe at least

it may be pronounced certain, that the patriarchal or paternal system of government is one to which they will not again be subject. That question ^w was decided, when they were taught to read, and allowed access to newspapers and political tracts ^x; when^x dissenting preachers were suffered to go among them, and appeal to their faculties and feelings in opposition to the creeds professed and countenanced by their superiors ^y; when^y they were brought together in numbers, to work socially under the same roof ^z; when^z railways enabled them to shift from place to place, and change their patrons and employers as easily as their ^acoats; when they were encouraged to seek a share in the government, by means of the electoral franchise.^a The working classes have taken their interests into their own hands, and are perpetually showing that they think the interests of their employers not identical with their own, but opposite to them. Some among the higher classes flatter themselves that these tendencies may be counteracted by moral and religious education: but they have let the time go by for giving an education which can serve their purpose. The principles of the Reformation have reached as low down in society as reading and writing, and the poor will ^bnot much^b longer accept morals and religion of other people's prescribing. I speak more particularly of ^cthis^c country, especially the town population, and the districts of the most scientific agriculture ^dor the^d highest wages, Scotland and the north of England. Among the more inert and less modernized agricultural population of the southern counties, it might be possible for the gentry to retain, for some time longer, something of the ancient deference and submission of the poor, by bribing them with high wages and constant employment; by insuring them support, and never requiring them to do anything which they do not like. But these are two conditions which never have been combined, and never can be, for long together. A guarantee of subsistence can only be practically kept up, when work is enforced and superfluous multiplication restrained by at least a moral compulsion. It is then, that the would-be revivers of old times which they do not understand, would feel practically in how hopeless a task they were engaged. The whole fabric of patriarchal or seignorial influence, attempted to be raised on the foundation of caressing the poor, would be shattered against the necessity of enforcing a stringent Poor-law.

^w48, 49   has been several times decided. It
^{x–x}48, 49   . It was decided when
^{y–y}48, 49   . It was decided when
^{z–z}48, 49   . It was decided when
^{a–a}48, 49   coats.] 52   coats; above all, when . . . as 71
^{b–b}48, 49, 52   no
^{c–c}48, 49   our own
^{d–d}48, 49, 52   and

§ 2. [*The future well-being of the labouring classes is principally depen-dent on their own mental cultivation*] It is on a far other basis that the well-being and well-doing of the labouring people must henceforth rest. The poor have come out of leading-strings, and cannot any longer be governed or treated like children. To their own qualities must now be commended the care of their destiny. Modern nations will have to learn the lesson, that the well-being of a people must exist by means of the justice and self-government, the δικαιοσύνη and σωφροσύνη, of the individual citizens. The theory of dependence attempts to dispense with the necessity of these qualities in the dependent classes. But now, when even in position they are becoming less and less dependent, and their minds less and less acquiescent in the degree of dependence which remains, the virtues of independence are those which they stand in need of. *ª*Whatever*ª* advice, exhortation, or guidance is held out to the labouring classes, must hence-forth be tendered to them as equals, and accepted *ᵇ*by them*ᵇ* with their eyes open. The prospect of the future depends on the degree in which they can be made rational beings.

There is no reason to believe that prospect other than hopeful. The progress indeed *ᶜ*has hitherto been, and still is,*ᶜ* slow. But there is a spon-taneous education going on in the minds of the multitude, which may be greatly accelerated and improved by artificial aids. The instruction obtained from newspapers and political tracts *ᵈ*may not be the most solid kind*ᵈ* of instruction, but it is *ᵉ*an immense improvement upon*ᵉ* none at all. *ᶠ*What it does for a people, has been admirably exemplified during the cotton crisis, in the case of the Lancashire spinners and weavers, who have acted with the consistent good sense and forbearance so justly applauded, simply because, being readers of newspapers, they understood the causes of the calamity which had befallen them, and knew that it was in no way imputable either to their employers or to the Government. It is not certain that their conduct would have been as rational and exemplary, if the distress had preceded the salutary measure of fiscal emancipation which gave existence to the penny press.*ᶠ* The institutions for lectures and dis-cussion, the collective deliberations on questions of common interest, the trades unions, the political agitation, all serve to awaken public spirit, to diffuse variety of ideas among the mass, and to excite *ᵍ* thought and reflec-

*ª-ª*48   These virtues it is still in the power of governments and of the higher classes greatly to promote; and they can hardly do anything which does not, by its own effects or those of its example, either assist or impede that object. But whatever
ᵇ-ᵇ+65, 71
*ᶜ-ᶜ*48, 49   must always be
*ᵈ-ᵈ*48, 49, 57, 62   is not the best sort] 52   may not be the best sort
*ᵉ-ᵉ*48, 49, 52, 57, 62   vastly superior to
ᶠ-ᶠ+65, 71
*ᵍ*48   real

tion in *h* the more intelligent *i*. Although the too early attainment of political
franchises by the least educated class might retard, instead of promoting,
their improvement, there can be little doubt that it *j*has been*j* greatly
stimulated by the attempt to acquire *k*them*k*. In the meantime, the working
classes are now part of thc public; in all discussions on matters of general
interest they, or a portion of them, are now partakers; all who use the
press as an instrument may, if it so *l*happens*l*, have them for an audience;
the avenues of instruction through which the middle classes acquire *m*such
ideas as*m* they have, are accessible to, at least, the operatives in the towns.
With these resources, it cannot be doubted that they will increase in intelligence, even by their own unaided efforts; while there is *n* reason to hope
that great improvements both in the quality and quantity of school education will be *o* effected by the exertions *p*either of government or*p* of individuals, and that the progress of the mass of the people in mental
cultivation, and in the virtues which are dependent on it, will take place
more rapidly, and with fewer intermittences and aberrations, than if left
to itself.

From this increase of intelligence, several effects may be confidently
anticipated. First: that they will become even less willing than at present
to be led and governed, and directed into the way they should go, by the
mere authority and *prestige* of superiors. If they have not now, still less
will they have hereafter, any deferential awe, or religious principle of
obedience, holding them in mental subjection to a class above them. The
theory of dependence and protection will be more and more intolerable
to them, and they will require that their conduct and condition shall be
essentially self-governed. It is, at the same time, quite possible that they
may demand, in many cases, the intervention of the legislature in their
affairs, and the regulation by law of various things which concern them,
often under very mistaken ideas of their interest. Still, it is their own will,
their own ideas and suggestions, to which they will demand that effect
should be given, and not rules laid down for them by other people. It is

---

*h*48   a few of
*i*48   , who become the leaders and instructors of the rest
*j-j*48, 49, 52   is
*k-k*48   those franchises. It is of little importance that some of them may, at a
certain stage of their progress, adopt mistaken opinions. Communists are already
numerous, and are likely to increase in number; but nothing tends more to the
mental developement of the working classes than that all the questions which Communism raises should be largely and freely discussed by them; nothing could be
more instructive than that some should actually form communities, and try practically
what it is to live without the institution of property] 49   those franchises
*l-l*48, 49, 52   chances
*m-m*48, 49   most of the ideas which
*n*48, 49   every
*o*48, 49   speedily   *p-p*48, 49   of government and

quite consistent with this, that they should feel ^{q} respect for superiority of intellect and knowledge, and defer much to the opinions, on any subject, of those whom they think well acquainted with it. Such deference is deeply grounded in human nature; but they will judge for themselves of the persons who are and are not entitled to it.

§ 3. [*Probable effects of improved intelligence in causing a better adjustment of population—Would be promoted by the social independence of women*] It appears to me impossible but that the increase of intelligence, of education, and of the love of independence among the working classes, must be attended with a corresponding growth of the good sense which manifests itself in provident habits of conduct, and that population, therefore, will bear a gradually diminishing ratio to capital and employment. This most desirable result would be much accelerated by another change, which lies in the direct line of the best tendencies of the time; the opening of industrial occupations freely to both sexes. The same reasons which make it no longer necessary that the poor should depend on the rich, make it equally unnecessary that women should depend on men; and the least which justice requires is that law and custom should not enforce dependence (when the correlative protection has become superfluous) by ordaining that a woman, who does not happen to have a provision by inheritance, shall have scarcely any means open to her of gaining a livelihood, except as a wife and mother. Let women who prefer that occupation, adopt it; but that there should be no option, no other *carrière* possible for the great majority of women, except in the humbler departments of life, is ^{a}a flagrant social injustice. The ideas and institutions by which the accident of sex is made the groundwork of an inequality of legal rights, and a forced dissimilarity of social functions, must ere long be recognised as the greatest hindrance to moral, social, and even intellectual improvement. ^{b} On the present occasion I shall only indicate, among the probable consequences of the industrial and social independence of women^a, a great diminution

^{q}48   real
$^{a-a}$48   one of those social injustices which call loudest for remedy. Among the salutary consequences of correcting it, one of the most probable would be] 49   *as* 48 . . . remedy. The ramifications of this subject are far too numerous and intricate to be pursued here. The social and political equality of the sexes is not a question of economical detail, but one of principle, so intimately connected with all the more vital points of human improvement, that none of them can be thoroughly discussed independently of it. But for this very reason it cannot be disposed of by way of parenthesis, in a treatise devoted to other subjects. It is sufficient for the immediate purpose, to point out, among . . . *as* 71
^{b}52   [*footnote:*] *It is truly disgraceful that in a woman's reign, not one step has been made by law towards removing even the smallest portion of the existing injustice to women. The brutal part of the population can still maltreat, not to say kill, their wives, with the next thing to impunity; and as to civil and social

of the evil of over-population. It is by devoting one-half of the human species to that exclusive function, by making it fill the entire life of one sex, and interweave itself with almost all the objects of the other, that the ᶜanimalᶜ instinct in question is nursed into the disproportionate preponderance which it has hitherto exercised in human life.

§ 4. [*Tendency of society towards the disuse of the relation of hiring and service*] The political consequences of the increasing power and importance of the operative classes, and of the growing ascendancy of numbers, which, even ᵃin England andᵃ under the present institutions, is rapidly giving to the will of the majority at least a negative voice in the acts of government, are too wide a subject to be discussed in this place. But, confining ourselves to economical considerations, and notwithstanding the effect which improved intelligence in the working classes, together with just laws, may have in altering the distribution of the produce to their advantage, I cannot think ᵇ that they will be permanently contented with the condition of labouring for wages as their ultimate state. ᶜ They may be willing to pass through the class of servants in their way to that of employers; but not to remain in it all their lives. To begin as hired labourers, then after a few years to work on their own account, and finally employ others, is the normal condition of labourers in a new country, rapidly increasing in wealth and population, like America or Australia. But ᵈin an old and fully peopled country, those who begin life as labourers for hire, as a general rule, continue such to the end, unless they sink into the still lower grade of recipients of public charity. In the present stage of

---

status, in framing a new reform bill for the extension of the elective franchise, the opportunity was not taken for so small a recognition of something like equality of rights, as would have been made by admitting to the suffrage, women of the same class and the same householding and tax-paying qualifications as the men who already possess it.] 57 *as* 52 . . . possess it. (Mr. Fitzroy's Act for the Better Protection of Women and Children against Assaults, is a well-meant though inadequate attempt to wipe off the former reproach. The second is more flagrant than ever, *another* Reform Bill having been since presented, largely extending the franchise among many classes of men, but leaving all women in their existing state of political as well as social servitude.) [*JSM's brackets*]   ᶜ⁻ᶜ+52, 57, 62, 65, 71

   ᵃ⁻ᵃ+49, 52, 57, 62, 65, 71   ᵇ48, 49   it probable

   ᶜ48, 49   To work at the bidding and for the profit of another, without any interest in the work—the price of their labour being adjusted by hostile competition, one side demanding as much and the other paying as little as possible—is not, even when wages are high, a satisfactory state to human beings of educated intelligence, who have ceased to think themselves naturally inferior to those whom they serve.

   ᵈ⁻ᵈ⁷⁶⁷⁴⁸, 49   something else is required when wealth increases slowly, or has reached the stationary state, when positions, instead of being more mobile, would tend to be much more permanent than at present, and the condition of any portion of mankind could only be desirable, if made desirable from the first.

human progress, when ideas of equality are daily spreading more widely among the poorer classes, and can no longer be checked by anything short of the entire suppression of printed discussion and even of freedom of speech, it is not to be expected that the division of the human race into two hereditary classes, employers and employed, can be permanently maintained. The relation is nearly as unsatisfactory to the payer of wages as to the receiver. If the rich regard the poor as, by a kind of natural law, their servants and dependents, the rich in their turn are regarded as a mere prey and pasture for the poor; the subject of demands and expectations wholly indefinite, increasing in extent with every concession made to them [e]. The total absence of regard for justice or fairness in the relations between the two, is as marked on the side of the employed as on that of the employers. We look in vain among the working classes in general for the just pride which will choose to give good work for good wages; for the most part, their sole endeavour is to receive as much, and return as little in the shape of service, as possible[e]. It will sooner or later become insupportable to the employing classes, to live in close and hourly contact with persons whose interests and feelings are in hostility to them. Capitalists are almost as much interested as labourers in placing the operations of industry on such a footing, that those who labour [f]for them[f] may feel the same interest in the work [g] , which is felt by those who labour [h]on their own account[h].[d]

The opinion expressed in a former part of this treatise respecting small landed properties and peasant proprietors, may have made the reader anticipate that a wide diffusion of property in land is the resource on which I rely for exempting at least the agricultural labourers from exclusive dependence on labour for hire. Such, however, is not my opinion. I indeed deem that form of agricultural economy to be most groundlessly [i]cried down[i], and to be greatly preferable, in its aggregate effects on human happiness, to hired labour in any form in which it exists at present; because the prudential check to population acts more directly, and is shown by experience to be more efficacious; and because, in point of security, of independence, of exercise [j]of any other than the animal faculties[j], the state of a peasant proprietor is far [k]superior to that of an agricultural labourer in this or any other old country[k]. Where the former system already exists,

[e-e]52 , while the return given in the shape of service is sought to be reduced to the lowest minimum

[f-f]+57, 62, 65, 71   [g]52   they perform
[h-h]52   for themselves   [i-i]48, 49, 52, 57   decried

[j-j]48, 49   for the moral faculties and for the intellect] 52, 57, 62   for any . . . as 71

[k-k]48, 49   nearer to what the state of the labourers should be, than the condition of an agriculturist in this or any other country of hired labour

and works on the whole satisfactorily, I should regret, in the present state of human intelligence, to see it abolished in order to make way for the other, under a pedantic notion of agricultural improvement as a thing necessarily the same in every diversity of circumstances. In a backward state of industrial improvement, as in Ireland, I should urge its introduction, in preference to an exclusive system of hired labour; as a more powerful instrument for raising a population from semi-savage listlessness and recklessness, to [l] persevering industry and prudent calculation.

But a people who have once adopted the large system of production, either in [m]manufactures[m] or in agriculture, are not likely to recede from it; [n]and[n] when population is kept in due proportion to the means of support, [o]it is not desirable that[o] they should. Labour is unquestionably more productive on the system of large industrial enterprises; the produce, if not greater absolutely, is greater in proportion to the labour employed: the same number of persons can be supported equally well with less toil and greater leisure; which will be wholly an advantage, as soon as civilization and improvement have so far advanced, that what is a benefit to the whole shall be a benefit to each individual composing it. [p]And in the moral aspect of the question, which is still more important than the economical, something better should be aimed at as the goal of industrial improvement, than to disperse mankind over the earth in single families, each ruled internally, as families now are, by a patriarchal despot, and having scarcely any community of interest, or necessary mental communion, with other human beings. The domination of the head of the family over the other members, in this state of things, is [q]absolute[q]; while [r]the effect on his own mind tends[r] towards concentration of all interests in the family, considered as an expansion of self, and absorption of all passions in that of exclusive possession, of all cares in those of preservation and acquisition. As a step out of the merely animal state into the human, out of reckless abandonment to brute instincts into prudential foresight and self-government, this moral condition may be seen without displeasure. But if public spirit, generous sentiments, or [s]true[s] justice and equality are desired, association, not isolation, of interests, is the school in which these excellences are nurtured. The aim of improvement should be not solely to place human beings in a condition in which they will be able to do without one another, but to enable them to work with or for one another in relations not involving dependence. Hitherto there has been no alternative for those who lived by

[l]48, 49   habits of
[m–m]57   manufacture [*printer's error?*]
[n–n]48, 49   nor,
[o–o]48, 49   is there any sufficient reason why
[p–p]76948, 49   The problem is, to obtain
[q–q]52   supreme   [r–r]52   in the chief, its tendency is   [s–s]52   even

their labour, but that of labouring either each for himself alone, or for a master. But the civilizing and improving influences of association, and*p* the efficiency and economy of production on a large scale, *t*may be obtained*t* without dividing the producers into two parties with hostile interests *u*and feelings*u*, the many who do the work being mere servants under the command of the one who supplies the funds, and having no interest of their own in the enterprise except to *v*earn their wages with as little labour as possible. The speculations and discussions of the last fifty years, and the events of the last *w*thirty*w*, are abundantly conclusive on this point. *x*If the improvement which even triumphant military despotism has only retarded, not stopped, shall continue its course*x*, there can be little doubt that the *status* of hired labourers will gradually tend to confine itself to the description of workpeople whose low moral qualities render them unfit for anything more independent: and that the relation of masters and workpeople will be gradually superseded by partnership, in one of two forms: *y* in some cases, association of the labourers with the capitalist; in *z*others, and perhaps finally*z* in all, association of labourers among themselves*v*.

§ 5. [*Examples of the association of labourers with capitalists*] *a* The first of these forms of association has long been practised, not indeed as a rule, but as an exception. In several departments of industry there are already cases in which every one who contributes to the work, either by labour or by pecuniary resources, has a partner's interest in it, proportional to the value of his contribution. It is already a common practice to remunerate those in whom peculiar trust is reposed, by means of a percentage on the profits: and cases exist in which the principle is, with *b* excellent success, carried down to the class of mere manual labourers.

In the American ships trading to China, it has long been the custom for every sailor to have an interest in the profits of the voyage; and to this has been ascribed the general good conduct of those seamen, and the extreme rarity of any collision between them and the government or people of the country. An instance in England, not so well known as it deserves to be, is that of the Cornish miners. "In Cornwall the mines are worked strictly on the system of joint adventure; gangs of miners contracting with the agent,

t-t+52, 57, 62, 65, 71
*u-u*48, 49   , employers and employed
*v-v*48, 49   fulfil their contract and earn their wages
*w-w*52   five] 57, 62   ten] 65   twenty
*x-x*52, 57   Unless the military despotism now triumphant on the Continent should succeed in its nefarious attempts to throw back the human mind
*y*52, 57, 62   temporarily and
*z-z*52, 57   other cases, and finally] 62   other cases, and perhaps finally
a[*for* 48, 49 *versions of the remainder of this chapter, see* Appendix D]
*b*52   the most

who represents the owner of the mine, to execute a certain portion of a vein and fit the ore for market, at the price of so much in the pound of the sum for which the ore is sold. These contracts are put up at certain regular periods, generally every two months, and taken by a voluntary partnership of men accustomed to the mine. This system has its disadvantages, in consequence of the uncertainty and irregularity of the earnings, and consequent necessity of living for long periods on credit; but it has advantages which more than counterbalance these drawbacks. It produces a degree of intelligence, independence, and moral elevation, which raise the condition and character of the Cornish miner far above that of the generality of the labouring class. We are told by Dr. Barham, that 'they are not only, as a class, intelligent for labourers, but men of considerable knowledge.' Also, that 'they have a character of independence, something American, the system by which the contracts are let giving the takers entire freedom to make arrangements among themselves; so that each man feels, as a partner in his little firm, that he meets his employers on nearly equal terms.' . . . With this basis of intelligence and independence in their character, we are not surprised when we hear that 'a very great number of miners are now located on possessions of their own, leased for three lives or ninety-nine years, on which they have built houses;' or that '281,541*l.* are deposited in *^c*saving*^c* banks in Cornwall, of which two-thirds are estimated to belong to miners.' " *

Mr. Babbage, who also gives an account of this system, observes that the payment to the crews of whaling ships is governed by a similar principle; and that "the profits arising from fishing with nets on the south coast of England are thus divided: one-half the produce belongs to the owner of the boat and net; the other half is divided in equal portions between the persons using it, who are also bound to assist in repairing the net when required." Mr. Babbage has the great merit of having pointed out the practicability, and the advantage, of extending the principle to manufacturing industry generally.†

Some attention has been excited by an experiment of this nature, commenced *^d*above thirty*^d* years ago by a Paris tradesman, a house-painter, M. Leclaire,‡ and described by him in a pamphlet published in the year 1842. M. Leclaire, according to his statement, employs on an average two

---

*This passage is from the Prize Essay on the Causes and Remedies of National Distress, by Mr. Samuel Laing [*Atlas Prize Essay. National Distress; its Causes and Remedies.* London: Longman, Brown, Green, and Longmans, 1844, pp. 40–1]. The extracts which it includes are from the Appendix to the Report of the Children's Employment Commission.

†*Economy of Machinery and Manufactures*, 3rd edition, ch. 26 [p. 259].

‡His establishment is [52, 57, 62   (or was)] 11, Rue Saint Georges.

^c–*^c*Source, 52, 57, 62   savings
^d–*^d*52   about ten] 57, 62, 65   about sixteen

hundred workmen, whom he pays in the usual manner, by fixed wages or salaries. He assigns to himself, besides interest for his capital, a fixed allowance for his labour and responsibility as manager. At the end of the year, the surplus profits are divided among the body, himself included, in the proportion of their salaries.* The reasons by which M. Leclaire was led to adopt this system are highly instructive. Finding the conduct of his workmen unsatisfactory, he first tried the effect of giving higher wages, and by this he managed to obtain a body of excellent workmen, who would not quit his service for any other. "Having thus succeeded" (I quote from an abstract of the pamphlet in Chambers' Journal,†) "in producing some sort of stability in the ᵉarrangementᵉ of his establishment, M. Leclaire expected, he says, to enjoy greater peace of mind. In this, however, he was disappointed. So long as he was able to superintend everything himself, from the general concerns of his business down to its minutest details, he did enjoy a certain satisfaction; but from the moment that, owing to the increase of his business, he found that he could be nothing more than the centre from which orders were issued, and to which reports were brought in, his former anxiety and discomfort returned upon him."[*] He speaks lightly of the other sources of anxiety to which a tradesman is subject, but describes as an incessant cause of vexation the losses arising from the misconduct of workmen. An employer "will find workmen whose indifference to his interests is such that they do not perform two-thirds of the amount of work which they are capable of; hence the continual fretting of masters, who, seeing their interests neglected, believe themselves entitled to suppose that workmen are constantly conspiring to ruin those from whom they derive their livelihood. If the journeyman were sure of constant employment, his position would in some respects be more enviable than that of the master, because he is assured of a certain amount of day's wages, which he will get whether he works much or little. He runs no risk, and has no other motive to stimulate him to do his best than his own sense of duty. The master, on the other hand, depends greatly on chance for his returns: his position is one of continual irritation and anxiety. This would no longer be the case to the same extent, if the interests of the master and those of the

*[49] It appears, however, that the workmen whom M. Leclaire had admitted to this participation of profits, were only a portion (rather less than half) of the whole number whom he employed. This is explained by another part of his system. M. Leclaire pays the full market rate of wages to all his workmen. The share of profit assigned to them is, therefore, a clear addition to the ordinary gains of their class, which he very laudably uses as an instrument of improvement, by making it the reward of desert, or the recompense for peculiar trust.

†For September 27, 1845. ["M. Leclaire of Paris," *Chamber's Edinburgh Journal*, n.s. IV, pp. 193–4.]

    [*Ibid., 193.]

ᵉ⁻ᵉSource, 52, 57, 62, 65   arrangements

workmen were bound up with each other, connected by some bond of mutual security, such as that which would be obtained by the plan of a yearly division of profits."[*]

Even in the first year during which M. Leclaire's experiment was in complete operation, the success was remarkable. Not one of his journeymen who worked as many as three hundred days, earned in that year less than 1500 francs, and some considerably more. His highest rate of daily wages being four francs, or 1200 francs for 300 days, the remaining 300 francs, or 12l., must have been the smallest amount which any journeyman, who worked that number of days, obtained as his proportion of the surplus profit. M. Leclaire describes in strong terms the improvement which was already manifest in the habits and demeanour of his workmen, not merely when at work, and in their relations with their employer, but at other times and in other relations, showing increased respect both for others and for themselves. [f]M. Chevalier, in a work published in 1848,† stated on M. Leclaire's authority,[f] that the increased zeal of the workpeople continued to be a full compensation to [g]him[g], even in a pecuniary sense, for the share of profit which he renounced in their favour. [h]And [i]Mr.[i] Villiaumé, in 1857‡ observes:—"Quoiqu'il ait toujours banni la fraude, qui n'est que trop fréquente dans sa profession, il a toujours pu soutenir la concurrence et acquérir une belle aisance, malgré l'abandon d'une si large part de ses profits. Assurément il n'y est parvenu que parce que l'activité inusitée de ses ouvriers, et la surveillance qu'ils exerçaient les uns sur les autres dans les nombreux chantiers, avaient compensé la diminution de ses profits personnels."§

[*"M. Leclaire of Paris," p. 194.]

†[49] Lettres sur l'Organisation du Travail [Paris: Capelle, 1848], par Michel Chevalier, lettre xiv [p. 298]. [49, 52   *"Je tiens de M. Leclaire que chez lui l'avantage du zèle extrême dont sont animés les ouvriers, depuis qu'il a adopté le système de la participation, fait plus que compenser le sacrifice représenté par la somme des parts qu'on leur alloue." Lettres . . . as 71] 57   as 49 . . . lettre xiv. [paragraph] A recent traveller describes a similar system to that of M. Leclaire, as practised by the Chinese at Manilla. "In these Chinese shops the owner . . . as II.774.n22–34 below] [49, 52, 57, 62   this footnote occurs at favour 3 lines below].

‡[62] Nouveau Traité d'Economie Politique [Paris: Guillaumin, 1857, Vol. II, p. 82].

§[65] At the present time [65   (1865)] M. Leclaire's establishment is conducted on a somewhat altered system, though the principle of dividing the profits is maintained. There are now three partners in the concern: M. Leclaire himself, one other person (M. Defournaux), and a Provident Society (Société de Secours Mutuels), of which all persons in his employment are the members. (This Society owns an excellent library, and has scientific, technical, and other

[f]–[f]52, 57 The system was still in operation in 1848; and we learn from M. Chevalier   [g]–[g]52, 57 M. Leclaire
      [h]–[h]77[3]+62, 65, 71   [i]–[i]62, 65 M.

The beneficent example set by M. Leclaire has been followed, with brilliant success, by other employers of labour on a large scale at Paris; and I annex, from the work last referred to (one of the ablest of the many able treatises on political economy produced by the present generation of the political economists of France), some signal examples of the economical and moral benefit arising from this admirable arrangement.*[h]

[j]Until the passing of the Limited Liability Act, it was held that an

_____

lectures regularly delivered to it.) Each of the three partners has 100,000 francs invested in the concern; M. Leclaire having advanced to the Provident Society as much as was necessary to supply the original insufficiency of their own funds. The partnership, on the part of the Society, is limited; on that of M. Leclaire and M. Defournaux, unlimited. These two receive 6000 francs (240*l*.) per annum each as wages of superintendence. Of the annual profits they receive half, though owning two-thirds of the capital. The remaining half belongs to the employés and workpeople; two-fifths of it being paid to the Provident Society, and the other three-fifths divided among the body. M. Leclaire, however, now reserves to himself the right of deciding who shall share in the distribution, and to what amount; only binding himself never to retain any part, but to bestow whatever has not been awarded to individuals, on the Provident Society. It is further provided that in case of the retirement of both the private partners, the goodwill and plant shall become, without payment, the property of the Society.

*[62] "En Mars 1847, M. Paul Dupont, gérant d'une imprimerie de Paris, eut l'idée d'associer ses ouvriers en leur promettant le dixième des bénéfices. Il en emploie habituellement trois cents, dont deux cents travaillent aux pièces et cent à la journée. Il emploie, en outre, cent auxiliaires, qui ne font pas partie de l'association.

"La part de bénéfice avenant aux ouvriers ne leur vaut guère, en moyenne, qu'une quinzaine de jours de travail; mais ils reçoivent leur salaire ordinaire suivant le tarif établi dans toutes les grandes imprimeries de Paris; et, de plus, ils ont l'avantage d'être soignés dans leurs maladies aux frais de la communauté, et de recevoir 1 fr. 50 cent. de salaire par jour d'incapacité de travail. Les ouvriers ne peuvent retirer leur part dans les bénéfices que quand ils sortent de l'association. Chaque année, cette part, qui est représentée tant en matériel qu'en rentes sur l'Etat, s'augmente par la capitalisation des intérêts, et crée ainsi une réserve à l'ouvrier.

"M. Dupont et les capitalistes, ses commanditaires, trouvent dans cette association un profit bien supérieur à celui qu'ils auraient; les ouvriers, de leur côté, se félicitent chaque jour de l'heureuse idée de leur patron. Plusieurs d'entre eux, encouragés à la réussite de l'établissement, lui ont fait obtenir une médaille d'or en 1849, une médaille d'honneur à l'Exposition Universelle de 1855; et quelques uns même ont reçu personellement la recompense de leurs découvertes et de leurs travaux. Chez un patron ordinaire, ces braves gens n'auraient pas eu le loisir de poursuivre leurs inventions, à moins que d'en laisser tout l'honneur à celui qui n'en était pas l'auteur: tandis qu'étant associés, si le patron eût été injuste, deux cents hommes eussent fait redresser ses torts.

"J'ai visité moi-même cet établissement, et j'ai pu m'assurer du perfectionnement que cette association apporte aux habitudes des ouvriers.

"M. Gisquet, ancien préfet de police, est propriétaire depuis long-temps d'une fabrique d'huile à Saint-Denis, qui est la plus importante de France, après celle

arrangement similar to M. Leclaire's would have been impossible in
England, as the workmen could not, in the previous state of the law, have
been associated in the profits, without being liable for losses. One of the
many benefits of that great legislative improvement has been to render
partnerships of this description possible, and we may now expect to see
them carried into practice. Messrs. Briggs, of the Whitwood and Methley
collieries, near Normanton in Yorkshire, have taken the first step. They
^{k}now^k work these mines by a company, two-thirds of the capital of which
they ^{l} themselves continue to hold, but ^{m}undertake^m, in the allotment of the
remaining third, ^{n}to^n give the preference to the "officials and operatives
employed in the concern;" and, what is of still greater importance, ^{o} whenever the annual profit exceeds 10 per cent, one-half the excess ^{p}is^p divided

de M. Darblay, de Corbeil. Lorsqu'en 1848 il prit le parti de la diriger lui-même,
il rencontra des ouvriers habitués à s'enivrer plusieurs fois par semaine, et qui,
pendant le travail, chantaient, fumaient, et quelquefois se disputaient. On avait
maintes fois essayé sans succès de changer cet état de choses: il y parvint par la
prohibition faite à tous ses ouvriers de s'enivrer les jours de travail, sous peine
d'exclusion, et par la promesse de partager entre eux, à titre de gratification
annuelle, 5 p. 100 de ses bénéfices nets, au *pro rata* des salaires, qui, du reste,
sont fixés, aux prix courants. Depuis ce moment, la reforme a été complète: il
se voit entouré d'une centaine d'ouvriers pleins de zèle et de dévouement. Leur
bien-être s'est accru de tout ce qu'ils ne dépensent pas en boissons, et de ce
qu'ils gagnent par leur exactitude au travail. La gratification que M. Gisquet
leur accorde, leur a valu, en moyenne, chaque année, l'équivalent de leur salaire
pendant six semaines. . . . .

"M. Beslay, ancien député de 1830 à 1839, et représentant du peuple à
l'Assemblée Constituante, a fondé un atelier important de machines à vapeur à
Paris, dans le Faubourg du Temple. Il eut l'idée d'associer dans ce dernier
établissement ses ouvriers, dès le commencement de 1847. Je transcris ici cet
acte d'association, que l'on peut regarder comme l'un des plus complets de tous
ceux faits entre patrons et ouvriers." [Villiaumé, Vol. II, pp. 80–1, 271.]

The practical sagacity of Chinese emigrants long ago suggested to them,
according to the report of a recent visitor to Manilla, a similar constitution of
the relation between an employer and labourers. "In these Chinese shops"
(at Manilla) "the owner usually engages all the activity of his countrymen
employed by him in them, by giving each of them a share in the profits of the
concern, or in fact by making them all small partners in the business, of which
he of course takes care to retain the lion's share, so that while doing good for
him by managing it well, they are also benefiting themselves. To such an extent
is this principle carried that it is usual to give even their coolies a share in the
profits of the business in lieu of fixed wages, and the plan appears to suit their
temper well; for although they are in general most complete eye-servants when
working for a fixed wage, they are found to be most industrious and useful ones
when interested even for the smallest share."—McMicking's [52, 57   M'Mick-
ing's] [MacMicking, Robert] Recollections of Manilla and the Philippines
during 1848, 1849, and 1850 [London: Bentley, 1851], p. 24.

$^{k-k}$65 have issued a proposal to	^{l}65 will
$^{m-m}$65 will	$^{n-n}$+71
^{o}65 will propose to the shareholders, that	$^{p-p}$65 shall be

among the workpeople and employés, whether shareholders or not, in proportion to their earnings during the year. It is highly honourable to these important employers of labour to have initiated a system so full of benefit both to the operatives employed and to the general interest of social improvement: and they express no more than a just confidence in the principle when they say, that "the adoption of the mode of appropriation thus recommended would, it is believed, add so great an element of success to the undertaking as to increase rather than diminish the dividend to the shareholders."[j]

§ 6. [*Examples of the association of labourers among themselves*] The form of association, however, which if mankind [a]continue[a] to improve, must be expected in the end to predominate, is not that which can exist between a capitalist as chief, and workpeople without a voice in the management, but the association of the labourers themselves on terms of equality, collectively owning the capital with which they carry on their operations, and working under managers elected and removable by themselves. So long as this idea remained in a state of theory, in the writings of Owen or of Louis Blanc, it may have appeared, to the common modes of judgment, incapable of being realized, and not likely to be tried unless by seizing on the existing capital, and confiscating it for the benefit of the labourers; which is even now imagined by many persons, and pretended by more, both in England and on the Continent, to be the meaning and purpose of Socialism. But there is a capacity of exertion and self-denial in the masses of mankind, which is never known but on the rare occasions on which it is appealed to in the name of some great idea or elevated sentiment. Such an appeal was made by the French Revolution of 1848. For the first time it then seemed to the intelligent and generous of the working classes of a great nation, that they had obtained a government who sincerely desired the freedom and dignity of the many, and who did not look upon it as their natural and legitimate state to be instruments of production, worked for the benefit of the possessors of capital. Under this encouragement, the ideas sown by Socialist writers, of an emancipation of labour to be effected by means of association, throve and fructified; and many working people came to the resolution, not only that they would work for one another, instead of working for a master tradesman or manufacturer, but that they would also free themselves, at whatever cost of labour or privation, from the necessity of paying, out of the produce of their industry, a heavy tribute for the use of capital; that they would extinguish this tax, not by robbing the capitalists of what they or their predecessors had acquired by labour and preserved by economy, but by honestly acquiring capital for themselves. If only a few operatives had attempted this arduous

[a]–[a]52   contrive [*printer's error?*]

task, or if, while many attempted it, a few only had succeeded, their success might have been deemed to furnish no argument for their system as a permanent mode of industrial organization. But, excluding all the instances of failure, there exist, or existed a *short time* ago, upwards of a hundred successful, and many eminently prosperous, associations of operatives in Paris alone, besides a considerable number in the departments. An instructive sketch of their history and principles has been published under the title of "L'Association Ouvrière Industrielle et Agricole, par H. Feugueray:"[*] and as it is frequently affirmed in English newspapers that the associations at Paris have failed, by writers who appear to mistake the predictions of their enemies at their first formation for the testimonies of subsequent experience, I think it important to show by quotations from M. Feugueray's volume, *strengthened by still later testimonies,* that these representations are not only wide of the truth, but the extreme contrary of it.

The capital of most of the associations was originally confined to the few tools belonging to the founders, and the small sums which could be collected from their savings, or which were lent to them by other work-people as poor as themselves. In some cases, however, loans of capital were made to them by the republican government: but the associations which obtained these advances, or at least which obtained them before they had already achieved success, are, it appears, in general by no means the most prosperous. The most striking instances of prosperity are in the case of those who have had nothing to rely on but their own slender means and the small loans of fellow-workmen, and who lived on bread and water while they devoted the whole surplus of their gains to the formation of a capital. "Souvent," says M. Feugueray,* "la caisse était tout-à-fait vide, et il n'y avait pas de salaire du tout. Et puis la vente ne marchait pas, les rentrées se faisaient attendre, les valeurs ne s'escomptaient pas, le magasin des matières premières était vide; et il fallait se priver, se restreindre dans toutes ses dépenses, se réduire quelquefois au pain et à l'eau . . . C'est au prix de ces angoisses et de ces misères, c'est par cette voie douloureuse, que des hommes, sans presque aucune autre ressource au début que leur bonne volonté et leurs bras, sont parvenus à se former une clientèle, à acquérir un crédit, à se créer enfin un capital social, et à fonder ainsi des associations dont l'avenir aujourd'hui semble assuré."

I will quote at length the remarkable history of one of these associations.†

"La nécessité d'un puissant capital pour l'établissement d'une fabrique de pianos était si bien reconnue dans la corporation, qu'en 1848 les délégués de plusieurs centaines d'ouvriers, qui s'étaient réunis pour la

_____

[*Paris: Havard, 1851.]

*[52] P. 112.

†[52] Pp. 113–6 [113–7].

*b–b*52   few months   *c–c*+62, 65, 71

formation d'une grande association, demandèrent en son nom au gouvernement une subvention de 300,000 fr., c'est-à-dire la dixième partie du fonds
total voté par l'Assemblée Constituante. Je me souviens d'avoir fait, en
qualité de membre de la commission chargée de distribuer ces fonds, des
efforts inutiles pour convaincre les deux délégués avec qui la commission
était en rapport, que leur demande était exorbitante. Toutes mes instances
restèrent sans succès; je prolongeai vainement la conférence pendant près
de deux heures. Les deux délégués me répondirent imperturbablement que
leur industrie était dans une condition spéciale; que l'association ne pouvait
s'y établir avec chance de réussite que sur une très grande échelle et avec
un capital considérable, et que la somme de 300,000 fr. était un minimum
au-dessous duquel ils ne pouvaient descendre; bref, qu'ils ne pouvaient pas
réduire leur demande d'un sou. La commission refusa.

"Or, après ce refus, et le projet de la grande association étant abandonné,
voici ce qui arriva: c'est que quatorze ouvriers, et il est assez singulier que
parmi eux se soit trouvé l'un des deux délégués, se résolurent à fonder entre
eux une association pour la fabrique des pianos. Le projet était au moins
téméraire de la part d'hommes qui n'avaient ni argent ni crédit; mais la foi
ne raissone pas, elle agit.

"Nos quatorze hommes se mirent donc à l'œuvre, et voici le récit de
leurs premiers travaux, que j'emprunte à un article du *National*, très bien
redigé par M. Cochut, et dont je me plais à attester l'exactitude.

"Quelques-uns d'entre eux, qui avaient travaillé à leur propre compte,
apportèrent, tant en outils qu'en matériaux, une valeur d'environ 2000 fr.
Il fallait, en outre, un fonds de roulement. Chacun des sociétaires opéra,
non sans peine, un versement de 10 fr. Un certain nombre d'ouvriers, non
intéressés dans la société, firent acte d'adhésion, en apportant de faibles
offrandes. Bref, le 10 mars 1849, une somme de 229 fr. 50 cent. ayant été
réalisée, l'association fut déclarée constituée.

"Ce fonds social n'était pas même suffisant pour l'installation, et pour
les menues dépenses qu'entraîne au jour le jour le service d'un atelier. Rien
ne restant pour les salaires, il se passa près de deux mois sans que les
travailleurs touchassent un centime. Comment vécurent-ils pendant cette
crise? Comme vivent les ouvriers pendant le chômage, en partageant la
ration du camarade qui travaille, en vendant ou en engageant pièce à pièce
le peu d'effets qu'on possède.

"On avait exécuté quelques travaux. On en toucha le prix le 4 mai 1849.
Ce jour fut pour l'association ce qu'est une victoire à l'entrée d'une cam-
pagne: aussi voulut-on le célébrer. Toutes les dettes exigibles étant payées,
le dividende de chaque sociétaire s'élevait à 6 fr. 61 cent. On convint
d'attribuer à chacun 5 fr. à valoir sur son salaire, et de consacrer le surplus
à un repas fraternel. Les quatorze sociétaires, dont la plupart n'avaient pas
bu de vin depuis un an, se réunirent, avec leurs femmes et leurs enfants. On

dépensa 32 sous par ménage. On parle encore de cette journée, dans les ateliers, avec une émotion qu'il est difficile de ne pas partager.

"Pendant un mois encore, il fallut se contenter d'une paie de 5 fr. par semaine. Dans le courant de juin, un boulanger, mélomane ou spéculateur, offrit d'acheter un piano payable en pain. On fit marché au prix de 480 fr. Ce fut une bonne fortune pour l'association. On eut du moins l'indispensable. On ne voulut pas évaluer le pain dans le compte des salaires. Chacun mangea selon son appétit, ou pour mieux dire, selon l'appétit de sa famille; car les sociétaires mariés furent autorisés à emporter du pain pour leurs femmes et leurs enfants.

"Cependant l'association, composée d'ouvriers excellents, surmontait peu à peu les obstacles et les privations qui avaient entravé ses débuts. Ses livres de caisse offrent les meilleurs témoignages des progrès que ses instruments ont faits dans l'estime des acheteurs. A partir du mois d'août 1849, on voit le contingent hebdomadaire s'élever à 10, à 15, à 20 fr. par semaine; mais cette dernière somme ne représente pas tous les bénéfices, et chaque associé a laissé à la masse beaucoup plus qu'il n'a touché.

"Ce n'est pas, en effet, par la somme que touche chaque semaine le sociétaire, qu'il faut apprécier sa situation, mais par la part de propriété acquise dans un établissement déjà considérable. Voici l'état de situation de l'association, tel que je l'ai relevé sur l'inventaire du 30 décembre 1850.

"A cette époque, les associés sont au nombre de trente-deux. De vastes ateliers ou magasins, loués 2000 fr., ne leur suffisent plus.

	Francs	Centimes
Indépendamment de l'outillage, évalué à	5,922	60
Ils possèdent en marchandises, et surtout en matières premières, une valeur de	22,972	28
Ils ont en caisse	1,021	10
Leurs effets en portefeuille montent à .	3,540	
Le compte des débiteurs s'élève à* . .	5,861	90
L'actif social est donc en totalité de . .	39,317	88
Sur ce total, il n'est dû que 4,737 fr. 86 c. à des créanciers, et 1,650 fr. à quatre-vingts adhérents;† ensemble . . .	6,387	86
Restent	32,930	2

formant l'actif réel, comprenant le capital indivisible et le capital de réserve des sociétaires. L'association, à la même époque, avait soixante-seize pianos en construction, et ne pouvait fournir à toutes les demandes."

*[52] "Ces deux derniers articles ne comprennent que de très bonnes valeurs, qui, presque toutes, ont été soldées depuis."
†[52] "Ces adhérents sont des ouvriers du métier qui ont commandité l'association dans ses débuts: une partie d'entre eux a été remboursée depuis le

*d*From a later report we learn that this society subsequently divided itself into two separate associations, one of which, in 1854, already possessed a circulating capital of 56,000 francs,*de* or 2240*l.* In 1863 its total capital was 6520*l.*e*

---

commencement de 1851. Le compte des créanciers a aussi beaucoup diminué; au 23 Avril, il ne s'élevait qu'à 1113 fr. 59 c."

*[62] Article by M. Cherbuliez on *Les Associations Ouvrières*, in the Journal des Economistes for November 1860 [Vol. XXVIII, pp. 161–95].

I subjoin, from M. Villiaumé and M. Cherbuliez, detailed particulars of other eminently successful experiments by associated workpeople.

"Nous citerons en première ligne," says M. Cherbuliez, "comme ayant atteint son but et présentant un résultat définitif, l'Association Remquet, de la Rue Garancière, à Paris, dont le fondateur était, en 1848, prote dans l'imprimerie Renouard. Cette maison ayant été forcée de liquider ses affaires, il proposa aux autres ouvriers de s'associer avec lui et de continuer l'entreprise pour leur propre compte, en demandant une subvention pour couvrir le prix d'achat et les premières avances. Quinze ouvriers acceptèrent cette proposition, et formèrent une société en nom collectif, dont les statuts fixaient le salaire de chaque espèce de travail et pourvoyaient à la formation graduelle du capital d'exploitation par un prélèvement de 25 pour 100 sur tous les salaires, prélèvement qui ne devait donner aucun dividende et aucun intérêt jusqu'à l'expiration des dix années que devait durer la société. Remquet demanda et obtint pour lui la direction absolue de l'entreprise, avec un salaire fixé très modéré. A la liquidation définitive, le bénéfice total devait se partager entre tous les associés, au *pro rata* de leur quote-part dans le fonds, c'est-à-dire, du travail que chacun aurait fourni. Une subvention de 80,000 francs fut accordée par l'Etat, non sans beaucoup de difficulté, et à des conditions très onéreuses. En dépit de ces conditions, et malgré les circonstances défavorables qui résultèrent de la situation politique du pays, l'Association Remquet a si bien prospéré, qu'elle s'est trouvée, à l'époque de la liquidation, et après avoir remboursé la subvention de l'Etat, en possession d'un capital net de 155,000 francs, dont le partage a produit en moyenne, 10,000 à 11,000 francs pour chaque associé: 7000 en minimum, 18,000 en maximum."

"La Société Fraternelle des Ouvriers Ferblantiers et Lampistes avait été fondée dès le mois de mars 1848 [62   1858], par 500 ouvriers, comprenant la presque totalité de ceux qui appartenaient alors à cette branche d'industrie. Ce premier essai, inspiré par des idées excentriques et inapplicables, n'ayant pas survécu aux fatales journées de juin, une nouvelle association se forma, après le rétablissement de l'ordre, sur des proportions plus modestes. Composée d'abord de quarante membres, elle entreprit ses affaires, en 1849, avec un capital formé par les cotisations de ses membres, sans demander aucune subvention. Après diverses péripéties, qui réduisirent à trois le nombre des associés puis le ramenèrent à quatorze, et le firent de nouveau retomber à trois, elle finit pourtant par se consolider entre quarante-six membres, qui réformèrent paisiblement leurs statuts dans les points que l'expérience avait signalés comme vicieux, et qui, leur nombre s'étant élevé jusqu'à 100 par des recrutements successifs, se trou-

d–d+62, 65, 71 [62   . . . francs.*]
e–e+65, 71

The same admirable qualities by which the associations were carried through their early struggles, maintained them in their increasing prosperity. Their rules of discipline, instead of being more lax, are stricter than those of ordinary workshops; but being rules self-imposed, for the manifest good of the community, and not for the convenience of an employer regarded as having an opposite interest, they are far more scrupulously

---

vèrent dès l'année 1858, en possession d'un avoir de 50,000 francs, et en état de se partager annuellement un dividende de 20,000 francs.

"L'association des ouvriers bijoutiers en doré, la plus ancienne de toutes, s'était formée dès l'année 1831, de huit ouvriers, avec un capital de 200 francs provenant de leurs épargnes réunies. Une subvention de 24,000 francs lui permit, en 1849, d'étendre beaucoup ses affaires, dont le chiffre annuel s'élevait déjà, en 1858, à 140,000 francs, et assurait à chaque associé un dividende égal au double de leur salaire."

The following are from M. Villiaumé:—

"Après les journées de juin 1848, le travail était suspendu dans le faubourg Saint-Antoine, occupé surtout, comme on le sait, par les fabricants de meubles. Quelques menuisiers en fauteuils firent un appel à ceux qui seraient disposés à travailler ensemble. Sur six à sept cents de cette profession, quatre cents se firent inscrire. Mais comme le capital manquait, neuf hommes des plus zélés commencèrent l'association avec tout ce qu'ils possédaient; savoir, une valeur de 369 francs en outils, et 135 francs 20 centimes en argent.

"Leur bon goût, leur loyauté et l'exactitude de leurs fournitures augmentant leurs débouchés, les associés furent bientôt au nombre de cent huit. Ils reçurent de l'Etat une avance de 25 mille francs, remboursables en quatorze ans par annuité, à raison de 3 fr. 75 c. pour cent d'intérêt.

"En 1857, le nombre des associés est de soixante-cinq, celui des auxiliaires de cent en moyenne. Tous les associés votent pour l'élection d'un conseil d'administration de huit membres, et d'un gérant, dont le nom représente la raison sociale. La distribution et la surveillance du travail dans les ateliers sont confiées à des contremaîtres choisis par le gérant et le conseil. Il y a un contremaître pour vingt ou vingt-cinq hommes.

"Le travail est payé aux pièces, suivant les tarifs arrêtés en assemblée générale. Le salaire peut varier entre 3 et 7 francs par jour, selon le zèle et l'habilité de l'ouvrier. La moyenne est de 50 francs par quinzaine. Ceux qui gagnent le moins touchent près de 40 francs par quinzaine. Un grand nombre gagnent 80 francs. Des sculpteurs et mouluriers gagnent jusqu'à 100 francs, soit 200 francs par mois. Chacun s'engage à fournir cent-vingt heures par quinzaine, soit dix heures par jour. Aux termes du réglement chaque heure de déficit soumet le délinquant à une amende de 10 centimes par heure en-deça de trente heures, et de 15 centimes au-delà. Cette disposition avait pour objet d'abolir l'habitude du lundi, et elle a produit son effet. Depuis deux ans, le système des amendes est tombé en désuetude, à cause de la bonne conduite des associés.

"Quoique l'apport des associés n'ait été que de 369 francs, le matériel d'exploitation appartenant à l'établissement* s'élevait déjà, en 1851, à 5713

---

*Il est situé dans la rue de Chavonne, cour Saint-Joseph, au faubourg Saint-Antoine.

obeyed, and the voluntary obedience carries with it a sense of personal worth and dignity. With wonderful rapidity the associated work-people have learnt to correct those of the ideas they set out with, which are in opposition to the teaching of reason and experience. Almost all the

francs, et l'avoir social, y compris les créances, à 24,000 francs. Depuis lors cette association est devenue plus florissante, ayant resisté à tous les obstacles qui lui ont été suscités. Cette maison est la plus forte de Paris dans son genre, et la plus considérée. Elle fait des affaires pour 400 mille francs par an. Voici son inventaire de décembre 1855.

Actif

Espèces	445	70
Marchandises	82,930	70 fait d'avance, ce qui empêche le chômage.
Salaires payés d'avance . . .	2,421	70
Matériel	20,891	35
Portefeuille	9,711	75
Meubles consignés	211	75
Loyer d'avance	4,933	10
Débiteurs divers	48,286	95
	169,831	55

Passif

Effets à payer	8,655	
Fonds d'association	133	
100 f. à chacun	7,600	ne la doivent qu'à eux-mêmes.
Fonds de retenue indivisible .	9,205	84 pour l'Etat, qui prend 10 p. 100 par an sur les bénéfices, le tout payable au bout de 14 ans.
Caisse de secours	1,544	30 ne la doivent qu'à eux-mêmes.
Prêt de l'Etat, principal et intérêt	27,053	30
Créanciers divers	12,559	51
	66,752	65

Différence active
100,398   90.   La société possède en réalité 123,000 fr."

But the most important association of all is that of the Masons:—

"L'association des maçons fut fondée le 10 août 1848. Elle a son siége rue Saint-Victor, 155. Le nombre de ses membres est de 85, et celui de ses auxiliaires de trois à quatre cents. Elle a deux gérants à sa tête; l'un, chargé spécialement des constructions; l'autre, de l'administration. Les deux gérants passent pour les plus habiles entrepreneurs de maçonnerie de Paris, et ils se contentent d'un modeste traitement. Cette association vient de construire trois ou quatre des plus remarquables hôtels de la capitale. Bien qu'elle travaille avec plus d'économie que les entrepreneurs ordinaires, comme on ne la rembourse qu'à des termes éloignés, c'est surtout pour elle qu'une banque serait nécessaire, car elle a des avances considérables à faire. Néanmoins elle prospère, et la preuve en est dans le dividende de 56 pour 100 qu'a produit cette année son propre capital, et

associations, at first, excluded piece-work, and gave equal wages whether
the work done was more or less. Almost all have abandoned this system,
and after allowing to every one a fixed minimum, sufficient for subsistence,
they apportion all further remuneration according to the work done: most

qu'elle a payé aux citoyens qui se sont associés à ses opérations.

"Cette association est formée d'ouvriers qui n'apportent que leur travail;
d'autres qui apportent leur travail et un capital quelconque; enfin de citoyens
qui ne travaillent point, mais qui se sont associés en fournissant un capital.

"Les maçons se livrent le soir à un enseignement mutuel. Chez eux, comme
chez les fabricants de fauteuils, le malade est soigné aux frais de la société, et
reçoit en outre un salaire durant sa maladie. Chacun est protégé par l'association
dans tous les actes de sa vie. Les fabricants de fauteuils auront bientôt chacun
un capital de deux ou trois mille francs à leur disposition, soit pour doter leurs
filles, soit pour commencer une réserve pour l'avenir. Quant aux maçons,
quelques-uns possèdent déjà 4000 francs d'épargnes qui restent au fonds social.

"Avant qu'ils fussent associés, ces ouvriers étaient pauvrement vêtus de la
veste et de la blouse; parce que, faute de prévoyance, et surtout à cause du
chômage, ils n'avaient jamais une somme disponible de 60 francs pour acheter
une redingote. Aujourd'hui, la plupart sont vêtus aussi bien que les bourgeois;
quelquefois même avec plus de goût. Cela tient à ce que l'ouvrier, ayant un
crédit dans son association, trouve partout ce dont il a besoin sur un bon qu'il
souscrit; et la caisse retient chaque quinzaine une partie de la somme à
éteindre. De la sorte, l'épargne se fait, pour ainsi dire, malgré l'ouvrier. Plusieurs
même, n'ayant plus de dettes, se souscrivent à eux-mêmes des bons de 100 francs
payables en cinq mois, afin de résister à la tentation des dépenses inutiles. On
leur retient 10 francs par quinzaine; et au bout des cinq mois, bon gré, mal gré,
ils trouvent ce petit capital épargné." [Villiaumé, Vol. II, pp. 87–93.]

The following Table; taken by M. Cherbuliez from a work (*Die gewerblichen
und wirthschaftlichen Genossenschaften der arbeitenden Classen in England,
Frankreich und Deutschland*), published at Tübingen in 1860 by Professor
Huber (one of the most ardent and high-principled apostles of this kind of
co-operation), shows the rapidly progressive growth in prosperity of the Masons'
Association up to 1858:—

Year	Amount of business done fr.	Profits realized fr.
1852	45,530	1,000
1853	297,208	7,000
1854	344,240	20,000
1855	614,694	46,000
1856	998,240	80,000
1857	1,330,000	100,000
1858	1,231,461	130,000

"Sur ce dernier dividende," adds M. Cherbuliez, "30,000 francs ont été
prélevés pour le fonds de réserve, et les 100,000 francs restant, partagés entre
les associés, ont donné pour chacun de 500 à 1500 francs, outre leur salaire, et

of them even dividing the profits at the end of the year, in the same proportion as the earnings.*

It is the declared principle *of most* of these associations, that they do not exist for the mere private benefit of the individual members, but for the promotion of the co-operative cause. With every extension, therefore, of their business, they take in additional members, not *(when they remain faithful to their original plan)* to receive wages from them as hired labourers, but to enter at once into the full benefits of the association, without being required to bring anything in, except their labour: the only condition imposed is that of receiving during a few years a smaller share in the annual division of profits, as some equivalent for the sacrifices of the founders. When members quit the association, which they are always at liberty to do, they carry none of the capital with them: it remains an indivisible property, of which the members for the time being have the use, but not the arbitrary disposal: by the stipulations of most of the contracts, even if the association breaks up, the capital cannot be divided, but must

---

leur part dans la propriété commune en immeubles et en matériel d'exploitation."

Of the management of the associations generally, M. Villiaumé says [Vol. II, p. 94], "J'ai pu me convaincre par moi-même de l'habileté des gérants et des conseils d'administration des associations ouvrières. Ces gérants sont bien supérieurs pour l'intelligence, le zèle, et même pour la politesse, à la plupart des patrons ou entrepreneurs particuliers. Et chez les ouvriers associés, les funestes habitudes d'intempérance disparaissent peu à peu, avec la grossièreté et la rudesse qui sont la conséquence de la trop incomplète education de leur classe." [62   *this footnote occurs at* 56,000 francs II.779.3.]

*[52] Even the association founded by M. Louis Blanc, that of the tailors of Clichy, after eighteen months' trial of this [52, 57, 62, 65   of his] system, adopted piece-work. One of the reasons given by them for abandoning the original system is well worth extracting. "En outre des vices dont j'ai parlé, les tailleurs lui reprochaient d'engendrer sans cesse des discussions, des querelles, à cause de l'intérêt que chacun avait à faire travailler ses voisins. La surveillance mutuelle de l'atelier dégénérait ainsi en un esclavage véritable, qui ne laissait à personne la liberté de son temps et de ses actions. Ces dissensions ont disparu par l'introduction du travail aux pièces." Feugueray, p. 88. [57] One of the most discreditable indications of a low moral condition given of late by part of the [57, 62   by the] English working classes, is the opposition to piece-work. When the payment per piece is not sufficiently high, that is a just ground of objection. But dislike to piece-work in itself, except under mistaken notions, must be dislike to justness [57, 62, 65   to justice] and fairness; a desire to cheat, by not giving work in proportion to pay. Piece-work is the perfection of contract; and contract, in all work, and in the most minute detail—the principle of so much pay for so much service, carried out to the utmost extremity—is the system, of all others, in the present state of society and degree of civilization, most favourable to the worker; though most unfavourable to the non-worker who wishes to be paid for being idle.

f-f+62, 65, 71   *g-g*+65, 71

be devoted entire to some work of beneficence or of public utility. A fixed, and generally a considerable, proportion of the annual profits is not shared among the members, but added to the capital of the association, or devoted to the repayment of advances previously made to it: another portion is set aside to provide for the sick and disabled, and another to form a fund for extending the practice of association, or aiding other associations in their need. The managers are paid, like other members, for the time which is occupied in management, usually at the rate of the highest paid labour: but the rule is adhered to, that the exercise of power shall never be an occasion of profit.

[h]Of the ability of the associations to compete successfully with individual capitalists, even at an early period of their existence, M. Feugueray* said, "Les associations qui[h] ont été fondées depuis deux années, avaient bien des obstacles à vaincre; la plupart manquaient presque absolument de capital; toutes marchaient dans une voie encore inexplorée; elles bravaient les périls qui menacent toujours les novateurs et les débutants. Et néanmoins, dans beaucoup d'industries où elles se sont établies, elles constituent déjà pour les anciennes maisons une rivalité redoutable, qui suscite même des plaintes nombreuses dans une partie de la bourgeoisie, non pas seulement chez les traiteurs, les limonadiers et les coiffeurs, c'est-à-dire dans les industries où la nature des produits permet aux associations de compter sur la clientèle démocratique, mais dans d'autres industries où elles n'ont pas les mêmes avantages. On n'a qu'à consulter par exemple les fabricants de fauteuils, de chaises, de limes, et l'on saura d'eux si les établissements les plus importants en leurs genres de fabrication ne sont pas les établissements des associés."[i]

*[52] Pp. 37–8. [52   *footnote to* associés." *14 lines below*]

[h-h]52   It is painful to think that these bodies, formed by the heroism and maintained by the public spirit and good sense of the working people of Paris, are in danger of being involved in the same ruin with everything free, popular, or tending to improvement in French institutions. The unprincipled adventurer who has for the present succeeded in reducing France to the political condition of Russia, knows that two or three persons cannot meet together to discuss, though it be only the affairs of a workshop, without danger to his power. He has therefore already suppressed most of the provincial associations, and many of those of Paris, and the remainder, instead of waiting to be dissolved by despotism, are, it is said, preparing to emigrate. Before this calamity overtook France, the associations could be spoken of not with the hope merely, but with positive evidence, of their being able to compete successfully with individual capitalists. "Les associations," says M. Feugueray, "qui] 57 *as* 52 . . . emigrate.* [*footnote:*] *It appears however from subsequent accounts that in 1854 twenty-five associations still existed at Paris, and several in the provinces, and that many of these were in a most flourishing condition. This number is exclusive of Cooperative Stores, which have greatly multiplied, especially in the South of France, and are not understood to be discouraged by the government. [*text:*] Before . . . *as* 52 . . . Feugueray, *[footnote:*] *Pp. 37–8. [*text:*] "qui

[i-i]52 [*paragraph*] Though the existing associations may be dissolved, or

The vitality of these associations must indeed be great, to have enabled about twenty of them to survive not only the anti-socialist reaction, which for the time discredited all attempts to enable workpeople to be their own employers—not only the *tracasseries* of the police, and the hostile policy of the government since the usurpation—but in addition to these obstacles, all the difficulties arising from the trying condition of financial and commercial affairs from 1854 to 1858. Of the prosperity attained by some of them even while passing through this difficult period, I have given examples which must be conclusive to all minds as to the brilliant future reserved for the principle of co-operation.*

It is not in France alone that these associations have commenced a

*[65] In the last few years [65   year or two] the co-operative movement among the French working-classes has taken a fresh start. An interesting account of the Provision Association (Association Alimentaire) of Grenoble has been given in a pamphlet by M. Casimir Périer (Les Sociétés de Co-opération); and in the *Times* of November 24, 1864, [p. 9] we read the following passage:—"While a certain number of operatives stand out for more wages, or fewer hours of labour, others who have also seceded, have associated for the purpose of carrying on their respective trades on their own account, and have collected funds for the purchase of instruments of labour. They have founded a society, 'Société Générale d'Approvisionnement et de Consommation.' It numbers between 300 and 400 members, who have already opened a 'co-operative store' at Passy, which is now within the limits of Paris. They calculate that by May next, fifteen new self-supporting associations of the same kind will be ready to commence operations; so that the number will be for Paris alone from 50 to 60."

driven to expatriate, their experience will not be lost. They have existed long enough to furnish the type of future improvement: they have exemplified the process for bringing about] 57 [*footnote:*] *Though this beneficent movement has been so seriously checked in the country in which it originated, it is rapidly spreading in those other countries which have acquired, and still retain, any political freedom. It forms already an important feature in the social improvement which is proceeding at a most rapid pace in Piedmont. In England also, under the impulse given by the writings and personal exertions of a band of friends, chiefly clergymen and barristers, the movement has made some progress. On the 15th of February, 1856, there had been registered under the Industrial and Provident Societies' Act, thirty-three associations, seventeen of which were industrial societies, the remainder being associations for cooperative consumption only: without reckoning Scotland, where, also, these associations were rapidly spreading. It is believed that all such societies are now registered under the Limited Liabilities Act. From later information it appears that the productive associations (excluding the flour mills, which partake more of the nature of stores) have fallen off in number since their first start; and their progress, in the present moral condition of the bulk of the population, cannot possibly be rapid. But those which subsist, continue to do as much business as they ever did: and there are in the North of England instances of brilliant and steadily progressive success. Cooperative stores are increasing both in number and prosperity, especially in the North; and they are the best preparation for a wider application of the principle. [*text:*] [*paragraph*] Though . . . as 52 [*cf.* In England . . . progress. *and* II.786.4–8] career of prosperity. To say nothing at present of [j]Germany, Piedmont, and Switzerland (where the Konsum-Verein of Zürich is one of the most prosperous co-operative associations in Europe)[j], England can produce cases of success rivalling even those which I have cited from France. Under the impulse commenced by Mr. Owen, and more recently propagated by the writings and personal efforts of a band of friends, chiefly clergymen and barristers, to whose noble exertions too much praise can scarcely be given, the good seed was widely sown; the necessary alterations in the English law of partnership were obtained from Parliament, on the benevolent and public-spirited initiative of Mr. Slaney; many industrial associations, and a still greater number of co-operative stores for retail purchases, were founded. Among these are already many instances of remarkable prosperity, the most signal of which are the Leeds Flour Mill, and the Rochdale Society of Equitable Pioneers. Of this last association, the most successful of all, the history has been written in a very interesting manner by Mr. Holyoake;* and the notoriety which by this and other means has been given to facts so encouraging, is causing a rapid extension of associations with similar objects in Lancashire [k], Yorkshire, London, and elsewhere[k].

The original capital of the Rochdale Society consisted of 28*l*., brought together by the unassisted economy of about forty labourers, through the slow process of a subscription of twopence (afterwards raised to threepence) per week. With this sum they established in 1844 a small shop, or store, for the supply of a few common articles for the consumption of their own families. As their carefulness and honesty brought them an increase of customers and of subscribers, they extended their operations to a greater number of articles of consumption, and in a few years were able to make a large investment in shares of a Co-operative Corn Mill. Mr. Holyoake thus relates the stages of their progress up to 1857.

"The Equitable Pioneers' Society is divided into seven departments: Grocery, Drapery, Butchering, Shoemaking, Clogging, Tailoring, Wholesale.

"A separate account is kept of each business, and a general account is given each quarter, showing the position of the whole.

"The grocery business was commenced, as we have related, in December

*[62] "Self-help by the People—History of Co-operation in Rochdale." [London: Holyoake, 1858.] [65] An instructive account of this and other co-operative associations has also been written in the "Companion to the Almanack" for 1862, by Mr. John Plummer, of Kettering; himself one of the most inspiring examples of mental cultivation and high principle in a self-instructed working man.

[j–j]62   Piedmont or of Germany   [k–k]62   and Yorkshire

1844, with only four articles to sell. It now includes whatever a grocer's shop should include.

"The drapery business was started in 1847, with an humble array of attractions. In 1854 it was erected into a separate department.

"A year earlier, 1846, the Store began to sell butcher's meat, buying eighty or one hundred pounds of a tradesman in the town. After a while the sales were discontinued until 1850, when the Society had a warehouse of its own. Mr. John Moorhouse, who has now two assistants, buys and kills for the Society three oxen, eight sheep, sundry porkers and calves, which are on the average converted into 130*l.* of cash per week.

"Shoemaking commenced in 1852. Three men and an apprentice make, and a stock is kept on sale.

"Clogging and tailoring commenced also in this year.

"The wholesale department commenced in 1852, and marks an important development of the Pioneers' proceedings. This department has been created for supplying any members requiring large quantities, and with a view to supply the co-operative stores of Lancashire and Yorkshire, whose small capitals do not enable them to buy in the best markets, nor command the services of what is otherwise indispensable to every store—*a good buyer*, who knows the markets and his business, who knows what, how, and where to buy. The wholesale department guarantees purity, quality, fair prices, standard weight and measure, but all on the never-failing principle, cash payment."[*]

In consequence of the number of members who now reside at a distance, and the difficulty of serving the great increase of customers, "Branch Stores have been opened. In 1856, the first Branch was opened, in the Oldham Road, about a mile from the centre of Rochdale. In 1857 the Castleton Branch, and another in the Whitworth Road, were established, and a fourth Branch in Pinfold."[†]

The warehouse, of which their original Store was a single apartment, was taken on lease by the Society, very much out of repair, in 1849. "Every part has undergone neat refitting and modest decoration, and now wears the air of a thoroughly respectable place of business. One room is now handsomely fitted up as a newsroom. Another is neatly fitted up as a library. . . . . Their newsroom is as well supplied as that of a London club."[‡] It is now "free to members, and supported from the Education Fund," [§] a fund consisting of 2½ per cent of all the profits divided, which is set apart for educational purposes. "The Library contains 2200 volumes

[*Holyoake, *Self-Help*, pp. 32-3.]
[†*Ibid.*, p. 35.]
[‡*Ibid.*, pp. 49-50.]
[§*Ibid.*, p. 49n.]

of the best, and among them, many of the most expensive books published. The Library is free. From 1850 to 1855, a school for young persons was conducted at a charge of twopence per month. Since 1855, a room has been granted by the Board for the use of from twenty to thirty persons, from the ages or fourteen to forty, for mutual instruction on Sundays and Tuesdays. . . .

"The corn-mill was of course rented, and stood at Small Bridge, some distance from the town—one mile and a half. The Society have since built in the town an entirely new mill for themselves. The engine and the machinery are of the most substantial and improved kind. The capital invested in the corn-mill is 8450*l.*, of which 3731*l.* 15*s.* 2*d.* is subscribed by the Equitable Pioneers' Society. The corn-mill employs eleven men."[*]

At a later period they extended their operations to the staple manufacture itself. From the success of the Pioneers' Society grew not only the co-operative corn-mill, but a co-operative association for cotton and woollen manufacturing. "The capital in this department is 4000*l.*, of which sum 2042*l.* has been subscribed by the Equitable Pioneers' Society. This Manufacturing Society has ninety-six power-looms at work, and employs twenty-six men, seven women, four boys, and five girls—in all forty-two persons. . . . ."

"In 1853 the Store purchased for 745*l.*, a warehouse (freehold) on the opposite side of the street, where they keep and retail their stores of flour, butcher's meat, potatoes, and kindred articles. Their committee-rooms and offices are fitted up in the same building. They rent other houses adjoining for calico and hosiery and shoe stores. In their wilderness of rooms, the visitor stumbles upon shoemakers and tailors at work under healthy conditions, and in perfect peace of mind as to the result on Saturday night. Their warehouses are everywhere as bountifully stocked as Noah's Ark, and cheerful customers literally crowd Toad Lane at night, swarming like bees to every counter. The industrial districts of England have not such another sight as the Rochdale Co-operative Store on Saturday night."* Since the disgraceful failure of the Rochdale Savings

[*Ibid., pp. 50, 37.]
*[62] [Ibid., pp. 37–8.] "But it is not," adds Mr. Holyoake, "the brilliancy of commercial activity in which either writer or reader will take the deepest interest; it is in the new and improved spirit animating this intercourse of trade. Buyer and seller meet as friends; there is no overreaching on one side, and no suspicion on the other. . . . . These crowds of humble working men, who never knew before when they put good food in their mouths, whose every dinner was adulterated, whose shoes let in the water a month too soon, whose waistcoats shone with devil's dust, and whose wives wore calico that would not wash, now buy in the markets like millionaires, and as far as pureness of food goes, live like lords." Far better, probably, in that particular; for assuredly

Bank in 1849, the Society's Store has become the virtual Savings Bank of the place.

The following Table, completed to 1860 from the Almanack published by the Society,[*] shows the pecuniary result of its operations from the commencement.

Year	No. of members	Amount of capital			Amount of cash sales in store (annual)			Amount of profit (annual)		
		£	s.	d.	£	s.	d.	£	s.	d.
1844	28	28	0	0	——			——		
1845	74	181	12	5	710	6	5	32	17	6
1846	86	252	7	1½	1,146	17	7	80	16	3½
1847	110	286	5	3½	1,924	13	10	72	2	10
1848	140	397	0	0	2,276	6	5½	117	16	10½
1849	390	1,193	19	1	6,611	18	0	561	3	9
1850	600	2,299	10	5	13,179	17	0	889	12	5
1851	630	2,785	0	1½	17,638	4	0	990	19	8½
1852	680	3,471	0	6	16,352	5	0	1,206	15	2½
1853	720	5,848	3	11	22,760	0	0	1,674	18	11½
1854	900	7,172	15	7	33,364	0	0	1,763	11	2½
1855	1400	11,032	12	10½	44,902	12	0	3,106	8	4½
1856	1600	12,920	13	1½	63,197	10	0	3,921	13	1½
1857	1850	15,142	1	2	79,788	0	0	5,470	6	8½
1858	1950	18,160	5	4	71,689	0	0	6,284	17	4½
1859	2703	27,060	14	2	104,012	0	0	10,739	18	6½
1860*	3450	37,710	9	0	152,063	0	0	15,906	9	11

lords are not the customers least cheated in the present race of dishonest competition. "They are weaving their own stuffs, making their own shoes, sewing their own garments, and grinding their own corn. They buy the purest sugar and the best tea, and grind their own coffee. They slaughter their own cattle, and the finest beasts of the land waddle down the streets of Rochdale

[footnote continued on p. 790]

[*Rochdale Equitable Pioneers' Co-operative Society's Almanack for 1861. Rochdale: Lawton (1862).]

*[65] The latest report to which I have access is that for the quarter ending September 20, 1864, of which I take the following abstract from the November number of that valuable periodical the "Co-operator," conducted by Mr. Henry Pitman, one of the most active and judicious apostles of the Co-operative Cause:—"The number of members is 4580, being an increase of 132 for the three months. The capital or assets of the society is 59,536l. 10s. 1d., or more than last quarter by 3687l. 13s. 7d. The cash received for sale of goods is 45,806l. 0s. 10½d., being an increase of 2283l. 12s. 5½d. as compared with the previous three months. The profit realized is 5713l. 2s. 7½d., which, after depreciating fixed stock account 182l. 2s. 4½d., paying interest on share capital 598l. 17s. 6d., applying 2½ per cent to an educational fund, viz. 122l. 17s. 9d., leaves a dividend to members on their purchases of 2s. 4d. in the pound. Non-members have received 261l. 18s. 4d., at 1s. 8d. in the pound on their purchases, leaving 8d. in the pound profit to the society, which increases the reserve fund 104l. 15s. 4d. This fund now stands at 1352l. 7s. 11½d., the accumulation of profits from the trade of the public with the store since September 1862, over and above the 1s. 8d. in the pound allowed to such purchasers."

I need not enter into similar particulars respecting the Corn-Mill Society, and will merely state that in 1860 its capital is set down, on the same authority, at 26,618*l*. 14*s*. 6*d*., and the profit for that single year at 10,164*l*. 12*s*. 5*d*. For the manufacturing establishment I have no certified information later than that of Mr. Holyoake, who states the capital of the concern, in 1857, to be 5500*l*. But a letter in the Rochdale Observer of May 26, 1860,[*] editorially announced as by a person of good information, says that the capital had at that time reached 50,000*l*.: and the same letter gives highly satisfactory statements respecting other similar associations; the Rossendale Industrial Company, capital 40,000*l*.; the Walsden Co-operative Company, capital 8000*l*.; the Bacup and Wardle Commercial Company, with a capital of 40,000*l*., "of which more than one-third is borrowed at 5 per cent, and this circumstance, during the last two years of unexampled commercial prosperity, has caused the rate of dividend to shareholders to rise to an almost fabulous height."

ᶦIt is not necessary to enter into any details respecting the subsequent history of English Co-operation; the less so, as it is now one of the recognised elements in the progressive movement of the age, and, as such, has latterly been the subject of elaborate articles in most of our leading periodicals, ᵐone of the most recent andᵐ best of which was in the Edinburgh Review for October 1864: and the progress of Co-operation from

for the consumption of flannel-weavers and cobblers. (Last year the Society advertised for a Provision Agent to make purchases in Ireland, and to devote his whole time to that duty.) When did competition give poor men these advantages! And will any man say that the moral character of these people is not improved under these influences? The teetotallers of Rochdale acknowledge that the Store has made more sober men since it commenced than all their efforts have been able to make in the same time. Husbands who never knew what it was to be out of debt, and poor wives who during forty years never had sixpence uncondemned in their pockets, now possess little stores of money sufficient to build them cottages, and go every week into their own market with money jingling in their pockets; and in that market there is no distrust and no deception; there is no adulteration, and no second prices. The whole atmosphere is honest. Those who serve neither hurry, finesse, nor flatter. *They have no interest in chicanery.* They have but one duty to perform—that of giving fair measure, full weight, and a pure article. In other parts of the town, where competition is the principle of trade, all the preaching in Rochdale cannot produce moral effects like these.

"As the Store has made no debts, it has incurred no losses; and during thirteen years' transactions, and receipts amounting to 303,852*l*., it has had no law-suits. The Arbitrators of the Societies, during all their years of office, have never had a case to decide, and are discontented that nobody quarrels."

[*"Co-operative Manufacturing Companies," p. 3.]

ᶦ⁻ᶦ791+65, 71   ᵐ⁻ᵐ65   the most recent, and one of the

month to month is regularly chronicled in the "Co-operator." I must not, however, omit to mention the last great step in advance in reference to the Co-operative Stores, the formation in the North of England (and another is in course of formation in London) of a Wholesale Society, to dispense with the services of the wholesale merchant as well as of the retail dealer, and extend to the Societies the advantage which each society gives to its own members, by an agency for co-operative purchases, of foreign as well as domestic commodities, direct from the producers.[1]

It is hardly possible to take any but a hopeful view of the prospects of mankind, when, in [n] two leading countries of the world, the obscure depths of society contain simple working men whose integrity, good sense, self-command, and honourable confidence in one another, have enabled them to carry these noble experiments to the triumphant issue which the facts recorded in the preceding pages attest.[o]

From the progressive advance of the co-operative movement, a great increase may be looked for even in the aggregate productiveness of industry. The sources of the increase are twofold. In the first place, the class of mere distributors, who are not producers but auxiliaries of production, and whose inordinate numbers, far more than the gains of capitalists, are the cause why so great a portion of the wealth produced does not reach the producers—will be reduced to more modest dimensions. Distributors differ from producers in this, that when producers increase, even though in any given department of industry they may be too numerous, they actually produce more: but the multiplication of distributors does not make more distribution to be done, more wealth to be distributed; it does but divide the same work among a greater number of persons, seldom even cheapening the process. By limiting the distributors to the number really required for making the commodities accessible to the consumers—which is the direct effect of the co-operative system—a vast number of hands will be set free for production, and the capital which feeds and the gains which remunerate them will be applied to feed and remunerate producers. This great economy of the world's resources would be realized even if co-operation stopped at associations for purchase and consumption, without extending to production.

The other mode in which co-operation tends, still more efficaciously, to

[n]62, 65   the
[o-o]793 62   Their admirable history shows how vast an increase might be made even in the aggregate productiveness of labour, if the labourers as a mass were placed in a relation to their work which would make it (what now it is not) their principle and their interest to do the utmost, instead of the least possible, in exchange for their remuneration. In the co-operative movement, the permanency of which may now be considered as ensured, we see exemplified the process for bringing about a [cf. II.792.1–5]

increase the productiveness of labour, consists in the vast stimulus given
to productive energies, by placing the labourers, as a mass, in a relation
to their work which would make it their principle and their interest—at
present it is neither—to do the utmost, instead of the least possible, in
exchange for their remuneration. It is scarcely possible to rate too highly
this material benefit, which yet is as nothing compared with the moral
revolution in society that would accompany it: the healing of the standing
feud between capital and labour; the transformation of human life, from
a conflict of classes struggling for opposite interests, to a friendly rivalry
in the pursuit of a good common to all; the elevation of the dignity of
labour; a new sense of security and independence in the labouring class;
and the conversion of each human being's daily occupation into a school
of the social sympathies and the practical intelligence.

Such is the noble idea which the promoters of Co-operation should have
before them. But to attain, in any degree, these objects, it is indispensable
that all, and not some only, of those who do the work should be identified
in interest with the prosperity of the undertaking. Associations which,
when they have been successful, renounce the essential principle of the
system, and become joint-stock companies of a limited number of shareholders, who differ from those of other companies only in being working
men; associations which employ hired labourers without any interest in the
profits (and I grieve to say that the Manufacturing Society even of Rochdale
has thus degenerated) are, no doubt, exercising a lawful right in honestly
employing the existing system of society to improve their position as
individuals, but it is not from them that anything need be expected towards
replacing that system by a better. Neither will such societies, in the long
run, succeed in keeping their ground against individual competition. Individual management, by the one person principally interested, has great
advantages over every description of collective management. Co-operation
has but one thing to oppose to those advantages—the common interest
of all the workers in the work. When individual capitalists, as they will
certainly do, add this to their other points of advantage; when, even if
only to increase their gains, they take up the practice which these co-operative societies have dropped, and connect the pecuniary interest of every
person in their employment with the most efficient and most economical
management of the concern; they are likely to gain an easy victory over
societies which retain the defects, while they cannot possess the full
advantages, of the old system.

Under the most favourable supposition, it will be desirable, and perhaps
for a considerable length of time, that individual capitalists, associating
their work-people in the profits, should coexist with even those co-operative
societies which are faithful to the co-operative principle. Unity of authority

makes many things possible, which could not or would not be under-taken subject to the chance of divided councils or changes in the manage-ment. A private capitalist, exempt from the control of a body, if he is a person of capacity, is considerably more likely than almost any association to run judicious risks, and originate costly improvements. Co-operative societies may be depended on for adopting improvements after they have been tested by success, but individuals are more likely to commence things previously untried. Even in ordinary business, the competition of capable persons who in the event of failure are to have all the loss, and in case of success the greater part of the gain, will be very useful in keeping the managers of co-operative societies up to the due pitch of activity and vigilance.

When, however, co-operative societies shall have sufficiently multiplied, it is not probable that any but the least valuable work-people will any longer consent to work all their lives for wages merely; both private capita-lists and associations will gradually find it necessary to make the entire body of labourers participants in profits. Eventually, and in perhaps a less remote future than may be supposed, we may, through the co-operative principle, see our way to^{oi} a change in society, which would combine the freedom and independence of the individual, with the moral, intellectual, and economical advantages of aggregate production; and which, without violence or spoliation, or even any sudden disturbance of existing habits and expectations, would realize, at least in the industrial department, the best aspirations of the democratic spirit, by putting an end to the division of society into the industrious and the idle, and effacing all social dis-tinctions but those fairly earned by personal services and exertions. Associations like those which we have described, by the very process of their success, are a course of education in those moral and active qualities by which alone success can be either deserved or attained. As associations multiplied, they would tend more and more to absorb all work-people, except those ^{p}who have too little understanding, or too little virtue, to be capable of learning to act on any other system than that of narrow selfishness^p. As this change proceeded, owners of capital would gradually find it to their advantage, instead of maintaining the struggle of the old system with work-people of only the worst description, to lend their capital to the associations; to do this at a diminishing rate of interest, and at last, perhaps, ^{q}even^q to exchange their capital for terminable annuities. In this or some such mode, the existing accumulations of capital might honestly, and by a kind of spontaneous process, become in the end the joint property of all who participate in their productive employment: a transformation

$^{p-p}$52   of an inferior class in capacity and in true morality
$^{q-q}$+62, 65, 71

which, thus effected, (and assuming of course that both sexes participate equally in the rights and in the government of the association)* would be the nearest approach to social justice, and the most beneficial ordering of industrial affairs for the universal good, which it is possible at present to foresee.

§ 7. [*Competition is not pernicious, but useful and indispensable*] I agree, then, with the Socialist writers in their conception of the form which industrial operations tend to assume in the advance of improvement; and I entirely share their opinion that the time is ripe for commencing this transformation, and that it should by all just and effectual means be aided and encouraged. But while I agree and sympathize with Socialists in this practical portion of their aims, I utterly dissent from the most conspicuous and vehement part of their teaching, their declamations against competition. With moral conceptions in many respects far ahead of the existing arrangements of society, they have in general very confused and erroneous notions of its actual working; and one of their greatest errors, as I conceive, is to charge upon competition all the economical evils which at present exist. They forget that wherever competition is not, monopoly is; and that monopoly, in all its forms, is the taxation of the industrious for the support of indolence, if not of *ᵃplunderᵃ*. They forget, too, that with the exception of competition among labourers, all other competition is for the benefit of the labourers, by cheapening the articles they consume; that competition even in the labour market is a source not of low but of high wages, wherever the competition *for* labour exceeds the competition *of* labour, as in America, in the colonies, and in the skilled trades; and never could be a cause of low wages, save by the overstocking of the labour market *ᵇthrough the too great numbers of the labourers' familiesᵇ*; while, if the supply of labourers is excessive, not even Socialism can prevent *ᶜtheirᶜ* remuneration

*[62] In this respect also the Rochdale Society has given an example of reason and justice, worthy of the good sense and good feeling manifested in their general proceedings. "The Rochdale Store," says Mr. Holyoake, "renders incidental but valuable aid towards realizing the civil independence of women. Women may be members of this Store, and vote in its proceedings. Single and married women join. Many married women become members because their husbands will not take the trouble, and others join in it in self-defence, to prevent the husband from spending their money in drink. The husband cannot withdraw the savings at the Store standing in the wife's name, unless she signs the order." [62, 65 order. Of course, as the law still stands, the husband could by legal process get possession of the money. But a process takes time, and the husband gets sober and thinks better of it before the law can move."] [*Self-Help*, p. 44.]

ᵃ⁻ᵃ52, 57   rapacity   ᵇ⁻ᵇ+57, 62, 65, 71   ᶜ⁻ᶜ52   its

from being low. Besides, if association ^dwere^d universal, there would be no competition between labourer and labourer; and that between association and association would be for the benefit of the consumers, that is, of the associations; of the industrious classes generally.

I do not pretend that there are no inconveniences in competition, or that the moral objections urged against it by Socialist writers, as a source of jealousy and hostility among those engaged in the same occupation, are altogether groundless. But if competition has its evils, it prevents greater evils. As M. Feugueray well says,* "La racine la plus profonde des maux et des iniquités qui couvrent le monde industriel, n'est pas la concurrence, mais bien l'exploitation du travail par le capital, et la part énorme que les possesseurs des instruments de travail prélèvent sur les produits. . . . Si la concurrence a beaucoup de puissance pour le mal, elle n'a pas moins de fécondité pour le bien, surtout en ce qui concerne le développement des facultés individuelles, et le succès des innovations." It is the common error of Socialists to overlook the natural indolence of mankind; their tendency to be passive, to be the slaves of habit, to persist indefinitely in a course once chosen. Let them once attain any state of existence which they consider tolerable, and the danger to be apprehended is that they will thenceforth stagnate; will not exert themselves to improve, and by letting their faculties rust, will lose even the energy required to preserve them from deterioration. Competition may not be the best conceivable stimulus, but it is at present a necessary one, and no one can foresee the time when it will not be indispensable to progress. Even confining ourselves to the industrial department, in which, more than in any other, the majority may be supposed to be competent judges of improvements; it would be difficult to induce the general assembly of an association to submit to the trouble and inconvenience of altering their habits by adopting some new and promising invention, unless their knowledge of the existence of rival associations made them apprehend that what they would not consent to do, others would, and that they would be left behind in the race.

Instead of looking upon competition as the baneful and anti-social principle which it is held to be by the generality of Socialists, I conceive that, even in the present state of society and industry, every restriction of it is an evil, and every extension of it, even if for the time injuriously affecting some class of labourers, is always an ultimate good. To be protected against competition is to be protected in idleness, in mental dulness; to be saved the necessity of being as active and as intelligent as other people; and if it is also to be protected against being underbid for employment by a less ^ehighly^e paid class of labourers, this is only where

*[52] P. 90.

^{d–d}52   was   ^{e–e}+57, 62, 65, 71

old custom, or local and partial monopoly, has placed some particular class
of artizans in a privileged position as compared with *f* the rest; and the
time has come when the interest of universal improvement is no longer
promoted by prolonging the privileges of a few. If the slopsellers and others
*g*of their class*g* have lowered the wages of tailors, and some other artizans,
by making them an affair of competition instead of custom, so much the
better in the end. What is now required is not to bolster up old customs,
whereby limited classes of labouring people obtain partial gains which
interest them in keeping up the present organization of society, but to
introduce new general practices beneficial to all; and there is reason to
rejoice at whatever makes the privileged classes of skilled artizans feel
that they have the same interests, and depend for their remuneration on the
same general causes, and must resort for the improvement of their condition
to the same remedies, as the less fortunately circumstanced and comparatively helpless multitude.

*f*52, 57   all
*g–g*52   , so unjustly and illiberally railed at—as if they were one iota worse in
their motives or practices than other people, in the existing state of society—

BOOK V

ON THE INFLUENCE OF GOVERNMENT

CHAPTER I

Of the Functions of Government
in General

§ 1. [*Necessary and optional functions of government distinguished*] One
of the most disputed questions both in political science and in practical
statesmanship at this particular period, relates to the proper limits of the
functions and agency of governments. At other times it has been a subject
of controversy how governments should be constituted, and according to
what principles and rules they should exercise their authority; but it is now
almost equally a question, to what departments of human affairs that
authority should extend. And when the tide sets so strongly towards
changes in government and legislation, as a means of improving the
condition of mankind, this discussion is more likely to increase than to
diminish in interest. On the one hand, impatient reformers, thinking it
easier and shorter to get possession of the government than of the intellects
and dispositions of the public, are under a constant temptation to stretch
the province of government beyond due bounds: while, on the other,
mankind have been so much accustomed by their rulers to interference for
purposes other than the public good, or under an erroneous conception of
what that good requires, and so many rash *ᵃproposalsᵃ* are made by sincere
lovers of improvement, for attempting, by compulsory regulation, the
attainment of objects which can only be effectually or only usefully
compassed by opinion and discussion, that there has grown up a spirit of
resistance *in limine* to the interference of government, merely as such, and
a disposition to restrict its sphere of action within the narrowest bounds.
From differences in the historical development of different nations, not
necessary to be here dwelt upon, the former excess, that of exaggerating the
province of government, prevails most, both in theory and in practice,
among the Continental nations, while in England the contrary spirit *ᵇhas
hitherto beenᵇ* predominant.

The general principles of the question, in so far as it is a question of
principle, I shall make an attempt to determine in a later chapter of this
Book: after first considering the effects produced by the conduct of government in the exercise of the functions universally acknowledged to belong

ᵃ⁻ᵃ48, 49, 52, 57 propositions   ᵇ⁻ᵇ48, 49 is decidedly

to it. For this purpose, there must be a specification of the functions which are either inseparable from the idea of a government, or are exercised habitually and without objection by all governments; as distinguished from those respecting which it has been considered questionable whether governments should exercise them or not. The former may be termed the *necessary*, the latter the *optional*, functions of government. ᶜBy the term optional it is not meant to imply, that it can ever be a matter of indifference, or of arbitrary choice, whether the government should or should not take upon itself the functions in question; but only that the expediency of its exercising them does not amount to necessity, and is a subject on which diversity of opinion does or may exist.ᶜ

§ 2. [*Multifarious character of the necessary functions of government*] In attempting to enumerate the necessary functions of government, we find them to be considerably more multifarious than most people are at first aware of, and not capable of being circumscribed by those very definite lines of demarcation, which, in the inconsiderateness of popular discussion, it is often attempted to draw round them. We sometimes, for example, hear it said that governments ought to confine themselves to affording protection against force and fraud: that, these two things apart, people should be free agents, able to take care of themselves, and that so long as a person practises no violence or deception, to the injury of others in person or property, ᵃlegislators and governments are in no way called on to concern themselves about himᵃ. But why should people be protected by their government, that is, by their own collective strength, against violence and fraud, and not against other evils, except that the expediency is more obvious? If nothing, but what people cannot possibly do for themselves, can be fit to be done for them by government, people might be required to protect themselves by their skill and courage even against force, or to beg or buy protection against it, as they actually do where the government is not capable of protecting them: and against fraud every one has the protection of his own wits. But without further anticipating the discussion of principles, it is sufficient on the present occasion to consider facts.

Under which of these heads, the repression of force or of fraud, are we to place the operation, for example, of the laws of inheritance? Some such laws must exist in all societies. It may be said, perhaps, that in this matter government has merely to give effect to the disposition which an individual makes of his own property by will. This, however, is at least extremely disputable; there is probably no country by whose laws the power of testamentary disposition is perfectly absolute. And suppose the very com-

ᶜ-ᶜ+49, 52, 57, 62, 65, 71
ᵃ-ᵃ48, 49, 52   he has a claim to do as he likes, without being molested or restricted by judges and legislators

mon case of there being no will: does not the law, that is, the government, decide on principles of general expediency, who shall take the succession? and in case the successor is in any manner incompetent, does it not appoint persons, frequently officers of its own, to collect the property and apply it to his benefit? There are many other cases in which the government under-takes the administration of property, because the public interest, or perhaps only that of the particular persons concerned, is thought to require it. This is often done in *b*case*b* of litigated property; and in cases of judicially declared insolvency. It has never been contended that in doing these things, a government exceeds its province.

Nor is the function of the law in defining property itself, so simple a thing as may be supposed. It may be imagined, perhaps, that the law has only to declare and protect the right of every one to what he has himself produced, or acquired by the voluntary consent, fairly obtained, of those who produced it. But is there nothing recognised as property except what has been produced? Is there not the earth itself, its forests and waters, and all other natural riches, above and below the surface? These are the inheritance of the human race, and there must be regulations for the common enjoyment of it. What rights, and under what conditions, a person shall be allowed to exercise over any portion of this common inheritance, cannot be left undecided. No function of government is less optional than the regulation of these things, or more completely involved in the idea of civilized society.

Again, the legitimacy is conceded of repressing violence or treachery; but under which of these heads are we to place the obligation imposed on people to perform their contracts? Non-performance does not necessarily imply fraud; the person who entered into the contract may have sincerely intended to fulfil it *c*: and the term fraud, which can scarcely admit of being extended even to the case of voluntary breach of contract when no decep-tion was practised, is certainly not applicable when the omission to perform is a case of negligence*c*. Is it no part of the duty of governments to enforce contracts? Here the doctrine of non-interference would no doubt be stretched a little, and it would be said, that enforcing contracts is not regu-lating the affairs of individuals at the pleasure of government, but giving effect to their own expressed desire. Let us acquiesce in this enlargement of the restrictive theory, and take it for what it is worth. But governments do not limit their concern with contracts to a simple enforcement. They take upon themselves to determine what contracts are fit to be enforced. It is not enough that one person, not being either cheated or compelled, makes a promise to another. There are promises by which it is not for the

---

*b-b*48, 49, 52, 57, 62, 65   cases [*printer's error?*]

*c-c*48, 49   ; his mind, or his circumstances, may have altered; or not even that, since the omission to perform may be a mere case of neglect

public good that persons should have the power of binding themselves. To say nothing of engagements to do something contrary to law, there are engagements which the law refuses to enforce, for reasons connected with the interest of the promiser, or with the general policy of the state. A contract by which a person sells himself to another as a slave, would be declared void by the tribunals of this and of most other European countries. There are few nations whose laws *d* enforce a contract for what *e*is*e* looked upon as prostitution, or any matrimonial engagement of which the conditions *f*vary*f* in any respect from those which the law *g*has*g* thought fit to prescribe. But when once it is admitted that there are any engagements which for reasons of expediency the law ought not to enforce, the same question is necessarily opened with respect to all engagements. Whether, for example, the law should enforce a contract to labour, when the wages are too low or the hours of work too severe: whether it should enforce a contract by which a person binds himself to remain, for more than a very limited period, in the service of a given individual: whether a contract of marriage, entered into for life, should continue to be enforced against the deliberate will of the persons, or of either of the persons, who entered into it. Every question which can possibly arise as to the policy of contracts, and of the relations which they establish among human beings, is a question for the legislator; and one which he cannot escape from considering, and in some way or other deciding.

Again, the prevention and suppression of force and fraud afford appropriate employment for soldiers, policemen, and criminal judges; but there are also civil tribunals. The punishment of wrong is one business of an administration of justice, but *h*the decision of disputes is another.*h* Innumerable disputes arise between persons, without *mala fides* on either side, through misconception of their legal rights, or from not being agreed about the facts, on the proof of which those rights are legally dependent. It is not for the general interest that the State should appoint persons to clear up these uncertainties and terminate these disputes? It cannot be said to be a case of absolute necessity. People might appoint an arbitrator, and engage to submit to his decision; and they do so where there are no courts of justice, or where the courts are not trusted, or where their delays and expenses, or the irrationality of their rules of evidence, deter people from resorting to them. Still, it is universally thought right that the State should establish civil tribunals; and if their defects often drive people to have recourse to substitutes, even then the power held in reserve of carrying the case before a legally constituted court, gives to the substitutes their principal efficacy.

*d*48, 49   would   *e–e*48, 49   was
*f–f*48, 49   varied   *g–g*48, 49   had
*h–h*48, 49   is not the decision of disputes another?

Not only does the State undertake to decide disputes, it takes precautions beforehand that disputes may not arise. The laws of most countries lay down rules for determining many things, not because it is of much consequence in what way they are determined, but in order that they may be determined somehow, and there may be no question on the subject. The law prescribes forms of words for many kinds of contract, in order that no dispute or misunderstanding may arise about their meaning: it makes provision that if a dispute does arise, evidence shall be procurable for deciding it, by requiring that the document be attested by witnesses and executed with certain formalities. The law preserves authentic evidence of facts to which legal consequences are attached, by keeping a registry of such facts; as of births, deaths, and marriages, of wills and contracts, and of judicial proceedings. In doing these things, it has never been alleged that government oversteps the proper limits of its functions.

Again, however wide a scope we may allow to the doctrine that individuals are the proper guardians of their own interests, and that government owes nothing to them but to save them from being interfered with by other people, the doctrine can never be applicable to any persons but those who are capable of acting in their own behalf. The individual may be an infant, or a lunatic, or fallen into imbecility. The law surely must look after the interests of such persons. It does not necessarily do this through officers of its own. It ʲoften devolvesʲ the trust upon some relative or connexion. But in doing so is its duty ended? Can it make over the interests of one person to the control of another, and be excused from supervision, or from holding the person thus trusted, responsible for the discharge of the trust?

There is a multitude of cases in which governments, with general approbation, assume powers and execute functions for which no reason can be assigned except the simple one, that they conduce to general convenience. We may take as an example, the ʲfunctionʲ (which is a monopoly too) of coining money. This is assumed for no more recondite purpose than that of saving to individuals the trouble, delay, and expense of weighing and assaying. No one, however, even of those most jealous of state interference, has objected to this as an improper exercise of the powers of government. Prescribing a set of standard weights and measures is another instance. Paving, lighting, and cleansing the streets and thoroughfares, is another; whether done by the general government, or as is more usual, and generally more advisable, by a municipal authority. Making or improving harbours, building lighthouses, making surveys in order to have accurate maps and charts, raising dykes to keep the sea out, and embankments to keep rivers in, are cases in point.

Examples might be indefinitely multiplied without intruding on any disputed ground. But enough has been said to show that the admitted

ⁱ⁻ⁱ48, 49   may devolve   ʲ⁻ʲ48, 49   power

functions of government embrace a much wider field than can easily be
included within the ring-fence of any restrictive definition, and that it is
hardly possible to find any ground of justification common to them all,
except the comprehensive one of general expediency; nor to limit the
interference of government by any universal rule, save the simple and
vague one, that it should never be admitted but when the case of expediency
is strong.

§ 3. [*Division of the subject*] Some observations, however, may be
usefully bestowed on the nature of the considerations on which the question
of government interference is most likely to turn, and on the mode of
estimating the comparative magnitude of the expediencies involved. This
will form the last of the three parts, into which our discussion of the
principles and effects of government interference may conveniently be
divided. The following will be our division of the subject.

We shall first consider the economical effects arising from the manner
in which governments perform their necessary and acknowledged functions.

We shall then pass to certain governmental interferences of what I have
termed the optional kind (*i.e.* overstepping the boundaries of the universally acknowledged functions) which have heretofore taken place, and in
some cases still take place, under the influence of false general theories.

It will lastly remain to inquire whether, independently of any false
theory, and consistently with a correct view of the laws which regulate
human affairs, there be any cases of the optional class in which governmental interference is really advisable, and what are those cases.

The first of these divisions is of an extremely miscellaneous character:
since the necessary functions of government, and those which are so
manifestly expedient that they have never or very rarely been objected to,
are, as already pointed out, too various to be brought under any very simple
classification. Those, however, which are of principal importance, which
alone it is necessary here to consider, may be reduced to the following
general heads.

First, the means adopted by governments to raise the revenue which is
the condition of their existence.

Secondly, the nature of the laws which they prescribe on the two great
subjects of Property and Contracts.

Thirdly, the excellences or defects of the system of means by which they
enforce generally the execution of their laws, namely, their judicature and
police.

We commence with the first head, that is, with the theory of Taxation.

CHAPTER II

^aOn^a the General Principles
of Taxation

§ 1. [*Four fundamental rules of taxation*] The qualities desirable, economically speaking, in a system of taxation, have been embodied by Adam Smith in four maxims or principles, which, having been generally concurred in by subsequent writers, may be said to have become classical, and this chapter cannot be better commenced than by quoting them.*

"1. The subjects of every state ought to contribute to the support of the government, as nearly as possible in proportion to their respective abilities: that is, in proportion to the revenue which they respectively enjoy under the protection of the state. In the observation or neglect of this maxim consists what is called the equality or inequality of taxation.

"2. The tax which each individual is bound to pay ought to be certain, and not arbitrary. The time of payment, the manner of payment, the quantity to be paid, ought all to be clear and plain to the contributor, and to every other person. Where it is otherwise, every person subject to the tax is put more or less in the power of the tax-gatherer, who can either aggravate the tax upon any obnoxious contributor, or extort by the terror of such aggravation, some present or perquisite to himself. The uncertainty of taxation encourages the insolence and favours the corruption of an order of men who are naturally unpopular, even when they are neither insolent nor corrupt. The certainty of what each individual ought to pay is, in taxation, a matter of so great importance, that a very considerable degree of inequality, it appears, I believe, from the experience of all nations, is not near so great an evil, as a very small degree of uncertainty.

"3. Every tax ought to be levied at the time, or in the manner, in which it is most likely to be convenient for the contributor to pay it. A tax upon the rent of land or of houses, payable at the same term at which such rents are usually paid, is levied at ^ba^b time when it is most likely to be convenient for the contributor to pay; or when he is most likely to have wherewithal

---

***Wealth of Nations*, book v. ch. ii. [Vol. IV, pp. 215–8.]

^{a–a}48, 49 Of   ^{b–b}Source, 48, 49, 52 the

to pay. Taxes upon such consumable goods as are articles of luxury, are all finally paid by the consumer, and generally in a manner that is very convenient to him. He pays them by little and little, as he has occasion to buy the goods. As he is at liberty, too, either to buy or not to buy, as he pleases, it must be his own fault if he ever suffers any considerable inconvenience from such taxes.

"4. Every tax ought to be so contrived as both to take out and to keep out of the pockets of the people as little as possible over and above what it brings into the public treasury of the state. A tax may either take out or keep out of the pockets of the people a great deal more than it brings into the public treasury, in the four following ways. First, the levying of it may require a great number of officers, whose salaries may eat up the greater part of the produce of the tax, and whose perquisites may impose another additional tax upon the people." Secondly, it may divert a portion of the labour and capital of the community from a more to a less productive employment. "Thirdly, by the forfeitures and other penalties which those unfortunate individuals incur who attempt unsuccessfully to evade the tax, it may frequently ruin them, and thereby put an end to the benefit which the community might have derived from the employment of their capitals. An injudicious tax offers a great temptation to smuggling. Fourthly, by subjecting the people to the frequent visits and the odious examination of the tax-gatherers, it may expose them to much unnecessary trouble, vexation, and oppression:" to which may be added, that the restrictive regulations to which trades and manufactures are often subjected to prevent evasion of a tax, are not only in themselves troublesome and expensive, but often oppose insuperable obstacles to making ᶜimprovementsᶜ in the ᵈprocessesᵈ.

The last three of these four maxims require little other explanation or illustration than is contained in the passage itself. How far any given tax conforms to, or conflicts with them, is a matter to be considered in the discussion of particular taxes. But the first of the four points, equality of taxation, requires to be more fully examined, being a thing often imperfectly understood, and on which many false notions have become to a certain degree accredited, through the absence of any definite principles of judgment in the popular mind.

§ 2. [*Grounds of the principle of Equality of Taxation*] For what reason ought equality to be the rule in matters of taxation? For the reason, that it ought to be so in all affairs of government. As a government ought to make

c–c48   any improvement
d–d48, 49, 52, 57   process

no distinction of persons or classes in the strength of their claims on it, whatever sacrifices it requires from them should be made to bear as nearly as possible with the same pressure upon all, which, it must be observed, is the mode by which least sacrifice is occasioned on the whole. If any one bears less than his fair share of the burthen, some other person must suffer more than his share, and the alleviation to the one is not, *cæteris paribus*, so great a good to him, as the increased pressure upon the other is an evil. Equality of taxation, therefore, as a maxim of politics, means equality of sacrifice. It means apportioning the contribution of each person towards the expenses of government, so that he shall feel neither more nor less inconvenience from his share of the payment than every other person experiences from his. This standard, like other standards of perfection, cannot be completely realized; but the first object in every practical discussion should be to know what perfection is.

There are persons, however, who are not content with the general principles of justice as a basis to ground a rule of finance upon, but must have something, as they think, more specifically appropriate to the subject. What best pleases them is, to regard the taxes paid by each member of the community as an equivalent for value received, in the shape of service to himself; and they prefer to rest the justice of making each contribute in proportion to his means, upon the ground, that he who has twice as much property to be protected, receives, on an accurate calculation, twice as much protection, and ought, on the principles of bargain and sale, to pay twice as much for it. Since, however, the assumption that government exists solely for the protection of property, is not one to be deliberately adhered to; some consistent adherents of the *quid pro quo* principle go on to observe, that protection being required for person as well as property, and everybody's person receiving the same amount of protection, a poll-tax of a fixed sum per head is a proper equivalent for this part of the benefits of government, while the remaining part, protection to property, should be paid for in proportion to property. There is in this adjustment a false air of nice adaptation, very acceptable to some minds. But in the first place, it is not admissible that the protection of *a*persons and that of*a* property are the sole purposes of government. The ends of government are as comprehensive as those of the social union. They consist of all the good, and all the immunity from evil, which the existence of government can be made either directly or indirectly to bestow. In the second place, the practice of setting definite values on things essentially indefinite, and making them a ground of practical conclusions, is peculiarly fertile in false views of social questions. It cannot be admitted, that to be protected in the ownership of ten

*a–a*48   person and

times as much property, is to be ten times as much protected. *b*Neither can it be truly said that the protection of 1000*l.* a year costs the state ten times as much as that of 100*l.* a year, rather than twice as much, or exactly as much. The same judges, soldiers, and sailors who protect the one protect the other, and the larger income does not necessarily, though it may sometimes, require even more policemen.*b* Whether the labour and expense of the protection, or the feelings of the protected person, or any other definite thing be made the standard, there is no such proportion as the one supposed, nor any other definable proportion. If we wanted to estimate the degrees of benefit which different persons derive from the protection of government, we should have to consider who would suffer most if that protection were withdrawn: to which question if any answer could be made, it must be, that those would suffer most who were weakest in mind or body, either by nature or by position. Indeed, such persons would almost infallibly be slaves. If there were any justice, therefore, in the theory of justice now under consideration, those who are least capable of helping or defending themselves, being those to whom the protection of government is the most indispensable, ought to pay the greatest share of its price: the reverse of the true idea of distributive justice, which consists not in imitating but in redressing the inequalities and wrongs of nature.

Government must be regarded as so pre-eminently a concern of all, that to determine who *c*are*c* most interested in it is of no real importance. If a person or class of persons receive so small a share of the benefit as makes it necessary to raise the question, there is something else than taxation which is amiss, and the thing to be done is to remedy the defect, *d*instead of recognising it and making*d* it a ground for demanding less taxes. As, in a case of voluntary subscription for a purpose in which all are interested, all are thought to have done their part fairly when each has contributed according to his means, that is, has made an equal sacrifice for the common object; in like manner should this be the principle of compulsory contributions: and it is superfluous to look for a more ingenious or recondite ground to rest the principle upon.

§ 3. [*Should the same percentage be levied on all amounts of income?*] Setting out, then, from the maxim that equal sacrifices ought to be demanded from all, we have next to inquire whether this is in fact done, by making each contribute the same percentage on his pecuniary means. Many persons maintain the negative, saying that a tenth part taken from a small income is a heavier burthen than the same fraction deducted from one much larger: and on this is grounded the very popular scheme of what

b-b+65, 71
*c-c*48, 49   is   *d-d*48, 49, 52, 57   not to recognize it and make

is called a graduated property tax, viz. an income tax in which the percentage rises with the amount of the income.

On the best consideration I am able to give to this question, it appears to me that the portion of truth which the doctrine contains, arises principally from the difference between a tax which can be saved from luxuries, and one which trenches, in ever so small a degree, upon the necessaries of life. To take a thousand a year from the possessor of ten thousand, would not deprive him of anything really conducive either to the support or to the comfort of existence; and if such *would* be the effect of taking five pounds from one whose income is fifty, the sacrifice required from the last is not only greater than, but entirely incommensurable with, that imposed upon the first. The mode of adjusting these inequalities of pressure, which seems to be the most equitable, is that recommended by Bentham, of leaving a certain minimum of income, sufficient to provide the necessaries of life, untaxed. Suppose 50*l.* a year to be *a*sufficient to provide the number of persons ordinarily supported from a single income,*a* with the requisites of life and health, and with protection against habitual bodily suffering, but not with any *b*indulgence*b*. This then should be made the minimum, and incomes exceeding it should pay taxes not upon their whole amount, but upon the surplus. If the tax be ten per cent, an income of 60*l.* should be considered as a net income of 10*l.*, and charged with 1*l.* a year, while an income of 1000*l.* should be charged as one of 950*l.* Each would then pay a fixed proportion, not of his whole means, but of his superfluities.* An income not exceeding 50*l.* should not be taxed at all, either directly or by taxes on necessaries; for as by supposition this is the smallest income which *c*labour ought to be able to command*c*, the government ought not to be a party to making it smaller. This arrangement however would constitute a reason, in addition to others which might be stated, for maintaining *d* taxes on articles of luxury consumed by the poor. The immunity extended to the income required for necessaries, should depend on its being actually expended for that purpose; and the poor who, not having more than enough for necessaries, divert any part of it to indulgences, should like other people contribute their quota out of those indulgences to the expenses of the state.

The exemption in favour of the smaller incomes should not, I think, be stretched further than to the amount of income needful for life, health, and

---

*[65] This principle of assessment has been partially adopted by Mr. Gladstone in renewing [65   at the last renewal of] the income-tax. From 100*l.*, at which the tax begins, up to 200*l.*, the income only pays tax on the excess above 60*l.*

*a–a*48, 49   an income ordinarily sufficient to provide a moderately numerous labouring family
*b–b*48, 49, 52   indulgences
*c–c*48, 49   a labouring family ought to have   *d*48, 49   indirect

immunity from bodily pain. [e]If 50*l*. a year is sufficient (which may be doubted) for these purposes, an[e] income of 100*l*. a year would, as it seems to me, obtain all the relief it is entitled to, compared with one of 1000*l*., by being taxed only on 50*l*. of its amount. It may be said, indeed, that to take 100*l*. from 1000*l*. (even giving back five pounds) is a heavier impost than 1000*l*. taken from 10,000*l*. (giving back the same five pounds). But this doctrine seems to me too disputable altogether, and even if true at all, not true to a sufficient extent, to be made the foundation of any rule of taxation. [f]Whether the person with 10,000*l*. a year cares less for 1000*l*. than the person with only 1000*l*. a year cares for 100*l*., and if so, how much less, does not appear to me capable of being decided with the degree of certainty on which a legislator or a financier ought to act.[f]

Some indeed contend that [g]the[g] rule of [h]proportional[h] taxation bears harder upon the moderate than upon the large incomes, because the same proportional payment has more tendency in the former case than in the latter, to reduce the payer to a lower grade of social rank. The fact appears to me more than questionable. But even admitting it, I object to its being considered incumbent on government to shape its course by such considerations, or to recognise the notion that social importance is or can be determined by amount of expenditure. Government ought to set an example of rating all things at their true value, and riches, therefore, at the worth, for comfort or pleasure, of the things which they will buy: and ought not to sanction the vulgarity of prizing them for the pitiful vanity of being known to possess them, or the [i] paltry shame of being suspected to be without them, the presiding motives of three-fourths of the expenditure of the middle classes. The sacrifices of real comfort or indulgence which government requires, it is bound to apportion among all persons with as much equality as possible; but their sacrifices of the imaginary dignity dependent on expense, it may spare itself the trouble of estimating.

Both in England and on the Continent a graduated property tax (*l'impôt progressif*) has been advocated, on the avowed ground that the state should use the instrument of taxation as a means of mitigating the inequalities of wealth. I am as desirous as any one, that means should be taken to diminish those inequalities, but not so as to [j]relieve the prodigal at the expense of the prudent[j]. To tax the larger incomes at a higher percentage than the

[e-e]48, 49, 52, 57   An

[f-f]48, 49   To tax all *incomes* in an equal ratio, would be unjust to those, the greater part of whose income is required for necessaries; but I can see no fairer standard of real equality than to take from all persons, whatever may be their amount of fortune, the same arithmetical proportion of their superfluities.

[g-g]48, 49   this

[h-h]+52, 57, 62, 65, 71   [i]48, 49   still more

[j-j]48, 49   impair the motives on which society depends for keeping up (not to say increasing) the produce of its labour and capital

smaller, is to lay a tax on industry and economy; to impose a penalty on people for having worked harder and saved more than their neighbours. It is *k*not the fortunes which are earned, but those which are unearned, that it is for the public good to place under limitation*k*. A just and wise legislation would *l* abstain from *m*holding out motives for dissipating rather than saving the earnings of*m* honest exertion. Its impartiality between competitors would consist in endeavouring that they should all start fair, and not *n*in hanging a weight upon the swift to diminish the distance between them and the slow*n*. Many, indeed, fail with greater efforts than those with which others succeed, not from difference of merits, but difference of opportunities; *o*but if all were done which it would be in the power of a good government to do, by instruction and by legislation, to *p*diminish*p* this inequality of opportunities, the differences*o* of fortune arising from people's own earnings could not justly give umbrage. With respect to the large fortunes acquired by gift or inheritance, the power of bequeathing *q* is one of those privileges of property which are fit subjects for regulation on grounds of general expediency; and I have already suggested,* as *r*a possible*r* mode of restraining the accumulation of large fortunes in the hands of those who have not earned them by exertion, a limitation of the amount which any one person should be permitted to acquire by gift, bequest, or inheritance. Apart from this, and from the proposal of Bentham (also discussed in a former chapter) that collateral inheritance *ab intestato* should cease, and the property escheat to the state, I conceive that inheritances and legacies, exceeding a certain amount, are highly proper subjects for taxation: and that the revenue from them should be as great as it can be made without giving rise to evasions, by donation *inter vivos* or concealment of property, such as it would be impossible adequately to check. The principle of graduation (as it is called,) that is, of levying a larger per-

*Supra, book ii. ch. 2. [48   ch. 1.] [Pp. 215–34.]

*k–k*48, 49   partial taxation, which is a mild form of robbery
*l*48, 49   scrupulously
*m–m*48, 49   opposing obstacles to the acquisition of even the largest fortune by
*n–n*48, 49   that, whether they were swift or slow, all should reach the goal at once
*o–o*48, 49   and it is the part of a good government to provide, that, as far as more paramount considerations permit, the inequality of opportunities shall be remedied. When all kinds of useful instruction shall be as accessible as they might be made, and when the cultivated intelligence of the poorer classes, aided so far as necessary by the guidance and co-operation of the state, shall obviate, as it might so well do, the major part of the disabilities attendant on poverty, the inequalities
*p–p*52, 57   remedy
*q*48, 49   is as much a part of the right of property as the power of using: that is not in the fullest sense a person's own, which he is not free to bestow on others. But this
*r–r*48, 49, 52, 57, 62   the most eligible

centage on a larger sum, though its application to general taxation would be *in my opinion objectionable, *seems to me* both just and expedient* as applied to legacy and inheritance duties.

The objection to a graduated property tax applies in an aggravated degree to the proposition of an exclusive tax on what is called "realized property," that is, property not forming a part of any capital engaged in business, or *rather* in business *under the superintendence of the owner*: as land, the public funds, money lent on mortgage, and shares (I presume) in joint stock companies. Except the proposal of applying a sponge to the national debt, no such palpable violation of common honesty has found sufficient support in this country, during the present generation, to be regarded as within the domain of discussion. It has not the palliation of a graduated property tax, that of laying the burthen on those best able to bear it; for "realized property" includes *the far larger portion of the* provision made for those who are unable to work, and consists, in great part, of extremely small fractions. I can hardly conceive a more shameless pretension, than that the major part of the property of the country, that of merchants, manufacturers, farmers, and shopkeepers, should be exempted from its share of taxation; that these classes should only begin to pay their proportion after retiring from business, and if they never retire should be excused from it altogether. But even this does not give an adequate idea of the injustice of the proposition. The burthen thus exclusively thrown on the owners of the smaller portion of the wealth of the community, would not even be a burthen on that *class* of persons in perpetual succession, but would fall exclusively on those who happened to compose it when the tax was laid on. As land and those particular securities would *thenceforth* yield a smaller net income, relatively to the general interest of capital and to the profits of trade; the balance would rectify itself by a permanent depreciation of those kinds of property. Future buyers would acquire land and securities at a reduction of price, equivalent to the peculiar tax, which tax they would, therefore, escape from paying; while the original possessors would remain burthened with it even after parting with the property, since they would have sold their land or securities at a loss of value equivalent to the fee-simple of the tax. Its imposition would thus be tantamount to the confiscation for public uses of a percentage of their property, equal to the percentage laid on their income by the tax. That such a proposition should find any favour, is a striking instance of the want of conscience in matters of taxation, resulting from the absence of any fixed principles in the public

---

s–s48, 49   a violation of first principles, is quite unobjectionable
t–t52, 57   is
u–u48, 49   (it should rather be said)
v–v48, 49   on the owner's account
w–w48, 49   almost every   x–x+62, 65, 71

mind, and of any indication of a sense of justice on the subject in the general conduct of *ʸgovernmentsʸ*. Should the scheme ever enlist a large party in its support, the fact would indicate a laxity of pecuniary integrity in national affairs, scarcely inferior to American repudiation.

§ 4. [*Should the same percentage be levied on perpetual and on terminable incomes?*] Whether the profits of trade may not rightfully be taxed at a *ᵃ* lower rate than incomes derived from interest or rent, is part of the more comprehensive question, so often mooted on the occasion of the present income tax, whether life incomes should be subjected to the same rate of taxation as perpetual incomes: whether salaries, for example, or annuities, or the gains of professions, should pay the same percentage as the income from inheritable property.

The existing tax treats all kinds of incomes exactly alike, taking *ᵇitsᵇ* *ᶜsevenpence (now fourpence)ᶜ* in the pound, as well from the person whose income dies with him, as from the *ᵈlandholderᵈ*, stockholder, or mortgagee, who can transmit his fortune undiminished to his descendants. This is a visible injustice: yet it does not arithmetically violate the rule that taxation ought to be in proportion to means. When it is said that a temporary income ought to be taxed less than a permanent one, the reply is irresistible, that it is taxed less; for the income which lasts only ten years pays the tax only ten years, while that which lasts for ever pays for ever. *ᵉ*On this point some financial reformers are guilty of a great fallacy. They contend that incomes ought to be assessed to the income tax not in proportion to their annual amount, but to their capitalized value: that, for example, if the value of a perpetual annuity of 100*l.* is 3000*l.*, and a life annuity of the same amount, being worth only half the number of years' purchase, could only be sold for 1500*l.*, the perpetual income should pay twice as much per cent income tax as the terminable income: if the one pays 10*l.* a year the other should pay only 5*l.* But in this argument there is the obvious oversight, that it values the incomes by one standard and the payments by another; it capitalizes the incomes, but forgets to capitalize the payments. An annuity worth 3000*l.* ought, it is alleged, to be taxed twice as highly as one which is only worth 1500*l.*, and no assertion can be more unquestionable; but it is forgotten that the income worth 3000*l.* pays to the supposed income tax 10*l.* a year in perpetuity, which is equivalent, by supposition, to 300*l.*, while the terminable income pays the same 10*l.* only during the

<hr>

*ʸ–ʸ*57 government   *ᵃ*48, 49 somewhat   *ᵇ–ᵇ*+62, 65, 71
*ᶜ–ᶜ*48, 49, 52, 57 sevenpence] 62 sevenpence (now ninepence)] 65 sevenpence (now sixpence)
*ᵈ–ᵈ*48, 49, 52 landowner
*ᵉ–ᵉ*⁸¹⁴48 But almost every one feels that this answer does not touch the real grievance; for in

life of its owner, which on the same calculation is a value of 150*l*. *ˡ*, and could actually be bought for that sum.*ˡ* Already, therefore, the income which is only half as valuable, pays only half as much to the tax; and if in addition to this its annual quota were reduced from 10*l*. to 5*l*., it would pay, not half, but a fourth part only of the payment demanded from the perpetual income. *ᵍ*To make it just that the one income should pay only half as much per annum as the other, it would be necessary that it should pay that half for the same period, that is, in perpetuity.*ᵍ*

*ʰ*The rule of payment which this school of financial reformers contend for, would be very proper if the tax were only to be levied once, to meet some national emergency. On the principle of requiring from all payers an equal sacrifice, every person who had anything belonging to him, reversioners included, would be called on for a payment proportioned to the present value of his property. I wonder it does not occur to the reformers in question, that precisely because this principle of assessment would be just in the case of a payment made once for all, it cannot possibly be just for a permanent tax. When each pays only once, one person pays no oftener than another; and the proportion which would be just in that case, cannot also be just if one person has to make the payment only once, and the other several times. This, however, is the type of the case which actually occurs. The permanent incomes pay the tax as much oftener than the temporary ones, as a perpetuity exceeds the certain or uncertain length of time which forms the duration of the income for life or years.*ʰ*

All attempts to establish a claim in favour of terminable incomes on numerical grounds—to make out, in short, that a proportional tax is not a proportional tax—are manifestly absurd. The claim does not rest on grounds of arithmetic, but of human *ⁱ*wants and feelings*ⁱ*. *ʲ*It is not because the temporary annuitant has smaller means, but because he has greater *ᵏ*necessities*ᵏ*, that he ought to be assessed at a lower rate.*ʲ*

In*ᵉ* spite of the nominal equality of income, A, an annuitant of 1000*l*. a year, cannot so well afford to pay 100*l*. out of it, as B who derives the same annual sum from heritable property; A having usually a demand on his income which B has not, namely, to provide by saving for children or others; to which, in the case of salaries or professional gains, must generally be added a provision for his own later years; while B may expend his whole income without injury to his old age, and still have it all to bestow on others after his death. If A, in order to meet these exigencies, must lay by 300*l*. of his income, to take 100*l*. from him as income tax is *ˡ*to take*ˡ*

ˡ–ˡ+65, 71
ᵍ–ᵍ+57, 62, 65, 71   *ʰ–ʰ*+62, 65, 71
*ⁱ–ⁱ*49, 52, 57   feelings and necessities   *ʲ–ʲ*+52, 57, 62, 65, 71
*ᵏ–ᵏ*52, 57   wants   *ˡ–ˡ*48   taking

100*l*. from 700*l*., since it must be retrenched from that part only of his means which he can afford to spend on his own consumption. Were he to throw it rateably on what he spends and on what he saves, abating 70*l*. from his consumption and 30*l*. from his annual saving, then indeed his immediate sacrifice would be *m*proportionately*m* the same as B's: but then his children or his old age would be worse provided for in consequence of the tax *n*. The capital sum which would be accumulated for them would be one-tenth less, and on the reduced income afforded by this reduced capital, they would be a second time charged with income tax *o*; while *p*B's*p* heirs would only be charged once*o*.*n*

The principle, therefore, of equality of taxation, interpreted in its only just sense, equality of sacrifice, requires that a person who has no means of providing for old age, or for those in whom he is interested, except by saving from *q* income, should have the tax remitted on all that part of his income which is really and *bonâ fide* applied to that purpose. *r*

*s*If, indeed, reliance could be placed on the conscience of the contributors, or sufficient security taken for the correctness of their statements by collateral precautions, the proper mode of assessing an income tax would be to tax only the part of income devoted to expenditure, exempting that which is saved. For when saved and invested (and all savings, speaking generally, are invested) it thenceforth pays income tax on the interest or

---

*m–m*48, 49, 52, 57, 62, 65   proportionally

*n–n*48   : and the plea ordinarily urged in vindication of its justice, that when the income ceases the tax ceases, would no longer be maintainable.

o–o+52, 57, 62, 65, 71   *p–p*52, 57 A's   *q*48, 49   his

*r*48, 49 I say really applied, because (as before remarked in the case of an income not more than sufficient for subsistence) an exemption grounded on an assumed necessity, ought not to be claimable by any one who practically emancipates himself from the necessity. One expedient might be, that the Income-Tax Commissioners should allow, as a deduction from income, all *bonâ fide* payments for insurance on life. This, however, would not provide for the case which most of all deserves consideration, that of persons whose lives are not insurable; nor would it include the case of savings made as a provision for age. The latter case might, perhaps, be met by allowing as a deduction from income all payments made in the purchase of deferred annuities; and the former by remitting income-tax on sums actually settled, and on sums paid into the hands of a public officer, to be invested in securities, and repaid only to the executor or administrator: the tax so remitted, with interest from the date of deposit, being retained (for the prevention of fraud) as a first debt chargeable on the deposit itself, before other debts could be paid out of it; but not demanded if satisfactory proof were given that all debts had been paid from other resources. I throw out these suggestions for the consideration of those whose experience renders them adequate judges of practical difficulties.]

52 [*footnote:*] *I say . . . *as text of* 48 . . . difficulties.] 57 *as* 52 . . . resources. (In the Income-Tax Act, as renewed and modified by Mr. Gladstone in 1853, the first two of these suggestions have been acted on.)

*s–s*81748, 49 [*no paragraph*] It is highly probable that there may be better modes of attaining the object. If no plan be found practicable by which the exemption can be confined to the portion of income actually saved, there still remains

profit which it brings, notwithstanding that it has already been taxed on the principal. Unless, therefore, savings are exempted from income tax, the contributors are twice taxed on what they save, and only once on what they spend. A person who spends all he receives, pays 7*d.* in the pound, or say three per cent, to the tax, and no more; but if he saves part of the year's income and buys stock, then in addition to the three per cent which he has paid on the principal, and which diminishes the interest in the same ratio, he pays three per cent annually on the interest itself, which is equivalent to an immediate payment of a second three per cent on the principal. So that while unproductive expenditure pays only three per cent, savings pay six per cent: or more correctly, three per cent on the whole, and another three per cent on the remaining ninety-seven. The difference thus created to the disadvantage of prudence and economy, is not only impolitic but unjust. To tax the sum invested, and afterwards tax also the proceeds of the investment, is to tax the same portion of the contributor's means twice over. The principal and the interest cannot both together form part of his resources; they are the same portion twice counted: if he has the interest, it is because he abstains from using the principal; if he ʰspendsʰ the principal, he does not receive the interest. Yet because he can do either of the two, he is taxed as if he could do both, and could have the benefit of the saving and that of the spending, ᵘconcurrentlyᵘ with one another.

ᵛIt has been urged as an objection to exempting savings from taxation, that the law ought not to disturb, by artificial interference, the natural competition between the motives for saving and those for spending. But we have seen that the law disturbs this natural competition when it taxes savings, not when it spares them; for as the savings pay at any rate the full tax as soon as they are invested, their exemption from payment in the earlier stage is necessary to prevent them from paying twice, while money spent in unproductive consumption pays only once. It has been further objected, that since the rich have the greatest means of saving, any privilege given to savings is an advantage bestowed on the rich at the expense of the poor. I answer, that it is bestowed on them only in proportion as they abdicate the personal use of their riches; in proportion as they divert their income from the supply of their own wants, to a productive investment, through which, instead of being consumed by themselves, it is distributed in wages among the poor. If this be favouring the rich, I should like to have it pointed out, what mode of assessing taxation can deserve the name of favouring the poor.ᵛ

No income tax is really just, from which savings are not exempted; and no income tax ought to be voted without that provision, if the form of the returns, and the nature of the evidence required, could be so arranged as to prevent the exemption from being taken fraudulent advantage of, by saving with one hand and getting into debt with the other, or by spending in the following year what had been passed tax-free as saving in the year preceding. If this difficulty could be surmounted, the difficulties and complexities arising from the comparative claims of temporary and permanent incomes, would disappear; for, since temporary incomes have no just claim to lighter taxation than permanent incomes, except in so far as their possessors are more called upon to save, the exemption of what they do save would fully satisfy the claim. But if no plan can be devised for the exemption of actual savings, sufficiently free from liability to fraud, it is necessary, as the next thing in point of justice, to take into account in assessing the tax, what the different classes of contributors *ought* to save. And there would probably be no other mode of doing this than[s] the rough expedient of two different rates of assessment. There would be great difficulty in taking into account differences of duration between one terminable income and another; and in the most frequent case, that of incomes dependent on life, differences of age and health would constitute such extreme diversity as it would be impossible to take proper cognizance of. It would probably be necessary to be content with one uniform rate for all incomes of inheritance, and another uniform rate for all those which necessarily terminate with the life of the individual. In fixing the proportion between the two rates, there must inevitably be something arbitrary; perhaps a deduction of one-fourth in favour of life-incomes would be as little objectionable as any which could be made, it being thus assumed that one-fourth of a life-income is, on the average of all ages and states of health, a suitable proportion to be laid by as a provision for successors and for old age.*

*[62] Mr. Hubbard, the first person who, as a practical legislator, has attempted the rectification of the income tax on principles of unimpeachable justice, and whose well-conceived plan wants little of being as near an approximation to a just assessment as it is likely that means could be found of carrying into practical effect, proposes a deduction not of a fourth but of a third, in favour of industrial and professional incomes. He fixes on this ratio, on the ground that, independently of all consideration as to what the industrial and professional classes ought [62   ought] to save, the attainable evidence goes to prove that a third of their incomes is what on an average they do [62   do] save, over and above the proportion saved by other classes. "The savings" (Mr. Hubbard observes) "effected out of incomes derived from invested property are estimated at one-tenth. The savings effected out of industrial incomes are estimated at four-tenths. The amounts which would be assessed under these two classes being nearly equal, the adjustment is simplified by striking off one-tenth on either side, and then reducing by three-tenths, or one-third, the assessable amount of industrial incomes." Proposed Report (p. xiv. of the Report and Evidence of the Committee of 1861 [*Parliamentary Papers*, 1861, VII]). In such an estimate there must be a large element of conjecture; but in so far as it

Of the net profits of persons in business, ^{w}a part, as before observed^w, may be considered as interest on capital, and of a perpetual character, and the ^{x}remaining part^x as remuneration for the skill and labour of superintendence ^{y}. The surplus beyond interest depends^y on the life of the individual, and even on his continuance in business ^{z}, and is entitled to the full amount of exemption allowed to terminable incomes. It has also, I conceive, a just claim to a further amount of exemption in consideration of its precariousness. An income which some not unusual vicissitude may reduce to nothing, or even convert into a loss, is not the same thing to the feelings of the possessor as a permanent income of 1000*l.* a year, even though on an average of years it may yield 1000*l.* a year. If life-incomes were assessed at three-fourths of their amount, the profits of business, after deducting

---

can be substantiated, it affords a valid ground for the practical conclusion which Mr. Hubbard founds on it.

[48] Several writers on the subject, including Mr. Mill in his Elements of Political Economy, and Mr. M'Culloch in his work on Taxation, have contended that as much should be deducted as would be sufficient to insure the possessor's life for a sum which would give to his successors for ever an income equal to what he reserves for himself; since this is what the possessor of heritable property can do without saving at all: in other words, that temporary incomes should be converted into perpetual incomes of equal present value, and taxed as such. [62] If the owners of life-incomes actually did [62 *did*] save this large proportion of their income, or even a still larger, I would gladly grant them an exemption from taxation on the whole amount, since, if practical means could be found of doing it, I would exempt savings altogether. But I cannot admit that they have a claim to exemption on the general assumption of their being obliged [62 *obliged*] to save this amount [48, 49, 52, 57   such. But this surely [52, 57   surely this]] is favouring them too much]. Owners of life-incomes are not bound to forego the enjoyment of them for the sake of leaving to a perpetual line of successors an independent provision equal to their own temporary one; and no one ever dreams of doing so. Least of all is it to be required or expected from those whose incomes are the fruits of personal exertion, that they should leave to their posterity for ever, without any necessity for exertion, the same incomes which they allow to themselves. All they are bound to do, even for their children, [48, 49   independently of any expectation they may themselves have raised,] is to place them in circumstances in which they will have favourable chances of earning their own living. To give, however, either to children or to others, by bequest, being a legitimate inclination, which these persons cannot indulge without laying by a part of their income, while the owners of heritable property can; this real inequality in cases where the incomes themselves are equal, should be considered, to a reasonable degree, in the adjustment of taxation, so as to require from both, as nearly as practicable, an equal sacrifice.

$^{w-w}$48, 49   one-half, perhaps
$^{x-x}$48, 49   other half
$^{y-y}$48, 49   ; depending therefore
$^{z-z}$81948, 49   . For profits, therefore, an intermediate rate might be adopted, one-half of the net income being taxed on the higher scale, and the other half on the lower.

interest on capital, should not only be assessed at three-fourths, but should pay, on that assessment, a lower rate. Or perhaps the claims of justice in this respect might be sufficiently met by allowing the deduction of a fourth on the entire income, interest included.*

These are the chief cases, of ordinary occurrence, in which any difficulty arises in interpreting the maxim of equality of taxation. The proper sense to be put upon it, as we have seen in the preceding example, is, that people should be taxed, not in proportion to what they have, but to what they can afford to spend. It is no objection to this principle that we cannot apply it consistently to all cases. A person with a life-income and precarious health, or who has many persons depending on his exertions, must, if he wishes to provide for them after his death, be more rigidly economical than one who has a life-income of equal amount with a strong constitution, and few claims upon him; and *if it be conceded that* taxation cannot accommodate itself to these distinctions, it is argued that there is no use in attending to any distinctions, where the absolute amount of income is the same. But the *difficulty* of doing perfect justice is no reason against doing as much as we can. Though it may be a hardship to an annuitant whose life is only worth five years' purchase, to be allowed no greater abatement than is granted to one whose life is worth twenty, it is better for him even so, than if neither of them were allowed any abatement at all.

§ 5. [*The increase of the rent of land from natural causes is a fit subject of peculiar taxation*] Before leaving the subject of Equality of Taxation, I must remark that there are cases in which exceptions may be made to it, consistently with that equal justice which is the groundwork of the rule. Suppose that there is a kind of income which constantly tends to increase, without any exertion or sacrifice on the part of the owners: those owners constituting a class in the community, whom the natural course of things progressively enriches, consistently with complete passiveness on their own part. In such a case it would be no violation of the principles on which private property is grounded, if the state should appropriate this increase of wealth, or part of it, as it arises. This would not properly be taking anything from anybody; it would merely be applying an accession of wealth, created by circumstances, to the benefit of society, instead of allowing it to become an unearned appendage to the riches of a particular class.

Now this is actually the case with rent. The ordinary progress of a society which increases in wealth, is at all times tending to augment the incomes of landlords; to give them both a greater amount and a greater proportion of the wealth of the community, independently of any trouble or outlay incurred by themselves. They grow richer, as it were in their sleep, without working, risking, or economizing. What claim have they, on the general ᵃprincipleᵃ of social justice, to this accession of riches? In what would they have been wronged if society had, from the beginning, reserved ᵇtheᵇ right of taxing the spontaneous increase of rent, to the highest amount required by financial exigencies? I admit that it would be unjust to come upon each individual estate, and lay hold of the increase which might be found to have taken place in its rental; because there would be no ᶜmeansᶜ of distinguishing in individual cases, between an increase owing solely to the general circumstances of society, and one which was the effect of skill and expenditure on the part of the proprietor. The only admissible mode of proceeding would be by a general measure. The first step should be a valuation of all the land in the country. The present value of all land should be exempt from the tax; but after an interval had elapsed, during which society had increased in population and capital, a rough estimate might be made of the spontaneous increase which had accrued to rent since the valuation was made. Of this the average price of produce would be some criterion: if that had risen, it would be certain that rent had increased, and (as already shown) even in a greater ratio than the rise of price. On this and other data, an approximate estimate might be made, how much value had been added to the land of the country by natural causes; and in laying on a general land-tax, which for fear of miscalculation should be considerably within the amount thus indicated, there would be an assurance of not touching any increase of income which might be the result of capital expended or industry exerted by the proprietor.

But though there could be no question as to the justice of taxing the increase of rent, if society had avowedly reserved the right, has not society waived that right by not exercising it? In England, for example, have not all who bought land for the last century or more, given value not only for the existing income, but for the prospects of increase, under an implied assurance of being only taxed in the same proportion with other incomes? This objection, in so far as valid, has a different degree of validity in different countries; depending on the degree of desuetude into which society has allowed a right to fall, which, as no one can doubt, it once fully possessed. In most countries of Europe, the right to take by taxation, as exigency might require, an indefinite portion of the rent of land, has never been allowed to slumber. In several parts of the Continent, the land-tax forms a large proportion of the public revenues, and has always been confessedly liable to be raised or lowered without reference to other taxes. In these countries no one can pretend to have become the owner of land on the faith of never being called upon to pay an increased land-tax. In England the land-tax has not varied since the early part of the last century.

ᵃ⁻ᵃ48, 49, 52, 57   principles   ᵇ⁻ᵇ48, 49, 52, 57   a   ᶜ⁻ᶜ48, 49   possibility

The last act of the legislature in relation to its amount, was to diminish it; and though the subsequent increase in the rental of the country has been immense, not only from agriculture, but from the growth of towns and the increase of buildings, the ascendency of landholders in the legislature has prevented any tax from being imposed, as it so justly might, upon the very large portion of this increase which was unearned, and, as it were, accidental. For the expectations thus raised, it appears to me that an amply sufficient allowance is made, if the whole increase of income which has accrued during this long period from a mere natural law, without exertion or sacrifice, is held sacred from any peculiar taxation. From the present date, or any subsequent time at which the legislature may think fit to assert the principle, I see no objection to declaring that the future increment of rent should be liable to special taxation; in doing which *all* injustice to the landlords would be obviated, if the present market-price of their land were secured to them; since that includes the present value of all future expectations. With reference to such a tax, perhaps a safer criterion than either a rise of rents or a rise of the price of corn, would be a general rise in the price of land. It would be easy to keep the tax within the amount which would reduce the market value of land below the original valuation: and up to that point, whatever the amount of the tax might be, no injustice would be done to the proprietors.

§ 6. [*A land tax, in some cases, is not taxation, but a rent-charge in favour of the public*] But whatever may be thought of the legitimacy of making the State a sharer in all future increase of rent from natural causes, the existing land-tax (which in this country unfortunately is very small) ought not to be regarded as a tax, but as a rent-charge in favour of the public; a portion of the rent, reserved from *the beginning* by the State, which has never belonged to or formed part of the income of the landlords, and should not therefore be counted to them as part of their taxation, so as to exempt them from their fair share of every other tax. As well might the tithe be regarded as a tax on the landlords: as well, in Bengal, where the State, *though* entitled to the whole rent of the land, gave away one-tenth of it to individuals, retaining the other nine-tenths, might those nine-tenths be considered as an unequal and unjust tax on the grantees of the tenth. That a person owns part of the rent, does not make the rest of it his just right, injuriously withheld from him. The landlords originally held their estates subject to feudal burthens, for which the present land-tax is an exceedingly small equivalent, and for their relief from which they should have been required to pay a much higher price. All who have bought land

d-d48, 49, 52   every shadow of
a-a48, 49   time immemorial   b-b48, 49 originally

since the tax existed have bought it subject to the tax. There is not the smallest pretence for looking upon it as a payment exacted from the existing race of landlords.

These observations are applicable to a land-tax, only in so far as it is a peculiar tax, and not when it is merely a mode of levying from the landlords the equivalent of what is taken from other classes. In France, for example, there are peculiar taxes on other kinds of property and income (the *mobilier* and the *patente*), and supposing the land-tax to be not more than equivalent to these, there would be no ground for contending that the state had reserved to itself a rent-charge on the land. But wherever and in so far as income derived from land is prescriptively subject to a deduction for public purposes, beyond the rate of taxation levied on other incomes, the surplus is not properly taxation, but a share of the property in the soil, reserved by the state. In this country there are no peculiar taxes on other classes, corresponding to, or intended to countervail, the land-tax. The whole of it, therefore, is not taxation, but a rent-charge, and is as if the state had retained, not a portion of the rent, but a portion of the land. It is no more a burthen on the landlord, than the share of one joint tenant is a burthen on the other. The landlords are entitled to no compensation for it, nor have they any claim to its being allowed for, as part of their taxes. Its continuance on the existing footing is no infringement of the principle of Equal Taxation.*

We shall hereafter consider, in treating of Indirect Taxation, how far, and with what modifications, the rule of equality is applicable to that department.

§ 7. [*Taxes falling on capital are not necessarily objectionable*] In addition to the preceding rules, another general rule of taxation is sometimes laid down, namely, that it should fall on income, and not on capital. That taxation should not encroach upon the amount of the national capital, is indeed of the greatest importance; but this encroachment, when it occurs, is not so much a consequence of any particular mode of taxation, as of its excessive amount. Over-taxation, carried to a sufficient extent, is quite capable of ruining the most industrious community, especially when it is in any degree arbitrary, so that the payer is never certain how much or how little he shall be allowed to keep; or when it is so laid on as to render

*[49] The same remarks obviously apply to those local taxes, of the peculiar pressure of which on landed property so much has been said [49 of late] by the remnant of the Protectionists. As much of these burthens as is of old standing, ought to be regarded as a prescriptive deduction or reservation, for public purposes, of a portion of the rent. And any recent additions have either been incurred for the benefit of the owners of landed property, or occasioned by their fault: in neither case giving them any just ground of complaint.

industry and economy a bad calculation. But if these errors be avoided, and the amount of taxation be not greater than it is at present even in the most heavily taxed country of Europe, there is no danger lest it should deprive the country of a portion of its capital.

To provide that taxation shall fall entirely on income, and not at all on capital, is beyond the power of any system of fiscal arrangements. There is no tax which is not partly paid from what would otherwise have been saved; no tax, the amount of which, if remitted, would be wholly employed in increased expenditure, and no part whatever laid by as an addition to capital. All taxes, therefore, are in some sense partly paid out of capital; and in a poor country it is impossible to impose any tax which will not impede the increase of the national wealth. But in a country where capital abounds, and the spirit of accumulation is strong, this effect of taxation is scarcely felt. Capital having reached the stage in which, were it not for a perpetual succession of improvements in production, any further increase would soon be stopped—and having so strong a tendency even to outrun those improvements, that profits are only kept above the minimum by emigration of capital, or by a periodical sweep called a commercial crisis; to take from capital by taxation what emigration would remove, or a commercial crisis destroy, is only to do what either of those causes would have done, namely, to make a clear space for further saving.

I cannot, therefore, attach any importance, in a wealthy country, to the objection made against taxes on legacies and inheritances, that they are taxes on capital. It is perfectly true that they are so. As Ricardo observes, if 100*l.* are taken from any one in a tax on houses or on wine, he will probably save it, or a part of it, by living in a cheaper house, consuming less wine, or retrenching from some other of his expenses; but if the same sum be taken from him because he has received a legacy of 1000*l.*, he considers the legacy as only 900*l.*, and feels no more inducement than at any other time (probably feels rather less inducement) to economize in his expenditure. The tax, therefore, is wholly paid out of capital: and there are countries in which this would be a serious objection. But in the first place, the argument cannot apply to any country which has a national debt, and devotes any portion of revenue to paying it off; since the produce of the tax, thus applied, still remains capital, and is merely transferred from the tax-payer to the fundholder. But the objection is never applicable in a country which increases rapidly in wealth. The amount which would be derived, even from a very high legacy duty, in each year, is but a small fraction of the annual increase of capital in such a country; and its abstraction would but make room for saving to an equivalent amount: while the effect of not taking it, is to prevent that amount of saving, or cause the savings, when made, to be sent abroad for investment. A country which, like England, accumulates capital not only for itself, but for half the world, may be said to defray the whole of its public expenses from its overflowings; and its wealth is probably at this moment as great as if it had no taxes at all. What its taxes really do is, to subtract from its means, not of production, but of enjoyment; since whatever any one pays in taxes, he could, if it were not taken for that purpose, employ in indulging his ease, or in gratifying some want or taste which at present remains unsatisfied.

CHAPTER III

Of Direct Taxes

§ 1. [*Direct taxes either on income or on expenditure*] Taxes are either direct or indirect. A direct tax is one which is demanded from the very persons who, it is intended or desired, should pay it. Indirect taxes are those which are demanded from one person in the expectation and intention that he shall indemnify himself at the expense of another: such as the excise or customs. The producer or importer of a commodity is called upon to pay a tax on it, not with the intention to levy a peculiar contribution upon him, but to tax through him the consumers of the commodity, from whom it is supposed that he will recover the amount by means of an advance in price.

Direct taxes are either on income, or on expenditure. Most taxes on expenditure are indirect, but some are direct, being imposed not on the producer or seller of an article, but immediately on the consumer. A house-tax, for example, is a direct tax on expenditure, if levied, as it usually is, on the occupier of the house. If levied on the builder or owner, it would be an indirect tax. *A* window-tax is a direct tax on expenditure; so are the taxes on horses and carriages, and the rest of what are called the assessed taxes.

The sources of income are rent, profits, and wages. This includes every *sort* of income, except gift or plunder. Taxes may be laid on any one of the three kinds of income, or an uniform tax on all of them. We will consider these in their order.

§ 2. [*Taxes on rent*] A tax on rent falls wholly on the landlord. There are no means by which he can shift the burthen upon any one else. It does not affect the value or price of agricultural produce, for this is determined by the cost of production in the most unfavourable circumstances, and in those circumstances, as we have so often demonstrated, no rent is paid. A tax on rent, therefore, has no effect, other than its obvious one. It merely takes so much from the landlord, and transfers it to the state.

This, however, is, in strict exactness, only true of the rent which is the result either of natural causes, or of improvements made by tenants. When

*a–a*48, 49 The   *b–b*48, 49, 52, 57 source

the landlord makes improvements which increase the productive power of
his land, he is remunerated for them by an extra payment from the tenant;
and this payment, which to the landlord is properly a profit on capital, is
blended and confounded with rent; which indeed it really is, to the tenant,
and in respect of the economical laws which determine its amount. A tax
on rent, if extending to this portion of it, would discourage landlords from
making improvements: but it does not follow that it would raise the price
of agricultural produce. The same improvements might be made with the
tenant's capital, or even with the landlord's if lent by him to the tenant;
provided he is willing to give the tenant so long a lease as will enable him
to indemnify himself before it expires. But whatever hinders improvements
from being made in the manner in which people prefer to make them, will
often prevent them from being made at all: and on this account a tax on
rent would be inexpedient, unless some means could be devised of excluding from its operation that portion of the nominal rent which may be
regarded as landlord's profit. This argument, however, is not needed for
the condemnation of such a tax. A peculiar tax on the income of any class,
not balanced by taxes on other classes, is a violation of justice, and amounts
to a partial confiscation. I have already shown grounds for excepting from
this censure a tax which, sparing existing rents, should content itself with
appropriating a portion of any future increase arising from the mere action
of natural causes. But even this could not be justly done, without offering
as an alternative the market price of the land. In the case of a tax on rent
which is not peculiar, but accompanied by an equivalent tax on other
incomes, the objection grounded on its reaching the profit arising from
improvements *is less applicable*: since, profits being taxed as well as
rent, the profit which assumes the form of rent *is liable to its share in
common with other profits; but since profits altogether ought, for reasons
formerly stated, to be taxed somewhat lower than rent properly so called,
the objection is only diminished, not removed*.

§ 3. [*Taxes on profits*] A tax on profits, like a tax on rent, must, at least
in its immediate operation, fall wholly on the payer. All profits being alike
affected, no relief can be obtained by a change of employment. If a tax
were laid on the profits of any one branch of productive employment, the
tax would be virtually an increase of the cost of production, and the value
and price of the article would rise accordingly; by which the tax would be
thrown upon the consumers of the commodity, and would not affect profits.
But a general and equal tax on all profits would not affect general prices,
and would fall, at least in the first instance, on capitalists alone.

*a–a*48, 49, 52 , does not apply
*b–b*48, 49, 52 merely pays its just share

There is, however, an ulterior effect, which, in a rich and prosperous country, requires to be taken into account. When the capital accumulated is so great and the rate of annual accumulation so rapid, that the country is only kept from attaining the stationary state by the emigration of capital, or by continual improvements in production; any circumstance which virtually lowers the rate of profit cannot be without a decided influence on these phenomena. It may operate in different ways. The curtailment of profit, and the consequent increased difficulty ^{a}in^a making a fortune or obtaining a subsistence by the employment of capital, may act as a stimulus to inventions, and to the use of them when made. If improvements in production are much accelerated, and if these improvements cheapen, directly or indirectly, any of the things habitually consumed by the labourer, profits may rise, and rise sufficiently to make up for all that is taken from them by the tax. In that case the tax will have been realized without loss to any one, the produce of the country being increased by an equal, or what would in that case be a far greater amount. The tax, however, must even in this case be considered as paid from profits, because the receivers of profits are those who would be benefited if it were taken off.

But though the artificial abstraction of a portion of profits would have a real tendency to accelerate improvements in production, no considerable improvements might actually result, or only of such a kind as not to raise general profits at all, or not to raise them so much as the tax had diminished them. If so, the rate of profit would be brought closer to that practical minimum, to which it is constantly approaching: and this diminished return to capital would either give a decided check to further accumulation, or would cause a greater proportion than before of the annual increase to be sent abroad, or wasted in unprofitable speculations. At its first imposition the tax falls wholly on profits: but the amount of increase of capital, which the tax prevents, would, if it had been allowed to continue, have tended to reduce profits to the same level; and at every period of ten or twenty years there will be found less difference between profits as they are, and profits as they would in that case have been: until at last there is no difference, and the tax is thrown either upon the labourer or upon the landlord. The real effect of a tax on profits is to make the country possess at any given period, a smaller capital and a smaller aggregate production, and to make the stationary state be attained earlier, and with a smaller sum of national wealth. It is possible that a tax on profits might even diminish the existing capital of the country. If the rate of profit is already at the practical minimum, that is, at the point at which all that portion of the annual increment which would tend to reduce profits is carried off either by exportation or by ^{b}speculation^b; then if a tax is imposed which

$^{a-a}$48, 49 of $\qquad\qquad\qquad$ $^{b-b}$48, 49, 52 speculations reduces profits still lower, the same causes which previously carried off the increase would probably carry off a portion of the existing capital. A tax on profits is thus, in a state of capital and accumulation like that in England, extremely detrimental to the national wealth. And this effect is not confined to the case of a peculiar, and therefore intrinsically unjust, tax on profits. The mere fact that profits have to bear their share of a heavy general taxation, tends, in the same manner as a peculiar tax, to drive capital abroad, to stimulate imprudent speculations by diminishing safe gains, to discourage further accumulation, and to accelerate the attainment of the stationary state. This is thought to have been the principal cause of the decline of Holland, or rather of her having ceased to make progress.

Even in countries which do not accumulate so fast as to be always within a short interval of the stationary state, it seems impossible that, if capital is accumulating at all, its accumulation should not be in some degree retarded by the abstraction of a portion of its profit; and unless the effect in stimulating improvements be a full counter-balance, it is inevitable that a part of the burthen will be thrown off the capitalist, upon the labourer or the landlord. One or other of these is always the loser by a diminished rate of accumulation. If population continues to increase as before, the labourer suffers: if not, cultivation is checked in its advance, and the landlords lose the accession of rent which would have accrued to them. The only ᶜcountriesᶜ in which a tax on profits seems likely to be permanently a burthen on capitalists exclusively, are those in which capital is stationary, because there is no new accumulation. In such countries the tax might not prevent the old capital from being kept up through habit, or from unwillingness to submit to impoverishment, and so the capitalist might continue to bear the whole of the tax. It is seen from these considerations that the effects of a tax on profits are much more complex, more various, and in some points more uncertain, than writers on the subject have commonly supposed.

§ 4. [*Taxes on wages*] We ᵃnow turnᵃ to Taxes on Wages. The incidence of these is very different, according as the wages taxed are those of ordinary unskilled labour, or are the remuneration of such skilled or privileged employments, whether manual or intellectual, as are taken out of the sphere of competition by a natural or ᵇ conferred monopoly.

I have already remarked, that in the present low state of popular education, all the higher grades of mental or educated labour are at a monopoly price; exceeding the wages of common workmen in a degree very far beyond that which is due to the expense, trouble, and loss of time required in qualifying for the employment. Any tax levied on these gains,

ᶜ⁻ᶜ57   country [*printer's error?*]
ᵃ⁻ᵃ48, 49, 52, 57   turn now   ᵇ48, 49, 52   a

which still leaves them above (or not below) their just proportion, falls on those who pay it; they have no means of relieving themselves at the expense of any other class. The same thing is true of ordinary wages, in cases like that of the United States, or of a new colony, where, capital increasing as rapidly as population can increase, wages are kept up by the increase of capital, and not by the adherence of the labourers to a fixed standard of comforts. In such a case some deterioration of their condition, whether by a tax or otherwise, might possibly take place without checking the increase of population. The tax would in that case fall on the labourers themselves, and would reduce them prematurely to that lower state to which, on the same supposition with regard to their habits, they would in any case have been reduced ultimately, by the inevitable diminution in the rate of increase of capital, through the occupation of all the fertile land.

Some will object that, even in this case, a tax on wages cannot be detrimental to the labourers, since the money raised by it, being expended in the country, comes back to the labourers again through the demand for labour. The fallacy, however, of this doctrine has been so completely exhibited in the First Book,* that I need do little more than refer to that exposition. It was there shown that funds expended unproductively have no tendency to raise or keep up wages, unless when expended in the direct purchase of labour. If the government took a tax of a shilling a week from every labourer, and laid it all out in hiring labourers for military service, public works, or the like, it would, no doubt, indemnify the labourers as a class for all that the tax took from them. That would really be "spending the money among the people." But if it expended the whole in buying goods, or in adding to the salaries of employés who bought goods with it, this would not increase the demand for labour, or tend to raise wages. Without ^c, however,^c reverting to ^dgeneral principles^d, we may rely on an obvious *reductio ad absurdum.* If to take money from the labourers and spend it in commodities is giving it back to the labourers, then, to take money from other classes, and spend it in the same manner, must be giving it to the labourers; consequently, the more a government takes in taxes, the greater will be the demand for labour, and the more opulent the condition of the labourers. A proposition the absurdity of which no one can fail to see.

In the condition of most communities, wages are regulated by the habitual standard of living to which the labourers adhere, and on less than which they will not multiply. Where there exists such a standard, a tax on wages will indeed for a time be borne by the labourers themselves; but unless this temporary depression has the effect of lowering the standard

*Supra, vol. i. pp. 78–88.

^{c–c}+52, 57, 62, 65, 71
^{d–d}48, 49   the proofs formerly given

itself, the increase of population will receive a check, which will raise wages, and restore the labourers to their previous condition. On whom, in this case, will the tax fall? According to Adam Smith, on the community generally, in their character of consumers; since the rise of wages, he thought, would raise general prices. We have seen, however, that general prices depend on other causes, and are never raised by any circumstance which affects all kinds of productive employment in the same manner and degree. A rise of wages occasioned by a tax, must, like any other increase of the cost of labour, be defrayed from profits. To attempt to tax day-labourers, in an old country, is merely to impose an extra tax upon all employers of common labour; unless the tax has the much worse effect of permanently lowering the standard of comfortable subsistence in the minds of the poorest class.

We find in the preceding considerations an additional argument for the opinion already expressed, that direct taxations should stop short of the class of incomes which do not exceed what is necessary for healthful existence. ^eThese^e very small incomes are ^fmostly^f derived from manual labour; and, as we now see, any tax imposed on these, either permanently degrades the habits of the labouring class, or falls on profits, and burthens capitalists with an indirect tax, in addition to their share of the direct taxes; which is doubly objectionable, both as a violation of the fundamental rule of equality, and for the reasons which, as already shown, render a peculiar tax on profits detrimental to the public wealth, and consequently to the means which society possesses of paying any taxes whatever.

§ 5. [*An Income Tax*] We now pass, from taxes on the separate kinds of income, to a tax attempted to be assessed fairly upon all kinds; in other words, an Income Tax. The discussion of the conditions necessary for making this tax consistent with justice, has been anticipated in the last chapter. We shall suppose, therefore, that ^athese^a conditions are complied with. They are, first, that incomes below a certain amount should be altogether untaxed. This minimum should not be higher than the amount which suffices for the necessaries of ^bthe existing population^b. The exemption from the present income tax, of all incomes under ^c100*l.*^c a year, ^dand the lower percentage ^eformerly^e levied on those between 100*l.* and 150*l.*, are^d only defensible on the ground that ^falmost all the indirect taxes^f press

^{e–e}48, 49   Almost all these
^{f–f}+52, 57, 62, 65, 71

^{a–a}48, 49, 52   those
^{b–b}48, 49   a labouring family of moderate numbers
^{c–c}48, 49, 52   150*l.*   ^{d–d}48, 49, 52   is   ^{e–e}+65, 71
^{f–f}48, 49, 52   some taxes on necessaries are still kept up, and that almost all the existing taxes on indulgences

more heavily on incomes between 50*l.* and 150*l.* than on any others whatever. The second condition is, that incomes above the limit should be taxed only in proportion to the surplus by which they exceed the limit. Thirdly, that *g*all sums saved from income and invested, should be exempt from the tax: or if this be found impracticable, that life incomes, and incomes from business and professions,*g* should be less heavily taxed than inheritable incomes, in a degree as nearly as possible equivalent to the increased need of economy arising from their terminable character *h*: allowance being also made, in the case of variable incomes, for their precariousness.*h*

An income-tax, fairly assessed on these principles, would be, in point of justice, the least exceptionable of all taxes. The objection to it, *i*in the present low state of public morality*i*, is the impossibility of ascertaining the real incomes of the contributors. The supposed hardship of compelling people to disclose the amount of their incomes, ought not, in my opinion, to count for much. One of the social evils of this country is the practice, amounting to a custom, of maintaining, or attempting to maintain, the appearance to the world of a larger income than is possessed; and it would be far better for the *j*interest*j* of those who yield to this weakness, if the extent of their means were universally and exactly known, and the temptation removed to expending more than they can afford, or stinting real wants in order to make a false show externally. At the same time, the reason of the case, even on this point, is not so exclusively on one side of the argument as is sometimes supposed. So long as the vulgar of any country are in the debased state of mind which this national habit presupposes—so long as their respect (if such a word can be applied to it) is proportioned to what they suppose to be each person's pecuniary means—it may be doubted whether anything which would remove all *k*uncertainty*k* as to that point, would not considerably increase the presumption and arrogance of the vulgar rich, and their insolence towards those above them in mind and character, but below them in *l*fortune*l*.

Notwithstanding, too, what is called the inquisitorial nature of the tax, no amount of inquisitorial power which would be tolerated by a people the most disposed to submit to it, could enable the revenue officers to assess the tax from actual knowledge of the circumstances of contributors. Rents, salaries, annuities, and all fixed incomes, can be exactly ascertained. But

---

*g–g*48, 49   life incomes
*h–h*48, 49   . Fourthly, that incomes which are jointly the result of capital and of personal exertion, should be taxed intermediately between the rate for inheritable and that for life incomes.
*i–i*48, 49   which, with much regret, I cannot help regarding as insuperable
*j–j*48, 49, 52, 57, 62   interests
*k–k*48, 49   doubt   *l–l*48, 49   circumstances

the variable gains of professions, and still more the profits of business, which the person interested cannot always himself exactly ascertain, can still less be estimated with any approach to fairness by a tax-collector. The main reliance must be placed, and always has been placed, on the returns made by the person himself. No production of accounts is of much avail, except against the more flagrant cases of falsehood; and even against these the check is very imperfect, for if fraud is intended, false accounts can generally be framed which it will baffle any means of inquiry possessed by the revenue officers to detect: the easy resource of omitting entries on the credit side being often sufficient without the aid of fictitious debts or disbursements. The tax, therefore, on whatever principles of equality it may be imposed, is in practice unequal in one of the worst ways, falling heaviest on the most conscientious. The unscrupulous succeed in evading a great proportion of what they should pay; even persons of integrity in their ordinary transactions are tempted to palter with their consciences, at least to the extent of deciding in their own favour all points on which the smallest doubt or discussion could arise: while the strictly veracious *may be* made to pay more than the state intended, by the powers of arbitrary assessment necessarily intrusted to the Commissioners, as the last defence against the tax-payer's power of concealment.

It is to be feared, therefore, that the fairness which belongs to the principle of an income tax, *cannot* be made to attach to it in practice: and that this tax, while apparently the most just of all modes of raising a revenue, is in effect more unjust than many others which are *primâ facie* more objectionable. This consideration would lead us to concur in the opinion which, until of late, has usually prevailed—that direct taxes on income should be reserved as an extraordinary resource for great national emergencies, in which the necessity of a large additional revenue overrules all *°* objections.

The difficulties of a fair income tax have *ᵖ* elicited a proposition for a direct tax of so much per cent, not on income but on expenditure; the aggregate amount of each person's expenditure being ascertained, as the amount of income now is, from statements furnished by the contributors themselves. The author of this suggestion, Mr. Revans, in a clever pamphlet on the subject,* contends that the returns which persons would furnish of their expenditure would be more trustworthy than those which they now make of their income, inasmuch as expenditure is in its own nature more public than income, and false representations of it more easily

*"A Percentage Tax on Domestic Expenditure to supply the whole of the Public Revenue." By John Revans. Published [London] by Hatchard, in 1847.

*ᵐ⁻ᵐ*48, 49, 52, 57   are often   *ⁿ⁻ⁿ*48, 49   can never
*°*48, 49   minor   *ᵖ*48, 49   lately

detected. He cannot, I think, have sufficiently considered, how few of the items in the annual expenditure of most families can be judged of with any approximation to correctness from the external signs. The only security would still be the veracity of individuals, and there is no reason for supposing that their statements would be more trustworthy on the subject of their expenses than *q* that of their revenues; especially as, the expenditure of most persons being composed of many more items than their income, there would be more scope for concealment and suppression in the detail of expenses than even of receipts.

The taxes on expenditure at present in force, either in this or in other countries, fall only on particular kinds of expenditure, and differ no otherwise from taxes on commodities than in being paid directly by the person who consumes or uses the article, instead of being advanced by the producer or seller, and reimbursed in the price. The taxes on horses and carriages, on dogs, on servants, are *rallr* of this nature. They evidently fall on the persons from whom they are levied—those who use the commodity taxed. A tax of a similar description, and more important, is a house-tax; which must be considered at somewhat greater length.

§ 6. [*A House Tax*] The rent of a house consists of two parts, the ground-rent, and what Adam Smith calls the building-rent. The first is determined by the ordinary principles of rent. It is the remuneration given for the use of the portion of land occupied by the house and its appurtenances; and varies from a mere equivalent for the rent which the ground would afford in agriculture, to the monopoly rents paid for advantageous situations in populous thoroughfares. The rent of the house itself, as distinguished from the ground, is the equivalent given for the labour and capital expended on the building. The fact of its being received in quarterly or half-yearly payments, makes no difference in the principles by which it is regulated. It comprises the ordinary profit on the builder's capital, and an annuity, sufficient at the current rate of interest, after paying for all repairs chargeable on the proprietor, to replace the original capital by the time the house is worn out, or by the expiration of the usual term of a building lease.

A tax of so much per cent on the gross rent, falls on both *a*those*a* portions alike. The more highly a house is rented, the more it pays to the tax, whether the quality of the situation or that of the house itself is the cause. The incidence, however, of these two portions of the tax must be considered separately.

As much of it as is a tax on building-rent, must ultimately fall on the consumer, in other words the occupier. For as the profits of building are already not above the ordinary rate, they would, if the tax fell on the owner and not on the occupier, become lower than the profits of untaxed employments, and houses would not be built. It is probable however that for some time after the tax was first imposed, a great part of it would fall, not on the renter, but on the owner of the house. A large proportion of the consumers either could not afford, or would not choose, to pay their former rent with the tax in addition, but would content themselves with a lower scale of accommodation. Houses therefore would be for a time in excess of the demand. The consequence of such excess, in the case of most other articles, would be an almost immediate diminution of the supply: but so durable a commodity as houses does not rapidly diminish in amount. New buildings indeed [b], of the class for which the demand had decreased,[b] would cease to be erected, except for special reasons; but in the meantime the temporary superfluity would lower rents, and the consumers would obtain perhaps nearly the same accommodation as formerly, for the same aggregate payment, rent and tax together. By degrees, however, as the existing houses wore out, or as increase of population demanded a greater supply, rents would again rise; until it became profitable to recommence building, which would not be until the tax was wholly [c]transferred to[c] the occupier. In the end, therefore, the occupier bears that portion of a tax on rent, which falls on the payment made for the house itself, exclusively of the ground it stands on.

[d]The case is partly[d] different with the portion which is a tax on ground-rent. As taxes on rent, properly so called, fall on the landlord, a tax on ground-rent, one would suppose, must fall on the ground-landlord, at least after the expiration of the building lease. [e]It will not however fall wholly on the landlord, unless with the tax on ground-rent there is[e] combined an equivalent tax on agricultural rent [f]. The [g]lowest[g] rent of land let for building is very little above the rent which the same ground would yield in agriculture: since it is reasonable to suppose that land, unless in case of exceptional circumstances, is let or sold for building as soon as it is decidedly worth more for that purpose than for [h]cultivation[h]. If, therefore, a tax were laid on ground-rents without being also laid on agricultural rents, it would, unless of [i] trifling amount, reduce the return from the lowest ground-rents below the ordinary return from land, and would [j]check[j] further building quite as effectually as if it were a tax on building-rents, until either the increased demand of a growing population, or a diminution

---

[b]–[b]48, 49 (at least of the more expensive class)   [c]–[c]48, 49 thrown upon
[d]–[d]48, 49, 52 At first sight one would be inclined to suppose the case to be
[e]–[e]48, 49, 52 And such would really be the case, if with the tax on ground-rent
there were   [f]48, 49, 52 ; but not otherwise
    [g]–[g]48 *lowest*   [h]–[h]48 agriculture
    [i]48, 49 quite   [j]–[j]48, 49 put a stop to

of supply by ^{k}the ordinary causes of destruction^k, had raised the rent by a full equivalent for the tax. But whatever raises the lowest ground-rents, raises all others, since each exceeds the lowest by ^{l} the market value of its peculiar advantages. ^{m}If, therefore, the tax on ground-rents were a fixed sum per square foot, the more valuable situations paying no more than those least in request, this fixed payment would ultimately fall on the occupier. Suppose the lowest ground-rent to be 10*l.* per acre, and the highest 1000*l.*, a tax of 1*l.* per acre on ground-rents would ultimately raise the former to 11*l.*, and the latter consequently to 1001*l.*, since the difference of value between the two situations would be exactly what it was before: the annual pound, therefore, would be paid by the occupier. But a tax on ground-rent is supposed to be a portion of a house-tax, which is not a fixed payment, but a percentage on the rent. The cheapest site, therefore, being supposed as before to pay 1*l.*, the dearest would pay 100*l.*, of which only the 1*l.* could be thrown upon the occupier, since the rent would still be only raised to 1001*l.* Consequently, 99*l.* of the 100*l.* levied from the expensive site, would fall on the ground-landlord. A house-tax thus requires to be considered in a double aspect, as a tax on all occupiers of houses, and a tax on ground-rents.

In the vast majority of houses, the ground-rent forms but a small proportion of the annual payment made for the house, and nearly all the tax falls on the occupier. It is only in exceptional cases, like that of the favourite situations in large towns, that the predominant element in the rent of the house is the ground-rent; and among the very few kinds of income which are fit subjects for peculiar taxation, these ground-rents hold the principal place, being the most gigantic example extant of enormous accessions of riches acquired rapidly, and in many cases unexpectedly, by a few families, from the mere accident of their possessing certain tracts of land, without their having themselves aided in the acquisition by the smallest exertion, outlay, or risk. So far therefore as a house-tax falls on the ground-landlord, it is liable to no valid objection.

In so far as it falls on the occupier^m, if justly proportioned to the value of the house, ^{n}it^n is one of the fairest and most unobjectionable of all taxes. No part of a person's expenditure is a better criterion of his means, or bears, on the whole, more nearly the same proportion to them. A house-tax

$^{k-k}$48, 49 wearing out ^{l}48, 49 precisely
$^{m-m}$48, 49, 52   There is thus no difference between the two component elements of house-rent, in respect to the incidence of the tax. Both alike fall ultimately on the occupier: while, in both alike, if the occupier in consequence reduces his demand by contenting himself with inferior accommodation, that is, if he prefers saving his tax from house-rent to saving it from other parts of his expenditure, he indirectly lowers ground-rent, or retards its increase; just as a diminished consumption of agricultural produce, by making cultivation retrograde, would lower ordinary rent.
    A house-tax $^{n-n}$+57, 62, 65, 71

is a nearer approach to a fair income tax, than a direct assessment on income can easily be; having the great advantage, that it makes spontaneously all the allowances which it is so difficult to make, and so impracticable to make exactly, in assessing an income tax: for if what a person pays in house-rent is a test of anything, it is a test not of what he possesses, but of what he thinks he can afford to spend. *o*The equality of this tax can only be seriously questioned on two grounds.*o* The first is, that a miser may escape it. This objection applies to all taxes on expenditure: nothing but a direct tax on income can reach a miser. But *p*as misers*p* do not now hoard their treasure, but invest it in *q*productive employments, it not only*q* adds to the national wealth, and consequently to the general means of paying taxes, *r*but the payment claimable from itself is only transferred from the principal sum to the income afterwards derived from it, which pays taxes as soon as it comes to be expended*r*. The second objection is, that a person may require a larger and more expensive house, not from having greater means, but from having a larger family. Of this, however, he is not entitled to complain; since having a large family is at a person's own choice: and, so far as concerns the public interest, is a thing rather to be discouraged than promoted.*

*[52] Another common objection is that large and expensive accommodation is often required, not as a residence, but for business. But it is an admitted principle that buildings or portions of buildings occupied exclusively for business, such as shops, warehouses, or manufactories, ought to be exempted from house-tax. The plea that persons in business may be compelled to live in situations, such as the great thoroughfares of London, where house-rent is at a monopoly rate, seems to me unworthy of regard: since no one does so but because the extra profit which he expects to derive from the situation, is more than an equivalent to him for the extra cost. [57] But in any case, the bulk of the tax on this extra rent will not fall on him, but on the ground-landlord.

[48] It has been also objected that house-rent in the rural districts is much lower than in towns, and lower in some towns and in some rural districts than in others: so that a tax proportioned to it would have a corresponding inequality of pressure. To this, however, it may be answered, that in places where house-rent is low, persons of the same amount of income usually live in larger and better houses, and thus expend in house-rent more nearly the same proportion of their incomes than might at first sight appear. Or if not, the probability will be, that many of them live in those places precisely because they are too poor to live elsewhere, and have therefore the strongest claim to be taxed lightly. In some cases, it is precisely because the people are poor, that house-rent remains low.

*o–o*48, 49, 52, 57   To the equality of this tax, there are but two decided objections.
*p–p*48, 49   this, though a real, is not a great defect; for there are few misers; and as they
*q–q*48, 49   employments in which it feeds productive labourers, and
*r–r*48, 49   the inconvenience of its paying no taxes of its own is in some degree compensated for

*ᵃA large*ᵃ portion of the taxation of ᵗthisᵗ country is ᵘ raised by a house-tax ᵛ. Theᵛ parochial taxation of the towns entirely, and of the rural districts partially, ʷconsistsʷ of an assessment on house-rent. The window-tax, which ˣwasˣ also a house-tax, but of a bad kind, operating as a tax on light, and a cause of deformity in building ʸ, was exchanged in 1851 for a house-tax properly so called, but on a much lower scale than that which existed previously to 1834. It is to be lamented that the new tax retainsʸ the unjust principle on which the old house-tax was assessed, and which contributed quite as much as the selfishness of the middle classes to produce the outcry against the tax ᶻ . The public were justly scandalized on learning that residences like Chatsworth or Belvoir were only rated on an imaginary rent of perhaps 200*l.* a year, under the pretext that owing to the great expense of keeping them up, they could not be let for more. Probably, indeed, they could not be let even for that, and if the argument were a fair one, they ought not to have been taxed at all. But a house-tax is not intended as a tax on incomes derived from houses, but on expenditure incurred for them. The thing which it is wished to ascertain is what a house costs to the person who lives in it, not what it would bring in if let to some one else. When the occupier is not the owner, ᵃand does not hold on a repairing lease,ᵃ the rent he pays is the measure of what ᵇthe houseᵇ costs him: ᶜbutᶜ when he is the owner, some other measure must be sought. A valuation should be made of the house, not at what it would sell for, but at what would be the cost of rebuilding it, and this valuation might be ᵈperiodically correctedᵈ by an allowance for what it had lost in value by time, or gained by repairs and improvements. The amount of the amended valuation would form a principal sum, the interest of which, at the current price of the public funds, would form the annual value at which the building should be assessed to the tax.

As incomes below a certain amount ought to be exempt from income tax, so ought houses below a certain value, from house-tax, on the universal principle of sparing from all taxation the absolute necessaries of healthful existence. In order that the occupiers of lodgings, as well as of houses, might benefit, as in justice they ought, by this exemption, it might be optional with the owners to have every portion of a house which is occupied by a separate tenant, valued and assessed separately, as is now usually the case with chambers.

ᵃ⁻ᵃ48, 49 Though the house-tax which formerly existed in this country has been repealed, a large   ᵗ⁻ᵗ48, 49, 52   the   ᵘ48, 49   still   ᵛ⁻ᵛ48, 49   ; the
ʷ⁻ʷ48, 49   consisting   ˣ⁻ˣ48, 49   is

ʸ⁻ʸ48, 49   . It would be a most advantageous exchange to abolish the window-tax and the present income-tax, and replace them by a house-tax of equivalent amount. In doing so, it would be necessary to avoid   ᶻ48, 49   in 1834

ᵃ⁻ᵃ+62, 65, 71   ᵇ⁻ᵇ48, 49, 52, 57   it
ᶜ⁻ᶜ+57, 62, 65, 71   ᵈ⁻ᵈ48, 49   corrected each year

CHAPTER IV

Of Taxes on Commodities

§ 1. [*A Tax on all Commodities would fall on profits*] By taxes on commodities are commonly meant, those which are levied either on the producers, or on the carriers or dealers who intervene between them and the final purchasers for consumption. Taxes imposed directly on the consumers of particular commodities, such as a house-tax, or the tax in this country on horses and carriages, might be called taxes on commodities, but are not; the phrase being by custom, confined to indirect taxes—those which are advanced by one person, to be, as is expected and intended, reimbursed by another. Taxes on commodities are either on production within the country, or on importation into it, or on conveyance or sale within it; and are classed respectively as excise, customs, or tolls and transit duties. To whichever class they belong, and at whatever stage in the progress of the *community* they may be imposed, they are equivalent to an increase of the cost of production; using that term in its most enlarged sense, which includes the cost of transport and distribution, or, in common phrase, of bringing the commodity to market.

When the cost of production is increased artificially by a tax, the effect is the same as when it is increased by natural causes. If only one or a few commodities are affected, their value and price rise, so as to compensate the producer or dealer for the peculiar burthen; but if there were a tax on all commodities, exactly proportioned to their value, no such compensation would be obtained: there would neither be a general rise of values, which is an absurdity, nor of prices, which depend on causes entirely different. There would, however, as Mr. M'Culloch has pointed out, be a disturbance of values, some falling, others rising, owing to a circumstance, the effect of which on values and prices we formerly discussed; the different durability of the capital employed in different occupations. The gross produce of industry consists of two parts; one portion serving to replace the capital consumed, while the other portion is profit. Now equal capitals in two branches of production must have equal expectations of profit; but if a greater portion of the one than of the other is fixed capital, or if that fixed

*a–a*48, 49, 52, 57   commodity [*printer's error?*]

capital is more durable, there will be a less consumption of capital in the year, and less will be required to replace it, so that the profit, *b*if absolutely the same, will*b* form a greater proportion of the annual returns. To derive from a capital of 1000*l*. a profit of 100*l*., the one producer may have to sell produce to the value of 1100*l*., the other only to the value of 500*l*. If on these two branches of industry a tax be imposed of five per cent *ad valorem*, the last will be charged only with 25*l*., the first with 55*l*.; leaving to the one 75*l*. profit, to the other only 45*l*. To equalize, therefore, their expectation of profit, the one commodity must rise in price, or the other must fall, or both: commodities made chiefly by immediate labour must rise in value, as compared with those which are chiefly made by machinery. It is unnecessary to prosecute this branch of the inquiry any further.

§ 2. [*Taxes on particular commodities fall on the consumer*] A tax on any one commodity, whether laid on its production, its importation, its carriage from place to place, or its sale, and whether the tax be a fixed sum of money for a given quantity of the commodity, or an *ad valorem* duty, will, as a general rule, raise the value and price of the commodity by at least the amount of the tax. There are few cases in which it does not raise them by more than that amount. In the first place, there are few taxes on production on account of which it is not found or deemed necessary to impose restrictive regulations on the manufacturers or dealers, in order to check evasions of the tax. These regulations are always sources of trouble and annoyance, and generally of expense, for all of which, being peculiar disadvantages, the producers or dealers must have compensation in the price of their commodity. These restrictions also frequently interfere with the processes of manufacture, requiring the producer to carry on his operations in the way most convenient to the revenue, though not the cheapest, or most efficient for purposes of production. Any regulations whatever, enforced by law, make it difficult for the producer to adopt new and improved processes. Further, the necessity of advancing the tax obliges producers and dealers to carry on their business with larger capitals than would otherwise be necessary, on the whole of which they must receive the ordinary rate of profit, though a part only is employed in defraying the real expenses of production or importation. The price of the article must be such as to afford a profit on more than its natural value, instead of a profit on only its natural value. A part of the capital of the country, in short, is not employed in production, but in advances to the state, repaid in the price of goods; and the consumers must give an indemnity to the sellers, equal to the profit which they could have made on the same capital if really

*b-b*48, 49   to be absolutely the same, must

employed in production.* Neither ought it to be forgotten, that whatever renders a larger capital necessary in any trade or business, limits the competition in that business; and by giving something like a monopoly to a few dealers, ᵃmay enableᵃ them either to keep up the price beyond what would afford the ordinary rate of profit, or to obtain the ordinary rate of profit with a less degree of exertion for improving and cheapening their commodity. In these several modes, taxes on commodities often cost to the consumer, through the increased price of the article, much more than they bring into the treasury of the state. There is still another consideration. ᵇThe higher price necessitatedᵇ by the tax, almost always checks the demand for the commodity; and since there are many improvements in production which, to make them practicable, require a certain extent of demand, such improvements are obstructed, and many of them prevented altogether. It is a well-known fact, that the branches of production in which fewest improvements are made, are those with which the revenue officer interferes; and that nothing, in general, gives a greater impulse to improvements in the production of a commodity, than taking off a tax which narrowed the market for it.

§ 3. [*Peculiar effects of taxes on necessaries*] Such are the effects of taxes on commodities, considered generally; but as there are some commodities (those composing the necessaries of the labourer) of which the values have an influence on the distribution of wealth among different classes of the community, it is requisite to trace the effects of taxes on those particular articles somewhat farther. If a tax be laid, say on corn, and the price rises in proportion to the tax, the rise of price may operate in two ways. First: it may lower the condition of the labouring classes; temporarily indeed it can scarcely fail to do so. If it diminishes their consumption of the produce of the earth, or ᵃmakes them resortᵃ to a food which the soil produces more abundantly, and therefore more cheaply, it to that extent contributes to throw back agriculture upon more fertile lands or less costly processes, and to lower the value and price of corn; which therefore ultimately ᵇsettlesᵇ at a price, increased not by the whole amount of the tax, but by only a part of its amount. Secondly, however, it may happen that the

*[65] It is true, this does not constitute, as at first sight it appears to do, a case of taking more out of the pockets of the people than the state receives; since if the state needs the advance, and gets it in this manner, it can dispense with an equivalent amount of borrowing in stock or exchequer bills. But it is more economical that the necessities of the state should be supplied from the disposable capital in the hands of the lending class, than by an artificial addition to the expenses of one or several classes of producers or dealers.

ᵃ⁻ᵃ48, 49, 52   enables   ᵇ⁻ᵇ48, 49, 52, 57,   The rise of price occasioned
ᵃ⁻ᵃ48, 49   reduces them   ᵇ⁻ᵇ48, 49   settle

dearness of the taxed food does not lower the habitual standard of the labourer's requirements, but that wages, on the contrary, through an action on population, rise, in a shorter or longer period, so as to compensate the labourers for their portion of the tax; the compensation being of course at the expense of profits. Taxes on necessaries must thus have one of two effects. Either they lower the condition of the labouring classes; or they exact from the owners of capital, in addition to the amount due to the state on their own necessaries, the amount due on those consumed by the labourers. In the last case, the tax on necessaries, like a tax on wages, is equivalent to a peculiar tax on profits; which is, like all other partial taxation, unjust, and is specially prejudicial to the increase of the national wealth.

It remains to speak of the effect on rent. Assuming (what is usually the fact,) that the consumption of food is not diminished, the same cultivation as before will be necessary to supply the wants of the community; the margin of cultivation, to use Dr. Chalmers' expression, remains where it was; and the same land or capital which, as the least productive, already regulated the value and price of the whole produce, will continue to regulate them. The effect which a tax on agricultural produce will have on rent, depends on its affecting or not affecting the difference between the return to this least productive land or capital, and the returns to other lands and capitals. Now this depends on the manner in which the tax is imposed. If it is an *ad valorem* tax, or what is the same thing, a fixed proportion of the produce, such as tithe for example, it evidently lowers corn-rents. For it takes more corn from the better lands than from the worse; and exactly in the degree in which they are better; land of twice the *°productiveness°* paying twice as much to the tithe. Whatever takes more from the greater of two quantities than from the less, diminishes the difference between them. The imposition of a tithe on corn would take a tithe also from corn-rent: for if *ᵈweᵈ* reduce a series of numbers by a tenth each, the differences between them are reduced one-tenth.

For example, let there be five qualities of land, which severally yield, on the same extent of ground, and with the same expenditure, 100, 90, 80, 70, and 60 bushels of wheat; the last of these being the lowest quality which the demand for food renders it necessary to cultivate. The rent of these lands will be as follows:—

The land producing 100 bushels will yield a rent of 100–60, or 40 bushels.
That producing 90 bushels will yield a rent of 90–60, or 30 bushels.
That producing 80 bushels will yield a rent of 80–60, or 20 bushels.
That producing 70 bushels will yield a rent of 70–60, or 10 bushels.
That producing 60 bushels will yield no rent.

ᶜ⁻ᶜ48, 49 fertility   ᵈ⁻ᵈ48, 49 you

Now let a tithe be imposed, which takes from these five pieces of land 10, 9, 8, 7, and 6 bushels respectively, the fifth quality still being the one which regulates the price, but returning to the farmer, after payment of tithe, no more than 54 bushels:—

The land producing } 100 bushels reduced to 90, will yield a rent of 90–54, or 36 bushels.

That producing } 90 bushels reduced to 81, will yield a rent of 81–54, or 27 bushels.

That producing } 80 bushels reduced to 72, will yield a rent of 72–54, or 18 bushels.

That producing } 70 bushels reduced to 63, will yield a rent of 63–54, or 9 bushels,

and that producing 60 bushels, reduced to 54, will yield, as before, no rent. So that the rent of the first quality of land has lost four bushels; of the second, three; of the third, two; and of the fourth, one: that is, each has lost exactly one-tenth. A tax, therefore, of a fixed proportion of the produce, lowers, in the same proportion, corn-rent.

But it is only corn-rent that is lowered, and not rent estimated in money, or in any other commodity. For, in the same proportion as corn-rent is reduced in quantity, the corn composing it is raised in value. Under the tithe, 54 bushels will be worth in the market what 60 were before; and nine-tenths will in all cases sell for as much as the whole ten-tenths previously sold for. The landlords will therefore be compensated in value and price for what they lose in quantity; and will suffer only so far as they consume their rent in kind, or after receiving it in money, expend it in agricultural produce: that is, they only suffer as consumers of agricultural produce, and in common with all ᵉtheᵉ other consumers. Considered as landlords, they have the same income as before; the tithe, therefore, falls on the consumer, and not on the landlord.

The same effect would be produced on rent, if the tax, instead of being a fixed proportion of the produce, were a fixed sum per quarter or per bushel. A tax which takes a shilling for every bushel, takes more shillings from one field than from another, just in proportion as it produces more bushels; and operates exactly like tithe, except that tithe is not only the same proportion on all lands, but is also the same proportion at all times, while a fixed sum of money per bushel will amount to a greater or ᶠaᶠ less proportion, according as corn is cheap or dear.

There are other modes of taxing agriculture, which would affect rent differently. A tax proportioned to the rent would fall wholly on the rent, and would not at all raise the price of corn, which is regulated by the portion of the produce that pays no rent. A fixed tax of so much per cultivated acre, without distinction of value, would have effects directly the reverse. Taking no more from the best qualities of land than from the worst, it would leave the differences the same as before, and consequently the same corn-rents, and the landlords would profit to the full extent of the rise of price. To put the thing in another manner; the price must ⁱrise sufficientlyⁱ to enable the worst land to pay the tax; thus enabling all lands which produce more than the worst, to pay not only the tax, but also an increased rent to the landlords. These, however, are not so much taxes on the produce of land, as taxes on the land itself. Taxes on the produce, properly so called, whether fixed or *ad valorem*, do not affect rent, but fall on the consumer: profits, however, generally bearing either the whole or the greatest part of the portion which is levied on the consumption of the labouring classes.

§ 4. [*How the peculiar effects of taxes on necessaries are modified by the tendency of profits to a minimum*] The preceding is, I apprehend, a correct statement of the manner in which taxes on agricultural produce operate when first laid on. When, however, they are of old standing, their effect may be different, as was first pointed out, I believe, by Mr. Senior. It is, as we have seen, an almost infallible consequence of any reduction of profits, to retard the rate of accumulation. Now the effect of accumulation, when attended by its usual accompaniment, an increase of population, is to increase the value and price of food, to raise rent, and to lower profits: that is, to do precisely what is done by a tax on agricultural produce, except that this does not raise rent. The tax, therefore, merely anticipates the rise of price, and fall of profits, which would have taken place ultimately through the mere progress of accumulation; while it at the same time prevents, or at least retards, that progress. If the rate of profit was such, previous to the imposition of a tithe, that the effect of the tithe reduces it to the practical minimum, the tithe will put a stop to all further accumulation, or cause it to take place out of the country; and the only effect which the tithe will then have had on the consumer, is to make him pay earlier the price which he would have had to pay somewhat later—part of which, indeed, in the gradual progress of wealth and population, he would have almost immediately begun to pay. After a lapse of time which would have admitted of a rise of one-tenth ᵃthroughᵃ the natural progress of wealth, the consumer will be paying no more than he would have paid if the tithe had never existed; he will have ceased to pay any portion of it, and the person who will really pay it is the landlord, whom it deprives of the increase of rent which would by that time have accrued to him. At every successive point in this interval of time, less of the burthen will rest on the

ⁱ⁻ⁱ48, 49 rise,   ᵃ⁻ᵃ48, 49, 52, 57, 62 from

consumer, and more of it on the landlord: and in the ultimate result, the minimum of profits will be reached with a smaller capital and population, and a lower rental, than if the course of things had not been disturbed by the imposition of the tax. If, on the other hand, the tithe or other tax on agricultural produce does not reduce profits to the minimum, but to something above the minimum, accumulation will not be stopped, but only slackened: and if population also increases, the two-fold increase will continue to produce its effects—a rise of the price of corn, and an increase of rent. These consequences, however, will not take place with the same rapidity as if the higher rate of profit had continued. At the end of twenty years the country will have a smaller population and capital, than, but for the tax, it would by that time have had; the landlords will have a smaller rent; and the price of corn, having increased less rapidly than it would otherwise have done, will *b*not be so much as*b* a tenth higher than what, if there had been no tax, it would by that time have *c*become*c*. A part of the tax, therefore, will already have ceased to fall on the consumer, and devolved upon the landlord; and the proportion will become greater and greater by lapse of time.

Mr. Senior illustrates *d*this*d* view of the subject by likening the effects of tithes, or other taxes on agricultural produce to those of natural sterility of soil. If the land of a country *e*without access to foreign supplies,*e* were suddenly smitten with a permanent deterioration of quality, to an extent which would make a tenth more labour necessary to raise the existing produce, the price of corn would undoubtedly rise one-tenth. But it cannot hence be inferred that if the soil of the country had from the beginning been one-tenth worse than it is, corn would at present have been one-tenth dearer than we find it. It is far more probable, that the smaller return to labour and capital, ever since the first settlement of the country, would have caused in each successive generation a less rapid increase than has taken place: that the country would now have contained less capital, and maintained a smaller population, so that notwithstanding the inferiority of the soil, the price of corn would not have been higher, nor profits lower, than at present; rent alone would certainly have been lower. We may suppose two islands, which, being alike in extent, in natural fertility, and industrial advancement, have up to a certain time been equal in population and capital, and have had equal rentals, and the same price of corn. Let us imagine a tithe imposed in one of these islands, but not in the other. There will be immediately a difference in the price of corn, and therefore probably in profits. While profits are not tending downwards in either country, that is, while improvements in the production of necessaries fully keep pace

*b-b*48, 49   no longer be   *c-c*48, 49   risen to
*d-d*48   his   *e-e*+52, 57, 62, 65, 71

with the increase of population, this difference of prices and profits between the islands may continue. But if, in the untithed island, capital increases, and population along with it, more than enough to counterbalance any improvements which take place, the price of corn will gradually rise, profits ᶠwillᶠ fall, and rent will increase; while in the tithed island capital and population will either not increase (beyond what is balanced by the improvements), or if they do, will increase in a less degree; so that rent and the price of corn will either not rise at all, or rise more slowly. Rent, therefore, will soon be higher in the untithed than in the tithed island, and profits not so much higher, nor corn so much cheaper, as they were on the first imposition of the tithe. These effects will be progressive. At the end of every ten years there will be a greater difference between the rentals and between the aggregate wealth and population of the two islands, and a less difference in profits and in the price of corn.

At what point will these last differences entirely cease, and the temporary effect of taxes on agricultural produce, in raising the price, have entirely given place to ᵍtheᵍ ultimate effect, that of limiting the total produce of the country? Though the untithed island is always verging towards the point at which the price of food would overtake that in the tithed island, its progress towards that point naturally slackens as it draws nearer to attaining it; since—the difference between the two islands in the rapidity of accumulation depending upon the difference in the rates of profit—in proportion as these approximate, the movement which draws them closer together, abates of its force. The one may not actually overtake the other, until both islands reach the minimum of profits: up to that point, the tithed island may continue more or less ahead of the untithed island in the price of corn: considerably ahead if it is far from the minimum, and is therefore accumulating rapidly; very little ahead if it is near the minimum, and accumulating slowly.

But whatever is true of the tithed and untithed islands in our hypothetical case, is true of any country having a tithe, compared with the same country if it had never had a tithe.

In England the great emigration of capital, and the almost periodical occurrence of commercial crises through the speculations occasioned by the habitually low rate of profit, are indications that profit has attained the practical, though not the ultimate minimum, and that all the savings which take place (beyond what improvements, tending to the cheapening of necessaries, make room for) are either sent abroad for investment, or periodically swept away. There can therefore, I think, be little doubt that if England had never had a tithe, or any tax on agricultural produce, the price of corn would have been by this time as high, and the rate of profits

as low, as at present. Independently of the more rapid accumulation which
would have taken place if profits had not been prematurely lowered by these
imposts; the mere saving of a part of the capital which has been wasted in
unsuccessful speculations, and the keeping at home a part of that which
has been sent abroad, would have been quite sufficient to produce the effect.
I think, therefore, with Mr. Senior, that the tithe, even before its commutation, had ceased to be a cause of high prices or low profits, and had become
a mere deduction from rent; its other effects being, that it caused the
country to have no greater capital, no larger production, and no more
numerous population than if it had been one-tenth less fertile than it is; or
let us rather say one-twentieth (considering how great a portion of the
land of Great Britain was tithe-free).

But though tithes and other taxes on agricultural produce, when of long
standing, *ʰeitherʰ* do not raise the price of food *ⁱandⁱ* lower profits at all, or
if at all, not in proportion to the tax; yet the abrogation of such taxes,
when they exist, does not the less diminish price, and, in general, raise the
rate of profit. The abolition of a tithe takes one-tenth from the cost of
production, and consequently from the price, of all agricultural produce;
and unless it permanently raises the labourer's requirements, it lowers the
cost of labour, and raises profits. Rent, estimated in money or in commodities, generally remains as before; estimated in agricultural produce, it is
raised. The country adds as much by the repeal of a tithe, to the margin
which intervenes between it and the stationary state, as *ʲisʲ* cut off from that
margin by *ᵏaᵏ* tithe when first imposed. Accumulation is greatly accelerated;
and if population also increases, the price of corn immediately begins to
recover itself, and rent to rise; thus gradually transferring the benefit of the
remission, from the consumer to the landlord.

The effects which thus result from abolishing tithe, result equally from
what has been done by the arrangements under the *ˡ* Commutation Act for
converting it into a rent-charge. When the tax, instead of being levied on
the whole produce of the soil, is levied only from the portions which pay
rent, and does not touch any fresh extension of cultivation, the tax no
longer forms any part of the cost of production of the portion of the
produce which regulates the price of all the rest. The land or capital which
pays no rent, can now send its produce to market one-tenth cheaper. The
commutation of tithe ought therefore to have produced a considerable fall
in the average price of corn. If it had not come so gradually into operation,
and if the price of corn had not during the same period been under the
influence of several other causes of change, the effect would probably have

ʰ⁻ʰ+52, 57, 62, 65, 71
ⁱ⁻ⁱ48, 49   or   ʲ⁻ʲ48, 49, 52, 57, 62   was
ᵏ⁻ᵏ48, 49, 52, 57, 62   the   ˡ48, 49   late

been markedly conspicuous. As it is, there can be no doubt that this circumstance has had its share in the fall which has taken place in the cost of production and in the price of home-grown produce; though the effects of the great agricultural improvements which have been simultaneously advancing, *and of the free admission of agricultural produce from foreign countries,* have masked those of the other cause. This fall of price would not in itself have any tendency injurious to the landlord, since corn-rents are increased in the same ratio in which the price of corn is diminished. But neither does it in any way tend to increase his income. The rent-charge, therefore, which is substituted for tithe, is a dead loss to him *at the expiration of existing leases*: and the commutation of tithe was not a mere alteration in the mode in which the landlord bore an existing burthen, but the imposition of a new one; relief being afforded to the consumer at the expense of the landlord, who, however, begins immediately to receive progressive indemnification at the consumer's expense, by the impulse given to accumulation and population.

§ 5. [*Effects of discriminating duties*] We have hitherto inquired into the effects of taxes on commodities, on the assumption that they are levied impartially on every mode in which the commodity can be produced or brought to market. Another class of considerations is opened, if we suppose that this impartiality is not maintained, and that the tax is imposed, not on the commodity, but on some particular mode of obtaining it.

Suppose that a commodity is capable of being made by two different processes; as a manufactured commodity may be produced either by hand or by steam-power; sugar may be made either from the sugar-cane or from beet-root, cattle fattened either on hay and green crops, or on oil-cake and the refuse of breweries. It is the interest of the community, that of the two methods, producers should adopt that which produces the best article at the lowest price. This being also the interest of the producers, unless protected against competition, and shielded from the penalties of indolence; the process most advantageous to the community is that which, if *not interfered with by government, they ultimately* find it to their advantage to adopt. Suppose however that a tax is laid on one of the processes, and no tax at all, or one of smaller amount, on the other. If the taxed process is the one which the producers would not have adopted, the measure is simply nugatory. But if the tax falls, as it is of course intended to do, upon the one which they would have adopted, it creates an artificial motive for preferring the untaxed process, though the inferior of the two. If, therefore, it has any effect at all, it causes the commodity to be produced of worse

m-m+57, 62, 65, 71
n-n+52, 57, 62, 65, 71   *a-a*48, 49   left to themselves, they generally

quality, or at a greater expense of labour; it causes so much of the labour of the community to be wasted, and the capital employed in supporting and remunerating *the* labour to be expended as uselessly, as if it were spent in hiring men to dig holes and fill them up again. This waste of labour and capital constitutes an addition to the cost of production of the commodity, which raises its value and price in a corresponding ratio, and thus the owners of the capital are indemnified. The loss falls on the consumers; though the capital of the country is also eventually diminished, by the diminution of their means of saving, and in some degree, of their inducements to save.

The kind of tax, therefore, which comes under the general denomination of a discriminating duty, transgresses the rule that taxes should take as little as possible from the tax-payer beyond what they bring into the treasury of the state. A discriminating duty makes the consumer pay two distinct taxes, only one of which is paid to the government, and that frequently the less onerous of the two. If a tax were laid on sugar produced from the cane, leaving the sugar from beet-root untaxed, then in so far as cane sugar continued to be used, the tax on it would be paid to the treasury, and might be as unobjectionable as *most other taxes*; but if cane sugar, having previously been cheaper than beet-root sugar, was now dearer, and beet-root sugar was to any considerable amount substituted for it, and fields laid out and manufactories established in consequence, the government would gain no revenue from the beet-root sugar, while the consumers of it would pay a real tax. They would pay for beet-root sugar more than they had previously paid for cane sugar, and the difference would go to indemnify producers for a portion of the labour of the country actually thrown away, in producing by the labour of (say) three hundred men, what could be obtained by the other process with the labour of two hundred.

One of the commonest cases of discriminating duties, is that of a tax on the importation of a commodity capable of being produced at home, unaccompanied by an equivalent tax on the home production. A commodity is never permanently imported, unless it can be obtained from abroad at a smaller cost of labour and capital on the whole, than is necessary for producing it. If, therefore, by a duty on the importation, it is rendered cheaper to produce the article than to import it, an extra quantity of labour and capital is expended, without any extra result. The labour is useless, and the capital is spent in paying people for laboriously doing nothing. All custom duties which operate as an encouragement to the home production of the taxed article, are thus an eminently wasteful mode of raising a revenue.

*b-b*48, 49, 52, 57, 62, 65   that
*c-c*48, 49   any other tax

This character belongs in a peculiar degree to custom duties on the produce of land, unless countervailed by excise duties on the home production. Such taxes bring less into the public treasury, compared with what they take from the consumers, than any other imposts to which civilized nations are *ᵈusually subjectᵈ*. If the wheat produced in a country is twenty millions of quarters, and the consumption twenty-one millions, a million being annually imported, and if on this million a duty is laid which raises the price ten shillings per quarter, the price which is raised is not that of the million only, but of the whole twenty-one millions. Taking the most favourable, but extremely improbable supposition, that the importation is not at all checked, nor the home production enlarged, the state gains a revenue of only half a million, while the consumers are taxed ten millions and a half; the ten millions being a contribution to the home growers, who are forced by competition to resign it all to the landlords. The consumer thus pays to the owners of land an additional tax, equal to twenty times that which he pays to the state. Let us now suppose that the tax really checks importation. Suppose importation stopped altogether in ordinary years; it being found that the million of quarters can be obtained, by a more elaborate cultivation, or by breaking up inferior land, at a less advance than ten shillings upon the previous price—say, for instance, five shillings a quarter. The revenue now obtains nothing, except from the extraordinary imports which may happen to take place in a season of scarcity. But the consumers pay every year a tax of five shillings on the whole twenty-one millions of quarters, amounting to $5\frac{1}{4}$ millions sterling. Of this the odd 250,000*l.* goes to compensate the growers of the last million of quarters for the labour and capital wasted under the compulsion of the law. The remaining five millions go to enrich the landlords as before.

Such is the operation of what are technically termed Corn Laws, when first laid on; and such continues to be their operation, so long as they have any effect at all in raising the price of corn. But I am by no means of opinion that in the long run they keep up either prices or rents in the degree which these considerations might lead us to suppose. What we have said respecting the effect of tithes and other taxes on agricultural produce, applies in a great degree to corn laws: they anticipate artificially a rise of price and of rent, which would at all events have taken place through the increase of population and of production. The difference between a country without corn laws, and a country which has long had corn laws, is not so much that the last has a higher price or a larger rental, but that it has the same price and the same rental with a smaller aggregate capital and a smaller population. The imposition of corn laws raises rents, but retards that progress of accumulation which would in no long period have raised

*ᵈ⁻ᵈ*48, 49   accustomed to submit

them fully as much. The repeal of corn laws tends to lower rents, but it unchains a force which, in a progressive state of capital and population, restores and even increases the former amount. There is every reason to expect that under the virtually free importation of agricultural produce, *at last* extorted from the ruling powers of this country, the price of food, if population goes on increasing *f* , will gradually but steadily rise; though this effect may for a time be postponed by the strong current which in this country has set in (and the impulse *g*is extending*g* itself to other countries) towards the *h*improvement*h* of agricultural science, and its increased application to practice.

What we have said of duties on importation generally, is equally applicable to discriminating duties which favour importation from one place or in one particular manner, in contradistinction to others: such as the preference given to the produce of a colony, or of a country with which there is a commercial treaty: or the higher duties *i*formerly imposed*i* by our navigation laws on goods imported in other than British shipping. Whatever else may be alleged in favour of such distinctions, whenever they are not nugatory, they are economically wasteful. They induce a resort to a more costly mode of obtaining a commodity, in lieu of one less costly, and thus cause a portion of the labour which the country employs in providing itself with foreign commodities, to be sacrificed without return.

§ 6. [*Effects produced on international exchange by duties on exports and on imports*] There is one more point relating to the operation of taxes on commodities conveyed from one country to another, which requires notice: the influence which they exert on international exchanges. Every tax on a commodity tends to raise its price, and consequently to lessen the demand for it in the market in which *a*it is*a* sold. All taxes on international trade tend, therefore, to produce a disturbance and a re-adjustment of what we have termed the Equation of International Demand. This consideration leads to some rather curious consequences, which have been pointed out in the separate essay on International Commerce, already several times referred to in this treatise.

Taxes on foreign trade are of two kinds—taxes on imports, and on exports. On the first aspect of the matter it would seem that both these taxes are paid by the consumers of the commodity; that taxes on exports consequently fall entirely on foreigners, taxes on imports wholly on the home consumer. The true state of the case, however, is much more complicated.

"By taxing exports, we may, in certain circumstances, produce a division of the advantage of the trade more favourable to ourselves. In some cases we may draw into our coffers, at the expense of foreigners, not only the whole tax, but more than the tax: in other cases, we should gain exactly the tax; in others, less than the tax. In this last case, a part of the tax is borne by ourselves: possibly the whole, possibly even, as we shall show, more than the whole."

Reverting to the suppositious case employed in the Essay, of a trade between Germany and England in broadcloth and linen, "suppose that England taxes her export of cloth, the tax not being supposed high enough to induce Germany to produce cloth for herself. The price at which cloth can be sold in Germany is augmented by the tax. This will probably diminish the quantity consumed. It may diminish it so much that, even at the increased price, there will not be required so great a money value as before. Or it may not diminish it at all, or so little, that in consequence of the higher price, a greater money value will be purchased than before. In this last case, England will gain, at the expense of Germany, not only the whole amount of the duty, but more; for, the money value of her exports to Germany being increased, while her imports remain the same, money will flow into England from Germany. The price of cloth will rise in England, and consequently in Germany; but the price of linen will fall in Germany, and consequently in England. We shall export less cloth, and import more linen, till the equilibrium is restored. It thus appears (what is at first sight somewhat remarkable) that by taxing her exports, England would, in some conceivable circumstances, not only gain from her foreign customers the whole amount of the tax, but would also get her imports cheaper. She would get them cheaper in two ways; for she would obtain them for less money, and would have more money to purchase them with. Germany, on the other hand, would suffer doubly: she would have to pay for her cloth a price increased not only by the duty, but by the influx of money into England, while the same change in the distribution of the circulating medium would leave her less money to purchase it with.

"This, however, is only one of three possible cases. If, after the imposition of the duty, Germany requires so diminished a quantity of cloth, that its total value is exactly the same as before, the balance of trade *would* be undisturbed; England will gain the duty, Germany will lose it, and nothing more. If, again, the imposition of the duty occasions such a falling off in the demand that Germany requires a less pecuniary value than before, our exports will no longer pay for our imports; money must pass from England into Germany; and Germany's share of the advantage of the trade will be increased. By the change in the distribution of money, cloth will fall in

*b–b*Source, 48, 49, 52   will

England; and therefore it will, of course, fall in Germany. Thus Germany will not pay the whole of the tax. From the same cause, linen will rise in Germany, and consequently in England. When this alteration of prices has so adjusted the demand, that the cloth and the linen again pay for one another, the result is that Germany has paid only a part of the tax, and the remainder of what has been received into our treasury has come indirectly out of the pockets of our own consumers of linen, who pay a higher price for that imported commodity in consequence of the tax on our exports, while at the same time they, in consequence of the efflux of money and the fall of prices, have smaller money incomes wherewith to pay for the linen at that advanced price.

"It is not an impossible supposition that by taxing our exports we might not only gain nothing from the foreigner, the tax being paid out of our own pockets, but might even compel our own people to pay a second tax to the foreigner. Suppose, as before, that the demand of Germany for cloth falls off so much on the imposition of the duty, that she requires a smaller money value than before, but that the case is so different with linen in England, that when the price rises the demand either does not fall off at all, or so little that the money value required is greater than before. The first effect of laying on the duty is, as before, that the cloth exported will no longer pay for the linen imported. Money will therefore flow out of England into Germany. One effect is to raise the price of linen in Germany, and consequently in England. But this, by the supposition, instead of stopping the efflux of money, only makes it greater, because the higher the price, the greater the money value of the linen consumed. The balance, therefore, can only be restored by the other effect, which is going on at the same time, namely, the fall of cloth in the English and consequently in the German market. Even when cloth has fallen so low that its price with the duty is only equal to what its price without the duty was at first, it is not a necessary consequence that the fall will stop; for the same amount of exportation as before will not now suffice to pay the increased money value of the imports; and although the German consumers have now not only cloth at the old price, but likewise increased money incomes, it is not certain that they will be inclined to employ the increase of their incomes in increasing their purchases of cloth. The price of cloth, therefore, must perhaps fall, to restore the equilibrium, more than the whole amount of the duty; Germany may be enabled to import cloth at a lower price when it is taxed, than when it was untaxed: and this gain she will acquire at the expense of the English consumers of linen, who, in addition, will be the real payers of the whole of what is received at their own custom-house under the name of duties on the export of cloth."

It is almost unnecessary to remark that cloth and linen are here merely representatives of exports and imports in general; and that the effect which a tax on exports might have in increasing the cost of imports, would affect the imports from all countries, and not peculiarly the articles which might be imported from the particular country to which the taxed exports were sent.

"Such are the extremely various effects which may result to ourselves and to our customers from the imposition of taxes on our exports; and the determining circumstances are of a nature so imperfectly ascertainable, that it must be almost impossible to decide with any certainty, even after the tax has been imposed, whether we have been gainers by it or losers." In general however there could be little doubt that a country which imposed such taxes would succeed in making foreign countries contribute something to its revenue; but unless the taxed article be one for which their demand is extremely urgent, they will seldom pay the whole of the amount which the tax brings in.* "In any case, whatever we gain is lost by somebody else, and there is the expense of the collection besides: if international morality, therefore, were rightly understood and acted upon, such taxes, as being contrary to the universal weal, would not exist."

Thus far of duties on exports. We now proceed to the more ordinary case of duties on imports. "We have had an example of a tax on exports, that is, on foreigners, falling in part on ourselves. We shall therefore not be surprised if we find a tax on imports, that is, on ourselves, partly falling upon foreigners.

"Instead of taxing the cloth which we export, suppose that we tax the linen which we import. The duty which we are now supposing must not be what is termed a protecting duty, that is, a duty sufficiently high to induce us to produce the article at home. If it had this effect, it would destroy entirely the trade both in cloth and in linen, and both countries would lose the whole of the advantage which they previously gained by exchanging those commodities with one another. We suppose a duty which might diminish the consumption of the article, but which would not prevent us from continuing to import, as before, whatever linen we did consume.

"The equilibrium of trade would be disturbed if the imposition of the tax diminished, in the slightest degree, the quantity of linen consumed. For, as the tax is levied at our own custom-house, the German exporter only receives the same price as formerly, though the English consumer pays a higher one. If, therefore, there be any diminution of the quantity bought, although a larger sum of money may be actually laid out in the article,

*Probably the strongest known instance of a large revenue raised from foreigners by a tax on exports, is the opium trade with China. The high price of the article under the Government monopoly (which is equivalent to a high export duty) has so little effect in discouraging its consumption, that it is said to have been occasionally sold in China for as much as its weight in silver.

a smaller one will be due from England to Germany: this sum will no longer be an equivalent for the sum due from Germany to England for cloth, the balance therefore must be paid in money. Prices will fall in Germany and rise in England; linen will fall in the German market; cloth will rise in the English. The Germans will pay a higher price for cloth, and will have smaller money incomes to buy it with; while the English will obtain linen cheaper, that is, its price will exceed what it previously was by less than the amount of the duty, while their means of purchasing it will be increased by the increase of their money incomes.

"If the imposition of the tax does not diminish the demand, it will leave the trade exactly as it was before. We shall import as much, and export as much; the whole of the tax will be paid out of our own pockets.

"But the imposition of a tax on a commodity almost always diminishes the demand more or less; and it can never, or scarcely ever, increase the demand. It may, therefore, be laid down as a principle, that a tax on imported commodities, when it really operates as a tax, and not as a prohibition either total or partial, almost always falls in part upon the foreigners who consume our goods; and that this is a mode in which a nation may appropriate to itself, at the expense of foreigners, a larger share than would otherwise belong to it of the increase in the general productiveness of the labour and capital of the world, which results from the interchange of commodities among nations."[*]

Those are, therefore, in the right who maintain that taxes on imports are partly paid by foreigners; but they are mistaken when they say, that it is by the foreign producer. It is not on the person from whom we buy, but on all those who buy from us, that a portion of our custom-duties spontaneously falls. It is the foreign consumer of our exported commodities, who is obliged to pay a higher price for them because we maintain revenue duties on foreign goods.

There are but two cases in which duties on commodities can in any degree, or in any manner, fall on the producer. One is, when the article is a strict monopoly, and at a scarcity price. The price in this case being only limited by the desires of the buyer; the sum obtained ᶜfromᶜ the restricted supply being the utmost which the buyers would consent to give rather than go without it; if the treasury interprets a part of this, the price cannot be further raised to compensate for the tax, and it must be paid from the monopoly profits. A tax on rare and high-priced wines will fall wholly on the growers, or rather, on the owners of the vineyards. The second case in which the producer sometimes bears a portion of the tax, is more impor-

[*Mill, J. S. *Essays on Some Unsettled Questions*, pp. 21–7.]

ᶜ⁻ᶜ48, 49, 52, 57, 62   for

tant: the case of duties on the produce of land or of mines. These might be so high as to diminish materially the demand for the produce, and compel the abandonment of some of the inferior qualities of land or mines. Supposing this to be the effect, the consumers, both in the country itself and in those which dealt with it, would obtain the produce at smaller cost; and a part only, instead of the whole, of the duty would fall on the purchaser, who would be indemnified chiefly at the expense of the land-owners or mine-owners in the producing country.

Duties on importation may, then, be divided "into two classes: those which have the effect of encouraging some particular branch of domestic industry, and those which have not. The former are purely mischievous, both to the country imposing them, and to those with whom it trades. They prevent a saving of labour and capital, which, if permitted to be made, would be divided in some proportion or other between the importing country and the countries which buy what that country does or might export.

"The other class of duties are those which do not encourage one mode of procuring an article at the expense of another, but allow interchange to take place just as if the duty did not exist, and to produce the saving of labour which constitutes the motive to international, as to all other commerce. Of this kind are duties on the importation of any commodity which could not by any possibility be produced at home; and duties not sufficiently high to counterbalance the difference of expense between the production of the article at home and its importation. Of the money which is brought into the treasury of any country by taxes of this last description, a part only is paid by the people of that country; the remainder by the foreign consumers of their goods.

"Nevertheless, this latter kind of taxes are in principle as ineligible as the former, though not precisely on the same ground. A protecting duty can never be a cause of gain, but always and necessarily of loss, to the country imposing it, just so far as it is efficacious to its end. A non-protecting duty, on the contrary, would in most cases be a source of gain to the country imposing it, in so far as throwing part of the weight of its taxes upon other people is a gain; but it would be a means which it could seldom be advisable to adopt, being so easily counteracted by a precisely similar proceeding on the other side.

"If England, in the case already supposed, sought to obtain for herself more than her natural share of the advantage of the trade with Germany, by imposing a duty upon linen, Germany would only have to impose a duty upon cloth, sufficient to diminish the demand for that article about as much as the demand for linen had been diminished in England by the tax. Things would then be as before, and each country would pay its own tax. Unless, indeed, the sum of the two duties exceeded the entire advantage of the trade; for in that case the trade, and its advantage, would cease entirely.

"There would be no advantage, therefore, in imposing duties of this kind, with a view to gain by them in the manner which has been pointed out. But when any part of the revenue is derived from taxes on commodities, these may often be as little objectionable as the rest. It is evident, too, that considerations of reciprocity, which are quite unessential when the matter in debate is a protecting duty, are of material importance when the repeal of duties of this other description is discussed. A country cannot be expected to renounce the power of taxing foreigners, unless foreigners will in return practise towards itself the same forbearance. The only mode in which a country can save itself from being a loser by the revenue duties imposed by other countries on its commodities, is to impose corresponding revenues duties on theirs. Only it must take care that those duties be not so high as to exceed all that remains of the advantage of the trade, and put an end to importation altogether, causing the article to be either produced at home, or imported from another and dearer market."[*]

[*Mill, J. S. *Essays on Some Unsettled Questions*, pp. 27–9.]

CHAPTER V

Of Some Other Taxes

§ 1. [*Taxes on contracts*] Besides direct taxes on income, and taxes on consumption, the financial systems of most countries comprise a variety of miscellaneous imposts, not strictly included in either class. The modern European systems retain many such taxes, though in much less number and variety than those semi-barbarous governments which European influence has not yet reached. In some of these, scarcely any incident of life has escaped being made an excuse for some fiscal exaction; hardly any act, not belonging to daily routine, can be performed by any one, without obtaining leave from some agent of government, which is only granted in consideration of a payment: especially when the act requires the aid or the peculiar guarantee of a public authority. In the present treatise we may confine our attention to such taxes as lately existed, or still exist, in countries usually classed as civilized.

In almost all nations a considerable revenue is drawn from taxes on contracts. These are imposed in various forms. One expedient is that of taxing the legal instrument which serves as evidence of the contract, and which is commonly the only evidence legally admissible. In England, scarcely any contract is binding unless executed on stamped paper, which has paid a tax to government; and *a*until very lately, when the contract related to property the tax was proportionally much heavier on the smaller than on the larger transactions; which is still true of some of those taxes*a*. There are also stamp-duties on the legal instruments which are evidence of the fulfilment of contracts; such as acknowledgments of receipt, and deeds of release. Taxes on contracts are not always levied by means of stamps. The duty on sales by auction, abrogated by Sir Robert Peel, was an instance in point. The taxes on transfers of landed property, in France, are another: in England *b*there*b* are stamp-duties. In some countries, contracts of many kinds are not valid unless registered, and their registration is made an occasion for a tax.

Of taxes on contracts, the most important are those on the transfer of

*a–a*48, 49   when the contract relates to property the tax rises, though in an irregular manner, with the pecuniary value of the property
*b–b*48, 49, 52, 57, 62, 65   these [*printer's error?*]

property; chiefly on purchases and sales. Taxes on the sale of consumable commodities are simply taxes on those commodities. If they affect only some particular commodities, they raise the prices of those commodities, and are paid by the consumer. If the attempt were made to tax all purchases and sales, which, however absurd, was for centuries the law of Spain, the tax, if it could be enforced, would be equivalent to a tax on all commodities, and would not affect prices: if levied from the sellers, it would be a tax on profits, if from the buyers, a tax on consumption; and neither class could throw the burthen upon the other. If confined to some one mode of sale, as for example by auction, it discourages recourse to that mode, and if of any material amount, prevents it from being adopted at all, unless in a case of emergency; in which case as the seller is under a necessity to sell, but the buyer under no necessity to buy, the tax falls on the seller; and this was the strongest of the objections to the auction duty: it almost always fell on a necessitous person, and in the ᶜ crisis of his necessities.

Taxes on the purchase and sale of land are, in most countries, liable to the same objection. Landed property in old countries is seldom parted with, except from reduced circumstances, or some urgent need: the seller, therefore, must take what he can get, while the buyer, whose object is an investment, makes his calculations on the interest which he can obtain for his money in other ways, and will not buy if he is charged with a government tax on the transaction.* It has indeed been objected, that this argument would not apply if all modes of permanent investment, such as the purchase of government securities, shares in joint-stock companies, mortgages, and the like, were subject to the same tax. But even then, if paid by the buyer, it would be equivalent to a tax on interest: if sufficiently heavy to be of any importance, it would disturb the established relation between interest and profit; and the disturbance would redress itself by a rise in the rate of interest, and a fall of the price of land and of all securities. It appears to me, therefore, that the seller is the person by whom such taxes, unless under peculiar circumstances, will ᵈgenerallyᵈ be borne.

All taxes must be condemned which throw obstacles in the way of the sale of land, or other instruments of production. Such sales tend naturally to render the property more productive. The seller, whether moved by necessity or choice, is probably some one who is either without the means,

---

*[65] The statement in the text requires modification in the case of countries where the land is owned in small portions. These, being neither a badge of importance, nor in general an object of local attachment, are readily parted with at a small advance on their original cost, with the intention of buying elsewhere; and the desire of acquiring land even on disadvantageous terms is so great, as to be little checked by even a high rate of taxation.

ᶜ48, 49, 52   very   ᵈ⁻ᵈ48, 49, 52, 57, 62   always

or without the capacity, to make the most advantageous use of the property for productive purposes; while the buyer, on the other hand, is at any rate not needy, and is *frequently* both inclined and able to improve the property, since, as it is worth more to such a person than to any other, he is likely to offer the highest price for it. All taxes, therefore, and all difficulties and expenses, annexed to such contracts, are decidedly detrimental; especially in the case of land, the source of subsistence, and the original foundation of all wealth, on the improvement of which, therefore, so much depends. Too great facilities cannot be given to enable land to pass into the hands, and assume the modes of aggregation or division, most conducive to its productiveness. If landed properties are too large, alienation should be free, in order that they may be subdivided; if too small, in order that they may be united. All taxes on the transfer of landed property should be abolished; but, as the landlords have no claim to be relieved from any reservation which the state has hitherto made in its own favour from the amount of their rent, an annual impost equivalent to the average produce of these taxes should be distributed over the land generally, in the form of a land-tax. *

*e-e*48, 49   probably a person
*f*48, 49   [*footnote:*] *In our own country, the taxes on contracts are the more objectionable, because, with that tendency to spare the rich which pervades our financial system, they are proportionally much heavier on the smaller transactions. Many stamp duties do not profess to be *ad valorem*, but are fixed charges, whether the amount of the transaction be great or small. With respect to those which do pretend to be *ad valorem*; "of the stamps on conveyances, the lowest, which attaches where the purchase money does not amount to 20*l.*, is 10*s.*; where the purchase money amounts to 20*l.* and not to 50*l.*, 1*l.*; where 50*l.*, and not amounting to 150*l.*, 1*l.* 10*s.*; and there are twenty-three other enumerated stamps, rising in amount by unequal steps, the highest being 1000*l.*, where the purchase money is 100,000*l.*, beyond which, however high the purchase money may rise, the tax does not increase. . . . In the case of a 20*l.* purchase of freehold, the duty is 2*l.*, or 10 per cent on the value; while on the 200,000*l.* or 300,000*l.* purchase (as on all conveyances of 150*l.* and upwards), the stamp is only 1*l.* 15*s.*, a fraction of the value too inconsiderable to deserve notice. It often happens also in conveyances of properties of small amount, that besides this conveyance, other deeds are required, as assignments or surrenders of terms, and covenants for the production of title deeds: and the stamps on these deeds are the same whether the purchase is 20*l.* or 20,000*l.*" In the stamp duties on bonds and mortgages, the inequality is still more glaring; the rate *ad valorem* being "eighty times as great on the security for 50*l.* as on that for 100,000*l.*" —*M'Culloch on Taxation*, [McCulloch, John R. *A Treatise on the Principles and Practical Influence of Taxation and the Funding System.* London: Longman, Brown, Green, and Longmans, 1845,] pp. 277–80. And in another place, "The stamp duties in their present form wholly want that compensating quality which has often been ascribed to them (and with which they might be endowed) of giving increased security to transactions. On the contrary, one would think they had been intended to serve as decoys with which to entrap parties, and force them into the courts. The difficulty which they create of determining what is and what is not a proper stamp, is itself a most prolific source of uncertainty, and consequently of litigation and expense." (p. 276[–7].) We may well add, with the same writer,

Some of the taxes on contracts are very pernicious, imposing a virtual penalty upon transactions which it ought to be the policy of the legislator to encourage. Of this sort is the stamp-duty on leases, which in a country of large properties are an essential condition of good agriculture; and the *ᵍtaxesᵍ* on insurances, a direct discouragement to prudence and fore-thought. *ʰ*

§ 2. [*Taxes on communication*] Nearly allied to the taxes on contracts are those on communication. The principal of these is the postage tax; to which may be added *ᵃtaxesᵃ* on advertisements, and *ᵇ* on newspapers, which are taxes on the communication of information.

The common mode of levying a tax on the conveyance of letters, is by making the government the sole authorized carrier of them, and demanding a monopoly price. When this price is so moderate as it is in this country under the uniform penny postage, scarcely if at all exceeding what would be charged under the freest competition by any private company, it can hardly be considered as taxation, but rather as the profits of a business; whatever excess there is above the ordinary profits of stock being a fair result of the saving of expense, caused by having only one establishment and one set of arrangements for the whole country, instead of many competing ones. The business, too, being one which both can and ought to be conducted on fixed rules, is one of the *ᶜ* few businesses which it is not unsuitable to a government to conduct. The post office, therefore, is at present one of the best of the sources from which this country derives its revenue. But a postage much exceeding what would be paid for the same service in a system of freedom, is not a desirable tax. Its chief weight falls on letters of business, and increases the expense of mercantile relations between distant places. It is like an attempt to raise a large revenue by

---

(p. 281) "it will be curious to see how long the present system will be permitted to continue."

It is a characteristic fact, that while the sale of land is taxed, its settlement, which prevents it from being sold, is one of the few legal transactions which are not liable to any tax.

*ᵍ⁻ᵍ*48, 49, 52, 57, 62, 65   tax

*ʰ*48, 49, 52, 62   In the case of fire insurances, the tax is exactly double the amount of the premium of insurance on common risks; so that the person insuring is obliged by the government to pay for the insurance just three times the value of the risk. If this tax existed in France, we should not see, as we do in some of her provinces, the plate of an insurance company on almost every cottage or hovel. This, indeed, must be ascribed to the provident and calculating habits produced by the dissemination of property through the labouring class: but a tax of so extravagant an amount would be a heavy drag upon any habits of providence.] 65 *as* 48 . . . the tax was until lately in all cases, and still is in most cases, exactly . . . *as* 48

*ᵃ⁻ᵃ*48, 49, 52   the tax   *ᵇ*48, 49, 52   that   *ᶜ*48, 49   very

heavy tolls: it obstructs all operations by which goods are conveyed from place to place, and discourages the production of commodities in one place for consumption in another; which is not only in itself one of the greatest sources of economy of labour, but is a necessary condition of almost all improvements in production, and one of the strongest stimulants to industry ^{d}, and promoters of civilization^d.

^{e}The^e tax on advertisements ^{f}was^f not free from the same objection, since in whatever degree advertisements are useful to business, by facilitating the coming together of the dealer or producer and the consumer, in that same degree, if the tax be high enough to be a serious discouragement to advertising, it prolongs the period during which goods remain unsold, and capital locked up in idleness. ^{g}

A tax on newspapers is objectionable, not so much where it does fall as where it does not, that is, where it prevents newspapers from being used. To the generality of those who ^{h} buy them, newspapers are a luxury which they can as well afford to pay for as any other indulgence, and which is as unexceptionable a source of revenue. But to that large part of the community who have been taught to read, but have received little other intellectual education, newspapers are the source of nearly all the general information which they possess, and of nearly all their acquaintance with the ideas and topics current among mankind; and an interest is more easily excited in newspapers, than in books or other more recondite sources of instruction. Newspapers ^{i}contribute so little, in a direct way to^i the origination of useful ideas, that many persons undervalue the importance of their office in disseminating ^{j}them. They correct many prejudices and superstitions, and keep up a^j habit of discussion, and interest in public concerns, the absence of which is a great cause of the stagnation of mind usually found in the lower and middle, if not in all, ranks, of those countries where newspapers of an important or interesting character do not exist. There ought to be no taxes ^{k}(as in this country there now are not)^k which render this great diffuser of ^{l}information^l, of mental excitement, and mental exercise, less accessible to that portion of the public which most needs to be carried ^{m} into a region of ideas and interests beyond its own limited horizon.

$^{d-d}$+52, 57, 62, 65, 71 $^{e-e}$48, 49, 52, 57, 62, 65   A
$^{f-f}$48, 49, 52, 57, 62, 65   is
^{g}48, 49   In this country the amount of the duty is moderate, and the abuse of advertising, which is quite as conspicuous as the use, renders the abolition of the tax, though right in principle, a matter of less urgency than it might otherwise be deemed. ^{h}48, 49, 52, 57   now
$^{i-i}$48, 49   do so little, and generally attempt so little, in
$^{j-j}$48, 49   those ideas; in correcting many prejudices and superstitions, and keeping up that $^{k-k}$+71
$^{l-l}$48, 49   ideas ^{m}48, 49   , as it were, out of itself,

§ 3. [*Law Taxes*] In the enumeration of bad taxes, a conspicuous place must be assigned to law taxes; which extract a revenue for the state from the various operations involved in an application to the tribunals. Like all needless expenses attached to law proceedings, they are a tax on redress, and therefore a premium on injury. Although such taxes have been abolished in this country as a general source of revenue, they still exist in the form of fees of court, for defraying the expense of the courts of justice; under the idea, apparently, that those may fairly be required to bear the expenses of the administration of justice, who reap the benefit of it. The fallacy of this doctrine was powerfully exposed by Bentham. As he remarked, those who are under the necessity of going to law, are those who benefit least, not most, by the law and its administration. To them the protection which the law affords has not been complete, since they have been obliged to resort to a court of justice to ascertain their rights, or maintain those rights against infringement: while the remainder of the public have enjoyed the immunity from injury conferred by the law and the tribunals, without the inconvenience of an appeal to them.

§ 4. [*Modes of taxation for local purposes*] Besides the general taxes of the State, there are in all or most countries local taxes, to defray any expenses of a public nature which it is thought best to place under the control or management of a local authority. Some of these expenses are incurred for purposes in which the particular locality is solely or chiefly interested; as the paving, cleansing, and lighting of the streets; or the making and repairing of roads and bridges, which may be important to people from any part of the country, but only in so far as they, or goods ^ain which they have an interest^a, pass along the roads or over the bridges. In other cases again, the expenses are of a kind as nationally important as any others, but are defrayed locally because supposed more likely to be well administered by local bodies; as, in England, the relief of the poor, and the support of gaols, and in some other countries, of schools. To decide for what public objects local superintendence is best suited, and what are those which should be kept immediately under the central government, or under a mixed system of local management and central superintendence, is a question not of political economy, but of administration. It is an important principle, however, that taxes imposed by a local authority, being less amenable to publicity and discussion than the acts of the government, should always be special—laid on for some definite service, and not exceeding the expense actually incurred in rendering the service. Thus limited, it is desirable, whenever practicable, that the burthen should fall on those to whom the service is rendered; that the expense, for instance,

*a–a*48, 49   belonging to them

of roads and bridges, should be defrayed by a toll on passengers and goods conveyed by them, thus dividing the cost between those who use them for pleasure or convenience, and the consumers of the goods which they enable to be brought to and from the market at a diminished expense. When, however, the tolls have repaid with interest the whole of the expenditure, the road or bridge should be thrown open free of toll, that it may be used also by those to whom, unless open gratuitously, it would be valueless; provision being made for repairs either from the funds of the state, or by a rate levied on the localities which reap the principal benefit.

In England, almost all local taxes are direct, (the coal duty of the City of London, and a few similar imposts, being the chief exceptions,) though the greatest part of the taxation for general purposes is indirect. On the contrary, in France, Austria, and other countries where direct taxation is much more largely employed by the state, the local expenses of towns are principally defrayed by taxes levied on commodities when entering them. These indirect taxes are much more objectionable in towns than on the frontier, because the things which the country supplies to the towns are chiefly the necessaries of life and the materials of manufacture, while, of what a country imports from foreign countries, the greater part usually consists of luxuries. An octroi cannot produce a large revenue, without pressing severely upon the labouring classes of the towns; unless their wages rise proportionally, in which case the tax falls in a great measure on the consumers of town produce, whether residing in town or country, since capital will not remain in the towns if its profits fall *below* their ordinary proportion as compared with the rural districts.

*b–b*48, 49 beyond

CHAPTER VI

Comparison between Direct and Indirect Taxation

§ 1. [*Arguments for and against direct taxation*] Are direct or indirect taxes the most eligible? This question, at all times interesting, has of late excited a considerable amount of discussion. In England there is a popular feeling, of old standing, in favour of indirect, or it should rather be said in opposition to direct, taxation. The feeling is not grounded on the merits of the case, and is of a *a* puerile kind. An Englishman *b*dislikes*b*, not so much the payment, as the act of paying. He dislikes seeing the face of the tax-collector, and being subjected to his peremptory demand. Perhaps, too, the money which he is required to pay directly out of his pocket is the only taxation which he is quite sure that he pays at all. That a tax of *c*one shilling*c* per pound on tea, or of *d*two*d* shillings per bottle on wine, raises the price of each pound of tea and bottle of wine which he consumes, by that and more than that amount, cannot indeed be denied; it is the fact, and is intended to be so, and he himself, at times, is perfectly aware of it; but it makes hardly any impression on his practical feelings and associations, serving to illustrate the distinction between what is merely known to be true and what is felt to be so. The *e*unpopularity*e* of direct taxation, contrasted with the easy manner in which the public consent to let themselves be fleeced in the prices of commodities, has generated in many friends of improvement a directly opposite mode of thinking to the foregoing. They contend that the very reason which makes direct taxation disagreeable, makes it preferable. Under it, every one knows how much he really pays; and if he votes for a war, or any other expensive national luxury, he does so with his eyes open to what it costs him. If all taxes were direct, taxation would be much more *f*perceived*f* than at present; and there would be a security which now there is not, for economy in the public expenditure.

*a*48, 49 rather
*b–b*48, 49 detests
*c–c*48, 49, 52, 57, 62 two shillings   *d–d*48, 49, 52, 57, 62 three
*e–e*48, 49 "ignorant impatience"   *f–f*48, 49 odious

Although this argument is not without force *g* , its weight is likely to be constantly diminishing. The real incidence of indirect taxation is every day more generally understood and more familiarly recognised: and whatever else may be said of the *h* changes which are taking place in the tendencies of the human mind, it can scarcely, I think, be denied, that things are more and more estimated according to their calculated value, and less according to their non-essential accompaniments. The mere distinction *i* between paying money directly to the tax-collector, and contributing the same sum through the intervention of the tea-dealer or the wine-merchant, *j*no longer makes*j* the whole difference between dislike or opposition, and passive acquiescence. But further, while *k*any such*k* infirmity of the popular mind subsists, the argument grounded on it tells partly on the other side of the question. If our present revenue of *l*about seventy*l* millions were all raised by direct taxes, an *m*extreme*m* dissatisfaction would certainly arise at having to pay so much; but while men's minds are so little guided by reason, as such a change of feeling from so irrelevant a cause would imply, *n* so great an aversion to taxation *o*might not be an unqualified*o* good. Of the *p*seventy*p* millions in question, nearly thirty are pledged, under the most binding obligations, to those whose *q*property*q* has been borrowed and spent by the state: and while this debt remains unredeemed, a greatly increased impatience of taxation would involve no little danger of a breach of faith, similar to that which, in the defaulting states of America, has been produced, and in some of them still continues, from the same cause. That part, indeed, of the public expenditure, which is devoted to the maintenance of civil and military establishments, *r*(that is, all except the interest of the national debt,) affords *s*, in many of its details,*s* ample scope for *t* retrenchment. But while *u* much of the revenue is wasted under the mere pretence of public service, so much of the most important business of government is left undone, that whatever can be rescued from useless expenditure is

*g*48, 49 , too much stress, I cannot but think, is laid on it: for, in the first place
*h*48, 49 progressive
*i*48, 49 , therefore,
*j–j*48, 49 will not continue to make
*k–k*48, 49 this
*l–l*48, 49, 52 above fifty] 57 above sixty] 62 above seventy
*m–m*48, 49 intense
*n*48, 49 it may be doubted if
*o–o*48, 49 would not produce more evil than
*p–p*48, 49, 52 fifty] 57 sixty   *q–q*48, 49 capital
*r–r*86*6*48 is still, in many cases, unnecessarily profuse, but though many of the items will bear great reduction, others certainly require increase. There is hardly any public reform or improvement of the first rank, proposed of late years, and still remaining to be effected, which would not probably require, at least for a time, an increased instead of a diminished appropriation of public money.] 49 *as* 48
. . . but though the total amount will . . . reduction, many items certainly . . . *as* 48
s–s+62, 65, 71   *t*52 the largest   *u*52, 57 so

urgently required for useful.[r] Whether the object be [v] education; [w]a more
efficient and accessible administration of justice [x] ;[w] reforms of any kind
which, like the Slave Emancipation, require compensation to individual
interests; or [y] what is as important as any of these, the entertainment of a
sufficient staff of able and [z]educated[z] public servants, to conduct in a better
than the present awkward manner the business of legislation and administration; every one of these things implies considerable expense, and many
of them have again and again been prevented by the reluctance which
[a]existed[a] to apply to Parliament for an increased grant of public money,
though [b](besides that the existing means would [c]probably be[c] sufficient if
applied to the proper purposes)[b] the cost would be repaid, often a hundred-
fold, in mere pecuniary advantage to the community generally. [d]If so great
an addition were made to the public dislike of taxation as might be the
consequence of confining it to the direct form, the classes who profit by the
misapplication of public money [e]might[e] probably succeed in saving that by
which they profit, at the expense of that which would only be useful to
the public.[d]

There is, however, a frequent plea in support of indirect taxation, which
must be altogether rejected, as grounded on a fallacy. We are often told
that taxes on commodities are less burthensome than other taxes, because
the contributor can escape from them by ceasing to use the taxed commodity. He certainly can, if that be his object, deprive the government of
the money: but he does so by a sacrifice of his own indulgences, which (if
he chose to undergo it) would equally make up to him for the same amount
taken from him by direct taxation. Suppose a tax laid on wine, sufficient to
add five pounds to the price of the quantity of wine which he consumes in
a year. He has only (we are told) to diminish his consumption of wine by
5l., and he escapes the burthen. True: but if the 5l., instead of being laid
on wine, had been taken from him by an income tax, he could, by expending 5l. less in wine, equally save the amount of the tax, so that the difference
between the two cases is really illusory. If the government takes from the
contributor five pounds a year, whether in one way or another, exactly that
amount must be retrenched from his consumption to leave him as well off

[v]48, 49   popular
[w-w]48, 49   emigration and colonization; a more efficient and accessible administration of justice; a more judicious treatment of criminals; improvement in the
condition of soldiers and sailors; a more effective police;
[x]52, 57, 62   ; emigration and colonization
[y]48, 49   , finally,
[z-z]48, 49   highly-educated   [a-a]48   exists
[b-b]+52, 57, 62, 65, 71   [c-c]52, 57, 62, 65   be more than
[d-d]48, 49   I fear that we should have to wait long for most of these things, if
taxation were as odious as it probably would be if it were exclusively direct.
[e-e]52   would

as before; and in either way the same amount of sacrifice, neither more nor less, is imposed on him.

On the other hand, it is *some* advantage on the side of indirect taxes, that what they exact from the contributor is taken at a time and in a manner likely to be convenient to him. It is paid at a time when he has at any rate a payment to make; it causes, therefore, no additional trouble, nor *(unless the tax be on necessaries)* any inconvenience but what is inseparable from the payment of the amount. He can also, except in the case of very perishable articles, select his own time for laying in a stock of the commodity, and consequently for payment of the tax. The producer or dealer who advances these taxes, is, indeed, sometimes subjected to inconvenience; but, in the case of imported goods, this inconvenience is reduced to a minimum by what is called the Warehousing System, under which, instead of paying the duty at the time of importation, he is only required to do so when he takes out the goods for consumption, which is seldom done until he has either actually found, or has the prospect of immediately finding, a purchaser.

The *strongest* objection, however, to raising the whole or the greater part of a large revenue by direct taxes, is the impossibility of assessing them fairly *without a conscientious co-operation on the part of the contributors, not to be hoped for in the present low state of public morality*. In the case of an income tax, *we have already seen that unless it be found practicable to exempt savings altogether from the tax, the burthen cannot* be apportioned with any tolerable approach to fairness upon those whose incomes are derived from *business or professions*; and this is in fact admitted by most of the advocates of direct taxation, who, I am afraid, generally get over the difficulty by leaving those classes untaxed, and confining their projected income tax to "realized property," in which form it certainly has the merit of being a very easy form of plunder. But enough has been said in condemnation of this expedient. We have seen, however, that a house tax is a form of direct taxation not liable to the same objections as an income tax, and indeed liable to as few objections of any kind as perhaps any of our indirect taxes. But it would be impossible to raise by a house tax alone, the greatest part of the revenue of Great Britain, without producing a very objectionable over-crowding of the population, through the strong motive which all persons would have to avoid the tax by restricting their house accommodation. Besides, even a house tax has inequalities, and *consequent* injustices; no tax is exempt from them, and it is neither

*f–f*48, 49   a real   *g–g*+52, 57, 62, 65, 71
*h–h*48, 49   decisive   *i–i*+52, 57, 62, 65, 71
*j–j*48, 49   I have pointed out that the burthen can never
*k–k*48, 49   a business or profession
*l–l*48, 49, 52, 57   consequently

just nor politic to make all the inequalities fall in the same places, by calling upon one tax to defray the whole or the chief part of the public expenditure. So much of the local taxation, in this country, being already in the form of a house tax, it is probable that ten millions a year would be fully as much as could beneficially be levied, through this medium, for general purposes.

A certain amount of revenue may, as we have seen, be obtained without injustice by a peculiar tax on rent. Besides the present land-tax, and an equivalent for the revenue now derived from stamp duties on the conveyance of land, some further taxation might, I have contended, at some future period be imposed, to enable the state to participate in the progressive increase of the incomes of landlords from natural causes. Legacies and inheritances, we have also seen, ought to be subjected to taxation sufficient to yield a considerable revenue. With these taxes, and a house tax of suitable amount, we should, I think, have reached the prudent limits of direct taxation, save in a national emergency so urgent as to justify the government in disregarding the *amount of* inequality and unfairness *which may ultimately be found inseparable from an* income tax. The remainder of the revenue would have to be provided by taxes on consumption, and the question is, which of these are the least objectionable.

§ 2. [*What forms of indirect taxation are most eligible*] There are some forms of indirect taxation which must be peremptorily excluded. Taxes on commodities, for revenue purposes, must not operate as protecting duties, but must be levied impartially on every mode in which the articles can be obtained, whether produced in the country itself, or imported. An exclusion must also be put upon all taxes on the necessaries of life, or on the materials or instruments employed in producing those necessaries. Such taxes are always liable to encroach on what should be left untaxed, the incomes barely sufficient for healthful existence; and on the most favourable supposition, namely, that wages rise to compensate the labourers for the tax, it operates as a peculiar tax on profits, which is at once unjust, and detrimental to national wealth.* What remain are taxes on luxuries. And

___

*Some argue that the materials and instruments of all production should be exempt from taxation; but these, when they do not enter into the production of necessaries, seem as proper subjects of taxation as the finished article. It is chiefly with reference to foreign trade, that such taxes have been considered injurious. Internationally speaking, they may be looked upon as export duties, and, unless in cases in which an export duty is advisable, they should be accompanied with an equivalent drawback on exportation. But there is no sufficient reason [48   no reason] against taxing the materials and instruments used in the production of anything which is itself a fit object of taxation.

m-m+52, 57, 62, 65, 71   *n-n*48, 49   inseparable from every practicable form of

these have some properties which strongly recommend them. In the first place, they can never, by any possibility, touch those whose whole income is expended on necessaries; while they do reach those by whom what is required for necessaries, is expended on indulgences. In the next place, they operate in some cases as an useful, and the only useful, kind of sumptuary law. I disclaim all asceticism, and by no means wish to see discouraged, either by law or opinion, any indulgence (consistent with the means and obligations of the person using it) which is sought from a genuine inclination for, and enjoyment of, the thing itself; but a great portion of the *a*expenses*a* of the higher and middle classes in most countries, and the greatest in this, is not incurred for the sake of the pleasure afforded by the things on which the money is spent, but from regard to opinion, and an idea that certain expenses are expected from them, as an appendage of station; and I cannot but think that expenditure of this sort is a most desirable subject of taxation. If taxation discourages it, some good is done, and if not, no harm; for in so far as taxes are levied on things which are desired and possessed from motives of this description, nobody is the worse for them. When a thing is bought not for its use but for its costliness, cheapness is no recommendation. As Sismondi remarks, the consequence of cheapening articles of vanity, is not that less is expended on such things, but that the buyers substitute for the cheapened article some other which is more costly, or a more elaborate quality of the same thing; and as the inferior quality answered the purpose of vanity equally well when it was equally expensive, a tax on the article *b*is really*b* paid by nobody: it *c*is*c* a creation of public revenue by which nobody *d*loses*d*.*

*"Were we to suppose that diamonds could only be procured from one particular and distant country, and pearls from another, and were the produce of the mines in the former, and of the fishery in the latter, from the operation of natural causes, to become doubly difficult to procure, the effect would merely be that in time half the quantity of diamonds and pearls would be sufficient to mark a certain opulence and rank, that it had before been necessary to employ for that purpose. The same quantity of gold, or some commodity reducible at last to labour, would be required to produce the now reduced amount, as the former larger amount. Were the difficulty interposed by the regulations of legislators . . . . . it could make no difference to the fitness of these articles to serve the purposes of vanity." Suppose that means were discovered whereby the physiological process which generates the pearl might be induced *ad libitum*, the result being that the amount of labour expended in procuring each pearl, came to be only the five hundredth part of what it was before. "The ultimate effect of such a change would depend on whether the fishery were free or not. Were it free to all, as pearls could be got simply for the labour of fishing for them, a string of them might be had for a few pence. The very poorest class of

*a–a*48, 49, 52, 57, 62, 65 expense	*b–b*48, 49, 52 would really be
*c–c*48, 49, 52 would be	*d–d*48, 49, 52 would lose

§ 3. [*Practical rules for indirect taxation*] In order to reduce as much as possible the inconveniences, and increase the advantages, incident to taxes on commodities, the following are the practical rules which suggest themselves. 1st. To raise as large a revenue as conveniently may be, from those classes of luxuries which have most connexion with vanity, and least with positive enjoyment; such as the more costly qualities of all kinds of personal equipment and ornament. 2ndly. Whenever possible, to demand the tax, not from the producer, but directly from the consumer, since when levied on the producer it raises the price always by more, and often by much more, than the mere amount of the tax. Most of the minor assessed taxes in this country are recommended by both these considerations. But with regard to horses and carriages, as there are many persons to whom, from health or constitution, these are not so much luxuries as necessaries, the tax paid by those who have but one riding horse, or but one carriage, especially of the cheaper descriptions, should be low; while taxation should rise very rapidly with the number of horses and carriages, and with their costliness. 3rdly. But as the only indirect taxes which yield a large revenue are those which fall on articles of universal or very general consumption, and as it is therefore necessary to have some taxes on real luxuries, that is, on things which afford pleasure in themselves, and are valued on that account rather than for their cost; these taxes should, if possible, be so adjusted as to fall with the same proportional weight on small, on moderate, and on large incomes. This is not an easy matter; since the things which are the subjects of the more productive taxes, are in proportion more largely consumed by the poorer members of the community than by the rich. Tea, coffee, sugar, tobacco, fermented drinks, can hardly be so taxed that the poor shall not bear more than their due share of the burthen. Something might be done by making the duty on the superior qualities, which are used by the richer consumers, much higher in proportion to the value (instead of much lower, as is almost universally the practice, under the present English system); but in some cases the difficulty of at all

society could therefore afford to decorate their persons with them. They would thus soon become extremely vulgar and unfashionable, and so at last valueless. If however we suppose that instead of the fishery being free, the legislator owns and has complete command of the place, where alone pearls are to be procured; as the progress of discovery advanced, he might impose a duty on them equal to the diminution of labour necessary to procure them. They would then be as much esteemed as they were before. What simple beauty they have would remain unchanged. The difficulty to be surmounted in order to obtain them would be different, but equally great, and they would therefore equally serve to mark the opulence of those who possessed them." The net revenue obtained by such a tax "would not cost the society anything. If not abused in its application, it would be a clear addition of so much to the resources of the community." —Rae, *New Principles of Political Economy*, pp. 369–71.

adjusting the duty to the value, so as to prevent evasion, is said, with what truth I know not, to be insuperable; so that it is thought necessary to levy the same fixed duty on all the qualities alike: a flagrant injustice to the poorer class of contributors, unless compensated by the existence of other taxes from which, as from the present income tax, they are altogether exempt. 4thly. As far as is consistent with the preceding rules, taxation should rather be concentrated on a few articles than diffused over many, in order that the expenses of collection may be smaller, and that as few employments as possible may be burthensomely and vexatiously interfered with. 5thly. Among luxuries of general consumption, taxation should by preference attach itself to stimulants, because these, though in themselves as legitimate *a* indulgences as any others, are more liable than most to be used in excess, so that the check to consumption, naturally arising from taxation, is on the whole better applied to them than to other things. 6thly. As far as other considerations permit, taxation should be confined to imported articles, since these can be taxed with a less degree of vexatious interference, and with fewer incidental bad effects, than when a tax is levied on the field or on the workshop. Custom-duties are, *cæteris paribus*, much less objectionable than excise: but they must be laid only on things which either cannot, or at least will not, be produced in the country itself; or else their production there must be prohibited (as in England is the case with tobacco), or subjected to an excise duty of equivalent amount. 7thly. No tax ought to be kept so high as to furnish a motive to its evasion, too strong to be counteracted by ordinary means of prevention: and especially no commodity should be taxed so highly as to raise up a class of lawless characters, smugglers, illicit distillers, and the like.

*b*Of*b* the excise and custom duties *c*lately*c* existing in this country, *d*all which are intrinsically unfit to form part of a good system of taxation, have, since the last reforms by Mr. Gladstone, been got rid of*d*. Among these are all duties on ordinary articles of food, *e* whether for human beings or for cattle; those on *f*timber,*f* as falling on the materials of lodging, which is one of the necessaries of life; all duties on the metals, and on implements made of them; *g*taxes*g* on soap, which is a necessary of cleanliness, and on tallow, the material both of that and of *h*some*h* other necessaries; the tax on paper,

*a*48, 49   and as beneficial
*b-b*48, 49, 52, 57   Among
*c-c*48, 49, 52   now] 57   now or lately
*d-d*48, 49, 52, 57   some must, on the principles we have laid down, be altogether condemned
*e*65 [*footnote:*] *Except the shilling per quarter duty on corn, ostensibly for registration and scarcely felt as a burthen.
*f-f*48, 49   bricks and timber, the former as being vexatious, and both
*g-g*48, 49, 52   the tax] 57   the (now abolished) tax
h-h+52, 57, 62, 65, 71

an indispensable instrument of almost all business and of most kinds of instruction ^{i} . The duties which ^{j}now^j yield ^{k}nearly the whole^k of the customs and excise revenue, those on sugar, coffee, tea, wine, beer, spirits, and tobacco, are in themselves, where a large amount of revenue is necessary, extremely proper taxes; but at present grossly unjust, from the disproportionate weight with which they press on the poorer classes; and some of them (those on spirits and tobacco) are so high as to cause ^{l}a considerable^l amount of smuggling. It is probable that most of these taxes ^{m}might^m bear a great reduction without any material loss of revenue. In what manner the finer articles of manufacture, consumed by the rich, might most advantageously be taxed, I must leave to be decided by those who have the requisite practical knowledge. The difficulty would be, to effect it without an inadmissible degree of interference with production. In countries which, like the United States, import the principal part of the finer manufactures which they consume, there is little difficulty in the matter: and even where nothing is imported but the raw material, that may be taxed, especially the qualities of it which are exclusively employed for the fabrics used by the richer class of consumers. Thus, in England a high custom-duty on raw silk would be consistent with principle; and it might perhaps be practicable to tax the finer qualities of cotton or linen yarn, whether spun in the country itself or imported.

^{i}48, 49, 52, 57 : but ornamental paper, for hangings, and similar purposes, might continue to be taxed
$^{j-j}$+62, 65, 71
$^{k-k}$48, 49, 52, 57   the greatest part
$^{l-l}$48, 49, 52, 57   an enormous
$^{m-m}$48, 49, 52   would

CHAPTER VII

Of a National Debt

§ 1. [*Is it desirable to defray extraordinary public expenses by loans?*] The question must now be considered, how far it is right or expedient to raise money for the purposes of government, not by laying on taxes to the amount required, but by taking a portion of the capital of the country in the form of a loan, and charging the public revenue with only the interest. Nothing needs be said about providing for temporary wants by taking up money; for instance, by an issue of exchequer bills, destined to be paid off, at furthest in a year or two, from the proceeds of the existing taxes. This is a convenient expedient, and when the government does not possess a treasure or hoard, is often a necessary one, on the occurrence of extraordinary expenses, or of a temporary failure in the ordinary sources of revenue. What we have to discuss is the propriety of contracting a national debt of a permanent character; defraying the expenses of a war, or of any season of difficulty, by loans, to be redeemed either very gradually and at a distant period, or not at all.

This question has *already been* touched upon in the First Book.* We *b* remarked, that if the capital taken in loans is abstracted from funds either engaged in production, or destined to be employed in it, their diversion from that purpose is equivalent to taking the amount from the wages of the labouring classes. Borrowing, in this case, is not a substitute for raising the supplies within the year. A government which borrows does actually take the amount within the year, and that too by a tax exclusively on the labouring classes: than which it could have done nothing worse, if it had supplied its wants by avowed taxation; and in that case the transaction, and its evils, would have ended with the emergency; while by the circuitous mode adopted, the value exacted from the labourers is gained, not by the state, but by the employers of labour, the state remaining charged with the debt besides, and with its interest in perpetuity. The system of public loans, in such circumstances, may be pronounced the very worst which, in the present state of civilization, is still included in the catalogue of financial expedients.

*Supra, vol. i. pp. 77–8.

*a-a*48, 49   been already   *b*48, 49, 52, 57   there

We however remarked that there are other circumstances in which loans are not chargeable with these pernicious consequences: namely, first, when what is borrowed is foreign capital, the overflowings of the general accumulation of the world; or, secondly, when it is capital which either would not have been saved at all unless this mode of investment had been open to it, or after being saved, would have been wasted in unproductive enterprises, or sent to seek employment in foreign countries. When the progress of accumulation has reduced profits either to the ultimate or to the practical minimum,—to the rate, less than which would either put a stop to the increase of capital, or send the whole of the new accumulations abroad; government may annually intercept ᶜtheseᶜ new accumulations, without trenching on the employment or wages of the labouring classes in the country itself, or perhaps in any other country. To this extent, therefore, the loan system may be carried, without being liable to the utter and peremptory condemnation which is due to it when it overpasses this limit. What is wanted is an index to determine whether, in any given series of years, as during the last ᵈgreatᵈ war for example, the limit has been exceeded or not.

Such an index exists, at once a certain and an obvious one. Did the government, by its loan operations, augment the rate of interest? If it only opened a channel for capital which would not otherwise have been accumulated, or which, if accumulated, would not have been employed within the country; this implies that the capital, which the government took and expended, could not have found employment at the existing rate of interest. So long as the loans do no more than absorb this surplus, they prevent any tendency to a fall of the rate of interest, but they cannot occasion any rise. When they do raise the rate of interest, as they did in a most extraordinary degree during the ᵉFrenchᵉ war, this is positive proof that the government is a competitor for capital with the ordinary channels of productive investment, and is carrying off, not merely funds which would not, but funds which would, have found productive employment within the country. To the full extent, therefore, to which the loans of government, during the ᶠ war, caused the rate of interest to exceed what it was before, and what it has been since, those loans ᵍare chargeable with all the evils which have been describedᵍ. If it be objected that interest only rose because profits rose, I reply that this does not weaken, but strengthens, the argument. If the government loans produced the rise of profits by the great amount of capital which they absorbed, by what means can they have had this effect, unless by lowering the wages of labour? It will perhaps be said, that what kept profits high during the war was not the drafts made on the

---

ᶜ⁻ᶜ48, 49, 52   those   ᵈ⁻ᵈ+57, 62, 65, 71
ᵉ⁻ᵉ48, 49   late] 52   last   ᶠ48, 49, 52   last
ᵍ⁻ᵍ48, 49, 52   cannot be relieved from the severest condemnation

national capital by the loans, but the rapid progress of industrial improvements. This, in a great measure, was the fact; and it no doubt alleviated the hardship to the labouring classes, and made the financial system which was pursued less actively mischievous, but not *less contrary to principle*. These very improvements in industry, made room for a larger amount of capital; and the government, by draining away a great part of the annual accumulations, did not indeed prevent that capital from existing ultimately, (for it started into existence with great rapidity after the peace,) but prevented it from existing at the time, and subtracted just so much, while the war lasted, from distribution among productive labourers. If the government had abstained from taking this capital by loan, and had allowed it to reach the labourers, but had raised the supplies which it required by a direct tax on the labouring classes, it would have produced *(in every respect but the expense and inconvenience of collecting the tax)* the very same economical effects *which it did produce, except that we should not now have had the debt. The course it actually took was therefore worse *than the very worst mode which it could possibly have adopted of raising the supplies within the year *: and the only excuse, or justification, which it admits of, (so far as that excuse could be truly pleaded,) was hard necessity; the impossibility of raising so enormous an annual sum by taxation, without resorting to taxes which from their odiousness, or from the facility of evasion, it would have been found impracticable to enforce*.

When government loans are limited to the overflowings of the national capital, or to those accumulations which would not take place at all unless suffered to overflow, they are at least not liable to this grave condemnation: they occasion no privation to any one at the time, except by the payment of the interest, and may even be beneficial to the labouring class during the term of their expenditure, by employing in the direct purchase of labour, as *that* of soldiers, sailors, &c., funds which might otherwise have quitted the country altogether. In this case therefore the question really is, what it is commonly supposed to be in all cases, namely, a choice between a great sacrifice at once, and a small one indefinitely prolonged. On this matter it seems rational to think, that the prudence of a nation will dictate the same conduct as the prudence of an individual; to submit to as much of the privation immediately, as can easily be borne, and only when any further burthen would distress or cripple them too much, to provide for the remainder by mortgaging their future income. It is an excellent maxim to make present resources suffice for present wants; the

*ʰ–ʰ*48, 49, 52   at all less indefensible
ⁱ–ⁱ+57, 62, 65, 71
*ʲ*48, 49, 52   , in every respect,
*ᵏ*48, 49, 52   , by the whole of that great fact,
ˡ–ˡ+57, 62, 65, 71   *ᵐ–ᵐ*+49, 52, 57, 62, 65, 71

future will have its own wants to provide for. On the other hand, it may reasonably be taken into consideration that in "a country increasing in wealth," the necessary expenses of government do not increase in the same ratio as capital or population; any burthen, therefore, is always less and less felt: and since those extraordinary expenses of government which are fit to be incurred at all, are mostly beneficial beyond the existing generation, there is no injustice in making posterity pay a part of the price, if the inconvenience would be extreme of defraying the whole of it by the exertions and sacrifices of the generation which first incurred it.

§ 2. [*Not desirable to redeem a national debt by a general contribution*] When a country, wisely or unwisely, has burthened itself with a debt, *is it* expedient to take steps for redeeming that debt? In principle it is impossible not to maintain the affirmative. It is true that the payment of the interest, when the creditors are members of the same community, is no national loss, but a mere transfer. The transfer, however, being compulsory, is a serious evil, and the raising a great extra revenue by any system of taxation necessitates so much expense, vexation, disturbance of the channels of industry, and other mischiefs over and above the mere payment of the money wanted by the government, that to get rid of the necessity of such taxation is at all times worth a considerable effort. The same amount of sacrifice which would have been worth incurring to avoid contracting the debt, it is worth while to incur, at any subsequent time, for the purpose of extinguishing it.

Two modes have been contemplated of paying off a national debt: either at once by a general contribution, or gradually by a surplus revenue. The first would be incomparably the best, if it were practicable; and *it would be practicable* if it could justly be done by *e* assessment on property alone. If property bore the whole interest of the debt, property might, with great advantage to itself, pay it off; since this would be merely surrendering to a creditor the principal sum, the whole annual proceeds of which were already his by law; *and* would be equivalent to what a landowner does when he sells part of his estate, to free the remainder from a mortgage. But property, it needs hardly be said, does not pay, and cannot justly be required to pay, the whole interest of the debt. Some indeed affirm that it can, on the *e* plea that the existing generation is only bound to pay the debts of its predecessors from the assets it has received from them, and not from the produce of its own industry. But has no one received anything from previous generations except those who have succeeded to property? Is the whole difference between the earth as it is, with its clearings and improvements, its roads

n-n48, 49   an improving country
b-b48, 49, 52, 57   practicable it would be
d-d48, 49, 52   or

a-a49   it is [*printer's error?*]
c48, 49, 52, 57   an
e48, 49   specious

and canals, its towns and manufactories, and the earth as it was when the first human being set foot on it, of no benefit to any but those who are called the owners of the soil? Is the capital accumulated by the labour and abstinence of all former generations, of no advantage to any but those who have succeeded to the legal ownership of part of it? And have we not inherited a mass of acquired knowledge, both scientific and empirical, due to the sagacity and industry of those who preceded us, the benefits of which are the common wealth of all? Those who are born to the ownership of property have, in addition to these common benefits, a separate inheritance, and to this difference it is right that advertence should be had in regulating taxation. *It belongs to the general financial system of the country to take* due account of this principle, and I have indicated, as in my opinion a proper mode of taking account of it, a considerable tax on legacies and inheritances. Let it be determined directly and openly what is due from property to the state, and from the state to property, and let the institutions of the state be regulated accordingly *g* . Whatever is the fitting contribution from property to the general expenses of the state, in the same and in no greater proportion should it contribute towards either the interest or the repayment of the national debt.

This, however, if admitted, is fatal to any scheme for the extinction of the debt by a general assessment on the community. Persons of property could pay their share of the amount by a sacrifice of property, and have the same net income as before; but if those who have no accumulations, but only incomes, were required to make up by a single payment the equivalent of the annual charge laid on them by the taxes maintained to pay the interest of the debt, they could only do so by incurring a private debt equal to their share of the public debt; while, from the insufficiency, in most cases, of the security which they could give, the interest would amount to a much larger annual sum than their share of that now paid by the state. Besides, a collective debt defrayed by taxes, has over the same debt parcelled out among individuals, the immense advantage, that it is virtually a mutual insurance among the contributors. If the fortune of a contributor diminishes, his taxes diminish; if he is ruined, they cease altogether, and his portion of the debt is wholly transferred to the solvent members of the community. If it were laid on him as a private obligation, he would still be liable to it even when penniless.

When the state possesses property, in land or otherwise, which there are not strong reasons of public utility for its retaining at its disposal, this

*f-f*48, 49   We are at liberty to assume that the general financial system of the country takes

*g*48, 49   ; but let not principles, admitted in theory, be wounded mortally by a back-handed blow

should be employed, as far as it will go, in extinguishing debt. Any casual gain, or godsend, is naturally devoted to the same purpose. Beyond this, the only mode which is both just and feasible, of extinguishing or reducing a national debt, is by means of a surplus revenue.

§ 3. [*In what cases it is desirable to maintain a surplus revenue for the redemption of debt*] The desirableness, *per se*, of maintaining a surplus for this purpose, does not, I think, admit of a doubt. We sometimes, indeed, hear it said that the amount should rather be left to "fructify in the pockets of the people." This is a good argument, as far as it goes, against levying taxes unnecessarily for purposes of unproductive expenditure, but not against paying off a national debt. For, what is meant by the word fructify? If it means anything, it means productive employment; and as an argument against taxation, we must understand it to assert, that if the amount were left with the people they would save it, and convert it into capital. It is probable, indeed, that they would save a part, but extremely improbable that they would save the whole: while if taken by taxation, and employed in paying off debt, the whole is saved, and made productive. To the fund-holder who receives the payment it is already capital, not revenue, and he will make it "fructify," that it may continue to afford him an income. The objection, therefore, is not only groundless, but the real argument is on the other side: the amount is much more certain of fructifying if it is *a*not*a* "left in the pockets of the people."

It is not, however, advisable in all cases to maintain a surplus revenue for the extinction of debt. The advantage of paying off the national debt of Great Britain, for instance, is that it would enable us to get rid of the worse half of our *b* taxation. But of this worse half some portions must be worse than others, and to get rid of those would be a greater benefit proportionally than to get rid of the rest. If renouncing a surplus revenue would enable us to dispense with a tax, we ought to consider the very worst of all our taxes as precisely the one which we are keeping up for the sake of ultimately abolishing taxes not so bad as itself. In a country advancing in wealth, whose increasing revenue gives it the power of ridding itself from time to time of the most inconvenient portions of its taxation, I conceive that the increase of revenue should rather be disposed of by taking off taxes, than by liquidating debt, as long as any very objectionable imposts remain. In the present state of England, therefore, I hold it to be good policy in the government, when it has a surplus of an apparently permanent character, to take off taxes, provided these are rightly selected. Even when no taxes remain but such as are not unfit to form part of a permanent system, it is wise to continue the same policy by experimental reductions

*a–a*48, 49, 52, 57 *not*   *b*48, 49, 52, 57 present

of those taxes, until the point is discovered at which a given amount of revenue can be raised with the smallest pressure on the contributors. After this, such surplus revenue as might arise from any further increase of the produce of the taxes, should not, I conceive, be remitted, but applied to the redemption of debt. Eventually, it might be expedient to appropriate the entire produce of particular taxes to this purpose; since there would be more assurance that the liquidation would be persisted in, if the fund destined to it were kept apart, and not blended with the general revenues of the state. The ^{c}succession duties^c would be peculiarly suited to such a purpose, since taxes paid as they are, out of capital, would be better employed in reimbursing capital than in defraying current expenditure. If this separate appropriation were made, any surplus afterwards arising from the increasing produce of the other taxes, and from the saving of interest on the successive portions of debt paid off, might form a ground for ^{d}a^d remission of taxation.

It has been contended that some amount of national debt is desirable, and almost indispensable, as an investment for the savings of the poorer or more inexperienced part of the community. Its convenience in that respect is undeniable; but (besides that the progress of industry is gradually affording other modes of investment almost as safe and untroublesome, such as the shares or obligations of great public companies) the only real superiority of an investment in the funds consists in the national guarantee, and this could be afforded by other means than that of a public debt, involving compulsory taxation. One mode which would answer the purpose, would be a national bank of deposit and discount, with ramifications throughout the country; which might receive any money confided to it, and either fund it at a fixed rate of interest, or allow interest on a floating balance, like the joint stock banks; the interest given being of course lower than the rate at which individuals can borrow, in proportion to the greater security of a government investment; and the expenses of the establishment being defrayed by the difference between the interest which the bank would pay, and that which it would obtain, by lending its deposits on mercantile, landed, or other security. There are no insuperable objections in principle, ^{e}nor, I should think,^{e} in practice, to an institution of this sort, as a means of supplying the same convenient mode of investment now afforded by the public funds. It would constitute the state a great insurance company, to insure that part of the community who live on the interest of their property, against the risk of losing it by the bankruptcy of those to whom they might otherwise be under the necessity of confiding it.

$^{c-c}$48, 49, 52   taxes on legacies and inheritances
$^{d-d}$+49, 52, 57, 62, 65, 71
$^{e-e}$48, 49, 52, 57   and I should think none

Of the Ordinary Functions of Government, Considered as to Their Economical Effects

§ 1. [*Effects of imperfect security of person and property*] Before we discuss the line of demarcation between the things with which government should, and those with which they should not, directly interfere, it is necessary to consider the economical effects, whether of a bad or of a good complexion, arising from the manner in which they acquit themselves of the duties which devolve on them in all societies, and which no one denies to be incumbent on them.

The first of these is the protection of person and property. There is no need to expatiate on the influence exercised over the economical interests of society by the degree of completeness with which this duty of government is performed. Insecurity of person and property, is as much as to say, uncertainty of the connexion between all human exertions or sacrifice, and the attainment of the ends for the sake of which they are undergone. It means, uncertainty whether they who sow shall reap, whether they who produce shall consume, and they who spare to-day shall enjoy to-morrow. It means, not only that labour and frugality are not the road to acquisition, but that violence is. When person and property are to a certain degree insecure, all the possessions of the weak are at the mercy of the strong. No one can keep what he has produced, unless he is more capable of defending it, than others who give no part of their time and exertions to useful industry are of taking it from him. The productive classes, therefore, when the insecurity surpasses a certain point, being unequal to their own protection against the predatory population, are obliged to place themselves individually in a state of dependence on some member of the predatory class, that it may be his interest to shield them from all depredation except his own. In this manner, in the Middle Ages, allodial property generally became feudal, and numbers of the poorer freemen voluntarily made themselves and their posterity serfs of some military lord.

Nevertheless, in attaching to this great requisite, security of person and property, the importance which is justly due to it, we must not forget that even for economical purposes there are other things quite as indispensable, the presence of which will often make up for a very considerable degree of imperfection in the protective arrangements of government. As was observed in a previous chapter,* the free cities of Italy, Flanders, and the Hanseatic league, were habitually in a state of such internal turbulence, varied by such destructive external wars, that person and property enjoyed very imperfect protection; yet during several centuries they increased rapidly in wealth and prosperity, brought many of the industrial arts to a high degree of advancement, carried on distant and dangerous voyages of exploration and commerce with extraordinary success, became an over-match in power for the greatest feudal lords, and could defend themselves even against the sovereigns of Europe: because in the midst of turmoil and violence, the citizens of those towns enjoyed a certain rude freedom, under conditions of union and co-operation, which, taken together, made them a brave, energetic, and high-spirited people, and fostered a great amount of public spirit and patriotism. The prosperity of these and other free states in a lawless age, shows that a certain degree of insecurity, in some combinations of circumstances, has good as well as bad effects, by making energy and practical ability the conditions of safety. Insecurity paralyzes, only when it is such in nature and in degree, that no energy of which mankind in general are capable, affords any tolerable means of self-protection. And this is a main reason why oppression by the government, whose power is generally irresistible by any efforts that can be made by individuals, has so much more baneful an effect on the springs of national prosperity, than almost any degree of lawlessness and turbulence under free institutions. Nations have acquired some wealth, and made some progress in improvement, in states of social union so imperfect as to border on anarchy: but no countries in which the people were ^aexposed without limit^a to arbitrary exactions from the officers of government, ever yet continued to have industry or wealth. A few generations of such a government never fail to extinguish both. Some of the fairest, and once the most prosperous, regions of the earth, have, under the Roman and afterwards under the Turkish dominion, been reduced to a desert, solely by that cause. I say solely, because they would have recovered with the utmost rapidity, as countries always do, from the devastations of war, or any other temporary calamities. Difficulties and hardships are often but an incentive to exertion: what is fatal to it, is the belief that it will not be suffered to produce its fruits.

*Supra, vol. i. pp. 113–4.

^{a–a}48, 49   habitually exposed

§ 2. [*Effects of over-taxation*] Simple over-taxation by government, though a great evil, is not comparable in the economical part of its mischiefs to exactions much more moderate in amount, *a* which either subject the contributor to the arbitrary mandate of government officers, or are so laid on as to place skill, industry, and frugality at a disadvantage. The burthen of taxation in our own country is very great, yet as every one knows its limit, and is seldom made to pay more than he expects and calculates on, and as the modes of taxation are not of such a kind as much to impair the motives to industry and economy, the sources of prosperity are little diminished by the pressure of taxation; they may even, as some think, be increased, by the extra exertions made to compensate for the pressure of the taxes. But in the barbarous despotisms of many countries of the East, where taxation consists in fastening upon those who have succeeded in acquiring something, in order to confiscate it, unless the possessor buys its release by submitting to give some large sum as a compromise, we cannot expect to find voluntary industry, or wealth derived from any source but plunder. And even in comparatively civilized countries, bad modes of raising a revenue have had effects similar in kind, though in an inferior degree. French writers before the Revolution represented the *taille* as a main cause of the backward state of agriculture, and of the wretched condition of the rural population; not from its amount, but because, being proportioned to the visible capital of the cultivator, it gave him a motive for appearing poor, which sufficed to turn the scale in favour of indolence. The arbitrary powers also of fiscal officers, of *intendants* and *subdélégués*, were more destructive of prosperity than a far larger amount of exactions, because they destroyed security: there was a marked superiority in the condition of the *pays d'états*, which were exempt from this scourge. The universal venality ascribed to Russian functionaries, must be an immense drag on the capabilities of economical improvement possessed so abundantly by the Russian empire: since the emoluments of public officers must depend on the success with which they can multiply vexations, for the purpose of being bought off by bribes.

Yet mere excess of taxation, even when not aggravated by uncertainty, is, independently of its injustice, a serious economical evil. It may be carried so far as to discourage industry by insufficiency of reward. Very long before it reaches this point, it prevents or greatly checks accumulation, or causes the capital accumulated to be sent for investment to foreign countries. Taxes which fall on profits, even though that kind of income may not pay more than its just share, necessarily diminish the motive to any saving, except *b* for investment in foreign countries where profits are higher. Holland, for example, seems to have long *c*ago*c* reached the practical

*a*48, 49   but   *b*48, 49   that which is made   *c–c*48, 49   since

minimum of profits: already in the last century her wealthy capitalists had a great part of their fortunes invested in the loans and joint-stock speculations of other countries: and this low rate of profit is ascribed to the heavy taxation, which had been in some measure forced on her by the circumstances of her position and history. The taxes indeed, besides their great amount, were many of them on necessaries, a kind of tax peculiarly injurious to industry and accumulation. But when the aggregate amount of taxation is very great, it is inevitable that recourse must be had for part of it to taxes of an objectionable character. And any taxes on consumption, when heavy, even if not operating on profits, have something of the same *d* effect, by driving persons of moderate means to live abroad, often taking their capital with them. Although I by no means join with those political economists who think no state of national existence desirable in which there is not a rapid increase of wealth, I cannot overlook the many disadvantages to an independent nation from being brought prematurely to a stationary state, while the neighbouring countries continue advancing.

§ 3. [*Effects of imperfection in the system of the laws, and in the administration of justice*] The subject of protection to person and property, considered as afforded by *a* government, ramifies widely, into a number of indirect channels. It embraces, for example, the whole subject of the perfection or inefficiency of the means provided for the ascertainment of rights and the redress of injuries. Persons and property cannot be considered secure where the administration of justice is imperfect, either from defect of integrity or capacity in the tribunals, or because the delay, vexation, and expense accompanying their operation impose a heavy tax on those who appeal to them, and make it preferable to submit to any endurable amount of the evils which they are designed to remedy. In England there is no fault to be found with the administration of justice, *b*in point of pecuniary integrity*b*; a result which the progress of social improvement may also be supposed to have brought about in several other nations of Europe. But legal and judicial imperfections of other kinds are abundant; and, in England especially, are a large abatement from the value of the services which the government renders back to the people in return for our enormous taxation. In the first place, the incognoscibility (as Bentham termed it) of the law, and its extreme uncertainty, even to those who best know it, render a resort to the tribunals often necessary for obtaining justice, when, there being no dispute as to facts, no litigation ought to be required. In the next place, the procedure of the tribunals is so replete with delay, vexation, and expense, that the price

*d*48, 49   injurious
*a*48, 49   a   *b–b*48, 49   so far as integrity is concerned

at which justice is at last obtained is an evil outweighing a very considerable amount of injustice; and the wrong side, even that which the law
considers such, has many chances of gaining its point, through the
abandonment of litigation by the other party for want of funds, or through
a compromise in which a sacrifice is made of just rights to terminate the
suit, or through some technical quirk, whereby a decision is obtained on
some other ground than the merits. This last detestable incident often
happens without blame to the judge, under a system of law, of which a
great part rests on no rational principles adapted to the present state of
society, but was originally founded partly on a kind of whims and con-
ceits, and partly on the principles and incidents of feudal tenure, (which
now survive only as legal fictions;) and has only been very imperfectly
adapted, as cases arose, to the changes which had taken place in society.
Of all parts of the English legal system, the Court of Chancery, which has
the best substantive law, ^{c}has been^c incomparably the worst as to delay,
vexation, and expense; and this is the only tribunal for most of the classes
of cases which are in their nature the most complicated, such as cases of
partnership, and the great range and variety of cases which come under
the denomination of trust. ^{d}The recent reforms in this Court have abated
the mischief, but are still far from having removed it.^{d}

Fortunately for the prosperity of England, the greater part of the
mercantile law is comparatively modern, and was made by the tribunals,
by the simple process of recognising and giving force of law to the usages
which, from motives of convenience, had grown up among merchants
themselves: so that this part of the law, at least, was substantially made
by those who were most interested in its goodness: while the defects of
the tribunals have been the less practically pernicious in reference to commercial transactions, because the importance of credit, which depends
on character, renders the restraints of opinion (though, as daily experience
proves, an insufficient) yet a very powerful, protection against those forms
of mercantile dishonesty which are generally recognised as such.

The imperfections of the law, both in its substance and in its procedure,
fall heaviest upon the interests connected with what is technically called
real property; in the general language of European jurisprudence, immoveable property. With respect to all this portion of the wealth of the community, the law fails egregiously in the protection which it undertakes to
provide. It fails, first, by the uncertainty, and the maze of technicalities,
which make it impossible for any one, at however great an expense, to
possess a title to land which he can positively know to be unassailable.
It fails, secondly, in omitting to provide due evidence of transactions, by

$^{c-c}$48, 49, 52   is] 57, 62   has hitherto been
$^{d-d}$+57, 62, 65, 71

a proper registration of legal documents. It fails, thirdly, by creating a necessity for operose and expensive instruments and formalities (independently of fiscal burthens) on occasion of the purchase and sale, or even the lease or mortgage, of immoveable property. And, fourthly, it fails by the intolerable expense and delay of law proceedings, in almost all cases in which real property is concerned. There is no doubt that the greatest sufferers by the defects of the higher courts of civil law are the landowners. Legal expenses, either those of actual litigation, or of the preparation of legal instruments, form, I apprehend, no inconsiderable item in the annual expenditure of most persons of large landed property, and the saleable value of their land is greatly impaired, by the difficulty of giving to the buyer complete confidence in the title; independently of the legal expenses which accompany the transfer. Yet the landowners, though they have been masters of the legislation of England, to say the least since 1688, have never made a single move in the direction of law reform, and have been strenuous opponents of some of the improvements of which they would more particularly reap the benefit; especially that great one of a registration of contracts affecting land, which when proposed by a Commission of eminent real property lawyers, and introduced into the House of Commons by Lord Campbell, was so offensive to the general body of landlords, and was rejected by so large a majority, as to have *long* discouraged any repetition of the attempt.* This irrational hostility to improvement, in a case in which their own interest would be the most benefited by it, must be ascribed to an intense timidity on the subject of their titles, generated by the defects of the very law which they refuse to alter; and to a conscious ignorance, and incapacity of judgment, on all legal subjects, which makes them helplessly defer to the opinion of their professional advisers, heedless of the fact that every imperfection of the law, in proportion as it is burthensome to them, brings gain to the lawyer.

In so far as the defects of legal arrangements are a mere burthen on the landowner, they do not much affect the sources of production; but the uncertainty of the *title* under which land is held, must often act as a great discouragement to the expenditure of capital in its improvement; and the expense of making transfers, operates to prevent land from coming into the hands of those who would use it to most advantage; often amounting, in the case of small purchases, to more than the price of the land, and tantamount, therefore, to a prohibition of the purchase and sale of land in small

*[65] Lord Westbury's recent Act is a material mitigation of this grievous defect in English law, and will probably lead to further improvements.

e-e+49, 52, 57, 62, 65, 71
*f-f*48   titles

portions, unless in exceptional circumstances. Such purchases, however, are almost everywhere extremely desirable, there being hardly any country in which landed property is not either too much or too little subdivided, requiring either that great estates should be broken down, or that small ones should be bought up and consolidated. To make land as easily transferable as stock, would be one of the greatest economical improvements which could be bestowed on a country; and has been shown, again and again, to have no insuperable difficulty attending it.

Besides the excellences or defects that belong to the law and judicature of a country as a system of arrangements for attaining direct practical ends, much also depends, even in an economical point of view, upon the moral influence of the law. Enough has been said in a former place,* on the degree in which both the industrial and all other combined operations of mankind depend for efficiency on their being able to rely on one another for probity and fidelity to engagements; from which we see how greatly even the economical prosperity of a country is liable to be affected, by anything in its institutions by which either integrity and trustworthiness, or the contrary qualities, are encouraged. The law everywhere ostensibly favours at least pecuniary honesty and the faith of contracts; but if it affords facilities for evading those obligations, by trick and chicanery, or by the unscrupulous use of riches in instituting unjust or resisting just litigation; if there are ways and means by which persons may attain the ends of roguery, under the apparent sanction of the law; to that extent the law is demoralizing, even in regard to pecuniary integrity. And such cases are, unfortunately, frequent under the English system. If, again, the law, by a misplaced indulgence, protects idleness or prodigality against their natural consequences, or dismisses crime with inadequate penalties, the effect, both on the prudential and on the social virtues, *g*is unfavourable*g*. When the law, by its own dispensations and injunctions, establishes injustice between individual and individual; as all laws do which recognise any form of slavery, as the laws of all countries do, though not all in the same degree, in respect to the family relations; and as the laws of many countries do, though in still more unequal degrees, as between rich and poor; the effect on the moral sentiments of the people is still more disastrous. But these subjects introduce considerations so much larger and deeper than those of political economy, that I only advert to them in order not to pass wholly unnoticed, things superior in importance to those of which I treat.

*Supra, vol. i. pp. 109–11.

*g–g*48, 49   requires no comment

CHAPTER IX

The Same Subject Continued

§ 1. [*Laws of Inheritance*] Having spoken thus far of the effects produced by the excellences or defects of the general system of the law, I shall now touch upon those resulting from the special character of particular parts of it. As a selection must be made, I shall confine myself to a few leading topics. The portions of the civil law of a country which are of most importance economically (next to those which determine the *status* of the labourer, as slave, serf, or free), are those relating to the two subjects of Inheritance and Contract. Of the laws relating to contract, none are more important economically, than the laws of partnership, and those of insolvency. It happens that on all these three points, there is just ground for condemning some of the provisions of the English law. *a*

With regard to Inheritance, I have, in an early *b*chapter*b*, considered the general principles of the subject, and suggested what appear to me to be, *c* putting all prejudice apart, the best dispositions which the law could adopt. Freedom of bequest as the general rule, but limited by two things: first, that if there are descendants, who, being unable to provide for themselves, would become burthensome to the state, the equivalent of whatever the state would accord to them should be reserved from the property for their benefit; and secondly, that no one person should be permitted to acquire, by inheritance, more than the amount of a moderate independence. In case of intestacy, the whole property to escheat to the state: which should be bound to make a just and reasonable provision for descendants, that is, such a provision as the parent or ancestor ought to have made, their circumstances, capacities, and mode of bringing up being considered.

The laws of inheritance, however, have probably several phases of improvement to go through, before ideas so far removed from present modes of thinking will be taken into serious consideration: and as, among the recognised modes of determining the succession to property, some must be better and others worse, it is necessary to consider which of them

*a*48, 49   I cannot, therefore, select topics more suitable to be touched upon in the present treatise.

*b–b*48, 49   part of this work

*c*48, 49   in themselves,

deserves the preference. As an intermediate course, therefore, *d* I would recommend the extension to all property, of the present English law of inheritance affecting personal property (freedom of bequest, and in case of intestacy, equal division): except that no rights should be acknowledged in collaterals, and that the property of those who have neither descendants nor ascendants, and make no will, should escheat to the state.

The laws of existing nations deviate from these maxims in two opposite ways. In England, and *e*in*e* most of the countries *f*where*f* the influence of feudality is still felt in the laws, one of the objects aimed at in respect to land and other immoveable property, is to keep it together in large masses: accordingly, in cases of intestacy, it passes, generally speaking (for the local custom of *g*a few*g* places is different), exclusively to the eldest son. And though the rule of primogeniture is not binding on testators, who in England have nominally the power of bequeathing their property as they please, any *h* proprietor may so exercise this power as to deprive his *i*immediate successor*i* of it, by entailing the property on one particular line of his descendants: which, besides preventing it from passing by inheritance in any other than the prescribed manner, is attended with the incidental consequence of precluding it from being sold; since each successive possessor, having only a life interest in the property, cannot alienate it for a longer period than his own life. In *j*some*j* other countries, such as France, the law, on the contrary, compels division of inheritances; not only, in case of intestacy, sharing the property, both real and personal, equally among all the children, or (if there are no children) among all relatives in the same degree of propinquity; but also not recognising any power of bequest, or recognising it over only a limited portion of the property, the remainder being subjected to compulsory equal division.

Neither of these systems, I apprehend, was introduced, or is *k*perhaps*k* maintained, in the countries where it exists, from any general considerations of justice, or any foresight of economical consequences, but chiefly from political motives; in the one case to keep up large hereditary fortunes, and a landed aristocracy; in the other, to break these down, and prevent their resurrection. The first object, as an aim of national policy, I conceive to be eminently undesirable: *l*with regard to the second*l*, I have pointed out what seems to me a better mode of attaining it. The merit, or demerit, however, of either purpose, belongs to the general science of politics, not

---

*d*48, 49   less eligible in itself, but better adapted to existing feelings and ideas,
e-e+52, 57, 62, 65, 71
*f-f*48, 49   in which
*g-g*48, 49, 52, 57   some
*h*48, 49   one
*i-i*48, 49, 52, 57, 62, 65   successors   *j-j*+62, 65, 71
k-k+49, 52, 57, 62, 65, 71   *l-l*48, 49   so far as the second is desirable

to the limited department of that science which ^{m}is here treated of^m. Each of the two systems is a real and efficient instrument for the purpose intended by it; but each, as it appears to me, achieves that purpose at the cost of much mischief.

§ 2. [*Law and Custom of Primogeniture*] There are two arguments of an economical character, which are urged in favour of primogeniture. One is, the stimulus applied to the industry and ambition of younger children, by leaving them to be the architects of their own fortunes. This argument was put by Dr. Johnson in a manner more forcible than complimentary to an hereditary aristocracy, when he said, by way of recommendation of primogeniture, that it "makes but one fool in a family." It is curious that a defender of aristocratic institutions should be the person to assert that to inherit such a fortune as takes away any necessity for exertion, is generally fatal to activity and strength of mind: in the present state of education, however, the proposition, with some allowance for exaggeration, may be admitted to be true. But whatever force there is in the argument, counts in favour of limiting the eldest, as well as all the other children, to a mere provision, and dispensing with even the "one fool" whom Dr. Johnson was willing to tolerate. If unearned riches are so pernicious to the character, one does not see why, in order to withhold the poison from the junior members of a family, there should be no way but to unite all their separate potions, and administer them in the largest possible dose to one selected victim. ^{a}It ^{b}cannot be^b necessary to inflict this great evil on the eldest son, for want of knowing what else to do with a large fortune.^{a}

Some writers, however, look upon the effect of primogeniture in stimulating industry, as depending, not so much on the poverty of the younger children, as on the contrast between that poverty and the riches of the elder; thinking it indispensable to the activity and energy of the hive, that there should be a huge drone here and there, to impress the working bees with a due sense of the advantages of honey. "Their inferiority in point of wealth," says Mr. M'Culloch, speaking of the younger children, "and their desire to escape from this lower ^{c}station^c, and to attain to the same level with their elder brothers, inspires them with an energy and vigour they could not otherwise feel. But the advantage of preserving large estates from being frittered down by a scheme of equal division, is not limited to its

$^{m-m}$48, 49   is the subject of the present treatise

$^{a-a}$48, 49   That it should be necessary to inflict this great evil on the eldest son, from sheer want of knowing what else to do with a large fortune, is surely the most arbitrarily conjured up of all embarrassments.

$^{b-b}$52   is not

$^{c-c}$Source, 48, 49, 52   situation

influence over the younger children of their owners. It raises universally the standard of competence, and gives new force to the springs which set industry in motion. The manner of living among the great landlords is that in which every one is ambitious of being able to indulge; and their habits of expense, though sometimes injurious to themselves, act as powerful incentives to the ingenuity and enterprise of the other classes, who never think their fortunes sufficiently ample, unless they will enable them to emulate the splendour of the richest landlords; so that the custom of primogeniture seems to render all classes more industrious, and to augment at the same time, the mass of wealth and the scale of enjoyment."*

The portion of truth, I ^{d}can hardly^d say contained in these observations, but recalled by them, I apprehend to be, that a state of complete equality of fortunes would not be favourable to ^{e}active exertion for the increase of wealth^e. Speaking of the mass, it is as true of wealth as of most other distinctions—of talent, knowledge, virtue—that those who already have, or think they have, as much of it as ^{f} their neighbours, will seldom ^{g} exert themselves to acquire more. But it is not therefore necessary that society should provide a set of persons with large fortunes, to fulfil the social duty of standing to be looked at, with envy and admiration, by the aspiring poor. The fortunes which people have acquired for themselves, answer the purpose quite as well, indeed much better; since a person is more powerfully stimulated by the example of somebody who has earned a fortune, than by the mere sight of somebody who possesses one; and the former is necessarily an example of prudence and frugality as well as industry, while the latter much oftener sets an example of profuse expense, which spreads, with pernicious effect, to the very class on whom the sight of riches is supposed to have so beneficial an influence, namely, those whose weakness of mind, and taste for ostentation, makes "the splendour of the richest landlords" attract them with the most potent spell. In America there are few or no ^{h} hereditary fortunes; yet industrial energy, and the ardour of accumulation, are not supposed to be particularly backward in that part of the world. When a country has once fairly entered into the industrial career, which is the ^{i}principal^i occupation of the modern, as war was that of the ancient and mediæval world, the desire of acquisition by industry needs no factitious stimulus: the advantages naturally inherent in riches, and the character they assume of a test by which talent and success in life are

---

*Principles of Political Economy, ed. 1843, p. 264. There is much more to [48   much to] the same effect in the more recent treatise by the same author, "On the Succession to Property vacant by Death."

$^{d-d}$48, 49, 52, 57   will not $^{e-e}$48, 49   industry
^{f}48, 49   any of ^{g}48, 49   greatly
^{h}48, 49   great $^{i-i}$+52, 57, 62, 65, 71

habitually measured, are an ample security for their being pursued with sufficient intensity and zeal. As to the deeper consideration, that the diffusion of wealth, and not its concentration, is desirable, and that the *more* wholesome state of society is not that in which immense fortunes are possessed by a few and coveted by all, but that in which the greatest possible numbers possess and are contented with a moderate competency, which all may hope to acquire: I refer to it in this place, only to show, how widely separated, on social questions, is the entire mode of thought of the *defenders* of primogeniture, from that which is partially promulgated in the present treatise.

The other economical argument in favour of primogeniture, has *special* reference to landed property. It is contended that the habit of dividing inheritances equally, or with an approach to equality, among children, promotes the subdivision of land into *portions* too small to admit of being cultivated in an advantageous manner. This argument, eternally reproduced, has again and again been refuted by English and Continental writers. It proceeds on a supposition entirely at variance with that on which all the theorems of political economy are grounded. It assumes that mankind in general will habitually act in a manner opposed to their immediate and obvious pecuniary interest. For the division of the inheritance does not necessarily imply division of the land; which may be held in common, as is not unfrequently the case in France and Belgium; or may become the property of one of the coheirs, being charged with the shares of the *others* by *o* way of mortgage; or they may sell it outright, and divide the proceeds. When the division of the land would diminish its productive power, it is the direct interest of the heirs to adopt some one of these arrangements. Supposing, however, what the argument assumes, that either from legal difficulties or from their own stupidity and barbarism, they would not, if left to themselves, obey the dictates of this obvious interest, but would insist upon cutting up the land bodily into equal parcels, with the effect of impoverishing themselves; this would be an objection to a law such as exists in France, of compulsory division, but can be no reason why testators should be discouraged from exercising the right of bequest in general conformity to the rule of equality, since it would always be in their power to provide that the division of the inheritance should take place without dividing the land itself. That the attempts of the advocates of primogeniture to make out a case by facts against the custom of equal division, are equally abortive, has been shown in a former *place*. In all countries, or parts of countries, in which

---

*ʲ-ʲ*48, 49   most
*ᵏ-ᵏ*48, 49, 52, 57   defender
*ᵐ-ᵐ*48, 49   occupations
*ᵒ*49, 52, 57, 62   the

*ˡ-ˡ*48, 49   especial
*ⁿ-ⁿ*52, 57, 62, 65   other
*ᵖ-ᵖ*48, 49   portion of this work

the division of inheritance is accompanied by small holdings, it is because small holdings are the general system of the country, even on the estates of the great proprietors.

Unless a strong case of social utility can be made out for primogeniture, it stands sufficiently condemned by the general principles of justice; being a broad distinction in the treatment of one person and of another, grounded solely on an accident. There is no need, therefore, to make out any case of economical evil *against* primogeniture. Such a case, however, and a very strong one, may be made. It is a natural effect of primogeniture to make the landlords a needy class. The object of the institution, or custom, is to keep the land together in large masses, and this it commonly accomplishes; but the legal proprietor of a large domain is not necessarily the *bonâ fide* owner of the whole income which it yields. It is usually charged, in each generation, with provisions for the other children. It is often charged still more heavily by the imprudent expenditure of the proprietor. Great land-owners are generally improvident in their expenses; they live up to their incomes when at the highest, and if any change of circumstances diminishes their resources, some time elapses before they make up their minds to retrench. Spendthrifts in other classes are ruined, and disappear from society; but the spendthrift landlord usually holds fast to his land, even when he has become a mere receiver of its rents for the benefit of creditors. The same desire to keep up the "splendour" of the family, which gives rise to the custom of primogeniture, indisposes the *owner* to sell a part in order to set free the remainder; their apparent are therefore habitually greater than their real means, and they are under a perpetual temptation to proportion their expenditure to the former rather than to the latter. From such causes as these, in almost all countries of great landowners, the majority of landed estates are deeply mortgaged; and instead of having capital to spare for improvements, it requires all the increased value of land, caused by *the* rapid increase of the wealth and population of the country, to preserve the class from being impoverished.

§ 3. [*Entails*] To avert this impoverishment, recourse was had to the contrivance of entails, whereby the order of succession was irrevocably fixed, and each holder, having only a life interest, was unable to burthen his successor. The land thus passing, free from debt, into the possession of the heir, the family could not be ruined by the improvidence of its existing representative. The economical evils arising from this disposition of property were partly of the same kind, partly different, but on the whole greater, than those arising from primogeniture. The possessor could not now ruin his successors, but he could still ruin himself: he was not at all more likely than in the former case to have the means necessary for improving the property: while, even if he had, he was still less likely to employ them for that purpose, when the benefit was to accrue to a person whom the entail made independent of him, while he had probably younger children to provide for, in whose favour he could not now charge the estate. While thus disabled from being himself an improver, neither could he sell the estate to somebody who would; since entail precludes alienation. In general he has even been unable to grant leases beyond the term of his own life; "for," says Blackstone, "if such leases had been valid, then, under cover of long leases, the issue might have been virtually disinherited;"[*] and it has been necessary in Great Britain to relax, by statute, the rigour of entails, in order to allow either of long leases, or of the execution of improvements at the expense of the estate. It may be added that the heir of entail, being assured of succeeding to the family property, however undeserving of it, and being aware of this from his earliest years, has much more than the ordinary chances of growing up idle, dissipated, and profligate.

In England, the power of entail is more limited by law, than in Scotland and in most other countries where it exists. A landowner can settle his property upon any number of persons successively who are living at the time, and upon one unborn person, on whose attaining the age of twenty-one, the entail expires, and the land becomes his absolute property. An estate may in this manner be transmitted through a son, or a son and grandson, living when the deed is executed, to an unborn child of that grandson. It has been maintained that this power of entail is not sufficiently extensive to do any mischief: in truth, however, it is much larger than it seems. Entails very rarely expire; the first heir of entail, when of age, joins with the existing possessor in resettling the estate, so as to prolong the entail for a further term. Large properties, therefore, are rarely free for any considerable period, from the restraints of a strict settlement; *though the mischief is in one respect mitigated, since in the renewal of the settlement for one more generation, the estate is usually charged with a *provision* for younger children*.

In an economical point of view, the best system of landed property is that in which land is most completely an object of commerce; passing readily from hand to hand when a buyer can be found to whom it is worth while to offer a greater sum for the land, than the value of the income

[*Blackstone, Sir William. *Commentaries on the Laws of England*. 4 vols. Oxford: Clarendon Press, 1766, II, 116.]

a–a48, 49, 52, 57   and English entails are not, in point of fact, much less injurious than those of other countries
b–b62   pension

drawn from it by its existing possessor. This of course is not meant of ornamental property, which is a source of expense, not profit; but only of land employed for industrial uses, and held for the sake of the income which it affords. Whatever facilitates the sale of land, tends to make it a more productive instrument ^cof^c the community at large; whatever prevents or restricts its sale, subtracts from its usefulness. Now, not only has entail this effect, but primogeniture also. The desire to keep land together in large masses, from other motives than that of promoting its productiveness, often prevents changes and alienations which would increase its efficiency as an instrument.

§ 4. [*Law of compulsory equal division of inheritances*] On the other hand, a law which, like the French, restricts the power of bequest to a narrow compass, and compels the equal division of the whole or the greater part of the property among the children, seems to me, though on different grounds, also very seriously objectionable. The only reason for recognising in the children any ^aclaim^a at all to more than a provision, sufficient to launch them ^bin^b life, and enable them to find a livelihood, is grounded on the expressed or presumed wish of the parent; whose claim to dispose of what is actually his ^c own, cannot be set aside by any pretensions of others to receive what is not theirs. To control the rightful owner's liberty of gift, by creating in the children a legal right superior to it, is to postpone a real claim to an imaginary one. To this great and paramount objection to the law, numerous secondary ones may be added. Desirable as it is that the parent should treat the children with impartiality, and not make an eldest son or a favourite, impartial division is not always synonymous with equal division. Some of the children may ^d, without fault of their own, be less capable than others of providing for themselves: some may, by other means than their own exertions, be already provided for:^d and impartiality may therefore require that the rule observed should not be one of equality, but of compensation. Even when equality is ^ethe object, there are sometimes better means of attaining it, than the inflexible rules by which law must necessarily proceed.^e If one of the coheirs, being of a quarrelsome ^for^f litigious disposition, stands upon his utmost rights, the law cannot make equitable adjustments; it cannot apportion the property as seems best for

---

^{c–c}48, 49, 52, 57, 62   for

^{a–a}48, 49   right

^{b–b}48, 49, 52, 57   into   ^c48, 49   (or her)

^{d–d}48, 49   be more capable than others of providing for themselves, or may have fewer wants, or possess other resources;

^{e–e}48, 49   desirable, it is not precise or pedantic equality. The law, however, must proceed by fixed rules.

^{f–f}+65, 71

the collective interest of ^{g}all concerned^g; if there are several parcels of land, and the heirs cannot agree about their value, the law cannot give a parcel to each, but every separate parcel must be either put up to sale or divided: if there is a residence, or a park or pleasure-ground, which would be destroyed, as such, by subdivision, it must be sold, ^{h}perhaps at a great sacrifice both of money and of feeling^h. But what the law could not do, the parent could. By means of the liberty of bequest, all these points might be determined according to reason and the general interest of the persons concerned; and the spirit of the principle of equal division might be the better observed, because the testator was emancipated from its letter. Finally, it would not then be necessary, as under the compulsory system it is, that the law should interfere authoritatively in the concerns of ^{i}individuals^i, not only on the occurrence of a death, but throughout life, in order to guard against the attempts of parents to frustrate the legal claims of their heirs, under colour of gifts and other alienations *inter vivos*.

In conclusion; all owners of property should, I conceive, have power to dispose by will of every part of it, but not to determine the person who should succeed to it after the ^{j}death^j of all who were living when the will was made. Under what restrictions it should be allowable to bequeath property to one person for life, with remainder to another person already in existence, is a question belonging to general legislation, not to political economy. Such settlements would be no greater hindrance to alienation than any case of joint ownership, since the consent of persons actually in existence is all that would be necessary for any new arrangement respecting the property.

§ 5. [*Laws of Partnership*] From the subject of Inheritance I now pass to that of Contracts, and among these, to the important subject of the Laws of Partnership. How much of good or evil depends upon these laws, and how important it is that they should be the best possible, is evident to all who recognise in the extension of the co-operative principle ^{a}in the larger sense of the term,^{a} the great economical necessity of modern industry. The progress of the productive arts requiring that many sorts of industrial occupation should be carried on by larger and larger capitals, the productive power of industry must suffer by whatever impedes the formation of large capitals through the aggregation of smaller ones. Capitals of the requisite magnitude belonging to single owners, do not, in most countries,

---

g–g48, 49   the family
h–h48, 49   possibly at a great pecuniary sacrifice, and with the destruction to the whole family of local ties and attachments] 52, 57   perhaps at a great pecuniary sacrifice
i–i48, 49   families
j–j48, 49   deaths a–a+65, 71

exist in the needful abundance, and would be still less numerous if the laws favoured the diffusion instead of the concentration of property: while it is most undesirable that all those improved processes, and those means of efficiency and economy in production, which depend on the possession of large funds, should be monopolies in the hands of a few rich individuals, through the difficulties experienced by persons of moderate or small means in associating their capital. Finally, I must repeat my conviction, that the industrial economy which divides society absolutely into two portions, the payers of wages and the receivers of them, the first counted by thousands and the last by millions, is neither fit for, nor capable of, indefinite duration: and the possibility of changing this system for one of combination without dependence, and unity of interest instead of organized hostility, depends altogether upon the future developments of the Partnership principle.

Yet there is scarcely any country whose laws do not throw great, and in most cases, intentional obstacles in the way of the formation of any numerous partnership. In England it is already a serious discouragement, that [b] differences among partners are, practically speaking, only capable of adjudication by the Court of Chancery: which is often worse than placing such questions out of the pale of all law; since any one of the disputant parties, who is either dishonest or litigious, can involve the others at his pleasure in the [c] expense, trouble, and anxiety, which are the unavoidable accompaniments of a [d] Chancery suit, without their having the power of freeing themselves from the infliction even by breaking up the association.*
Besides this, it required, until lately, a separate Act of the legislature before

*[52] Mr. Cecil Fane, the Commissioner of the Bankruptcy Court, in his evidence before the Committee on the Law of Partnership, says: "I remember a short time ago reading a written statement by two eminent solicitors, who said that they had known many partnership accounts go into Chancery, but that they never knew one come out. . . . Very few of the persons who would be disposed to engage in partnerships of this kind" (co-operative associations of working men) "have any idea of the truth, namely, that the decision of questions arising amongst partners is really impracticable.
"Do they not know that one partner may rob the other without any possibility of his obtaining redress?—The fact is so; but whether they know it or not, I cannot undertake to say."
This flagrant injustice is, in Mr. Fane's opinion, wholly attributable to the defects of the tribunal. "My opinion is, that if there is one thing more easy than another, it is the settlement of partnership questions, and for the simple reason, that everything which is done in a partnership is entered in the books; the evidence therefore is at hand; if therefore a rational mode of proceeding were once adopted, the difficulty would altogether vanish."—Minutes of Evidence annexed to the Report of [52 for] the Select Committee on the Law of Partnership [*Parliamentary Papers*] (1851), [XVIII,] pp. 85–7.

[b]48, 49   all or most
[c]48, 49, 52   endless   [d]48, 49   prolonged

any joint-stock association could legally constitute itself, and be empowered to act as one body. By a statute passed [e] a few years ago, this necessity is done away [f]; but the statute in question is described by competent authorities as a "mass of confusion," of which they say that there "never was such an infliction" on persons entering into partnership[f].* When a number of persons, whether few or many, freely desire to unite their funds for a common undertaking, not asking any peculiar privilege, nor the power to dispossess any one of property, the law can have no good reason for throwing difficulties in the way of the realization of the project. On compliance with a few simple conditions of publicity, any body of persons ought to have the power of constituting themselves into a joint-stock company, or *société en nom collectif*, without asking leave either of any public officer or of parliament [g]. As an association of many partners must practically be under the management of a few, every facility [h] ought to be afforded to the body for exercising the necessary control and check over those few, whether they be themselves members of the association, or merely its hired servants: and in this point the English system is still at a lamentable distance from the standard of perfection [i].

§ 6. [*Partnerships with limited liability. Chartered Companies*] Whatever facilities, however, English law [a]might[a] give to associations formed on the principles of ordinary partnership, there is one sort of joint-stock association which [b]until the year 1855[b] it absolutely [c]disallowed[c], and which [d]could only be[d] called into existence by a special act either of the legislature or of the crown. I mean, associations with limited liability.

Associations with limited liability are of two kinds: in one, the liability of all the partners is limited, in the other that of some of them only. The first is the *société anonyme* of the French law, which in England [e]had until lately[e] no other name than that of "chartered company:" meaning thereby a joint-stock company whose shareholders, by a charter from the crown or a special enactment of the legislature, [f]stood[f] exempted from any liability for the debts of the concern, beyond the amount of their subscrip-

*[52] Report, ut supra, p. 167.

[e]48, 49   only
[f-f]48, 49   , and the formalities which have been substituted for it are not sufficiently onerous to be very much of an impediment to such undertakings
[g]48   : and this liberty, in England, they cannot now be fairly said not to have, though they have had it but for a little more than three years.] 49   *as* 48 . . . to have.
[h]48, 49   which law can give
[i]48, 49   , though less, I believe, owing to the defects of the law, than to those of the courts of judicature

[a-a]48, 49, 52 may	[b-b]+57, 62, 65, 71
[c-c]48, 49, 52 disallows	[d-d]48, 49, 52 can still be only
[e-e]48, 49, 52 has	[f-f]48, 49, 52 stand

tions. *g* The other species of limited partnership is that known to the French law under the name of *commandite*; of this, which in England is *h*still*h* unrecognised and illegal, I shall speak presently.

If a number of persons choose to associate for carrying on any operation of commerce or industry, agreeing among themselves and announcing to those with whom they deal that the members of the association do not undertake to be responsible beyond the amount of the subscribed capital; is there any reason that the law should raise objections to this proceeding, and should impose on them the unlimited responsibility which they disclaim? For whose sake? Not for that of the partners themselves; for it is they whom the limitation of responsibility benefits and protects. It must therefore be for the sake of third parties; namely, those who may have transactions with the association, and to whom it may run in debt beyond what the subscribed capital suffices to pay. But nobody is obliged to deal with the association: still less is any one obliged to give it unlimited credit. The class of persons with whom such associations have dealings are in general perfectly capable of taking care of themselves, and there seems no reason that the law should be more careful of their interests than they will themselves be; provided no false representation is held out, and they are aware from the first what they have to trust to. The law is warranted in requiring from all joint-stock associations with limited responsibilities, not only that the amount of capital on which they profess to carry on business should either be actually paid up or security given for it (if, indeed, with complete publicity, such a requirement would be necessary), but also that such accounts should be kept, accessible to individuals, and if needful, published to the world, as shall render it possible to ascertain at any time the existing state of the company's affairs, and to learn whether the capital which is the sole security for the engagements into which they enter, still subsists unimpaired: the fidelity of such accounts being guarded by sufficient penalties. When the law has thus afforded to individuals all practicable means of knowing the circumstances which ought to enter into their prudential calculations in dealing with the company, there seems no more need for interfering with individual judgment in this sort of transactions, than in any other part of the private business of life.

The reason usually urged for such interference is, that the managers of an association with limited responsibility, not risking their whole fortunes in the event of loss, while in case of gain they *i*might*i* profit largely, are not sufficiently interested in exercising due circumspection, and are under the temptation of exposing the funds of the association to improper hazards.

*g*48, 49, 52. This form of association, though unknown to the general law of this country, exists in many particular cases by special *privilegium*.
  *h–h*48, 49, 52 entirely   *i–i*48, 49 may

^{j}It ^{k}is, however, well ascertained^k that associations with unlimited responsibility, if they have rich shareholders, can obtain, even when known to be reckless in their transactions, improper credit to an extent far exceeding what would be given to companies equally ill-conducted whose creditors had only the subscribed capital to rely on.* To whichever side the balance of evil inclines^j, it is a consideration of more importance to the shareholders themselves than to third parties; since, with proper securities for publicity, the capital of ^{l}an association with limited liability^l could not be engaged in hazards beyond those ordinarily incident to the business it carries on, without the facts being known, and becoming the subject of comments by which the credit of the body would be likely to be affected in quite as great a degree as the circumstances would justify. If, under securities for publicity, it were found in practice that companies, formed on the principle of unlimited responsibility, ^{m}were more skilfully and more cautiously managed^m, companies with limited liability would be unable to maintain an equal competition with them; and would therefore rarely be formed, unless when such limitation was the only condition on which the necessary amount of capital could be raised: and in that case it would be very unreasonable to say that their formation ought to be prevented.

It may further be remarked, that although, with equality of capital, a company of limited liability offers a somewhat less security to those who deal with it, than one in which every shareholder is responsible with his whole fortune, yet even the weaker of these two securities is in some respects stronger than that which an individual capitalist can afford. In the case of an individual, there is such security as can be founded on his unlimited liability, but not that derived from publicity of transactions, or from a known and large amount of paid-up capital. This topic is well treated in an able paper by M. Coquelin, published in the Revue des Deux Mondes for July 1843.†

"While third parties who trade with individuals," says this writer, "scarcely ever know, except by approximation, and even that most vague and uncertain, what is the amount of capital responsible for the performance of contracts made with them, those who trade with a *société anonyme*

*See the Report already referred to [*Parliamentary Papers*, 1851, XVIII], pp. 145–158.

†The quotation is from a translation published by Mr. H. C. Carey, in [48 published in] an American periodical, Hunt's Merchant's Magazine, for May and June 1845 [Vol. XII, pp. 514–5] [48 , by Mr. H. C. Carey of Philadelphia, to whose writings I have before had occasion to advert].

$^{j-j}$48, 49 Admitting that this is one of the disadvantages of such associations
$^{k-k}$52, 57 has however been proved by the evidence of several experienced witnesses before a late committee of the House of Commons,
$^{l-l}$48, 49 the association
$^{m-m}$48, 49 obtained, with equal capital, greater credit

can obtain full information if they seek it, and perform their operations with a feeling of confidence that cannot exist in the other case. Again, nothing is easier than for an individual trader to conceal the extent of his engagements, as no one can know it certainly but himself. Even his confidential clerk may be ignorant of it, as the loans he finds himself compelled to make may not all be of a character to require that they be entered in his day-book. It is a secret confined to himself; one which transpires rarely, and always slowly; one which is unveiled only when the catastrophe has occurred. On the contrary, the *société anonyme* neither can nor ought to borrow, without the fact becoming known to all the world—directors, clerks, shareholders, and the public. Its operations partake in some respects, of the nature of those of governments. The light of day penetrates in every direction, and there can be no secrets from those who seek for information. Thus all is fixed, recorded, known, of the capital and debts in the case of the *société anonyme*, while all is uncertain and unknown in the case of the individual trader. Which of the two, we would ask the reader, presents the most favourable aspect, or the surest guarantee, to the view of those who trade with them?

"Again, availing himself of the obscurity in which his affairs are shrouded, and which he desires to increase, the private trader is enabled, so long as his business appears prosperous, to produce impressions in regard to his means far exceeding the reality, and thus to establish a credit not justified by those means. When losses occur, and he sees himself threatened with bankruptcy, the world is still ignorant of his condition, and he finds himself enabled to contract debts far beyond the possibility of payment. The fatal day arrives, and the creditors find a debt much greater than had been anticipated, while the means of payment are as much less. Even this is not all. The same obscurity which has served him so well thus far, when desiring to magnify his capital and increase his credit, now affords him the opportunity of placing a part of that capital beyond the reach of his creditors. It becomes diminished, if not annihilated. It hides itself, and not even legal remedies, nor the activity of creditors, can bring it forth from the dark corners in which it is placed. . . . Our readers can readily determine for themselves if practices of this kind are equally easy in the case of the *société anonyme*. We do not doubt that such things are possible, but we think that they will agree with us that from its nature, its organization, and the necessary publicity that attends all its actions, the liability to such occurrences is very greatly diminished."

The laws of most countries, England included, have erred in a twofold manner with regard to joint-stock companies. While they have been most unreasonably jealous of allowing such associations to exist, especially with limited responsibility, they have generally neglected the enforcement of publicity; the best security to the public against any danger which might arise from this description of partnerships; and a security quite as much required in the case of those associations of the kind in question, which, by an exception from their general practice, they suffered to exist. Even in the instance of the Bank of England, which holds a monopoly from the legislature, and has had partial control over a matter of so much public interest as the state of the circulating medium, it is only within these few years that any publicity [n] has been enforced; and the publicity was at first of an extremely incomplete character, though now, for most practical purposes, probably at length sufficient.

§ 7. [*Partnerships in* commandite] The other kind of limited partnership which demands our attention, is that in which the managing partner or partners are responsible with their whole fortunes for the engagements of the concern, but have others associated with them who contribute only definite sums, and are not liable for anything beyond, though they participate in the profits according to any rule which may be agreed on. This is called partnership *en commandite*: and the partners with limited liability (to whom, by the French law, all interference in the management of the concern is interdicted) are known by the name *commanditaires*. Such partnerships are not [a]allowed[a] by English law: [b]in all private partnerships,[b] whoever shares in the profits is liable for the debts, to as plenary an extent as the managing partner.

For such prohibition no [c]satisfactory[c] defence has ever, so far as I am aware, been made. Even the insufficient reason given against limiting the responsibility of shareholders in a joint-stock company, does not apply here; there being no diminution of the motives to circumspect management, since all who take any part in the direction of the concern are liable with their whole fortunes. To third parties, again, the security is improved by the existence of commandite; since the amount subscribed by commanditaires is all of it available to creditors, the commanditaires losing their whole investment before any creditor can lose anything; while, if instead of becoming partners to that amount, they had lent the sum at an interest equal to the profit they derived from it, they would have shared with the other creditors in the residue of the estate, diminishing *pro rata* the dividend obtained by all. While the practice of commandite thus conduces to the interest of creditors, it is often highly desirable for the contracting parties themselves. The managers are enabled to obtain the aid of a much greater amount of capital than they could borrow on their own security; and persons are induced to aid useful undertakings, by embarking limited

[n]48, 49   at all
[b-b]+65, 71

[a-a]48, 49   permitted
[c-c]48, 49   rational

portions of capital in them, when they would not, and often could not prudently, have risked their whole fortunes on the chances of the enterprise.

It may perhaps be thought that where due facilities are afforded to joint-stock companies, commandite partnerships are not required. But there are classes of cases to which the commandite principle must always be better adapted than the joint-stock principle. "Suppose," says M. Coquelin, "an inventor seeking for a capital to carry his invention into practice. To obtain the aid of capitalists, he must offer them a share of the anticipated benefit; they must associate themselves with him in the chances of its success. In such a case, which of the forms would he select? Not a common partnership, certainly;" for various reasons, and especially *d*the extreme difficulty of finding*d* a partner with capital, willing to risk his whole fortune on the success of *e*the*e* invention.* "Neither would he select the *société anonyme*," or any other form of joint-stock company, "in which he might be superseded as manager. He would stand, in such an association, on no better footing than any other shareholder, and he might be lost in the crowd; whereas, the association existing, as it were, by and for him, the management would appear to belong to him as a matter of right. Cases occur in which a merchant or a manufacturer, without being precisely an inventor, has undeniable claims to the management of an undertaking,

*[52] "There has been a great deal of commiseration professed," says Mr. Duncan, solicitor, "towards the poor inventor; he has been oppressed by the high cost of patents; but his chief oppression has been the partnership law, which prevents his getting any one to help him to develop his invention. He is a poor man, and therefore cannot give security to a creditor; no one will lend him money; the rate of interest offered, however high it may be, is not an attraction. But if by the alteration of the law he could allow capitalists to take an interest with him and share the profits, while the [Source, 52, 57   their] risk should be confined to the capital they embarked, there is very little doubt at all that he would frequently get assistance from capitalists; whereas at the present moment, with the law as it stands, he is completely destroyed, and his invention is useless to him; he struggles month after month; he applies again and again to the capitalist without avail. I know it practically in two or three cases of patented inventions; especially one where parties with capital were desirous of entering into an undertaking of great moment in Liverpool, but five or six different gentlemen were deterred from doing so, all feeling the strongest objection to what each one called the cursed partnership law." Report, [*Parliamentary Papers*, 1851, XVIII,] p. 155.

Mr. Fane says, "In the course of my professional life, as a Commissioner of the Court of Bankruptcy, I have learned that the most unfortunate man in the world is an inventor. The difficulty which an inventor finds in getting at capital involves him in all sorts of embarrassments, and he ultimately is for the most part a ruined man, and somebody else gets possession of his invention." Ib. p. 82.

*d–d*48, 49   because it would often be very difficult to find
*e–e*48   another person's

from the possession of qualities peculiarly calculated to promote its success. So great, indeed," continues M. Coquelin, "is the necessity, in many cases, for the limited partnership, that it is difficult to conceive how we could dispense with or replace it:"[*] and in reference to his own country he is probably in the right.

Where there is so great a readiness as in England, on the part of the public, to form joint-stock associations, even without the encouragement of a limitation of responsibility; commandite partnership, though its prohibition is in principle quite indefensible, cannot be deemed to be, in a merely economical point of view, of the imperative necessity which M. Coquelin ascribes to it. Yet the inconveniences are not small, which arise indirectly from those provisions of the law by which every one who shares in the profits of a concern is subject to the full liabilities of an unlimited partnership. It is impossible to say how many or what useful modes of combination are rendered impracticable by this state of the law. It is sufficient for its condemnation that, unless in some way relaxed, it is inconsistent with *f* the payment of wages in part by a percentage on profits; in other words, the association of the operatives as virtual partners with the capitalist.†

It is, above all, with reference to the improvement and elevation of the working classes that complete freedom in the conditions of partnership is indispensable. *g*Combinations such as the associations of workpeople, described in a former chapter, *h* are the most powerful means of effecting the social emancipation of the labourers through their own moral qualities. Nor is the liberty of association*g* important solely for its examples of success, but fully as much so for the sake of attempts which would not succeed; but by their failure would give instruction more impressive than can be afforded by anything short of actual experience. *i*Every*i* theory of social improvement, the worth of which is capable of being brought to an experimental test, should be permitted, and even encouraged, to submit itself to that test. From such experiments the *j*active portion of*j* the working classes would derive lessons, which they would be slow to learn from the

[*Hunt's Merchants' Magazine, XII (May, 1845), 412.]

†[65] It is considered possible to effect this through the Limited Liability Act, by erecting the capitalist and his workpeople into a Limited Company; as proposed by Messrs. Briggs (supra, vol. ii. pp. 774–5).

*f*48, 49 the system of which M. Leclaire has set so useful an example,

*g–g*48, 49 It is only by combining, that the small means of many can be on anything like an equality of advantage with the great fortunes of a few. The liberty of association is not

*h*52, 57 which have been so eminently successful in France,

*i–i*48 Socialism, Communism, every

*j–j*48, 49 aspiring among

teaching of persons supposed to have interests and prejudices adverse to their good; [k]would obtain the means of correcting, at no cost to society, [l]whatever[l] is now erroneous in their notions of the means of establishing their independence; and of discovering the conditions, moral, intellectual, and industrial, which are indispensably necessary for effecting without injustice, or for effecting at all, the social regeneration they aspire to[k].*

The French law of partnership is superior to the English in permitting commandite; and superior, in having no such unmanageable instrument as the Court of Chancery, all cases arising from commercial transactions being adjudicated in a comparatively cheap and expeditious manner by a tribunal of merchants. In other respects the French system is far worse than the English. A [m]joint-stock[m] company with limited responsibility cannot be formed without the express authorization of the department of government called the *Conseil d'Etat*, a body of administrators, generally entire strangers to industrial transactions, who have no interest in promoting enterprises, and are apt to think that the purpose of their institution is to restrain them; whose consent cannot in any case be obtained without an amount of time and labour which is a very serious hindrance to the commencement of an enterprise, while the extreme uncertainty of obtaining that consent at all is a great discouragement to capitalists who would be willing to subscribe. In regard to joint-stock companies without limitation of responsibility, which in England exist in such numbers and are formed with such facility, [n]these[n] associations cannot, in France, exist at all; for, in cases of unlimited partnership, the French law does not permit the division of the capital into transferable shares.

The best existing laws of partnership appear to be those of the New

---

*[52] By an Act of the year 1852, [52   the present session (1852)]] called the Industrial and Provident Societies [52, 57   Provident Partnerships] Act, for which the nation is indebted to the public-spirited exertions of Mr. Slaney, industrial associations of working people are admitted to the statutory privileges of Friendly Societies. This not only exempts them from the formalities applicable to joint-stock companies, but provides for the settlement of disputes among the partners without recourse to the Court of Chancery. [62] There are still some defects in the provisions of this Act, which hamper the proceedings of the Societies in several respects; as is pointed out in the Almanack of the Rochdale Equitable Pioneers for 1861.

[k-k]48, 49   and would discover, at no cost to society, the limits of the practical worth of their ideas of social regeneration, as applicable to the present stage of human advancement

[l-l]52, 57, 62   what

[m-m]+52, 57, 62, 65, 71

[n-n]48, 49   as to reduce (in a merely economical point of view) the jealousy which the law entertains of the principle of limitation to the rank of a very minor inconvenience, such

England States. According to Mr. Carey,* "nowhere is association so little trammelled by regulations as in New England; the consequence of which is, that it is carried to a greater extent there, and particularly in Massachusetts and Rhode Island, than in any other part of the world. In these states, the soil is covered with *compagnies anonymes*—chartered companies—for almost every conceivable purpose. Every town is a corporation for the management of its roads, bridges, and schools: which are, therefore, under the direct control of those who pay for them, and are consequently well managed. Academies and churches, lyceums and libraries, saving-fund societies, and trust companies, exist in numbers proportioned to the wants of the people, and all are corporations. Every district has its local bank, of a size to suit its wants, the stock of which is owned by the small capitalists of the neighbourhood, and managed by themselves; the consequence of which is, that in no part of the world is the system of banking so perfect—so little liable to vibration in the amount of loans—the necessary effect of which is, that in none is the value of property so little affected by changes in the amount or value of the currency resulting from the movements of *their own* banking institutions. In the two states to which we have particularly referred, they are almost two hundred in number. Massachusetts, alone, offers to our view fifty-three insurance offices, of various forms, scattered through the state, and all incorporated. [o]Factories are incorporated, and are owned in shares[o]; and [p]every one that has any part in the management[p] of their concerns, from the purchase of the raw material to the sale of the manufactured article, [q]is a part owner[q]; while every one employed in them has a prospect of becoming one, by the use of prudence, exertion, and economy. Charitable associations exist in large numbers, and all are incorporated. [r]Fishing vessels are owned in shares[r] by those who navigate them; and [s]the sailors of a whaling ship depend[s] in a great degree, if not altogether, [t]upon the success of the voyage for their compensation[t]. Every master of a vessel trading in the Southern Ocean is a part owner, and the interest he possesses is a strong inducement to exertion and economy, by aid of which the people of New England are rapidly driving out the competition of other nations for the trade of that part of the world. Wherever settled, they exhibit the same tendency to combination of action. In New York they are the chief owners of [u]the lines of packet ships[u], which [v]are divided into shares, owned by the shipbuilders, the merchants, the master, and the mates[v]; which last generally acquire the

*In a note appended to his translation of M. Coquelin's paper. [*Hunt's Merchants' Magazine*, XII (June, 1845), 517–9.]

[o-o]48, 49 [*in italics*]
[p-p]48, 49 [*in italics*]
[q-q]48, 49 [*in italics*]
[r-r]48, 49 [*in italics*]
[s-s]48, 49 [*in italics*]
[t-t]48, 49 [*in italics*]
[u-u]48, 49 [*in italics*]
[v-v]48, 49 [*in italics*]

means of becoming themselves masters, and to this is due their great success. The system is the most perfectly democratic of any in the world. ʷIt affords to every labourer, every sailor, every operative, male or female, the prospect of advancementʷ; and its results are precisely such as we should have reason to expect. In no part of the world are talent, industry, and prudence, so certain to be largely rewarded."

ˣ The cases of insolvency and fraud on the part of chartered companies in America, which have caused so much loss and so much scandal in Europe, did not occur in the part of the Union to which this extract refers, but in other States, in which the right of association is much more fettered by legal restrictions, and in which, accordingly, joint-stock associations are not comparable in number or variety to those of New England. Mr. Carey adds, "A careful examination of the systems of the several states, can scarcely, we think, fail to convince the reader of the advantage resulting from permitting men to determine among themselves the terms upon which they will associate, and allowing the associations that may be formed to contract with the public as to the terms upon which they will trade together, whether of the limited or unlimited liability of the partners ᵛ."[*] This principle has been adopted as the foundation of all recent English legislation on the subjectᵛ.

§ 8. [*Laws relating to Insolvency*] I proceed to the subject of Insolvency Laws.

Good laws on this subject are important, first and principally, on the score of public morals; which are on no point more under the influence of the law, for good and evil, than in a matter belonging so pre-eminently to the province of law as the preservation of pecuniary integrity. But the subject is also, in a merely economical point of view, of great importance. First, because the economical well-being of a people, and of mankind, depends in an especial manner upon their being able to trust each other's engagements. Secondly, because one of the risks, or expenses, of industrial operations is the risk or expense of what are commonly called bad debts, and every saving which can be effected in this liability is a diminution of cost of production; by dispensing with an item of outlay which in no way conduces to the desired end, and which must be paid for either by the

[*Hunt's *Merchants' Magazine*, XII (June, 1845), 520.]

ʷ⁻ʷ48, 49 [*in italics*]
ˣ48, 49   To this state might England also be brought, but not without giving the same plenitude of liberty to voluntary association.
ᵛ⁻ᵛ48, 49   ;" and I concur in thinking that to this conclusion, science and legislation must ultimately come] 52, 57, 62 *as* 48 . . . must come

consumer of the commodity, or from the general profits of capital, according as the burthen is peculiar or general.

The laws and practice of nations on this subject have almost always been in extremes. The ancient laws of most countries *were* all severity to the debtor. They *b* invested the creditor with a power of coercion, more or less tyrannical, which he might use against his insolvent debtor, either to extort the surrender of hidden property, or to obtain satisfaction of a vindictive character, which might console him for the non-payment of the debt. This arbitrary power has extended, in some countries, to making the insolvent debtor serve the creditor as his slave: in which plan there were *at least* some grains of common sense, since it might possibly be regarded as a scheme for making him work out the debt by his labour. In England the coercion assumed the milder form of ordinary imprisonment. The one and the other were the barbarous expedients of a rude age, repugnant to justice, as well as to humanity. Unfortunately the reform of them, like that of the criminal law generally, has been taken in hand as an affair of humanity only, not of justice: and the modish humanity of the present time, which is essentially a thing of one idea, *d* has in this as in other cases, gone into a violent reaction against the ancient severity, and *might almost be supposed to see* in the fact of having lost or squandered other people's property, a peculiar title to indulgence. Everything in the law which attached disagreeable consequences to that fact, *was* gradually relaxed, *or* entirely got rid of *h*: until the demoralizing effects of this laxity became so evident as to determine, by *more recent legislation, a salutary though very insufficient* movement in the reverse direction.*h*

The indulgence of the *j* laws to those who have made themselves unable to pay their just debts, is usually defended, on the plea that the sole object of the law should be, in case of insolvency, not to coerce the person of the debtor, but to get at his property, and distribute it fairly among the creditors. Assuming that this is and ought to be the sole object, *kthe mitigation of the law was in the first instance carried so far as to sacrifice that object*k. Imprisonment at the discretion of a creditor was really a

---

*a–a*48, 49, 52, 57   have been   *b*48, 49, 52, 57   have   *c–c*+62, 65, 71
*d*48, 49   (and is indeed little better than a timid shrinking from the infliction of anything like pain, next neighbour to the cowardice which shrinks from necessary endurance of it,)
*e–e*48, 49   sees
*f–f*48, 49   has been   *g–g*48, 49   and much of it
*h–h*48, 49   . Because insolvency was formerly treated as if it were necessarily a crime, everything is now done to make it, if possible, not even a misfortune.
*i–i*52, 57   a recent enactment, a partial but very salutary
*j*48, 49   present
*k–k*48, 49   that object, in the present state of the law, is not attained

powerful engine for extracting from the debtor any property which he had concealed or otherwise made away with [l]; and it remains to be shown by experience whether, in[l] depriving creditors of this instrument, the law [m], even as last amended, has furnished them with a[m] sufficient equivalent. [n] But the doctrine, that the law has done all that ought to be expected from it, when it has put the creditors in [o] possession of the property of an insolvent, is in itself a totally inadmissible piece of spurious humanity. It is the business of law to prevent wrong-doing, and not simply to patch up the consequences of it when it has been committed. The law is bound to take care that insolvency shall not be a good pecuniary speculation; that men shall not have the privilege of hazarding other people's property without their knowledge or consent, taking the profits of the enterprise if it is successful, and if it fails throwing the loss upon the [p]rightful[p] owners; [q]and[q] that they shall not find it answer to make themselves unable to pay their just debts, by spending the money of their creditors in personal indulgence. [r]It is admitted[r] that what is technically called fraudulent bankruptcy, the false pretence of inability to pay, [s]is[s], when detected, [t]properly[t] subject to punishment. But does it follow that insolvency is not the consequence of misconduct because the inability to pay may be real? If a man has been a spendthrift, or a gambler, with property on which his creditors had a prior claim, shall he pass scot-free because the mischief is consummated and the money gone? Is there any very material difference [u]in point of morality[u] between this conduct, and those other kinds of dishonesty which go by the names of fraud and embezzlement?

Such cases are not a minority, but a large majority among insolvencies. The statistics of bankruptcy prove the fact. "By far the greater part of all insolvencies arise from notorious misconduct; the proceedings of the Insolvent Debtors Court and of the Bankruptcy Court will prove it. Excessive and unjustifiable overtrading, or most absurd speculation in commodities, merely because the poor speculator 'thought they would get up,' but why he thought so he cannot tell; [v]speculation[v] in hops, in tea, in

[l-l]48, 49   . In

[m-m]48, 49   has not furnished them with any

[n]48   And it is seldom difficult for a dishonest debtor, by an understanding with one or more of his creditors, or by means of pretended creditors set up for the purpose, to abstract a part, perhaps the greatest part, of his assets, from the general fund, through the forms of the law itself. The facility and frequency of such frauds is a subject of much complaint, and their prevention demands a vigorous effort of the legislature, under the guidance of judicious persons practically conversant with the subject. [paragraph]] 49   as 48 . . . frauds are . . . as 48

[o]48   the   [p-p]48, 49   lawful

[q-q]+52, 57, 62, 65, 71   [r-r]48, 49   The humanitarians do not deny

[s-s]48, 49   may reasonably   [t-t]48, 49   be

[u-u]+52, 57, 62, 65, 71   [v-v]Source, 48, 49   speculations

silk, in corn—things with which he is altogether unacquainted; wild and absurd investments in foreign funds, or in joint-stocks; these are among the most innocent causes of bankruptcy."* The experienced and intelligent writer from whom I quote, corroborates his assertion by the testimony of several of the official assignees of the Bankruptcy Court. One of them says, "As far as I can collect from the books and documents furnished by the bankrupts, it seems to me that" in the whole number of cases which occurred during a given time in the court to which he was attached, "fourteen have been ruined by speculations in things with which they were unacquainted; three by *w*neglecting*w* book-keeping; ten by trading beyond their capital and means, and the consequent loss and expense of accommodation-bills; forty-nine by expending more than they could reasonably hope their profits would be, though their business yielded a fair return; none by any general distress, or the falling off of any particular branch of trade." Another of these officers says *x*that, during a period of eighteen months, "*x*fifty-two cases of bankruptcy have come under my care. It is my opinion that thirty-two of these have arisen from an imprudent expenditure, and five partly from that cause, and partly from a pressure on the business in which the bankrupts were employed. Fifteen I attribute to improvident speculations, combined in many instances with an extravagant mode of life."

To these citations the author adds the following statements from his personal means of knowledge *y* . "Many insolvencies are produced by tradesmen's indolence; they keep no books, or at least imperfect ones, which they never balance; they never take stock; they employ servants, if their trade be extensive, whom they are too indolent even to supervise, and then become insolvent. It is not too much to say, that one-half of all the persons engaged in trade, even in London, never take stock at all: they go on year after year without knowing how their affairs stand, and at last, like the child at school, they find to their surprise, but one halfpenny left in their pocket. I will venture to say that not one-fourth of all the persons in the provinces, either manufacturers, tradesmen, or farmers, ever take stock; nor in fact does one-half of them ever keep account-books, deserving any other name than memorandum books. I know sufficient of the concerns of five hundred small tradesmen in the provinces, to be enabled to say, that not one-fifth of them ever take stock, or keep even the most ordinary

*From a volume published in 1845, entitled, "Credit the Life of Commerce," by Mr. J. H. Elliott. [London: Madden and Malcolm, pp. 48–50.]

*w–w*Source, 48, 49 neglected
*x–x*Source, 48, 49, 52, 57 , "The new Court has been open upwards of eighteen months, during which period
*y*48, 49 , which are considerable

accounts. I am prepared to say of such tradesmen, from carefully prepared tables, giving every advantage where there has been any doubt as to the causes of their insolvency, that where nine happen from extravagance or dishonesty, one" at most "may be referred to misfortune alone."*

Is it rational to expect among the trading classes any high sense of justice, honour, or integrity, ᶻifᶻ the law enables men who act in this manner to shuffle off the consequences of their misconduct upon those who have been so unfortunate as to trust them; and practically proclaims that it looks upon insolvency thus produced, as a "misfortune," not an offence?

It is, of course, not denied, that insolvencies do arise from causes beyond the control of the debtor, and that, in many more cases, his culpability is not of a high order; and the law ought to make a distinction in favour of such cases, but not without a searching investigation; nor should the case ever be let go without having ascertained, in the most complete manner practicable, not the fact of insolvency only, but the cause of it. To have been trusted with money or money's worth, and to have lost or spent it, is *primâ facie* evidence of something wrong: and it is not for the creditor to prove, which he cannot do in one case out of ten, that there has been criminality, but for the debtor to rebut the presumption, by laying open the whole state of his affairs, and showing either that there has been no misconduct, or that the misconduct has been of an excusable kind. If he fail in this, he ought never to be dismissed without a punishment proportioned to the degree of blame which seems justly imputable to him; which punishment, however, might be shortened or mitigated in proportion as he appeared likely to exert himself in repairing the injury done.

It is a common argument with those who approve a relaxed system of insolvency laws, that credit, except in the great operations of commerce, is an evil; and that to deprive creditors of legal redress is a judicious means of preventing credit from being given. That which is given by retail dealers to unproductive consumers is, no doubt, to the excess to which it is carried, a considerable evil. This, however, is only true of large, and especially of long, credits; for there is credit whenever goods are not paid for before they quit the shop, or, at least, the custody of the seller; and there would be much inconvenience in putting an end to this sort of credit. But a large proportion of the debts on which insolvency laws take effect, are those due by small tradesmen to the dealers who supply them: and on no class of debts does the demoralization occasioned by ᵃa badᵃ state of the law, operate more perniciously. These are commercial credits, which no one

*Pp. 50–1.

ᶻ⁻ᶻ48, 49   when
ᵃ⁻ᵃ48, 49   the present

wishes to see curtailed; their existence is of great importance to the general industry of the country, and to numbers of honest, well-conducted persons of small means, to whom it would be a *h*great*h* injury that they should be prevented from obtaining the accommodation they need, and would not abuse, through the omission of the law to provide just remedies against dishonest or reckless borrowers.

But though it were granted that retail transactions, on any footing but that of ready money payment, are an evil, and their entire suppression a fit object for legislation to aim at; a worse mode of compassing that object could scarcely be invented, than to permit those who have been trusted by others to cheat and rob them with impunity. The law does not *c*generally*c* select the vices of mankind as the appropriate instrument for inflicting chastisement on the comparatively innocent *d*. When*d* it seeks to discourage any course of action, it does so by applying inducements of its own, not by outlawing those who act in the manner it deems objectionable, and letting loose the predatory instincts of the worthless part of mankind to feed upon them. If a man has committed murder, the law *e*condemns*e* him to death; but it does not promise impunity to anybody who may kill him for the sake of taking his purse. The offence of believing another's word, even rashly, is not so heinous that for the sake of discouraging it, the spectacle should be brought home to every door, of triumphant rascality, with the law on its side, mocking the victims it has made. This pestilent example *f*has been*f* very widely exhibited since the relaxation of the insolvency laws. It is idle to expect that, even by absolutely depriving creditors of all legal redress, the kind of credit which is considered objectionable would really be very much checked. Rogues and swindlers are still an exception among mankind, and people will go on trusting each other's promises. Large dealers, in abundant business, would refuse credit, as many of them already do: but in the eager competition of a great town, *g*or the dependent position of a village shopkeeper,*g* what can be expected from the tradesman to whom a single customer is of importance, the beginner, perhaps, who is striving to get into business? He will take the risk, even if it were still greater; he is ruined if he cannot sell his goods, and he can but be ruined if he is defrauded. Nor does it avail to say, that he ought to make proper inquiries, and ascertain the character of those to whom he supplies goods on trust. In some of the most flagrant cases of profligate debtors which have come

*b–b*48, 49   grievous
c–c+52, 57, 62, 65, 71
*d–d*48, 49, 52, 57, 62   : when
*e–e*48, 49   puts
*f–f*48, 49   is already
g–g+65, 71

before the Bankruptcy Court, the swindler had been able to give, and had given, excellent references.*

*The following extracts from the French Code de Commerce, (the translation is that of Mr. [Cecil] Fane [*Bankruptcy Reform.* London: Sweet, 1838, pp. 44–7],) show the great extent to which the just distinctions are made, and the proper investigations provided for, by French law. The word *banqueroute*, which can only be translated by bankruptcy, is, however, confined in France to *culpable* insolvency, which is distinguished into *simple* bankruptcy and *fraudulent* bankruptcy. The following are cases of simple bankruptcy:—

"Every insolvent who, in the investigation of his affairs, shall appear chargeable with one or more of the following offences, shall be proceeded against as a simple bankrupt.

"If his house expenses, which he is bound to enter regularly in a [Source, 48, 49, 52 his] day-book, appear excessive.

"If he has spent considerable sums at play, or in operations of pure hazard.

"If it shall appear that he has borrowed largely, or resold merchandize at a loss, or below the current price, after it appeared by his last account-taking that his debts exceeded his assets by one-half.

"If he has issued negotiable securities to three times the amount of his available assets, according to his last account-taking.

"The following *may* also be proceeded against as simple bankrupts:—

"He who has not declared his own insolvency in the manner prescribed by law:

"He who has not come in and surrendered within the time limited, having no legitimate excuse for his absence:

"He who either produces no books at all, or produces such as have been irregularly kept, and this although the irregularities may not indicate fraud."

The penalty for "simple bankruptcy" is imprisonment for a term of not less than one month, nor more than two years. The following are cases of fraudulent bankruptcy, of which the punishment is *travaux forcés* (the galleys) for a term:

"If he has attempted to account for his property by fictitious expenses and losses, or if he does not fully account for all his receipts:

"If he has fraudulently concealed any sum of money or any debt due to him, or any merchandize or other movables:

"If he has made fraudulent sales or gifts of his property:

"If he has allowed fictitious debts to be proved against his estate:

"If he has been entrusted with property, either merely to keep, or with special directions as to its use, and has nevertheless appropriated it to his own use: [48, 49, 52, 57, 62 " (for such acts of peculation by trustees there is generally in England only a civil remedy, and that too through the Court of Chancery:)]

"If he has purchased real property in a borrowed name:

"If he has concealed his books.

"The following *may* also be proceeded against in a similar way:—

"He who has not kept books, or whose books shall not exhibit his real situation as regards his debts and credits:

"He who, having obtained a protection (*sauf-conduit*), shall not have duly attended."

These various provisions relate only to commercial insolvency. The laws in regard to ordinary debts are considerably more rigorous to the debtor.

CHAPTER X

Of Interferences of Government
Grounded on Erroneous Theories

§ 1. [*Doctrine of Protection to Native Industry*] From the necessary functions of government, and the effects produced on the economical interests of society by their good or ill discharge, we proceed to the functions which belong to what I have termed *[a]*, for want of a better designation,*[a]* the optional class; those which are sometimes assumed by governments and sometimes not, and which it is not unanimously admitted that they ought to exercise.

Before entering on the general principles of the question, it will be advisable to clear from our path all those cases, in which government interference works ill because grounded on false views of the subject interfered with. Such cases have no connexion with any theory respecting the proper limits of interference. There are some things with which governments ought not to meddle, and other things with which they ought; but whether right or wrong in itself, the interference must work for ill, if government, not understanding the subject which it meddles with, meddles to bring about a result which would be mischievous. We will therefore begin by passing in review various false theories, which have from time to time formed the ground of acts of government more or less economically injurious.

Former writers on political economy have found it needful to devote much trouble and space to this department of their subject. It has now happily become possible, at least in our own country, greatly to abridge this purely negative part of our discussions. The false theories of political economy which have done so much mischief in times past, are entirely discredited among all who have not lagged behind the general progress of opinion; and few of the enactments which were once grounded on those theories still help to deform the statute-book. As the principles on which their condemnation rests have been fully set forth in other parts of this Treatise, we may here content ourselves with a few brief indications.

Of these false theories, the most notable is the doctrine of Protection to

[a-a]+49, 52, 57, 62, 65, 71

Native Industry; a phrase meaning the prohibition, or the discouragement by heavy duties, of such foreign commodities as are capable of being produced at home. If the theory involved in this system had been correct, the practical conclusions grounded on it would not have been unreasonable. The theory was, that to buy things produced at home was a national benefit, and the introduction of foreign commodities generally a national loss. It being at the same time evident that the interest of the consumer is to buy foreign commodities in preference to domestic whenever they are either cheaper or better, the interest of the consumer appeared in this respect to be contrary to the public interest; he was certain, if left to his own inclinations, to do what according to the theory was injurious to the public.

It was shown, however, in our analysis of the effects of international trade, as it had been often shown by former writers, that the importation of foreign commodities, in the common course of traffic, never takes place, except when it is, economically speaking, a national good, by causing the same amount of commodities to be obtained at a smaller cost of labour and capital to the country. To prohibit, therefore, this importation, or impose duties which prevent it, is to render the labour and capital of the country less efficient in production than they would otherwise be; and compel a waste, of the difference between the labour and capital necessary for the home production of the commodity, and that which is required for producing the things with which it can be purchased from abroad. The amount of national loss thus occasioned is measured by the excess of the price at which the commodity is produced over that at which it could be imported. In the case of manufactured goods, the whole difference between the two prices is absorbed in indemnifying the producers for waste of labour, or of the capital which supports that labour. Those who are supposed to be benefited, namely, the makers of the protected articles, (unless they form an exclusive company, and have a monopoly against their own countrymen as well as against foreigners,) do not obtain higher profits than other people. All is sheer loss, to the country as well as to the consumer. When the protected article is a product of agriculture—the waste of labour not being incurred on the whole produce, but only on what may be called the last instalment of it—the extra price is only in part an indemnity for waste, the remainder being a tax paid to the landlords.

The restrictive and prohibitory policy was originally grounded on what is called the Mercantile System, which representing the advantage of foreign trade to consist solely in bringing money into the country, gave artificial encouragement to exportation of goods, and discountenanced their importation. The only exceptions to the system were those required by the system itself. The materials and instruments of production were the subjects of a contrary policy, directed however to the same end; they were freely imported, and not permitted to be exported, in order that manufacturers, being more cheaply supplied with the requisites of manufacture, might be able to sell cheaper, and therefore to export more largely. For a similar reason, importation was *allowed* and even favoured, when confined to the productions of countries which were supposed to take from *the country* still more than *it* took from them, thus enriching *it* by a favourable balance of trade. As part of the same system, colonies were founded, for the supposed advantage of compelling them to buy our commodities, or at all events not to buy those of any other country: in return for which restriction, we were generally willing to come under an equivalent obligation with respect to the staple productions of the colonists. The consequences of the theory were pushed so far, that it was not unusual even to give bounties on exportation, and induce foreigners to buy from us rather than from other countries, by a cheapness which we artificially produced, by paying part of the price for them out of our own taxes. This is a stretch beyond the point yet reached by any private tradesman in his competition for business. No shopkeeper, I should think, ever made a practice of bribing customers by selling goods to them at a permanent loss, making it up to himself from other funds in his possession.

The principle of the Mercantile Theory is now given up even by writers and governments who still cling to the restrictive system. Whatever hold that system has over men's minds, independently of the private interests *f* exposed to real or apprehended loss by its abandonment, is derived from fallacies other than the old notion of the benefits of heaping up money in the country. The most effective of these is the specious plea of employing our own countrymen and our national industry, instead of feeding and supporting the industry of foreigners. The answer to this, from the principles laid down in former chapters, is evident. Without reverting to the fundamental theorem discussed in an early part of the present treatise,* respecting the nature and sources of employment for labour, it is sufficient to say, what has usually been said by the advocates of free trade, that the alternative is not between employing our own *people* and foreigners, but between employing one class and another of our own *people*. The imported commodity is always paid for, directly or indirectly, with the produce of our own industry: that industry being, at the same time rendered more productive, since, with the same labour and outlay, we are enabled to possess ourselves of a greater quantity of the article. Those who have not

*Supra, vol. i. pp. 78 et seqq.

*b–b*48, 49	permitted		
*c–c*48, 49	us	*d–d*48, 49	we
*e–e*48, 49	the country	*f*48, 49	which would be
*g–g*48, 49	country-people	*h–h*48, 49	country-people

well considered the subject are apt to suppose that our exporting an
equivalent in our own produce, for the foreign articles we consume, depends
on contingencies—on the consent of foreign countries to make some
corresponding relaxation of their own restrictions, or on the question
whether those from whom we buy are induced by that circumstance to buy
more from us; and that, if these things, or things equivalent to them, do
not happen, the payment must be made in money. Now, in the first place,
there is nothing more objectionable in a money payment than in payment
by any other medium, if the state of the market makes it the most advantageous remittance; and the money itself was first acquired, and would
again be replenished, by the export of an equivalent value of our own
products. But, in the next place, a very short interval of paying in money
would so lower prices as either to stop a part of the importation, or raise
up a foreign demand for our produce, sufficient to pay for the imports. I
grant that this disturbance of the equation of international demand would be
in some degree to our disadvantage, in the purchase of other imported
articles; and that a country which prohibits some foreign commodities,
does, *cæteris paribus*, obtain those which it does not prohibit, at a less
price than it would otherwise have to pay. To express the same thing in
other words; a country which destroys or prevents altogether certain
branches of foreign trade, thereby annihilating a general gain to the world,
which would be shared in some proportion between itself and other countries—does, in some circumstances, draw to itself, at the expense of
foreigners, a larger share than would else belong to it of the gain arising
from that portion of its foreign trade which it suffers to subsist. But even
this it can only be enabled to do, if foreigners do not maintain equivalent
prohibitions or restrictions against its commodities. In any case, the justice
or expediency of destroying one of two gains, in order to engross a rather
larger share of the other, does not require much discussion: the gain, too,
which is destroyed, being, in proportion to the magnitude of the transactions, the larger of the two, since it is the one which capital, left to itself,
is supposed to seek by preference.

   Defeated as a general theory, the Protectionist doctrine finds support in
some particular cases, from considerations which, when really in point,
involve greater interests than mere saving of labour; the interests of
national subsistence and of national defence. The discussions on the Corn
Laws have familiarized everybody with the plea, that we ought to be
independent of foreigners for the food of the people; and the Navigation
Laws ʲwereʲ grounded, in theory and profession, on the necessity of keeping
up a "nursery of seamen" for the navy. On this last subject I at once admit,
that the object is worth the sacrifice; and that a country exposed to invasion

ʲ⁻ʲ48, 49   are

by sea, if it cannot otherwise have sufficient ships and sailors of its own to secure the means of manning on an emergency an adequate fleet, is quite right in obtaining those means, even at ᶨanᶨ economical sacrifice in point of cheapness of transport. When the English Navigation Laws were enacted, the Dutch, from their maritime skill and their low rate of profit at home, were able to carry for other nations, England included, at cheaper rates than those nations could carry for themselves: which placed all other countries at a great comparative disadvantage in obtaining experienced seamen for their ships of war. The Navigation Laws, by which this deficiency was remedied, and at the same time a blow struck against the maritime power of a nation with which England was then frequently engaged in hostilities, were probably, though economically disadvantageous, politically expedient. But English ships and sailors can now navigate as cheaply as those of any other country; maintaining at least an equal competition with the other maritime nations even in their own trade. The ends which may once have justified Navigation Laws, require them no longer, and ᵏaffordedᵏ no reason for maintaining this invidious exception to the general rule of free trade.

With regard to subsistence, the plea of the Protectionists has been so often and so triumphantly met, that it requires little notice here. That country is the most steadily as well as the most abundantly supplied with food, which draws its supplies from the largest surface. It is ridiculous to found a general system of policy on so ᶧimprobableᶧ a danger as that of being at war with all the nations of the world at once; or to suppose that, even if inferior at sea, a whole country could be blockaded like a town, or that the growers of food in other countries would not be as anxious not to lose an advantageous market, as we should be not to be deprived of their corn. On the subject, however, of subsistence, there is one point which deserves more ᵐespecialᵐ consideration. In cases of actual or apprehended scarcity, many countries of Europe are accustomed to stop the exportation of food. Is this, or not, sound policy? There can be no doubt that in the present state of international morality, a people cannot, any more than an individual, be blamed for not starving itself to feed others. But if the greatest amount of good to mankind on the whole, were the end aimed at in the maxims of international conduct, such collective churlishness would certainly be condemned by them. Suppose that in ordinary circumstances the trade in food were perfectly free, so that the price in one country could not habitually exceed that in any other by more than the cost of carriage, together with a moderate profit to the importer. A general scarcity ensues, affecting all countries, but in unequal degrees. If the price rose in one

ᶨ⁻ᶨ48, 49   some
ᶧ⁻ᶧ48, 49   chimerical

ᵏ⁻ᵏ48, 49   there seems
ᵐ⁻ᵐ48, 49, 52   special

country more than in others, it would be a proof that in that country the scarcity was severest, and that by permitting food to go freely thither from any other country, it would be spared from a less urgent necessity to relieve a greater. When the interests, therefore, of all countries are considered, free exportation is desirable. To the exporting country considered separately, it may, at least on the particular occasion, be an inconvenience: but taking into account that the country which is now the giver, will in some future season be the receiver, and the one that is benefited by the freedom, I cannot but think that even to the apprehension of food rioters it might be made apparent, that in such cases they should do to others what they would wish done to themselves.

In countries in which the [n]Protection theory[n] is declining, but not yet [o] given up, such as the United States, a doctrine has come into notice which is a sort of compromise between free trade and restriction, namely, that protection for protection's sake is improper, but that there is nothing objectionable in having as much protection as may incidentally result from a tariff framed solely for revenue. Even in England, regret is sometimes expressed that a "moderate fixed duty" was not preserved on corn, on account of the revenue it would yield. Independently, however, of the general impolicy of taxes on the necessaries of life, this doctrine overlooks the fact, that revenue is received only on the quantity imported, but that the tax is paid on the entire quantity consumed. To make the public pay much that the treasury may receive a little, is [p]not an[p] eligible mode of obtaining a revenue. In the case of manufactured articles the doctrine involves a palpable inconsistency. The object of the duty as a means of revenue, is inconsistent with its affording, even incidentally, any protection. It can only operate as protection in so far as it prevents importation; and to whatever degree it prevents importation, it affords no revenue.

The only case in which, on mere principles of political economy, protecting duties can be defensible, is when they are imposed temporarily (especially in a young and rising nation) in hopes of naturalizing a foreign industry, in itself perfectly suitable to the circumstances of the country. The superiority of one country over another in a branch of production, often arises only from having begun it sooner. There may be no inherent advantage on one part, or disadvantage on the other, but only a present superiority of acquired skill and experience. A country which has this skill and experience yet to acquire, may in other respects be better adapted to the production than those which were earlier in the field: and besides, it is a just remark [q]of Mr. Rae[q], that nothing has a greater tendency to promote

[n-n]48, 49, 52, 57, 62, 65 system of Protection
[o]48, 49, 52, 57, 62, 65 wholly
[p-p]48, 49, 52, 57, 62 no
[q-q]+62, 65, 71

improvements in any branch of production, than its trial under a new set of conditions. But it cannot be expected that individuals should, at their own risk, or rather to their certain loss, introduce a new manufacture, and bear the burthen of carrying it on until the producers have been educated up to the level of those with whom the processes are traditional. A protecting duty, continued for a reasonable time, *might* sometimes be the least inconvenient mode in which the nation can tax itself for the support of such an experiment. But *it is essential that* the protection should be confined to cases in which there is good ground of assurance that the industry which it fosters will after a time be able to dispense with it; nor should the domestic producers ever be allowed to expect that it will be continued to them beyond the time *t* necessary for a fair trial of what they are capable of accomplishing.

*The only writer, of any reputation as a political economist, who now adheres to the Protectionist doctrine, Mr. H. C. Carey, rests its defence, in an economic point of view, principally on two reasons. One is, the great saving in cost of carriage, consequent on producing commodities at or very near to the place where they are to be consumed. The whole of the cost of carriage, both on the commodities imported and on those exported in exchange for them, he regards as a direct burthen on the producers, and not, as is obviously the truth, on the consumers. On whomsoever it falls, it is, without doubt, a burthen on the industry of the world. But it is obvious (and that Mr. Carey does not see it, is one of the many surprising things in his book) that the burthen is only borne for a more than equivalent advantage. If the commodity is bought in a foreign country with domestic produce in spite of the double cost of carriage, the fact proves that, heavy as that cost may be, the saving in cost of production outweighs it, and the collective labour of the country is on the whole better remunerated than if the article were produced at home. Cost of carriage is a natural protecting duty, which free trade has no power to abrogate: and unless America gained more by obtaining her manufactures through the medium of her corn and cotton than she loses in cost of carriage, the capital employed in producing corn and cotton in annually increased quantities for the foreign market, would turn to manufactures instead. The natural *advantages* attending a mode of industry in which there is less cost of carriage to pay, can at most be only a justification for a temporary and merely tentative protection. The expenses of production being always greatest at first, it may happen that the home production, though really the most advantageous, may not become so until after a certain duration of pecuniary loss, which

r–r48, 49, 52, 57, 62, 65   will
s–s+71
u–u921+65, 71

t48, 49   strictly
v–v65   advantage

it is not to be expected that private speculators should incur in order that their successors may be benefited by their ruin. I have therefore conceded that in a new country a temporary protecting duty may sometimes be economically defensible; on condition, however, that it be strictly limited in point of time, and provision be made that during the latter part of its existence it be on a gradually decreasing scale. Such temporary protection is of the same nature as a patent, and should be governed by similar conditions.

The remaining argument of Mr. Carey in support of the economic benefits of Protectionism, applies only to countries whose exports consist of agricultural produce. He argues, that by a trade of this description they actually send away their soil: the distant consumers not giving back to the land of the country, as home consumers would do, the fertilizing elements which they abstract from it. This argument deserves attention on account of the physical truth on which it is founded; a truth which has only lately come to be understood, but which is henceforth destined to be a permanent element in the thoughts of statesmen, as it must always have been in the destinies of nations. To the question of Protectionism, however, it is irrelevant. That the immense growth of raw produce in America to be consumed in Europe, is progressively exhausting the soil of the Eastern, and even of the older Western States, and that both are already far less productive than formerly, is credible in itself, even if no one bore witness to it. But what I have already said respecting cost of carriage, is true also of the cost of manuring. Free trade does not compel America to export corn: she would cease to do so if it ceased to be to her advantage. As, then, she would not persist in exporting raw produce and importing manufactures, any longer than the labour she saved by doing so exceeded what the carriage cost her, so when it became necessary for her to replace in the soil the elements of fertility which she had sent away, if the saving in cost of production were more than equivalent to the cost of carriage and of manure together, manure would be imported; and if not, the export of corn would cease. It is evident that one of these two things would already have taken place, if there had not been near at hand a constant succession of new soils, not yet exhausted of their fertility, the cultivation of which enables her, whether judiciously or not, to postpone the question of manure. As soon as it no longer answers better to break up new soils than to manure the old, America will either become a regular importer of manure, or will, without protecting duties, grow corn for herself only, and manufacturing for herself, will make her manure, as Mr. Carey desires, at home.*

*[65] To this Mr. Carey would reply (indeed he has already so replied in advance) that of all commodities manure is the least susceptible of being conveyed to a distance. This is true of sewage, and of stable manure, but not true of

For these obvious reasons, I hold Mr. Carey's economic arguments for Protectionism to be totally invalid. The economic, however, is far from being the strongest point of his case. American Protectionists often reason extremely ill; but it is an injustice to them to suppose that their Protectionist creed rests upon nothing superior to an economic blunder. Many of them have been led to it, much more by consideration for the higher interests of humanity, than by purely economic reasons. They, and Mr. Carey at their head, deem it a necessary condition of human improvement that towns should abound; that men should combine their labour, by means of interchange—with near neighbours, with people of pursuits, capacities, and mental cultivation different from their own, sufficiently close at hand for mutual sharpening of wits and enlarging of ideas—rather than with people on the opposite side of the globe. They believe that a nation all engaged in the same, or nearly the same, pursuit—a nation all agricultural—cannot attain a high state of civilization and culture. And for this there is a great foundation of reason. If the difficulty can be overcome, the United States, with their free institutions, their universal schooling, and their omnipresent press, are the people to do it; but whether this is possible or not is still a problem. So far, however, as it is an object to check the excessive dispersion of the population, Mr. Wakefield has pointed out a better way; to modify the existing method of disposing of the unoccupied lands, by raising the price, instead of lowering it, or giving away the land gratuitously, as is largely done since the passing of the Homestead Act. To cut the knot in Mr. Carey's fashion, by Protectionism, it would be necessary that Ohio and Michigan should be protected against Massachusetts as well as against England: for the manufactories of New England, no more than those of the old country, accomplish his desideratum of bringing a manufacturing population to the doors of the Western farmer. Boston and New York do not supply the want of local towns to the Western prairies, any better than Manchester; and it is as difficult to get back the manure from the one place as from the other.[u]

---

the ingredients to which those manures owe their efficiency. These, on the contrary, are chiefly substances containing great fertilizing power in small bulk; substances of which the human body requires but a small quantity, and hence peculiarly susceptible of being imported; the mineral alkalies and the phosphates. The question indeed mainly concerns the phosphates, for of the alkalies, soda is procurable everywhere; while potass, being one of the constituents of granite and the other feldspathic rocks, exists in many subsoils, by whose progressive decomposition it is renewed, a large quantity also being brought down in the deposits of rivers. As for the phosphates, they, in the very convenient form of pulverized bones, are a regular article of commerce, largely imported into England; as they are sure to be into any country where the conditions of industry make it worth while to pay the price.

There is only one part of the Protectionist scheme which requires any further notice: its policy towards colonies, and foreign dependencies; that of compelling them to trade exclusively with the dominant country. A country which thus secures to itself an extra foreign demand for its commodities, undoubtedly gives itself some advantage in the distribution of the general gains of the commercial world. Since, however, it causes the industry and capital of the colony to be diverted from channels, which are proved to be the most productive, inasmuch as they are those into which industry and capital spontaneously tend to flow; there is a loss, on the whole, to the productive powers of the world, and the mother country does not gain so much as she makes the colony lose. If, therefore, the mother country refuses to acknowledge any reciprocity of obligation, she imposes a tribute on the colony in an indirect mode, greatly more oppressive and injurious than the direct. But if, with a more equitable spirit, she submits herself to corresponding restrictions for the benefit of the colony, the result of the whole transaction is the ridiculous one, that each party loses much, in order that the other may gain a little.

§ 2. [*Usury Laws*] Next to the system of Protection, among mischievous interferences with the spontaneous course of industrial transactions, may be noticed certain interferences with contracts. One instance is that of the Usury Laws. These originated in a religious prejudice against receiving interest on money, derived from that fruitful source of mischief in modern Europe, the attempted adaptation to Christianity of doctrines and precepts drawn from the Jewish law. In Mahomedan nations the receiving of interest is formally interdicted, and rigidly abstained from: and Sismondi has noticed, as one among the causes of the industrial inferiority of the Catholic, compared with the Protestant parts of Europe, that the Catholic Church in the middle ages gave its sanction to the same prejudice; which subsists, impaired but not destroyed, wherever that religion is acknowledged. Where law or conscientious scruples prevent lending at interest, the capital which belongs to persons not in business is lost to productive purposes, or can be applied to them only in peculiar circumstances of personal connexion, or by a subterfuge. Industry is thus limited to the capital of the undertakers, and to what they can borrow from persons not bound by the same laws or religion as themselves. In Mussulman countries the bankers and money dealers are either Hindoos, Armenians, or Jews.

In more improved countries, legislation no longer discountenances the receipt of an equivalent for money lent; but it *a*has everywhere interfered*a* with the free agency of the lender and borrowers, by fixing a legal limit to the rate of interest, and making the receipt of more than the appointed

*a–a*48, 49, 52   everywhere interferes

maximum a penal offence. This restriction, though approved by Adam Smith, has been condemned by all enlightened persons since the triumphant onslaught made upon it by Bentham in his "Letters on Usury," which may still be referred to as the best extant writing on the subject.

Legislators may enact and maintain Usury Laws from one of two motives: ideas of public policy, or concern for the interest of the parties *b*in*b* the contract; in this case, of one party only, the borrower. As a matter of policy, the notion may possibly be, that it is for the general good that interest should be low. *c* It is *d*however*d* a misapprehension of the causes which influence commercial transactions, to suppose that the rate of interest is really made lower by law, than it would be made by the spontaneous play of supply and demand. If the competition of borrowers, left unrestrained, would raise the rate of interest to six per cent, this proves that at five there would be a greater demand for loans, than there is capital in the market to supply. If the law in these circumstances permits no interest beyond five per cent, there will be some lenders, who not choosing to disobey the law, and not being in a condition to employ their capital otherwise, will content themselves with the legal rate: but others, finding that in a season of pressing demand, more may be made of their capital by other means than they are permitted to make by lending it, will not lend it at all; and the loanable capital, already too small for the demand, will be still further diminished. Of the disappointed candidates there will be many at such periods, who must have their necessities supplied at any price, and these will readily find a third section of lenders, who will not be averse to join in a violation of the law, either by circuitous transactions partaking of the nature of fraud, or by relying on the honour of the borrower. The extra expense of the roundabout mode of proceeding, and an equivalent for the risk of non-payment and of legal penalties, must be paid by the borrower, over and above the extra interest which would *e* have been required of him by the general state of the market. The laws which were intended to lower the price paid by him for pecuniary accommodation, end thus in greatly increasing it. These laws have also a directly demoralizing tendency. Knowing the difficulty of detecting an illegal pecuniary transaction between two persons, in which no third person is involved, so long as it is the interest of both to keep the secret, legislators have adopted the expedient of tempting the borrower to become the informer, by making the annulment of the debt a part of the penalty for the offence; thus rewarding men for *f*first*f*

*b–b*48, 49, 52   to

*c*48, 49   It is for the good certainly of borrowers. For preferring, however, their advantage to that of lenders, it would be difficult to give any better reason than that in most countries the governing classes are borrowers.

*d–d*48, 49   besides

*e*48, 49, 52   at any rate   *f–f*+71

obtaining the property of others by false promises, and then not only refusing payment, but invoking legal penalties on those who have helped them in their need. The moral sense of mankind very rightly infamizes those who resist an otherwise just claim on the ground of usury, and tolerates such a plea only when resorted to as the best legal defence available against an attempt really considered as partaking of fraud or extortion. But this very severity of public opinion renders the enforcement of the laws so difficult, and the infliction of the penalties so rare, that when it does occur it merely victimizes an individual, and has no effect on general practice.

In so far as the motive of the restriction may be supposed to be, not public policy, but regard for the interest of the borrower, it would be difficult to point out any case in which such tenderness on the legislator's part is more misplaced. A person of sane mind, and of the age at which persons are legally competent to conduct their own concerns, must be presumed to be a sufficient guardian of his pecuniary interests. If he may sell an estate, or grant a release, or assign away all his property, without control from the law, it seems very unnecessary that the only bargain which he cannot make without its intermeddling, should be a loan of money. The law seems to presume that the money-lender, dealing with necessitous persons, can take advantage of their necessities, and exact conditions limited only by his own pleasure. It might be so if there were only one money-lender within reach. But when there is the whole monied capital of a wealthy community to resort to, no borrower is placed under any disadvantage in the market merely by the urgency of his need. If he cannot borrow at the interest paid by other people, it must be because he cannot give such good security: and competition will limit the extra demand to a fair equivalent for the risk of his proving insolvent. Though the law intends favour to the borrower, it is to him above all that injustice is, in this case, done by it. What can be more unjust than that a person who cannot give perfectly good security, should be prevented from borrowing of persons who are willing to lend money to him, by their not being permitted to receive the rate of interest which would be a just equivalent for their risk? Through the mistaken kindness of the law, he must either go without the money which is perhaps necessary to save him from much greater losses, or be driven to expedients of a far more ruinous description, which the law either has not found it possible, or has not happened, to interdict.

Adam Smith rather hastily expressed the opinion, that only two kinds of persons, "prodigals and projectors,"[*] could require to borrow money at more than the market rate of interest. He should have included all persons who are in any pecuniary difficulties, however temporary their necessities

[*Smith, *Wealth of Nations*, Vol. II, p. 409.]

may be. It may happen to any person in business, to be disappointed of the resources on which he had calculated for meeting some engagement, the non-fulfilment of which on a fixed day would be bankruptcy. In periods of commercial difficulty, this is the condition of many prosperous mercantile firms, who become competitors for the small amount of disposable capital which, in a time of general distrust, the owners are willing to part with. ^{g}Under the English usury laws, now happily abolished^g, the limitations imposed by those laws were felt as a most serious aggravation of every commercial crisis. Merchants who could have obtained the aid they required at an interest of seven or eight per cent for short periods, were obliged to give 20 or 30 ^{h}per cent^h, or to resort to forced sales of goods at a still greater loss. Experience having obtruded these evils on the notice of Parliament, the sort of compromise took place, of which English legislation affords so many instances, and which helps to make our laws and policy the mass of inconsistency that they are. ^{i}The law was reformed^i as a person reforms a tight shoe, who cuts a hole in it where it pinches hardest, and continues to wear it. Retaining the erroneous principle as a general rule, Parliament allowed an exception in the case in which the practical mischief was most flagrant. It left the usury laws unrepealed, but exempted bills of exchange, of not more than three months date, from their operation. Some years afterwards the laws were repealed in regard to all other contracts, but left in force as to all those which relate to land. Not a particle of reason could be given for making this extraordinary distinction: but the "agricultural mind" was of opinion that the interest on mortgages, though it hardly ever ^{j}came^j up to the permitted point, would come up to a still higher point; and the ^{k}usury^k laws ^{l}were^l maintained that the landlords ^{m}might^m as they ^{n}thought^n, be enabled to borrow below the market rate, as the corn-laws were ^{o} kept up that the same class might be able to sell corn above the market rate. The modesty of the pretension ^{p}was^p quite worthy of the intelligence which ^{q}could^q think that the end aimed at ^{r}was^r in any way forwarded by the means used.

With regard to the "prodigals and projectors" spoken of by Adam Smith; no law can prevent a prodigal from ruining himself, unless it lays him or his property under actual restraint, ^{s}according to the unjustifiable practice of the Roman Law and some of the Continental systems founded on it^s. The

---

$^{g-g}$48, 49, 52, 57, 62   Up to the relaxation of the usury laws a few years ago
$^{h-h}$+52, 57, 62, 65, 71
$^{i-i}$48, 49   We reformed the laws $^{j-j}$48, 49, 52, 57   comes
$^{k-k}$+52, 57, 62, 65, 71 $^{l-l}$48, 49, 52   are
$^{m-m}$48, 49, 52   may $^{n-n}$48, 49, 52   think
^{o}48, 49   so long $^{p-p}$48, 49, 52   is
$^{q-q}$48, 49, 52   can $^{r-r}$48, 49, 52   is
$^{s-s}$48, 49   which, on the requisition of his relations, the Roman Law and some of the Continental systems founded on it give power in certain cases to do

only effect of usury laws upon a prodigal, is to make his ruin rather more expeditious, by driving him to a disreputable class of money-dealers, and rendering the conditions more onerous by the extra risk created by the law. As for projectors, *(a term, in its unfavourable sense, rather unfairly applied to every person who has a project)*; such laws may put a veto upon the prosecution of the most promising enterprise, when planned, as it generally is, by a person who does not possess capital adequate to its successful completion. Many of the greatest improvements were at first looked shyly on by capitalists, and had to wait long before they found one sufficiently adventurous to be the first in a new path: many years elapsed before Stephenson could convince even the enterprising mercantile public of Liverpool and Manchester, of the advantage of substituting railways for turnpike roads; and plans on which great labour and large sums have been expended with little visible result, (the epoch in their progress when predictions of failure are *u* most rife,) may be indefinitely suspended, or altogether dropped, and the outlay all lost, if, when the original funds are exhausted, the law will not allow more to be raised on the terms on which people are willing to expose it to the chances of an enterprise not yet secure of success.

§ 3. [*Attempts to regulate the prices of commodities*] Loans are not the only kind of contract, of which governments have thought themselves qualified to regulate the conditions better than the persons interested. There is scarcely any commodity which they have not, at some place or time, endeavoured to make either dearer or cheaper than it would be if left to itself. The most plausible case for artificially cheapening a commodity, is that of food. The desirableness of the object is in this case undeniable. But since the average price of food, like that of other things, conforms to the cost of production, with the addition of the usual profit; if this price is not expected by the farmer, he will, unless compelled by law, produce no more than he requires for his own consumption: and the law, therefore, if absolutely determined to have food cheaper, must substitute, for the ordinary motives to cultivation, a system of penalties. If it shrinks from doing this, it has no resource but that of taxing the whole nation, to give a bounty or premium to the grower or importer of corn, thus giving everybody cheap bread at the expense of all: in reality a largess to those who do not pay taxes, at the expense of those who do; one of the *a* forms of a practice essentially bad, that of converting the working classes into unworking classes by making them a present of subsistence.

It is not however so much the general or average price of food, as its

t-t48, 49, 52, 57, 62, 65   a term ... *as* 71 ... project
*u*48, 49   sure to be the   *a*48, 49   worst

occasional high price in times of emergency, which governments have studied to reduce. In some cases, as for example the famous "maximum" of the revolutionary government of 1793, the compulsory regulation was an attempt by the ruling powers to counteract the necessary consequences of their own acts; to scatter an indefinite abundance of the circulating medium with one hand, and keep down prices with the other; a thing manifestly impossible under any régime except one of unmitigated terror. In case of actual scarcity, governments are often urged, as they were in the Irish emergency of 1847, to take measures of some sort for moderating the price of food. But the price of a thing cannot be raised by deficiency of supply, beyond what is sufficient to make a corresponding reduction of the consumption; and if a government prevents this reduction from being brought about by a rise of price, there remains no mode of effecting it unless by taking possession of all the food, and serving it out in rations, as in a besieged town. In a real scarcity, nothing can afford general relief, except a determination by the richer classes to diminish their own consumption. If they buy and consume their usual quantity of food, and content themselves with giving money, they do no good. The price is forced up until the poorest competitors have no longer the means of competing, and the privation of food is thrown exclusively upon the indigent, the other classes being only affected pecuniarily. When the supply is insufficient, somebody must consume less, and if every rich person is determined not to be that somebody, all they do by subsidizing their poorer competitors is to force up the price so much the higher, with no effect but to enrich the corn-dealers, the very reverse of what is desired by those who recommend such measures. All that governments can do in these emergencies, is to counsel a general moderation in consumption, and to interdict such kinds of it as are not of primary importance. Direct measures at the cost of the state, to procure food from a distance, are expedient when from peculiar reasons the thing is not likely to be done by private speculation. In any other case they are a great error. Private speculators will not, in such cases, venture to compete with the government; and though a government can do more than any one merchant, it cannot do nearly so much as all merchants.

§ 4. [*Monopolies*] Governments, however, are oftener chargeable with having attempted, *a* too successfully, to make things dear, than with having aimed by wrong means at making them cheap. The usual instrument for producing artificial dearness is monopoly. To confer a monopoly upon a producer or dealer, or upon a set of producers or dealers *b*not too*b* numerous to combine, is to give them the power of levying any amount of taxation on the public, for their individual benefit, which will not make the

*a*48, 49 but   *b–b*48, 49 sufficiently

public forego the use of the commodity. When the sharers in the monopoly are so numerous and so widely scattered that they are prevented from combining, the evil is considerably less: but even then the competition is not so active among a limited as among an unlimited number. Those who feel assured of a fair average proportion in the general business, are seldom eager to get a larger share by foregoing a portion of their profits. A limitation of competition, however partial, may have mischievous effects quite disproportioned to the apparent cause. The mere exclusion of foreigners, from a branch of industry open to the free competition of every native, has been known, even in *c* England, to render that branch a conspicuous exception to the general industrial energy of the country. The silk manufacture of England remained far behind that of other countries of Europe, so long as the foreign fabrics were prohibited. In addition to the tax levied for the profit, real or imaginary, of the monopolists, the consumer thus pays an additional tax for their laziness and incapacity. When relieved from the immediate stimulus of competition, producers and dealers grow indifferent to the dictates of their ultimate pecuniary interest; preferring to the most hopeful prospects, the present ease of adhering to routine. A person who is already thriving, seldom puts himself out of his way to commence even a lucrative improvement, unless urged by the additional motive of fear lest some rival should supplant him by getting possession of it before him.

The condemnation of monopolies ought not to extend to patents, by which the originator of an improved process is *ᵈallowedᵈ* to enjoy, for a limited period, the exclusive privilege of using his own improvement. This is not making the commodity dear for his benefit, but merely postponing a part of the increased cheapness which the public owe to the inventor, in order to compensate and reward him for the service. That he ought to be both compensated and rewarded for it, will not be denied, and also that if all were at once allowed to avail themselves of his ingenuity, without having shared the labours or the expenses which he had to incur in bringing his idea into a practical shape, either such expenses and labours would be undergone by nobody except *e* very opulent and very public-spirited persons, or the state must put a value on the service rendered by an inventor, and make him a pecuniary grant. This has been done in some instances, and may be done without inconvenience in cases of very conspicuous public benefit; but in general an exclusive privilege, of temporary duration, is preferable; because it leaves nothing to any one's discretion; because the reward conferred by it depends upon the invention's being found useful, and the greater the usefulness the greater the reward; and because it is paid by the very persons to whom the service is rendered, the consumers of the

*c*48, 49   enterprising
*ᵈ⁻ᵈ*48, 49   permitted   *e*48   by

commodity. So decisive, indeed, are 'these' considerations, that if the system of patents were abandoned for that of rewards by the state, the best shape which these could assume would be that of a small temporary tax, imposed for the inventor's benefit, on all persons making use of the invention. *To this, however, or to any other system which would vest in the state the power of deciding whether an inventor should derive any pecuniary advantage from the public benefit which he confers, the objections are evidently stronger and more fundamental than the strongest which can possibly be urged against patents *. It is generally admitted that the present Patent Laws need much improvement; but in this case, as well as in the closely analogous one of Copyright, it would be a gross immorality in the law to set everybody free to use a person's work without his consent, and without giving him an equivalent.* I have seen with real alarm several recent attempts, in quarters carrying some authority, to impugn the principle of patents altogether; attempts which, if practically successful, would enthrone free stealing under the prostituted name of free trade, and make the men of brains, still more than at present, the needy retainers and dependents of the men of money-bags.*

§ 5. [*Laws against Combination of Workmen*] I pass to another kind of government interference, in which the end and the means are alike odious, but which existed in England until not *more than* *a generation* ago, and *in France up to the year 1864*. I mean the laws against combinations of workmen to raise wages; laws enacted and maintained for the declared purpose of keeping wages low, as the famous Statute of Labourers was passed by a legislature of employers, to prevent the labouring class, when its numbers had been thinned by a pestilence, from taking advantage of the diminished competition to obtain higher wages. Such laws exhibit the infernal spirit of the slave master, when to retain the working classes in avowed slavery has ceased to be practicable.

If it were possible for the working classes, by combining among themselves, to raise or keep up the general rate of wages, it needs hardly be said that this would be a thing not to be punished, but to be welcomed and rejoiced at. Unfortunately the effect is quite beyond attainment by such means. The multitudes who compose the working class are too numerous and too widely scattered to combine at all, much more to combine effectually. If they could do so, they might doubtless succeed in diminishing the

*f–f*62, 65   those
g–g+62, 65, 71
*h–h*62   : and
*a–a*48, 49, 52   much more than] 57, 62, 65   so much as
*b–b*48, 49   twenty years] 52   twenty-five years
*c–c*48, 49, 52, 57, 62   is in full vigour at this day in some other countries

hours of labour, and obtaining the same wages for less work. *They would also have a limited power of obtaining, by combination, an increase of general wages at the expense of profits. But the limits of this power are narrow; and were they to attempt to strain it beyond those limits,* this could only be accomplished by keeping a part of their number permanently out of employment. As support from public charity would of course be refused to those who could get work and would not accept it, they would be thrown for support upon the trades union of which they were members; and the *workpeople* collectively would be no better off than before, having to support the same numbers out of the same aggregate wages. In this way, however, the class would have its attention forcibly drawn to the fact of a superfluity of numbers, and to the necessity, if they would have high wages, of proportioning the supply of labour to the demand.

Combinations to keep up wages are sometimes successful, in trades where the workpeople are few in number, and collected in a small number of local centres. It is questionable if combinations ever had the smallest effect on the permanent remuneration of spinners or weavers; but the journeymen type-founders, by a close combination, are able, it is said, to keep up a rate of wages much beyond that which is usual in employments of equal hardness and skill; and even the tailors, a much more numerous class, are understood to have had, to some extent, a similar success. A rise of wages, thus confined to particular employments, is not (like a rise of general wages) defrayed from profits, but raises the value and price of the particular article, and falls on the consumer; the capitalist who produces the commodity being only injured in so far as the high price tends to narrow the market; and not even then, unless it does so in a greater ratio than that of the rise of price: for though, at higher wages, he employs, with a given capital, fewer *workpeople*, and obtains less of the commodity, yet if he can sell the whole of this diminished quantity at the higher price, his profits are as great as before.

This partial rise of wages, if not gained at the expense of the remainder of the working class, ought *not* to be regarded as *an evil*. The consumer, indeed, must pay for it; but cheapness of goods is desirable only when the cause of it is that their production costs little labour, and not when occasioned by that labour's being ill remunerated. It may appear, *indeed*, at first sight, that the high wages of the type-founders (for example) are obtained at the general cost of the labouring class. This high remuneration

---

*d–d*48, 49, 52, 57, 62, 65   But if they aimed at obtaining actually higher wages than the rate fixed by demand and supply—the rate which distributes the whole circulating capital of the country among the entire working population—
    *e–e*48, 49   workmen
    *f–f*48, 49   workmen   *g–g*+52, 57, 62, 65, 71
    *h–h*48, 49   a benefit   *i–i*48, 49, 52, 57   however

either causes fewer persons to find employment in the trade, or if not, must lead to the investment of more capital in it, at the expense of other trades: in the first case, it throws an additional number of labourers on the general market; in the second, it withdraws from that market a portion of the demand: effects, both of which are injurious to the working classes. Such, indeed, would really be the result of a successful combination in a particular trade or trades, for some time after its formation [j]; but[j] when it is a permanent thing, the principles so often insisted upon in this treatise, show that it can have no such effect. The habitual earnings of the working classes at large can be affected by nothing but the habitual requirements of the labouring people: these indeed may be altered, but while they remain the same, wages never fall permanently below the standard of these requirements, and [k]do not[k] long remain above that standard. If there had been no combinations in particular trades, and the wages of those trades had never been kept above the [l]common[l] level, there is no reason [m] to suppose that the [n]common[n] level would have been at all higher than it now is. There would merely have been a [o]greater[o] number of people altogether, and a smaller number of exceptions to the ordinary low rate of wages.

[p]If, therefore, no improvement were to be hoped for in the general circumstances of the working classes, the success of a portion of them, however small, in keeping their wages by combination above the market rate, would be wholly a matter of satisfaction. But when the elevation of the character and condition of the entire body has at last become a thing not beyond the reach of rational effort, it is time that the better paid classes of skilled artisans should seek their own advantage in common with, and not by the exclusion of, their fellow-labourers. While they continue to fix their hopes on hedging themselves in against competition, and protecting their own wages by shutting out others from access to their employment, nothing better can be expected from them than that total absence of any large and generous aims, that almost open disregard of all other objects than high wages and little work for their own small body, which were so deplorably evident in the proceedings and manifestoes of the Amalgamated Society of Engineers during their [q] quarrel with their employers. Success, even if attainable, in raising up a protected class of working people, would now be a hindrance, instead of a help, to the emancipation of the working classes at large.

But though combinations to keep up wages are seldom effectual, and

[j-j]48 . But
[k-k]48, 49 cannot
[l-l]48, 49, 52, 57 universal
[m]48, 49 whatever
[n-n]48, 49, 52, 57 universal
[o-o]49 great [*printer's error?*]
[p-p933]48, 49 Combinations to keep up wages are therefore not only permissible, but useful, whenever really calculated to have that effect. [*no paragraph*]
[q]52, 57 late

when effectual, are, for the reasons which I have assigned, seldom desirable, the right of making the attempt is one which cannot be refused to any portion of the working population without great injustice, or without the probability of fatally misleading them respecting the circumstances which determine their condition. So long as combinations to raise wages were prohibited by law, the law appeared to the operatives to be the real cause of the low wages which there was no denying that it had done its best to produce. Experience of strikes has been the best teacher of the labouring classes on the subject of the relation between wages and the demand and supply of labour: and it is most important that this course of instruction should not be disturbed.

᾿It is a great error to condemn, *per se* and absolutely, either trades unions or the collective action of strikes. ᵃEven assuming that a strike must inevitably failᵃ whenever it attempts to raise wages above that market rate which is ᵗfixedᵗ by the demand and ᵘsupply;ᵘ demand and supply are not physical agencies, which thrust a given amount of wages into a labourer's hand without the participation of his own will and actions. The market rate is not fixed for him by some self-acting instrument, but is the result of bargaining between human beings—of what Adam Smith calls "the higgling of the market;"[*] and those who do not "higgle" will long continue to pay, even over a counter, more than the market price for their purchases. Still more might poor labourers who have to do with rich employers, remain long without the amount of wages which the demand for their labour would justify, unless, in vernacular phrase, they stood out for it: and how can they stand out for terms without organized concert? What chance would any labourer have, who struck singly for an advance of wages? How could he even know whether the state of the market admitted of a rise, except by consultation with his fellows, naturally leading to concerted action? I do not hesitate to say that associations of labourers, of a nature similar to trades unions, far from being a hindrance to a free market for labour, are the necessary instrumentality of that free market; the indispensable means of enabling the sellers of labour to take due care of their own interests under a system of competition. There is an ulterior consideration of much importance, to which attention was for the first time drawn by ᵛProfessorᵛ Fawcett, in an article in the *Westminster Review*.[†] Experience has at length enabled the more intelligent trades to take a tolerably correct

[*Smith, *Wealth of Nations*, Vol. I, p. 102.]
[†"Strikes, Their Tendencies and Remedies," *Westminster Review*, n.s. XVIII (July, 1860), 1–23, especially 5 ff.]

ʳ–ʳ933+62, 65, 71
ˢ–ˢ62, 65   I grant that a strike is wrong whenever it is foolish, and it is foolish
ᵗ–ᵗ62, 65   rendered possible
ᵘ–ᵘ62, 65   supply. But   ᵛ–ᵛ62   Mr. Henry

measure of the circumstances on which the success of a strike for an advance of wages depends. The workmen are now nearly as well informed as the master, of the state of the market for his commodities; they can calculate his gains and his expenses, they know when his trade is or is not prosperous, and only when it is, are they ever again likely to strike for higher wages; which wages their known readiness to strike makes their employers for the most part willing, in that case, to concede. The tendency, therefore, of this state of things is to make a rise of wages in any particular trade usually consequent upon a rise of profits, which, as Mr. Fawcett observes, is a commencement of that regular participation of the labourers in the profits derived from their labour, every tendency to which, for the reasons stated in a previous chapter,* it is so important to encourage, since to it we have chiefly to look for any radical improvement in the social and economical relations between labour and capital. Strikes, therefore, and the trade societies which render strikes possible, are for these various reasons not a mischievous, but on the contrary, a valuable part of the existing machinery of society.^{pr}

^{w} It is, however, an indispensable condition ^{x}of tolerating combinations, that they^x should be voluntary. No severity, necessary to the purpose, is too great to be employed against attempts to compel workmen to join a union, or take part in a strike by threats or violence. Mere moral compulsion, by the expression of opinion, the law ought not to interfere with; it belongs to more enlightened opinion to restrain it, by rectifying the moral sentiments of the people. Other questions arise when the combination, being voluntary, proposes to itself objects really contrary to the public good. High wages and short hours are generally good objects, or, at all events, may be so ^{y}: but^y in many trades unions, it is among the rules that there shall be no task work, or no difference of pay between the most expert workmen and the most unskilful, or that no member of the union shall earn more than a certain sum per week, in order that there may be more employment for the rest ^{z}; and the abolition of piece work, under more or less of modification, held a conspicuous place among the demands of the Amalgamated Society^z. These are combinations to effect objects which are pernicious. Their success, even when only partial, is a public mischief; and

*Supra, book v. chap. vii. [? IV, vii, pp. 758–96.]

^{w}52, 57 [*no paragraph*] $^{x-x}$48, 49   that the combination
$^{y-y}$48, 49   , and a limitation of the number of persons in employment may be a necessary condition of these. Combinations, therefore, not to work for less than certain wages, or for more than a certain number of hours, or even not to work for a master who employs more than a certain number of apprentices, are, when voluntary on the part of all who engage in them, not only unexceptionable, but would be desirable, were it not that they almost always fail of their effect. But
$^{z-z}$+52, 57, 62, 65, 71

were it complete, would be equal in magnitude to almost any of the evils arising from bad *economical* legislation. Hardly anything worse can be said of the worst laws on the subject of *industry and its remuneration, consistent with the personal freedom of the labourer*, than that they place the energetic and the idle, the skilful and the incompetent, on a level: and this *, in so far as it is in itself possible, it is the direct tendency* of the regulations of these unions to do. *It does not, however, follow as a consequence that* the law would be warranted in making the formation of such associations illegal and punishable *. Independently of all considerations of constitutional liberty, the best interests of the human race *ʲ* imperatively require that all economical experiments, voluntarily undertaken, should have the fullest licence, and that force and fraud should be the only means of attempting to benefit themselves, which are interdicted to the less fortunate classes of the community.*e

§ 6. [*Restraints on opinion or on its publication*] Among the modes of undue exercise of the power of government, on which I have commented in this chapter, I have included only such as rest on theories which have

*[62] Whoever desires to understand the question of Trade Combinations as seen from the point of view of the working people, should make himself acquainted with a pamphlet published in 1860, under the title "Trades Unions and Strikes, their Philosophy and Intention; by T. J. Dunning, Secretary to the London Consolidated Society of Bookbinders." [London: Dunning, 1860.] There are many opinions in this able tract in which I only partially, and some in which I do not at all, coincide. But there are also many sound arguments, and an instructive exposure of the common fallacies of opponents. Readers of other classes will see with surprise, not only how great a portion of truth the Unions have on their side, but how much less flagrant and condemnable even their errors appear, when seen under the aspect in which it is only natural that the working classes should themselves regard them.

a–a+49, 52, 57, 62, 65, 71
*b–b*48   property and industry] 49   industry and its remuneration
*c–c*48, 49, 52, 57   it is the avowed object
*d–d*48   Every society which exacts from its members obedience to rules of this description, and endeavours to enforce compliance with them on the part of employers by refusal to work, is a public nuisance. Whether] 49   Any society . . . *as* 48 . . . work, incurs the inconveniences of Communism, without getting rid of any of those of individual property. It does not follow, however, that
*e–e*48   , depends upon the difficult question of the legitimate bounds of constitutional liberty. What are the proper limits to the right of association? To associate for the purpose of violating the law, could not of course be tolerated under any government. But among the numerous acts which, although mischievous in themselves, the law ought not to prohibit from being done by individuals, are there not some which are rendered so much more mischievous when people combine to do them, that the legislature ought to prohibit the combination, though not the act itself? When these questions have been philosophically answered, which belongs to a different branch of social philosophy from the present, it may be determined whether the kind of associations here treated of can be a proper subject of any other than merely moral repression.   *f*49   now

still more or less of footing in the most enlightened countries. I have not spoken of some which have done still greater mischief in times not long past, but which are now generally given up, at least in theory, though enough of them still remains in practice to make it impossible as yet to class them among exploded errors.

The notion, for example, that a government should choose opinions for the people, and should not suffer any doctrines in politics, morals, law, or religion, but such as it approves, to be printed or publicly professed, may be said to be altogether abandoned as a general thesis. It is now well understood that a régime of this sort is fatal to all prosperity, even of an economical kind: that the human mind when prevented either by fear of the law or by fear of opinion from exercising its faculties freely on the most important subjects, acquires a general torpidity and imbecility, by which, when they reach a certain point, it is disqualified from making any considerable advances even in the common affairs of life, and which, when greater still, make it gradually lose even its previous attainments. There cannot be a more decisive example than Spain and Portugal, *a*for two centuries after the Reformation*a*. The decline of those countries in national greatness, and even in material civilization, while almost all the other nations of Europe were uninterruptedly advancing, has been ascribed to various causes, but there is one which lies at the foundation of them all: the Holy Inquisition, and the system of mental slavery of which it is the symbol.

Yet although these truths are very widely recognised, and freedom both of opinion and of discussion is admitted as an axiom in all free countries, this apparent liberality and tolerance has acquired so little of the authority of a principle, that it is always ready to give way to the dread or horror inspired by some particular sort of opinions. Within the last *b*fifteen or twenty*b* years several individuals have suffered imprisonment, for the public profession, sometimes in a very temperate manner, of *c*disbelief in religion*c*; and it is probable that both the public and the government, at the first panic which arises on the subject of Chartism or Communism, will fly to similar means for checking the propagation of democratic or anti-property doctrines. In this country, however, the effective restraints on mental freedom proceed much less from the law or the government, than from the intolerant temper of the national mind; arising no longer from even *d*as*d* respectable a source as bigotry or fanaticism, but rather from the general habit, both in opinion and conduct, of making adherence to custom the rule of life, and enforcing it, by social penalties, against all persons who, without a party to back them, assert their individual independence.

*a–a*48, 49, 52, 57 from the Reformation to the present time
*b–b*48, 49 two or three] 52 five or six] 62, 65 ten or fifteen
*c–c*48, 49 infidel opinions   *d–d*48, 49 so

CHAPTER XI

Of the Grounds and Limits
of the *Laisser-Faire* or
Non-Interference Principle

§ 1. [*Governmental intervention distinguished into authoritative and unauthoritative*] We have now reached the last part of our undertaking; the discussion, so far as suited to this treatise (that is, so far as it is a question of principle, not detail) of the limits of the province of government: the question, to what objects governmental intervention in the affairs of society may or should extend, over and above those which necessarily appertain to it. No subject has been more keenly contested in the present age: the contest, however, has chiefly *a*taken place*a* round certain select points, with only flying excursions *b*into*b* the rest of the field. Those indeed who have discussed any particular question of government interference, such as state education (spiritual or secular), regulation of hours of labour, a public provision for the poor, &c., have often dealt largely in general arguments, far outstretching the special application made of them, and have shown a sufficiently strong bias either in favour of letting things alone, or in favour of meddling; but have seldom declared, or apparently decided in their own minds, how far they would carry either principle. The supporters of interference have been content with asserting a general right and duty on the part of government to intervene, wherever its intervention would be useful: and when those who have been called the *laisser-faire* school have attempted any definite limitation of the province of government, they have usually restricted it to the protection of person and property against force and fraud; a definition to which neither they nor any one else can deliberately adhere, since it excludes, as has been shown in a preceding chapter,* some of the most indispensable and unanimously recognised of the duties of government.

*Supra, book v. ch. 1. [Pp. 799–804.]

*a–a*48, 49, 52   been carried on
*b–b*62, 65   in

Without professing entirely to supply this deficiency of a general theory, on a question which does not, as I conceive, admit of any universal solution, I shall attempt to afford some little aid towards the resolution of this class of questions as they arise, by examining, in the most general point of view in which the subject can be considered, what are the advantages, and what the evils or inconveniences, of government interference.

We must set out by distinguishing between two kinds of intervention by the government, which, though they may relate to the same subject, differ widely in their nature and effects, and require, for their justification, motives of a very different degree of urgency. The intervention may extend to controlling the free agency of individuals. Government may interdict all persons from doing certain things; or from doing them without its authorization; or may prescribe to them certain things to be done, or a certain manner of doing things which it is left optional with them to do or to abstain from. This is the *authoritative* interference of government. There is another kind of intervention which is not authoritative: when a government, instead of issuing a command and enforcing it by penalties, adopts the course so seldom resorted to by governments, and of which such important use might be made, that of giving advice, and promulgating information; or when, leaving individuals free to use their own means of pursuing any object of general interest, the government, not meddling with them, but not trusting the object solely to their care, establishes, side by side with their arrangements, an agency of its own for a like purpose. Thus, it is one thing to maintain a Church Establishment, and another to refuse toleration to other religions, or to persons professing no religion. It is one thing to provide schools or colleges, and another to require that no person shall act as an instructor of youth without a government licence. There might be a national bank, or a government manufactory, without any monopoly against private banks and manufactories. There might be a post-office, without penalties against the conveyance of letters by other means. There may be a corps of government engineers for civil purposes, while the profession of a civil engineer is free to be adopted by every one. There may be public hospitals, without any restriction upon private medical or surgical practice.

§ 2. [*Objections to government intervention—the compulsory character of the intervention itself, or of the levy of funds to support it*] It is evident, even at first sight, that the authoritative form of government intervention has a much more limited sphere of legitimate action than the other. It requires a much stronger necessity to justify it in any case; while there are large departments of human life from which it must be unreservedly and imperiously excluded. Whatever theory we adopt respecting the foundation of the social union, and under whatever political institutions we live, there is a circle around every individual human being, which no government, be it that of one, of a few, or of the many, ought to be permitted to overstep: there is a part of the life of every person who has come to years of discretion, within which the individuality of that person ought to reign uncontrolled either by any other individual or by the public collectively. That there is, or ought to be, some space in human existence thus entrenched ªaroundª, and sacred from authoritative intrusion, no one who professes the smallest regard to human freedom or dignity will call in question: the point to be determined is, where the limit should be placed; how large a province of human life this reserved territory should include. I apprehend that it ought to include all that part which concerns only the life, whether inward or outward, of the individual, and does not affect the interests of others, or affects them only through the moral influence of example. With respect to the domain of the inward consciousness, the thoughts and feelings, and as much of external conduct as is personal only, involving no consequences, none at least of a painful or injurious kind, to other people; I hold that it is allowable in all, and in the more thoughtful and cultivated often a duty, to assert and promulgate, with all the force they are capable of, their opinion of what is good or bad, admirable or contemptible, but not to compel others to conform to that opinion; whether the force used is that of extra-legal coercion, or exerts itself by means of the law.

Even in those portions of conduct which do affect the interest of others, the onus of making out a case always lies on the defenders of legal prohibitions. It is not a merely constructive or presumptive injury to others, which will justify the interference of law with individual freedom. To be prevented from doing what one is inclined to, or from acting according to one's own judgment of what is desirable, is not only always irksome, but always tends, *pro tanto*, to starve the development of some portion of the bodily or mental faculties, either sensitive or active; and unless the conscience of the individual goes freely with the legal restraint, it partakes, either in a great or in a small degree, of the degradation of slavery. Scarcely any degree of utility, short of absolute necessity, will justify a prohibitory regulation, unless it can ᵇalsoᵇ be made to recommend itself to the general conscience; unless persons of ordinary good intentions either believe already, or can be induced to believe, that the thing prohibited is a thing which they ought not to wish to do.

It is otherwise with governmental interferences which do not restrain individual free agency. When a government provides means for fulfilling a certain end, leaving individuals free to avail themselves of different means

ª–ª48, 49, 52   round   ᵇ–ᵇ+52, 57, 62, 65, 71 if in their opinion preferable, there is no infringement of liberty, no irksome or degrading restraint. One of the principal objections to government interference is then absent. There is, however, in almost all forms of government agency, one thing which is compulsory; the provision of the pecuniary means. These are derived from taxation; or, if existing in the form of an endowment derived from public property, they are still the cause of as much compulsory taxation as the sale or the annual proceeds of the property would enable to be dispensed with.* And the objection necessarily attaching to compulsory contributions, is almost always greatly aggravated by the expensive precautions and onerous restrictions, which are indispensable to prevent evasion of a compulsory tax.

§ 3. [*Objections to government intervention—increase of the power and influence of government*] A second general objection to government agency, is that every increase of the functions devolving on the government is an increase of its power, both in the form of authority, and still more, in the indirect form of influence. The importance of this consideration, in respect to political freedom, has in general been quite sufficiently recognised, at least in England; but many, in latter times, have been prone to think that limitation of the powers of the government is only essential when the government itself is badly constituted; when it does not represent the people, but is the organ of a class, or coalition of classes: and that a government of sufficiently popular constitution might be trusted with any amount of power over the nation, since its power would be only that of the nation over itself. This might be true, if the nation, in such cases, did not practically mean a mere majority of the nation, and if minorities were only capable of oppressing, but not of being oppressed. Experience, however, proves that the depositaries of power who are mere delegates of the people, that is of a majority, are quite as ready (when they think they can count on popular support) as any organs of oligarchy, to assume arbitrary power, and encroach unduly on the liberty of private life. The public collectively is abundantly ready to impose, not only its generally narrow views of its interests, but its abstract opinions, and even its tastes, as laws binding upon individuals. And ªtheª present civilization tends so strongly to make the

---

*The only cases in which government agency involves nothing of a compulsory nature, are the rare cases in which, without any artificial monopoly, it pays its own expenses. A bridge built with public money, on which tolls are collected sufficient to pay not only all current expenses, but the interest of the original outlay, is one case in point. The government railways in Belgium and Germany are another example. The Post Office, if its monopoly were abolished, and it still paid its [48, 49, 52, 57   own] expenses, would be another.

ª–ª48, 49   our

power of persons acting in masses the only substantial power in society, that there never was more necessity for surrounding individual independence of thought, speech, and conduct, with the most powerful defences, in order to maintain that originality of mind and individuality of character, which are the only source of any real progress, and of most of the qualities which make the human race much superior to any herd of animals. Hence it is no less important in a democratic than in any other government, that all tendency on the part of public authorities to stretch their interference, and assume a power of any sort which can easily be dispensed with, should be regarded with unremitting jealousy. Perhaps this *is even more* important in a democracy than in any other form of political society; because where public opinion is sovereign, an individual who is oppressed by the sovereign does not, as in most other states of things, find *a* rival power to which he can appeal for relief *d*, or, at all events, for sympathy*d*.

§ 4. [*Objections to government intervention—increase of the occupations and responsibilities of government*] A third general objection to government agency, rests on the principle of the division of labour. Every additional function undertaken by the government, is a fresh occupation imposed upon a body already overcharged with duties. A natural consequence is that most things are ill done; much not done at all, because the government is not able to do it without delays which are fatal to its purpose; that the more troublesome, and less showy, of the functions undertaken, are postponed or neglected, and an excuse is always ready for the neglect; while the heads of the administration have their minds so fully taken up with official details, in however perfunctory a manner superintended, that they have no time or thought to spare for the great interests of the state, and the preparation of enlarged measures of social improvement.

But these inconveniences, though real and serious, result much more from the bad organization of governments, than from the extent *and* variety of the duties undertaken by them. Government is not a name for some one functionary, or definite number of functionaries: there may be almost any amount of division of labour within the administrative body itself. The evil in question is felt in great magnitude under some of the governments *of* the Continent, where six or eight men, living at the capital and known by the name of ministers, demand that the whole public business of the country shall pass, or be supposed to pass, under their individual eye. But the inconvenience would be reduced to a very manageable compass, in a country in which there was a proper distribution of

---

*b–b*49   is more
*c–c*48, 49   some other and   *d–d*+62, 65, 71
   *a–a*48, 49, 52, 57   or   *b–b*48, 49, 52   on

functions between the central and local officers of government, and in which the central body was divided into a sufficient number of departments. When Parliament thought it expedient to confer on the government an inspecting and partially controlling authority over railways, it did not add railways to the department of the Home Minister, but created a Railway Board. When it determined to have a central superintending authority for pauper administration, it established the Poor Law Commission. There are few countries in which a greater number of functions are discharged by public officers, than in some states of the American Union, particularly the New England States: but the division of labour in public business is extreme; most of these officers being not even amenable to any common superior, but performing their duties freely, under the double check of election by their townsmen, and civil as well as criminal responsibility to the tribunals.

It is, no doubt, indispensable to good government that the chiefs of the administration, whether permanent or temporary, should extend a commanding, though general, view over the *ensemble* of all the interests confided, in any degree, to the responsibility of the central power. But with a skilful internal organization of the administrative machine, leaving to subordinates, and as far as possible, to local subordinates, not only the execution, but to a great degree the control, of details; holding them accountable for the results of their acts rather than for the acts themselves, except where these come within the cognizance of the tribunals; taking the most effectual securities for honest and capable appointments; opening a broad path to promotion from the inferior degrees of the administrative scale to the superior; leaving, at each step, to the functionary, a wider range in the origination of measures, so that, in the highest grade of all, deliberation ᶜmightᶜ be concentrated on the great collective interests of the country in each department; if all this were done, the government would not probably be overburthened by any business, in other respects fit to be undertaken by it; though the overburthening would remain as a serious addition to the inconveniences incurred by its undertaking any which was unfit.

§ 5. [*Objections to government intervention—superior efficiency of private agency, owing to stronger interest in the work*] But though a better organization of governments would greatly diminish the force of the objection to the mere multiplication of their duties, it would still remain true that in all the more advanced communities, the great majority of things are worse done by the intervention of government, than the individuals most interested in the matter would do them, or cause them to be done, if left to themselves. The grounds of this truth are expressed with

ᶜ⁻ᶜ48, 49, 52   may

tolerable exactness in the popular dictum, that people understand their own business and their own interests better, and care for them more, than the government does, or can be expected to do. This maxim holds true throughout the greatest part of the business of life, and wherever it is true we ought to condemn every kind of government intervention that conflicts with it. The inferiority of government agency, for example, in any of the common operations of industry or commerce, is proved by the fact, that it is hardly ever able to maintain itself in equal competition with individual agency, where the individuals possess the requisite degree of industrial enterprise, and can command the necessary assemblage of means. All the facilities which a government enjoys of access to information; all the means which it possesses of remunerating, and therefore of commanding, the best available talent in the market—are not an equivalent for the one great disadvantage of an inferior interest in the result.

It must be remembered, besides, that even if a government were superior in intelligence and knowledge to any single individual in the nation, it must be inferior to all the individuals of the nation taken together. It can neither possess in itself, nor enlist in its service, more than a portion of the acquirements and capacities which the country contains, applicable to any given purpose. There must be many persons equally qualified for the work with those whom the government employs, even if it selects its instruments with no reference to any consideration but their fitness. Now these are the very persons into whose hands, in the cases of most common occurrence, a system of individual agency naturally tends to throw the work, because they are capable of doing it better ᵃorᵃ on cheaper terms than any other person. So far as this is the case, it is evident that government, by excluding or even by superseding individual agency, either substitutes a less qualified instrumentality for one better qualified, or at any rate substitutes its own mode of accomplishing the work, for all the variety of modes which would be tried by a number of equally qualified persons aiming at the same end; a competition by many degrees more propitious to the progress of improvement, than any uniformity of system.

§ 6. [*Objections to government intervention—importance of cultivating habits of collective action in the people*] I have reserved for the last place one of the strongest of the reasons against the extension of government agency. Even if the government could comprehend within itself, in each department, all the most eminent intellectual capacity and active talent of the nation, it would not be the less desirable that the conduct of a large portion of the affairs of ᵃtheᵃ society should be left in the hands of the

ᵃ⁻ᵃ48, 49, 52, 57 and
ᵃ⁻ᵃ+65, 71

persons immediately interested in them. The business of life is an essential part of the practical education of a people; without which, book and school instruction, though most necessary and salutary, does not suffice to qualify them for conduct, and for the adaptation of means to ends. Instruction is only one of the desiderata of mental improvement; another, almost as indispensable, is a vigorous exercise of the active energies; labour, contrivance, judgment, self-control: and the natural stimulus to these is the difficulties of life. This doctrine is not to be confounded with the complacent optimism, which represents the *b*evils*b* of life as desirable things, because they call forth qualities adapted to combat with *c*evils*c*. It is only because the difficulties exist, that the qualities which combat with them are of any value. As practical beings it is our business to free human life from as many as possible of its difficulties, and not to keep up a stock of them as hunters preserve game, for the exercise of pursuing it. But since the need of active talent and practical judgment in the affairs of life can only be diminished, and not, even on the most favourable supposition, done away with, it is important that those endowments should be cultivated not merely in a select few, but in all, and that the cultivation should be more varied and complete than most persons are able to find in the narrow sphere of their merely individual interests. A people among whom there is no habit of spontaneous action for a collective interest—who look habitually to their government to command or prompt them in all matters of joint concern—who expect to have everything done for them, except what can be made an affair of mere habit and routine—have their faculties only half developed; their education is defective in one of its most important branches.

Not only is the cultivation of the active faculties by exercise, diffused through the whole community, in itself one of the most valuable of national possessions: it is rendered, not less, but more, necessary, *d*when*d* a high degree of that indispensable culture is systematically kept up in the chiefs and functionaries of the state. There cannot be a combination of circumstances more dangerous to human welfare, than that in which intelligence and talent are maintained at a high standard within a governing corporation, but starved and discouraged outside the pale. Such a system, more completely than any other, embodies the idea of despotism, by arming with intellectual superiority as an additional weapon, those who have already the legal power. It approaches as nearly as the organic difference between human beings and other animals admits, to the government of sheep by their shepherd, without anything like so strong an interest as the shepherd has in the thriving condition of the flock. The only security against political

*b–b*48, 49   difficulties
*c–c*48, 49   difficulties
*d–d*48, 49   by the fact, that

slavery, is the check maintained over governors, by the diffusion of intelligence, activity, and public spirit among the governed. Experience proves the extreme difficulty of permanently keeping up a sufficiently high standard of those qualities; a difficulty which increases, as the advance of civilization and security removes one after another of the hardships, embarrassments, and dangers against which individuals had formerly no resource but in their own strength, skill, and courage. It is therefore of supreme importance that all classes of the community, down to the lowest, should have much to do for themselves; that as great a demand should be made upon their intelligence and virtue as it is in any respect equal to; that the government should not only leave as *far* as possible to their own faculties the conduct of whatever concerns themselves alone, but should suffer them, or rather encourage them, to manage as many as possible of their joint concerns by voluntary co-operation; since *this* discussion and management of collective interests is the great school of that public spirit, and the great source of that intelligence of public affairs, which are always regarded as the distinctive character of the public of free countries.

A democratic constitution, not supported by democratic institutions in detail, but confined to the central government, not only is not political freedom, but often creates a spirit precisely the reverse, carrying down to the lowest grade in society the desire and ambition of political domination. In some countries the desire of the people is for not being tyrannized over, but in others it is merely for an equal chance to everybody of tyrannizing. Unhappily this last state of the desires is fully as natural to mankind as the former, and in many of the conditions even of civilized humanity, is far more largely exemplified. In proportion as the people are accustomed to manage their affairs by their own active intervention, instead of leaving them to the government, their desires will turn to repelling tyranny, rather than to tyrannizing: while in proportion as all real initiative and direction resides in the government, and individuals habitually feel and act as under its perpetual tutelage, popular institutions develope in them not the desire of freedom, but an unmeasured appetite for place and power; diverting the intelligence and activity of the country from its principal business, to a wretched competition for the selfish prizes and the petty vanities of office.

§ 7. [Laisser-faire *the general rule*] The preceding are the principal reasons, of a general character, in favour of restricting to the narrowest compass the intervention of a public authority in the business of the community: and few will dispute the more than sufficiency of these reasons, to throw, in every instance, the burthen of making out a strong case, not on those who resist, but on those who recommend, government interference.

*e–e*48, 49, 52   much   *f–f*48, 49, 52, 57   the

Laisser-faire, in short, should be the general practice: every departure from it, unless required by some great good, is a certain evil.

The degree in which the maxim, even in the cases to which it is most manifestly applicable, has heretofore been infringed by governments, future ages will probably have difficulty in crediting. Some idea may be formed of it from the description *ª*of*ª* M. Dunoyer* of the restraints imposed on the operations of manufacture under the old government of France, by the meddling and regulating spirit of legislation.

"La société exerçait sur la fabrication la juridiction la plus illimitée et la plus arbitraire: elle disposait sans scrupule des facultés des fabricants; elle décidait qui pourrait travailler, quelle chose on pourrait faire, quels matériaux on devrait employer, quels procédés il faudrait suivre, quelles formes on donnerait aux produits, etc. Il ne suffisait pas de faire bien, de faire mieux, il fallait faire suivant les règles. Qui ne connaît ce règlement de 1670, qui préscrivait de saisir et de clouer au poteau, avec le nom des auteurs, les marchandises non conformes aux règles tracées, et qui, à la seconde récidive, voulait que les fabricants y fussent attachés eux-mêmes? Il ne s'agissait pas de consulter le goût des consommateurs, mais de se conformer aux volontés de la loi. Des légions d'inspecteurs, de commissaires, de contrôleurs, de jurés, de gardes, étaient chargés de les faire exécuter; on brisait les métiers, on brûlait les produits qui n'y étaient pas conformes: les améliorations étaient punies; on mettait les inventeurs à l'amende. On soumettait à des règles différentes la fabrication des objets destinés à la consommation intérieure et celle des produits destinés au commerce étranger. Un artisan n'était pas le maître de choisir le lieu de son établissement, ni de travailler en toute saison, ni de travailler pour tout le monde. Il existe un décret du 30 Mars 1700, qui borne à dix-huit villes le nombre des lieux où l'on pourra faire des bas au métier; un arrêt du 18 Juin 1723 enjoint aux fabricants de Rouen de suspendre leurs travaux du 1er Juillet au 15 Septembre, afin de faciliter ceux de la récolte; Louis XIV., quand il voulut entreprendre la colonnade du Louvre, défendit aux particuliers d'employer des ouvriers sans sa permission, sous peine de 10,000 livres d'amende, et aux ouvriers de travailler pour les particuliers, sous peine, pour la première fois, de la prison, et pour la seconde, des galères."

That these and similar regulations were not a dead letter, and that the officious and vexatious meddling was prolonged down to the French Revolution, we have the testimony of Roland, the Girondist minister.† "I have seen," says he, "eighty, ninety, a hundred pieces of cotton or woollen stuff

De la Liberté du Travail, vol. ii. pp. 353–4.

†I quote at second hand, from Mr. Carey's *Essay on the Rate of Wages* [Philadelphia: Carey, Lea and Blanchard, 1835], pp. 195–6 [195n–196n].

*ª–ª*48, 49, 52, 57, 62, 65   by

cut up, and completely destroyed. I have witnessed similar scenes every week for a number of years. I have seen manufactured goods confiscated; heavy fines laid on the manufacturers; some pieces of fabric were burnt in public places, and at the hours of market: others were fixed to the pillory, with the name of the manufacturer inscribed upon them, and he himself was threatened with the pillory, in case of a second offence. All this was done under my eyes, at Rouen, in conformity with existing regulations, or ministerial orders. What crime deserved so cruel a punishment? Some defects in the materials employed, or in the texture of the fabric, or even in some of the threads of the warp.

"I have frequently seen manufacturers visited by a band of satellites who put all in confusion in their establishments, spread terror in their families, cut the stuffs from the frames, tore off the warp from the looms, and carried them away as proofs of infringement; the manufacturers were summoned, tried, and condemned: their goods confiscated; copies of their judgment of confiscation posted up in every public place; fortune, reputation, credit, all was lost and destroyed. And for what offence? Because they had made of worsted, a kind of cloth called shag, such as the English used to manufacture, and even sell in France, while the French regulations stated that that kind of cloth should be made with mohair. I have seen other manufacturers treated in the same way, because they had made camlets of a particular width, used in England and Germany, for which there was a great demand from Spain, Portugal, and other countries, and from several parts of France, while the French regulations prescribed other widths for camlets."

The time is gone by, when such applications as these of the principle of "paternal government" would be attempted, in even the least enlightened country of the European commonwealth of nations. In such cases as those cited, all the general objections to government interference are valid, and several of them in nearly their highest degree. But we must now turn to the second part of our task, and direct our attention to cases, in which some of those general objections are altogether absent, while those which can never be got rid of entirely, are overruled by counter-considerations of still greater importance.

We have observed that, as a general rule, the business of life is better performed when those who have an immediate interest in it are left to take their own course, uncontrolled either by the mandate of the law or by the meddling of any public functionary. The persons, or some of the persons, who do the work, are likely to be better judges than the government, of the means of attaining the particular end at which they aim. Were we to suppose, what is not very probable, that the government has possessed itself of the best knowledge which had been acquired up to a given time by the persons most skilled in the occupation; even then, the individual ^{b}agents have^b so much stronger and more direct an interest in the result, that the means are far more likely to be improved and perfected if left to ^{c}their^c uncontrolled choice. But if the workman is generally the best selector of means, can it be affirmed with the same universality, that the consumer, or person served, is the most competent judge of the end? Is the buyer always qualified to judge of the commodity? If not, the presumption in favour of the competition of the market does not apply to the case; and if the commodity be one, in the quality of which society has much at stake, the balance of advantages may be in favour of some mode ^{d}and^d degree of intervention, by the authorized representatives of the collective interest of the state.

§ 8. [*Large exceptions to* laisser-faire. *Cases in which the consumer is an incompetent judge of the commodity. Education*] Now, the proposition that the consumer is a competent judge of the commodity, can be admitted only with numerous abatements and exceptions. He is generally the best judge (though even this is not true universally) of the material objects produced for his use. These are destined to supply some physical want, or gratify some taste or inclination, respecting which wants or inclinations there is no appeal from the person who feels them; or they are the means and appliances of some occupation, for the use of the persons engaged in it, who may be presumed to be judges of the things required in their own habitual employment. But there are other things, of the worth of which the demand of the market is by no means a test; things of which the utility does not consist in ministering to inclinations, nor in serving the daily uses of life, and the want of which is least felt where the need is greatest. This is peculiarly true of those things which are chiefly useful as tending to raise the character of human beings. The uncultivated cannot be competent judges of cultivation. Those who most need to be made wiser and better, usually desire it least, and if they desired it, would be incapable of finding the way to it by their own lights. It will continually happen, on the voluntary system, that, the end not being desired, the means will not be provided at all, or that, the persons requiring improvement having an imperfect or altogether erroneous conception of what they want, the supply called forth by the demand of the market will be anything but what is really required. Now any well-intentioned and tolerably civilized government may think, without presumption, that it does or ought to possess a degree of cultivation above the average of the community which it rules, and that it should therefore be capable of offering better education and better instruction to

$^{b-b}$48, 49   agent has $^{c-c}$48, 49   his $^{d-d}$48, 49   or

the people, than the greater number of them would spontaneously ᵃdemandᵃ. Education, therefore, is one of those things which it is admissible in principle that a government should provide for the people. The case is one to which the reasons of the non-interference principle do not necessarily or universally extend.*

With regard to elementary education, the exception to ordinary rules may, I conceive, justifiably be carried still further. There are certain primary elements and means of knowledge, which it is in the highest degree desirable that all human beings born into the community should acquire during childhood. If their parents, or those on whom they depend, have the power of obtaining for them this instruction, and fail to do it, they commit a double breach of duty, towards the children themselves, and towards the members of the community generally, who are all liable to suffer seriously from the consequences of ignorance and want of education in their fellow-citizens. It is therefore an allowable exercise of the powers of government, to impose on parents the legal obligation of giving elemen-

*In opposition to these opinions, a writer, with whom on many points I agree, but whose hostility to government intervention seems to me too indiscriminate and unqualified, M. Dunoyer, observes, that instruction, however good in itself, can only be useful to the public in so far as they are willing to receive it, and that the best proof that the instruction is suitable to their wants is its success as a pecuniary enterprise. This argument seems no more conclusive respecting instruction for the mind, than it would be respecting medicine for the body. No medicine will do the patient any good if he cannot be induced to take it; but we are not bound to admit as a corollary from this, that the patient will select the right medicine without assistance. Is it not probable [48, 49, 52, 57, 62   possible] that a recommendation, from any quarter which he respects, may induce him to accept a better medicine than he would spontaneously have chosen? This is, in respect to education, the very point in debate. Without doubt, instruction which is so far in advance of the people that they cannot be induced to avail themselves of it, is to them of no more worth than if it did not exist. But between what they spontaneously choose, and what they will refuse to accept when offered, there is a breadth of interval proportioned to their deference for the recommender. Besides, a thing of which the public are bad judges, may require to be shown to them and pressed on their attention for a long time, and to prove its advantages by long experience, before they learn to appreciate it, yet they may learn at last; which they might never have done, if the thing had not been thus obtruded upon them in act, but only recommended in theory. Now, a pecuniary speculation cannot wait years, or perhaps generations for success; it must succeed rapidly, or not at all. Another consideration which M. Dunoyer seems to have overlooked, is, that institutions and modes of tuition which never could be made sufficiently popular to repay, with a profit, the expenses incurred on them, may be invaluable to the many by giving the highest quality of education to the few, and keeping up the perpetual succession of superior minds, by whom knowledge is advanced, and the community urged forward in civilization.

ᵃ⁻ᵃ48, 49   select

tary instruction to children. This, however, cannot fairly be done, without taking measures to insure that such instruction shall be always accessible to them, either gratuitously or at a trifling expense.

It may indeed be objected that the education of children is one of those expenses which parents, even of the labouring class, ought to defray; that it is desirable that they should feel it incumbent on them to provide by their own means for the fulfilment of their duties, and that by giving education at the cost of others, just as much as by giving subsistence, the standard of necessary wages is proportionally lowered, and the springs of exertion and self-restraint in so much relaxed. *b*This argument could, at best, be only valid*b* if the question were that of substituting a public provision for what individuals would otherwise do for themselves; if all parents in the labouring class recognised and practised the duty of giving instruction to their children at their own expense *c*. But inasmuch as*c* parents do not practise this duty, and do not include education among those necessary expenses which their wages must provide for, *d*therefore*d* the general rate of wages is not high enough to bear those expenses, and *e* they must be borne from some other source. And this is not one of the cases in which the tender of help perpetuates the state of things which renders help necessary. Instruction, when it is really such, does not enervate, but strengthens as well as enlarges the active faculties: in whatever manner acquired, its effect on the mind is favourable to the spirit of independence: and when, unless had gratuitously, it would not be had at all, help in this form has the opposite tendency to that which in so many other cases makes it objectionable; it is help towards doing without help.

In England, and most European countries, elementary instruction cannot be paid for, at its full cost, from the common wages of unskilled labour, and would not if it could. The alternative, therefore, is not between government and private speculation, but between a government provision and voluntary charity: between interference by government, and interference by associations of individuals, subscribing their own money for the purpose, like the two great School Societies. It is, of course, not desirable that anything should be done by funds derived from compulsory taxation, which is already sufficiently well done by individual liberality. How far this is the case with school instruction, is, in each particular instance, a question of fact. The education provided in this country on the voluntary principle has of late been so much discussed, that it is needless in this place to criticise it minutely, and I shall merely express my conviction, that even in quantity

*b-b*48   To this argument there could be no reply,

*c-c*48   , no one would seek to undermine so virtuous a habit by volunteering a needless assistance. It is because

*d-d*48   that

*e*48   that

it is, and is likely to remain, altogether insufficient, while in quality, though with some slight tendency to improvement, it is never good except by some rare accident, and generally so bad as to be little more than nominal. I hold it therefore the duty of the government to supply the defect, by *giving pecuniary support to elementary schools, such as to render them* accessible to all the children of the poor, either freely, or for a payment too inconsiderable to be sensibly felt *g* .

One thing must be strenuously insisted on; that the government must claim no monopoly for its education, either in the lower or in the higher branches; must exert neither authority nor influence to induce the people to resort to its teachers in preference to others, and must confer no peculiar advantages on those who have been instructed by them. Though the government teachers will probably be superior to the average of private instructors, they will not embody all the knowledge and sagacity to be found in all instructors taken together, and it is desirable to leave open as many roads as possible to the desired end. *It is not endurable* that a government should, either *de jure* or *de facto*, have a complete control over the education of the *i* people. To possess such a control, and actually exert it, is to be *despotic*. A government which can mould the opinions and sentiments of the people from their youth upwards, can do with them whatever it pleases. Though a government, therefore, may, and in many cases ought to, establish schools and colleges, it must neither compel nor bribe any person to come to them; nor ought the power of individuals to set up rival establishments, to depend in any degree upon its authorization. It *would* be justified in requiring from all the people that they shall possess instruction in certain things, but not in prescribing to them how or from whom they shall obtain it.

§ 9. [*Case of persons exercising power over others. Protection of children and young persons; of the lower animals. Case of women not analogous*] In the matter of education, the intervention of government is justifiable, because the case is not one in which the interest and judgment of the consumer are a sufficient security for the goodness of the commodity. Let us now consider another class of cases, where there is no person in the situation of a consumer, and where the interest and judgment to be relied

---

*f-f*48, 49, 52   providing elementary schools,

*g*48   , but which it might be proper to demand, merely in recognition of a principle: the remainder of the cost to be defrayed, as in Scotland, by a local rate, that the inhabitants of the locality might have a stronger interest in watching over the management, and checking negligence and abuse] 49, 52   : the remainder . . . *as* 48

*h-h*48, 49, 52, 57   Nor is it to be endured

*i*48, 49   whole

*j-j*48, 49   a despot

*k-k*48, 49, 52   may

on are those of the agent himself; as in the conduct of any business in which he is exclusively interested, or in entering into any contract or engagement by which he himself is to be bound.

The ground of the practical principle of non-interference must here be, that most persons take a juster and more intelligent view of their own interest, and of the means of promoting it, than can either be prescribed to them by a general enactment of the legislature, or pointed out in the particular case by a public functionary. The maxim is unquestionably sound as a general rule; but there is no difficulty in perceiving some very large and conspicuous exceptions to it. These may be classed under several heads.

First:—The individual who is presumed to be the best judge of his own interests may be incapable of judging or acting for himself; may be a lunatic, an idiot, an infant: or though not wholly incapable, may be of immature years and judgment. In this case the foundation of the *laisser-faire* principle breaks down entirely. The person most interested is not the best judge of the matter, nor a competent judge at all. Insane persons are everywhere regarded as proper objects of the care of the state.* In the case of children and young persons, it is common to say, that though they cannot judge for themselves, they have their parents or other relatives to judge for them. But this removes the question into a different category; making it no longer a question whether the government should interfere with individuals in the direction of their own conduct and interests, but whether it should leave absolutely in their power the conduct and interests of somebody else.

*[52] The practice of the English law with respect to insane persons, especially on the all-important point of the ascertainment of insanity, most urgently demands reform. At present no persons, whose property is worth coveting, and whose nearest relations are unscrupulous, or on bad terms with them, are secure against a commission of lunacy. At the instance of the persons who would profit by their being declared insane, a jury may be impanelled and an investigation held at the expense of the property, in which all their personal peculiarities, with all the additions made by the lying gossip of low servants, are poured into the credulous ears of twelve petty shopkeepers, ignorant of all ways of life except those of their own class, and regarding every trait of individuality in character or taste as eccentricity, and all eccentricity as either insanity or wickedness. If this sapient tribunal gives the desired verdict, the property is handed over to perhaps the [52   very] last persons whom the rightful owner would have desired or suffered to possess it. Some recent instances of this kind of investigation have been a scandal to the administration of justice. Whatever other changes in this branch of law may be made, two at least are imperative: first, that, as in other legal proceedings, the expenses should not be borne by the person on trial, but by the promoters of the inquiry, subject to recovery of costs in case of success: and secondly, that the property of a person declared insane, should in no case be made over to heirs while the proprietor is alive, but should be managed by a public officer until his death or recovery.

Parental power is as susceptible of abuse as any other power, and is, as a matter of fact, constantly abused. If laws do not succeed in preventing parents from brutally ill-treating, and even from murdering their children, far less ought it to be presumed that the interests of children will never be sacrificed, in more commonplace and less revolting ways, to the selfishness or the *ignorance* of their parents. Whatever it can be clearly seen that parents ought to do or forbear for the interest of children, the law is warranted, if it is able, in compelling to be done or forborne, and is generally bound to do so. To take an example from the peculiar province of political economy; it is right that children, and young persons not yet arrived at maturity, should be protected, so far as the eye and hand of the state can reach, from being over-worked. Labouring for too many hours in the day, or on work beyond their strength, should not be permitted to them, for if permitted it may always be compelled. Freedom of contract, in the case of children, is but another word for freedom of coercion. Education also, the best which circumstances admit of their receiving, is not a thing which parents or relatives, from indifference, jealousy, or avarice, should have it in their power to withhold.

The reasons for legal intervention in favour of children, apply not less strongly to the case of those unfortunate slaves and victims of the most brutal part of mankind, the lower animals. It is by the grossest misunderstanding of the principles of liberty, that the infliction of exemplary punishment on ruffianism practised towards these defenceless creatures, has been treated as a meddling by government with things beyond its province; an interference with domestic life. The domestic life of domestic tyrants is one of the things which it is the most imperative on the law to interfere with; and it is to be regretted that metaphysical scruples respecting the nature and source of the authority of government, should induce many warm supporters of laws against cruelty to animals, to seek for a justification of such laws in the incidental consequences of the indulgence of ferocious habits to the interests of human beings, rather than in the intrinsic merits of the case itself. What it would be the duty of a human being, possessed of the requisite physical strength, to prevent by force if attempted in his presence, it cannot be less incumbent on society generally to repress. The existing laws of England on the subject are chiefly defective in the trifling, often almost nominal, maximum, to which the penalty even in the worst cases is limited *b* .

Among those members of the community whose freedom of contract ought to be controlled by the legislature for their own protection, on account (it is said) of their dependent position, it is frequently proposed to include

*a–a*48, 49, 52, 57   mistakes
*b*48, 49   ; a fortnight's imprisonment, or a fine of forty shillings

women: and in the *c*existing*c* Factory *d*Acts*d*, their labour, in common with that of young persons, has been placed under peculiar restrictions. But the classing together, for this and other purposes, of women and children, appears to me both indefensible in principle and mischievous in practice. Children below a certain age *cannot* judge or act for themselves; up to a considerably greater age they are inevitably more or less disqualified for doing so; but women are as capable as men of appreciating and managing their own concerns, and the only hindrance to their doing so arises from the injustice of their present social position. *e*When*e* the law makes every-thing which the wife acquires, the property of the husband, while by com-pelling her to live with him it forces her to submit to almost any amount of moral and even physical tyranny which he may choose to inflict, there is some ground for regarding every act done by her as done under coercion: but it is the great error of reformers and philanthropists in our time, to nibble at the consequences of unjust power, instead of redressing the injustice itself. If women had as absolute a control as men have, over their own persons and their own patrimony or acquisitions, there would be no plea for limiting their hours of labouring for themselves, in order that they might have time to labour for the husband, in what is called, by the advocates of restriction, *his* home. Women employed in factories are the only women in the labouring rank of life whose position is not that of slaves and drudges; precisely because they cannot easily be compelled to work and earn wages in factories against their will. For improving the condition of women, it should, on the contrary, be an object to give them the readiest access to independent industrial employment, instead of closing, either entirely or partially, that which is already open to them.

§ 10. [*Case of contracts in perpetuity*] A second exception to the doc-trine that individuals are the best judges of their own interest, is when an individual attempts to *a*decide*a* irrevocably now, what will be best for his interest at some future and distant time. The presumption in favour of individual judgment is only legitimate, where the judgment is grounded on actual, and especially on present, personal experience; not where it is formed antecedently to experience, and not suffered to be reversed even after experience has condemned it. When persons have bound themselves by a contract, not simply to do some one thing, but to continue doing something for ever or for a prolonged period, without any power of revok-ing the engagement, the presumption which their perseverance in that course of conduct would otherwise raise in favour of its being advantageous to them, does not exist; and any such presumption which can be grounded

*c–c*48, 49, 52, 57   recent   *d–d*48, 49, 52, 57, 62, 65   Act
*e–e*48, 49, 52, 57, 62, 65   So long as   *a–a*48, 49, 52   judge

on their having voluntarily entered into the contract, perhaps at an early age, and without any real knowledge of what they undertook, is commonly next to null. The practical maxim of leaving contracts free, is not applicable without great limitations in case of engagements in perpetuity; and the law should be extremely jealous of such engagements; should refuse its sanction to them, when the obligations they impose are such as the contracting party cannot be a competent judge of; if it ever does sanction them, it should take every possible security for their being contracted with foresight and deliberation; and in compensation for not permitting the parties themselves to revoke their engagement, should grant them a release from it, on a sufficient case being made out before an impartial authority. *b*These considerations are eminently applicable to marriage, the most important of all cases of engagement for life.*b*

§ 11. [*Cases of delegated management*] The third exception which I shall notice, to the doctrine that government cannot manage the affairs of individuals as well as the individuals themselves, has reference to the great class of cases in which the individuals can only manage the concern by delegated agency, and in which the so-called private management is, in point of fact, hardly better entitled to be called management by the persons interested, than administration by a public officer. Whatever, if left to spontaneous agency, can only be done by joint-stock associations, will often be as well, and sometimes better done, as far as the actual work is concerned, by the state. Government management is, indeed, proverbially jobbing, careless, and ineffective, but so likewise has generally been joint-stock management. The directors of a joint-stock company, it is true, are always shareholders; but also the members of a government are invariably taxpayers; and in the case of directors, no more than in that of governments, is their proportional share of the benefits of good management, equal to the interest they may possibly have in mismanagement, even without reckoning the interest of their ease. It may be objected, that the shareholders, in their collective character, exercise a certain control over the directors, and have almost always full power to remove them from office. Practically, however, the difficulty of exercising this power is found to be so great, that it is hardly ever exercised except in cases of such flagrantly unskilful, or, at least, unsuccessful management, as would generally produce the ejection from office of managers appointed by the government. Against the *a*very ineffectual*a* security afforded by meetings of shareholders, and by their individual inspection and inquiries, may be placed the greater publicity and more active discussion and comment, to be expected in free countries with regard to affairs in which the general government takes part.

b-b+52, 57, 62, 65, 71   *a-a*+62, 65, 71

The defects, therefore, of government management, do not seem to be necessarily much greater, if necessarily greater at all, than those of management by joint-stock.

The true reasons in favour of leaving to voluntary associations all such things as they are competent to perform, would exist in equal strength if it were certain that the work itself would be as well or better done by public officers. These reasons have been already pointed out: the mischief of overloading the chief functionaries of government with demands on their attention, and diverting them from duties which they alone can discharge, to objects which can be sufficiently well attained without them; the danger of unnecessarily swelling the direct power and indirect influence of government, and multiplying occasions of collision between its agents and private citizens; and the [b] inexpediency of concentrating in a dominant bureaucracy, all the skill and experience in the management of large interests, and all the power of organized action, existing in the community; a practice which keeps the citizens in a relation to the government like that of children to their guardians, and is a main cause of the inferior capacity for political life which has hitherto characterized the over-governed countries of the Continent, whether with or without the forms of representative government.*

But although, for these reasons, most things which are likely to be even tolerably done by voluntary associations, should, generally speaking, be left to them; it does not follow that the manner in which those associations perform their work should be entirely uncontrolled by the government. There are many cases in which the agency, of whatever nature, by which a service is performed, is certain, from the nature of the case, to be virtually single; in which a practical monopoly, with all the power it confers of taxing the community, cannot be prevented from existing. I have already more than once adverted to the case of the gas and water companies, among which, though perfect freedom is allowed to competition, none really takes place, and practically they are found to be even more irresponsible, and

---

*A parallel case may be found in the distaste for politics, and absence of public spirit, by which women, as a class, are characterized in the present state of society, and which is often felt and complained of by political reformers, without, in general, making them willing to recognise, or desirous to remove, its cause. It obviously arises from their being taught, both by institutions and by the whole of their education, to regard themselves as entirely apart from politics. Wherever they have been politicians, they have shown as great interest in the subject, and as great aptitude for it, according to the spirit of their time, as the men with whom they were cotemporaries: in that period of history (for example) in which Isabella of Castile and Elizabeth of England were, not rare exceptions, but merely brilliant examples of a spirit and capacity very largely diffused among women of high station and cultivation in Europe.

[b]48, 49   still greater

unapproachable by individual complaints, than the government. There are the expenses without the advantages of plurality of agency; and the charge made for services which cannot be dispensed with, is, in substance, quite as much compulsory taxation as if imposed by law; there are few house-holders who make any distinction between their "water rate" and their other local taxes. In the case of these particular services, the reasons preponderate in favour of their being performed, like the paving and cleansing of the streets, not certainly by the general government of the state, but by the municipal authorities of the town, and the expense defrayed, as even now it in fact is, by a local rate. But in the many analogous cases which it is best to resign to voluntary agency, the community needs some other security for the fit performance of the service than the interest of the managers; and it is the part of government, either to subject the business to reasonable conditions for the general advantage, or to retain such power over it, that the profits of the monopoly may at least be obtained for the public. This applies to the case of a road, a canal, or a railway. These are always, in a great degree, practical monopolies; and a government which concedes such monopoly unreservedly to a private company, does much the same thing as if it allowed an individual or an association to levy any tax they chose, for their own benefit, on all the malt produced in the country, or on all the cotton imported into it. To make the concession for a limited time is generally justifiable, on the principle which justifies patents for inventions: but the state should either reserve to itself a reversionary property in such public works, or should retain, and freely exercise, the right of fixing a maximum of fares and charges, and, from time to time, varying that maximum. It is perhaps necessary to remark, that the state may be the proprietor of canals or railways without itself working them; and that they will almost always be better worked by means of a company, renting the railway or canal for a limited period from the state.

§ 12. [*Cases in which public intervention may be necessary to give effect to the wishes of the persons interested. Examples: hours of labour; disposal of colonial lands*] To a fourth case of exception I must request particular attention, it being one to which, as it appears to me, the attention of politi-cal economists has not yet been sufficiently drawn. There are matters in which the interference of law is required, not to overrule the judgment of individuals respecting their own interest, but to give effect to that judgment: they being unable to give effect to it except by concert, which concert again cannot be effectual unless it receives validity and sanction from the law. For illustration, and without prejudging the particular point, I may advert to the question of diminishing the hours of labour. Let us suppose, what is at least supposable, whether it be the fact or not—that a general reduction of the hours of factory labour [a], say from ten to nine[a], would be for the advantage of the work-people: that they would receive as high wages, or nearly as high, for [b]nine[b] hours' labour as they receive for [c]ten[c]. If this would be the result, and if the operatives generally are convinced that it would, the limitation, some may say, will be adopted spontaneously [d] . I answer, that it will not be adopted unless the body of operatives bind themselves to one another to abide by it. A workman who refused to work more than [e]nine[e] hours while there were others who worked [f]ten[f], would either not be employed at all, or if employed, must submit to lose [g]one-tenth[g] of his wages. However convinced, therefore, he may be that it is the interest of the class to work short time, it is contrary to his own interest to set the example, unless he is well assured that all or most others will follow it. But suppose a general agreement of the whole class: might not this be effectual without the sanction of law? Not unless enforced by opinion with a rigour practically equal to that of law. For however beneficial the observance of the regulation might be to the class collectively, the immediate interest of every individual would lie in violating it: and the more numerous those were who adhered to the rule, the more would individuals gain by departing from it. If nearly all restricted themselves to [h]nine[h] hours, those who chose to work for [i]ten[i] would gain all the [j]advantages[j] of the restriction, together with the profit of infringing it; they would get [k]ten[k] hours' wages for [l]nine[l] hours' work, and [m]an hour's[m] wages besides. I grant that if a large majority adhered to the [n]nine[n] hours, there would be no harm done: the benefit would be, in the main, secured to the class, while those individuals who preferred to work harder and earn more, would have an opportunity of doing so. This certainly would be the state of things to be wished for; and assuming that a reduction of hours without any diminution of wages could take place without expelling the commodity from some of its markets—which is in every particular instance a question of fact, not of principle—the manner in which it would be most desirable that this effect should be brought about, would be by a quiet change in the general custom of the trade; short hours becoming, by spontaneous choice, the general practice, but those who chose to deviate from it having the fullest liberty to do so. Probably, however, so many would prefer the [o]ten[o] hours' work

[a-a]48, 49, 52, 57   from twelve to ten
[b-b]48, 49, 52, 57   ten
[c-c]48, 49, 52, 57   twelve
[d]48, 49   , and there cannot be any need for enforcing it by a legal prohibition]
52, 57   *as* 48 . . . by legal . . . *as* 48
[e-e]48, 49, 52, 57   ten
[f-f]48, 49, 52, 57   twelve
[g-g]48, 49, 52, 57   one-sixth
[h-h]48, 49, 52, 57   ten
[i-i]48, 49, 52, 57   twelve
[j-j]48, 49, 52, 57, 62, 65   advantage
[k-k]48, 49, 52, 57   twelve
[l-l]48, 49, 52, 57   ten
[m-m]48, 49, 52, 57   two hours'
[n-n]48, 49, 52, 57   ten
[o-o]48, 49, 52, 57   twelve

on the improved terms, that the limitation could not be maintained as a general practice: what some did from choice, others would soon be obliged to do from necessity, and those who had chosen long hours for the sake of increased wages, would be forced in the end to work long hours for no greater wages than before. Assuming then that it really would be the interest of each to work only *p*nine*p* hours if he could be assured that all others would do the same, there might be no means of their attaining this object but by converting their supposed mutual agreement into an engagement under penalty, by consenting to have it enforced by law. I *q*am not expressing any*q* opinion in favour of such an enactment, *r*which has never *s*in this country*s* been demanded, and which I certainly should not, in present circumstances, recommend:*r* but it serves to exemplify the manner in which classes of persons may need the assistance of law, to give effect to their deliberate collective opinion of their own interest, by affording to every individual a guarantee that his competitors will pursue the same course, without which he cannot safely adopt it himself.

Another exemplification of the same principle *t* is afforded by what is known as the Wakefield system of colonization. This system is grounded on the important principle, that the degree of productiveness of land and labour depends on their being in a due proportion to one another; that if a few persons in a newly-settled country attempt to occupy and appropriate a large district, or if each labourer becomes too soon an occupier and cultivator of land, there is a loss of productive power, and a great retardation of the progress of the colony in wealth and civilization: that nevertheless the instinct (*u*as it may almost*u* be called) of appropriation, and the feelings associated in old countries with landed proprietorship, induce almost every emigrant to take possession of as much land as he has the means of acquiring, and every labourer to become at once a proprietor, cultivating his own land with no other aid than that of his family. If this propensity to the immediate possession of land could be in some degree restrained, and each labourer induced to work a certain number of years on hire before he became a landed proprietor, a perpetual stock of hired labourers could be maintained, available for roads, canals, works of irrigation, &c., and for the establishment and carrying on of the different branches of town industry; whereby the labourer, when he did at last become a landed proprietor, would find his land much more valuable, through access to markets, and facility of obtaining hired labour. Mr.

*p–p*48, 49, 52, 57   ten
*q–q*48, 49, 52, 57   do not mean to express an
r–r+62, 65, 71
s–s+71
*t*48, 49   , and one of great practical moment,
*u–u*48, 49, 52, 57   if such it may

Wakefield therefore proposed to check the premature occupation of land, and dispersion of the people, by putting upon all unappropriated lands a rather high price, the proceeds of which were to be expended in conveying emigrant labourers from the mother country.

This salutary provision, however, has been objected to, in the name and on the authority of what was represented as the great principle of political economy, that individuals are the best judges of their own interest. It was said, that when things are left to themselves, land is appropriated and occupied by the spontaneous choice of individuals, in the quantities and at the times most advantageous to each person, and therefore to the community generally; and that to interpose artificial obstacles to their obtaining land, is to prevent them from adopting the course which in their own judgment is most beneficial to them, from a self-conceited notion of the legislator, that he knows what is most for their interest, better than they do themselves. Now this is a complete misunderstanding, either of the system itself, or of the principle with which it is alleged to conflict. The oversight is similar to that which we have just seen exemplified on the subject of hours of labour. However beneficial it might be to the colony in the aggregate, and to each individual composing it, that no one should occupy more land than he can properly cultivate, nor become a proprietor until there are other labourers ready to take his place in working for hire; it can never be the interest of an individual to exercise this forbearance, unless he is assured that others will do so too. Surrounded by settlers who have each their thousand acres, how is he benefited by restricting himself to fifty? or what does ^{v}a labourer^v gain by deferring the acquisition altogether for a few years, if all other labourers rush to convert their first earnings into estates in the wilderness, several miles apart from one another? If they, by seizing on land, prevent the formation of a class of labourers for wages, he will not, by postponing the time of his becoming a proprietor, be enabled to employ the land with any greater advantage when he does obtain it; to what end therefore should he place himself in what will appear to him and others a position of inferiority, by remaining a ^{w}hired^w labourer, when all around him are proprietors? It is the interest of each to do what is good for all, but only if others will do likewise.

The principle that each is the best judge of his own interest, understood as these objectors understand it, would prove that governments ought not to fulfil any of their acknowledged duties—ought not, in fact, to exist at all. It is greatly the interest of the community, collectively and individually, not to rob or defraud one another: but there is not the less necessity for laws to punish robbery and fraud; because, though it is the interest of each that nobody should rob or cheat, it ^{x}is not^x any one's interest to refrain

$^{v-v}$48   he $^{w-w}$+49, 52, 57, 62, 65, 71 $^{x-x}$48   cannot be from robbing and cheating others when all others are permitted to rob and cheat him. Penal laws exist at all, chiefly for this *reason—* because *even an* unanimous opinion that a certain line of conduct is for the general interest, does not *always* make it people's individual interest to adhere to that line of conduct.

§ 13. [*Case of acts done for the benefit of others than the persons concerned. Poor Laws*] Fifthly; the argument against governmental interference grounded on the maxim that individuals are the best judges of their own interest, cannot apply to the very large class of cases, in which those acts of individuals *with which the government claims to interfere*, are not done by those individuals for their own interest, but for the interest of other people. This includes, among other things, the important and much agitated subject of public charity. Though individuals should, in general, be left to do for themselves whatever it can reasonably be expected that they should be capable of doing, yet when they are at any rate not to be left to themselves, but to be helped by other people, the question arises whether it is better that they should receive this help exclusively from individuals, and therefore uncertainly and casually, or by systematic arrangements, in which society acts through its organ, the state.

This brings us to the subject of Poor Laws; a subject which would be of very minor importance if the habits of all classes of the people were temperate and prudent, and the diffusion of property satisfactory; but of the greatest moment in a state of things so much the reverse of this, in both points, as that which the British islands present.

Apart from any metaphysical considerations respecting the foundation of morals or of the social union, it will be admitted to be right that human beings should help one another; and the more so, in proportion to the urgency of the need: and none needs help so urgently as one who is starving. The claim to help, therefore, created by destitution, is one of the strongest which can exist; and there is *primâ facie* the amplest reason for making the relief of so extreme an exigency as certain to those who require it, as by any arrangements of society it can be made.

On the other hand, in all cases of helping, there are two sets of consequences to be considered; the consequences of the assistance itself, and the consequences of relying on the assistance. The former are generally beneficial, but the latter, for the most part, injurious; so much so, in many cases, as greatly to outweigh the value of the benefit. And this is never more likely to happen than in the very cases where the need of help is the most intense.

*ᵛ–ᵛ*48, 49, 52, 57, 62   reason,
*ᶻ–ᶻ*48   an even   *ᵃ–ᵃ*+57, 62, 65, 71
*ᵃ–ᵃ*48, 49, 52, 57   over which the government claims control

There are few things for which it is more mischievous that people should rely on the habitual aid of others, than for the means of subsistence, and unhappily there is no lesson which they more easily learn. The problem to be solved is therefore one of peculiar nicety as well as importance; how to give the greatest amount of needful help, with the smallest encouragement to undue reliance on it.

Energy and self-dependence are, however, liable to be impaired by the absence of help, as well as by its excess. It is even more fatal to exertion to have no hope of succeeding by it, than to be assured of succeeding without it. When the condition of any one is so disastrous that his energies are paralyzed by discouragement, assistance is a tonic, not a sedative: it braces instead of *deadening* the active faculties: always provided that the assistance is not such as to dispense with self-help, by substituting itself for the person's own labour, skill, and prudence, but is limited to affording him a better hope of attaining success by those legitimate means. This accordingly is a test to which all plans of philanthropy and benevolence should be brought, whether intended for the benefit of individuals or of classes, and whether conducted on the voluntary or on the government principle.

In so far as the subject admits of any general doctrine or maxim, it would appear to be this—that if assistance is given in such a manner that the condition of the person helped is as desirable as that of the person who succeeds in doing the same thing without help, the assistance, if ᵒ capable of being previously calculated on, is mischievous: but if, while available to everybody, it leaves to every one a strong motive to do without it if he can, it is then for the most part beneficial. This principle, applied to a system of public charity, is that of the Poor Law of 1834. If the condition of a person receiving relief is made as eligible as that of the labourer who supports himself by his own exertions, the system strikes at the root of all individual industry and self-government; and, if fully acted up to, would require as its supplement an organized system of compulsion, for governing and setting to work like cattle, those who had been removed from the influence of the motives that act on human beings. But if, consistently with guaranteeing all persons against absolute want, the condition of those who are supported by legal charity can be kept considerably less desirable than the condition of those who find support for themselves, none but beneficial consequences can arise from a law which renders it impossible for any person, except by his own choice, to die from insufficiency of food. That in England at least this supposition can be realized, is proved by the experience of a long period preceding the close of the last century, as well as by that of many highly pauperized districts in more recent times, which have been dispauperized by adopting strict rules of poor-law administration,

ᵇ⁻ᵇ48, 49, 52, 57   relaxing   ᵒ48, 49   systematic and

to the great and permanent benefit of the whole labouring class. There is probably no country in which, by varying the means suitably to the character of the people, a legal provision for the destitute might not be made compatible with the observance of the conditions necessary to its being innocuous.

Subject to these conditions, I conceive it to be highly desirable, that the certainty of subsistence should be held out by law to the destitute able-bodied, rather than that their relief should depend on voluntary charity. In the first place, charity almost always does too much or too little: it lavishes its bounty in one place, and leaves people to starve in another. Secondly, since the state must necessarily provide subsistence for the criminal poor while undergoing punishment, not to do the same for the poor who have not offended is to give a premium on crime. And lastly, if the poor are left to individual charity, a vast amount of mendicity is inevitable [d] . What the state may and should abandon to private charity, is the task of distinguishing between one case of real necessity and another. [e]Private charity can give more to the more deserving.[e] The state must act by general rules. It cannot undertake to discriminate between the deserving and the undeserving indigent. It owes no more than subsistence to the first, and [f] can give no less to the last. What is said about the injustice of a law which has no better treatment for the merely unfortunate poor than for the ill-conducted, is founded on a misconception of the province of law and public authority. The dispensers of public relief have no business to be inquisitors. Guardians and overseers are not fit to be trusted to give or withhold other people's money according to their verdict on the morality of the person soliciting it; and it would show much ignorance of the ways of mankind to suppose that such persons, even in the almost impossible case of their being qualified, will take the trouble of ascertaining and sifting the past conduct of a person in distress, so as to form a rational judgment on it. Private charity can make these distinctions; and in bestowing its own money, is entitled to do so according to its own judgment. It should understand that this is its peculiar and appropriate province, and that it is commendable or the contrary, as it exercises the function with more or [g] less discernment. But the administrators of a public fund ought not to be required to do more for anybody, than that minimum which is due even to the worst. If they are, the indulgence very speedily becomes the rule, and refusal the more or less capricious or tyrannical exception.

§ 14. [*Case of acts done for the benefit of others. Colonization*] Another class of cases which fall within the same general principle as the case of

---

[d]48, 49 ; and to get rid of this is important, even as a matter of police [policy? *printer's error?*]   [e-e]+52, 57, 62, 65, 71   [f]48 it   [g]48, 49, 52, 57 with

public charity, are those in which the acts done by individuals, though intended solely for their own benefit, involve consequences extending indefinitely beyond them, to interests of the nation or of posterity, for which society in its collective capacity is alone able, and alone bound, to provide. One of these cases is that of Colonization. If it is desirable, as no one will deny it to be, that the planting of colonies should be conducted, not with an exclusive view to the private interests of the first founders, but with a deliberate regard to the permanent welfare of the nations afterwards to arise from these small beginnings; such regard can only be secured by placing the enterprise, from its commencement, under regulations constructed with the foresight and enlarged views of philosophical legislators; and the government alone has power either to frame such regulations, or to enforce their observance.

The question of government intervention in the work of Colonization involves the future and permanent interests of civilization itself, and far outstretches the comparatively narrow limits of purely economical considerations. But even with a view to those considerations alone, the removal of population from the overcrowded to the unoccupied parts of the earth's surface is one of those works of eminent social usefulness, which most require, and which at the same time best repay, the intervention of government.

To appreciate the benefits of colonization, it should be considered in its relation, not to a single country, but to the collective economical interests of the human race. The question is in general treated too exclusively as one of distribution; of relieving one labour market and supplying another. It is this, but it is also a question of production, and of the most efficient employment of the productive resources of the world. Much has been said of the good economy of importing commodities from the place where they can be bought cheapest; while the good economy of producing them where they can be produced cheapest, is comparatively little thought of. If to carry consumable goods from the places where they are superabundant to those where they are scarce, is a good pecuniary speculation, is it not an equally good speculation to do the same thing with regard to labour and instruments? The exportation of labourers and capital from old to new countries, from a place where their productive power is less, to a place where it is greater, increases by so much the aggregate produce of the labour and capital of the world. It adds to the joint wealth of the old and the new country, what amounts in a short period to many times the mere cost of effecting the transport. There needs be no hesitation in affirming that Colonization, in the present state of the world, is the [a] best affair of business, in which the capital of an old and wealthy country can [b] engage.

[a]48, 49   very   [b]48, 49   possibly

It is equally obvious, however, that Colonization on a great scale can be undertaken, as an affair of business, only by the government, or by some combination of individuals in complete understanding with the government ^c; except under such very peculiar circumstances as those which succeeded the Irish famine^c. Emigration on the voluntary principle ^drarely has^d any material influence in lightening the pressure of population in the old country, though as far as it goes it is doubtless a benefit to the colony. Those labouring persons who voluntarily emigrate are seldom the very poor; they are small farmers with some little capital, or labourers who have saved something, and who, in removing only their own labour from the crowded labour-market, withdraw from the capital of the country a fund which maintained and employed more labourers than themselves. Besides, this portion of the community is so limited in number, that it might be removed entirely, without making any sensible impression upon the numbers of the population, or even upon the annual increase. Any considerable emigration of labour is only practicable, when its cost is defrayed, or at least advanced, by others than the ^eemigrants^e themselves. Who then is to advance it? Naturally, it may be said, the capitalists of the colony, who require the labour, and who intend to employ it. But to this there is the obstacle, that a capitalist, after going to the expense of carrying out labourers, has no security that he shall be the person to derive any benefit from them. If all the capitalists of the colony were to combine, and bear the expense by subscription, they would still have no security that the labourers, when there, would continue to work for them. After working for a short time and earning a few pounds, they always, unless prevented by the government, squat on unoccupied land, and work only for themselves. The experiment has been repeatedly tried whether it was possible to enforce contracts for labour, or the repayment of the passage money of emigrants to those who advanced it, and the trouble and expense have always exceeded the advantage. The only other resource is the voluntary contributions of parishes or individuals, to rid themselves of surplus labourers who are already, or who are likely to become, locally chargeable on the poor-rate. Were this speculation to become general, it might produce a sufficient amount of emigration to clear off the existing unemployed population, but not to raise the wages of the ^femployed^f: and the same thing would require to be done over again in less than another generation.

One of the principal reasons why Colonization should be a national undertaking, is that in this manner alone ^g, save in highly exceptional cases,^g can emigration be self-supporting. The exportation of capital and labour

c–c+62, 65, 71
d–d48, 49   cannot have   e–e48, 49, 52, 57   labourers
f–f52   unemployed [*printer's error?*]   g–g+52, 57, 62, 65, 71

to a new country being, as before observed, one of the best of all affairs of business, it is absurd that it should not, like other affairs of business, repay its own expenses. Of the great addition which it makes to the produce of the world, there can be no reason why a sufficient portion should not be intercepted, and employed in reimbursing the outlay incurred in effecting it. For reasons already given, no individual, or body of individuals, can reimburse themselves for the expense; the government, however, can. It can take from the annual increase of wealth, caused by the emigration, the fraction which suffices to repay with interest what the emigration has cost. The expenses of emigration to a colony ought to be borne by the colony; and this, in general, is only possible when they are borne by the colonial government.

Of the modes in which a fund for the support of colonization can be raised in the colony, none is comparable in advantage to that which was first suggested, and [h] so ably and perseveringly advocated, by Mr. Wakefield: the plan of putting a price on all unoccupied land, and devoting the proceeds to emigration. The unfounded and pedantic objections to this plan have been answered in a former part of this chapter: we have now to speak of its advantages. First, it avoids the difficulties and discontents incident to raising a large annual amount by taxation; a thing which it is almost useless to attempt with a scattered population of settlers in the wilderness, who, as experience proves, can seldom be compelled to pay direct taxes, except at a cost exceeding their amount; while in an infant community indirect taxation soon reaches its limit. The sale of lands is thus by far the easiest mode of raising the requisite funds. But it has other and still greater recommendations. It is a beneficial check upon the tendency of a population of colonists to adopt the tastes and inclinations of savage life, and to disperse so widely as to lose all the advantages of commerce, of markets, of separation of employments, and combination of labour. By making it necessary for those who emigrate at the expense of the fund, to earn a considerable sum before they can become landed proprietors, it keeps up a perpetual succession of labourers for hire, who in every country are a most important auxiliary even to peasant proprietors: and by diminishing the eagerness of agricultural speculators to add to their domain, it keeps the settlers within reach of each other for purposes of co-operation, arranges a numerous body of them within easy distance of each centre of foreign commerce and non-agricultural industry, and insures the formation and rapid growth of towns and town products. This concentration, compared with the dispersion which uniformly occurs when unoccupied land can be had for nothing, greatly accelerates the attainment of prosperity, and enlarges the fund which may be drawn upon for further emigration. Before the adoption of the Wakefield system, the early years of all new colonies

[h]48, 49, 52, 57, 62, 65   has since been

were full of hardship and difficulty: the last colony founded on the old principle, the Swan River settlement, being one of the most characteristic instances. In all subsequent colonization, the Wakefield principle has been acted upon, though imperfectly, *i* a part only of the proceeds *j*of the sale of land*j* being devoted to emigration: yet wherever it has been introduced at all, as in South Australia, *k*Victoria*k*, and New Zealand, the restraint put upon the dispersion of the settlers, and the influx of capital caused by the assurance of being able to obtain hired labour, has, in spite of many difficulties and much mismanagement, produced a suddenness and rapidity of prosperity more like fable than reality. *l* *

The self-supporting system of colonization, once established, would increase in efficiency every year; its effect would tend to increase in geometrical progression: for since every able-bodied emigrant, until the country is fully peopled, adds in a very short time to its wealth, over and above his own consumption, as much as would defray the expense of bringing out another emigrant, it follows that the greater the number already sent, the greater number might continue to be sent, each emigrant laying the foundation of a succession of other emigrants at short intervals without fresh expense, until the colony is filled up. It would therefore be worth while, to the mother country, to accelerate the early stages of this progression, by loans to the colonies for the purpose of emigration, repayable from the fund formed by the sales of land. In thus advancing the means of accomplishing a large immediate emigration, it would be investing that amount of capital in the mode, of all others, most beneficial to the colony; and the labour and savings of these emigrants would hasten the period at which a large sum would be available from sales of land. It would be necessary, in order not to overstock the labour market, to act in concert with the persons disposed to remove their own capital to the colony. The knowledge

*[57] The objections which have been made, with so much virulence, in some of these colonies, to the Wakefield system, apply, in so far as they have any validity, not to the principle, but to some provisions which are no part of the system, and have been most unnecessarily and improperly engrafted on it; such as the offering only a limited quantity of land for sale, and that by auction, and in lots of not less than 640 acres, instead of selling all land which is asked for, and allowing to the buyer unlimited freedom of choice, both as to quantity and situation, at a fixed price.

*i*48, 49   the price of land being generally fixed too low, and
j-j+52, 57, 62, 65, 71
*k-k*48, 49, 52, 57   Port Philip
*l*48   The oldest of the Wakefield colonies, South Australia, is scarcely twelve years old; Port Philip is still more recent; and they are probably at this moment the two places, in the known world, where labour on the one hand, and capital on the other, are the most highly remunerated.]   49 *as* 48 . . . is little more than twelve . . . *as* 48

that a large amount of hired labour would be available, in so productive a field of employment, would insure a large emigration of capital from a country, like England, of low profits and rapid accumulation: and it would only be necessary not to send out a greater number of labourers at one time, than this capital could absorb and employ at high wages.

Inasmuch as, on this system, any given amount of expenditure, once incurred, would provide not merely a single emigration, but a perpetually flowing stream of emigrants, which would increase in breadth and depth as it flowed on; this mode of relieving overpopulation has a recommendation, not possessed by any other plan ever proposed for making head against the consequences of increase without restraining the increase itself: there is an element of indefiniteness in it; no one can perfectly foresee how far its influence, as a vent for surplus population, might possibly reach. There is hence the strongest obligation on the government of a country like our own, with a crowded population, and unoccupied continents under its command, to build, as it were, and keep open, *m*in concert with the colonial governments,*m* a bridge from the mother country to those continents, by establishing the self-supporting system of colonization on such a scale, that as great an amount of emigration as the colonies can at the time accommodate, may at all times be able to take place without cost to the emigrants themselves.

*n*The importance of these considerations, *o* as regards the British islands, *p*has been of late*p* considerably diminished by the unparalleled amount of spontaneous emigration from Ireland; an emigration not solely of small farmers, but of the poorest class of agricultural labourers, and which is at once voluntary and self-supporting, the succession of emigrants being kept up by funds contributed from the earnings of their relatives and connexions who *q*had*q* gone before. *r*To this has been added a large amount of voluntary emigration to the seats of the gold discoveries, which has partly supplied the wants of our most distant colonies, where, both for local and national interests, it was most of all required. But the stream of both these emigrations has already considerably slackened, and *s*though that from Ireland has since partially revived,*s* *t*it is not certain*t* that the aid of government in a systematic form, and on the self-supporting principle, *u*will not again become*u* necessary to keep the communication open between the hands needing work in England, and the work which needs hands elsewhere.*r n*

m–m+71
n–n+52, 57, 62, 65, 71   *o*52   at the present moment,
*p–p*52   is   *q–q*52   have
*r–r*52   While the stream of this emigration continues flowing, as broad and deep as at present, the principal office required from government would be to direct a portion of it to quarters (such as Australia), where, both for local and national interests, it is most of all required, but which it does not sufficiently reach in its spontaneous course.   *s–s*+65, 71
    *t–t*57   there are indications   *u–u*57   is again becoming

§ 15. [*Case of acts done for the benefit of others. Miscellaneous examples*] The same principle which points out colonization, and the relief of the indigent, as cases to which the principal objection to government interference does not apply, extends also to a variety of cases, in which important public services are to be performed, while yet there is no individual specially interested in performing them, nor would any adequate remuneration naturally or spontaneously attend their performance. Take for instance a voyage of geographical or scientific exploration. The information sought may be of great public value, yet no individual would derive any benefit from it which would repay the expense of fitting out the expedition; and there is no mode of intercepting the benefit on its way to those who profit by it, in order to levy a toll for the remuneration of its authors. Such voyages are, or might be, undertaken by private subscription; but this is a rare and precarious resource. Instances are more frequent in which the expense has been borne by public companies or philanthropic associations; but in general such enterprises have been conducted at the expense of government, which is thus enabled to entrust them to the persons in its judgment best qualified for the task. Again, it is a proper office of government to build and maintain lighthouses, establish buoys, &c. for the security of navigation: for since it is impossible that the ships at sea which are benefited by a lighthouse, should be made to pay a toll on the occasion of its use, no one would build lighthouses from motives of personal interest, unless indemnified and rewarded from a compulsory levy made by the state. There are many scientific researches, of great value to a nation and to mankind, requiring assiduous devotion of time and labour, and not unfrequently great expense, by persons who can obtain a high price for their services in other ways. If the government had no power to grant indemnity for expense, and remuneration for time and labour thus employed, such researches could only be undertaken by the very few persons who, with an independent fortune, unite technical knowledge, laborious habits, and either great public spirit, or an ardent desire of scientific celebrity.

*a*Connected with this subject is the question of providing, by means of endowments or salaries, for the maintenance of what has been called a learned class. The cultivation of speculative knowledge, though one of the most useful of all employments, is a service rendered to *b*a*b* community collectively, not individually, and one *c*consequently for which*c* it is, *primâ facie*, reasonable that the community collectively should pay; since it gives no claim on any individual for a pecuniary remuneration; and unless a provision is made for such services from some public fund, there is not only

---

*a–a*96948, 49, 52, 57, 62   [*in footnote*]
*b–b*48   the
*c–c*62   consequently which [*printer's error?*]

no encouragement to them, but there is as much discouragement as is implied in the impossibility of gaining a living by such pursuits, and the necessity consequently imposed on most of those who would be capable of them, to employ the greatest part of their time in gaining a subsistence. The evil, however, is greater in appearance than in reality. The greatest things, it has been said, have generally been done by those who had the least time at their disposal; and the occupation of some hours every day in a routine employment, has often been found compatible with the most brilliant achievements in literature and philosophy. Yet there are investigations and experiments which require not only a long but a continuous devotion of time and attention: there are also occupations which so engross and fatigue the mental faculties, as to be inconsistent with any vigorous employment of them upon other subjects, even in intervals of leisure. It is highly desirable, therefore, that there should be a mode of insuring to the public the services of scientific discoverers, and perhaps of some other classes of savants, by affording them the means of support consistently with devoting a sufficient portion of time to their peculiar pursuits. The fellowships of *d*the*d* Universities are an institution excellently adapted for such a purpose; but are hardly ever applied to it, being bestowed, at the best, as a reward for past proficiency, in committing to memory what has been done by others, and not as the salary of future labours in the advancement of knowledge. In some countries, Academies of science, antiquities, history, &c., have been formed, with emoluments annexed. The most effectual plan, and at the same time *e* least liable to abuse, seems to be that of conferring Professorships, with duties of instruction attached to them. The occupation of teaching a branch of knowledge, at least in its higher departments, is a help rather than an impediment to the systematic cultivation of the subject itself. The duties of a professorship almost always leave much time for original researches; and the greatest advances which have been made in the various sciences, both moral and physical, have originated with those who were public teachers of them; from *f*Plato and Aristotle*f* to the great names of the Scotch, French, and German Universities. I do not mention the English, because *g*until very lately*g* their professorships *h*have been*h*, as is well known, little more than nominal. In the case, too, of a lecturer in a great institution of education, the public at large has the means of judging, if not the quality of the teaching, at least the talents and industry of the teacher; and it is more difficult to misemploy the power of appointment to such an office, than to job in pensions and salaries to persons not so directly before the public eye.*a*

*d–d*48, 49   our
*e*48, 49, 52, 57, 62   the
g–g+65, 71

*f–f*48, 49   Aristotle and Plato
*h–h*48, 49, 52   are

It may be said generally, that anything which it is desirable should be done for the general interests of mankind or of future generations, or for the present interests of those members of the community who require external aid, but which is not of a nature to remunerate individuals or associations for undertaking it, is in itself a suitable thing to be undertaken by government: though, before making the work their own, governments ought always to consider if there be any rational probability of its being done on what is called the voluntary principle, and if so, whether it is likely to be done in a better or more effectual manner by government agency, than by the zeal and liberality of individuals.

§ 16. [*Government intervention may be necessary in default of private agency, in cases where private agency would be more suitable*] The preceding heads comprise, to the best of my judgment, the whole of the exceptions to the practical maxim, that the business of society can be best performed by private and voluntary agency. It is, however, necessary to add, that the intervention of government cannot always practically stop short at the limit which defines the cases intrinsically suitable for it. In the particular circumstances of a given age or nation, there is scarcely anything really important to the general interest, which it may not be desirable, or even necessary, that the government should take upon itself, not because private individuals cannot effectually perform it, but because they will not. At some times and places, there will be no roads, docks, harbours, canals, works of irrigation, hospitals, schools, colleges, printing-presses, unless the government establishes them; the public being either too poor to command the necessary resources, or too little advanced in intelligence to appreciate the ends, or not sufficiently practised in *ᵃ*joint*ᵃ* action to be capable of the means. This is true, more or less, of all countries inured to despotism, and particularly of those in which there is a very wide distance in civilization between the people and the government: as in those which have been conquered and are retained in subjection by a more energetic and more cultivated people. In many parts of the world, the people can do nothing for themselves which requires large means and combined action: all such things are left undone, unless done by the state. In these cases, the mode in which the government can most surely demonstrate the sincerity with which it intends the greatest good of its subjects, is by doing the things which are made incumbent on it by the helplessness of the public, in such a manner as shall tend not to increase and perpetuate, but to correct, that helplessness. A good government will give all its aid in such a shape, as to encourage and nurture any rudiments it may find of a spirit of individual exertion. It will be assiduous in removing obstacles and discouragements to voluntary enter-

ᵃ⁻ᵃ48, 49, 52, 57   conjoint

prise, and in giving whatever facilities and whatever direction and guidance may be necessary: its pecuniary means will be *b*applied*b*, when practicable, in aid of private efforts rather than in supersession of them, and it will call into play its machinery of rewards and honours to elicit such efforts. Government aid, when given merely in default of private enterprise, should be so given as to be as far as possible a course of education for the people in the art of accomplishing great objects by individual energy and voluntary co-operation.

I have not thought it necessary here to insist on that part of the functions of government which all admit to be indispensable, the function of prohibiting and punishing such conduct on the part of individuals in the exercise of their freedom, as is clearly injurious to other persons, whether the case be one of force, fraud, or negligence. Even in the best state which society has yet reached, it is lamentable to think how great a proportion of all the efforts and talents in the world are employed in merely neutralizing one another. It is the proper end of government to reduce this wretched waste to the smallest possible amount, by taking such measures as shall cause the energies now spent by mankind in injuring one another, or in protecting themselves against injury, to be turned to the legitimate employment of the human faculties, that of compelling the powers of nature to be more and more subservient to physical and moral good.

*b–b*48   supplied

APPENDICES

Appendix A

Book II, Chapter i ("Of Property"), §§ 3–6, 2nd edition (1849), collated
with the 1st edition and the MS[1]

§ 3. [*Examination of Communism*] It would be too much to affirm that
communities constituted on *any* of these principles could not permanently
subsist. That a country of any large extent could be formed into a single
"Co-operative Society," is indeed not easily conceivable. The nearest
approach to it ever realized seems to have been the government of Peru
under the Incas, a despotism held together by a superstition; not likely to
be erected into a type for modern aspirations, although it appeared mild
and beneficent to those who contrasted it with the iron rule which took its
place.* But a country might be covered with small Socialist communities,
and these might have a Congress to manage their joint concerns. The
scheme is not what is commonly meant by impracticable. Supposing that
the soil and climate were tolerably propitious, and that the several communities, possessing the means of all necessary production within themselves, had not to contend in the general markets of the world against the
competition of societies founded on private property, I doubt not that by a
very rigid system of repressing population, they might be able to live and
hold together, without positive discomfort. This would be a considerable
improvement, so far as the great majority are concerned, over those existing
states of society in which no restraint at all is placed on population, or in
which the restraint is very inadequate.

[The objection ordinarily made to a system of community of property
and equal distribution of the produce, that each person would be incessantly

*See [William H.] Prescott's History of the Conquest of Peru [*with a
Preliminary View of the Civilization of the Incas*. 2 vols. London: Bentley,
1847].

*a–a*MS, 48   either

[1]The method of footnoting is the same as that used in the text proper: i.e., the MS
and 48 variants are indicated by superscript letters and given in footnotes. The places
where the 49 text *agrees* with the 71 text are surrounded by square brackets to
simplify comparison; references to the 71 text are given in numbered footnotes to the
end of bracketed passages.

occupied in evading his fair share of the work,]² is, I think, in general considerably overstated. There is a kind of work, hitherto more indispensable than most others, that of fighting, which is never conducted on any other than the co-operative system; and neither in a rude nor in a civilized society has the supposed difficulty been experienced. Education and the current of opinion having adapted themselves to the exigency, the sense of honour and the fear of shame have as yet been found to operate with sufficient strength; and common sentiment has sanctioned the enforcement by adequate penalties, upon those not sufficiently influenced by other motives, of rules of discipline certainly not deficient in rigidity. The same sanctions would not fail to attach themselves to the operations of industry, and to secure, as indeed they are found to do in the Moravian and similar establishments, a tolerable adherence to the prescribed standard of duty. The deficiency would be of motives to exceed that minimum standard. In war, the question lies between great success and great failure, between losing a battle and gaining it, perhaps between being slaves and conquerors; and the circumstances of the case are stirring and stimulating to the feelings and faculties. The common operations of industry are the reverse of stirring and stimulating, and the only direct result of extra exertion would be a trifling addition to the common stock shared out among the mass. Mankind are capable of a far greater amount of public spirit than the present age is accustomed to suppose possible. But if the question were that of taking a great deal of personal trouble to produce a very small and unconspicuous public benefit, the love of ease would preponderate. Those who made extra exertions would expect and demand that the same thing should be required from others and made a duty; and in the long run, little more work would be performed by any, than could be exacted from all: the limit to all irksome labour would be the amount which the majority would consent to have made compulsory on themselves. But the majority, even in our present societies, where the intensity of competition and the exclusive dependence of each on his own energies tend to give a morbid strength to the industrial spirit, are almost everywhere indolent and unambitious; content with little, and unwilling to trouble themselves in order to make it more. The standard of industrial duty would therefore be fixed extremely low. There are, no doubt, some kinds of useful exertion to which the stimulus would not be weakened in the same degree. Invention is one of these. Invention is in itself an agreeable exercise of the faculties; and when applied successfully to the diminution of labour or the satisfaction of the physical wants of the community, it would in any society be a source of considerable *éclat*. But though to invent is a pleasant operation, to perfect an invention and render it practical is a dull and toilsome one; requiring also means and appliances

[²See I.203.37—204.2 *above*.]

which, in a society so *b*constructed,*b* no one would possess of his own. The many and long-continued trials by which the object is at last attained, could only be made by first persuading the majority that the scheme would be advantageous: and might be broken off at the very time when the work approached completion, if the patience of the majority became exhausted. We might expect therefore that there would be many projects conceived, and very few perfected; while, the projects being prosecuted, if at all, at the public expense and not at the projector's, if there was any disposition to encourage them, the proportion of bad schemes to good would probably be even greater than at present.

It must be further observed, that the perfect equality contemplated in the theory of the scheme could not be really attained. The produce might be divided equally, but how could the labour? There are many kinds of work, and by what standard are they to be measured one against another? Who is to judge how much cotton spinning, or distributing goods from the stores, or bricklaying, or chimney sweeping, is equivalent to so much ploughing? In the existing system of industry these things do adjust themselves with some, though but a distant, approach to fairness. If one kind of work is harder or more disagreeable than another, or requires a longer practice, it is better paid, simply because there are fewer competitors for it; and an individual generally finds that he can earn most by doing the thing which he is fittest for. I admit that this self-adjusting machinery does not touch some of the grossest of the existing inequalities of remuneration, and in particular the unjust advantage possessed by almost the commonest mental over almost the hardest and most disagreeable bodily labour. Employments which require any kind of technical education, however simple, have hitherto been the subject of a real monopoly as against the mass. But as popular instruction advances, this monopoly is already becoming less complete, and every increase of prudence and foresight among the people encroaches upon it more and more. On the Communist system the impossibility of making the adjustment between different qualities of labour is so strongly felt, that the advocates of the scheme usually find it necessary to provide that all should work by turns at every description of useful labour; an arrangement which, by putting an end to the division of employments, would sacrifice the principal advantage which co-operative production possesses, and would probably reduce the amount of production still lower than in our supposition. And after all, the nominal equality of labour would be so great a real inequality, that justice would revolt against its being enforced. All persons are not equally fit for all labour; and the same quantity of labour is an unequal burthen on the weak and the strong, the hardy and the delicate, the quick and *c* slow, the dull and the intelligent.

*b–b*MS constituted   *c*MS the

Assuming, however, all the success which is claimed for this state of society by its partisans, it remains to be considered how much would be really gained for mankind, and whether the form that would be given to life, and the character which would be impressed on human nature, *d*would be such as to*d* satisfy any but a *e* low estimate of the capabilities of the species. *f*On the Communistic scheme, supposing it to be successful, there would be an end to all anxiety concerning the means of subsistence; and this would be much gained for human happiness. But it is perfectly possible to realize this same advantage in a society grounded on private property; and to this point the tendencies of political speculation are rapidly converging. Supposing this attained, it is surely a vast advantage on the side of the individual system, that it is compatible with a far greater degree of personal liberty.*f* The perfection of social arrangements would be to secure to all persons complete independence and freedom of action, subject to no restriction but that of not doing injury to others *g*. The*g* scheme which we are considering *h*(at least as it is commonly understood)*h* abrogates this freedom entirely, and places every action of every member of the community under command.

Communism, it is true, might exist without forcing the members of the community to live together, or controlling them in the disposal of their appointed rations, and of such leisure as might be left to them; but it is of the essence of the scheme, that the association, through its managing body, should have absolute power over every one of its members during working hours, and that no one could choose either at what, or with whom, or

*d–d*MS, 48   can

*e*MS, 48   very

*f–f*MS, 48   Those who have never known freedom from anxiety as to the means of subsistence, are apt to overrate what is gained for positive enjoyment by the mere absence of that uncertainty. The necessaries of life, when they have always been secure for the whole of life, are scarcely more a subject of consciousness or a source of happiness than the elements. There is little attractive in a monotonous routine, without vicissitudes, but without excitement; a life spent in the enforced observance of an external rule, and performance of a prescribed task: in which labour would be devoid of its chief sweetener, the thought that every effort tells perceptibly on the labourer's own interests or those of some one with whom he identifies himself; in which no one could by his own exertions improve his condition, or that of the objects of his private affections; in which no one's way of life, occupations, or movements, would depend on choice, but each would be the slave of all: a social system in which identity of education and pursuits would impress on all the same unvarying type of character, to the destruction of that multiform developement of human nature, those manifold unlikenesses, that diversity of tastes and talents, and variety of intellectual points of view, which by presenting to each innumerable notions that he could not have conceived of himself, are the great stimulus to intellect and the mainspring of mental and moral progression. [*Cf.* p. 979. 13–19.]

*g–g*MS, 48   : but the

h–h+49   *i–1979*+49

generally in what method, he would work. Let us add, that the work would be devoid of all feeling of interest, except that which might be conferred on it by a principle of duty to the community. All the interest which it now derives from the hope of advancement, or of increased gain to the labourer himself, or to the objects of his private affections, would cease; and it remains to be shown that any equally powerful source of excitement would be substituted for these, or that the feeling of duty, even if strong enough to ensure performance of the work, would have the power of rendering it agreeable. What was done, would probably be done as men do the things, which are not done from choice but from necessity: and a life passed in the enforced observance of an external rule, and performance of a prescribed task, would sink into a monotonous routine. Lastly, the identity of education and pursuits would tend to impress on all the same unvarying type of character; to the destruction of that multiform development of human nature, those manifold unlikenesses, that diversity of tastes and talents, and variety of intellectual points of view, which not only form a great part of the interest of human life, but by bringing intellects into stimulating collision, and by presenting to each innumerable notions that he could not have conceived of himself, are the mainspring of mental and moral progression.[i]

I am aware it may be said that the great majority of the species already suffer, in the existing state of society, all the disadvantages which I ascribe to the Communist system. The factory labourer has as monotonous, indeed a more monotonous existence, than a member of an Owenite community; working a greater number of hours, and at the same dull occupation, without the alternation of employment which the Socialist scheme provides. The generality of labourers, in this and most other countries, have as little choice of occupation or freedom of locomotion, are practically as dependent on fixed rules and on the will of others, as they could be on any system short of actual slavery; to say nothing of the entire domestic subjection of one half the species, to whom it is the signal honour of Owenism and most other forms of ʲSocialismʲ that they assign equal rights, in all respects, with those of the hitherto dominant sex. Again, it may be said of almost all labourers, on the present system, namely of all who work by the day, or for a fixed salary, that labouring for the gain of others, not for their own, they have no interest in doing more than the smallest quantity of work which will pass as a fulfilment of the mere terms of their engagement. Production, therefore, it may be said, should be at least as inefficient on the present plan, as it would be from a similar cause under the other.

To take the last argument first, it is true that, for the very reason assigned, namely the insufficient interest which day-labourers have in the result of their labour, there is a natural tendency in such labour to be extremely

ʲ–ʲMS, 48   Communism

inefficient: a tendency only *to be* overcome by *l* vigilant superintendence on the part of persons who *are* interested in the result. The "master's eye" is notoriously the only security to be relied on. If a delegated and hired superintendence is found effectual, it is when the superintendents themselves are well superintended, and have a high salary and a privileged situation to lose on being found neglectful of their trust. Superintend them as you will, day-labourers are so much inferior to those who work by the piece, that the latter system is practised in all industrial occupations to which it is conveniently applicable. And yet it is by no means true that day-labourers, under the present arrangements, have no inducements of private interest to energetic action. They have a strong inducement, that of gaining a character as workmen, which may secure them a preference in employment; and they have often a hope of promotion and of rising in the world, nor is that hope always disappointed. Where no such possibility is open to the labouring classes, their condition is confessedly wrong, and demands a remedy. With respect to the other objections which I have anticipated, I freely admit them. I believe that the condition of the operatives in a well-regulated manufactory, with a great reduction of the hours of labour and a considerable variety of the kind of it, is very like what the condition of all would be in *m*an Owenite*m* community. *n* But to maintain even this state, the limitation of the propagative powers of the community must be as much a matter of public regulation as everything else; since under the supposed arrangements prudential restraint would no longer exist. Now, if we suppose an equal degree of regulation to take place under the present system, either compulsorily, or, what would be so much preferable, voluntarily; a condition at least equal to what the *o*Communist*o* system offers to all, would fall to the lot of the least fortunate, by the mere action of the competitive principle. Whatever of pecuniary means or freedom of action any one obtained beyond this, would be so much to be counted in favour of the competitive system. It is an abuse of the principle of equality to demand that no individual be permitted to be better off than the rest, when his being so makes none of the others worse off than they otherwise would be.

§ 4. [*Examination of St. Simonism*] These arguments *a* against Communism are not applicable to St. Simonism, a system of far higher intellectual pretensions than the *b*former:*b* constructed with greater foresight of

---

k–k+48, 49   *l*MS   most   *m–m*MS, 48   a Socialist
*n*MS, 48   I believe that the majority would not exert themselves for any thing beyond this, and that unless they did, nobody else would; and that on this basis human life would settle itself into one invariable round.
*o–o*MS, 48   Socialist
*a*MS   conclusive] 48   , to my mind conclusive
*b–b*MS, 48   other;

objections, and juster appreciation of them; grounded on views of human nature much less limited, and the work altogether of larger and more accomplished minds, by most of whom accordingly, what was erroneous in their theory has long ago been seen and abandoned. [The St. Simonian scheme does not contemplate an equal, but an unequal division of the produce; it does not propose that all should be occupied alike, but differently, according to their vocation or capacity; the function of each being assigned, like grades in a regiment, by the choice of the directing authority, and the remuneration being by salary, proportioned to the importance, in the eyes of that authority, of the function itself, and the merits of the person who fulfils it. For the constitution of the ruling body, different plans might be adopted, consistently with the essentials of the system. It might be appointed by popular suffrage. In the idea of the original authors, the rulers were supposed to be persons of genius and virtue, who obtained the voluntary adhesion of the rest by][1] mere [force of mental superiority],[2] through a religious feeling of reverence and subordination. Society, thus constituted, would wear as diversified a face as it does now; would be still fuller of interest and excitement, would hold out even more abundant stimulus to individual exertion, and would nourish, it is to be feared, even more of rivalries and animosities than at present. [That the scheme might in some peculiar states of society work with advantage,][3] I will not deny. [There is indeed a successful experiment, of a somewhat similar kind, on record, to which I have once alluded, that of the Jesuits, in Paraguay. A race of savages, belonging to a portion of mankind more averse to consecutive exertion for a distant object than any other authentically known to us, was brought under the mental dominion of civilized and instructed men who were united among themselves by a system of community of goods. To the absolute authority of these men they reverentially submitted themselves, and were induced by them to learn the arts of civilized life, and to practise labours for the community which no inducement that could have been offered would have prevailed on them to practise for themselves. This social system was of short duration, being prematurely destroyed by diplomatic arrangements and foreign force. That it could be brought into action at all was probably owing to the immense distance in point of knowledge and intellect which separated the few rulers from the whole body of the ruled, without any intermediate orders, either social or intellectual. In any other circumstances it would probably have been a complete failure][4]; and we may venture to say that in no European community could it have even the

[1*See* I.210.37—211.7 *above.*]
[2*See* I.211.7–8 *above.*]
[3*See* I.211.8–9 *above.*]
[4*See* I.211.9–25 *above.*]

partial success which might really be obtained by an association on the principle of Communism. [It supposes an absolute despotism in the heads of the association; which would probably not be much improved if the depositaries of the despotism (contrary to the views of the authors of the system) were varied from time to time according to the result of a popular canvass. But to suppose that one or a few human beings, howsoever selected, could, by whatever machinery of subordinate agency, be qualified to adapt each person's work to his capacity, and proportion each person's remuneration to his merits—to be, in fact, the dispensers of distributive justice to every member of a community][5], were it even the smallest that ever had a separate political existence—[or that any use which they could make of this power would give general satisfaction, or would be submitted to without the aid of force—is a supposition almost too chimerical to be reasoned against. A fixed rule, like that of equality, might be acquiesced in, and so might chance, or an external necessity; but that a handful of human beings should weigh everybody in the balance, and give more to one and less to another at their sole pleasure and judgment, would not be borne unless from persons believed to be more than men, and backed by supernatural terrors.

§ 5. [*Examination of Fourierism*] [a]The most skilfully combined, and][1] in every respect the least open to objection, of [the forms of Socialism, is that commonly known as Fourierism. This system does not contemplate the abolition of private property, nor even of inheritance: on the contrary, it avowedly takes into consideration, as an element in the distribution of the produce, capital as well as labour. It proposes that the operations of industry should be carried on by associations of about two thousand members, combining their labour on a district of about a square league in extent, under the guidance of chiefs selected by themselves. In the distribution, a certain minimum is first assigned for the subsistence of every member of the community, whether capable or not of labour. The remainder of the produce is shared in certain proportions, to be determined beforehand, among the three elements, Labour, Capital, and Talent. The capital of the

---

[a-a]986MS, 48   There has never been imagined any mode of distributing the produce of industry, so well adapted to the requirements of human nature on the whole, as that of letting the share of each individual (not in a state of bodily or mental incapacity,) depend in the main on that individual's own energies and exertions, and on such furtherance as may be obtained from the voluntary good offices of others. It is not the subversion of the system of individual property that should be aimed at; but the improvement of it, and the participation of every member of the community in its benefits.

[5See I.211.25–9 above.]
[1See I.211.33–42 above.]

community may be owned in unequal shares by different members, who would in that case receive, as in any other joint-stock company, proportional dividends. The claim of each person on the share of the produce apportioned to talent, is estimated by the grade or rank which the individual occupies in the several groups of labourers to which he or she belongs; these grades being in all cases conferred by the choice of his or her companions. The remuneration, when received, would not of necessity be expended or enjoyed in common; there would be separate *ménages* for all who preferred them, and no other community of living is contemplated, than that all the members of the association should reside in the same pile of buildings; for saving of labour and expense not only in building, but in every branch of domestic economy; and in order that, the whole]² [buying and selling operations of the community being performed by a single agent, the enormous portion of the produce of industry now carried off by the profits of mere distributors might be reduced to the smallest amount possible.]³

Thus far it is apparent that this [system, unlike Communism, does not, in theory at least, withdraw any of the motives to exertion which exist in the present]⁴ system [of society. On the contrary, if the arrangement]⁵ could be supposed to work [according to the intentions of its contrivers, it would even strengthen those motives, since each person would have much more certainty of reaping individually the fruits of increased skill or energy, bodily or mental, than under the present social arrangements can be felt by any but those who are in the most advantageous positions, or to whom the chapter of accidents is more than ordinarily favourable. The Fourierists, however, have still another resource. They believe that they have solved the great and fundamental problem of rendering labour attractive. That this is not impracticable, they contend by very strong arguments; in particular by one which they have in common with the Owenites, viz., that scarcely any labour, however severe, undergone by human beings for the sake of subsistence, exceeds in intensity that which other human beings, whose subsistence is already provided for, are found ready and even eager to undergo for pleasure. This certainly is a most significant fact, and one from which the student in social philosophy may draw important instruction. But the argument founded on it may easily be stretched too far. If occupations full of discomfort and fatigue are freely pursued by many persons as amusements, who does not see that they are amusements exactly because they are pursued freely, and may be discontinued at pleasure? The liberty of quitting

[²*See* I.212.1–24 *above.*]
[³*See* I.212.24–7 *above.*]
[⁴*See* I.212.28–9 *above.*]
[⁵*See* I.212.29–30 *above.*]

a position often makes the whole difference between its being painful and pleasurable. Many a person remains in the same town, street, or house from January to December, without a wish or a thought tending towards removal, who if confined to that same place by the mandate of authority, would find the imprisonment absolutely intolerable.

According to the Fourierists, scarcely any kind of useful labour is naturally and necessarily disagreeable, unless it is either regarded as dishonourable, or is immoderate in degree, or destitute of the stimulus of sympathy and emulation.][6] The few kinds of useful employment which are inherently distasteful to either the physical or the moral sense, or which would be so to persons in as high a state of cultivation as the Fourierists rightly aspire to confer upon all, they propose to surround with marks of honour, and to remunerate on the highest scale. [Excessive toil needs not, they contend, be undergone by any one, in a society in which there would be no idle class, and no labour wasted, as so enormous an amount of labour is now wasted, in useless things; and where full advantage would be taken of the power of association, both in increasing the efficiency of production, and in economizing consumption. The other requisites for rendering labour attractive would, they think, be found in the execution of all labour by social groups, to any number of which the same individual might simultaneously belong, at his or her own choice; their grade in each being determined by the degree of service which they were found capable of rendering, as appreciated by the suffrages of their comrades. It is inferred from the diversity of tastes and talents, that every member of the community would be attached to several groups, employing themselves in various kinds of occupation, some bodily, others mental, and would be capable of occupying a high place in some one or more; so that a real equality, or][7] a [something more nearly approaching to it than might at first be supposed, would practically result: not][8] (as in Communism) [from the compression, but, on the contrary, from the largest possible developement, of the various natural superiorities residing in each individual.

Even from so brief an outline, it][9] will be perceived [that this system does no violence to any of the general laws by which human action, even in the present imperfect state of moral and intellectual cultivation, is influenced][10]. All persons would have a prospect of deriving individual advantage from every degree of labour, of abstinence, and of talent, which they individually exercised. The impediments to success would not be in the principles of the system, but in the unmanageable nature of its machinery.

[6See I.212.30—213.17 above.]
[7See I.213.17–31 above.]
[8See I.213.31–3 above.]
[9See I.213.33–5 above.]
[10 See I.213.35–7 above.]

Before large bodies of human beings could be fit to live together in such close union, and still more, before they would be capable of adjusting, by peaceful arrangement among themselves, the relative claims of every class or kind of labour and talent, and of every individual in every class, a vast improvement in human character must be presupposed. When it is considered that each person who would have a voice in this adjustment would be a party interested in it, in every sense of the term—that each would be called on to take part by vote in fixing both the relative remuneration, and the relative estimation, of himself as compared with all other labourers, and of his own class of labour or talent as compared with all others; the degree of disinterestedness and of freedom from vanity and irritability, which would be required in such a community from every individual in it, would be such as is now only found in the élite of humanity: while if these qualities fell much short of the required standard, either the adjustment could not be made at all, or if made by a majority, would engender jealousies and disappointments destructive of the internal harmony on which the whole working of the system avowedly depends. These, it is true, are difficulties, not impossibilities: and the Fourierists, who alone among Socialists are in a great degree alive to the true conditions of the problem which they undertake to solve, are not without ways and means of contending against these. With every advance in education and improvement, their system tends to become less impracticable, and the very attempt to make it succeed would cultivate in those making the attempt, many of the virtues which it requires. But we have only yet considered the case of a single Fourierist community. When we remember that the communities themselves are to be the constituent units of an organised whole, (otherwise competition would rage as actively between rival communities as it now does between individual merchants or manufacturers,) and that nothing less would be requisite for the complete success of the scheme, than the organisation from a single centre, of the whole industry of a nation, and even of the world; we may, without attempting to limit the ultimate capabilities of human nature, affirm, that the political economist, for a considerable time to come, will be chiefly concerned with the conditions of existence and progress belonging to a society founded on private property and individual competition; and that, rude as is the manner in which those two principles apportion reward to exertion and to merit, they must form the basis of the principal improvements which can for the present be looked for in the economical condition of humanity.

§ 6. [*The institution of property requires, not subversion, but improvement*] And those improvements will be found to be far more considerable than the adherents of the various Socialist systems are willing to allow.

Whatever may be the merit or demerit of their own schemes of society, they have hitherto shown themselves extremely ill acquainted with the economical laws of the existing social system; and have, in consequence, habitually assumed as necessary effects of competition, evils which are by no means inevitably attendant on it. It is from the influence of this erroneous interpretation of existing facts, that many Socialists of high principles and attainments are led to regard the competitive system as radically incompatible with the economical well-being of the mass.^a

[The principle of private property has never yet had a fair trial in any country; and less so, perhaps, in this country than in some others. The social arrangements of modern Europe commenced from a distribution of property which was the result, not of ^ajust partition, or acquisition by industry,^a but of conquest and violence: and notwithstanding what industry has been doing for many centuries to modify the work of force, the system still retains many ^band large^b traces of its origin. The laws of property have never yet conformed to the principles on which the justification of private property rests. They have made property of things which never ought to be property, and absolute property where only a qualified property ought to exist. They have not held the balance fairly between human beings, but have heaped impediments upon some, to give advantage to others; they have purposely fostered inequalities, and prevented all from starting fair in the race. That all should indeed start on perfectly equal terms, is inconsistent with any law of private property: but if as much pains as has been taken to aggravate the inequality of chances arising from the natural working of the principle, had been taken to temper that inequality by every means not subversive of the principle itself; if the tendency of legislation had been to favour the diffusion, instead of the concentration of wealth— to encourage the subdivision of the large masses, instead of striving to keep them together; the principle of individual property would have been found to have no ^cnecessary^c connexion with the physical and social evils which][1] have made so many minds turn eagerly to any prospect of relief, however desperate.

^d[We are][2] as yet [too ignorant either of what individual agency in its best form, or Socialism in its best form can accomplish, to be qualified to decide which of the two will be the ultimate form of human society.][3] In

a–aMS   justice or industry
b–b+49   c–c48   real
d–d987MS   It is, at the same time, undeniable that an increasing power of co-operation in any common undertaking, is one of the surest fruits, and most accurate tests,

[1*This passage appears in 71.§3; see I.207.25—208.8 above.]
[2*Ibid., I.208.29–30.]
[3*Ibid., I.208.30–2. The next sentence ("In . . . benefits.") appears in altered form in 71.§4 (see I.214.9–12 above), and in MS, 48.§5 (see II.982a–a above).]

the present stage of human improvement at least, it is not (I conceive) the subversion of the system of individual property that should be aimed at, but the improvement of it, and the participation of every member of the community in its benefits. Far, however, from looking upon the various classes of Socialists with any approach to disrespect, I honour the intentions of almost all who are publicly known in that character, the acquirements and talents of several, and I regard them, taken collectively, as one of the most valuable elements of human improvement now existing; both from the impulse they give to the reconsideration and discussion of all the most important questions, and from the ideas they have contributed to many; ideas from which the most advanced supporters of the existing order of society have still much to learn.[d]

---

of the progress of civilization: and we may expect, as mankind improve, that joint enterprises of many kinds, which would now be impracticable, will be successively numbered among possibilities, thus augmenting, to an indefinite extent, the powers of the species. But the proper sphere for collective action lies in the things which cannot be done by individual agency, either because no one can have a sufficiently strong personal interest in accomplishing them, or because they require an assemblage of means surpassing what can be commanded by one or a few individuals. In things to which individual agency is at all suitable, it is almost always the most suitable; working, as it does, with so much greater intensity of motive when the object is personal, with so much stronger a sense of responsibility when it is public, and in either case with a feeling of independence and individual power, unknown to the members of a body under joint government.] 48   *as* MS . . . few individuals. Where individual agency . . . *as* MS

Appendix B

Book II, Chapter x ("Means of Abolishing Cottier Tenancy"), §§ 1–7, 2nd edition (1849), collated with the 1st edition and the MS[1]

§ 1. [*Mode of disposing of a cottier population is the vital question for Ireland*] The question, what is to be done with a cottier population? which in any case would have been a fit subject for consideration in a work like the present, is to the English Government at this time [the most urgent of practical questions. The majority of a population of eight millions, having long grovelled in helpless inertness and abject poverty under the cottier system; reduced by its operation to mere food, of the cheapest description, and to an incapacity of either doing or willing anything for the improvement of their lot]² ; have [at last, by the failure of that lowest quality of food, been plunged into a state *ᵃ* in which the alternative]³ is [death, or to be permanently supported by other people, or a radical change in the economical arrangements under which it]⁴ has [hitherto been their misfortune to live. Such an emergency]⁵ has [compelled attention to the subject from the legislature and from the nation, but it]⁶ can [hardly] as yet [be said, with much result; for, the evil having originated in a system of land tenancy which withdrew from the people every motive to industry or thrift except the fear of starvation, the remedy provided by Parliament was to take away even that, by conferring on them a legal claim to eleemosynary support: while, towards correcting the cause of the mischief, nothing was done, beyond vain complaints, though at the price to the national treasury of ten millions sterling for] one year's [delay.]⁷

ᵃMS worse than the worst in which it is physically possible for human beings to exist—a state

[1]The method of footnoting is the same as that used in the text proper: i.e., the MS and 48 variants are indicated by superscript letters and given in footnotes. The places where the 49 text *agrees* with the 71 text are surrounded by square brackets to simplify comparison; references to the 71 text are given in numbered footnotes to the end of bracketed passages.

[²*See* I.324.3–8 *above.*]   [³*See* I.324.8–9 *above.*]
[⁴*See* I.324.10–11 *above.*]   [⁵*See* I.324.12 *above.*]
[⁶*See* I.324.12–13 *above.*]   [⁷*See* I.324.14–20 *above.*]

I presume it [is needless] [to expend any argument in proving that the very foundation of the economical evils of Ireland is the cottier system: that while peasant rents fixed by competition are the practice of the country, to expect industry, useful activity, any restraint on population but death, or any the smallest diminution of poverty, is to look for figs on thistles and grapes on thorns. If our practical statesmen are not ripe for the recognition of this fact; or if while they acknowledge it in theory, they have not a sufficient feeling of its reality, to be capable of founding upon it any course of conduct; there is still another, and a purely physical consideration, from which they will find it impossible to escape. If the one crop on which the people have hitherto supported themselves continues to be precarious, either some new and great impulse must be given to agricultural skill and industry, or the soil of Ireland can no longer feed any thing like its present population. The whole produce of the western half of the island, leaving nothing for rent, will not now keep permanently in existence the whole of its people: and they will necessarily remain an annual charge on the taxation of the empire, until they are reduced either by emigration or by starvation to a number corresponding with the low state of their industry, or unless the means are found of making that industry much more productive.][8]

Cottiers, therefore, must cease to be. Nothing can be done for Ireland without transforming her rural population from cottier tenants into something else. But into what? [Those who, knowing neither Ireland nor any foreign country, take as their sole standard of social and economical excellence, English practice, propose as the single remedy for Irish wretchedness, the transformation of the cottiers into hired labourers.][9] I contend that the object should be their transformation, as far as circumstances admit, into landed proprietors. Either, indeed, would be a most desirable exchange from the present nuisance; but as a practical object the latter of the two seems to me preferable in an almost incalculable degree to the former, both as the most desirable in itself, and very much the easiest to effect.

§ 2. [*To convert the cottiers into hired labourers is not desirable or practicable*] To convert the cottiers into hired labourers [is rather a scheme for the improvement of Irish agriculture, than of the condition of the Irish people. The status of a day labourer has no charm for infusing forethought, frugality, or self-restraint, into a people devoid of them.][1] It is not necessarily injurious to those qualities where they exist, but it seldom engenders them where they are absent. [If the Irish peasantry could be] instantane-

[8*See* I.324.21—325.8 *above.*]
[9*See* I.326.20–3 *above.*]   [1*See* I.326.23–7 *above.*]

ously [changed into receivers of wages,]² the wages being no higher than they now are, or than there is any reason to hope that they would be, and the present [habits and mental characteristics of the people remaining, we should merely see] five or six [millions of people living as day labourers in the same wretched manner in which as cottiers they lived before; equally passive in the absence of every comfort, equally reckless in multiplication, and even, perhaps, equally listless at their work; since they could not be dismissed] *en masse* [, and if they could, dismissal would now be simply remanding them to the poor-rate. Far other would be the effect of making them peasant proprietors. A people who in industry and providence have everything to learn—who are confessedly among the most backward of European populations in the industrial virtues—require for their regeneration the most powerful incitements by which those virtues can be stimulated: and there is no stimulus] [comparable to property in land. A permanent interest in the soil to those who till it, is almost a guarantee for the most unwearied laboriousness: against over-population, though not infallible, it is the best preservative yet known; and where it failed, any other plan would probably fail much more egregiously; the evil would be beyond the reach of merely *ᵃeconomicᵃ* remedies.]³ Having already insisted so strongly on these topics, I feel it needless to argue any further, that the conversion of the Irish peasantry, or of some considerable portion of them, into small landed proprietors, is a more beneficial object than the transformation of all of them indiscriminately into labourers for hire.

But besides being more desirable, it is, above all, more attainable. The other plan, as a measure standing by itself, is wholly impracticable. It involves contradictory conditions. The conversion of the cottiers into hired labourers implies the introduction, all over Ireland, of capitalist farmers, in lieu of the present small tenants. These farmers, or their capital at least, must come from England. But to induce capital to come in, the cottier population must first be peaceably got rid of: in other words, that must be already accomplished, which English capital is proposed as the means of accomplishing. Why is Ireland the only country in the world to which English capital does *not* go? Because it cannot go to any purpose without turning out the people, and the people refuse to be turned out. I presume it is not seriously proposed that they should be turned out *en masse*, without being otherwise provided for. With their own consent they never will be dislodged from their holdings until something better is given to them. They will not be got rid of by merely telling them that something better will follow.

ᵃ⁻ᵃMS, 48   economical

[²*See* I.326.27–8 *above.*]   [³*See* I.326.28—327.5 *above.*]

It is necessary however in the next place to consider, what is the condition of things which would follow. The ineffective Irish agriculture is to be converted into an effective English agriculture, by throwing together the small holdings into large farms, cultivated by combined labour, with the best modern improvements. On the supposition of success, Ireland would be assimilated, in her agriculture, to the most improved parts of England. But what are the most improved parts of England? Those in which fewest labourers are employed, in proportion to the extent of the soil. Taking the number of Irish peasants to the square mile, and the number of hired labourers on an equal space in the model counties of Scotland or England, the former number is commonly computed to be about three times the latter. Two-thirds, therefore, of the Irish peasantry, would be absolutely dispensed with. What is to be done with them? Is it supposed that they would find employment in manufacturing labour? They are at present unfit for it; and even if fit, capital would require to be imported for that purpose too; and is it likely that manufacturing capital will resort to Ireland, abandoning Leeds and Manchester? Under a more efficient cultivation of her soil, Ireland would require a greatly increased amount of manufactured goods, but these would still be most advantageously manufactured in Lancashire or Yorkshire; and even if Ireland became, as to agricultural improvement, an English county, she would be but a larger Devonshire, drawing everything which she consumed, except the products of agriculture, from elsewhere. All the excess of Irish population above the Devonshire standard would be a local surplus, which must migrate to England, or to America, or subsist on taxation or *b* charity, or must be enabled to raise its own food from its own soil. The plan therefore of turning the cottiers into labourers for wages, even if it fulfilled its utmost promise, only disposes of a third of the population; with respect to the remaining two-thirds, the original difficulty recurs in its full force.

The question, what system of agriculture is best in itself, is, for Ireland, of purely theoretical interest: the people are there, and the problem is not how to improve the country, but how it can be improved by and for its present inhabitants. It is not probable that England will undertake a simultaneous removal of two millions—the smallest number which in the opinion of any person acquainted with the subject, would make a clear field for the introduction of English agriculture. But unless she does, the soil of Ireland must continue to employ and feed the people of Ireland: and since it cannot do this on the English system, or on any system whatever of large farming, all idea of *c*that*c* species of agricultural improvement as an exclu-

*b*MS, 48 on
*c–c*MS *that*

sive thing must be abandoned: the *petite culture* ^din some one of its shapes^d will continue, and a large proportion of the peasants, ^eif they do not become small proprietors, will remain^e small farmers. In the few cases in which comprehensive measures of agricultural improvement have been undertaken by large capitals, the capitalists have not, as some might perhaps suppose, employed themselves in creating large farms, and cultivating them by hired labour; their farms are of a size only sufficient for a single family: it was by other expedients that the improvement, which was to render the enterprise profitable, was brought about: these were, advances of capital, and a temporary security of tenure. There is a Company called the Irish Waste Land Improvement Society, of whose operations, in 1845, the following report was made, by their intelligent manager, Colonel Robinson.*

[*f* "Two hundred and forty-five tenants, many of whom were a few years since in a state bordering on pauperism, the occupiers of small holdings of from ten to twenty plantation acres each, have, by their own free labour, with the Society's aid, improved their farms to the value of 4396*l.*; 605*l.* having been added during the last year, being at the rate of 17*l.* 18*s.* per tenant for the whole term, and 2*l.* 9*s.* for the past year; the benefit of which improvements each tenant will enjoy during the unexpired term of a] *thirty-one years lease.*

["These 245 tenants and their families, have, by spade] husbandry [, reclaimed and brought into cultivation 1032 plantation acres of land, previously unproductive mountain waste, upon which they grew, last year, crops valued by competent practical persons at 3896*l.*, being in the proportion of 15*l.* 18*s.*, each tenant; and their live stock, consisting of cattle, horses, sheep, and pigs, now actually upon the estates, is valued, according to the present prices of the neighbouring markets, at 4162*l.*, of which 1304*l.* has been added since February 1844, being at the rate of 16*l.* 19*s.* for the whole period, and 5*l.* 6*s.* for the last year; during which time their stock has thus increased in value a sum equal to their present annual rent; and by the statistical] table [and returns referred to in previous reports, it is proved that the tenants, in general, improve their little farms, and increase their cultivation and crops, in nearly direct proportion to the number of available working persons of both sexes of which their families consist."

There cannot be a stronger testimony to the superior amount of] *gross* [produce raised by small farming, under any tolerable system of landed

*In the *Appendix to the Report of Lord Devon's Commission,* [*Parliamentary Papers,* 1845, XX,] p. 84[–5].

^{d–d}MS   must, and indubitably
^{e–e}MS   will & must be, either small proprietors or
^f[*The following quotation occurs in a footnote in 71; see* I.331n *above*]

tenure: and it is worthy of attention, that the industry and zeal] are [greatest among the smaller holders: Colonel Robinson noticing as exceptions to the remarkable and rapid progress of improvement, some tenants] "who are [occupants of larger farms than twenty acres, a class too often deficient in the enduring industry indispensable for the successful prosecution of mountain improvements."]*⁴

§ 3. [*Limitation of rent, by law or custom, is indispensable*] [The case of Ireland is similar in its requirements to that of India. In India, though great errors have from time to time been committed, no one ever proposed, under the name of agricultural improvement, to eject the ryots or peasant farmers from their possession;] all [the improvement that has been looked for, has been through making their tenure more secure to them, and the sole difference of opinion is between those who contend for *ᵃ* perpetuity, and those who think that long leases will suffice. The same question] may exist [as to Ireland];¹ and with the case of the Waste Lands Improvement Society before us, as well as many other instances of reclamation of land, recorded by Lord Devon's Commission, [it would be idle to deny that long leases, under such landlords as are sometimes to be found, do effect wonders, even in Ireland. But then, they must be leases at a low rent. Long leases are in no way to be relied on for getting rid of cottierism. During the existence of cottier tenancy, leases have always been long; twenty-one years and three lives concurrent, was a usual term. But the rent being fixed by competition, at a higher amount than could be paid, so that the tenant neither had, nor could by any exertion acquire, a beneficial interest in the land, the advantage of a lease was] merely [nominal. In India, the government]² [is able to prevent this evil, because, being itself the landlord, it can fix the rent according to its own judgment; but under individual landlords, while rents are fixed by competition, and the competitors are a peasantry struggling for subsistence, nominal rents are inevitable, unless the population is so thin, that the competition itself is only nominal. The majority of landlords will grasp at immediate money and immediate power; and so long as they find cottiers eager to offer them every thing, it is useless to rely on them for tempering the vicious practice by a considerate self-denial.

*[49] I have recently seen, with much regret, an announcement that this most useful Society is under the necessity of winding up its affairs. In the state to which Ireland has been reduced by the poor law and the famine, such a fact detracts nothing from the evidence which the previous success of the Society afforded in favour of its plan of operations.

ᵃMS, 48   a

[⁴See I.331.n4—332.n12 *above.*]
[¹See I.327.6–13 *above.*]   [² See I.327.13–21 *above.*]

A perpetuity is a]³ preferable tenure to a long lease; it is a far stronger stimulus to improvement[: not only because the longest lease, before coming to an end, passes through all the varieties of short leases down to no lease at all; but for more fundamental reasons. It is very shallow, even in pure economics, to take no account of the influence of imagination: there is a virtue in "for ever" beyond the longest term of years; even if the term is long enough to include children, and all whom a person individually cares for,]⁴ [he will not exert himself with the same ardour to increase the value of an estate, his interest in which diminishes in value every year.]⁵ A lease, therefore, is never a complete substitute for a perpetuity. [But where a country is under cottier tenure, the question of perpetuity is quite secondary to the more important point, a limitation of the rent. Rent paid by a ᵇcapitalist who farmsᵇ for profit, and not for bread, may safely be abandoned to competition; rent paid by labourers cannot, unless the labourers were in a state of civilization and improvement which labourers have nowhere yet reached, and cannot easily reach under such a tenure. Peasant rents ought never to be arbitrary, never at the discretion of the landlord: either by custom or law, it is imperatively necessary that they should be fixed; and where no mutually advantageous custom, such as the metayer system of Tuscany, has established itself, reason and experience recommend that they should be fixed] in perpetuity[: thus changing the rent into a quit-rent, and the farmer into a peasant proprietor.]⁶

§ 4. [*Fixity of Tenure considered*] Let us, then, examine what means are afforded by the economical circumstances of Ireland, for [carrying this change into effect on a sufficiently large scale to accomplish the complete abolition of cottier tenancy]. The [mode which] first [suggests itself is the] obvious and [direct one, of doing the thing outright by Act of Parliament; making the whole land of Ireland the property of the tenants, subject to the rents now really paid (not the nominal] rents[), as a fixed rent charge. This, under the name of "fixity of tenure," was one of the demands of the Repeal Association during the most successful period of their agitation; and was better expressed by Mr. Conner, its earliest, most enthusiastic, and most indefatigable apostle,* by the words, "a valuation and a perpetuity." In] this [measure there would not], strictly speaking, be [any injustice,

*Author of numerous pamphlets, entitled "True Political Economy of Ireland," "Letter to the Earl of Devon," "Two Letters [MS Letters to the Editor of the Times] on the Rackrent Oppression of Ireland," and others. Mr. Conner has been an agitator on the subject since 1832.

ᵇ⁻ᵇMS capitalists, who farm

[³*See* I.327.22–31 *above.*]   [⁴*See* I.327.31–7 *above.*]
[⁵*See* I.328.1–3 *above.*]   [⁶*See* I.328.7–19 *above.*]

provided the landlords were compensated for the present value of the chances of increase which they] would be [prospectively required to forego. The rupture of existing social relations would hardly] be [more violent than that effected by the ministers Stein and Hardenberg, when, by a series of edicts, in the early part of the present century, they revolutionized the state of landed property in the Prussian monarchy, and left their names to posterity among the greatest benefactors of their country. To enlightened foreigners writing on Ireland, Von Raumer and Gustave de Beaumont, a remedy of this sort] seems [so exactly and obviously what the disease] requires[, that they] have [some difficulty in comprehending how it] is [that the thing] is [not yet done.][1]

But though this measure is not beyond the competence of a just legislature, and would be no infringement of property if the landlords had the option allowed them of giving up their lands at the full value, reckoned at the ordinary number of years purchase; it is *only fit to be adopted if the nature of the case admitted of no milder remedy*. In the first place, it is [a complete expropriation of the higher classes of Ireland: which, if there is any truth in the principles we have laid down, would be perfectly warrantable, but only if it were the sole means of effecting a great public good. *In* the second place, that there should be none but peasant-proprietors, is in itself far from desirable. Large farms, cultivated by large] capitals[, and owned by persons of the best education which the country can give, persons qualified by instruction to *appreciate scientific discoveries*, and able to bear the delay and risk of costly experiments, are an important part of a good agricultural system. Many such landlords there are even in Ireland; and it would be a public misfortune to drive them from their][2] post. Other objections might be added; a [large proportion] [of the present holdings are] [too small to try the proprietary system under the greatest advantages: nor are the tenants always the persons one would desire to select, as the first occupants of peasant-properties. There are numbers of them on whom it would have a more beneficial effect to give them the hope of acquiring a landed property by industry and frugality, than the property itself in immediate possession.][3]

§ 5. [*Tenant Right*] Some persons who desire to avoid the term fixity of tenure, but who cannot be satisfied without some measure co-extensive with the whole country, have proposed the universal adoption of "tenant-

*a–a*MS   open to objections which I cannot but regard as decisive
*b–b*MS   But, in
*c–c*MS   be the earliest recipients of new ideas

[[1]*See* I.328.20—329.9 *above.*]
[[2]*See* I.329.10–20 *above.*]   [[3]*See* I.329.20–6 *above.*]

right." Under this equivocal phrase, two things are confounded. What it commonly stands for in Irish discussion, is the Ulster practice, which is in fact, fixity of tenure. It supposes a customary, though not a legal, limitation of the rent; without which the tenant evidently could not acquire a beneficial and saleable interest. Its existence is highly salutary, and is one principal cause of the superiority of Ulster in efficiency of cultivation, and in the comfort of the people, notwithstanding a minuter subdivision of holdings than in the other provinces. But to convert this customary limitation of rent into a legal one, and to make it universal, would be to establish *a*a fixity of tenure by law, the objections to which have already been stated.

The same appellation *b*(tenant right)*b* has of late years been applied, more particularly in England, to something altogether different, and falling as much short of the exigency, as the enforcement of the Ulster custom would exceed it. This English tenant right, with which a high agricultural authority has connected his name by endeavouring to obtain for it legislative sanction, amounts to no more than this, that on the expiration of a lease, the landlord should make compensation to the tenant for "unexhausted improvements." This is certainly very desirable, but provides only for the case of capitalist farmers, and of improvements made by outlay of money; of the worth and cost of which, an experienced land agent or a jury of farmers could accurately judge. The improvements to be looked for from peasant cultivators are the result not of money but of their labour, applied at such various times and in such minute portions as to be incapable of judicial appreciation. For such labour, compensation could not be given on any principle but that of paying to the tenant the whole difference between the value of the property when he received it, and when he gave it up: which would as effectually annihilate the right of property of the landlord as if the rent had been fixed in perpetuity, while it would not offer the same inducements to the cultivator, who improves from affection and passion as much as from calculation, and to whom his own land is a widely different thing from the most liberal possible pecuniary compensation for it.

§ 6. [*Location of peasant proprietors on the waste lands*] There are then strong objections, as well as great difficulties, opposed to the attempt to make peasant properties universal. But, fortunately, that they should be universal is not necessary to their usefulness. There is no need to extend them to all the population, or all the land. It is enough if there be land available, on which to locate so great a portion of the population, that the remaining area of the country shall not be required to maintain greater numbers than are compatible with large farming and hired labour. For this

a–a+48, 49
*b–b*MS   of tenant right,

purpose there is an obvious resource in the waste lands; which are happily so extensive, and a large proportion of them so improvable, as to afford a means by which, without making the present tenants proprietors, nearly the whole surplus population might be converted into peasant proprietors elsewhere. This plan has been strongly pressed upon the public by several writers: but the first to bring it prominently forward in England was Mr. William Thornton, in a work* honourably distinguished from most others which have been recently published, by its rational treatment of the great questions affecting the economical condition of the labouring classes. *a*

The detailed estimate of an irrefragable authority, Mr. Griffith, annexed to the Report of Lord Devon's Commission, shows nearly a million and a half of acres reclaimable for the spade or plough, some of them with the promise of great fertility, and about two millions and a half more, reclaimable for pasture:† the greater part being in most convenient proximity to the principal masses of destitute population. Besides these four millions of

---

Over Population and its Remedy. By William Thomas Thornton. Pp. 429–34. [49] In his subsequent work, "A Plea for Peasant Proprietors," Mr. Thornton has restated his former arguments and suggestions, with many additions and improvements.

†Mr. Griffith's numbers are 1,425,000 and 2,330,000. See p. 53 of the Report [*Parliamentary Papers*, 1845, XIX].

*a*MS [*paragraph*] "The present exorbitance of rents & want of leases are owing" says Mr Thornton "to the keenness of competition for land, which enables proprietors to dictate their own terms. Better conditions would of course be obtainable if the competitors were less numerous; & if those who are unable to procure adequate settlements on the land already occupied were removed to a distance, the rest would no longer have to outbid each other, or to submit to any outrageous demands. Is it then possible that an asylum can anywhere be found for the crowds who are at present without any certain means of support? The question is a difficult one, but there is at least one spot in Ireland where a satisfactory answer has already been made to it. Two miles from the little town of Kilculler, in Kildare, is a tract of excessively green land, dotted over with brilliant white cottages, each with its couple of trim acres of garden, where you see thick potato ridges covered with blossom, great blue plots of comfortable cabbages & such pleasant plants of the poor man's garden. Two or three years since, the land was a marshy common, which had never since the days of the Deluge fed any being bigger than a snipe, & into which the poor people descended, draining & cultivating & rescuing the marsh from the water, & raising their cabins, & setting up their little enclosures of two or three acres upon the land which they had thus created. . . . There are now two hundred flourishing little homesteads upon this rescued land, & as many families in comfort & plenty*. Now, if two or three acres of reclaimed marsh can furnish plentiful subsistence to one family, 600,000 acres would do as much for 200,000 families; that is to say, for one-fourth part of the Irish peasantry. . Mr Nicholls tells us that most of the recently recovered bog which he saw in the western counties was reclaimed by small occupiers, who drained & enclosed an acre or two at a time." [*footnote:*] *The facts mentioned are extracted by Mr Thornton from Mr Thackeray's "Irish Sketch Book." [Thornton, *Over-population*, pp. 429–31.]

acres, there are above two millions and a half,* pronounced by Mr. Griffith to be unimprovable; but he is only speaking of reclamation for profit: it is doubtful if there be any land, in a temperate climate, which cannot be reclaimed and rendered productive by labourers themselves, under the *b*inducement*b* of a permanent property. Confining ourselves to the one and a half million of arable first mentioned, it would furnish properties averaging five acres each to three hundred thousand persons, *c*which*c* at the rate of five persons to a family, a rather low rate for Ireland, *d*answers*d* to a population of fifteen hundred thousand. Suppose such a number drafted off to a state of independence and comfort, together with a very moderate additional relief by emigration; and the introduction of English capital and farming, over the remaining surface of Ireland, would at once cease to be chimerical.†

"The improvement of wastes," Mr. Thornton *e*observes*e*, "may perhaps be thought to require a good deal of capital; but capital is principally useful for its command of labour, and the Irish peasantry have quite labour enough at their own disposal. Their misfortune is, that they have so much. Their labour would not be the worse applied because they worked for

*2,535,000.

†If instead of throwing small farms into large, and exchanging peasant for capitalist farmers, the "clearing" were limited to such a consolidation of small holdings as would make [MS as should make] them correspond in size to the admirable small farms of Belgium, the adequacy of the resource is still more clear and unquestionable. "There are at present," says the Digest of Evidence to Lord Devon's Report, ([Vol. I,] p. 399,) "326,084 occupiers of land (more than one-third of the total number returned in Ireland) whose holdings vary from seven acres to less than one acre, and are therefore inadequate to support the families residing upon them." It is shown by calculation, "that the consolidation of these small holdings, up to eight acres, would require the removal of about 192,368 families, and that the first class of improvable waste land in Ireland would furnish to those removed families locations of about eight acres each; or the first and second qualities of improvable waste land, taken together, would furnish them with locations of about twenty acres each." It is computed (p. 565) that by these arrangements 500,000 labourers, equivalent to at least two millions and a half of population, would be abstracted from competition in the labour market, while, on the waste land alone, an addition of nearly twenty-two millions sterling would be made to the gross produce of the country; "and that the first three or four years' crops would return the cost requisite to bring about this change." [*Ibid.*, p. 565.]

[49] Mr. Griffith and the other witnesses no doubt made their calculations on the supposition of potato culture. But the small farms in Belgium are a proof that the cultivation of hemp and flax (the latter in particular completely suited to the climate of Ireland) may be profitably conducted on soil originally as barren as most of the Irish wastes, and in farms of five or six acres.

*b–b*MS inducements	*c–c*MS who
*d–d*MS answer	*e–e*MS continues

themselves, instead of for a paymaster. So far is [large] capital from being indispensable for the cultivation of barren tracts, that schemes of this kind, which could only bring loss to a rich speculator, are successfully achieved by his penniless rival. A capitalist must have a certain return for the money he lays out, but the poor man expends nothing but his own superabundant labour, which would be valueless if not so employed, so that his returns, however small, are all clear profit. No man in his senses would ever have thought of wasting money upon the original sand of the Pays de Waes; but the hard-working boors who settled there two hundred years ago, without any other stock than their industry, contrived to enrich both themselves and the land, and indeed to make the latter the richest in Europe. There is no soil so worthless that an English labourer will not eagerly accept an allotment of it; and while the green valley, from which some Highland community has been driven, is fast relapsing under the superintendence of a wealthy sheep-farmer into its primitive wildness, its former tenants are forming new patches of arable land on the rock-strewn moors along the sea-coast."[*]

"The profit of reclaiming waste land," says the Digest of Evidence to Lord Devon's Commission,† "will be best understood from a practice not uncommon in Ireland, to which farmers sometimes resort. This consists in giving the use of a small portion of it to a poor cottier or herdsman for the first three crops, after which this improved portion is given up to the farmer, and a fresh piece of the waste land is taken on the same terms by the cottier." Well may the compiler say, "Here we have the example of the very poorest class in Ireland obtaining a livelihood by the cultivation of waste land under the most discouraging and the least remunerative circumstances that can well be imagined."

It is quite worthy of the spirit which pervades the wretched attempts as yet made to do good to Ireland, that this spectacle of the poorest of mankind making the land valuable by their labour for the profit of other people, who have done nothing to assist them, does not once strike Lord Devon and his Commission as a thing which ought not to be. Mr. Thornton strongly urges the claims of common justice and common sense.

"The colonists ought to be allowed to retain permanent possession of the spots reclaimed by them. To employ them as labourers in bringing the land into a remunerative condition, (see Report of Land Occupation Commissioners), in order that it may then be let to some one else, while they are sent to shift for themselves where they can, may be an excellent mode of enriching the landlord, but must eventually aggravate the sufferings of the poor. It is probably because this plan has been generally practised, that

[*Over-population, pp. 431–2.] [JSM's square brackets around large]
†[Vol. I,] P. 570.

the reclamation of waste land has hitherto done nothing for the benefit of the Irish peasantry. If the latter are to derive any advantage from it, such of them as may be located on the waste, should receive perpetual leases of their respective allotments—should be made freeholders, in fact, or at least perpetual tenants at a quit-rent. Such an appropriation of waste land would of course require that compensation should be made to all who previously possessed any interest in it. But the value of a legal interest in land which cannot be enclosed or cultivated without permission of the legislature, can only be proportionate to the actual yearly produce; and as land in a natural state yields little or nothing, all legal claims upon it might be bought up at a trifling expense, or might be commuted for a very small annual payment to be made by the settlers. Of the perfect competence of Parliament to direct some arrangement of this kind, there can be no question. An authority which compels individuals to part with their most valued property on the slightest pretext of public convenience, and permits railway projectors to throw down family mansions and cut up favourite pleasure grounds, need not be very scrupulous about forcing the sale of boggy meadows or mountain pastures, in order to obtain the means of curing the destitution and misery of an entire people."[*]

It would be desirable, and in most cases necessary, that the tracts of land should be prepared for the labours of the peasant, by being drained and intersected with roads at the expense of Government; the interest of the sums so expended, and of the compensation paid for existing rights to the waste land, being charged on it when reclaimed as a perpetual quit-rent, redeemable at a moderate number of years' purchase. The state would thus incur no loss, while the advances made would give that immediate employment to the surplus labour of Ireland, which if not given in this manner, will assuredly have to be given in some other, not only less useful, but far less likely to repay its cost. The millions lavished during the famine in the almost nominal execution of useless works, without any result but that of keeping the people alive, would, if employed in a great operation on the waste lands, have been quite as effectual for relieving immediate distress, and would have laid the foundation broad and deep for something really deserving the name of social improvement. But, as usual, it was thought better to throw away money and exertion in a beaten track, than to take the responsibility of the most advantageous investment of them in an untrodden one.

§ 7. [*Resources supplementary to the waste lands*] If after the superabundant evidence elicited in the Irish inquiries, of the extent and capability of improvement of the waste lands, the reader can doubt their sufficiency for

[*Over-population, pp. 432–4.]

home colonization on such a scale as to effect with benefit to everybody the "clearing" of all Ireland; there are yet other means, by which not a little could be done in the dissemination of peasant proprietors over even the existing area of cultivation. There is at the present time an experiment in progress, in more than one part of England, for the creation of peasant proprietors. The project is of Chartist origin, and its first colony is now in full operation near Rickmansworth, in Hertfordshire. The plan is as follows:—Funds were raised *a*by subscription, and vested in*a* a joint-stock company. With part of these funds an estate of several hundred acres was bought. This estate was divided into portions of two, three, and four acres, on each of which a house was erected by the Association. These holdings were let to select labourers, to whom also such sums were advanced as were thought to amount to a sufficient capital for cultivation by spade labour. An annual payment, affording to the Company an interest of five per cent on their outlay, was laid on the several holdings as a fixed quit-rent, never in any circumstances to be raised. The tenants *b*are*b* thus proprietors from the first, and their redemption of the quit-rent, by saving from the produce of their labour, is desired and calculated upon.

*c*The originator of this experiment appears to have successfully repelled (before a tribunal by no means prepossessed in his favour, a Committee of the House of Commons) the imputations which were lavished upon his project, and upon his mode of executing it. Should its issue ultimately*c* be unfavourable, *d* the cause of failure will be in the details of management, not in the principle. These well-conceived arrangements afford [a mode in which private capital may] co-operate [in renovating the social and agricultural economy of Ireland, not only without sacrifice but with considerable profit to its owners. The remarkable success of the Waste Land Improvement Society, which proceeded on a plan far less advantageous to the tenant, is an instance of what an Irish peasantry can be stimulated to do, by a sufficient assurance that what they do will be for their own advantage. It is not] [indispensable to]¹ begin at once with a perpetuity[; long leases at moderate rents, like those of the Waste Land Society, would suffice, if a prospect were held out to the farmers of being allowed to purchase their farms with the capital which they might acquire, as the Society's tenants were so rapidly acquiring under the influence of its beneficent system.]² It would be a boon to allow them to become purchasers of the land even

a–aMS, 48   , in shares, by
b–bMS, 48   were
c–cMS, 48   Should the issue of this experiment
dMS, 48   which at present there seems no reason to believe,

[¹See I.330.14–20 above.]
[²See I.330.21–5 above.]

at the value given to it by their own labour: and though, on the part of government, to take such an advantage of their exertions would be most ungenerous and illiberal, it would be allowable in private capitalists undertaking a work of national benefit as an advantageous investment of capital. [*When the lands were* sold, the funds of the association would be liberated, and it might recommence operations in some other quarter.]³

Nor is it only by joint-stock associations, and the introduction of English capital, that this system might be acted upon: it would be most advantageous to every individual landowner in the distressed counties, who has any funds which he can freely dispose of. Under the new Irish poor law, there are no means for the landlords of escaping ruin, unless, by some potent stimulant to the industrial energies of the people, they can largely increase the produce of agriculture: and since there is no stimulant available, so potent as a permanent interest in the soil, either the present landlords, or those English mortgagees to whom the estates of the more impoverished landowners must inevitably pass, would find it to their advantage, if not to grant at once this permanent interest to their tenants, at least to hold out to them the prospect of acquiring it. The government, too, into whose hands no small portion of the land of Ireland may be expected to fall, in consequence of unrepaid advances, either past or yet to come, will have a noble opportunity of rendering the acquisition instrumental to the formation of a peasant proprietary: but, to the state, it would be most discreditable to seek for profit at the expense of the peasantry; and whether the ʃownershipsʃ were granted immediately or only held out in prospect, the rent or price should be no more than sufficient to repay the state for its advances.

*e–e*MS   The lands thus
*f–f*MS   ownership

[³*See* I.330.25–7 *above.*]

Appendix C

Book II, Chapter x ("Means of Abolishing Cottier Tenancy"), § 3, 4th edition (1857), collated with the earlier editions and the MS[1]

a§ 3.*a* [*Probable consequences of the measures recommended*] When the *b*difficulties of governing a country whose social system requires not ordinary amendment but radical change,*b* shall be met instead of *c*being*c* evaded, by men capable of rising superior both to their own indolence and prejudices and to those of others; we may hope to see, from the present lazy, apathetic, reckless, improvident and lawless Ireland, a new Ireland arise, consisting of peasant proprietors with something to lose, and of hired labourers with something to gain; the former *d*peaceful and industrious*d* through the possession of property, the latter through the hope of it; while the agriculture of *e* Ireland would be *f*partly*f* conducted on the best system of small cultivation, *g*and partly*g* on the best principles of large farming and combination of labour. *h*Nor would*h* it be too much to hope, that when the number of hired labourers was duly proportioned to the soil on which they were employed, and a peaceful "clearing" had made the country safe for English capital to dwell in, the rate of wages would be sufficient to establish a tolerably high standard of living; and *i*that*i* the spirit of saving, fostered by the desire of acquiring land, *j*might*j* prevent that standard from being again depressed through an imprudent increase of *k*population.*k*

*a–a*MS, 48, 49 §8.
*b–b*MS, 48, 49 formidable difficulties in which the government of this country is becoming more and more deeply involved by the condition of Ireland,
c–c+49, 52, 57
*d–d*MS, 48, 49 attached to peace and law
*e*MS, 48, 49 one-half of   *f–f*+52, 57
*g–g*MS that of the other half] 48, 49 and that . . . *as* MS
*h–h*MS, 48, 49 Would   *i–i*+52, 57
*j–j*MS, 48, 49 would   *k–k*MS, 48, 49 population?

[1]The method of footnoting is the same as that used in the text proper: i.e., the MS, 48, 49, and 52 variants are indicated by superscript letters and given in footnotes. The places where the 57 text *agrees* with the 71 text are surrounded by square brackets to simplify comparison; references to the 71 text are given in numbered footnotes to the end of bracketed passages.

In the complication of human affairs, the actual effects of causes, whether salutary or injurious, remain always far short of their tendencies. But history is not without examples of changes, similar in kind to that which I have been sketching, and the results of them are not uninstructive. ['Three times during the course of] French history, [the peasantry have been purchasers of land; and these times immediately preceded the three principal eras of French agricultural prosperity.

"Aux temps les plus mauvais," says the historian Michelet,* "aux moments de pauvreté universelle, où le riche même est pauvre et vend par force, alors le pauvre se trouve en état d'acheter; nul acquéreur ne se présentant, le paysan en guenilles arrive avec sa pièce d'or, et il acquiert un bout de terre. Ces moments de désastre où le paysan a pu acquérir la terre à bon marché, ont toujours été suivis d'un élan subit de fécondité qu'on ne s'expliquait pas. Vers 1500, par exemple, quand la France épuisée par Louis XI. semble achever sa ruine en Italie, la noblesse qui part est obligée de vendre; la terre, passant à de nouvelles mains, refleurit tout-à-coup; on travaille, on bâtit. Ce beau moment (dans le style de l'histoire monarchique) s'est appelé *le bon Louis XII.*

"Il dure peu, malheureusement. La terre est à peine remise en bon état, le fisc fond dessus; les guerres de religion arrivent, qui semblent raser tout jusqu'au sol, misères horribles, famines atroces où les mères mangeaient leurs enfants. Qui croirait que le pays se relève de là? Eh bien, la guerre finit à peine, de ce champ ravagé, de cette chaumière encore noire et brulée, sort l'épargne du paysan. Il achète; en dix ans, la France a changé de face; en vingt ou trente, tous les biens ont doublé, triplé de valeur. Ce moment encore baptisé d'un nom royal, s'appelle *le bon Henri IV.* et le grand Richelieu."

Of the third era it is needless ᵐagainᵐ to speak: it was that of the Revolution.

Whoever would study the reverse of the picture, may compare these historic periods, characterized by the dismemberment of large and the construction of small properties, with the wide-spread national suffering which accompanied, and the permanent deterioration of the condition of the labouring classes which followed, the "clearing" away of small yeomen to make room for large grazing farms, which was the grand economical event of English history during the sixteenth century.ᴵ][2]

[I have concluded a discussion, which has] already [occupied a space almost disproportioned to the dimensions of this work; and I here close the

Le Peuple, 1re partie, ch. 1.

ᴸ⁻ᴸ[*In* II, vii, § 5; *see* I.296n *above*]   ᵐ⁻ᵐ+52, 57

[[2]*See* I.296.n2–31 *above*.]

examination of those simpler forms of social economy in which the produce of the land either belongs undividedly to one class, or is shared only between two classes. We now proceed to the hypothesis of a threefold division of the produce, among labourers, landlords, and capitalists: and in order to connect the coming discussions as closely as possible with those which have now for some time occupied us, I shall commence with the subject of Wages.][3]

[[3]*See* I.336.27–36 *above.*]

Appendix D

Book IV, Chapter vii ("On the Probable Futurity of the Labouring Classes"), §§ 5–6, 2nd edition (1849), collated with the 1st edition.[1]

§ 5. [*Examples of the association of the labourers in the profits of industrial undertakings*] *a*It is this feeling, almost as much as despair of the improvement of the condition of the labouring masses by other means, which has caused so great a multiplication of projects for the "organization of industry" by the extension and development of the co-operative or joint stock principle: some of the more conspicuous of which have been described and characterized in an early chapter of this work. It is most desirable that all these schemes should have opportunity and encouragement to test their capabilities by actual experiment. There are, in almost all of them, many features, in themselves well worth submitting to that test; while, on the other hand, the exaggerated expectations entertained by large and growing multitudes in all the principal nations of the world, concerning what it is possible, in the present state of human improvement, to effect by such means, have no chance of being corrected except by a fair trial in practice. The French Revolution of February 1848, at first seemed to have opened a fair field for the trial of such experiments, on a perfectly safe scale, and with every advantage that could be derived from the countenance of a government which sincerely desired their success. It is much to be regretted that these prospects have been frustrated, and that the reaction of the middle class against anti-property doctrines has engendered for the present an unreasoning and undiscriminating antipathy to all ideas, however harmless or however just, which have the smallest savour of Socialism.

*a–a*100748   A solution of this problem is afforded by the extension and developement of which the co-operative or joint-stock principle is susceptible. That principle supplies means by which

[1]The method of footnoting is the same as that used in the text proper: i.e., the 48 variants are indicated by superscript letters and given in footnotes. The places where the 49 text *agrees* with the 71 text are surrounded by square brackets to simplify comparison; references to the 71 text are given in numbered footnotes to the end of bracketed passages.

This is a disposition of mind, of which the influential classes, both in France and elsewhere, will find it necessary to divest themselves. Socialism has now become irrevocably one of the leading elements in European politics. The questions raised by it will not be set at rest by merely refusing to listen to it; but only by a more and more complete realization of the ends which Socialism aims at, not neglecting its means so far as they can be employed with advantage.

On the particular point specially considered in the present chapter, those means have been, to a certain extent, put in practice in several departments of existing industry; by arrangements giving to*a* [every one who contributes to the work,][2] whether [by labour or by pecuniary resources,][3b] [a partner's interest in it,][4] proportionally [to the value of his contribution. It is already a common practice to remunerate those in whom peculiar trust is reposed by means of a percentage on the profits; and cases exist in which the principle is, with][5] the most [excellent success, carried down to the class of mere manual labourers.

In the American ships trading to China, it has long been the custom for every sailor to have an interest in the profits of the voyage; and to this has been ascribed the general good conduct of those seamen, and the extreme rarity of any collision between them and the government or people of the country. An instance in England][6] itself[, not so well known as it deserves to be, is that of the Cornish miners. "In Cornwall the mines are worked strictly on the system of joint adventure; gangs of miners contracting with the agent, who represents the owner of the mine, to execute a certain portion of a vein, and fit the ore for market, at the price of so much in the pound of the sum for which the ore is sold. These contracts are put up at certain regular periods, generally every two months, and taken by a voluntary partnership of men accustomed to the mine. This system has its disadvantages, in consequence of the uncertainty and irregularity of the earnings, and consequent necessity of living for long periods on credit; but it has advantages which more than counterbalance these drawbacks. It produces a degree of intelligence, independence, and moral elevation, which raise the condition and character of the Cornish miner far above that of the generality of the labouring class. We are told by Dr. Barham, that 'they are not only, as a class, intelligent for labourers, but men of considerable knowledge.' Also, that 'they have a character of independence, something American, the system by which the contracts are let giving the takers entire freedom to make arrangements among them-

b48   may have

[*2See* II.769.21 *above.*]
[*3See* II.769.21–2 *above.*]   [*4See* II.769.22 *above.*]
[*5See* II.769.23–5 *above.*]   [*6See* II.769.25–31 *above.*]

selves; so that each man feels, as a partner in his little firm, that he meets his employers on nearly equal terms.' . . . With this basis of intelligence and independence in their character, we are not surprised when we hear that 'a very great number of miners are now located on possessions of their own, leased for three lives or ninety-nine years, on which they have built houses;' or that '281,541*l*. are deposited in]⁷ savings [banks in Cornwall, of which two-thirds are estimated to belong to miners.' "*

Mr. Babbage, who also gives an account of this system, observes† that the payment to the crews of whaling ships is governed by a similar principle; and that "the profits arising from fishing with nets on the south coast of England are thus divided: one-half the produce belongs to the owner of the boat and net; the other half is divided in equal portions between the persons using it, who are also bound to assist in repairing the net when required." Mr. Babbage has the great merit of having pointed out the practicability, and the advantage, of extending the principle to manufacturing industry generally.]⁸ I venture to quote the principal part of his observations on the subject.

"The general principles on which the proposed system is founded, are—1st. That a considerable part of the wages received by each person employed, should depend on the profits made by the establishment; and 2nd. That every person connected with it should derive more advantage from applying any improvement he might discover, to the factory in which he is employed, than he could by any other course.

"It would be difficult to prevail on the large capitalist to enter upon any system, which would change the division of the profits arising from the employment of his capital in setting skill and labour in action; any alteration, therefore, must be expected rather from the small capitalist, or from the higher class of workmen, who combine the two characters; and to these latter classes, whose welfare will be first affected, the change is most important. I shall therefore first point out the course to be pursued in making the experiment; and then, taking a particular branch of trade as an illustration, I shall examine the merits and defects of the proposed system as applied to it.

"Let us suppose, in some large manufacturing town, ten or twelve of the most intelligent and skilful workmen to unite, whose characters for sobriety

*This passage is from the Prize Essay on the Causes and Remedies of National Distress, [pp. 40–1,] by Mr. Samuel Laing. The extracts which it includes are from the Appendix to the Report of the Children's Employment Commission.

†*Economy of Machinery and Manufactures*, 3rd edition, ch. 26 [p. 259]. [52, 57, 62, 65, 71 [*this footnote occurs at the end of the paragraph*]]

[⁷*See* II.769.31—770–21 *above*.]   [⁸*See* II.770.21–31 *above*.]

and steadiness are good, and are well known among their class. Such persons will each possess some small portion of capital; and let them join with one or two others who have raised themselves into the class of small master-manufacturers, and therefore possess rather a larger portion of capital. Let these persons, after well considering the subject, agree to establish a manufactory of fire-irons and fenders; and let us suppose that each of the ten workmen can command forty pounds, and each of the small capitalists possesses two hundred pounds: thus they have a capital of 800*l.*, with which to commence business, and for the sake of simplifying, let us further suppose the labour of each of these twelve persons to be worth two pounds a week. One portion of their capital will be expended in procuring the tools necessary for their trade, which we shall take at 400*l.*, and this must be considered as their fixed capital. The remaining 400*l.* must be employed as circulating capital, in purchasing the iron with which their articles are made, in paying the rent of their workshops, and in supporting themselves and their families until some portion of it is replaced by the sale of the goods produced.

"Now the first question to be settled is, what proportion of the profit should be allowed for the use of capital, and what for skill and labour? It does not seem possible to decide this question by any abstract reasoning: if the capital supplied by each partner is equal, all difficulty will be removed; if otherwise, the proportion must be left to find its level, and will be discovered by experience; and it is probable that it will not fluctuate much. Suppose it to be agreed that the capital of 800*l.* shall receive the wages of one workman. At the end of each week, every workman is to receive one pound as wages, and one pound is to be divided amongst the owners of the capital. After a few weeks the returns will begin to come in; and they will soon become nearly uniform. Accurate accounts should be kept of every expense and of all the sales; and at the end of each week the profit should be divided. A certain portion should be laid aside as a reserved fund, another portion for repair of the tools, and the remainder being divided into thirteen parts, one of these parts would be divided amongst the capitalists and one belong to each workman. Thus each man would, in ordinary circumstances, make up his usual wages of two pounds weekly. If the factory went on prosperously, the wages of the men would increase; if the sales fell off, they would be diminished. It is important that every person employed in the establishment, whatever might be the amount paid for his services, whether he act as labourer or porter, or as the clerk who keeps the accounts, or as book-keeper employed for a few hours once a week to superintend them, should receive one-half of what his service is worth in fixed salary, the other part varying with the success of the undertaking.

"The result of such arrangements in a factory would be,

"1. That every person engaged in it would have a direct interest in its prosperity; since the effect of any success, or falling off, would almost immediately produce a corresponding change in his own weekly receipts.

"2. Every person concerned in the factory would have an immediate interest in preventing any waste or mismanagement in all the departments.

"3. The talents of all connected with it would be strongly directed to improvement in every department.

"4. None but workmen of high character and qualifications could obtain admission into such establishments, because when any additional hands were required, it would be the common interest of all to admit only the most respectable and skilful, and it would be far less easy to impose upon a dozen workmen than upon the single proprietor of a factory.

"5. When any circumstance produced a glut in the market, more skill would be directed to diminishing the cost of production; and a portion of the time of the men might then be occupied in repairing and improving their tools, for which a reserved fund would pay, thus checking present, and at the same time facilitating future production.

"6. Another advantage, of no small importance, would be the total removal of all real or imaginary causes for combinations. The workmen and the capitalist would so shade into each other—would so evidently have a common interest, and their difficulties and distresses would be mutually so well understood, that instead of combining to oppress one another, the only combination which could exist would be a most powerful union between both parties to overcome their common difficulties.

"One of the difficulties attending such a system is, that capitalists would at first fear to embark in it, imagining that the workmen would receive too large a share of the profits: and it is quite true that the workmen would have a larger share than at present: but at the same time, it is presumed the effect of the whole system would be, that the total profits of the establishment being much increased, the smaller proportion allowed to capital under this system would yet be greater in actual amount, than that which results to it from the larger share in the system now existing.

"A difficulty would occur also in discharging workmen who behaved ill, or who were not competent to their work; this would arise from their having a certain interest in the reserved fund, and perhaps from their possessing a certain portion of the capital employed; but without entering into detail, it may be observed, that such cases might be determined on by meetings of the whole establishment; and that if the policy of the laws favoured such establishments, it would scarcely be more difficult to enforce just regulations than it now is to enforce some which are unjust, by means of combinations either amongst the masters or the men."[*]

[*Babbage, pp. 253-9.]

In this imaginary case, it is supposed that each labourer brings some small portion of capital into the concern: but the principle is equally applicable to the ordinary case, in which the whole capital belongs to an individual capitalist. An application of it to such a case is actually in progress, by a Paris tradesman, a house-painter, M. Leclaire.* The intelligent author of this meritorious experiment, published a pamphlet in the year 1842, descriptive of his system of operations; to which attention was first directed by M. Duveyrier, in his Lettres Politiques, and a full abstract of which has been published in Chambers' Journal.† M. Leclaire [employs on an average two hundred workmen, whom he pays in the usual manner, by fixed wages or salaries. He assigns to himself, besides interest for his capital, a fixed allowance for his labour and responsibility as manager. At the end of the year, the surplus profits are divided among the ^{c} body, himself included, in the proportion of their ^{d} salaries.‡ The reasons by which M. Leclaire was led to adopt this system are][9] interesting and [instructive. Finding the conduct of his workmen unsatisfactory, he first tried the effect of giving higher wages, and by this he managed to obtain a body of excellent workmen, who would not quit his service for any other. "Having thus succeeded" (I quote from][10] the [abstract] [in Chambers' Journal,) "in producing some sort of stability in the] arrangements [of his establishment, M. Leclaire expected, he says, to enjoy greater peace of mind. In this, however, he was disappointed. So long as he was able to superintend everything himself, from the general concerns of his business down to its minutest details, he did enjoy a certain satisfaction; but from the moment that, owing to the increase of his business, he found that he could be nothing more than the centre from which orders were issued, and to which reports were brought in, his former anxiety and discomfort returned upon him." He speaks lightly of the other sources of anxiety to which a tradesman is subject, but describes as an incessant cause of vexation the losses arising from the misconduct of workmen. An employer "will find workmen whose indifference to his interests is such

*[His establishment is] (or was) [11, Rue Saint Georges.] [See II.770n above.]
†[For September 27, 1845.] [See II.771n above.]
‡[49] [It appears, however, that the workmen whom M. Leclaire] admits [to this participation of profits,] are as yet [only a portion (rather less than half) of the whole number whom he] employs. [This is explained by another part of his system. M. Leclaire pays the full market rate of wages to all his workmen. The share of profit assigned to them is, therefore, a clear addition to the ordinary gains of their class, which he very laudably uses as an instrument of improvement, by making it the reward of desert, or the recompense for peculiar trust.] [See II.771n above.]

^{c}48   whole ^{d}48   fixed

[^{9}See II.770.35—771.6 above.]
[^{10}See II.771.6–9 above.]

that they do not perform two-thirds of the amount of work which they are capable of; hence the continual fretting of masters, who, seeing their interests neglected, believe themselves entitled to suppose that workmen are constantly conspiring to ruin those from whom they derive their livelihood. If the journeyman were sure of constant employment, his position would in some respects be more enviable than that of the master, because he is assured of a certain amount of day's wages, which he will get whether he works much or little. He runs no risk, and has no other motive to stimulate him to do his best than his own sense of duty. The master, on the other hand, depends greatly on chance for his returns: his position is one of continual irritation and anxiety. This would no longer be the case to the same extent, if the interests of the master and those of the workmen were bound up with each other, connected by some bond of mutual security, such as that which would be obtained by the plan of a yearly division of profits."

*e*Even in the first year during which M. Leclaire's experiment was in complete operation, the success was*e* remarkable. Not one of his journeymen who worked as many as three hundred days, earned in that year less than 1500 francs, and some considerably more. His highest rate of daily wages being four francs, or 1200 francs for 300 days, the remaining 300 francs or 12*l*. must have been the smallest amount which any journeyman, who worked that number of days, obtained as his proportion of the surplus profit. M. Leclaire describes in strong terms the improvement which was already manifest in the habits and demeanour of his workmen, not merely when at work, and in their relations with their employer, but at other times and in other relations, showing increased respect both for others and for themselves.][11] *f*The system is still in operation; and we learn from [M. Chevalier][12] [that the increased zeal of the workpeople][13] continues [to be a full compensation to][14] M. Leclaire[, even in a pecuniary sense, for the share of profit which he][15] foregoes [in their favour.]*f*[16]

Under this system, as well as under that recommended by Mr. Babbage,

---

*[49] "Je tiens de M. Leclaire que chez lui l'avantage du zèle extrême dont sont animés les ouvriers, depuis qu'il a adopté le système de la participation, fait plus que compenser le sacrifice représenté par la somme des parts qu'on leur alloue." Lettres sur l'Organisation du Travail, par Michel Chevalier, (1848,) lettre xiv [p. 298].

*e-e*48 It is to be regretted that we are only in possession of the result of M. Leclaire's experiment in the first year during which it was in complete operation. Already, however, the success had been
f-f+49

[11*See* II.771.10—772.15 *above.*] [12*See* II.772.15 *above.*]
[13*See* II.772.16 *above.*] [14*See* II.772.17 *above.*]
[15*See* II.772.17–18 *above.*] [16*See* II.772.18 *above.*]

the labourers are, in reality, taken into partnership with their employer. Bringing nothing into the common concern but their labour, while he brings not only his labour of direction and superintendence but his capital also, they have justly a smaller share of the profits; this, however, is a matter of private arrangement in all partnerships: one partner has a large, another a small share, according to their agreement, grounded on the equivalent which is given by each. The essence, however, of a partnership is obtained, since each benefits by all things that are beneficial to the concern, and loses by all which are injurious. It is, in the fullest sense, the common concern of all.

§ 6. [*Probable future developement of this principle*] To this principle, in whatever form embodied, it seems to me that futurity has to look for obtaining the benefits of co-operation, without constituting the numerical majority of the co-operators an inferior caste. The objections that apply to a "co-operative society," in the Communist or Owenite sense, in which, by force of giving to every member of the body a share in the common interest, no one has a greater share in it than another, are not applicable to what is now suggested. It is expedient that those, whose performance of the part assigned to them is the most essential to the common end, should have a greater amount of personal interest in the issue of the enterprise. If those who supply the funds, and incur the whole risk of the undertaking, obtained no greater reward or more influential voice than the rest, few would practise the abstinence through which those funds are acquired and kept in existence. Up to a certain point, however, the principle of giving to every person concerned an interest in the profits is an actual benefit to the capitalist, not only (as M. Leclaire has testified) in point of ease and comfort, but even in pecuniary advantage. And after the point of greatest benefit to the employers has been attained, the participation of the labourers may be carried somewhat further without any material abatement from that maximum of benefit. At what point, in each employment of capital, this ultimatum is to be found, will one day be known and understood from experience; and up to that point it is not unreasonable to expect that the partnership principle will be, at no very distant time, extended.

The value of this "organization of industry," for healing the widening and embittering feud between the class of labourers and the class of capitalists, must, I think, impress itself by degrees on all who habitually reflect on the condition and tendencies of modern society. I cannot conceive how any such person can persuade himself that the majority of the community will for ever, or even for much longer, consent to hew wood and draw water all their lives in the service and for the benefit of others;

or can doubt, that they will be less and less willing to co-operate as sub-ordinate agents in any work, when they have no interest in the result, and that it will be more and more difficult to obtain the best work-people, or the best services of any work-people, except on conditions similar in principle to those of M. Leclaire. Although, therefore, arrangements of this sort are now in their infancy, their multiplication and growth, when once they enter into the general domain of popular discussion, are among the things which may most confidently be expected.

Appendix E

Appendix to Volume II in the 4th edition (1857). The information contained in this Appendix came to John Stuart Mill's notice too late for incorporation into the text of the 4th edition;[1] in the 5th and subsequent editions it was incorporated into Book IV, Chapter vii ("On the Probable Futurity of the Labouring Classes"), §§ 5–6.[2]

Latest Information on the French Industrial Associations. (From "Nouveau Traité d'Economie Politique," by M. Villiaumé. Paris, 1857.)

1. Associations between the labourers and the employer.

["En Mars 1847, M. Paul Dupont, gérant d'une imprimerie de Paris, eut l'idée d'associer ses ouvriers en leur promettant le dixième des bénéfices. Il en emploie habituellement trois cents, dont deux cents travaillent aux pièces et cent à la journée. Il emploie, en outre, cent auxiliaires, qui ne font pas partie de l'association.

"La part de bénéfice avenant aux ouvriers ne leur vaut guère, en moyenne, qu'une quinzaine de jours de travail; mais ils reçoivent leur salaire ordinaire suivant le tarif établi dans toutes les grandes imprimeries de Paris; et, de plus, ils ont l'avantage d'être soignés dans leurs maladies aux frais

---

[1]In a letter thanking Villiaumé for a copy of his *Nouveau traité d'économie politique*, in return for which JSM sent a copy of the 4th edition of his *Principles*, JSM says: "Vous avez probablement deviné que l'impression de ma nouvelle édition se trouvait trop avancée pour que j'eûsse pû [*sic*] la faire profiter de votre ouvrage autrement qu'en y ajoutant, en forme d'appendice, les renseignements importants que vous avez donnés sur l'état actuel des associations ouvrières." A.L.s. in the Hollander Collection, item 4017, University of Illinois. I would like to thank Professor Jack Stillinger for a copy of this letter.

[2]The variants within IV, vii, §§5–6 are given in the normal way as footnotes to the text at the relevant places; as this Appendix is arranged differently, and contains linking passages from Villiaumé not contained in those variants, it is reprinted here as a unit, with the places where the 57 text of the Appendix *agrees* with the 71 text surrounded by square brackets to simplify comparison; references to the 71 text are given in numbered footnotes to the end of each bracketed passage.

de la communauté, et de recevoir 1 fr. 50 cent. de salaire par jour d'incapacité de travail. Les ouvriers ne peuvent retirer leur part dans les
bénéfices que quand ils sortent de l'association. Chaque année, cette part,
qui est représentée tant en matériel qu'en rentes sur l'Etat, s'augmente
par la capitalisation des intérêts, et crée ainsi une réserve à l'ouvrier.

"M. Dupont et les capitalistes, ses commanditaires, trouvent dans cette
association un profit bien supérieur à celui qu'ils auraient; les ouvriers, de
leur côté, se félicitent chaque jour de l'heureuse idée de leur patron.
Plusieurs d'entre eux, encouragés à la réussite de l'établissement, lui ont fait
obtenir une médaille d'or en 1849, une médaille d'honneur à l'Exposition
Universelle de 1855; et quelques-uns même ont reçu personellement la
récompense de leurs découvertes et de leurs travaux. Chez un patron
ordinaire, ces braves gens n'auraient pas eu le loisir de poursuivre leurs
inventions, à moins que d'en laisser tout l'honneur à celui qui n'en était
pas l'auteur; tandis qu'étant associés, si le patron eût été injuste, deux
cents hommes eussent fait redresser ses torts.

"J'ai visité moi-même cet établissement, et j'ai pu m'assurer du perfectionnement que cette association apporte aux habitudes des ouvriers.

"M. Gisquet, ancien préfet de police, est propriétaire depuis long-temps
d'une fabrique d'huile à Saint-Denis, qui est la plus importante de France,
après celle de M. Darblay, de Corbeil. Lorsqu'en 1848 il prit le parti de
la diriger lui-même, il rencontra des ouvriers habitués à s'enivrer plusieurs
fois par semaine, et qui, pendant le travail, chantaient, fumaient, et quelquefois se disputaient. On avait maintes fois essayé sans succès de changer
cet état de choses; il y parvint par la prohibition faite à tous ses ouvriers
de s'enivrer les jours de travail, sous peine d'exclusion, et par la promesse
de partager entre eux, à titre de gratification annuelle, 5 p. 100 de ses
bénéfices nets, au *pro rata* des salaires, qui, du reste, sont fixés aux prix
courants. Depuis ce moment, la réforme a été complète; il se voit entouré
d'une centaine d'ouvriers pleins de zèle et de dévouement. Leur bien-être
s'est accru de tout ce qu'ils ne dépensent pas en boissons, et de ce qu'ils
gagnent par leur exactitude au travail. La gratification que M. Gisquet
leur accorde, leur a valu, en moyenne, chaque année, l'équivalent de leur
salaire pendant six semaines.][3]

"L'un des patrons qui comprirent le mieux l'association avec les ouvriers
est M. Leclaire, entrepreneur de peinture en bâtiments, à Paris. Dès 1842,
sur les conseils de quelques économistes, il associa ses deux cents ouvriers,
en leur promettant la moitié du bénéfice net outre leur salaire, qui était
toujours au moins égal au taux courant. Une amélioration extraordinaire

[[3]*See* II.773.n15—774.n13 *above.*]

se manifesta tout à coup dans les habitudes de ses ouvriers, qui devinrent des modèles d'exactitude et de probité. M. Leclaire introduisit l'usage du blanc de zinc au lieu du blanc de céruse, qui était souvent mortel pour les ouvriers. Les immenses travaux que lui nécessita cette heureuse innovation l'ont tellement fatigué, qu'il se vit forcé de s'adjoindre deux associés en titre, qu'il choisit parmi ses anciens ouvriers; et depuis 1853, la part du bénéfice partagée entre les ouvriers n'est plus que du quart, ce dont ceux-ci sont encore satisfaits. Quant à M. Leclaire, quoiqu'il [ait toujours banni la fraude, qui n'est que trop fréquente dans sa profession, il a toujours pu soutenir la concurrence et acquérir une belle aisance, malgré l'abandon d'une si large part de ses profits. Assurément, il n'y est parvenu que parce que l'activité inusitée de ses ouvriers, et la surveillance qu'ils exerçaient les uns sur les autres dans les nombreux chantiers, avaient compensé la diminution de ses profits personnels."]⁴

["M. Beslay, ancien député de 1830 à 1839, et représentant du peuple à l'Assemblée constituante, a fondé un atelier important de machines à vapeur à Paris, dans le faubourg du Temple. Il eut l'idée d'associer dans ce dernier établissement ses ouvriers, dès le commencement de 1847. Je transcris ici cet acte d'association, que l'on peut regarder comme l'un des plus complets de tous ceux faits entre patrons et ouvriers."]⁵

2. Associations of labourers among themselves.

"Dès 1851, il existait à Paris environ cent cinquante associations d'ouvriers qui avaient réussi, la plupart même sans aucun secours. Les événements politiques de la fin de cette année, et les rivalités de patrons jaloux, en firent dissoudre le plus grand nombre. L'on n'en compte plus en 1857 que vingt-trois à Paris, qui, presque toutes, prospèrent. Je vais brièvement examiner la situation de quelques-unes.

["Après les journées de juin 1848, le travail était suspendu dans le faubourg Saint-Antoine, occupé surtout, comme on le sait, par les fabricants de meubles. Quelques menuisiers en fauteuils firent un appel à ceux qui seraient disposés à travailler ensemble. Sur six à sept cents de cette profession, quatre cents se firent inscrire. Mais comme le capital manquait, neuf hommes des plus zélés commencèrent l'association avec tout ce qu'ils possédaient; savoir, une valeur de 369 francs en outils, et 135 francs 20 centimes en argent.

"Leur bon goût, leur loyauté et l'exactitude de leurs fournitures augmentant leurs débouchés, les associés furent bientôt au nombre de cent huit.

[⁴*See* II.772.19–25 *above*.]   [⁵*See* II.774.n14–19 *above*.]

Ils reçurent de l'Etat une avance de 25 mille francs, remboursables en quatorze ans par annuité, à raison de 3 fr. 75 c. pour cent d'intérêt.

"En 1857, le nombre des associés est de soixante-cinq, celui des auxiliaires de cent en moyenne. Tous les associés votent pour l'election d'un conseil d'administration de huit membres, et d'un gérant, dont le nom représente la raison sociale. La distribution et la surveillance du travail dans les ateliers sont confiées à des contremaîtres choisis par le gérant et le conseil. Il y a un contre-maître pour vingt ou vingt-cinq hommes.

"Le travail est payé aux pièces, suivant les tarifs arrêtés en assemblée générale. Le salaire peut varier entre 3 et 7 francs par jour, selon le zèle et l'habileté de l'ouvrier. La moyenne est de 50 francs par quinzaine. Ceux qui gagnent le moins touchent près de 40 francs par quinzaine. Un grand nombre gagnent 80 francs. Des sculpteurs et mouluriers gagnent jusqu'à 100 francs, soit 200 francs par mois. Chacun s'engage à fournir cent-vingt heures par quinzaine, soit dix heures par jour. Aux termes du règlement chaque heure de déficit soumet le délinquant à une amende de 10 centimes par heure en-deça de trente heures, et de 15 centimes au-delà. Cette disposition avait pour objet d'abolir l'habitude du lundi, et elle a produit son effet. Depuis deux ans, le système des amendes est tombé en désuetude, à cause de la bonne conduite des associés.

"Quoique l'apport des associés n'ait été que de 369 francs, le matériel d'exploitation appartenant à l'établissement* s'élevait déjà, en 1851, à 5713 francs, et l'avoir social, y compris les créances, à 24,000 francs. Depuis lors cette association est devenue plus florissante, ayant resisté à tous les obstacles qui lui ont été suscités. Cette maison est la plus forte de Paris dans son genre, et la plus considérée. Elle fait des affaires pour 400 mille francs par an. Voici son inventaire de décembre 1855.

Actif

Espèces	445	70	
Marchandises	82,930	70	fait d'avance, ce qui empêche le chômage.
Salaires payés d'avance	2421	70	
Matériel	20,891	35	
Portefeuille	9711	75	
Meubles consignés	211	75	
Loyer d'avance	4933	10	
Débiteurs divers	48,286	95	
	169,831	55	

*[Il est situé dans la rue de Chavonne, cour Saint-Joseph, au faubourg Saint-Antoine.] [See II.780n above.]

Passif

Effets à payer 8655			
Fonds d'association 133		ne la doivent qu'à eux-mêmes.
100 fr. à chacun 7600		pour l'Etat, qui prend 10
Fonds de retenue indivisible 9205	84	p. 100 par an sur les
		bénéfices, le tout payable
		au bout de 14 ans.
Caisse de secours 1544	30	ne la doivent qu'à eux-
Prêt de l'Etat, principal et intérêt 27,053	30	mêmes.
Créanciers divers 12,559	51	
66,752	65	

Différence active

100,398   90.   La société possède en réalité 123,000 fr.][6]

["L'association des maçons fut fondée le 10 août 1848. Elle a son siége rue Saint-Victor, 155. Le nombre de ses membres est de 85, et celui de ses auxiliaires de trois à quatre cents. Elle a deux gérants à sa tête; l'un, chargé spécialement des constructions; l'autre, de l'administration. Les deux gérants passent pour les plus habiles entrepreneurs de maçonnerie de Paris, et ils se contentent d'un modeste traitement. Cette association vient de construire trois ou quatre des plus remarquables hôtels de la capitale. Bien qu'elle travaille avec plus d'économie que les entrepreneurs ordinaires, comme on ne la rembourse qu'à des termes éloignés, c'est surtout pour elle qu'une banque serait nécessaire, car elle a des avances considérables à faire. Néanmoins elle prospère, et la preuve en est dans le dividende de 56 pour 100 qu'a produit cette année son propre capital, et qu'elle a payé aux citoyens qui se sont associés à ses opérations.

"Cette association est formée d'ouvriers qui n'apportent que leur travail; d'autres qui apportent leur travail et un capital quelconque; enfin de citoyens qui ne travaillent point, mais qui se sont associés en fournissant un capital."

"Les maçons se livrent le soir à un enseignement mutuel. Chez eux, comme chez les fabricants de fauteuils, le malade est soigné aux frais de la société, et reçoit en outre un salaire durant sa maladie. Chacun est protégé par l'association dans tous les actes de sa vie. Les fabricants de fauteuils auront bientôt chacun un capital de deux ou trois mille francs à leur disposition, soit pour doter leurs filles, soit pour commencer une

[[6]*See* II.780.n10—781.n30 *above.*]

réserve pour l'avenir. Quant aux maçons, quelques-uns possèdent déjà 4000 francs d'épargnes qui restent au fonds social.

"Avant qu'ils fussent associés, ces ouvriers étaient pauvrement vêtus de la veste et de la blouse; parce que, faute de prévoyance, et surtout à cause du chômage, ils n'avaient jamais une somme disponible de 60 francs pour acheter une redingote. Aujourd'hui, la plupart sont vêtus aussi bien que les bourgeois; quelquefois même avec plus de goût. Cela tient à ce que l'ouvrier, ayant un crédit dans son association, trouve partout ce dont il a besoin sur un bon qu'il souscrit; et la caisse retient chaque quinzaine une partie de la somme à éteindre. De la sorte, l'épargne se fait, pour ainsi dire, malgré l'ouvrier. Plusieurs même, n'ayant plus de dettes, se souscrivent à eux-mêmes des bons de 100 francs payables en cinq mois, afin de résister à la tentation des dépenses inutiles. On leur retient 10 francs par quinzaine; et au bout des cinq mois, bon gré, mal gré, ils trouvent ce petit capital épargné."][7]

["J'ai pu me convaincre par moi-même de l'habileté][8] du choix [des gérants et des conseils d'administration des associations ouvrières. Ces gérants sont bien supérieurs pour l'intelligence, le zèle, et même pour la politesse, à la plupart des patrons ou entrepreneurs particuliers. Et chez les ouvriers associés, les funestes habitudes d'intempérance disparaissent peu à peu, avec la grossièreté et la rudesse qui sont la conséquence de la trop incomplète éducation de leur classe."][9]

[[7]*See* II.781.n32—782.n23 *above.*]
[[8]*See* II.783.n4 *above.*]
[[9]*See* II.783.n4—10 *above.*]

Appendix F

The MS of the *Principles*

THE ONLY KNOWN MS of the *Principles* is that in the Pierpont Morgan Library, New York.* It is the press-copy MS of Vol. I of the 1st edition, bound in three volumes, half-green morocco, the MS volumes containing, respectively, Book I; Book II; and Chapters i–vi of Book III, with the Appendix to Vol. I. The folios of MS Vols. I and II are watermarked 1846; those of Vol. III are watermarked 1829 and 1833, but were undoubtedly prepared at the same time as those of the other volumes. The binding paper, however, is watermarked 1878 (five years after Mill's death), and the original folios may not have been cut to their present size (*circa* 24c. × 18.5c.) until that time.

The text is written on recto, with the verso sheets reserved for notes and revisions. (This is one of the two methods usually employed by Mill, the other being to write on the right-hand side of both recto and verso, reserving the left-hand side for notes and revisions.) The sheets are gathered usually into groups of twenty which are lettered sequentially in Mill's hand from A to Bb (L, which would occur on the first folio of Vol. II, does not appear, as the folio is missing). The first volume is numbered 1–66, 66x, 67–187, and 1–40. Neither the Table of Contents nor the Preface is here, and the "Preliminary Remarks" of the printed editions appear as Chapter i, so the chapter numbers differ. The second volume is numbered 2–139, 1–60, and 1–58, the first folio, as noted above, being missing; also ff135 and 136 have been misbound between ff129 and 130. The third volume is numbered 1–60, and 1–16, the last 16ff being the Appendix to Vol. I of the printed text, consisting here of pasted-up columns from the *Morning Chronicle,* linked and altered in ink by Mill. Printers' marks and signatures are found throughout.

As indicated in the Textual Introduction, the MS is heavily revised, almost every folio containing cancellations and interlineations. Most of

*It was bought in 1919 for £225 from Bernard Quaritch Limited, who had obtained it from Sotheby's sale (6 May, 1919) of Alfred Morrison's autograph collection.

the cancellations are trivial (many are false starts); many are virtually indecipherable. In the following illustrative examples the early readings are sometimes tentative.

The longest revision evidently took place in Book I, Chapter ix, §2 (on joint-stock management), which appears in the MS on slightly smaller sheets in a different pen. The earlier version must have been rejected in full, as the beginning of this first version of §2 is cancelled on the last full-sized folio, and the beginning of §3 is found on the last of the smaller folios, where the last line does not reach the margin. (These folios are watermarked like those in MS Vol. III.)

Trivial changes are very frequent; I.97.35, "considerable", will serve as example. The final MS reading is "material", but Mill wrote and then cancelled "great" and "large", interlined and cancelled "considerable", and finally interlined "material". There are other places where Mill restored cancelled readings (evidently) in proof; for example at I.135.31, where the cancelled "advantages" replaces the MS "recommendations" in the printed version. In a few places proof corrections were necessary to clear up tangles created by the MS revisions. For example at I.187.34–5, in altering by cancellation and interlineation "the improvements which in the arts of production" to "the improvements which facilitate production", Mill forgot to cancel "of" in the MS, but it was caught in proof. A similar change which was not caught in proof, and so is recorded as a variant,] may be seen at I.188^{l-i}, where Mill cancelled "properties of the soil" and interlined "niggardliness of nature" without altering the verb "are" to the singular. A printer's error which led to a revision is seen at I.110^{k-k}, where Mill wrote "the direst waste of wealth", which the typesetter read as "the direct waste of wealth"; in looking over the passage in 1852 (and probably puzzling over his apparent choice of words), Mill must have seen "direct" used again six lines lower in the next sentence, and so changed the reading to the final "the most obvious part of the waste of wealth".

One typical example of the extent of revision will illustrate Mill's habits. At I.67, a paragraph ends: "I conceive this to be one of the many errors arising in political economy, from the practice of not beginning with the examination of simple cases, but rushing at once into the complexity of concrete phenomena." The earliest MS version read, after "rushing", "at once into the complication of concrete phenomena, without having obtained a clue to disentangle them, & hence seeing only a part of the facts which are relevant to the point in consideration." A first revision altered "point in consideration" to "matter"; a second resulted in the reading, "into the complexity of concrete phenomena, without first obtaining a clue to disentangle it"; and the final reading was reached in proof. (Such passages were often altered again in later editions.)

The most interesting cancellations are, of course, the longer ones. In the 1st edition is found the following passage (an interesting anticipation of *On Liberty*), which was altered in the 3rd edition:

The perfection of social arrangements would be to secure to all persons complete independence and freedom of action, subject to no restriction but that of not doing injury to others: but the scheme which we are considering abrogates this freedom entirely, and places every action of every member of the community under command. [*See* I.978.13–18.]

In the MS (II.f9v) that sentence is added to replace the following cancelled one:

Deprive human life of all which this system would take away from it, & it would be reduced as I said before, to a sort of sentient vegetation; a state not so much superior as may be thought, to the condition of any of the other gregarious animals when they have enough to eat. [*In these two passages I ignore internal revisions.*]

An example of a cancelled passage not replaced will seem, to those who know Mill's habits, even more typical. At I.368.20, between the sentences ending with "discussed" and beginning with "People," the following sentences were cancelled in the MS:

The maladies of society are like the physical ailments of the wealthy Turk, whom the Swedish traveller Hasselquist was asked to prescribe for at Smyrna. The patient was dying of marasmus, & Hasselquist learning that he had a numerous harem, well knew what advice he needed, but forbore to give it, & prescribed some trifling palliative, knowing that any allusion to such a subject, besides being entirely useless, would be regarded as a mortal affront. [MS II.ii.51–2.]

A longer example, tentatively reproducing all the stages of revision (ignoring only a few false starts), shows Mill in difficulty over one of his key notions, the distinction between Production and Distribution. Towards the end of his "Preliminary Remarks," he first wrote the following sentences:

But though governments or nations can in some measure determine what institutions shall be established, it is not in their power to make those institutions have any other effects, than those which naturally belong to them. What are the effects of human institutions is as much a question of necessary laws & of strict science, as what are the effects of natural agencies. The laws, therefore, of the Distribution of Wealth, are as susceptible of scientific treatment as those of its production: the latter however are universal, & belong to all states of society equally, while the former are in a great measure different, according to the artificial circumstances of different societies; to ascertain the relation between these artificial circumstances & the differences in the distribution of wealth which are consequent on it, is the very scientific object which Political Economy, in this branch of it, proposes to itself. If mankind will produce wealth, they can do so according to invariable laws: the manner in which they will distribute it, is partly, & would on the supposition of perfect wisdom be wholly, in their own power to determine: but the necessary conditions of the power they can exercise over the distribution, & the manner in which it is affected by the various modes of conduct which society may think fit to adopt, are determined by laws as rigid, & as independent of human control, as the laws of Production itself. [MS Vol. I.27r, 28r.]

The words "in their power" were altered to "in the power of either", and then altered again to produce, with other revisions, the reading:

But though governments or nations can in some measure determine what institutions shall be established, they cannot arbitrarily determine how those institutions shall work; their operation when established is a question of necessary laws & strict science & quite as susceptible of scientific treatment as are the operation of natural agencies. Though [*illegible word*] difference is [*illegible word*], the laws of Production are universal, & belong equally to all states of society, while those of Distribution are in a great measure different, according to the artificial circumstances of different societies. Mankind can produce wealth only by conforming to the natural laws of its production; the manner in which they will distribute it, is partly, & would on the supposition of perfect knowledge be wholly, in their own power to determine, but the conditions of the power which they can exercise over the distribution, & the manner in which it is affected by the various modes of conduct which society may think fit to adopt, are determined by laws as rigid, & as independent of human control, as those of Production itself.

Immediately after this revision, Mill carried the beginning of the sentence starting "Mankind can" over to the verso of f26, writing:

Mankind can produce wealth, only by conforming to the natural laws of its production, while the manner in which they will distribute it,

Then, apparently going through the passage yet again, he cancelled all between "strict science" and "to the laws of Production", and then decided to cancel the middle part of the account totally by drawing vertical lines through it; he then rewrote the final sentence, producing the last MS version, which is reproduced in the 1st edition with only one change (", & as independent of human control," being omitted from the last clause). Here is the 1848 version, with subsequent changes indicated in square brackets:

But though governments or nations can in some measure determine [*3rd to 7th eds.* nations have the power of deciding] what institutions shall be established [*3rd to 7th eds.* shall exist], they cannot arbitrarily determine how those institutions shall work. The conditions on which the power they possess over the distribution of wealth is dependent, and the manner in which the distribution is affected [*5th to 7th eds.* effected] by the various modes of conduct which society may think fit to adopt, are determined by laws as rigid as those of Production itself [*3rd to 7th eds.* are as much a subject for scientific enquiry as any of the physical laws of nature]. [*See* I.21.18–25.]

Chapter IV.
Of Unproductive Labour.

The beginning of Book I, Chapter iv, from the MS in the Pierpont Morgan Library

One final example will show the difficulty of reconstructing the heavily revised passages. The passage below, which is reproduced on the opposite page, is an attempt at reconstruction: the final reading is given in bold-face; the first two readings are given in italic, with square brackets to indicate the cancellations which led (with the italic interlineation) to the second reading; further revisions are given in ordinary roman type. (It should be realized that none of the readings but the last may have existed in complete form.)

of the matter in dispute.

this seems to me a decided **misunderstanding** *is intended to any of*
But *no* [*one intends any*] *disparagement* [*to*] *these classes*

not being

of words, if not of things. **Production is not the sole end of human existence, & the term**
of persons by refusing to their labour the name of productive, nor are

nor

unproductive, therefore, does not necessarily imply any stigma; It is not in   was never
their respective functions in the economy of society at all in question

intended to do so in the present case. The question is one of mere language & classification.
here.   [I.45.20–4; MS I.56]

The assumption is that the first reading was:

But no one intends any disparagement to these classes of persons by refusing to their labour the name of productive, nor are their respective functions in the economy of society at all in question here.

The second reading was:

But no disparagement is intended to any of these classes of persons by refusing to their labour the name of productive, nor are their respective functions in the economy of society at all in question here.

The third reading was:

But this seems to me a decided misunderstanding of words, if not of things. Production is not the sole end of human existence & the term unproductive, therefore, does not necessarily imply any stigma. It was never intended to do so in the present case. The question is one of mere language & classification.

(Here a false start in the penultimate sentence is ignored: Mill wrote "It is not in" and then cancelled "is not in".) Finally he reached the ultimate MS reading:

But this seems to me a misunderstanding of the matter in dispute. Production not being the sole end of human existence, the term unproductive does not necessarily imply any stigma; nor was ever intended to do so in the present case. The question is one of mere language & classification.

The complexity and uncertainty of this reconstruction should illustrate the inutility of any attempt to reproduce in full the MS cancellations.

Appendix G

John Stuart Mill—Harriet Taylor Mill Correspondence

IN VIEW OF John Stuart Mill's account of Harriet Taylor's part in the writing of the *Principles*,[1] his dedication of the work to her,[2] and his description of it as a "joint production" with her,[3] it seems useful to include here those passages in their correspondence which refer specifically to the *Principles*.[4] Unfortunately, Harriet Taylor's side of the correspondence is lost, except for isolated items not here germane, and only part of John Stuart Mill's survives. The passages printed below include all references in these letters to revisions for the 2nd and 4th editions. There is no record of the specific part she played in the writing of the first draft, in the revision for the press copy, or for the 3rd edition.[5] (The revisions for the 5th, 6th, and 7th were made, of course, after her death.) This is not the place to consider in detail John Stuart Mill's account of her role as co-author of the *Principles*, but it might be pointed out that the

[1]*Autobiography* (Columbia University Press, 1924), 173–6. An early draft of part of this passage is in the Sterling Library, Yale.

[2]This dedication, not included in the 1st edition because Harriet's husband, John Taylor, objected, was pasted into gift copies of the 1st and 2nd editions. (Cf. F. A. Hayek, *John Stuart Mill and Harriet Taylor* [London: Routledge and Kegan Paul, 1951], 121–2, and M. St. J. Packe, *The Life of John Stuart Mill* [London: Secker and Warburg, 1954], 309–10.) The only one I have seen is in JSM's copy of the 2nd edition, in the library of Somerville College, Oxford. It reads: "TO/MRS JOHN TAYLOR,/AS THE MOST EMINENTLY QUALIFIED/OF ALL PERSONS KNOWN TO THE AUTHOR/EITHER TO ORIGINATE OR TO APPRECIATE/SPECULATIONS ON SOCIAL IMPROVEMENT,/THIS ATTEMPT TO EXPLAIN AND DIFFUSE IDEAS/MANY OF WHICH WERE FIRST LEARNED FROM HERSELF,/IS/WITH THE HIGHEST RESPECT AND REGARD,/DEDICATED."

[3]N. MacMinn, J. McCrimmon, and J. Hainds (eds.), *Bibliography of the Published Writings of John Stuart Mill* (Northwestern University Press, 1945), 69.

[4]Most of the passages are quoted or referred to by Professor Hayek in *John Stuart Mill and Harriet Taylor*; they are printed here, in corrected form, from the MSS.

[5]Actually, except for the two brief references in letters dated 1857 (quoted below), the revisions for the 4th edition apply not to the edition itself, but to the preliminary rewriting done in 1854 with a view to the proposed reprint of IV, vii by the Christian Socialists as working-class propaganda. See II.1032–7.

evidence given below concerns the revision of two important chapters (II, i and IV, vii), both of which were subject to major revisions again after the editions to which this evidence applies.

The letters quoted are all in the Sterling Library at Yale, except that quoted at II.1032n, which is in the Huntington Library. The numbers at the upper left of each letter are those used by the correspondents to indicate the sequence. The letters have no salutations; the dates have been regularized in form; a series of seven dots has been used to indicate omitted passages not dealing with the revisions. Superscript letters (for example, in "2ᵈ," "Messʳˢ," etc.) have been lowered.

The 1st edition having sold quickly, Mill was urged into revision at the beginning of 1849, when Harriet (to be widowed in July) was at Pau.

15   19 Feb., 1849

I received your dear letter 11 on Saturday & this morning the first instalment of the Pol. Ec. This last I will send again (or as much of it as is necessary) when I have been able to make up my mind about it. The objections are I think very inconsiderable as to quantity—much less than I expected—but that paragraph, p. 248,[6] in the first edit. which you object to so strongly & totally, is what has always seemed to me the strongest part of the argument (it is only what even Proudhon says against Communism)—& as omitting it after it has once been printed would imply a change of opinion, it is necessary to see whether the opinion has changed or not—yours has, in some respects at least, for you have marked strong dissent from the passage that "the necessaries of life when secure for the whole of life are scarcely more a subject of consciousness"[7] &c. which was inserted on your proposition & very nearly in your words. This is probably only the progress we have been always making, & by thinking sufficiently I should probably come to think the same—as is almost always the case, I believe *always* when we think long enough. But here the being unable to discuss verbally stands sadly in the way, & I am now almost convinced that as you said at first, we cannot settle this 2d edit. by letter. We will try, but I now feel almost certain that we must adjourn the publication of the 2d edit. to November. In the new matter one of the sentences that you have cancelled is a favorite of mine, viz "It is probable that this will finally depend upon considerations not to be measured by the coarse standard which in the present state of human improvement is the only one that can be applied to it."[8] What I meant was that whether individual

[6]48.I.247–8; see II.978.1–18.

[7]In 48 the passage actually reads: "The necessaries of life, when they have always been secure for the whole of life, are scarcely more a subject of consciousness. . . ." (48.I.247.34ff.) It was altered in 49; see II.978*f–f*.

[8]This passage does not occur in any edition, and its intended place cannot be accurately determined. The most likely place is in 49.I.254.31—255.4 (see II.978*f–f*, and the next letter below, II.1028.note 11); other possibilities are 49.I.265.26ff. (suggested by Professor Hayek, 300.n44), and 49.I.264 (see II.986–7).

agency or Socialism would be best ultimately—(*both* being necessarily very imperfect now, & *both* susceptible of immense improvement) will depend on the comparative attractions they will hold out to human beings with all their capacities, both individual & social, infinitely more developed than at present. I do not think it is English improvement only that is too backward to enable this point to be ascertained for if English character is starved in its social part I think Continental is as much or even more so in its individual, & Continental people incapable of entering into the feelings which make very close contact with crowds of other people both disagreeable & mentally & morally lowering. I cannot help thinking that something like what I meant by the sentence, ought to be said though I can imagine good reasons for your disliking the way in which it is put. Then again if the sentence "the majority would not exert themselves for anything beyond this & unless they did nobody else would &c"[9] is not tenable, then all the two or three pages of argument which precede & of which this is but the summary, are false, & there is nothing to be said against Communism at all—one would only have to turn round & advocate it—which if done would be better in a separate treatise & would be a great objection to publishing a 2d edit. until *after* such a treatise. I think I agree in all the other remarks. Fourrier[10] if I may judge by Considerant is perfectly right about women both as to equality & marriage—& I suspect that Fourier himself went farther than his disciple thinks prudent in the directness of his recommendations. Considerant sometimes avails himself as Mr Fox used, of the sentimentalities & superstitions about purity, though asserting along with it all the right principles. But C. says that the Fourrierists are the *only* Socialists who are not orthodox about marriage—he forgets the Owenites, but I fear it is true of all the known Communist leaders in France—he says it specially of Buchez, Cabet, & what surprises one in Sand's "guide, philosopher & friend" of Leroux. This strengthens one exceedingly in one's wish to prôner the Fourrierists besides that their scheme of association seems to me much nearer to being practicable at present than Communism.

. . . .

16   21 Feb., 1849

I despatched yesterday to the dear one an attempt at a revision of the objectionable passages.[11] I saw on consideration that the objection to Communism on the ground of its making life a kind of dead level might admit of being weakened, (though I think it never could be taken away) consistently with the principle of Communism, though the Communistic plans now before the public could not do it. The statement of objections was moreover too vague & general. I have made it more explicit as well as more moderate; you will judge whether it is now sufficiently either one or the other; & altogether

[9]In 48 the passage actually reads: "I believe that the majority would not exert themselves for any thing beyond this, and that unless they did, nobody else would. . . ." (48.I.250.5–7.) The sentence is deleted in 49; see II.980[n].

[10]JSM's inconsistency in spelling Fourier's name may indicate that at the time he knew his work only at second-hand.

[11]The reference here is undoubtedly to the passage referred to in the previous letter; see II.1027. note 8.

whether any objection can be maintained to Communism, except the amount of objection which, in the new matter I have introduced, is made to the present applicability of Fourierism.[12] I think there can—& that the objections as now stated to Communism are valid: but if *you* do not think so, I certainly will not print it, even if there were no other reason than the certainty I feel that I never should long continue of an opinion different from yours on a subject which you have fully considered. I am going on revising the book: not altering much, but in one of the purely political economy parts which occurs near the beginning, viz. the discussion as to whether buying goods made by labour gives the same employment to labour as hiring the labourers themselves, I have added two or three pages of new explanation & illustration which I think make the case much clearer.[13]

. . . .

22   14 March, 1849

What a nuisance it is having anything to do with printers—Though I had no reason to be particularly pleased with Harrison, I was alarmed at finding that Parker had gone to another, & accordingly, though the general type of the first edition is exactly copied, yet a thing so important as the type of the headings at the top of the page cannot be got right—you know what difficulty we had before—& now the headings, & everything else which is in that type, they first gave much too close & then much too wide, & say they have not got the exact thing, unless they have the types cast on purpose. Both the things they have produced seem to me detestable & the worst is that as Parker is sole owner of this edition I suppose I have no voice in the matter at all except as a point of courtesy. I shall see Parker today & tell him that I should have much preferred waiting till another season rather than having either of these types—but I suppose it is too late now to do any good—& perhaps Parker dragged out the time in useless delays before, on purpose that all troublesome changes might be avoided by hurry now. It is as disagreeable as a thing of the sort *can* possibly be—because it is necessary that something should be decided immediately without waiting for the decision of my only guide & oracle. If the effect should be to make the book an unpleasant object to the only eyes I wish it to please, how excessively I shall regret not having put off the edition till next season.

. . . .

23   17(?) March, 1849

. . . .

The bargain with Parker is a good one & that it is so is entirely your doing— all the difference between it & the last being wholly your work, as well as all the best of the book itself so that you have a redoubled title to your joint ownership of it. While I am on the subject I will say that the difficulty with

12 49.I.263.5—264.18; see II.984.37—985.38.
13 49.I.102.1—105.2 (I.84n—86n).

the printer is surmounted—both he & Parker were disposed to be accommodating & he was to have the very same type from the very same foundry today—in the meantime there has been no time lost, as they have been printing very fast without the headings, & will I have no doubt keep their engagement as to time. You do not say anything this time about the bit of the P.E.— I hope you did not send it during the week, as if so it has miscarried—at the rate they are printing, both volumes at once, they will soon want it.

. . . .

24   21 March, 1849

The Pol. Ec. packet came on Monday for which a thousand thanks. I have followed to the letter every recommendation. The sentence which you objected to in toto of course has come quite out.[14] In explanation however of what I meant by it—I was not thinking of any mysterious change in human nature— but chiefly of this—that the best people now are necessarily so much cut off from sympathy with the multitudes that I should think they must have difficulty in judging how they would be affected by such an immense change in their whole circumstances as would be caused by having multitudes whom they could sympathize with—or in knowing how far the social feelings might then supply the place of that large share of solitariness & individuality which they cannot now dispense with. I meant one thing more, viz. that as, hereafter, the more obvious & coarser obstacles & objections to the community system will have ceased or greatly diminished, those which are less obvious & coarse will then step forward into an importance & require an attention which does not now practically belong to them & that we can hardly tell without trial what the result of that experience will be. I do not say that *you* cannot realize & judge of these things—but if you, & perhaps Shelley & one or two others in a generation can, I am convinced that to do so requires both great genius & great experience & I think it quite fair to say to common readers that the present race of mankind (speaking of them collectively) are not competent to it. I cannot persuade myself that you do not greatly overrate the ease of making people unselfish. Granting that in "ten years" the children of a community might by teaching be made "perfect" it seems to me that to do so there must be perfect people to teach them. You say "if there were a desire on the part of the cleverer people to make them perfect it would be easy— but how to produce that desire in the cleverer people? I must say I think that if we had absolute power tomorrow, though we could do much to improve people by good laws, & could even give them a very much better education than they have ever had yet, still, for effecting in our lives anything like what we aim at, all our plans would fail from the impossibility of finding fit instruments. To make people really good for much it is so necessary not merely to give them good intentions & conscientiousness but to unseal their eyes—to prevent self flattery, vanity, irritability & all that family of vices from warping their moral judgments as those of the very cleverest people are almost always warped now. But we shall have all these questions out together & they will all require to be entered into to a certain depth, at least, in the

[14]See II.1027. note 8.

new book which I am so glad you look forward to as I do with so much interest.

· · · · · · ·

27   *c.* 31 March, 1849

· · · · · · ·

The alteration I had made in that sentence of the P.E. was instead of "placard their intemperance" to say "placard their enormous families"—it does not read so well, but I think it may do, especially as the previous sentence contains the words "this sort of incontinence"—but your two sentences are so very good that as that sheet is not yet printed, get them in I must & will.[15]— Are you not amused with Peel about Ireland? He sneers down the waste lands plan, two years ago, which the timid ministers, timid because without talent, give up at a single sarcasm from him, & now he has enfanté a scheme containing that & much more than was then proposed—& the Times supports him & Ireland praises him. I am extremely glad he has done it—I can see that it is working as nothing else has yet worked to break down the superstition about property—& it is the only thing happening in England which promises a step forward—a thing which one may well welcome when things are going so badly for the popular cause in Europe—not that I am discouraged by this— progress of the right kind seems to me quite safe now that Socialism has become *inextinguishable.* I heartily wish Proudhon dead however—there are few men whose state of mind, taken as a whole, inspires me with so much aversion, & all his influence seems to me mischievous except as a potent *dissolvent* which is good so far, but every single thing which he would substitute seems to me the worst possible in practice & mostly [?] in principle. I have been reading another volume of Considerant lately published[16]—he has got into the *details* of Fourierism, with many large extracts from Fourier himself. It was perhaps necessary to enter into details in order to make the thing look practicable, but many of the details *are,* & all *appear,* passablement ridicules. As to their system, & general mode of thought there is a great question at the root of it which must be settled before one can get a step further. Admitting the omnipotence of education, is not the very pivot & turning point of that education a *moral sense*—a feeling of duty, or conscience, or principle, or whatever name one gives it—a feeling that one *ought* to do, & to wish for, what is for the greatest good of all concerned. Now Fourier, & all his followers, leave this out entirely, & rely wholly on such an arrangement of social circumstances[17] as without any inculcation of duty or of "right," will make every one, by the spontaneous action of the passions, intensely zealous for all the interests of the whole. Nobody is ever to be made to do anything but act just as they like, but it is calculated that they will always, in a phalanstere, like what is best. This of course leads to the freest

---

[15]See I.368*c–c*. The phrase "this species [*not* sort] of incontinence" occurs two sentences above; Harriet's sentences presumably are those in the note added in 49 (I.368n).

[16]V. P. Considerant, *Le socialisme devant le vieux monde, ou, le vivant devant les morts.* Paris: 1848. Cf. Hayek, 302. note 72.

[17]Page ripped; MS reads only "circumstance".

notions about personal relations of all sorts, but is it, in other respects, a foundation on which people would be able to live & act together [?][18] *Owen* keeps in generals & only says that education can make everybody perfect, but the Fourierists attempt to shew how, & exclude, as it seems to me, one of the most indispensable ingredients.

. . . .

The next references to the *Political Economy* in the correspondence between John Stuart Mill and Harriet occur in the series of letters written early in 1854 when Harriet was at Hyères. As the letters indicate, Mill was approached by Frederick J. Furnivall, on behalf of the Christian Socialists, with a request to reprint "On the Probable Futurity of the Labouring Classes" (IV, vii) as a pamphlet. Mill, with Harriet's and his publisher's approval, acceded to the request, and made extensive alterations to the chapter. Although he sent the proofs to Furnivall, no copy of the pamphlet has been located, and there is considerable doubt as to whether it was printed. In fact, Furnivall approached him again in 1860 with the same request, to which Mill replied almost exactly as he had done six years earlier.[19]

16   4 Feb., 1854

. . . .

While I write, in comes a note from one of the Kingsley set who has written before, as you probably remember. I send his affected note which asks leave to

[18]Page ripped.
[19]Were the date on the letter not so clear, and the last paragraph omitted, one would assume that it was written in 1854. It reads:

> Saint Véran
> near Avignon
> Dec. 10. 1860.

DEAR SIR

I would with great pleasure accede to your proposal with respect to a reprint of the chapter on the Futurity of the Labouring Classes for separate sale, if it rested with me to do so. The current edition however of the Pol. Economy is the property of the publisher Mr Parker, and he alone has the power of authorizing what you propose. Your application therefore should be to him, unless you prefer waiting till the present edition is out of print, which is likely to be, I believe, in a few months. I propose making some additions to the chapter for another edition, so as to bring up the facts of Cooperation to the latest date, and if I have anything to say worth saying in the way of advice to Cooperators, that will be, I think, the most suitable occasion.

I am very glad to hear such good news of the progress of Cooperation. The publicity given to the brilliant results of the Rochdale and Leeds experiments, by Mr Holyoake's book, by Bright's speech, and otherwise, was likely to encourage others to do the same. I am

> Dear Sir
> very truly yours
> J. S. MILL

reprint the Chapter on the Future of the Labouring Classes. Of course I must tell him that he must ask leave of Parker, but I should perhaps tell him also, & certainly should be prepared to tell Parker, whether I have any objection myself. I should think I have not: what does my angel think? I did not expect the Xtian Socialists would wish to circulate the chapter as it is in the 3d edit. since it stands up for Competition against their one-eyed attacks & denunciations of it.

. . . .

19   13 Feb., 1854

. . . .

I will answer Furnivall as you say. I do not know what alterations the chapter requires & cannot get at it as the last edition is locked up in the plant room. I can of course get from Parker another copy, or even those particular sheets from the "waste". I imagine that if I tell Furnivall of making alterations he will be willing to give me time enough—besides I could send you the chapter by post.

. . . .

21   18 Feb., 1854

. . . .

I wrote to Furnivall in the manner you wished, & have had two notes from him since—the first short—"I am very much obliged to you for your kind letter of yesterday, & will communicate forthwith with Messrs Parker & Son, & then again with you as to the additions to the chapter." The other which came this morning "Messrs P. & Son have given me their consent to your chapter on" &c. "being reprinted, If you will be kind enough to send me the additions you said you would be so good as to make, as soon as is convenient to you, I will have the chapter as revised set up immediately on receipt of them, & send you a proof." I wrote a short answer asking for a few days time to consider how I could improve it, & wrote to Parker for the sheets—they will come I suppose on Monday & I will send them to my precious guide philosopher & friend by that day's post. I have not the least idea at present what additions they require, but between us we shall I am sure manage to improve them very much.

. . . .

22   20 Feb., 1854

. . . .

The chapter of the P.E. I shall send by the post which takes this letter. If the post office tells me right, a penny stamp will cover it & you will have nothing to pay. I do not know where to begin or where to stop in attempting to improve it. One would like to write a treatise instead. As for minor additions I wish I could get some more recent facts as to the French Associations

Ouvrières. I must also say something about the English ones (though a very little will suffice) as Furnivall suggests in another note he has written to me which I inclose. The note at p. 331[20] now requires modification so far as concerns the first half of it. I shall not attempt any alterations till I hear from you.

. . . .

24   28 Feb., 1854

. . . .

You have by this time got the chapter—As so much is said of the French associations I must put in a few words about the English, of which Furnivall has sent me a long list[21]—especially as it is going among the very people—but I shall take care not to commit myself to anything complimentary to them. F. has also from Nadaud some later intelligence about the French,[22] nearly all of which are put down.

. . . .

26   6 March, 1854

. . . .

The Pol. Ec. was put into the post 21 Feb. being Tuesday, instead of Monday, the day I wrote—the reason being that Parker did not send it till I was just leaving the I.H. at near five oclock, & as I had no other copy I wished to read it quietly at home before sending it. It certainly dear was very wrong to send it without making that sentence illegible,[23] for it was wrong to run any risk of that kind—the risk happily was small, as they were not likely to take the trouble of looking into letters or packets addressed to unsuspected persons, nor if they did were they likely to see that sentence, nor if they saw it to make the receiver answerable for a sentence in a printed paper forming part of an English book. Still it was a piece of criminal rashness which might have done mischief though it probably has not. Did it arrive with a penny stamp, attached half to the cover & half to the blank page, so as to be a sort of cachet? If it did not, however, it would not prove it to have been opened, as the stamp might come off. It was another piece of thoughtlessness not to say that I had no other copy. It is, however, probable, though not certain, that I could get another from Parker, & I would have applied to him for one now if you had said that you would not send yours until you receive this; but as you will probably have sent it after receiving my next letter, & it is therefore probably on its way, I will wait to see. I quite agree with you about the inexpediency of adding anything like practical advice, or anything at all which alters the character of the chapter—the working men ought to see that it was not written *for* them—any attempt to mingle the two characters would be

[20]57.II.335n. Deleted in 62; see II.765[b].

[21]See 57.II.352n.–353n. Passage rewritten in 62; see II.784[i–i793].

[22]See II.784[i–i793], and II.1036.23–30.

[23]Probably one of the sentences in the paragraph at 52.II.347.10ff., beginning "It is painful to think. . . ." See II.784[h–h].

sure to be a failure & is not the way in which we should do the thing even if we had plenty of time & were together.

. . . .

27   9 March, 1854

. . . .

About the P.E. I shall write immediately to Parker for another copy. I do not intend to say anything in praise of the English Associations but solely to state the fact that they are now very numerous & increasing—perhaps stating *how many*, according to a list which F. gave me. Whatever I do write I will send you & it will cause no or but little delay as the thing can go to press meanwhile & alterations be made when it is in proof.

. . . .

28   11 March, 1854

I have not yet any answer from Parker to my application for another copy of the chapter.

. . . .

30   14 March, 1854

. . . .

I find a good deal of difficulty in adding much to the chapter of the P. Econ. without altering its character, which must be maintained, in the main, as it is, as something written *of* but not *to* the working classes. I think I agree in all your remarks & have adopted them almost all—but I do not see the possibility of bringing in the first two pages (from the preceding chapter)[24]—I see no place which they would fit. Not having your copy, I do not know what sentence you would omit from page 330.[25] I do not see how to bring in anything about short hours bills well; does it seem necessary to do so here?—& I have not yet succeeded in bringing in your remark on page 346.[26] I have translated (with some omissions) all the French. I give on the next page all the additions I have made. If I make any more I will send them. I shall keep it back from Furnivall for a few days—if he is not urgent, till I hear from you.

. . . .

Additional note, in brackets, to p. 331[27]
[Mr Fitzroy's Act for the better protection of women & children against assaults, is a well meant though inadequate attempt to remove the first re-

[24]The reference is not clear; probably IV.vi.2 is intended; see II.753–7. No such change was made in any subsequent edition.

[25]No alterations were made to this passage, see II.764–5.

[26]The only alteration to this page is that indicated in the note by JSM added to this letter; see II.1036, note to p. 346.

[27]See II.765[b] (the wording was altered before the 4th ed.).

proach. The second is more flagrant than ever, *another* Reform Bill having been presented this year, which largely extends the franchise among many classes of men, but leaves all women in their existing state of political as well as social servitude.]

Page 332 near the bottom.[28] "The rich in their turn are regarded as a mere prey & pasture for the poor & are the subject of demands & expectations wholly indefinite, increasing in extent with every concession made to them. The total absence of regard for justice or fairness in the relations between the two, is at the least as marked on the side of the employed as on that of the employers. We look in vain among the working classes for the just pride which will choose to give good work for good wages: for the most part their sole endeavour is to receive as much, & return as little in the shape of service, as possible."

Page 346, continuation of note.[29] "One of the most discreditable indications of a low moral condition, given of late by the English working classes, is the opposition to piece work. Dislike to piecework, except under mistaken notions, must be dislike to justice & fairness, or desire to cheat, by not giving work in proportion to the pay. Piecework is the perfection of *contract*; & contract, in all work, & in the most minute detail—the principle of so much pay for so much service carried to the utmost extremity—is the system, of all others, in the present state of society, most favorable to the worker, though most unfavourable to the non-worker who wishes to be paid for being idle."

Note to p. 347.[30] "According to the latest accounts which have reached us (March 1854) seven of these associations are all which are now left. But Cooperative stores (associations pour la consommation) have greatly developed themselves, especially in the S. of France, & are at least not forbidden (we know not whether discouraged) by the Government."

Note to p. 348.[31] "Though this beneficent movement has been so fatally checked in the country in which it originated, it is rapidly spreading in those other countries which have acquired, & still retain, any political freedom. It forms already an important feature in the social improvement which is proceeding at a most rapid pace in Piedmont: & in England on the 15th of Feb. of the present year 1854 there had been registered under the Indl & Provt Societies Act, 33 associations, 17 of which are Industrial Societies, the remainder being associations for cooperative consumption only. This does not include Scotland, where also these assns are rapidly multiplying. The Societies which have registered under this new Act are only a portion of the whole. A list dated in June 1852 gives 41 assns for productive industry in E. & Sc. besides a very much greater number of flour mill societies & cooperative stores."

[28]See II.767*e–e* and the variants therein.
[29]See II.783n and the variants therein.
[30]This passage was almost completely rewritten for the 57 edition; see II.784*h–h*.
[31]See II.784*i–i793* and the variants therein.

31   18 March, 1854

. . . .

My letter to Avignon also contained copies of all the new matter of any importance in the Chapter of the Pol. Ec. & asked what was the sentence in page 330 that you had marked to come out—but the chapter itself has arrived since & there is *no* sentence marked in that page—I suppose the dear one altered her mind & rubbed out the marks.[32] I still hold to keeping it back from Furnivall till I hear your opinion of the additional matter which will be in a few days now.

. . . .

34   3 April, 1854

. . . .

When I got her approval of the alterations in the chapter, I inserted a saving clause about piece work[33] & sent the whole to Furnivall who promises a proof shortly.

. . . .

The last references to the *Political Economy* in the correspondence between John Stuart Mill and Harriet occur in 1857, when he was revising for the 4th edition while she was in Glasgow.

                                                          18 Feb., 1857

. . . .

I get on quickly with the Pol. Econ. as there is but little to add or alter.

. . . .

                                                          19 Feb., 1857

. . . .

I pass the evening always at the Pol. Economy, with now & then a little playing to rest my eyes & mind. There will be no great quantity to alter, but now & then a little thing is of importance. One page I keep for consideration when I can shew it to you. It is about the qualities of English workpeople, & of the English generally. It is not at all as I would write it now, but I do not, in reality, know how to write it.[34]

. . . .

[32]See II.1035. note 25.

[33]See II.783n, and JSM's note to 52.346 (II.1036). Cf. Hayek, 203, who says that Harriet suggested the added clause.

[34]The reference is probably to I.104*f-f* (I.vii.3); cf. Hayek, who suggests I.viii [? vii]. 5.

Appendix H

John Stuart Mill—John E. Cairnes Correspondence and Notes

THE CENTRAL and most detailed part of the long and friendly correspondence between John Stuart Mill and John E. Cairnes concerns the
suggestions which Cairnes made, on Mill's request, about the revision
for the 6th edition of the *Principles*. This appendix draws on that
correspondence (both sides of which are in the Mill-Taylor Collection,
London School of Economics),[1] and on two sets of notes written by
Cairnes to accompany his letters. The first of these, hereafter called
"Notes on the Principles" (Mill-Taylor Collection) deals with technical
criticisms of isolated passages in the 5th edition; the second, hereafter
called "Notes on Ireland" (National Library of Ireland), supplies information about land tenure and population in Ireland.

The "Notes on the Principles" were sent in two batches, with Cairnes'
letters of 29 Nov. and 6 Dec., 1864. The "Notes on Ireland" were also
sent in two batches, on 23 and 24 Dec., 1864. The material is arranged
below in chronological order, with the Notes attached at the end of the
relevant letters. It has been necessary to limit quotation from the letters
to passages concerning the revision of the *Principles*, although other economic and political matters are discussed at great length in this very
interesting correspondence. All the letters between 3 Oct., 1864, and
27 March, 1865, are here represented in part, except for Cairnes' letters
of 17 and 20 March, which contain no reference to revision. The passage
from Cairnes' letter of 2 June, 1865, is given merely as a conclusion. As in
Appendix G, the form of the dates has been regularized; a series of seven
dots has been used to indicate omitted passages not dealing with the
revisions, and superscripts have been lowered.

The "Notes on the Principles" are given in full, with editorial notes
in square brackets at the end of each note, indicating the relevant pas-

[1]An account of this correspondence, with quotations, is given in George O'Brien,
"J. S. Mill and J. E. Cairnes," *Economica*, n.s. X (Nov., 1943), 273–85.

sages in the present edition, and noting (by the words "Altered" and "Unaltered") whether Mill changed the passage as a result of Cairnes' criticism. The following editorial liberties have been taken: the separate notes are each headed by a centred number, and the page reference to the present edition is given at the beginning of each note, followed by Cairnes' reference to the 5th edition in parentheses. Cairnes' numbering of his folios has been ignored; his square brackets have been altered to round; punctuation has been supplied where necessary for abbreviations; and superscripts (as in "wᵈ" and "shᵈ") have been lowered. Square brackets within the text, unless otherwise noted, indicate tears in the manuscript or (as there is no chance of confusion) references to the present edition where Cairnes has references to the 5th edition. (At two places references to the present edition replace Cairnes' references to folios in this manuscript.) Cairnes' footnotes are given at the bottom of the page; occasionally the exact placing of the footnote indicator in the text has been difficult, because Cairnes places them in the margin against passages; they are here placed after the most appropriate word. One curious matter: the manuscript is very delicate, and the British Library of Political Science and Economics has a photostat copy which actually contains readings no longer preserved in the manuscript, because of the latter's deterioration.

The "Notes on Ireland" have not been reproduced in full; most of them are summaries of books and articles on Ireland (a list is given at II.1075n), and what appears below is Cairnes' final version of his own opinions and findings, which appears in the collection as a discrete item. (There is also an earlier version.) The same editorial liberties have been taken, where appropriate, as in the case of the "Notes on the Principles," and footnotes added to indicate the passages incorporated by Mill into the 6th edition.

1. MILL TO CAIRNES

Saint Véran, Avignon
3 Oct., 1864.

. . . .

We shall be here till January. I have much work cut out for me to do during this autumn and winter, part of which is that of correcting my Political Economy for a new edition. I should be very glad to make any improvement in it which you can suggest, and especially to know if there is anything which you think it would be useful to say on the present state of Ireland. My speculations on the means of improvement there have been in a state of suspended animation, from which it is almost time that they should emerge.

. . . .

2. CAIRNES TO MILL

Stameen, Drogheda
13 Oct., 1864.

. . . .

I assure you I feel very deeply gratified by your wish for suggestions from me for the forthcoming edition of your Political Economy, with which I shall be only too happy to comply. In about a month I go down to Galway to put in a course of lectures there, and I purpose to take that opportunity to make a careful perusal of your Political Economy. I shall then make notes of any points that occur to me as at all deserving of your consideration, and will send them to you. I do not anticipate, however, that I can make any suggestion of the least importance. There is one portion of the subject indeed in which I should like to see the nomenclature considerably recast—that which deals with the causes affecting the phenomena of the Money Market, including the subjects of the loan fund, credit &c., but even should you approve of my views on this point, the gain from the change would form no kind of compensation for the trouble it would involve. I have a paper on this subject partly written[2] (which I had intended as one of the essays which were to form that volume of which I spoke to you some time ago) and, as soon as I can find time to finish it, I should be very glad to submit it to you. I shall hope to have both it and the notes ready before Xmas. With regard to Ireland, I think you have exactly hit the true state of the case in the remark in the last edition of your Pol. Economy in which you say that the time has passed for heroic remedies.[3] Further improvement is I think to be effected by such measures as Land Law reform, with a view principally to facilitating the transfer and acquisition of land in small portions, diffusion of agricultural knowledge, and lastly—a point to which I attach some importance—the inculcation through the press and otherwise of sound opinions on the subject of land tenure with a view to the creation of a public opinion capable of controlling landlords in the exercise of their legal rights. All such measures, however, appear to me to be quite as much needed for England as for this country. As for land-compensation schemes I have no faith in them.

As regards the actual condition of Ireland, I hope to be able in the course of a month to furnish you with at least the materials for forming a sound opinion. My friend Judge Longfield, of whom I have just spoken, is at present preparing an address for the opening of the approaching Session of our Statistical Society on this subject;[4] and I know no one on whose judgment, from his long and extended acquaintance with the subject, the soundness of his economic views (he was the first Whately Professor) and his entire freedom from prejudice, I should for my part be more disposed to rely. I expect a very valuable address from him, and you may depend upon me to lose no time in sending you a copy.

. . . .

[2]This paper does not appear to have been published.
[3]See I.331c-c336.
[4]Mountifort Longfield, "Address by the President, Hon. Judge Longfield, at the Opening of the Eighteenth Session," *Journal of the Statistical and Social Inquiry Society of Ireland*, IV, Part 24 (January, 1865), 129–46; "Appendix to the foregoing Address," *ibid.*, 146–54. The address was given on 26 November, 1864.

3. MILL TO CAIRNES

Saint Véran, Avignon
8 Nov., 1864.

. . . .

Your letter of the 13th October was as your letters always are, extremely interesting to me. I am very desirous of any suggestions that may occur to you for the improvement of this edition of my Political Economy, as it will be the foundation of a cheap popular edition which will be stereotyped. I have just heard from the publisher that the old edition is so nearly out, as to require that the new one should be got on with sooner than I expected when I wrote to you, and I am therefore obliged to lay aside what I was writing (a paper on Comte for the Westminster Review)[5] to set about the revision. Consequently, the sooner I can have even a part of your remarks, the better: but what is not ready for the revision may easily be in time to be made use of in the proofs.

I expect to learn much respecting the state of Ireland from Judge Longfield's address. But I at present feel considerably puzzled what to recommend for Ireland. It cannot be said any longer that the English system of landlords, tenant farmers, and hired labourers is impossible in Ireland, as it was in the days before the famine. But it does not seem to me to suit the ideas, feelings, or state of civilization of the Irish. And I cannot see that the changes, great as they are, have abolished cottierism. They have diminished competition for land, and the evil of rackrents, and tenants always in arrear. But I do not see that the tenant has an atom more of motive to improve, or inducement to industry and frugality than he had. He finds all this in America: if he could find it at home, he probably would not emigrate.

. . . .

4. CAIRNES TO MILL

Galway
29 Nov., 1864.

. . . .

You will think it strange that you have not heard from me sooner in reply to your letter of the 8th inst. It reached me at a time when I was working under much pressure, and, not having any notes in such a state that I could send them to you, I have deferred writing till I could get some material ready. I now send you some ten pages of notes set down in the order which I happened to have them most forward in preparation. You will see that I have in several instances made bold to criticise you: for the most part my criticisms do not pass beyond verbal questions; but even when they go no further than this I offer them with the most sincere deference: much more do I feel distrust of my conclusions when I venture to differ from you on

[5]"The Positive Philosophy of Auguste Comte," *Westminster Review*, LXXXIII (Apr., 1865), 339–405, and "Later Speculations of Auguste Comte," *ibid.*, LXXXIV (July, 1865), 1–42; republished together as *Auguste Comte and Positivism* (London: Trübner, 1865).

points of doctrine. I hope to send you another batch of notes in about a week, the remainder will consist in what I have to say on Ireland & on the theory of money and interest.[6]

Ere this reaches you, you will probably have seen Judge Longfield's address, and possibly will detect my hand in some articles in the Daily News,[7] setting forth his views. I expect you will be somewhat disappointed with his address. I certainly do not agree with much of his argument on the subject of "fixity of tenure," which I think is pervaded by the fallacy of transferring what is true from an individual point of view to a point of view of a general kind. However his suggestions are I think very valuable. I have just received from him a bundle of M.S., from which I hope to extract a good deal of information to send you with my next despatch.

. . . .

Notes on the Principles of Political Economy (*Fifth Edition*)

1

I.58.6–7 (I.71). "This mode of levying taxes, therefore, limits unnecessarily the industry of the country." This, I think, is only true where the Govt keeps in hand larger funds than the requirements of the public service call for; and where the Govt does this, the observation holds in whatever way taxation be imposed. [This note cancelled by Cairnes. Unaltered.]

2

I.65–6 (I.81). To the instances given here of industry falling short of the development rendered possible by the state of capital might perhaps be added the case of "unemployed capital" referred to ante p. 70 [I.57]. [Unaltered.]

3

I.70.11 (I.87). "To consume less than is produced, is saving".—Might it not be well to add "the balance being employed productively"—with a view to distinguish "saving" from "hoarding". Without this distinction two good terms seem to be thrown away in expressing the same conception. (I observe in the next paragraph this distinction is maintained.) [Unaltered. The "next paragraph" is at I.70.17ff.]

4

I.78.32 (I.98). Fourth fundamental theorem:—"Demand for commodities is not demand for labour." It seems to me that this is rather a different mode of stating the third fundamental theorem (p. 87 [I.70.20–3])—"that the result of saving is consumed, though by persons other than he who saves", than a separate and distinct proposition, and that there wd, with a view to clearness of exposition, be an advantage in connecting the discussion of this doctrine with that—the third theorem. I say with a view to clearness; because if the fact be once firmly seized, that saving, as compared with unproductive spending, involves the distinction, that in the former case [pro]ductive labourers consume, while in the latter the consumption is performed by the owner of the

[6]See below, II.1058ff.
[7]Unheaded leading articles, *Daily News*, 1 Dec., 1864, 4, and 3 Dec., 1864, 4.

wealth (and the fact is so simple that it has only need to be fairly presented to the mind in order to be apprehended)—I say if this simple distinction be once firmly seized, I think all that follows with the important consequences which attach to it cannot but be accepted. In short to establish the doctrine that "demand for commodities is not demand for labour"—i.e. does not benefit the labouring classes—all that is needed is the two assumptions 1. that he who profits by (i.e. enjoys) wealth is he who consumes it, and 2. that productive labourers consume saved wealth, while wealth unproductively spent is consumed wholly by the unproductive consumers.

Perhaps the best practical *reductio ad absurdum* of the opposite doctrine is afforded by the Poor Law. If it be equally for the benefit of the poorer classes whether I consume my wealth unproductively or set aside a portion in the form of wages or alms for their direct consumption, then on what ground can the policy be justified of taking my money from me to support paupers? wd not my unproductive expenditure have equally benefitted *them*, while *I* shd have enjoyed it too? If society can both eat its cake and have its cake, why shd it not be permitted to indulge in the double luxury? Whately said somewhere[8] that the only difference between giving money in alms and spending it for one's own pleasure, was, that in one case you paid a man for doing something, while in the other you paid him for doing nothing. Now let us test this by a simple case. I have a sixpence and am in doubt whether to purchase a cake with it for my own eating or to give it to a beggar. By purchasing the cake, according to Whately, I pay a man for making a cake; by giving it to the beggar I pay a man for doing nothing; therefore on the principle of encouraging industry, I am bound to eat the cake. But suppose the beggar were to plead that he meant to purchase & consume the very same sweetmeat? &c &c

[Altered. At I.84^r-r Mill adopts, mostly in Cairnes' words, the material contained in the paragraph beginning: "Perhaps the best practical. . . . " The passage above in quotation marks, beginning: "that the result of saving . . ." is not a direct quotation.]

5

I.8.26–8 (I.9). "Wealth as applied to the possessions of an individual, and to those of a nation or of mankind". The distinction might be carried further— to capital, and even to the subdivisions of capital. Thus the rent paid by the farmer is a portion of *his* capital, but it is not capital to the nation or to mankind. Again Surplus Wages—i.e. wages in excess of what is necessary "for the strictly indispensable" requirements of the labourer, is capital to his employer, but not in the general sense;—in short all the limitations specified at pp. 70–71 [I.57–8] wd be met by this distinction.* Further the same

---

*Had the distinction been kept in view by Senior it wd have saved his readers the tedious and unprofitable discussion on the question whether "houses and other articles of slow consumption" were "capital"—a discussion in which I think Adam Smith was plainly in the right.[9]

[8]Richard Whately, *Introductory Lectures on Political Economy* (London: Fellowes, 1831), 164.
[9]Nassau William Senior, *An Outline of the Science of Political Economy* (London: Clowes, 1836), 155ff.

distinction may be traced in the subdivisions. e.g. Money is, regarded from an *individual* point of view, "circulating capital", but it is "fixed capital" in a *national* sense. (I rather think Adam Smith has made a remark to this effect).[10] It may be regarded as a machine for effecting the exchanges of the nation. To that portion however which passes from country to country, and which in times like the present when gold & silver are increasing is very large the remark of course does not apply. [Unaltered in specified places.]

6

I.97^{b-b} (I.120). "I doubt if there could be found a single example of a great increase of fixed capital at a time and place where circulating capital was not rapidly increasing also." I think Ireland during the last four years wd furnish such a case. That her total agricultural wealth has greatly diminished is proved by the Registrar General's returns—Mr Gladstone estimated the loss at £27,000,000—and during the same time the conver[sion] of tillage into pasture has been rapidly progressing. The coincidence of the two occurrences has no doubt powerfully stimulated the emigration. [Altered.]

7

I.99.18–19 (I.122). "Capital as to its destination" which "is not yet capital in actual exercise":—Might we not conveniently distinguish the former as "potential capital"? "Potential capital" in the largest sense wd include all the capital which the credit of an individual or of a nation, if forced to the utmost, cd command. [Unaltered.]

8

I.100–15 (I.124–41). Should not the strength of "abstinence", or (what is the positive aspect of the same principle) of the "effective desire of accumulation" have a place among the causes on which "the degrees of productiveness" depend? [Unaltered.]

9

I.120.1–3 (I.147). "There is no inconsistency between this doctrine and the proposition we before maintained that a market for commodities does not constitute employment for labour." This statement appears irreconcileable with the admission made in note * to p. 107. [I.87^{x-x}] where this very case is regarded as "a limitation" of the proposition in question.* [The] latter seems to me the more correct view, and with this limitation I think might be combined others. I wd state the doctrine and its limitations thus:—*The general*

---

*The conclusion from the illustration given at pp. 146–47 [I.119–20] seems to me, *so far as it reaches* directly to negative the general doctrine laid down at pp. 98–110 [I.78–89]. Substantially that doctrine amounted to this, that it is only by what a man *abstains* from consuming that he can benefit the labouring classes; while the illustration shows that those classes may be benefitted by the unproductive demand (or, to be more accurate, the demand for their *own* consumption) of other people.

[10]*Wealth of Nations*, Book II, Chap. ii; in Wakefield's ed., II, 266–340.

principle is, that demand for coms determines merely the *direction* of labour and the *kind* of wealth produced, not the quantity or efficiency of the labour or the aggregate of wealth. *The exceptions* are:—

1. Where labour is supported but not fully occupied, an increase of demand may stimulate the labour thus supported to increased exertions—to full activity—of which the result may be an increase of wealth; the producers obtaining a share of this increase. But *note*—even in the supposed case this result will only happen when the new demand is based upon a new creation of commodities *directly applicable to human purposes.* An increase of demand based on an increase of money (whether paper or gold) wd not have this effect:* it wd only issue in a general rise of prices; the motives to industry being the same as before. An increase of money might indeed have the effect of stimulating partially employed labour into increased exertion *if money were* an *object* of *desire for its own sake,* as in hoarding countries (it would here become "directly applicable to human purposes"). It is probable that the increased production of the precious metals of late years may have in this way contributed to the augmentation of wealth in certain semi-civilized countries— e.g. India.

2. There is another case in which increase of demand may increase the aggregate of wealth and benefit the productive classes—namely, where this increase renders possible an increased development of the principle of division of labour, and thus a more effective distribution of the productive forces of society.

Communities having a certain density of population are more favourably situated for the production of wealth and therefore for the remuneration of the productive classes than some in which population is extremely sparse. The benefit obtained in this case is effected *through an increased demand for commodities. Note* This is not identical with the last exception: the advantage in that case was obtained by calling into greater activity labour which had previously been but partially employed: in the latter instance the labour may have been all fully employed, but exerted inefficiently through lack of that market for its products which was requisite to allow of its due division.

3. A third exception occurs in the case noticed post p. 410 [I.338]—the case described by the common saying that "wages are high when trade is good". It is true that in this case the proximate agency in the benefit conferred on the labouring classes is the capital applied to the purchase of their labour, but this capital is called into activity through the demand for commodities. [Unaltered at I.120, but I.87 altered and moved to text, incorporating Cairnes' wording; see I.87^{x-x}. For Cairnes' second case, see I.87^{y-y}88; the passage indicated in his third case (I.338) is unaltered.]

10

I.119.17ff. (I.146). If an actual illustration be preferred to a hypothetical one, one will be found in Vol. IV, pp. 11–12 of Grote's History of Greece (*new ed.*),[11] where the historian describes the stimulating effect on Athenian agriculture of the accession of a large number of "metics" to the population of

---

*It is important I think to insist on this by way of precaution against the popular currency fallacy.

[11]George Grote, *History of Greece*, IV (London, 1862), 11–12 (i.e., Chap. xliv).

Athens and its neighbourhood on the occasion of the building the fortifications of the Piræus after the expulsion of the Persians. [Unaltered.]

11

I.118–22 (I.145–50). It seems to me that in this passage more is attributed to "separation of employments" than is fairly due to it. In the imaginary case of the settlement, a separation of empls is no doubt coincident with the advantages which arise from the accession of new settlers; but I cannot see that separation of employments is the cause of this gain in such a sense as wd justify one in saying that the separation being effected the result must follow. The true cause, I should prefer to say, was the increase of population coupled with an accession of industrial skill and knowledge. Now with a view to the practical application of the illustration this is an important distinction; for if we adopt the former view, that the benefit is the result of separation of emplts, the natural conclusion wd be that, in order to secure the benefit, we have only to effect the separation. This was the conclusion which Wakefield drew, and he consistently advocated measures which had for their object to compel the population of new settlements into towns, overlooking, or at least regarding as of subordinate importance, their aggregate increase. But if we adopt the latter [view] the practical conclusion will be very different. Recognizing in the advantages gained the effect of increased numbers and superior industrial skill, we should direct our attention, as the main business, to rendering by every means the colony attractive, and attractive especially to persons in possession of industrial skill, trusting that when the conditions of society occurred in which separation of employments was profitable, separation wd take place. Thus in considering the question of a "sufficient price" for colonial land, we should decide it exclusively with a view to what wd render the colony attractive to the greatest number of the right sort of people, without complicating the problem by introducing the consideration of "separation of employments." I am fully alive to the immense services which Wakefield has rendered to the cause of colonization; but his system, as he himself conceived it, appears to me to commit the mistake of seeking to accomplish by giving increased complexity to the machinery of society—multiplying the social valves and cranks—what can only be accomplished and can be completely and effectually accomplished by augmenting the motive power. It may be added that, with a view to the end contemplated by Wakefield, even granting the importance of separation of employments, there wd be no necessity in the present state of the world for the *local* separation of employments which he was anxious to enforce. The *"territorial"* separation—foreign trade—wd furnish the stimulus in an intensified form. This is in truth contained in the remarks on the best means of promoting the prosperity of India pp. 149–50. [I.121–2.] [Unaltered.]

12

I.135–7 (I.168–9). Among the advantages which the Joint Stock plan enjoys over individual management is its incident of *publicity*. In banking especially publicity is, I should think, a most important a [*sic*] condition towards securing confidence—perhaps as much so as a large subscribed capital. A heavy loss occurring to a private bank may be kept secret; even though it were of such magnitude as to occasion the ruin of the bank, the copartners may nevertheless go on for years trying to retrieve its position, only to fall in the end with a greater crash; but this cannot happen in the case of a joint stock company whose accounts are published periodically. The accounts indeed may be, as they often are, cooked; but they *do* exercise *some* check. Hence the public repose greater confidence in joint stock management in the case of banks. I observe it stated in a financial article in the *D. News* that nearly all new accounts are opened with the joint stock banks. The most striking testimony to the superiority of the joint stock principle in banking yet furnished has been furnished within the present year, by the amalgamation of three of the oldest private banking houses in London—those of Messrs Masterman & Co., of Messrs Hankey & Co. and Heywood & Kennard & Co., and of Messrs Jones Lloyd & Co., with joint stock concerns—viz. the first with "the Agra & United Service Bank", the two next with "the Consolidated Bank", and the last with "the London & Westminster Bank". See *Daily News*, 18 April 1864.[12] [Altered; see I.136*g-g*.]

13

I.155.19ff. (I.194). "ephemeral theories of a different law of increase &c." I observe the *Spectator* frequently of late[13] bringing forward what it regards as a "decisive fact" against the practical deduction from the doctrine of Malthus— namely that even where men defer marriage they generally choose young wives; and that such marriages—the man say being 40 and the woman 20—are as prolific—indeed I believe the statement is are *more* prolific—than where both parties are young: hence the *Spectator* argues the deferring of marriage tends to accelerate the rate of human increase. The insufficiency of the premiss for the conclusion based on it is obvious enough; but how far are there physiological grounds for the statement? And wd it be worth while to dispose of the so called "refutation" in a foot note? [Unaltered.]

14

I.172.12–15 (I.214) as compared with p. 230 [I.186.3]. There seems to be here a verbal contradiction. In the former passage are the words:—"the second requisite, increase of capital, shows no tendency to become deficient. So far as that element is concerned, production is susceptible of an increase without assignable limits"; while in the latter "the limit to the increase of production" is stated as "twofold; *from deficiency of capital* or of land." The context in the former passage shows that, in speaking of capital you there had in view the *mental principle* on which the accumulation of capital depends—abstinence or the effective desire of accumulation; which, as you show, becomes stronger with the advance of human society; while in the latter passage the reference is obviously to the *material substances* which form the prerequisites of production. The verbal difficulty appears to me to arise from the imperfect analysis of the agents of production contained in the formula—"land, capital, and labour"—capital being itself wealth in its most complex form: to explain the law of its increase is to explain the law of the increase of wealth; and, were the word throughout chap. XI employed in the sense in which it had been previously defined, nothing wd be gained by the analysis towards the

---

[12]"Trade and Finance," *Daily News*, 18 Apr., 1864, 4. The *Daily News* correctly reads "Loyd" not "Lloyd."

[13]Reference not located.

simplification of the problem; but the word is throughout the argument I think plainly used as convertible with the principle of the "effective desire of accumulation." This is so manifestly the case that I do not think any intelligent reader cd be led astray: still perhaps it wd be better—it wd certainly I think be more accurate—to make the analysis of industrial agents into land, the effective desire of accumulation, and labour. All verbal confusion wd thus be avoided. What we want I think is some word which wd express both the purpose and the self-denial—the desire to accumulate and the sacrifice in the form of abstinence which the satisfaction of that desire entails. [Unaltered.]

15

I.414.22–5 (I.503). "The cost of labour is a function of three variables: the efficiency of labour; the wages of labour (meaning thereby the real reward of the labourer); and the greater or less cost at which the articles composing that real reward can be produced or *purchased."

The analysis here, it seems to me, is incomplete; "the cost of the real reward of the labourer" involving the very conception—"cost of labour"—which it is the purpose of the analysis to elucidate. Or look at it in this way—The "cost of the real reward" depends in part on "the efficiency of labour", which element forms the first branch of the division, and is thus included twice. I have always found great difficulty in getting students to take in this statement of the theory of profits, so much so that I have attempted to throw it into another form, which I will here state for what it is worth.

I Take first the simplest conceivable case—an act of production in which the whole process is performed by labour, and in which the return from that labour is in commodities *the same in kind* as that of which the outlay is composed. For example, 100 quarters of corn are applied to the support of workmen who, while consuming them, produce 120 quarters. Here it is plain the rate of profit, which is obviously 20 per cent, depends upon *two conditions and upon two conditions only*—1. the real wages necessary to command the labour of the men who produce the 120 quarters†; and 2. the productiveness of their industry in raising corn. Diminish the productiveness of their industry, their real wages remaining the same, and you will diminish the rate of profit; and *vice versa*.

II Take now a slightly more complex case:—another set of workmen, who also receive 100 qrs of corn, are employed in producing not corn, but silk: while consuming those 100 qrs they produce, say, 200 lbs of manufactured silk. What will determine the rate of profit in this case? The outlay and the return not being homogeneous, they cannot be directly compared: we must look at them through their values. The rate of profit will plainly depend on the ratio which the *value* of the 200 lbs of silk will bear to the *value* of the 100 qrs of corn which formed the means of effecting their production. What will determine the value of the silk? The cost of its production; but this by hypothesis is equal to the cost of 120 qrs of corn; for it required the same

---

*"purchased": this word appears to me to have a disturbing effect, suggesting the idea of *price* as equivalent to, or connected with, the "cost" just mentioned: perhaps "obtained" mi[ght] answer the purpose, & be free from this objection.

†i.e., in other words, "proportional wages"—the statement is therefore entirely equivalent to the doctrine of Ricardo.

outlay to produce both—viz. 100 qrs of corn. Hence it follows that the rate of profit in the silk manufacture will be the same as in agriculture. And this will be the case whatever may be the productiveness of industry in the former branch of production. For if the silk weavers in the supposed case were only to produce 100 lbs of silk instead of 200, or were to produce 400, this wd not affect the question; since in all cases alike the cost of production being the same, the value of the return, large or small, wd be the same: its ratio to the value of the outlay wd therefore be the same; and, therefore, also the rate of profit.

It thus appears that the law of profit which we found to operate in the simplest case operates also in that which we may describe as of the first degree of complexity: the rate still depends on the real remuneration of the labourer as compared with the productiveness of his industry in producing his own remuneration.

III   We may now introduce a second element of complication. Suppose the outlay to consist only partly in advances to labourers, and for the rest in the purchase of raw materials & machinery. I then proceed to show, as in pp. 500–501 [I.412], that the latter advances are resolvable into wages.

IV   Lastly, Suppose a portion of the outlay to consist in the purchase of a natural agent—e.g. the rent paid by the farmer to the landowner. This is then shown not to alter the case, rent representing merely surplus profits—the diffce between the returns on the worst soils cultivated and the return from the better. Rent, in short, merely brings down the rate of profit on the better soils to the general level.

The law of profit is thus found under all circumstances to be that which we found it in the simplest case: it varies inversely—other things being the same—with the real remuneration of the labourer; directly with the productiveness of his industry in producing that real remuneration. But the latter condition—the productiveness of the labourer's industry—is resolvable into two elements—1. the efficiency of his industry, & 2. the fertility of the natural agents to which it is applied; or since rent, for the reason stated, must be eliminated, rather the fertility of *the least fertile* of the natural agents &c. I am thus brought by my method to the conclusion that the rate of profit is "a function of three variables"—viz. 1. the real remuneration of the labourer; 2. the efficiency of his industry in producing his own remuneration; and 3. the fertility of the [least fertile] natural agents to which *this* industry is applied. It seems to me that these three elements contain all that is included in your "cost of labour", while they are at the same time, so far as I see, independent and distinct.

A further case of complication arises through foreign trade. By this means the efficiency of industry in obtaining labourers' commodities may be increased by improvements in industry in *other* departments of production, or by occurrences in foreign countries which may affect foreign demand. Increased efficiency of industry in manufacturing *silk*, or in raising the more *expensive wines*, might thus tend to raise profits in the country in which this occurred, if by means of the cheapened silk or wine, the industry of the country was made more efficient in obtaining labourer's [*sic*] coms. So also the discovery of gold in one country might lead to a rise of profits in another.

The only objection, I see, to the above mode of stating the theory of profits is that it presupposes a knowledge of the laws of value and rent. And in reply to this I can only say that I have found it much easier to state the latter laws without reference to the law of profits, than to reverse the process. In fact I have never yet succeeded in making the law of profits intelligible to a student till I had first made him familiar with the doctrine of value; and I accordingly now always send my students to your chapter on value before bringing them to grapple with the former problem. I do not at all think that it wd be desirable on this account to alter the general arrangement of your book; but perhaps it might be worth considering—supposing you shd concur in the above criticisms—whether it wd not be well to confine the exposition of the doctrine in Chap. XV to the simplest case of production (No. I on the other side),[14] and reserve the full exposition till after the chapter on "Value". You have adopted a similar course in other instances. [The text is unaltered at this point. The word "purchased" objected to in Cairnes' footnote is changed to "procured".]

16

I.422.7 (I.512). "The truths of political economy are truths only in the rough." Would it not be better to say that they express tendencies which are liable to be counteracted? The expression "truths only in the rough" seems to give up the scientific pretension of political economy. [Altered; see I.422^{t-t}.]

17

II.459.33–7ff. (I.531). "A general rise or general fall of prices. . . . is a matter of complete indifference save in so far as it affects existing contracts &c."— save also in so far as it affects the interests of those who produce money—e.g. Australia & California are interested in maintaining a low range of general prices. Whatever tends to keep up the value of money benefits them, and in the same degree injures the rest of the world—so far at least as its trade with those countries is concerned. The point may be turned to account in showing the way in which the gold discoveries affect the world within and without the auriferous regions. [Altered; see II.459^{d-d}.]

18

II.808–9 (II.387–8). I ventured to advocate (*Economist* 4 May 1861)[15] the principle of a graduated property tax as a set off against the undue pressure of indirect taxation on the lower class of incomes. Considering that the bulk of our indirect taxation is raised from a few leading articles—tea, sugar, tobacco, malt liquor, and spirits—all of which are staple articles of consumption with the lower middle class, it must be allowed that our *indirect* taxation presses with undue weight on this section of the people. The proportion of an income of £3 or £400 a year which is spent on such commodities is plainly much larger than that of an income of £3 or £4000. Quoad *indirect* taxation, therefore, the lower class of incomes are mulcted more heavily than the higher; and this, I think, constitutes for the lower incomes a claim for special con- sideration in the imposition of *direct* taxation. The principle has already been recognized in the distinction made in favour of incomes below £200 in laying on the income tax; but the allowance seems to me to be altogether inadequate to meet the justice of the case. I should be disposed to exempt altogether

[14]See above, II.1048.

[15]"The Cause of the Inequalities in the Pressure of the Income Tax," *Economist*, XIX (4 May, 1861), 481–3.

incomes under £200 a year, and carry the reduced rate of charge up at least to £500 a year. This of course wd necessitate a higher rate on the incomes above this level; and this is only I think what the principle of equality demands. I regard this as the most important reform now to be effected in the direction of financial equality. [Unaltered. The date of Cairnes' article in the *Economist* is supplied by JSM in pencil.]

19

II.813 (II.390–1). I must confess myself unable to go with you here in your concessions to the popular argument in favour of the justice of a uniform income tax: it seems to me that such a tax *does* "arithmetically violate the rule that taxation ought to be in proportion to means". What are a man's "means"? Surely they are not to be confined to *that portion* of his possessions which he decides to apply to his expenditure in a given year. I cannot understand on what principle it can be said that a man making £1000 a year at a profession or in trade has in a given year the same "means" as a man in possession of a fee simple property which yields the same annual sum. Suppose the latter were to make up his mind to sell his estate and to expend the proceeds in a single year, this determination cd scarcely be said to add to his "means"; yet in this case, tried by what standard you please, his "means" in this year wd exceed the "means" during the same period of the professional man or trader earning yearly £1000. [Unaltered.]

20

II.813.31 (II.390). "It capitalizes the incomes,. but forgets to capitalize the payments." But why shd the payments be capitalized? The reason for capitalizing the income is to ascertain what its owner is worth *in a given year*: the thing to be compared with this is the payment *in that year—not* the capitalized value of the payments in future years. [Unaltered; but see II.814*ᶠ⁻ᶠ*.]

21

II.814.14–17 (II.391). "I wonder it does not occur . . . that precisely because this principle of assessment wd be just in the case of a payment made once for all, it cannot possibly be just for a permanent tax". Here again I am unable to follow: on the contrary my inference is exactly the reverse. If a deduction from all incomes in proportion to their capitalized values produce an equality of sacrifice this year, I cannot see why a deduction carried out on the same principle next year shd not produce the same result for that year; nor why this argument may not be applied to all future years. [Unaltered.]

22

II.814.27–9 (II.392). "It is not because the temporary annuitant has smaller means, but because he has greater necessities, that he ought to be assessed at a lower rate." But why has the temporary annuitant greater necessities? I see no answer to this except "because he has smaller means". The means of the perpetual annuitant has enabled him to make the provision for his posterity which the means of the temporary annuitant has not yet allowed him to make. The necessity of the temporary annuitant to provide for his family seems to me to be merely another way of saying that he is wanting in the means which the perpetual annuitant commands.

At the risk of appearing dense or perverse I have stated broadly my inability to follow your reasoning on this doctrine of capitalization of incomes; at the same time I do not adopt that principle as affording a solution of the practical problem of equalizing direct taxation. Its grand defect, as it seems to me, is that it fails to distinguish between human requirements of very different urgency—the portion of income which goes for necessaries or comforts which, if not strictly necessaries in a physical sense, are at least essential to the maintenance of a standard of decent living among the masses, and that which is expended on mere superfluities. "Equality of sacrifice" is I am sure the sound principle; and this can only be attained by resolving income into its parts—that required for necessaries, that for comforts, that for luxuries &c., and dealing with each portion on a distinct principle; the sacrifice, as you point out, involved in a curtailment of necessaries being quite incommensurable with that which a curtailment of mere luxuries involves. For such distinctions the "capitalization" plan affords no field: the *whole* means of every man is regarded as standing in the *same* relation to his happiness—which is I think palpably a fallacious position. [Unaltered.]

23

II.831.35–6 (II.413). "Rents, salaries, annuities, and all fixed incomes, can be exactly ascertained"; and these, it is important to note, yield, I think, more than three-fourths of the proceeds from the tax. This fact, I think, considerably attenuates the practical force of the objection founded on the demoralizing tendency of the tax. [Unaltered.]

24

II.839.30–2 (II.423). "The necessity of advancing the tax obliges producers and dealers to carry on their business with larger capitals than wd otherwise be necessary". Ricardo I think has pointed out[16] that this does not constitute (as it might at first sight seem to do) a case of "taking more out of the pockets of taxpayers than the State receives"; since the State gets the benefit of the advance: it is thus enabled to dispense with Exchequer bills to the same amount, the interest of which is saved to the community. [Altered by the addition of footnote (II.840n) incorporating Cairnes' wording.]

25

II.841.4–5 (II.424). "the compensation being of course at the expense of profits". It appears to me that the compensation wd be partly at the expense of rent. The rise in wages, taking place through an action on population, less food wd be required; the area of cultivation wd be curtailed; corn rents wd fall—but, on consideration, corn being more valuable by reason of the tax, money rents wd I believe remain as before. I suppose profits *would* bear the whole compensation. [This note cancelled by Cairnes. Unaltered.]

26

II.850ff. (II.437). § 6. I venture to point out what appears to me to be an important condition overlooked in the reasoning in this section,—a condition

[16]David Ricardo, *Principles of Political Economy and Taxation*, in *The Works of David Ricardo, Esq., M.P., with a Notice of the Life and Writings of the Author*, by J. R. McCulloch (London: Murray, 1846), 230–1.

which, taken account of, invalidates I think altogether, or nearly altogether, the application here made of the principle of the "Equation of International Demand" to the subject of taxation.

In reasoning on taxation—at all events on taxation as it imposed [*sic*] in civilized countries—it is proper I think to assume that a tax is only imposed or retained where the revenue it yields is indispensable. It follows that, in discussing the effects of a tax, we are not at liberty to consider those effects apart from the indispensableness of the revenue which the tax yields—in other words we are bound always to take account of this, that the imposition or retention of any given tax will relieve the community from taxation in some other direction. Now if this be admitted, the conclusion seems to follow that a rise in the price of a commodity consequent on the imposition of a tax does not necessarily (and as I think I can show will not generally) "lessen the demand for it."

Let us suppose that the country requires an additional million of revenue, and that in raising it the choice lies between an increased duty on beer and an increased duty on tobacco. By adopting the latter method, it is said, we should raise the price and thus check the demand for a foreign commodity, alter international demand in our favour, and thereby obtain our imports from the foreign country which produces tobacco on better terms: we shd in short by this means throw a portion of our taxation [on] a foreign country. Now granting that this reasoning is sound, the question still remains whether precisely the same result wd not be reached by laying the tax upon beer. Supposing the tax laid on beer, the price of tobacco no doubt wd not rise, but the margin of the consumer's means available for the purchase of tobacco wd be diminished in the same proportion as the rise in the price of tobacco in the former case. The price of his tobacco was then higher, but he had an undiminished income to meet it: he has now his tobacco at an unenhanced price, but then his available means of purchase have been reduced by the necessity of paying more for his beer.

Let me state the principle in a more general form. A man has £1000 a year, and with this sum he obtains annually necessaries comforts and luxuries in certain proportions. His power of commanding these things is curtailed to a certain extent by taxation; but the amount thus deducted from his income being given, I contend that the character of his expenditure will not be affected by the mode in which the deduction is made. If £50 a year be taken in the form of remitted taxes from the price of necessaries, and placed in the form of new taxes on the price of luxuries; or if both necessaries and luxuries are relieved at the expense of a direct deduction from his income—*so long as the total amount taken from him is the same*, I cannot see (apart from objections to particular taxes on *other* grounds) why this shd affect the proportions in which he consumes commodities. His means of commanding commodities remains in all cases the same, and if his tastes also remain the same, why shd the mode of taxation affect the quality of his demand? It is conceivable indeed that for a time, the expenditure of people on particular commodities having been regulated with reference to a certain scale of prices, any sudden change in relative prices might induce them to alter the character of their expenditure; but I imagine they wd very soon ascertain what their most urgent wants were, and find also the means of distributing their expenditure in such a way as most effectually to satisfy them.

The above argument proceeds upon the assumption that the taxes, between which the alternative lies, *fall upon the same persons*. In practice this is substantially the case in this country (unless where the alternative lies between direct & indirect taxation); our indirect taxation now being confined to a few grand staples which are consumed by all above the worst paid classes. So far as this is the case I think it must be allowed, that the inference contended for in §6 [II.850ff.] cannot be sustained. A given revenue being indispensable, it cannot be admitted that a tax on a foreign commodity will lessen the demand for it, nor therefore that it will alter the "Equation of International Demand."

Even in the other case—where the option lies between taxes which fall upon different classes in the community—or in different proportions on different classes—say between a tax on wine and a tax on paper—even in this case the soundness of the inference, at least with a view to a practical policy, is I think more than questionable. For 1st. Suppose a customs' duty on wine were substituted for an excise duty on paper—the wine drinkers not being identical with the paper consumers, the substitution, it may be granted, wd check the demand for wine; but then the effects of the substitution wd not end here: as the expenses of the wine drinkers increased, those of the consumers of paper wd be diminished: a portion of the income of the latter wd be set free, of which portion it is possible, and I suppose not improbable, that a share wd be applied to the purchase of foreign commodities—say tea and sugar. [So] far as this was the case, what was gained for the Equation of International Demand [by(?)] the retrenchment on wine wd be lost in the increased expenditure on the foreign articles of a different [kind thus(?)] brought into increased requisition. Further, even supposing something were gained for [the(?) Equa]tion of International Demand by this mode of distributing taxation, still I think it [might be(?)] questioned if this wd be a gain to the community. To show this, let us take the case which wd be most favourable for your argument—a tax transferred from a commodity of domestic production to one of foreign, so similar in its nature that one may become a substitute for the other; a substitution of a customs' duty on cheap French wines in lieu of an excise duty on light ale will furnish an example in point. Now the effect of such a change wd probably be to check the demand for the foreign commodity, and so far as this was the case to alter international demand in our favour. We shd get consequently our imports on better terms; but this wd not be clear gain. It wd be accomplished at the expense of forcing people by an artificial arrangement of price, to consume an inferior liquor, or one at least less suited to their tastes: it wd be an artificial interference with the natural course of human desires. The case wd not, so far as I can see, differ in principle from a protective duty: the distinction wd be this, that whereas a protective duty gives artificial encouragement to the production at home of a commodity which cd be obtained more cheaply from abroad, an import duty of the kind we are considering wd encourage the home production, not indeed of a commodity which cd better be obtained from foreign countries, but of an inferior substitute for such a commodity.

The principle, of which I have endeavoured to exhibit some of the applications—the principle that the operation of a tax must properly be regarded in relation to the whole income of the community as affected by taxation—has other important bearings in connexion with the theory of taxation. If the position which I have taken be sound it leads to this conclusion, that the question of encouraging particular modes of expenditure is not one which it is competent to a financial minister to entertain; for, as I have shown, this can only be done by shifting the burden of taxation from one class to another;

and as regards the relative pressure of taxation, the rule for him is equality. It seems to me therefore that the objection to a tax that it is a tax on knowledge is not a sound objection; for supposing the persons affected by the paper duty paid no more than their fair proportion to the revenue, justice wd require that the tax [removed?] from paper shd be reimposed on the same persons in another form; and provided this were done the increased cheapness of paper wd not in the least increase their ability to acquire knowledge. In practice I believe that the abolition of the paper duty was a good financial measure; because, the duty *not* being reimposed on them at least not to its full extent in any other form—the real substitution for the duty being the retention of a higher rate of income tax than wd otherwise have been necessary —the effect of the abolition was to relieve the classes who were the chief payers of the duty. But I think the true grounds on which to have put the case wd have been the undue pressure of taxation on the lower middle classes. Equal encouragement to knowledge wd I believe have been afforded by a reduction of the duty on tea and sugar.

I think it therefore important to insist on this principle, as enabling us to clear financial discussions from many irrelevant topics.

See Ricardo's Works (McCulloch's edition), pp. 141–142, more particularly note to p. 142.[17] [Unaltered at indicated place. The square brackets at II.1054.25 indicate a faded word, and at II.1053.21 "[on]", which was mistakenly cancelled by Cairnes in a minor revision, has been inserted.]

5. MILL TO CAIRNES

Saint Véran, Avignon
1 Dec., 1864.

. . , ...

Am I right in thinking that among the improvements consequent on the Irish famine and emigration, the desuetude of cottier tenancy is *not* one? My impression is that the land is still mainly let direct to the labourer, without the intervention of a capitalist farmer—and if so, other things in Ireland being as they are, all the elements of the former overpopulation are still there, though for the present neutralized by the emigration. I very much wish to hear from you whether I am right.

Have you formed any opinion, or can you refer me to any good authority, respecting the ordinary rate of mercantile and manufacturing profit in the United States? I have hitherto been under the impression that it is much higher than in England, because the rate of interest is so. But I have lately been led to doubt the truth of this impression, because it seems inconsistent with known facts respecting wages in America. High profits are compatible with a high reward of the labourer through low prices of necessaries, but they are not compatible with a high cost of labour; and it seems to me that the very high *money* wages of labour in America, the precious metals not being of lower value there than in Europe, indicates a high *cost* as well as a high remuneration of labour. Supposing profits to be lower than in Europe instead of higher, it is yet quite intelligible that interest might be higher. There is, I apprehend, in

[17]Ricardo, *Works* (ed. McCulloch), 141–2. At 142n Ricardo quotes Say's argument that a tax, by raising the price of a commodity, necessarily reduces its consumption.

America, scarcely any unoccupied class, living on interest: almost everybody is in active business, needing all his own capital and more too. In New England even the banks have scarcely any deposits, the class who in England would be depositors being there shareholders. Consequently the loan market is hardly supplied at all from native sources, except the capital and notes of the banking companies: and when there is a great demand for loans it has to be supplied from the European money market, and therefore at a rate of interest so high as to be a temptation to foreigners. I should be much indebted to you if you could help me on this subject, as, if I have been misleading the readers of my Political Economy, it is very desirable that the error should be corrected in this edition.

I have been obliged to read, with a view to my new edition, the most recent & most voluminous of Carey's writings, his "Principles of Social Science":[18] because his attacks on the Ricardo political economy and on free trade are, some of them, if not new, at least made in a new shape, and I have thought it good to give a brief refutation of them, the rather as the book is a good deal thought of by some of the French political economists, and is helping to muddle their ideas. The parts of his speculations which I have had to attack are really the best parts, as it was not worth while to notice any of his errors but those which had some affinity with truths. But it really would be a useful exercise for any clearheaded and painstaking student of political economy to shew up the book, for I think I never met with any modern treatise with such an apparatus of facts and reasonings, in which the facts were so untrustworthy and the interpretations of fact so perverse and absurd. I do not imagine that it would be worth your while any more than mine to take the trouble of reviewing it, but I should very much like to see it properly done. To give a really adequate exposure of the book would be out of the question, for there would be something requiring comment in every page: but a selection might be made, in a moderate compass, which would suffice to destroy any authority the book might have. Withal I cannot dislike the man, for his feelings, and his way of thinking on general subjects, so far as I can perceive, are usually right.

I have not yet had any application from Longman to begin printing, but I think it will not be long before I have.

. . . .

6. CAIRNES TO MILL

Galway
6 Dec., 1864.

. . . .

Your letter of the 1st. inst. reached me here yesterday. I hope in about a week to be able to answer your questions pretty fully and accurately. Meantime, however, I will state my impression on the points to which you refer. I believe there is no doubt that the class of cottier tenants has been immensely reduced in Ireland, and that the causes now in operation are tending rapidly to its

[18]Henry Charles Carey, *Principles of Social Science*, 3 vols. (London: Trübner, 1858). This is the unnamed work by Carey referred to by JSM at II.919-21, in a passage added in 1865.

entire extinction. I gave some figures from the census of 1861 illustrating this point in an article on "Ireland" in the Edin. Review of last Jany—;[19] and it is quite certain that the movement has made great progress since 1861. That "the elements of over population" however, still exist in Ireland is, I regret to say, but too undeniable. They exist in the wretched *morale* of the agricultural population brought almost to the level of the brute by centuries of neglect and oppression, and which I fear it will take more than one generation of good influences to effect any substantial change in; and they exist also in that recklessness of mind which dependence on the labour market—the condition of all the ex-cottiers who have not died or emigrated—seems in my mind inevitably to engender. So much so that I see for my part no hope of effectually elevating the mass of the Irish working population than by measures which may ultimately have the effect of dissociating them altogether from their present mode of life. Something may I think be done in this way by facilitating the acquisition of land in small parcels—i.e. by encouraging the growth of a peasant proprietary; more by developing manufactures or other non-agricultural pursuits, such as mining, and bringing to bear upon the people thus brought together the influences which are now working such wonders in the manufacturing districts of England. Lastly the extensive conversion of the land to grass will render a smaller population necessary; and, now that the emigration movement is in full swing, this may be effected without severe suffering. By such means I think the number of the population dependent on the agricultural labour market may be greatly reduced, while those which are drawn off will be brought within the range of ameliorative influences. Up to the present, however, I think you may take this for granted that, so far as cottiers have been converted into labourers, *no good has been done*. For the present the rate of wages may be somewhat higher than formerly; but if it were not for the emigration it might be confidently predicted that within a generation it would be reduced once more to the starvation point—even with the emigration I dont feel very sanguine that they will be avoided. In these remarks I speak of the cottier & labouring class: with the class above them— the farmer class, and such a class is beyond question growing up in Ireland, the case is much more hopeful. Real progress has I think already been made here; and I think it only needs such measures as Judge Longfield has advocated to accelerate this progress greatly. But on this, as well as the former point I hope to write to you more fully and with greater confidence after I have returned to Dublin and conversed with the Judge and some others whose practical acquaintance with the country is far more extensive than mine.

As to the rate of mercantile and manufacturing profit in the U.S., I have written to a quarter from which I have good hopes of getting information. I have indeed hitherto taken the supposed high rate of profit in the U.S. for granted. The high rate of *money* wages certainly would make one suspect the correctness of this view, but the fact is not conclusive. The precious metals may not be lower *in value* in America than in Europe, but their *cost* is certainly lower; the only question is whether it is so much lower as to render the high rate of money wages which prevails consistent with a rate of profit also higher than, or as high as, in this country. In what you say on the rate of interest in its relation to profit I entirely concur. You will find something on this point in my notes.[20]

[19]"Ireland," *Edinburgh Review*, CXIX (Jan., 1864), 279–304.
[20]See below, II.1060.

I send by this post a second batch of notes which I submit to you for what they are worth—I do not at all expect you will find them of any real use, but I rejoice at the opportunity of passing my speculations under your eye. I shall learn whether there is any value in them: should you think so, and turn it to account in any way, it will be to me a source of real gratification.

I should like to write to you on other topics you refer to, but I am anxious not to lose this post, and will therefore bring this to a close. . . .

. . . .

I hope you received the batch of notes sent with a letter about a week ago. With those now sent I send also a number of the N. British Review with an article of mine on Capital & Currency,[21] which perhaps you will do me the favour of reading.

[Further Notes on the Fifth Edition of the *Principles*]

1

II.647–59 (Book III, Chap. xxiii). The doctrine laid down here is that the rate of interest is "a question of demand and supply" [II.647.22] . . . "The rate of interest will be such as to equalize the demand for loans with the supply of them" [II.647.24–5]. Thus far I agree; but loans of what? You say of "capital"—Here I join issue with you. It cannot be denied that the thing lent is money—the medium of exchange; but you say that, though money passes formally, in reality it is "capital" which in such transactions is passed from hand to hand. I maintain, on the contrary, *1.* that in the case of a large class of loans "capital" does not pass in *any* sense other than that in which the word is identified *either* with the medium of exchange *or* with commodities consumed unproductively—that is to say, in which *either* "capital" and "currency" *or* "capital" and "non-capital" are confounded; *2.* that where in a certain sense "capital" may be said to pass—i.e., where the money borrowed is employed in the purchase of "capital"—this does not entitle us to call the money, "capital",—to say that the transaction is one in which "capital", not money, is borrowed, or, if it does, then in an ordinary sale we ought to speak of the commodity sold being exchanged for capital, when the money obtained in exchange is applied in the same manner—in short according to this way of speaking, all that portion of the circulating medium which is employed in effecting exchanges of "capital" shd be called "capital"; *3.* that the straining of nomenclature, as is done in such explanations, is prejudicial to a clear apprehension of the monetary phenomena, introducing verbal inconsistencies which react on our conceptions, and preventing us from perceiving, or causing us to perceive but obscurely, the operation of some powerful, but not obvious, influences on the course of the Money Market.

I will take these points in order, and set down what occurs to me on each head.

1. I say that in a large class of loans "capital" does not pass in any sense other than &c. This, I think, is involved in your admission at p. 192 [II.648] where you distinguish loans into those for productive and those for unproductive uses. Taking the case of money lent to a Govt to be expended in war, or to a spendthrift to be expended in profligacy—the money itself is here not "capital",

[21]Cairnes, "Capital and Currency," *North British Review*, XXVIII (Feb., 1858), 191–230.

if any distinction between capital and currency is to be preserved; nor are the things on which it is spent "capital", unless we obliterate the distinction between productive and unproductive wealth. Apply your own test—"the *mind*" of the person owning the wealth—and I think you must admit that the loan belongs to the category—"*not capital*". (Vol. I, pp. 68–70 [I.55–7]). I can imagine still another ground taken: it may be said that the money borrowed by Govt or by the spendthrift wd, but for their competition, have passed into the hands of productive borrowers, and that it may therefore be regarded as so much capital withdrawn from the market. But, first, the statement is not strictly true: a portion—I fancy no inconsiderable portion—of the money obtained by Govt is attracted to the loan market by the enhanced rate of interest caused by Govt demand, and wd but for this inducement have been employed unproductively: so far as this is the case, the effect of the Govt loan is merely to substitute one kind of unproductive expenditure for another; and, secondly, this way of describing the operation appears to me to obscure its real character, for an analysis of which see N.B. article pp. 204–205.[22]

2. I cannot see why, because the money borrowed is afterwards applied to the purchase of "capital", it shd therefore be said that "capital" is borrowed. We do not use language in this way in speaking of purchase and sale, why shd we do so in speaking of loans. Besides the way of using language is open to the serious of [*sic*] objection of comprising, and in fact confounding, under the same description two perfectly distinct acts—acts which are often separated by a considerable interval of time. The lending of the money produces a certain effect—an effect which is realized whether the subsequent purchase takes place or not: the purchase also when it takes place produces an effect, but this effect wd be quite the same though the money had not been borrowed. A nomenclature which precludes the possibility of distinguishing effects distinct in their character, and separated in point of time must I think be pronounced especially vicious.

3. I say the received mode of stating the doctrine involves verbal inconsistencies which react on our conceptions, and are prejudicial to a clear apprehension of monetary phenomena. I will give a few instances. In describing at pp. 37–38 [II.528–9] the nature of the service performed by banks of deposit, you say that they collect together the scattered "sums" which individuals wd otherwise have to keep as reserves; the aggregate of which being more than sufficient, when collected into one fund, as a reserve against the liabilities it has to provide for, the greater part is lent out to producers and dealers; "thereby", you say, "adding the amount, not indeed to the capital in existence, but to that in employment, and making a corresponding addition to the aggregate production of the community." Now here it seems to me there is verbal inconsistency. The "sums" which individuals hold in reserve against liabilities are clearly money, not capital; and all that your description proves is that Banks of deposit add to the *money* in employment, yet, without assigning reason for the change in the phraseology, you substitute the word "capital" for "sums", which I think must be regarded as meaning "money". But further it seems to me that this use of language not merely obscures the real nature of the function performed by banks of deposit, but has even led you into a slight inaccuracy of doctrine. For the true nature of the process, I take it, is this. The Banks by collecting together the stagnant money of the country and

[22]*Ibid.*, 204–5.

rendering it active, cause an effect on prices, which results in increased importation, the money rendered redundant, through the economy effected by the banks, passing out of the country. The result of the whole is a larger amount of consumable commodities in the country and less money. The addition of consumable commodities *may* be employed productively, or they [*sic*] may not:* if they are *not*, then the banks have neither increased capital in the country, nor have they rendered it more active: if the new commodities *are* employed productively, then the banks *have added* to the *aggregate amount* of capital in the country. In no case can I see that banks have any tendency to render "capital" more active. They render *"money"* more active, by this means economize *"money"*, thereby enable us to dispense with a portion and get capital in exchange, and add to the aggregate amount of capital in the country in which they are established: ultimately, if the cause be traced to its last result, as it is in another passage by you, they add to the capital in existence by superseding the necessity of a portion of that which is employed in producing money, & thus setting it free for other purposes. Perfectly analogous is the effect of the economy of credit—e.g. bank notes. The credit instruments cannot [like coin(?)] go abroad; but in proportion as they are economized or as cheaper forms of credit are substituted for dearer, a smaller amount of capital is required for carrying on the business of circulation in a country, and the portion saved is set free for other occupations.

Further I have said that this straining of nomenclature prevents us from perceiving, or causes us to perceive but obscurely, the operation of some powerful influences on the Money Market.—On consideration I will reserve this topic till I have stated my view of the causes governing the rate of interest, or rather my view of the best mode of *stating* those laws.

The first point, and that which is the most fundamental in the whole matter, is to establish the relation in which the rate of interest stands to the productive powers of capital. That relation is this: (1) the productive powers of capital are the condition which render [*sic*] it possible that interest should be permanently paid: consequently the productiveness of capital sets the limit within which the rate of interest over long periods must confine itself; (2) since "more will be given for the use of money when more can be made with money", the rate of interest will *tend*† to rise and fall with the rate of profit. These two propositions, I think, express adequately the relation in which the rate of interest stands to capital. The fundamental importance of appreciating that relation I fully admit; but I do *not* admit that the importance of securing this result justifies in [*sic*] so stating the doctrine as to shut out from view the

---

*On consideration it is fair to suppose that the new commodities wd be employed productively; since the money, rendered active by the banks, wd get into the hands of "producers & dealers". The prices first & principally affected wd be those of coms required by "producers & dealers": the new commodities therefore wd chiefly belong to this class.

†A tendency, however, which, as you point out in your letter of the 1st Dec. (just received) [23] need not by any means necessarily be realized in fact, since other causes, such as those existing in the U.S. to which you advert, may more than neutralize it, leaving as the result a rate of interest in some places higher than in others where profits are higher.

[23] See above, II.1055–6.

relation in which the same phenomenon stands to money. This I think the received formula does. The rate of interest, then, though *permanently* limited by the productiveness of capital, and though *tending* to follow the variations in that productiveness, is *temporarily* not limited by any thing, but the actual pecuniary means of borrowers at the time of effecting the loan, and does not, with any general conformity follow the fluctuations in the rate of profit, often rising when profit—i.e. the productiveness of capital—is falling, & *vice versa*; the *tendency* noticed being constantly more or less neutralized and frequently wholly overcome by influences of an opposite kind. What then are the proximate causes on which the rate of interest depends?—I answer simply—on *"the demand & supply of the community in relation to the amount of its money** (using the word in a large sense to include circulating medium of every kind which *practically* possesses purchasing or paying power according to the purpose for which the loan is made) *disposable on loan."* (This statement of the doctrine differs in words only from that given by Tooke in his tract on the Currency 1826—for my view of which I refer you to N.B. Review, pp. 199–201.)[24] This mode of stating the doctrine brings me directly into conflict with the proposition which you lay down p. 197 [II.653^{b-b657}]—viz. "An increase of the currency has in itself no effect, and is incapable of having any effect on the rate of interest." I venture to maintain as against this, that "an increase of the currency *is* capable of affecting the rate of interest, and as a matter of fact almost invariably does affect it in one direction or the other." Let us consider this point.

An increase of the currency (understanding by currency for the present simply circulating medium in any form which practically possesses purchasing & paying power) must take effect in one or other of two ways:—either through the medium of a loan, or through that of purchase: the persons into whose hands the new currency first comes either *lend* it, or *spend* it. Now in either case I contend that the augmentation will tend to affect the rate of interest. I observe you draw a distinction (p. 198 [II.653^{b-b657}]) between issues "as currency" and issues "as loans." But this distinction seems to me exactly to beg the question in dispute. You say the issue are "loans"—no doubt—but loans of what?—of capital? This I deny and refer you back on this point to my previous arguments. I say that they are "loans of currency" just as truly as money handed over the counter in exchange for a commodity is payment in currency. Well if I am right in this it certainly follows that an increase of currency is capable of affecting the rate of interest—further the illustration shows, that, when the increase takes place by way of loan, its tendency is to depress the rate of interest. In conformity with the doctrine as stated above:—the supply of money disposable on loan being increased, while the demand by hypothesis remains the same, the rate of interest falls. Now take the other case, suppose the increase of the currency to take place through the medium of purchase, here again the rate of interest will be affected, though in an opposite direction. For the effect of an augmentation of the currency by means of purchase is to raise prices. Now as prices rise, the pecuniary needs of borrowers will increase, the demand for money on loan will therefore increase; but the supply of disposable money, according to our hypothesis, remaining as before, the rate

---

*"Money". See as to this word *post* II.1064ff.

[24]Thomas Tooke, *Considerations on the State of the Currency* (London: Murray, 1826); Cairnes, "Capital and Currency," 199–201.

of interest will rise. Another consideration, noticed by you, will tend to strengthen this tendency: if the depreciation of the circulating medium be so rapid as to be perceptible, this will affect the inclination of those in possession of money to lend: thus at the same time that the demand for money on loan will increase, the supply will diminish; both changes operating in the same direction—towards an elevation of the rate.

And now, reverting to the question as I left it at [II.1060.22ff.], let us try the two theories by the only effective test—the ability of each to explain the phenomena, and for this purpose let us take first the effect of the gold discoveries on the rate of interest. Viewing the occurrence through the received theory the judgment of economists was I think in general to the effect, that the increased supplies of gold wd have no tendency to disturb the rate of interest. The argument urged by you p. 197 [II.653^{b-b657}] was employed. The theory directed attention to "capital", as distinguished from currency; and it not being apparent that the increased supplies of gold wd have any speedy effect in altering the demand for capital as compared with the supply, the decision was as I have stated. Now I think it cannot be denied that the increased supplies of gold have in the event profoundly affected the money-markets of the world; and further I think the doctrine, as I have stated it above, wd if applied to the known facts of the case, have indicated generally the course which the fluctuations have taken. Thus that doctrine wd at once have suggested this inquiry:—into whose hands will the new money first come?—into the hands of persons who will *spend* it, or into the hands of persons who will *lend* it? So far as it promised to fall into the possession of the former class we might have expected the rate of interest to rise—so far as it promised to fall into the possession of the latter, we might have expected it to fall. Now in the gold countries, whither people went, not to live on their income, but to make money rapidly, *spending* wd clearly be the rule; and in these we might accordingly have expected the rate of interest rapidly to rise and to remain constantly nearly as high as the productiveness of capital wd admit: this in fact is what happened both in Australia & California: in the latter country especially money on loan was scarcely to be had on any terms: in both countries interest was for a time computed by the *month*, not by the year. I do not know whether this is still the case. On the other hand, we might have expected the rates for loans to have taken an opposite course in Gt Britain. The new money first reached this country principally through the hands of large capitalists. The rising demand in the gold countries wd of course lead them to extend their operations; but meanwhile the new gold wd find its way to the banks and show itself in an increase of their reserves. Even when their operations had reached the full limits of the expanding demand, still, economized as coin is in this country, the extended business wd be far from absorbing the whole of the new money, which wd still continue a dead weight on the loan market. This is, as you will remember what happened. From 1852 down to the breaking out of the Russian war the rate of interest in England was quite abnormally low—so low as to tempt Mr Gladstone to attempt a conversion of the 3 per cents into 2½ per cent stock—an operation in which he failed solely through the unexpected turn of our relations with Russia. No doubt it may be said that all this is merely wisdom after the event; but I submit that there is nothing in the above beyond the reach of fair inference from the theory of the rate of interest as I have stated it taken in connexion with the known facts of the case.

Again, I will give another example of the way in which, as it seems to me, the received mode of stating the law of interest the real operation of causes affecting the money market [*sic*]. Take a case which has occurred lately in which, owing to the sudden failure of a leading staple, there has happened a great derangement in the course of trade. The effect of such a derangement invariably is to cause a rise in the rate of interest. Why? I really do not clearly see how the fact wd be explained on the principles of the received doctrine. I do not think it cd be done at all without a very violent straining of words. But I will state how I wd explain it on my mode of conceiving the theory. In the case supposed—a derangement of trade from the failure of a leading staple—the rate of interest tends to rise chiefly from a diminution in the supply of lendable money, but this tendency may be strengthened by a simultaneous increase of demand; though it is possible also that the effect on demand may be in the opposite direction; and may in some degree neutralize the tendency of the other agent in the change. The effect on the demand for money on loan depends upon this—will the aggregate sum applied to the purchase of the staple be increased or the contrary? The price may so rise as to check the demand very greatly, so that on the whole the sum applied to the purchase of the scarce article will be less than before: this was I believe the case for some time with cotton on the first breaking out of the American war; but, speaking from memory, the Board of Trade returns have lately shown a larger aggregate expenditure on cotton than in the times of its abundance. In the latter state of affairs, the pecuniary requirements of borrowers in cotton manufacturing will be augmented; consequently the effect of the failure must be to increase the demand for money on loan: in the former state, of course the effect wd be the opposite. So far as to demand. But in all circumstances a derangement of trade from the cause supposed, indeed from any cause, wd be to diminish for a considerable time the supply of lendable money. For its effect is to send us to other countries in search of the staple which has failed us in its usual field. Now when a trade is opened for the first time with a new country it is an almost invariable rule that for a time, more or less extended, it is carried on, on one side, in the precious metals. It wd be an extraordinary circumstance if the failure which in 1856 & 57 sent us to China for silk shd have synchronized with an accident which shd have sent the Chinese to us for goods to the same value. It may therefore be assumed as a rule that a derangement in trade necessitates a larger use of gold and silver international transactions. Where is this gold & silver to come from? In the main it must come from the stocks which are held as the disposable reserve in commercial countries. The supply of money on loan is thus diminished, and a rise in the rate of interest is the natural result.* The above conditions supply I think all the elements for a solution of the problem: can it be said that the received doctrine supplies those elements? That doctrine wd, I think, direct the attention of the inquirer to the loss of "capital" incident to the failure of the staple. Now though the phenomena which result may no doubt be traced back to this fact, these phenomena take their shape & character, not

---

*A rise in the rate may, I think, be taken as the most usual result of a commercial derangement; but it is quite conceivable that it might have the opposite effect, and, so far as my memory now serves me, the *early* effect of the cotton famine was to depress the rate of interest. This will happen when the check given to demand by the advance in price is so great that the diminished requirements for money on loan more than balance the diminution in the

at all from the fact itself, but from the way in which the occurrence happens to affect the pecuniary apparatus by which trade is carried on. For example, supposing the loss were one which could be repaired by a diversion of production within the limits of our own country, or within some civilized country, not given to hoarding and with tastes already formed for our commodities—in this case, although we were quite as slow in repairing the loss, the effect on the rate of interest wd be very different from that which wd be experienced if we were obliged to resort for the deficient article to a semi-barbarous country. Nor wd the circumstance that the failing staple were an element of "capital" affect the result in the least: if it were a finished manufacture suited only to luxurious consumption the effect wd, or at least might be, quite the same.

I could multiply these illustrations very considerably, but probably I have now said enough to give you a fair idea of the view for which I seek to obtain a hearing. If I were asked to characterize it by a word I should say that it regards the rate of interest as essentially a "*monetary*" phenomenon; whereas it has hitherto been represented as expressing a relation of "*capital*", as distinguished from money. Monetary science in short, as a department of political economy, resolves itself, according to my notion, into two leading departments —prices and the rate of interest—or, as we might describe them, the value of money in relation to commodities at a given time, and its value in relation to itself at different times. All classifications of the circulating medium shd I think be made with reference to the convenience of interpretation in regard to these two classes of phenomena.

As an example of what I mean I will venture to lay before you a speculation as to the definition of money, which I had hoped before now to have brought before the Pol. Economy Club.

Let me first state what I understand to be the true criteria of a definition in Political Economy. The purpose of definition in P.E. is, I think, altogether analogous to its purpose in the physical sciences, say in Chemistry—namely to classify phenomena with a view to their interpretation. That classification of economic phenomena will be best, & therefore those definitions will be best, which mark those relations in the facts of wealth which are most important in determining the laws of its production and distribution. (I may observe here by the way that, if this view be sound, definitions in Pol. Economy should not be regarded, as Senior regards them, as the *bases* of our reasoning, and as *final*, but merely as *provisional expedients* to be constantly modified with the progress of our economic knowledge—as, in short, registers of the state of that knowledge.) The business of defining in P.E., therefore, is more than a verbal affair: it involves a question as to the relative importance of external facts. It is also indeed in some degree a question of words, inasmuch as P.E. deals in popular language, and it will always be desirable, as far as possible, to use words in such a sense that they shall suggest the right ideas. Well, keeping these two criteria of sound definition in view the question I have to consider is—What is the best definition of money?

The purpose of a definition of money, agreeably to the foregoing view, will be to assist the interpretation of monetary phenomena: these phenomena resolve themselves into two grand divisions—prices, and (according to my notions)

---

supply. Further it shd be considered that the falling off in the demand will occur in a very early stage; while that in the supply will not happen till the new sources for repairing the deficiency in the staple have been opened.

the rate of interest. Confining ourselves, for the present, to the first class of phenomena, let us observe the relation in which the several portions of the circulating medium stand to them. And first we may note this fact, that in one point all the elements of the circulating medium agree;—they are all capable of affecting prices; and further none of them affect prices unless so far as they are actually employed as instruments of purchase. I need not illustrate this position as I know you will accept it. But, secondly, there is this difference between certain elements of the circulation and others, that the action of some upon prices is what, for want of a better word, I will call "unconditional", while that of others is "conditional". One condition indeed must be satisfied in all cases— the circulating medium, whatever its nature, must be used—used I mean as an instrument of demand. But assuming this condition to be fulfilled, one portion of the circulating medium is capable, not only of raising prices but of permanently sustaining them at the enhanced level; while other portions may raise prices, but whether they are capable of keeping them up or not depends on the fulfilment of a condition which has no place in the former case. Thus an increase of coin (on the assumption only that the persons into whose hands it comes be willing to use it) will, other things being the same, not merely raise prices for once, or keep them up for a time, but will permanently maintain them at the level to which it has raised them; the same may be said of incon- vertible bank notes; but it is otherwise with credit in all its forms. So long as the credit circulation is trusted, it is perfectly efficacious in its action on price, but distrust at once smites it with impotence. The power of the credit circula- tion in every form (bank notes included) to uphold price depends upon the condition that the promise which it implies be performed, or at least that there be belief that this shall be done.

Now this distinction suggests some important inferences. It follows from it, for example, that, while any cause calculated to cheapen coin or to augment the supply of inconvertible notes tends to raise *permanently* the level of prices over the field throughout which these media circulate, and thus permanently to depreciate the currency over this area; an increased facility of creating credit instruments, even though resulting in an increased supply of these instruments, has no such tendency. Temporarily indeed an effect on prices may be produced, but whether that effect be permanently sustained depends, not on the facilities of creating credit media of exchange, but on the possibility of maintaining a sufficient supply of that commodity—gold or silver—in which the credit instru- ments are made payable, to enable the promises embodied in those instruments to be made good. Thus a discovery of gold or silver mines tends with certainty to raise prices and to depreciate those metals. But improvements in banking have no tendency permanently to depreciate the currency in the country in which they occur. They may indeed depreciate it slightly for a time till the excess in the circulation be got rid of; but so soon as this happens prices will return to their ordinary gold or silver level. The distinction again will throw light upon a point around which in the early days of the Bank Charter Act discussion much vehement controversy took place. In those days the stereo- typed explanation of the monetary phenomena incident to all periods of specu- lative excitement was—the banks *forced* their issues into circulation; prices were driven up &c., &c. The evidence indeed of all competent bankers showed con- clusively that the banks had no power of the kind attributed to them; but in spite of reiterated denials, the explanation was still put forward, still apparently believed in by those who advanced it, and I think was generally accepted by loose thinkers as satisfactory. The plausibility of the explanation consisted, I think, in this:—It was certain that the banks were anxious to find employment for their reserves: the low rate of interest proved this: now this anxiety on the part of the banks implied the power on the part of all persons in fair credit to obtain the command of purchasing power. In fact the credit, whether of the banks or of individuals, represented purchasing power; and it was assumed that this undefined store of purchasing power being left free from all legislative restraint wd surely be used. Such an inference wd be perfectly just if the purchasing power consisted in gold and silver. If the Banks, for example, had each a gold mine in its vault, and the large capitalists each a Fortunatus' purse in his pocket, purchasing power of this sort wd quite certainly be brought into exercise and force up prices; but purchasing power resting on credit differed from purchasing power resting on coin in this, that it cd not be put in operation without bringing those who employed it under an obligation to make good the amt at some time or other in specie. Individuals and institutions, accordingly, who were in good credit, sensible of this, wd of course refuse to employ their credit in unproductive expenditure, and were deterred from employing it in productive operation unless where they saw their way or thought they saw their way to turning their capital with a profit. Hence the justification of the position maintained with so much ability by Tooke, that overtrading and speculative extravagance were due, not to the facilities afforded by credit establishments, but to the prospects, well-founded or delusive, of turning increased capital (I use the word in the received sense) with a profit.

There is also another position of Tooke, in his treatment of it assuming sometimes I think a paradoxical character, which receives elucidation from the same distinction. Tooke maintained that "the prices of commodities do not depend on the quantity of money as indicated by the amount of bank notes, nor upon the amount of the whole circulating medium, but, on the contrary, that the amount of bank notes & of the circulating medium is the consequence of prices."[25] The doctrine encountered abundant ridicule from Colonel Torrens and other writers of his school: nevertheless I have not the least doubt that the principle laid down is both true and important. The whole plausibility of the objection to the doctrine depends upon one ignoring the distinction which I am contending for. The statement wd be palpably absurd if made with regard to coin, or inconvertible currency: it seems to me to be not less clearly true when the allegation is confined to a credit circulation. The truth which the proposition embodies is this, that in a country like England, where the great mass of the circulation consists of instruments of credit, the proximate cause of prices is opinion—the opinion of merchants and dealers as to the value of commodities estimated in *gold*: when, for example the price of a given commodity rises, the fact indicates that, in the opinion of the dealers in that commodity, its value, until the present stock of it be consumed or until an increased supply be obtained, may be maintained at that level in relation to gold and silver or, what comes to the same thing, paper convertible into gold or silver: the judgment to this effect once being formed by those who have credit at their command, this credit is (to borrow an expression of yours) "coined" into bills, cheques and other convenient forms. The advance in price is thus not *caused* by an increase of the circulating medium, but on the contrary the increase in the circulating medium is *caused* by the advance of price. (I think, by the way, that this analysis shows that credit may influence prices *potentially*—I mean without being

[25]Tooke, *Considerations*; exact location not found, but cf. pp. 31 and 62.

actually offered for commodities: the belief that it wd be offered or that at some future time it will be offered is sufficient to induce the holders of the commodity to raise their terms. The same qualification must, I rather think, be applied also in the case of coin.)

Once more, the distinction for which I contend enables us to answer a question about which much confused argument was put forward some years ago—the question whether in estimating the probable effects of the gold discoveries we should compare the new increments of gold with the stock of the metal in existence, or with the composite aggregate of *metal, circulating paper*, and *credit of all kinds*. I remember M. Leon Faucher[26] maintained that it was with the latter body that the comparison shd be made; and the same position was maintained in the *Times* no longer ago than a year[27] by less known names. But with the distinction which I have stated in view, it is quite plain that the position is fallacious. The (gold & silver) prices which at present prevail in commercial countries are, as *permanent* phenomena, the consequence of the quantity of gold & silver which is maintained there, not at all of the quantity of credit in circulation; this being, on the contrary as we have seen, the effect, instead of the cause of prices.

I have now pointed out one important distinction between coin and inconvertible notes on the one hand, & credit media of circulation on the other—the circumstance that the one class act "*unconditionally*" on prices and are therefore capable of "*permanently*" sustaining them, while the sustaining power of the other is conditional & liable at any moment to break down. Closely connected with this is another important distinction—the *elasticity* of credit as compared with coin (as compared also with inconvertible notes). This elasticity may conduce, in a certain state of public feeling, to intensify oscillations of price; but it may also, (and this is its more frequent though less noticed effect), be made the means of moderating such oscillations.* By following up this line of speculation we shd be led to the true conditions on which the stability of a credit system depends—those conditions being—(1) sound views amongst the mercantile community as to the causes affecting the supply and demand of commodities, (2) entire freedom in the use of credit, and lastly (3) the habitual maintenance of a large reserve of gold or silver. The Bank Act of 1844, founded as it is on a theory of currency essentially unsound, so far as it has any operation, tends, as I conceive, to aggravate all the causes which conduce to instability. On this point I refer to *N.B. Review*, pp. 211 et seq.[28]

The result of the foregoing investigation has been, to show that, as regards the phenomena of price, the most important distinction among the elements of the circulating medium lies between coin and inconvertible notes† on the one

---

*The *elasticity* of a credit currency, and the power which in virtue of this quality it possesses of moderating the fluctuations in the value of a mixed currency of metal and paper, seems to have wholly escaped the "currency school" of writers. I observe you call attention to it at p. 211 [II.666–7].

†I have not thought it necessary to apply the reasoning to inconvertible notes, both because the application is very obvious, and because the argument will be found in the 4th Volume of Tooke's History of Prices.[29]

[26]Léon Faucher, *Recherches sur l'or et sur l'argent considérés comme étalons de la valeur* (Paris: Librairie de Paulin, 1843).
[27]Reference not located.
[28]Cairnes, "Capital and Currency," 211ff.
[29]Tooke, *History of Prices*, IV, 171–97.

hand and instruments of credit on the other. This distinction I wd mark by confining the term "money" to the two former; of money therefore there wd be two sorts—*metallic* and *paper* money (the latter being inconvertible notes): all the rest wd come under the general head of "credit." We might, agreeably with this view, define money as consisting of those kinds of exchange media of which the purchasing & paying power is *unconditional,* or of which the power of sustaining prices can never suffer defalcation. I have treated the question so far solely with reference to the phenomena of price, but it is plain that an examination of it with reference to those of the rate of interest wd lead us to precisely the same conclusion; the purposes for which circulating medium is borrowed having always direct regard to its purchasing and paying power. (Supposing this definition to be adopted, it wd be necessary to substitute in the statement of the law governing the rate of interest (as given ante II.1060-1) for "money", the words circulating medium possessing at the time of the loan purchasing or paying power.) [Altered; see e.g. II.650^{c-c}, 651^{a-a}, 651^{c-c}, 651^{d}, 651^{f-f652}, 653^{a-a}, 653^{b-b657}.]

2

II.665 (II.208-9). I understand you to admit here that the contrivance of the Act—i.e. the separation of departments combined with the restriction placed on the power of issue—*does* in some degree "prevent the ultimate aggravation of the severity" of a commercial crisis. I cannot but think that in doing so you make a concession which the facts of the case do not call for. I cannot see that the "retardation" of a crisis must necessarily or would probably, aggravate its severity. If the retardation occurred during the "ascending period", obviously enough it wd have this effect. Doubtless too it wd have this effect if it took place during the "quiescent state". But the highest point having been reached and the descent having commenced, I should expect that the more gradual the descent, the more it wd allow time for the disentangling of sound from unsound speculation; and that, on the contrary, a very abrupt collapse of the markets wd be well calculated to bring down solvent and insolvent houses, solid and bubble schemes, in one general ruin—in fact to produce a crisis which otherwise might never have happened. There is a phrase that is frequently in the mouths of the admirers of the Act—that of "clearing the air"; but experience seems to show that those sudden oscillations in the rate of interest which the Act produces, while they are quite sufficient to send into the Gazette men who are afterwards able to pay 20s. in the £, are very far from being certainly efficacious in searching out the rotten parts of our commercial economy. How many bubble schemes have been exploded in times of commercial quiescence; while the very worst and most disgraceful speculations which the country has seen have lived through all the rigours of the most violent crisis. To mention one instance, that gigantic scheme of complicated fraud organized in the leather trade survived the crisis of 1857, though now known to have been at that time in a state of bankruptcy—survived "the clearing of the air" of that time to succumb in the comparatively mild season of some years ago. The truth, as I fancy, is, that the detection and explosion of rotten schemes depends less upon the stringency of the money market than on the private knowledge of creditors as to the position of persons and houses with whom they have transactions. In a period of alarm suspicion is generally undiscriminating, so that it becomes a good deal a matter of chance on whom the pressure falls. In connexion with the point now under discussion I venture to think that you do not sufficiently advert to the fact, that neither at this stage—the commencement of the decline—any more than at any other stage, does the Act make any provision that the Bank shall not continue its advances until its reserve is absolutely exhausted: if the Bank contracts its operations a moment before this consummation is reached, it is in deference to its own *discretion, not at all to any restraint imposed by the law.* This is in truth a vital point in connexion with the theoretical justification of the Act, because the doctrine originally laid down, and still frequently assumed as realized in practice, was that the Act took the management of the currency out of the reach of individual discretion and placed it under a self-acting law: in fact nothing is more certain than that the stability of our currency rests now as much on the discretion of individuals as it ever did. This has indeed become so apparent that the defence of the Act is now generally shifted—at least by its more judicious advocates—from theoretical to practical grounds—practical grounds which directly negative its theoretical pretensions. It is said that the Act virtually compels the Bank to raise the rate of interest under a drain at an earlier period than it otherwise wd do. Doubtless it does: if the Bank did not raise the rate of interest sooner now than under the old system, the certain result wd be that it wd find itself, at what under the old system wd be an early stage of the movement, at the end of its resources. But does this constitute a practical justification of the Act? It creates an artificial pitfall, and because efforts are made, more or less successfully, to avoid the snare, its admirers take credit for having added to our security, and point triumphantly to the strainings of the endangered parties as conclusive evidence of the wisdom and benevolence of the law! What those who undertake to defend the Act on practical grounds ought to show, is, either that it renders the task of maintaining the stability of our credit system more easy than formerly, or, failing this, that it provides for the exercise on the part of the Bank directors of a larger and surer discretion. The former end it certainly has not accomplished: on the contrary the separation of the departments by splitting the reserve in two combined with the restriction on issue has enormously enhanced the difficulty of the problem; while, as regards the latter point, though public criticism has done something towards quickening the discretion of the Bank directors (as it wd with the progress of monetary knowledge under any system), this cannot be ascribed in any degree to the influence of the Act of 1844, the teaching of whose promoters was, as the *Times* once put it, that "it was for bankers to look to their own interest, leaving the currency under Sir. R. Peel's Act, to take care of itself."[30] [Unaltered in specified place.]

3

II.649–50 and 667–8 (II.194 and 212–13). In the former passage p. 194 [II.649–50], you enumerate, as constituting the elements of "the general loan fund of the country"—"the disposable capital deposited in banks or represented by banknotes (I am not quite clear whether the expression "or represented by bank notes" is intended to qualify *"disposable capital"*, or *"disposable capital deposited in banks"*—in other words whether you intend it as an equivalent expression for "deposited in banks", or as denoting *a particular* form in which such deposits may be made), together with the funds of those who . . . live upon the interest of their property" [II.649.42–650.5]; and in the reasoning in pp. 212–13 [II.667–8] these seems [*sic*] to be the only elements of the loan fund

[30]Quotation not located.

which you contemplate. But surely there is another very important one—the *credit of bankers*,* as distinct both from the sums lodged with them on deposit, and from the notes which they hold, or under the present law, may issue. The reasoning in pp. 212–13 [II.667–8] appears to proceed upon the assumption that when a bank discounts a bill, it must either *issue notes* to the person from whom the bill is obtained, or encroach (in order to discount the bill) on the money lying with them in deposit. But, as I understand the matter, the bank may, and in the great majority of instances does, adopt neither of these courses: may it not simply place the amount to the credit of the person from whom it receives the bill, leaving him to draw against it at his convenience; and may not the cheques thus drawn be lodged again in the bank, the amt being simply transferred from the credit of drawer to that of the drawee? or if not lodged in the bank which originally discounted the bill, it might be lodged in [some (?)] other, with whom an exchange wd be effected through the Clearing House. If I correctly conceive the process, it seems to me that the banks possess an indefinite fund from [wh (?)] to extend monetary accomodation to the public, without sensibly increasing their issue, or touching the funds left with them in deposit—a fund of which the only limit is the prudence [of (?)] the managers of each institution. Supposing my notion to be right as to what happens in a large class of [cases when (?)] a bill is discounted, I presume the sum, written down by the bank to the credit of [the (?)] person presenting the bill, wd be regarded as a "*deposit*". I have no authoritat[ive] knowledge as to how the matter stands, but I presume this is so. If so, it is a ver[y im]portant consideration; for "deposits" are commonly supposed to represent *reso[urces*(?)] of the bank as well as *liabilities*; but a deposit occurring in the way I hav[e] described wd represent a *liability* only. I think it wd be very desirable if this point were cleared up, but I have not here access to any one sufficiently informe[d] to enlighten me. [Altered; see II.650^{c-c} and $^{b-b}$ (referring to "disposable capital").]

4

II.668.4ff. (II.212). "But the mode in which they are really objectionable &c &c . . . The rate of interest is [not] prevented from rising." I do not follow this reasoning: it seems to me the effect on the rate [of] interest wd be the same in either case. What really happens, and happens alike in bo[th] cases, is this:—a certain amt of circulating medium formerly existing in the state of mo[ney(?)] disposable on loan is withdrawn from this state and employed in circulating commo[———] Supposing the bank to make the loan *out of actual funds lodged with it*, the lending abili[ty(?)] of the bank and of the country is diminished by so much, and a certain portion of [———] demand for purchasing or paying power is satisfied: supposing the depositors to draw the funds out themselves, an equal encroachment is made on the loan fund of the bank and of the country, and an equal portion of the demand for loans is satisfied. I cannot see that either the demand or the supply of money on loan wd be affected by the mode in which this result—the same in each case—was brought about; nor therefore why, one course shd affect the rate of interest more than

---

*I observe that in the following paragraph p. 196[5?] [II.650.24–5] you take account of this element where you say "in speculative times money lenders, as well as other people, are inclined to extend their business by stretching their credit."

the other. *In practice* I believe there wd be a difference; *because* I believe that *in practice the bank wd make the loan not out of funds actually in its posses-sion, but out of its general credit* in the way indicated above. Made in this way the rate of interest wd not be affected in the same degree as if made in the other; but why? because a refusal to [discount(?)] by the bank wd be a refusal to extend its credit further: it wd therefore be equivalent to a curtailment effected in the available loan fund of the country.

Supposing I am right in the view above advanced I think it must be admitted that the considerations urged attenuate indefinitely, if they do not entirely remove, the force of the concession made to the supporters of the Act on pp. 213–14 [II.670.12ff.]. "I am compelled to think that the being restricted from increasing their issues is a real impediment" &c. . . . If the restrictions of the Act of 1844 were no obstacle to the advances of the banks in the interval preceding the crisis, why were they found an insuperable obstacle during the crisis"? I answer, because in the former period a credit with the Bank—to be used by means of cheques and not involving any important increase of issue—answered the purpose of those who borrowed; whereas in the latter period—owing to the extensive collapse in the mean time in the ordinary media of circu-lation—actual notes were required. See the quotation from Fullarton p. 216. [II.671.17ff.] [Altered; see II.668^{q-q} and $^{r-r}$, and 670^{y-y}.]

5

II.678 (II.225). "Every drain for exportation. . . . . is now compulsorily drawn from that source alone—the bank-note circulation." [II.678^{o-o}.] This I think is only true when we include as part of the "circulation" the notes or gold held in the banking department of the bank, as well as other "reserves" existing through the country; but these "reserves" are *not* "circulation" in the sense in which the word is used by Mr Fullarton in the passages previously quoted. In those passages the word "circulation" is restricted to "that portion of the metallic wealth of the nation *which really circulates*" (224 [II.677.7–8]), as distinguished from "the hoards", or stagnant metallic wealth only to be called into activity by the attraction of a high rate of interest. Restrict the term "circulation" equally in its application to our monetary system, and it is *not* true that every drain for exportation is drawn from "the bank-note circulation". As you point out in the next paragraph "the first operation (and I venture to add not merely the first but almost the *entire* operation) of the drain is *on the banking depart-ment*, "the deposits" in [sic] which, as you add, "constitute the bulk of the *unemployed and disposable capital* of the country." The drain therefore does not fall on the "circulation" in Fullarton's sense of that word. The true analogue in our system for the hoards which exist under a metallic currency are clearly I think the bank reserves, or more generally lendable money wherever it is to be found. The objection to the Act of '44, it seems to me, is, *not* that it throws a drain upon a part of the currency on which it wd not fall under a metallic system, but that it curtails the dimensions of the available reserve: this it does by the separation of departments; the effect of which is to lock up in the Issue department a vast quantity of gold which really answers no practical purpose whatever. In the passage (p. 224 [II.677.24]) beginning "In a country &c . . . [sic] the word "reserve" of the Bank of England seems [to be(?)] used to cover the gold in *both* departments. *Reasoning on the principles of the Act* I do not [think(?)] this use of "reserve" is justifiable. The gold in the Issue department wd not I think be regarded by those who framed the Act, as "reserve", but as "circulation"—the notes actually circulating being mere tickets representing it. [Altered; see II.678^{o-o}.]

7. MILL TO CAIRNES

Saint Véran, Avignon
12 Dec., 1864.

. . . .

I do not know how sufficiently to thank you for all you have done for me. That you should have taken the trouble to write out your thoughts so fully on so many points, only for my use, is a favour such as I should never have presumed to ask from you. It is like nothing but the philosophic correspondences in which the thinkers of the 16th and 17th centuries used to compare notes and discuss each other's opinions before or after publication—of which we have so many interesting specimens in the published works of Descartes. I shall keep the notes carefully and return them to you, for I do not like that so much thought, so clearly worked out on paper, should have no reader but me: besides, it enables me with a better conscience to use their contents.

On most of the minor points I think you are right, and shall profit by your suggestions. On Ireland I shall cancel all I had newly written on that subject, and wait for the further communication you kindly promise.[31] On the few points of doctrine on which our opinions differ, you have not, thus far, convinced me, though you have taught me much. Among these I do not count the theory of the rate of interest, for I agree entirely with your explanation of the phenomena, and the article in the North British Review appears to me excellent. I had, even before I heard from you, inserted a passage pointing out how the new gold, as long as it continues to flow in, must tend to keep down the rate of interest [II.651^{f-f}652]. We differ, I believe, only on a question of nomenclature, and at present it seems to me that the objections to your phraseology are stronger than to mine. But I have not done thinking on the subject, and I shall in any case have to modify several expressions, if nothing more.

In the matter of the operation of duties on international values, I see that I have omitted one of the elements of the question, viz. the competing demands of other commodities on the purse of the consumer; but it does not seem to me that this omission materially affects the conclusion. Suppose that I have a given sum, say £10 a year, the expenditure of which I am determined, whatever happens, to divide between two commodities, A and B. I conceive that even then, if A rises in price and B falls, the effect in the average of cases will be that I shall buy more of B and less of A.

On the Wakefield system I scarcely understand your argument. In the supposed case of the settlers, and in every other, I apprehend the separation of employments to be a real cause and indispensable condition of a larger production. It is true that territorial separation of employments, by international trade, often suffices: but the main justification of Wakefield's system is, that this trade does not take effect when families settle, each of them many miles from its next neighbour in the wilderness.

[31]See below, II.1074ff.

The point on which we seem to differ most, & to be least likely to come to an agreement, is the income tax. You think it fair to take from different people in a single year, an equal percentage of what their incomes, whether permanent or temporary, would sell for in that year: because (you say) the payment in each year should be compared with what the income is worth in that year to its owner. In this I agree; but I answer, that the income is, in that year, worth *to him* its capitalized value only on the supposition that he actually capitalizes it, and spends the whole value within the year. Then, indeed, he will have been fairly taxed: but then, he will not have to pay the tax in any future year, for the income will have passed into other hands. On any other supposition the income is only worth to him its capitalized value spread over the whole of its duration, that is, in each year the total amount divided by the number of years. I agree in what you say about equality of sacrifice, but in estimating this, I only exclude necessaries. I do not think a distinction can be fairly made between comforts and luxuries, or that I am entitled to call my tea and coffee by the one name, and another person's melons and champagne by the other. I allow for nothing but what is needed to keep an average person alive and free from physical suffering.

· · · · · · ·

I have read with the greatest interest Judge Longfield's address, and two of your articles on it in the Daily News.[32] There may be others which I have missed, as the paper is often stopped at the French post office. Though I thought the Judge wrong in much of what he said on fixity of tenure, I agreed with, I think, every part of his address which was praised in your articles, and I think it altogether a most important paper. I give him the greatest credit for speaking out so plainly, and so much to the purpose. It is particularly timely, coming so soon after the speech in which Gladstone included remedial measures for Ireland among the things which he put in the front of his policy.[33] We see there, as usual in Gladstone, the man who speaks from his own convictions, and not from external influences. No other minister would have put forward Ireland, any more than Reform, just at this time, when there is no public outcry about it.

8. MILL TO CAIRNES

Saint Véran, Avignon
20 Dec., 1864.

· · · · · · ·

I wrote to you some days ago a letter addressed Dublin and "to be forwarded", thanking you for the two packets of notes you kindly sent and remarking generally on their purport. I have since carefully revised all the passages you referred to, and there are very few of the notes by which I have not, to some extent, profited. In a great many cases I have entirely adopted your view. I have rewritten the fourth section of the chapter on the Rate of Interest and

[32]See note 7 above; JSM presumably read the reports of Longfield's paper in the *Daily News* ("Statistical Society of Dublin," *DN*, 29 Nov., 1864, 5, and "Judge Longfield on Ireland," *DN*, 1 Dec., 1864, 2).
[33]Reference not located.

have much enlarged it [II.653–8]; completing my exposition of the causes on which the rate of interest depends, by adopting nearly all you have said on the subject that involves doctrine. In what merely involves the mode of stating the theory, I still prefer my own: but I see that the whole truth of the subject may be expressed in either way, and may usefully be so in both. Your remarks on the definition of money I have not used, for a different reason: I cannot, in conscience, take without necessity what belongs to you. When it is for the correction of an error I have less scruple, but all I have said on this matter tended to your opinion, though less thorough and conclusive. Even on the Interest question, I should like, if you will permit me, to acknowledge my obligations to you in a note.

. . . .

9. CAIRNES TO MILL
74 Lower Mount St. (Dublin)
23 Dec., 1864.

. . . .

I have received both your letters—that of the 20th inst. this day—which have caused me, I needly not say, very sincere gratification. That you should have modified your book in any degree in deference to suggestions of mine is a compliment which I shall never cease to prize, coming as it does from one to whom I lie under the deepest intellectual obligations. It brings me the comforting assurance that I have so appropriated your principles and methods that I can now apply them for myself. I shall not affect to deny that I shall be proud of any reference you may make to me in your work; but be assured that whatever I have done (and in truth you very greatly overrate this) has been a labour of love, for which I have thought of no other acknowledgment than its being received and considered by you.

I must apologize for the delay which I have allowed to elapse in forwarding you the results of my inquiries into the state of Ireland. You will accept my assurance that it has been quite unavoidable. I have now got on paper, and hope to forward you by next post [sic], the most material items of such information as I have been able to obtain. So far as the facts go, I think you may accept them as trustworthy. When not taken from official documents or from my own experience they are given on the authority of informants in whom I have every confidence, of whom the principal have been Judge Longfield, Mr Thom (of Thom's Almanack)[34] and Mr Jonathan Pim[35]—the last a merchant of this city connected with the Quaker body & author of a very good book on Ireland which, together with another in the compiling of which he took part, he has (as you will see by his letter which I enclose) requested me to forward to you. I have also had the advantage of conversing much with an intimate friend, Mr McDonnell,[36] Examiner in Judge L's Court,

[34]Alexander Thom, *Thom's Irish Almanac and Official Directory of the United Kingdom of Great Britain and Ireland, for the year 1863* (Dublin: Thom, 1863).

[35]Jonathan Pim, of Pim Bros. and Co., author of *On the Connection between the Condition of Tenant Farmers and the Laws respecting the Ownership and Transfer of Land in Ireland* (Dublin, 1853), and *The Land Question in Ireland* (Dublin, 1867).

[36]A Randal McDonnell is mentioned in the accompanying material sent by Cairnes.

than whom I dont know any one more thoroughly familiar with the present state of land tenure in Ireland or more anxious to impart his knowledge truthfully. A good deal of what I send is in the nature of speculation, and of the value of this you will judge yourself.

I have read with great interest what you have said on my criticisms, but before replying to this part of your letter, I prefer to wait till I have time to consider some of the points you have urged more carefully than since the receipt of your letter I have had time to do.

. . . .

Notes on the State of Ireland (1864) for J.S.M.[37]

That cottierism has undergone an extensive reduction in Ireland is quite beyond question. The fact is conclusively indicated in the statistics of holdings quoted at p. 18 of the article sent herewith.[38] The causes which have brought about this reduction are numerous and powerful, and are still in active operation. At the head of these I would place free trade. The cottier class, on the scale on which it has been known in modern Irish history, had its origin in the transition of Ireland from a grazing to a corn-producing country, which occurred in the latter half of the 18th century: the phenomenon was connected with the same group of causes under the influence of which England from being an exporter became an importer of grain: and the cottiers have always been identified with the system of agriculture under which they arose. Free trade has effectually shattered, and already in great part overthrown, that system, by throwing the country upon its special capabilities which (speaking generally) are pastoral. It is curious to note how exactly the process which was in operation a century ago is now being reversed. Tillage was then rapidly taking the place of pasture; the labourers employed in this conversion being paid (in the absence of circulating capital) in land. At the commencement of the movement, which we may date at 1754, the population of Ireland, which for quarter [*sic*] of a century had scarcely moved, having been 2,309,000 in 1726, was 2,372,634

[37]In addition to the two versions of the "Notes on Ireland," MS 8983 in the National Library of Ireland also has notes by Cairnes derived from (a) Thornton's *A Plea for Peasant Proprietors*, (b) the notes Judge Longfield sent to Cairnes, (c) Lavergne's *Essai sur l'économie rurale de l'Angleterre, de l'Ecosse et de l'Irlande*, (d) Edmund Spenser's *A View of the State of Ireland, Written Dialogue-Wise Betweene Eudoxus and Irenæus* (Cairnes was probably using the reprint in *A Collection of Tracts and Treatises, Illustrative of the Natural History, Antiquities, and the Political and Social State of Ireland*, I [Dublin: Thom, 1860], 417–592), (e) Goldwin Smith's *Irish History and Irish Character* (London: Parker, 1861), (f) William Henry Hardinge's "Observations on the earliest known Manuscript Census Returns of the People of Ireland," read 16 Mar., 1865, and printed in *Transactions of the Royal Irish Academy, Part III, Antiquities*, XXIV (1873), 317–28, (g) the Devon Commission's Report and Evidence, Part I, (h) Henry Fawcett's *Manual of Political Economy* (London: Macmillan, 1863), (i) various accounts of the Irish labouring population, drawn from the *Social Science Transactions* for 1859, 1860, 1862, 1863, and (j) "Co-operative Societies in 1864," *Edinburgh Review*, CXX (Oct., 1864), 407–36. The surrounding MSS in the National Library of Ireland contain related material.

[38]Article not identified.

persons: by 1788 it was upwards of 4,000,000; in 1805 it was 5,395,456.*
Now a contrary impulse is causing tillage to give way to pasture: the labour†
of the cottiers is every year less and less required; on the other hand the land
which they hold can be turned to good account in grass. The circulating capital
which came into existence a century ago contemporaneously with the cottier
system is now going back into the fixed form; and with the decline in the
country's circulating capital, the population is also declining. Free trade, it
must be confessed, has been injurious to Ireland if the maintenance of an
immense agricultural population in the condition of the cottiers was a good.

I have placed free trade at the head of the causes tending to the reduction
of cottierism, because I think that it is the fundamental agency in the movement, and would even alone have led sooner or later to this result. Of course
the tendency thus developed was immensely accelerated by the famine: it
has also been aided by other causes:—Amongst these the principal are the
lesson of experience; the universal breakdown of the system in 1847 has shown
landlords that the system is as ruinous to them as it is demoralizing to the
peasantry; 2. the commercial ideas infused into agricultural society through
the medium of the new men who have purchased land in the Encumbered
and Landed Estates Court. Land is every day coming more and more to be
looked at in the light of an investment; and from this point of view cottiers
are an abomination. Lastly, the increased facilities of intercourse and communication with America and other new countries have opened the door of
escape to the superfluous population, and allowed the movement to go forward
at a rate which without this wd be impossible. It may be too much to say that
cottierism is tending towards entire extinction; but I think there need be no
hesitation in saying that the dimensions of the phenomenon will soon be so
reduced that it will cease to be important.

What is the state of things that is taking its place? This is indicated by the
statistics already referred to. The farms between 15 and 30 acres and those
above 30, have increased *pari passu* with the diminution of those below 15
acres. The usual course of proceeding is much as follows:—A landlord finds
his estate encumbered with a number of small cottiers holding from 1 to 9
or 10 acres. He has no occasion for their services as labourers; for he finds he
can turn what land he farms himself to better account in grass; nor for the
same reason can he procure employment from the larger farmers in the
neighbourhood. For any other purpose than that of mere labourers they are
utterly unfit: they are ignorant unenterprising and generally largely in arrear of
rent. Improvement of his estate, or the rendering of it profitable in any way,
is manifestly impossible while they are on it. He comes to the most hopeless
amongst them, urges them to give up the land, offers to remit all arrears of
rent, suggests emigration, and occasionally offers to contribute something
towards the expenses of the journey. While this is going forward those poor

---

*These figures are taken from Shaw Mason's population returns of 1821 [?].[39]

†The movement towards pasture is also favoured by the extreme inefficiency
of the cottier's labour—indeed of agricultural labour in every form in Ireland:
this gives capital in the *fixed* form a constant pull as against capital in the
circulating: it enhances the *relative* superiority of Ireland in respect to pasture.

[39]William Shaw Mason, *A Statistical Account or Parochial Survey of Ireland,
Drawn Up From the Communications of the Clergy*. 3 vols. (Dublin: Cumming,
1814ff.).

people are probably plied at the same time with invitations from their friends on the other side of the Atlantic to join them; their invitations being seconded by remittances to pay their passage money out. Then the movement once set on foot is contagious. The cottiers are thus rapidly passing away, and the landlord, once rid of them, will not be anxious to submit his back again to the burden. He will proceed to consolidate several of the small holdings, and, according to circumstances, will either take the land into his own hands, or look out for a solvent tenant of some substance to whom he can let the whole: very frequently the plan adopted is to add the land thus liberated to the holdings of the most promising of the existing tenants.*

I have referred above to the beneficial influence exercised on land tenure in Ireland through the commercial ideas of the new proprietory: it must be confessed that this agency is not without its drawbacks.[41] A class of men, not very numerous, but sufficiently so to do much mischief, have through the Landed Estates Court, got into possession of land in Ireland who of all classes are least likely to recognize the duties of a landlord's position. These are small traders in towns, who by dint of sheer parsimony frequently combined with money lending at usurious rates have succeeded in the course of a long life in scraping together as much money as will enable them to buy 50 or 100 acres of land. These people never think of turning farmers, but proud of their position as landlords, proceed to turn it to the utmost account. An instance of this kind came under my notice lately in the neighbourhood of Drogheda. The tenants on the property were at the time of the purchase, some 12 years ago, in a tolerably comfortable state. Within that period their rent has been raised three several times; and it is now, as I was informed last night by the priest of the district, nearly double its amount at the commencement of the present proprietor's reign. The result is that the people who were formerly in tolerable comfort, are now reduced to poverty: two of them have left the property and squatted near an adjacent turf bog where they exist trusting for support to occasional jobs. In the end, if this man is not shot, he will injure himself through the deterioration of his property, but meantime he has been getting 8 or 10 per cent on his purchase money. This is by no means a rare case. The worst evil is that the scandal which such occurrences cause casts its reflection on transactions of a wholly different & perfectly legitimate kind, such as I have described above, where the removal of the tenants is simply an act of mercy for all parties.

---

*Since writing the above I have been shown a letter in *Gardener's Chronicle* which describes an actual case.[40] I shall endeavour to obtain it, and if so will send it herewith. (The paper is sent.)

[40]"An Irish Landlord," "Twenty-five Years' Work in Ireland," *The Gardener's Chronicle and Agricultural Gazette,* 3 Dec., 1864, 1162–4.

[41]The following passage, to "mercy for all parties." (II.1077.36), and (omitting the next two sentences) from "The anxiety of landlords" to "in every lease." (II.1078.23), is quoted by JSM at I.332n–333n. JSM alters the punctuation and spelling, and makes the following alterations: omits "in the neighbourhood of Drogheda"; substitutes "as I am informed" for "as I was informed last night"; omits "In the end"; omits "The worst evil is that"; omits "such as I have described above"; adds "also" after "cottiers is"; omits "To understand this it should be remembered that"; substitutes "rent received" for "rent reserved"; substitutes "Some of these leases are always" for "These leases are constantly"; substitutes "For this purpose" for "In this purpose"; substitutes "general tendency" for "general tendencies"; substitutes "Perhaps it may be thought" for "Perhaps it will here occur".

I have indicated above the causes which are conducing to the decline of cottierism. Simultaneously with the movement thus induced, there is an opposite process going on. The anxiety of landlords to get rid of cottiers is to some extent neutralized by the anxiety of middlemen to get them. To understand this it should be remembered that about one fourth of the whole land of Ireland is held under long leases; the rent reserved, where the lease is of long standing, being generally greatly under the real value of the land. It rarely happens that the land thus held is cultivated by the owner of the lease: instead of this he sublets it at a rack rent to small men, and lives on the excess of the rent which he receives over that which he pays. These leases are constantly running out; and as they draw towards their close, the middleman has no other interest in the land than at any cost of permanent deterioration to get the utmost out of it during the unexpired period of the term. In this purpose the small cottier tenants precisely answer his turn. Middlemen in this position are as anxious to obtain cottiers as tenants as the landlords are to be rid of them; and the result is a transfer of this sort of tenant from one class of estates to the other. The movement is of limited dimensions, but it does exist, and so far as it exists, neutralizes the general tendencies. Perhaps it will here occur that this system will reproduce itself; that the same motives which led to the existence of middlemen will perpetuate the class; but there is no danger of this. Landowners are now perfectly alive to the ruinous consequences of this system however convenient for a time; and a clause against subletting is now becoming a matter of course in every lease.

We see then that the cottier class are rapidly diminishing in Ireland, absorbed chiefly in the emigration; not however altogether: to some extent they pass into the position of ordinary labourers. So far as the latter lot has been theirs, I do not believe that any sensible improvement has been effected in their condition. For a time their wages may rise under the influence of a good harvest and the drain of population to America: in the last 20 years the rates at large over the country have probably risen from 20 to 40 or 50 per cent; but this mode of stating the case is I believe misleading; the improvement in *real* wages not at all corresponding to this nominal rise. Potatoes, which was almost their sole subsistence in former years, and is still their main subsistence, have in recent times sold at 2 or 3 or 4 times their former price. In this year potatoes are exceptionally low, but are probably twice their price as it stood 20 years ago, or nearly so. The 4d or 6d a day which in remote parts of the country was a common rate of wage twenty years ago cd not now by any means subsist a man. Money wages, therefore, have necessarily risen: I dare say too that on the whole looking at the lowered prices of tea sugar and clothing during the time in question, real wages have risen; but I see no indications in any direction of an advance in the *standard of comfort*. In the part of the country that I know best—the Co. Meath & more especially the neighbourhood of Drogheda—the ordinary course of things is for men to marry at the age of three or four and twenty, often earlier, the women being somewhat younger, and their joint wage frequently not exceeding 1s/6d a day, rarely exceeding 2s/6d. A man of good character earning 2s/6d a day is thought to be a catch. Any hope of permanent improvement therefore by the conversion of cottiers into labourers I regard as quite chimerical.*

---

*I observe the Irish landlord writing in the *Gardener's Chronicle* represents the change as resulting in a marked improvement. His evidence should certainly go for what it is worth; and I do not desire that mine shd go for more. My

The cottier class, as the statistics of holdings show are giving place in a large degree to the class of farmers immediately above them—those holding from 15 to 30 or 40 acres. What are the prospects of improvement amongst these? One cannot represent them as very hopeful: still the horison in this direction is not altogether dark. One fact is noteworthy. Within the last 20 years a very large increase has taken place in the private balances and deposits in the banks of the country. In 1840 the aggregate of these moneys was, on the last day of the year, £5,568,000: in 1862 it had risen to £14,389,000: it is probably now more than three times its amount at the former date. During this period the deposits in savings banks, after falling at the time of the famine from nearly three to little over one million, have on the whole undergone little change: In 1861 they stood almost exactly at the same amount as in 1841. With regard to the former item—the deposits in banks—there seems good reason for believing that the increase is mainly due to the accumulations of the small farmers. The banks in which the increase has been most marked are, as I have been informed by Mr. Jon. Pim, the Provincial and National banks, which are also the banks of which the branches in the rural districts are most numerous. Now it is not likely that these accumulations wd come from the larger class of farmers—the so called "gentlemen-farmers":—these, when they have made money, look out for investments of a different kind—as railways mining speculations and stocks of various kinds: on the other hand the rural traders, accustomed to larger profits, wd be dissatisfied with the low rate of interest allowed by the banks. The small farmer class is the only one whose ideas on the subject of pecuniary return are so limited and moderate as to be content with this sort of investment. For the most part they look upon the bank as the only alternative to the thatch.

The last remark will suggest a qualification of the inference which wd at first view suggest itself on contemplating the statistics just quoted. A good part of the ten millions added in the last fourteen years to the aggregate of bank deposits has been undoubtedly merely transferred from hoards—the form which the savings of the same class formerly assumed; and this process is still going on. A priest—the same to whom I have referred as my informant on another point—told me that, only a few months ago, he received 600 sovereigns from a small farmer to be lodged in a bank at Drogheda: these had all been concealed in the thatch of his cottage—the sum of the savings of a life time. Nevertheless, making all due allowance for accessions from this source, a considerable portion of the ten millions of new deposits will doubtless represent new accumulations. We are justified therefore in concluding, notwithstanding the symptoms of poverty that still everywhere abound, that wealth is growing among this class.

And here the question occurs, why with agriculture in its present backward state, do not these people invest their savings in the most obvious way—the improvement of their farms? The tenant-righter has a reply at hand—want of security. But, plausible as this solution is, it may be met by a practical answer. It is an unquestionable fact that many of the worst cultivated farms in the country are held under long and profitable leases; it is a common

---

statements are based upon experience of two localities in Meath, the town of Galway, and the confirmatory observation of friends with whom I have conversed on the subject: I shd state however that some of those with whom I have talked take a more favourable view of the labourer's position than I do—Judge Longfield for one.

saying amongst country people—such a man can "afford" to farm badly—
i.e. even below the low standard which generally prevails. Further, though it
is probably true that in the Northern districts where "tenant-right" prevails,
cultivation is on the whole somewhat better than in other parts of the country,
the superiority after all is not very great; while, such as it is, it may be
sufficiently accounted for by the superior energy which generally characterises
the people in the Northern part of the island. This view of the case is confirmed by what I am told is an admitted fact—admitted even by R. Catholic
landlords—that Protestants form the best tenants, and are invariably preferred.
In dealing with the case I think we should distinguish between proximate
and ultimate causes. Proximately I think it is beyond question that the bad
state of cultivation is to be referred to the low industrial morale of the farming
population. With the vast majority the one idea of farming which prevails is
to take as much as they can out of the land and to put as little as they can
into it. The notion of considerable outlay with a view to improvement of a
permanent kind, whatever be the interest of the cultivator in the land, hardly
occurs to an Irish farmer. But I think it is not the less true that this low
conception of the farmer's functions—this fear to cast his bread upon the
waters—is the result of causes among which insecurity of tenure holds a
prominent place. Insecurity of tenure has long been and is still the rule in
Ireland; and the state of feeling generated under this condition of things, has
not only, as frequently happens, in a great degree detached itself from and
become independent of its original cause, but has influenced opinion far beyond
the reach of its direct action. The standard of farming which prevails generally
becomes the standard for the few who are placed under circumstances more
favourable than those which generally prevail. The conclusion to which I come
is that the remedy is to be sought in many directions. Security of tenure I
regard as an indispensable condition, and this I think an improved public
opinion in connexion with the reforms suggested by Judge Longfield wd substantially accomplish;* but this should go hand in hand with general and
specific instruction. As regards instruction, the National Board have attempted
something in this direction: in 1862 altogether 134 agricultural school farms
were in operation, of which 19 were school farms of the first class under the
exclusive control of the Commissioners; but, so far as I can discover, the
instruction imparted in these schools has not yet reached the farming classes
to any sensible extent:† the function which these schools have hitherto performed has been the training of stewards for the gentry, through whom it is
possible some knowledge may have trickled down to the classes beneath

---

*Substantial security of tenure, coupled I would add with the extinction, once
for all, of the hopes constantly kept alive by tenant-right agitation (in the
revolutionary sense) of a wholesale confiscation of property in favour of
existing cultivators. Judge Longfield's treatment of this project seemed to me,
as a matter of speculation, to be profoundly fallacious; but I do not think he
has at all overstated the practical mischief which the constant agitation of
these schemes produces in the unsettling of people's minds.

†I find it is Judge Longfield's opinion (he is a member of the National
Board) that the instruction given in these schools has been hitherto too high,
and that simpler and more strictly practical courses, with a view to the actual
exigencies of the small farmers, should be established. Some such change,
it is probable, will soon be made.

them. The means of instruction which has hitherto been found most efficacious is that described in the "Irish Landlords" letter in *The Gardener's Chronicle*—a combination of example, precept, and coercion. Another mode which has been tried, but not with success, is the introduction of Irish & Scotch farmers on the lands obtained from the emigrating cottiers. The want of local knowledge, both of places and character, and the jealousy of the native population of "foreigners" has generally succeeded in defeating experiments of this kind.

In connexion with this part of the subject—the condition of the small farmers in the rank above the cottiers—you will be curious to know what is the prospect of a class of peasant proprietors arising in Ireland. The prevailing opinion amongst those with whom I have conversed on the subject is that there is no likelihood of this. This is Judge Longfield's opinion, who founds himself upon the following considerations:—1. that, wherever in Ireland substantial interests exist in land, the owner of such interests almost invariably sublets; 2—(and this is plainly but another aspect of the fact just mentioned)—that the natural disposition of the Irish people is careless improvident given to dash and show—in a word the opposite in all respects of that mental type which is the characteristic of peasant proprietors, and which seems to be indispensable to the keeping up of peasant-properties; 3. that the peasant-proprietor *régime* belongs to an early and primitive condition of society, and may be expected to disappear before the influences developed by the increase of intercourse amongst peoples, commercial progress and other modern forces; and that therefore the introduction of peasant proprietors wd be a movement antagonistic to strong modern tendencies. These reasons do not seem to me to be conclusive: 1. The disposition evidenced by the practice of subletting is only the natural and inevitable consequence of former social and political conditions—conditions which are now rapidly passing away. Landlords have admittedly felt the force of this change, and are every day coming to look at their estates less and less through the medium of feudal and mediæval, and more and more through that of commercial and modern, ideas. Why should not the same influences reach the classes below them, and neutralize in them too the mere "landlord" passion? 2. No doubt the Irish disposition is careless and improvident; but why are we to suppose that these qualities are ineradicable? Has there not been quite enough in the history of the country to account for them? And if they be eradicable, what more effectual means of accomplishing their extirpation than by bringing the Irish people under the influence of a system which in every quarter of Europe among various races of men is found invariably accompanied with exactly opposite traits of mind? Regarded from this point of view, peasant proprietorship appears to me to be exactly the specific for the prevailing Irish disease. With regard to the third consideration adverted to above, it wd certainly seem, if we confined our view to a few countries, as if the pursuits connected with land moved in a sort of cycle, commencing with pastoral industry, passing into agriculture carried on by peasant proprietors, and issuing in the large farm system carried on by capitalist farmers, and in which pasture wd in Ireland at least occupy a large place. Thornton has traced this course of things in the case of the Jews, Greeks, Romans and English.[42] But there are patent facts which suggest the doubt whether there be any thing normal or necessary in this sequence of affairs. Peasant proprietorship exists extensively all over the Continent of

[42]William Thornton, *A Plea for Peasant Proprietors*, 60ff.

Europe: in France its definitive establishment and greatest extension have been directly connected with the triumph and growth of democratical ideas— emphatically a modern power. In the United States, industrially the most advanced country in the world, the cultivators of the soil are I believe every where throughout the free states its owners. I am not aware that in the more advanced countries of Europe where peasant proprietorship exists, there are any indications of a decline of this form of tenure. The greatly higher prices obtained for land when sold in small than when sold in large quantities seems, on the contrary, to point to a tendency towards increased growth. I do not think therefore that experience wd warrant us in assuming the existence of a law in social progress inconsistent with the permanence (or at all events the maintenance for some generations) of a peasant-proprietory system: indeed I should rather be inclined to regard the tenor of affairs in England as an exception to the prevailing order of democratic progress than as indicating the rule. But, however this may be, the state of Ireland is so backward as compared with countries which are now cultivated by peasant proprietors that, even supposing the ultimate tendency was as is alleged, it might, and I conceive would, still be good policy to encourage this system as a transitional expedient to help Ireland forward in its course.

But leaving these general considerations, what are the prospects in the actual state of things in Ireland of the land getting in any large extent into the hands of the actual cultivators? To some, but I believe to a very limited extent, this has been, or at least was, realized.[43] On the sale some eight or ten years ago of the Thomond, Portarlington, and Kingston estates in the Encumbered Estates Court, it was observed that a considerable number of occupying tenants purchased the fee of their farms. I have no knowledge of the localities where these properties are situated, and have not been able to obtain any information as to what followed that proceeding—whether the purchasers continued to farm their small properties, or under the mania of landlordism tried to escape from their former mode of life. But there are other facts which have a bearing on this question which I will mention here. In those parts of the country where tenant-right prevails, the prices given for the good will of a farm are enormous. The following figures, taken from the

---

[43]The following passage, to "disposition of the people." (II.1083.49), is quoted by JSM at I.334–6. As above, JSM alters the punctuation and spelling, and here rewrites more freely, as follows: omits "have no knowledge of the localities where these properties are situated, and"; omits "which I will mention here"; substitutes "Newry was sold" for "Newry sold"; substitutes "gives but an inadequate" for "wd give but an altogether inadequate"; substitutes "It is a remarkable" for "Now here is a very remarkable"; substitutes "Why, it will be asked, do they . . . ?" for "why is it, it will be asked, that they do. . . . "; substitutes "The answer to this question, I believe, is to be found in the state of our land laws. The cost" for "I believe the true answer is that the cost"; substitutes "portions is, relatively to the purchase money, very inconsiderable, even in the Landed Estates Court" for "parcels is even in the Landed Estates Court very great, very great that is to say as compared with the purchase money"; substitutes "in that Court, where the utmost economy, consistent with the present mode of remunerating legal services, is strictly enforced, would" for "in the Landed Estates Court wd"; substitutes "10*l.*—a very sensible addition to the purchase" for "£ 10, which would represent a year's or two year's purchase"; four sentences "But, in truth . . . of the evil." replace the sentence "This is the case . . . lots."; the changes in the last two sentences are so complex as to make direct comparison necessary.

schedule of an estate in the neighbourhood of Newry, now passing through the Landed Estates Court, will give an idea, but a very inadequate one, of the prices which this mere customary right generally fetches.

Statement showing the prices at which the tenant-right of certain farms near Newry sold.

	acres	rent	purchase money of tenant-right
Lot 1	23	£ 74	£ 33
2	24	77	240
3	13	39	110
4	14	34	85
5	10	33	172
6	5	13	75
7	8	26	130
8	11	33	130
9	2	5	5
	110	£334	£980

The prices here represent on the whole about three years purchase of the rental; but this, as I have said, wd give but an altogether inadequate idea of that which is frequently, indeed of that which is ordinarily, paid. The right being purely customary will vary in value with the confidence generally reposed in the good faith of the landlord. In the present instance circumstances have come to light in the course of the proceedings connected with the sale of the estate which give reason to believe that the confidence in this case was not high: consequently the rates above given may be taken as considerably under those which ordinarily prevail. Cases, as I am informed on the highest authority, have in other parts of the country come to light, also in the Landed Estates Court, in which the price given for the tenant right was equal to that of the whole fee of the land. Now here is a very remarkable fact, that people shd be found to give say 20 or 25 year's purchase for land which is still subject to a good round rent: why is it, it will be asked, that they do not purchase land out and out for the same or a slightly larger sum. I believe the true answer is that the cost of transferring land in small parcels is even in the Landed Estates Court very great, very great that is to say as compared with the purchase money; while the good will of a farm may be transferred without any cost at all. The cheapest conveyance that cd be drawn in the Landed Estates Court wd, irrespective of stamp duties, cost £10, which wd represent a year's or two year's purchase of a small peasant estate: a conveyance to transfer a thousand acres might not cost more, and wd probably not cost much more. This is the case of land sold in the Landed Estates Court, where all expenses of investigating title are avoided: where those must be incurred, of course the expense is wholly inconsistent with the transfer of property in any but large lots.

The heavy expenses incident to the sale & purchase of land have thus obviously the effect of placing an immense premium upon large dealings in land; and while this is the state of the law, the experiment of peasant proprietorship it is plain cannot fairly be tried. The facts, however, which I have stated, show I think conclusively that there is no obstacle to the introduction of this system in the disposition of the people.

That the fortunes of Ireland must, at all events for a considerable future, turn upon her agriculture is manifest on looking to the limited extent to which her other industries have yet been carried. Taking manufacturing industry proper, including cotton, woollen and worsted, flax, jute, silk,—the total number of persons (i.e. of males & females, old & young—[sic] employed in all these branches was in 1862 only 37,872. Of these 33,525 were employed in Flax factories, situated almost exclusively in Ulster, and chiefly in the counties of Antrim, Down and Armagh; 2,734 in Cotton factories (one half of these—viz. 1,412 being employed in one factory in Waterford, and the rest in the North); 1,039 in Woollen and Worsted factories; the remainder being distributed among the Jute and Silk factories. The only other industry of any moment is mining, and this is of moment rather for the possibilities it may have in store, than for any results which it has yet achieved. The following figures will give some idea of the present state of mining industry in Ireland.* In 1861 the number of collieries at work in Ireland were 46: these turned out altogether 123,070 tons of coal. Of iron almost nothing has been produced. Copper in the same year (1861) was raised, chiefly in Cork and Waterford, to the value of £132,535. Of lead ore in the same year 2,403 tons were turned out, yielding 1,592 tons of metal. Lastly silver was raised, chiefly in Wicklow, to the value of £14,575. So inconsiderable are the results yet accomplished. As to the future all is conjecture & speculation. I have not been able to obtain any opinion on the subject on which I am disposed to place the least reliance; there being a general disposition among those who know most of the matter to conceal their knowledge.

Such, as nearly as I have been able to ascertain it, is our present position. The direction in which we are moving seems to be indicated with sufficient clearness. The figures already given show the large reduction which had been effected in the cottier class up to 1861. I have just learned from Mr. Thom that returns obtained within the last year show that since that time, the movement has gone forward with an accelerated pace. (A summary of these returns Mr Thom has promised to send me, and I hope to be able to transmit them with these notes). The emigration steadily increases. It nearly reached last year the figure of 90,000: this year it had up to October reached 90,000: there can be no doubt that before the year closes it will have exceeded 100,000. This has occurred in the face of the American civil war, and all the alarm which has been excited about compulsory enlistment. There can be little doubt that the effect of peace, whenever it comes, will be to swell considerably the tide. In view of these facts I look for a further considerable decrease in the population; this consummation seems to me at once inevitable and desirable: it is the effect of all those causes which are shortening the distance and facilitating the intercourse between nations acting upon a country surcharged with population under the influence of a bad economic and a worse moral and political system. The new and best parts of the world have, for the first time in history, been brought into practical competition with the old and exhausted portions. The result, I think, must be, as I have said elsewhere, "a greater dispersion and mixing of populations and a greater equalization of the conditions of wealth. It will no longer be a few favoured and conveniently situated spots on the earth's surface, but the whole earth, that will be turned to the purposes of man."[44]

---

*These figures are taken from Thom's Almanack.

[44]Cairnes, "Fragments on Ireland," in *Political Essays* (London: Macmillan, 1873), 147.

The same tendencies, which in the emigration exhibit themselves on a cosmopolitan scale, are traceable also in the internal economy of the country. Those portions of the country in which the natural advantages are greatest are advancing, not merely relatively to, but in some degree at the expense of, the less favoured parts. For example, Galway—the place in the West with which I am best acquainted—has beyond all question seriously retrograded within the last twenty years, and I think is still going back. The population has greatly declined, and I have no doubt the present reduced population is, man for man, poorer than the larger population of former years. I will mention a few facts connected with this town. When I first went to Galway some fifteen years ago —1849—things at that time having greatly declined from their former state under the shock of the famine—there were at work three distilleries, three breweries, several large grain storing establ[ishments,] several large corn mills, a paper manufactory, and I am sure other industrial establishments which now escape my memory. Every one of these has now either closed, or is carrying on a business so diminished that its closing is only a question of time. There was at this time an export trade in cattle, and previous to the famine there had been a considerable export trade in grain, chiefly oats. Both these branches of trade have wholly disappeared, and the sole seaward trade of Galway at present is an import of coal, chiefly for unproductive consumption; the return cargo being taken in ballast. Now this collapse is the more remarkable, as on no town in Ireland has the outlay of public money been so large as on Galway—this outlay occurring exactly during the period of its decline. 1. The Queen's College was built, having been commenced about 1846. Besides the original outlay this has entailed a permanent expenditure in the town from the residence there of at the lowest computation some 200 persons of the better-off classes, connected with the College, some of these being persons maintaining domestic establishments on a considerable scale. 2. A very fine dry dock, and, connected with this, a ship canal (connecting Lough Corrib with the sea), both executed in the mostly [?] costly style, have been made during the same time by the Board of Works—both for all practical purposes as useless as the Irish round towers. 3. An extensive drainage was carried out during the same time all round the shores of Lough Corrib, also under the management of the Board of Works. Lastly (though it is true the funds in this case did not come from the public revenue) the Galway end of the Gt. Western Railway was made, in connexion with which an enormous hotel was built at the Galway terminus, the largest I believe in Ireland,—built in expectation of requirements which have never come to pass. Yet in spite of such adventitious aids Galway has retrograded. The causes are not far to seek. The grain export was the creature of the monopoly of the English market secured under the protective system. Free trade, followed by a succession of good harvests between 1849 & 53 gave the *coup de grace* to the corn growing interest in this part of the country. What free trade did for the export trade in grain the railway has done for the export trade in cattle. The live stock of all that part of the country westward of Roscommon which formerly found a port at Galway or Limerick is now carried by the railways to the Eastern coast. These two facts involved all the rest: the small cottiers who were identified with the grain-growing *régime* were the chief customers of the distilleries; the better class of farmers who dealt in cattle, and the merchants and traders whom this conflux of people supported, were the chief stays of the breweries. The larger population, from all these causes, supplied the paper manufactory with rags, for lack of which, I heard the other day, it was preparing to close.

Galway is perhaps a palmary instance, but it is only an instance of a very general tendency. At Limerick, which I visited lately,—though things there are greatly better, two or three large manufactories being now maintained there in a flourishing condition—I heard also complaints of decay, and saw evidences of it. For example, what was once a staple export from Limerick—butter—is now all carried off to Cork by railway, from whence it is shipped to England, and largely to Australia.

Contemporaneously, therefore, with the decline of population in Ireland, I think there is going forward a redistribution of it—a redistribution which will be effected in a large degree at the expense of those parts of the country of which the natural advantages are least. This latter circumstance should be borne in mind, as it will serve to explain a good deal of what is conflicting in the accounts of the country.

10. CAIRNES TO MILL

74 Lower Mount St.
25 Dec., 1864.

. . . .

In writing to you yesterday I omitted in my haste to refer to your question respecting the rate of profit in the United States. I am sorry to say I am not able as yet to give you any satisfactory information upon this point. On receiving your letter I communicated with Mr. Ashworth of Bolton[45] with whom I occasionally correspond, and from whom,—as he is a thoughtful man, with large experience in business, and who has spent some time in the U. States on which he has also written a book—I had great hopes I should have been able to obtain the information I desired. I have had two letters from him on the subject: in the last referring to this point, he writes as follows:—"Your inquiry relating to the ordinary rate of mercantile profit in N. York and the other cities of the U. States is difficult to answer:—indeed I do not find from all the inquiries I have made that any definite answer can be given." He then proceeds to describe a method by which the risk in mercantile transactions is provided against in N. York, which complicates in some degree the question of profit, and concludes with the remark that "The rates of profit on sale of goods and the fluctuations on the current credit of the buyer admit of no general estimate." Let me state that the way I put the question was as to the rate of profit which a person about to engage in a business would regard as "fair"; his conception of "fairness" would of course be founded on his knowledge of what in that business was ordinarily obtained.

I wrote also to Mr Moran of the U. States Legation[46] on the subject, and have had a reply to this effect. "At this time I have no documents bearing upon the subject of the ordinary rate of mercantile & manufacturing profits in the U.S., but I will write this week (his letter is dated the 9th Dec.) to a friend at home for all the data he may be able to furnish." He adds "Nearly all the

[45]Henry Ashworth, author of *A Tour in the United States, Cuba, and Canada* (London: Bennett and Pitman, [1861]).
[46]Benjamin Moran, Secretary of the United States Legation in London from 1857 to 1875.

manufactories of N. England are Joint Stock Concerns, and reports are furnished annually of their dividends. These I think I can get, & they may be useful." Supposing that in striking these dividends an adequate reserve fund against risk is maintained, might they not be taken to represent the *net* profit on manufacturing undertakings? and would not railway reports give us the same element for this kind of investment? Combining these with the returns of a few more industrial departments, might we not obtain the average *net* profit on investments of a *permanent* kind (which of course would be quite distinct from the interest on mercantile bills?; and, this obtained, should we not have a basis for comparing American with English profits? For gross profits being made up of the reward to abstinence, indemnity for risk, & wages of superintendence, we should by this process obtain the first quantity, and the two latter—at all events the last—there would not be much difficulty in ascertaining with approximate accuracy. But, without going into a complicated calculation, if we know the net profit on a few of the leading investments of capital, we might I fancy with sufficient accuracy for your purposes, infer the rest. Supposing, for example, that railway dividends were found to be on the whole same for the U. S. & England, I think it would be a sound inference that profits are higher in the former country, since the wages of superintendance [*sic*], which net profit does not cover are certainly higher, & the indemnity for risk is I suppose not less. The information promised by Mr Moran may be expected in about three weeks from this.

Having thought over your remarks in reply to my criticisms I may as well say now what occurs to me on the points between us. You say—"Suppose I have a given sum, £10 a year, the expenditure of which I am determined whatever happens to divide between two commodities A & B, I conceive that even then, if A rises in price and B falls, the effect in the average of cases will be that I shall buy more of B and less of A. If this position be sound I admit my point fails—at least to the extent of the "more" and "less". But I cannot think that it is sound. Substitute for A & B, beer & tobacco. Suppose a man has £10 to spend on these luxuries, & that after the transference of the tax from one commodity to the other, his money will enable him to consume them in the same quantities & in the same proportion as before, is it conceivable that he will continue permanently to regulate the proportion of his smoking and drinking not by his tastes—his means being by hypothesis sufficient—but by the relative prices? I conceive that he might do so for a time under the influence of association; but this influence would be constantly diminishing, while his tastes & means would remain constant forces.

What I intended to say with reference to the Wakefield system was that the forcible separation of employments was unnecessary, and for this reason, that where the density of the population and the variety of industrial skill and knowledge are such as to render expedient a separation of employments, *there* a separation of employments will *naturally* take place; it seems to me that the tendency of Wakefield's scheme for requiring a "sufficient-price" for land was to force on an artificial separation of employments at the cost of these conditions—density of population &c—under which alone separation of employments is expedient or indeed permanently possible; his test of "sufficiency" having reference, *not* to the satisfying of the requirements of the colony (on which its attractiveness to emigrants depends) but to the checking of the purchase of land. So far as this latter end is obtained without full compensation in the increased attractiveness of the colony, the effect must be to repel immigration—

i.e. to prevent the realization of the conditions in which the separation of employment becomes expedient.

Lastly, with regard to the income tax question I do not think my position was (or if it was I did not correctly state my ideas) that "the payment in each year should be compared with what the income is worth in that year to the owner". My position is that the payment in each year should be compared with what the payer is worth in that year; and that the payer is worth, not merely his income —that portion of his wealth which he allocates to current expenses, but also, that which he invests, or allows to remain invested. The latter, no less than the former, appears to me to be to the owner a real source of pecuniary power, as well as of present enjoyment—that enjoyment which arises from the sense of having provided against future contingencies. Were it not that you so decidedly reject what I have said on this point, I should be inclined to feel confident in it, and for this reason, that applying the principle, subject to a deduction for necessaries, it would I imagine bring us to precisely the same practical conclusion as your principle of "equality of sacrifice". With regard to this, I should not think of insisting on the distinction between comfort & luxuries. In practice it could not evidently be carried out, though I think something might be said for it in speculation.

. . . .

Pray do not think of troubling yourself by replying further to what I have said: in the end I dare say my errors will find me out. I hope the parcels sent yesterday & the day before will reach you safely.

11. MILL TO CAIRNES

Saint Véran, Avignon
5 Jan., 1865.

. . . .

I have been too long in acknowledging the receipt of the very interesting things you last sent; but I was working against time on another subject, and had unwillingly to put by your last notes unread until this morning. I thank you most heartily for them. They are a complete Essay on the state and prospects of Ireland, and are so entirely satisfactory that they leave me nothing to think of except how to make the most use of them. For my new edition I must confine myself chiefly to the general results; but if I find it advantageous to transcribe certain paragraphs entire, will you allow me to name their real author? The article is a valuable supplement to the notes. The letter in the Gardener's Chronicle I was already acquainted with, having read it in I forget what newspaper.[47] I beg you to offer my sincere thanks to Mr Pim for the books he so kindly sent, which I shall immediately read. His letter, inclosed [sic] in yours, is full of good sense.

Respecting the rate of profits in the United States, we must hope to learn something through the kind offices of Mr Moran. But it is, I imagine, very difficult to ascertain the real average rate of profit, or expectation of profit, in any country. It would, however, be something to have an answer to the more vague question, whether, in the opinion of Mr Ashworth, or other persons to

[47]Reference not located.

whom business in both countries is familiar, the profits of capital in the United States are or are not, higher than in England.

Of the two or three points which we differ about, I will only touch upon one—the influence of price on demand. You say, if a tax is taken off beer and laid on tobacco in such a manner that the consumer can still, at the same total cost as before, purchase his usual quantity of both, his tastes being supposed unaltered, he will do so. Does not this assume that his taste for each is a fixed quantity? or at all events that his comparative desire for the two is not affected by their comparative prices. But I apprehend the case to be otherwise. Very often the consumer cannot afford to have as much as he would like of either: and if so, the ratio in which he will share his demand between the two may depend very much on their price. If beer grows cheaper and tobacco dearer, he will be able to increase his beer more, by a smaller sacrifice of his tobacco, than he could have done at the previous prices: and in such circumstances it is surely probable that some will do so. His apportionment of self-denial between his two tastes is likely to be modified, when the obstacle that confined them is in the one case brought nearer, in the other thrown farther off.

. . . .

I take Macmillan, and was much interested by your article,[48] which makes more distinct the idea I already had of the contract system in the mining districts. Laing, in his Prize Essay, brought it forward many years ago as an example of the cooperative principle.

. . . .

I have had a visit here from a rather remarkable American, Mr Hazard, of Peacetown, Rhode Island.[49] Do you know him, or his writings? If not, I shall have a good deal to tell you about him that will interest you.

. . . .

12. CAIRNES TO MILL

74 Lower Mount St., Dublin
9 Jan., 1865

. . . .

I am sincerely happy that you are pleased with my notes on the state of Ireland. As I said before, I shall not affect to deny that I shall be gratified by the appearance of my name on your pages wherever it may occur; at the same time I should be sorry that you introduced it if there were no other object for doing this but my gratification.

I will write to Mr. Ashworth putting the question respecting the rate of profit in the U. States in the relative form in which you suggest.

Touching the taxation question, after weighing carefully what you say I am still inclined to think that the position is *substantially* sound that "a man's comparative desire for two commodities is not affected by their comparative

[48]Cairnes, "Co-operation in the Slate Quarries of North Wales," *Macmillan's Magazine*, XI (Jan., 1865), 181–90; reprinted in *Essays in Political Economy, Theoretical and Applied* (London: Macmillan, 1873), 166–86.

[49]Rowland Gibson Hazard, of Peacedale, Rhode Island, had just published *Our Resources. A Series of Articles on the Financial and Political Condition of the United States* (London, 1864). He later wrote *Two Letters on Causation and Freedom in Willing, addressed to J. S. Mill* (Boston, 1869).

prices". The animal propensity towards beer and tobacco in certain proportions to each other depends on physical conditions: I can conceive that these may be overborne in some degree by the force of mental impressions; but then I think the mental impressions depending for their force on the principle of association are liable to become weak, while the force of the former is a constant quantity. At all events we have, I think, brought the question to a point at which it can only be decided by experiment, which, next to agreement, is the most satisfactory issue of an economic argument.

. . . .

Mr. Hazard I am not acquainted with, or his writings, but I shall look forward to learning something of both from you at your leisure.

. . . .

It occurs to me to call your attention to that passage in your Political Economy (I cannot this moment put my finger on it) in which you allow that Protection may in a conceivable case be justifiable as a means of helping manufacturing industry through its initial stage [II.918–19]. I know you have expressed yourself very guardedly: still it would seem that the concession is frequently turned to bad account. In a recent letter from the *Times*' Australian correspondent,[50] the writer represents the protectionist party there as founding themselves on your authority. It occurs to me as questionable whether the theoretic value of the admission is worth the practical evil which its perversion involves.

I intended in a former letter to have suggested to you the advisability of adding an index to the new edition. I often myself feel the want of one.

13. CAIRNES TO MILL

74 Lower Mount St., Dublin
24 Jan., 1865.

. . . .

I received the enclosed from Mr. Moran two days ago, and have waited in hopes of getting the further information he promises; but as it has not yet arrived I think it better to forward you what has reached me. I have also had a letter from Mr. Ashworth in which he says:—"I make no doubt that the rate of profit upon commercial capital is greater in the United States than it is in this country, and this may be inferred not only from the higher rate of interest which prevails, but also from the extent of mercantile losses by bad debts which require to be covered by compensating profits, and by the evidence afforded in the household extravagance which prevails amongst the mercantile classes." The reasoning is somewhat shaky, but I send you the remarks for what they are worth. He adds that he had, at the time of writing, written to an "eminent merchant and manufacturer in Boston who has long been engaged in business there, and has also resided 20 years in this country engaged in trading pursuits," and that he hoped in a month or six weeks to be able to send me the opinion on the point in question of this gentleman. You may depend on my forwarding it the moment it is received.

. . . .

[50]"Australia," *The Times*, 14 Dec., 1864, 4. For JSM's reaction, see Letter 14 below, and II.919*u–u*921.

14. MILL TO CAIRNES

Blackheath
4 Feb., 1865.

. . . .

I have delayed answering your last letter, until I could at the same time inform you of my return here.

The Political Economy has gone to press, considerably improved as I think, and indebted to you for much of the improvement. I have availed myself of your permission to acknowledge this in the preface, and also in the chapter on the Irish question, a good deal of which I have given in inverted commas as a communication from you. I have endeavoured to correct the effect of the passage which has been used by Australian protectionists, not by omitting it, but by giving a fuller expression of my meaning [II.919–21]. The subject of an Index I had thought of, but most Indexes of philosophical treatises are so badly and stupidly done, that unless I could have made it myself or got it made by a political economist, I thought it better let alone. An index is less wanted for a systematic treatise than for a book of a miscellaneous character, as the general arrangement of topics, aided by the analytical table of contents, shews where to find the things most likely to be wanted.

. . . .

15. CAIRNES TO MILL

74 Lower Mount St., Dublin
5 Feb., 1865.

. . . .

I have just received your letter informing me of your arrival in England. I am not certain from it whether you received mine in which I enclosed a communication from Mr. Moran (of the U. S. Legation) on the subject of profits in the U. States, and also sent an extract from a letter of Mr. Ashworth on the same subject. The opinion expressed by both writers was not very definite, and probably would be late for the purpose for which you desired it, but I may as well state that, in reply to your question as to the relative state of manufacturing and mercantile profits here and in the U. States, Mr. Ashworth expressed the opinion that the rate in the U. States was decidedly higher than here. The communication from Mr. Moran came from a correspondent in Chicago who said that mercantile profits in that town & district had been very high since the war had broken out—I forget the precise figures he named. Mr. Moran promised further information as did also Mr. Ashworth. In a letter since received from Mr. Ashworth he suggests Messrs Brown or Messrs Rathbone of Liverpool[51] as the persons in this country most competent to give an opinion on the point in question. All this I expect will be quite late for any practical purpose; but should you wish for any further inquiries to be made I shall be happy to make them.

[51]Brown, Shipley and Co., merchant bankers, and Rathbone Bros. and Co., cotton and general merchants.

I am glad to hear that you have got the Political Economy to press. I have already said how gratified I shall feel for your reference in it to me, though I expect from what you tell me that it will not be without some sense of shame at the disproportion of my slender services to your acknowledgment.

What you say on the subject of an Index is quite true: it is no doubt far better there should be none than a bad one. Were there time, and had I a little more leisure than I am likely to have for the next two or three months I should have been very happy to have undertaken it, could you have entrusted it to me.

. . . .

16. MILL TO CAIRNES

Blackheath
9 Feb., 1865.

. . . .

As you supposed, your letter of Jan. 24 had not reached me when I last wrote to you, but it has been sent from Avignon since. I am much obliged to you for the trouble you have taken to get information respecting the rate of profit in the U. States, but I fear it is next to impossible to obtain any conclusive evidence on the subject. There is no more difficult point to ascertain in the whole field of statistics. The scientific question remains as great a puzzle to me as ever. Hitherto I have left the passage of my Pol. Economy exactly as it was; but I shall have to alter it more or less in the proof sheet.

I may perhaps get some light on the subject from Mr Hazard, (himself a New England manufacturer of great experience) whom I shall see tomorrow. I wish you had been already here, that I might have asked you to meet him. He leaves for America on the 25th.

. . . .

17. CAIRNES TO MILL

Galway
1 March, 1865.

. . . .

I have just received the enclosed from Mr. Pim. I send it to you, as he seems to wish that I should do so, though I do not expect that you will derive much new light from his remarks, even if it should reach you in time to enable you to turn it to practical account. Much of his criticism appears to me to be irrelevant, and more to be answered by reference to the date of the publication (for you will see that he writes from the 3rd edition) some of his remarks indeed—as for example his demand for an explanation of "cottier tenure"— would seem to argue that he had read the book with but little attention. However I send you his comments such as they have come to me.

. . . .

18. MILL TO CAIRNES

Blackheath
5 March, 1865.

. . . .

Your two letters, with their inclosures, arrived in time; the former of them only just in time. Mr. Pim's remarks, as you anticipated, do not change any of my opinions, but they have enabled me to correct one or two inaccuracies, not so much of fact as of expression. On reading the proofs of the new matter I have inserted respecting Ireland for most of which I am indebted to you, and in which consequently your name is mentioned, I feel unwilling that it should see the light without your *imprimatur*. I have therefore taken the liberty of sending you by this post the two sheets of which it forms a part, and I shall not have them struck off until I hear from you that you do not object to anything they contain. Any addition or improvement you may kindly suggest will be most welcome.

The American information is very valuable, and I can hardly be thankful enough to Mr Ashworth and to his Boston correspondent for the trouble they have taken and the service they have done me. I beg you will convey to Mr Ashworth my grateful acknowledgements. From their statements it is clear that the ordinary notion of the extravagantly high rate of profit in the U. States is an exaggeration, and there seems some doubt whether the rate is at all higher than in England. But that does not resolve the puzzle, as even equality of profits, in the face of the higher cost of labour, indicated by higher money wages, is as paradoxical as superiority. This is the scientific difficulty I mentioned, and I cannot yet see my way through it. I have framed a question for the purpose of bringing it before the P. Ec. Club, which will perhaps be discussed at the April meeting & if not, at the July. I hope you may be present in either case. You were greatly missed on Friday last. Had not I shone in plumes borrowed from you, we should not have made much of it, and I regretted your absence the more, as the Chancellor of the Exchequer[52] was present, and spoke.

. . . .

19. MILL TO CAIRNES

Blackheath Park
11 March, 1865.

. . . .

I thank you sincerely for your further favours in regard to my Political Economy. I have sent your new matter to press, and have profited to the full by your observations on what I had myself written. I am indebted to you for nearly all which will give to that chapter of the book, any present value.

Your solution of the difficulty as to American profits is perfectly scientific, and was the one which had occurred to myself. As far as it goes, I fully admit it; but my difficulty was, and still is, in believing that there can be *so great* a difference between the cost of obtaining the precious metals in America and in

[52]Gladstone.

England, as to make the enormous difference which seems to exist in money wages, consistent with a difference the contrary way in the cost of labour. It is impossible to *approfondir* the subject in time for the present edition. I have contented myself, therefore, with qualifying the opinion I had previously expressed [I.414.20–1], so as to leave the subject open for further inquiry.

. . . .

20. CAIRNES TO MILL

Galway
13 March, 1865.

. . . .

You very much overrate my small services in reference to the "Political Economy"; but I should not easily exaggerate the satisfaction it has given me to have rendered even these small services. Had I thought of recompense, which I trust you will acquit me of, I have received it in copious measure in the terms in which you speak of me in the portion of your book of which you sent me the proof—terms of which I cannot help saying that one epithet included in them appears to me so disproportioned to its subject that, were the omission of this epithet easily feasible, I could almost wish it made: as for the latter you could have used none which I should have prized so highly. It is the highest compliment I have ever received; but it is much more than a compliment, it is a rich reward; and will be a powerful incentive. Pray excuse my having said this much on what perhaps I had better not to have referred to.

I see my observations on American wages and profits in their connexion with the theory of profit did not hit the mark; and I fear I must now relinquish the hope—I might say the ambition—of doing this, as on the assumption that the exposition I gave was correct—which you concede to me—I am unable to perceive where the difficulty lies: in short the scientific problem seems to me to be solved. For the rest, it is (to my apprehension) merely a matter of evidence whether money wages and profits *are*, at one and the same time, so high as is alleged: if they *are*—then the fact on the assumption that my exposition was correct is conclusive, as it seems to me, that the difference between the cost of obtaining the precious metals in America and in England *is* great enough to produce the results which we see. Am I guilty of arrogance in suspecting that the difference between us here—my inability to perceive the difficulty of which you are sensible—is due to the greater simplicity of the theory of profit through which I look at the phenomena?—I refer to that mode of stating the doctrine—differing from yours and Ricardo's only in form—of which a sketch was contained in the papers I sent you.[53] Of course if the theory, thus stated, failed to embrace any essential condition, this would be simply its condemnation; but it appears to me to embrace all the conditions included in your doctrine of "cost of labour", and it renders the phenomena in the case with which we are now concerned unless I deceive myself perfectly intelligible. Might I ask as a favour, when you come to deal with this question at your leisure, that you would consider once again that mode of stating the theory.

. . . .

[53]See above, II.1060ff.

21. MILL TO CAIRNES

Blackheath
22 March, 1865.

. . . .

I have again gone through your exposition of profits in the papers you so kindly took the trouble of writing for me; and I think, as before, that your mode of putting the doctrine is very good as one among others, and that there is no difference of opinion between us. I still, however, prefer my own mode of statement, for reasons which it would be long to state, and which I have not time at present to reconsider from the foundations. I am inclined to think that the real solution of the difficulty, and the only one it admits of, has been given by myself in a subsequent place, Book III, ch. xix, § 2 (vol. ii. p. 156 of the fifth edition.) [II.620.]

. . . .

22. CAIRNES TO MILL

3, Martello Terrace, Holywood, Belfast
27 March, 1865.

. . . .

Thank you for looking over my note on profits again: I suppose it must be that I overrate the importance of my form of stating the theory, which indeed is in itself not unlikely—I have not a copy of the "Political Economy" at hand, but will not neglect to look up the passage you refer to.

23. CAIRNES TO MILL

8 Duke St., St. James's, S.W.
2 June, 1865.

. . . .

Accept my warm thanks for your kind letter. I had frequently lately thought of writing to you, amongst other reasons to thank you for the much prized present of your "Political Economy"—the second copy of that work you have given me. . . .

. . . .

Appendix I

Bibliographic Index of Persons and Works Cited in the *Principles*, with Variants and Notes

MILL, like most nineteenth-century authors, is very cavalier in his approach to sources, seldom identifying them with sufficient care, and very frequently quoting them inaccurately and without indicating omissions.[1] This Appendix is intended to help correct these deficiencies, and also to serve as an index of names and titles (which are consequently omitted in the Index proper). The material is arranged in alphabetical order, with an entry for each author and work quoted or referred to in the *Principles* and Appendices A–H.

The entries take the following form:

1. Identification: author, title, etc., in the usual bibliographic form.

2. A list of the places in the *Principles* where the author or work is quoted, and a separate list of the places where there is reference only.

3. Notes (if required) giving information about JSM's use of the source, and any other relevant information.

4. A list of substantive variants between the *Principles* and the source, in this form: Page and line reference to the *Principles*. Reading in the *Principles*] Reading in the source (page reference in the source).

The list of substantive variants also attempts to place quoted remarks in their contexts by giving the beginnings and endings of sentences. Omissions of two sentences or less are given in full; only the length of other omissions is given. Following the page reference to the source, cross-references to substantive variants within editions (i.e., those recorded in footnotes to the present text) are given, where applicable. (These help identify places where inaccuracies may be blamed on the printer.) Only surnames are given in cases of simple reference.

AESCHYLUS. Referred to: 16

ALFIERI. Referred to: 310n

[1]See my remarks in the Textual Introduction, pp. lxxvi–lxxvii.

AMPÈRE. Referred to: 42

ANDERSON, JAMES. *An Enquiry into the Nature of the Corn-Laws; with a View to the New Corn-Bill proposed for Scotland.* Edinburgh: Mundell, 1777.

REFERRED TO: 419

ANON. "Australia," *The Times*, 14 Dec., 1864, 4.

REFERRED TO: 1090–1

ANON. "Co-operative Manufacturing Companies," *Rochdale Observer*, 26 May, 1860, 3.

QUOTED: 790

ANON. "Foreign Intelligence: France," *The Times*, 24 November, 1864, 9.

QUOTED: 785n

785.n6 operatives stand] operatives still stand (9)
785.n7 who have also] who also (9)

ANON. "Trade and Finance," *Daily News*, 18 Apr., 1864, 4.

REFERRED TO: 1047

NOTE: The *Daily News* correctly reads "Loyd" not "Lloyd".

ANON. Unheaded article, *Le Siècle*, 29 Dec., 1847, 2.

REFERRED TO: 437

NOTE: JSM reduces to round numbers, and uses the figures for the Département de la Seine rather than those for Paris. The article gives the population of Paris in 1846 as 1,053,907; that of the Département de la Seine in 1846 as 1,356,907, in 1841 as 1,181,425, in 1836 as 1,106,000, and in 1832 as 935,000.

ANON. Unheaded leading articles, *Daily News*, 1 Dec., 1864, 4, and 3 Dec., 1864, 4.

REFERRED TO: 1042

ARISTOPHANES. Referred to: 16

ARISTOTLE. Referred to: 969

ARKWRIGHT. Referred to: 96, 189, 344

ASHWORTH, HENRY. *A Tour in the United States, Cuba, and Canada.* London: Bennett and Pitman, [1861].

REFERRED TO: 1086–7, 1089–91, 1093

ATTWOOD. Referred to: 563–4

BABBAGE, CHARLES. *On the Economy of Machinery and Manufactures.*
3rd ed. London: Knight, 1832 [1833].

QUOTED: 106, 111, 111n–113n, 124–6, 128–9, 131–2, 770, 1008–10 REFERRED TO:
1012

NOTE: Babbage's text is broken into numbered sections, with other (not subsidiary)
numbers as required: JSM ignores these. In the passages he quotes, they occur
at 126.17, 132.8, 132.16, 132.24, 1008.24, 1008.34, 1009.18, 1010.1 (twice),
1010.26, 1010.34 (twice). Italics and quotation marks distinguishing 'doctoring,'
'single-press,' 'double-press,' and 'warp-lace' are ignored.

111.7   At] To such an extent is this confidence in character carried in England, that,
at (219)
111.n5.112.n2   The cost . . . contracts] [*in italics*] (134)
112.n10   customers. The] customers. [*paragraph*] The (135)
112.n12–13   Government . . . themselves] [*in italics*] (135)
112.n24   it by] it with (135)
113.n6   articles,] article; (136) [*see* 140n]
124.6   it is] is (202) [*see* 124^{d–d}]
125.13   process.] process; in this view of the subject, therefore, the division of
labour will diminish the price of production. (171)
131.20   person] servant (214) [*see* 131^{b–b}]
132.8   When] Where (215) [*see* 132^{c–c}]
132.15–16   order. [*paragraph*] Pursuing] order. One of the first results will be, that
the looms can be driven by the engine nearly twice as fast as before: and as
each man, when relieved from bodily labour, can attend to two looms, one
workman can now make almost as much cloth as four. This increase of
producing power is, however, greater than that which really took place at
first; the velocity of some of the parts of the loom being limited by the strength
of the thread, and the quickness with which it commences its motion: but an
improvement was soon made, by which the motion commenced slowly, and
gradually acquired greater velocity than it was safe to give it at once; and
the speed was thus increased from 100 to about 120 strokes per minute.
[*paragraph*] Pursuing (215–6)
770.25   "the] Some approach to this system is already practised in several trades:
the mode of conducting the Cornish mines has already been alluded to; the
payment to the crew of whaling ships is governed by this principle; the (259)
770.29   required] injured (259)
1008.10–14   "the . . . required."] [*as in* 770.25 *and* 770.29 *above*]
1008.19–23   1st. That . . . course.] [*except for ordinals, in italics with paragraph
breaks at* 1st. *and* 2d.] (253–4)
1009.1   their class] their own class (254)
1009.24   Suppose] Let us suppose (255)
1009.42–1010.1   undertaking. [*paragraph*] "The] [*one paragraph omitted*] (256–7)
1010.2   direct] *direct* (257)
1010.8   to improvement] to its improvement (257)
1010.21   evidently] *evidently* (258)
1010.25   between] *between* (258)
1010.33–4   existing. [*paragraph*] "A] existing. [*paragraph*] It is possible that the
present laws relating to partnerships might interfere with factories so conducted. If this interference could not be obviated by confining their purchases
under the proposed system to ready money, it would be desirable to consider
what changes in the law would be necessary to its existence:—and this

furnishes another reason for entering into the question of limited partnerships. [*paragraph*] A (258)

BARHAM. Referred to: 770, 1007

BASTIAT, FRÉDÉRIC. "Considérations sur le métayage," *Journal des Économistes*, 2ᵉ Série, XIII (Feb., 1846), 225–39.
QUOTED: I, 299n–300n
300.n3   fait bien] fait également bien (236)
300.n7   redoutable. C'est] redoutable. [*paragraph*] C'est (236)
300.n9   salariat] *salariat* (236)
300.n14   opére] opère (237)

———— *Harmonies économiques*. Paris: Guillaumin, 1850.
REFERRED TO: 424

BEAUMONT. Referred to: 329, 995

BENTHAM, JEREMY. Referred to: 220, 392, 809, 811, 862, 883

———— "Letters on Usury." [*Defence of Usury*. London, 1816.] Referred to: 923

BÉRANGER, CHARLES. "La liberté et le monopole," *La République*, 1 Jan., 1851, 2.
QUOTED: 446n–7n
446.n4   "La consommation] [paragraph] Or, tandis que la consommation de la viande de boucherie diminuait ainsi, un fait opposé se produisait dans la consommation des autres denrées: celle du (2)
446.n10   presque] près de (2)
446.n11   fr. C'est] fr. [*paragraph*] C'est (2)
446.n24—447.1   1835 . . . Nous] 1835, pour l'habitant de la banlieue, tandis que de 1812 à 1847, la consommation individuelle des habitans de Paris a diminué de 10 kilog. Si la boucherie eût été libre à Paris, il est impossible de douter que la consommation parisienne ne se fût développée dans des proportions égales à celle de la banlieue. [*paragraph*] Nous (2)
447.n5   constaté. Nous] constaté. [*paragraph*] Nous (2)
447.6–7   1835 . . . L'accroissement] 1835; mais ceux que nous avons cités suffisent amplement pour démontrer que la cherté de la viande et la diminution relative de la consommation n'ont point d'autres causes que la constitution de boucherie en monopole. L'accroissement (2)
447.n7–8   corréspond] correspond (2)

BERTIN, AMÉDÉE, and MAUPILLÉ, LÉON. *Notice historique et statistique sur la Baronie, la Ville et l'Arrondissement de Fougères*. Rennes: Marteville and Lefas, 1846.
QUOTED: 450   REFERRED TO: 450–1

NOTE: JSM draws broadly from pp. 350–414.

450.26–30 "It . . . period."] [*translated from:*] C'est seulement depuis la paix que l'agriculture a fait quelques progrès dans l'arrondissement de Fougères: à partir de 1815, le mouvement d'amélioration de son agriculture a toujours été de plus en plus rapide. On peut dire que si, de 1815 à 1825 ce mouvement a été comme 1, il a été comme 3 de 1825 à 1835, et qu'il est comme 6 depuis 1835. (352)

BESLAY. Referred to: 774n, 1017

BLACKER, WILLIAM. *Prize Essay, Addressed to the Agricultural Committee of the Royal Dublin Society. On the Management of Landed Property in Ireland; the Consolidation of Small Farms, Employment of the Poor, Etc. Etc.* Dublin: Curry, 1834.

QUOTED: 144

144.17 plough and] plough or (23n)
144.18–19 if . . . house] *if . . . house* (23n)
144.21–2 subject . . . The] subject, and I think it will not appear extraordinary, that such should be the case, to any one who reflects that the (23n)
144.23 farmer. He] farmer in this country. He (23n)
144.26 acres." After . . . adds, "Besides] acres. Add to this, he must appear himself, and have his family also to appear in a superior rank, and his farm must not only enable him to pay his rent, and yield him the support he requires, but it must also be chargeable with the interest of the large capital which is necessary to its cultivation; besides (23n)
144.30 children. And] children; and (23n)
144.33 difference."] difference perfectly. (24n)

BLACKSTONE, SIR WILLIAM. *Commentaries on the Laws of England.* Vol. II. Oxford: Clarendon Press, 1766.

NOTE: JSM gives no indication of edition.

QUOTED: 893

893.9 "for] Children grew disobedient when they knew they could not be set aside: farmers were ousted of their leases made by tenants in tail; for (116)
893.10 cover] colour (116)
893.10 disinherited;"] disinherited: creditors were defrauded of their debts; for, if the tenant in tail could have charged his estate with their payment, he might also have defeated his issue, by mortgaging it for as much as it was worth: innumerable latent entails were produced to deprive purchasers of the lands they had fairly bought; of suits in consequence of which our antient books are full: and treasons were encouraged; as estates-tail were not liable to forfeiture, longer than for the tenant's life. (116)

BLANC, JEAN JOSEPH LOUIS. Referred to: 203, 210, 775, 783n
———— *Organisation du travail.* Paris: Société de l'industrie fraternelle, 1839.

REFERRED TO: 1012.n4

BRIGGS, HENRY (MESSRS.) Referred to: 774–5, 903

NOTE: JSM is evidently citing the prospectus of the Company's reconstitution in 1865. No such prospectus has been located.

BRIGHT. Referred to: 1032n

BROWN. Referred to: 1091

BROWNE. Referred to: 287, 295n

BUCHEZ. Referred to: 1028

BYRON. Referred to: 392

CABET, ÉTIENNE. Referred to: 203

——— *Voyage en Icarie, Roman philosophique et social.* 2nd ed. Paris: Mallet, 1842.
REFERRED TO: 1028

CAIRNES, JOHN E. "Capital and Currency," *North British Review*, XXVIII (Feb., 1858), 191–230.
REFERRED TO: 1058, 1059, 1067

——— "Co-operation in the Slate Quarries of North Wales," *Macmillan's Magazine*, XI (Jan., 1865), 181–190; reprinted in *Essays in Political Economy, Theoretical and Applied.* London: Macmillan, 1873, 166–186.
REFERRED TO: 1089

——— "The Cause of the Inequalities in the Pressure of the Income Tax," *Economist*, XIX (4 May, 1861), 481–3.
REFERRED TO: 1050
NOTE: The date of Cairnes' article is supplied by JSM in pencil.

——— "Fragments on Ireland," in *Political Essays.* London: Macmillan, 1873, 147.
REFERRED TO: 1084

——— "Ireland," *Edinburgh Review*, CXIX (Jan., 1864), 279–304.
REFERRED TO: 1057

——— Personal communication to JSM.
QUOTED: 332n–333n, 334–6, 1038–95

CAMPBELL. Referred to: 885

CAREY, HENRY CHARLES. "Commercial Associations of France and England," *Hunt's Merchants' Magazine*, XII (May, 1845), 403–20; *ibid.*
(June, 1845), 499–520.

QUOTED: 899–900, 902–3, 905–6, 906   REFERRED TO: 904, 919–21, 1056

NOTE: Carey is translating from Charles Coquelin, "Des Sociétés Commerciales en
France et en Angleterre," *Revue des Deux Mondes*, n.s. III (Aug., 1843), 397–
437. Carey adds "Remarks and Notes."

899.30   "While] Thus, while (514)
899.31   even that] that even (514)
900.2   case. Again] case. [*paragraph*] Again (514)
900.4–5 Even his confidential clerk] His confidential clerk, even, (514)
900.14   information. Thus] information. [*paragraph*] Thus (514)
900.33   placed. . . . Our] placed; and thus are the parties doubly deceived. Our (515)
900.35   possible] *possible* (515)
902.6   "Suppose] Would the reader see the action of a limited partnership in its most
         rigorous form, let him suppose (412)
902.7   to carry] to enable him to carry (412)
902.11–13 certainly;" . . . "Neither] certainly! for who would call in a third person
         to take part in the management of a business, the secret of which belonged
         exclusively to himself? What advantage, indeed, would result from the unlimited
         liability of the partners, where there was no reciprocity? Neither (412)
902.14   *anonyme*," or any other form of joint-stock company, "in] *anonyme*, or
         chartered company, in (412)
902.18   right. Cases] right. [*paragraph*] Cases (412)
905.1   "nowhere] No where (517)
905.4   these] those (517)
905.11   Every district] Every little district (517)
905.13   neighbourhood,] neighborhood,* [*footnote:*] *In the banking laws of both
         Massachusetts and Rhode Island, there are provisions in relation to a liability
         of the shareholders for the payment of their notes, in case of bankruptcy; but
         they are of such a character as to be of scarcely any importance, whatever. It is
         nearly impossible that they should ever become operative, and consequently they
         do little injury. (517)
905.18   institutions.] [*footnote containing list of types of shareholders in New
         England small companies omitted*] (517–18)
905.21   through] throughout (518)
905.26   economy. Charitable] economy. All are, therefore, interested in the success
         of the concern; the consequence of which is, that the manufactures of New
         England are gradually superseding those of Great Britain, in the markets of the
         world. Charitable (518)
905.34   world.] [*4-paragraph footnote omitted*] (518)

——— *Essay on the Rate of Wages: with an examination of the causes of
the differences in the condition of the labouring population throughout
the world.* Philadelphia: Carey, Lea and Blanchard, 1835.

QUOTED: 945–6

946.10   warp.] warp! (195)
946.16   fortune, reputation] future reputation (195)

946.18   shag] *shag* (195)
946.20   mohair. I] mohair. [*paragraph*] I (195)

———— *The Past, the Present, and the Future.* London: Longman, Brown, Green, and Longmans, 1848.

QUOTED: 426^{o-o}

427.n4   We find the settler] If we find him
427.n5   requiring] requring [*sic*]
427.n8   increase. . . . . When] increase: then will the theory we have offered be confirmed by practice: American practice at least. If, however, we can thence follow him into Mexico, and through South America; into Britain, and through France, Germany, Italy, Greece and Egypt, into Asia and Australia, and show that such has been his invariable course of action, then may it be believed that when
427.n9   soils. With] soils: that with (25)
427.n12 them."] them; and that with this change there is a steady diminution in the proportion of the population required for producing the means of subsistence, and as steady an increase in the proportion that may apply themselves to producing the other comforts, conveniences and luxuries of life. (25)

———— *Principles of Political Economy. Part the First: of the laws of the production and distribution of wealth.* Philadelphia: Carey, Lea and Blanchard, 1837.

REFERRED TO: 424^{c-c}

———— *Principles of Social Science.* 3 vols. London: Trübner, 1858.

REFERRED TO: 919–21, 1056

CHALMERS, THOMAS. Referred to: 67n, 75–7, 418, 570–1, 576, 697, 725, 735–6, 741, 841.

———— *On Political Economy in connexion with the Moral State and Moral Prospects of Society.* 2nd ed. Glasgow: Collins, 1832.

NOTE: JSM does not indicate edition. Chalmers' Chapter iii is "On the Increase and Limit of Capital."

REFERRED TO: 735

CHARLEVOIX. Referred to: 166–7

CHÂTEAUVIEUX, JACOB FRÉDÉRIC LULLIN DE. *Italy, its Agriculture, &c. From the French of Mons. Châteauvieux, being Letters written by him in Italy, in the years 1812 & 1813.* Trans. Edward Rigby. Norwich: Hunter, 1819.

QUOTED: 303–4, 304–5, 305, 306, 306–7   REFERRED TO: 298, 435, 443

NOTE: The letters are presumably addressed to Charles Pictet.

303.14   "an extent] This farm, like all others in Lombardy, displays an extent (19)

303.15   rarely] scarcely (19) [see 302^{d-d}]
303.16   "affords] [*paragraph*] This is a perfect model of all the farm-houses in Lombardy, with nearly their dimensions, and should be that of every one in Europe; for it is a plan which affords (20)
303.19   "exhibits a] To secure the purpose of cleanliness, the dung of the cattle is thrown on the outside of the court, which exhibits, among its symmetrical columns, a (20)
303.24   "the] [*paragraph*] The (25)
303.24   great."] great in Piedmont; and this country, in whose limited extent a considerable space is occupied by mountains, supplies, in corn and cattle, the riviere of Genoa, Nice, and as far as the port of Toulon. (25)
303.26   plough works] plough thus works (27)
303.27   season. . . . . Nothing] season. You have, yourself, some years ago, so well described the excellent Piedmont plough, and the skill with which the active laborers manage it, that it would be superfluous to repeat it here. I cannot, however, avoid mentioning to you the method they have acquired of executing, with a single plough, all the work necessary for putting in the grain and earthing up the plants, for which, in England, so many implements have been invented. Nothing (27–8)
303.34   grain. . . . . In] grain. [*paragraph*] [*5-sentence omission*] It will be obvious, that in (30–1)
304.10   amphitheatre. The] amphitheatre. [*paragraph*] The (73)
304.11   other. . . . . They] other; they are built of brick, and in a justness of proportion, and with an elegance of form unknown in our country. They consist of only one story, which has often but a single door and two windows in the front. They (74)
304.15   vines. . . . . . Before] vines, so that during the summer it is difficult to determine whether they are green pavilions, or houses for winter. [*paragraph*] Before (74)
304.17   flowers. . . . . These] flowers, and placed on one side of the head. [*10-sentence omission*] [*paragraph*] These (74–6)
304.23–4 vine. . . . . These] vine, the branches of which are twined round, in various directions. [*paragraph*] These (76)
304.24   arrayed] arranged (76) [see 304^{f-f}]
304.25   oxen] them (76) [see 304^{g-g}]
304.27   farms . . . . . Almost] farms. The oxen come from the neighbourhood of Rome and the maremmes. They are of the Hungarian breed, extremely well kept, and covered with embroidered white linen and red ornaments. [*paragraph*] Almost (76)
305.3   which] that (78) [see 305^{h-h}]
305.4   small. I] small. [*paragraph*] I (79)
305.30   fifteen to twenty pence] thirty to forty sous (75) [*not quoted directly*]
306.3–4   society. The] society. [*paragraph*] The (295)
306.10   hills: gradual] hills. Gradual (295)
306.13   interested. Thus] interested. [*paragraph*] Thus (296)
306.16   labour] labors (296) [see 306^{j-j}]

CHERBULIEZ, ANTOINE ÉLISÉE. "Des associations ouvrières," *Journal des Économistes*, 2e Série, XXVIII (Nov., 1860), 161–95.

QUOTED: 779n–780n, 782n–783n

779.n15   et aucun] ni aucun (168)
779.n21   très onéreuses. En] très-onéreuses. [*paragraph*] En (168)
779.n27   maximum." [*paragraph*] "La] [*4-paragraph omission*] (168–9)
780.n2–3 francs. [*paragraph*] "L'association] [*4-sentence omission*] (170)

782.n35   344,240] 344,210 (170)
782.n36   46,000] 16,000 (170)

CHEVALIER, MICHEL. *Lettres sur l'organisation du travail, ou études sur les principales causes de la misère et sur les moyens proposés pour y remédier*. Paris: Capelle, 1848.

QUOTED: 772n, 1012

NOTE: 772n is identical with Appendix D, 1012; therefore the entry is not duplicated.

772.n4   l'avantage du] l'avantage qui résulte du (298)

———— "Rapport verbal sur un ouvrage de M. Armand Husson, intitulé: Les Consommations de Paris," *Journal des Économistes*, 2ᵉ Série, XI (July, 1856), 121–7.

QUOTED: 448n—449n

NOTE: Chevalier heads the extract: "En résumé, chaque Parisien absorbe annuellement en denrées animales un poids total de 95 kilog. 561 grammes, savoir:" (124)

CLÉMENT, A. *Recherches sur les causes de l'indigence*. Paris: Guillaumin, 1846.

QUOTED: 290n

290.n4   "Les] Pour démontrer combien les évaluations au moyen desquelles on prétend prouver que l'accroissement de l'indigence suit les progrès industriels méritent peu d'attention, il suffit de leur opposer un fait incontestable et reconnu de tous: l'industrie a fait en France, pendant les quarante dernières années, plus de progrès qu'à aucune autre époque, et les (84)
290.n5   les] le (84)
290.n7   siècle. . . . On] siècle. [*paragraph*] Ce fait ne peut être traduit en chiffres, mais il prouve évidemment le contraire de ce que l'on a voulu établir par les données statistiques dont il s'agit, et comme on (84–5)
290.n7   appuyer] l'appuyer (85)
290.n8   [ce fait]] [*JSM's addition*] (85)
290.n9   comparées. . . . S'il] comparées, il est assurément beaucoup plus concluant que des évaluations fondées, en grande partie, sur l'imagination de leurs auteurs.* [*footnote:*] *S'il (85, 85n)
290.n11   nous-mêmes] nous-même (85n)
290.n13   exact, M.] exact, déjà cité, M. (85n)
290.n17   "la] On peut raisonnablement conclure, des observations que nous avons présentées, que la (118)
290.18   journaliers;"] journaliers, doit être attribuée, en partie, au fractionnement des vastes propriétés territoriales qui existaient à cette epoque. (118)
290.n23–4   parure. . . . . . Les] parure. On doit s'applaudir, sans doute, de ce que les (164)
290.n24–6   Lyon," . . . "ne] Lyon, par exemple, ne (164)
290.n27   haillons."] haillons; mais peut-être eût-il mieux valu, dans leur intérêt, que le développement de leurs besoins ne se portât pas aussi exclusivement sur cet objet; des vêtements propres, mais simples, et composés de ces étoffes grossières et durables dont se revêtent encore les travailleurs de nos campagnes, auraient assuré leur bien-être, sous ce rapport, aussi bien et mieux que ne peuvent le faire les habits d'un prix élevé et de peu de durée dont ils font trop généralement usage. (164)

COBBETT. Referred to: 576

COCHUT. Referred to: 777

COMTE. Referred to: 1041

CONNER, WILLIAM. *A Letter to the Right Honourable the Earl of Devon, Chairman of the Land Commission, on the Rackrent System of Ireland: showing its Cause, its Evils, and its Remedy.* Dublin: Machen, 1843.

REFERRED TO: 328n

NOTE: This pamphlet and the two following are bound in JSM's own collection of Conner's pamphlets on the Irish Land Question, now in the Goldsmith's Library, University of London. In the Pierpont Morgan MS, the footnote listing Conner's writings (II.ii.lv) includes a cancelled title, "The Cane laid to the root of Irish oppression," which may have been cancelled because of its oddness: the correct title is *The Axe Laid to the Root of Irish Oppression.*

———— *The True Political Economy of Ireland: or Rack-rent the one great cause of all her evils: with its remedy. Being a speech delivered at a meeting of the Farming and Laboring Classes, at Inch, in the Queen's County.* Dublin: Wakeman, 1835.

REFERRED TO: 328n

———— *Two Letters to the Editor of the Times, on the Rackrent Oppression of Ireland, its Source—its Evils—and its Remedy, in reply to the Times Commissioner, with prefatory strictures on public men and parties in Ireland, showing their perfidy to the People. Also, on Lord Lincoln's three Bills, showing their unfairness and utter futility.* Dublin: Machen, 1846.

QUOTED: 328, 994

CONSIDERANT, VICTOR PROSPER. *Le socialisme devant le vieux monde, ou, le vivant devant les morts.* Paris: Librairie Phalanstérienne, 1848.

REFERRED TO: 1028, 1031

CONWAY, DERWENT. *See* Inglis, Henry David.

COOPER, WILLIAM. "Report from Rochdale. Free Speech and the Wholesale Society," *The Co-operator,* LVII (Nov., 1864), 89–90.

QUOTED: 789.n11

789.n19   to an educational] to educational (89)

COQUELIN, CHARLES. Referred to: 899–900, 902–4, 905n. *See also* Carey, Henry Charles, "Commercial Associations of France and England."

CORRY. Referred to: 113n

CROKER, J. W. "Agriculture in France," *Quarterly Review*, LXXIX (Dec., 1846), 202–38.

QUOTED: 433, 436   REFERRED TO: 433n, 438

433.14   "in] The law has no limits—though the land has; and in (217)
433.14   Napoleon will] Napoleon—still in all its power and vigour—will (217)
436.34–5   "on . . . inheritance,"] But however that may be, it is obvious that under the unremitting action of the law, the *ten thousand* 690*l*. incomes of one generation must become in the next (on . . . inheritance), *thirty thousand* of 230*l*.; and although there is at work an antagonist process of reconstruction or accumulation by marriage, purchase, and collateral inheritance, it is altogether inadequate to stem the dispersing torrent. (212)
438.7 & 8   600,000] In the ten years from 1826 to 1835 the *Côtes Foncières* exhibit an increase of 60,000 properties. (212)

CUNIN-GRIDAINE. Referred to: 445

Daily News. See Anon., "Trade and Finance"; and Anon., Unheaded leading articles, *Daily News*.

DARBLAY. Referred to: 774n

DEFOURNAUX. Referred to: 772n–773n

DE L'ISLE BROCK. Referred to: 272–3

DE PERSIGNY, F. "Rapport au Prince Président de la République Française," *Le Moniteur Universel*, CLV, 14 May, 731.

REFERRED TO: 437n

DE QUINCEY, THOMAS. *The Logic of Political Economy.* Edinburgh: Blackwood and Sons, 1844.

QUOTED: 462–4, 474   REFERRED TO: 456–7, 466, 468

462.7   "Any] Indeed, it is evident to common sense, that any (13)
462.10   secondly, even] secondly, that even (13)
462.17   not] *not* (14)
462.24   "Walk] Thus, by way of illustration, walk (24)
462.26   the ninety-nine] ninety-nine (24) [*see* 462*a–a*]
462.26   cases out] cases (24)
463.11   for the] for a (25)
463.11   come. One] come: one (25) [*see* 463*b–b*]
463.21   guineas] [*18-sentence footnote omitted*] (25–7)

463.36   under a] under the (28)
474.6   cheaper. Silk] cheaper: silk (230) [*see* 474*g–g*]
474.18   stationary? . . . . Offer] stationary? The articles and the manufacturing interests are past counting which conform to the case here stated; viz. which are so interorganized with other articles or other interests, that apart from that relation—standing upon their own separate footing—they *cannot* be diminished in price through any means or any motive depending upon the extension of sale. Offer (231)
474.22   whose habits and] whose rank, habits, and (231)
474.24   Oxford."] Oxford, or the separate costume for Cantabs. (231)

DESCARTES. Referred to: 1072

DESTUTT-TRACY. Referred to: 302

DEVON, WILLIAM COURTENAY, EARL OF. "Report from Her Majesty's Commissioners of Inquiry into the State of the Law and Practice in Respect to the Occupation of Land in Ireland," *Parliamentary Papers*, 1845, XIX–XXII.
QUOTED: 318, 330n–1n, 992–3, 997–1000   REFERRED TO: 992n, 993, 994n, 997, 999
NOTE: for specific passages, see Griffith, R., Hurley, J., and Robinson, Colonel. See also Kennedy, J. P.

DOUBLEDAY. Referred to: 155n–156n

DUNCAN. Quoted: 902n (*see* Fane)

DUNNING, T. J. *Trades' Unions and Strikes: their Philosophy and Intention.* London: Dunning, 1860.
REFERRED TO: 934n

DUNOYER, CHARLES B. *De la liberté du travail ou simple exposé des conditions dans lesquelles les forces humaines s'exercent avec le plus de puissance.* Vol. II. Paris: Guillaumin, 1845.
QUOTED: 111*v*, 945–6   REFERRED TO: 35, 948n
NOTE: the passage referred to in 948n occurs in Dunoyer, Vol. III, Book ix, Chapter iv.
945.13   etc.] etc.* [*footnote:*] *V. dans Chaptal, t. II, p. 250 à 280, le détail des règlements aux-quels étaient assujétis une multitude de métiers.
945.34   galères] galères* [*footnote:*] *Dulaure, *Hist. de Paris*, t. IV, p. 443.

DUPONT. Referred to: 773n, 1015–16

DUVEYRIER. Referred to: 1011

ELIZABETH I (of England). Referred to: 233n, 955n

ELLIOTT, J. H. *Credit the Life of Commerce: being a defence of the British Merchant against the unjust and demoralizing tendency of the recent alterations in the Laws of Debtor and Creditor; with an outline of remedial measures.* London: Madden and Malcolm, 1845.

QUOTED: 908–9, 910

908.28–9   it. Excessive] it. It is asserted by a gentleman, one of the able officers of the latter court, whose business it is, as an official assignee, to investigate the cases that come before it, that a case of bankruptcy, arising from misfortune,— unavoidable misfortune,—is extremely rare. By far the great majority arise from excessive (49)

908.29   speculation] speculations (49)

908.31   speculation] speculations (49)

909.3   innocent] [*in italics*] (49)

909.10   neglecting] neglected (49)

909.11   and means] and facile means (49)

909.16   "fifty-two] "The New Court has been open upwards of eighteen months, during which period fifty-two (49) [*see* 509^{x-x}]

909.16   care. It] care. To the best of my judgment, not one of them can be attributed to what may be termed general distress. It (49)

909.31   not one-fourth] [*in italics*] (50)

910.4   alone."] alone; but it is possible that if further examination were made, some delinquency could be made out against that one. (51)

ELLIS, WILLIAM. "Employment of Machinery," *Westminster Review*, V (Jan., 1826), 101–30.

REFERRED TO: 736n

ESCHER, ALBERT G. "Evidence of Employers of Labourers on the Influence of Training and Education on the Value of Workmen, and on the Comparative Eligibility of Educated and Uneducated Workmen for Employment," in "Report to the Secretary of State for the Home Department, from the Poor Law Commissioners, on the Training of Pauper Children," *House of Lords Sessional Papers*, 1841, XXXIII, 15–21.

QUOTED: 108, 108^{d-d}, 109–110, 110

NOTE: Escher's answers were in response to questions probably put by the Secretary to the Poor Law Commission, Edwin Chadwick. JSM omits these questions, which read:

108.13   The] [*paragraph*] What are the more particular natural characteristics of the several classes of workmen?—The (16)

108.19   As] [*paragraph*] What, however, do you find to be the differences of acquirements imparted by specific training and education?—As (16)

108.34   JSM here omits one question and its answer. (16)

108.36   The] [*paragraph*] But is the superior general usefulness of the Saxon, or workman of superior education, accompanied by any distinction of superiority as to moral habits?—Decidedly so. The (16)

109.10   Whilst] [*paragraph*] In respect to order and docility what have you found to be the rank of your English workmen?—Whilst (19)

In the following places JSM departs in substance from his source:

108.14 , in a power] [*not in Source*] (16) [*see* 108*e-e*]
108.30 else; and] else; he will understand only his steam-engine, and (16)
108.33 work] works (16)
109.3   kind; they have] kind; they are more refined themselves, and they have (17)

EURIPIDES. Referred to: 16

FANE, ROBERT GEORGE CECIL. *Bankruptcy Reform: in a series of Letters addressed to Sir Robert Peel, Bart. Letters IV. V. VI. VII.* London: Sweet, 1838.

QUOTED: 912n

NOTE: Fane uses numbered sections drawn from his source; JSM omits these numbers at the following places: 912.n7, 912.n11, 912.n13, 912.n14, 912.n17, 912.n19, 912.n22, 912.n29, 912.n31, 912.n41.

912.n8   in the investigation of his affairs] [*in italics*] (44)
912.n9   shall be] *shall be** [*footnote:*] *There seems to be some distinction between the cases provided for by clause 587; and that distinction seems to be expressed in the French, by the words "sera poursuivi," applied to the first class of cases, and "pourra être poursuivi" applied to the second, which I understand to be, the one *imperative* and the other *permissive*. I have translated the first "shall be," and the second "may be." (44)
912.n11 in a] in his (44) [*see* 912n]
912.n19 may] may* [*same footnote as in* 912.n9 *above*] (44)
912.n22 time limited] limited time (45)
912.n26-8 [*JSM's information drawn from Fane's translation of* Section 592 (p. 45) *and* Section 596 (pp. 46-7)]
912.n29 expenses and] expenses or (45)
912.n41 may] may* [*footnote:*] *See note, p. 44. [*i.e.,* 912.n9] (46)
912.n46-7 [*JSM's note*]

———— "Report from the Select Committee on the Law of Partnership; together with the Proceedings of the Committee, Minutes of Evidence, Appendix, and Index," *Parliamentary Papers*, 1851, XVIII, 66–113.

QUOTED: 896, 896n, 897, 902n   REFERRED TO: 899n

NOTE: JSM omits the question numbers in the ellipsis at 896.n5, and at 896.n9. The "competent authorities" cited at 897.4 would appear to be H. Bellenden Ker, in his "Reply to Queries, Appendix 5," in the above Report (and see *Parliamentary Papers*, 1851, XLIV, 165-7). In 899.n1, the reference is to the evidence of E. W. Field (pp. 145–50) and John Duncan (pp. 151–8).

896.n5   out. . . . Very] [*ellipsis indicates omission of 3 questions and answers, and also:*] I have no doubt that the difficulty of getting judicial decisions in partnership disputes does operate to prevent persons from engaging in partnership; but still I do not think that is the thing which prevents them, because I believe that very (86)
896.n10 it or not, I] it I (86)
896.n16 therefore is] is therefore (87)
897.4   "mass of confusion,"] After years of discussion, reports, committees, &c., that mass of confusion the Joint Stock Companies Act was passed. (167)
897.4-5 "never was such an infliction"] Never was such an infliction on parties entering into partnership as these Acts; and yet the registrar and his staff go on putting, in my opinion, the most absurd construction, on the inconsistent and

contrarient clauses of these Acts, whilst one would have thought it would have been the duty of the head of the office, long before this, to have furnished such information as would have led to a reasonable and plain law. (167)

902.n9 the risk] their risk (155) [*see* 902n]

FAUCHE. Referred to: 287, 295n

FAUCHER, LÉON. *Recherches sur l'or et sur l'argent considérés comme étalons de valeur* (Paris: Librairie de Paulin, 1843).

REFERRED TO: 1067

FAWCETT, HENRY. "Strikes, their Tendencies and Remedies," *Westminster Review*, n.s. XVIII (July, 1860), 1–23.

REFERRED TO: 932–3

NOTE: the relevant passages are on 5ff.

FEUGUERAY, H. *L'association ouvrière, industrielle et agricole.* Paris: Havard, 1851.

QUOTED: 776, 776–9, 783n, 784, 784^{h-h}, 795

NOTE: from 777.22 to 778.17, Feugueray is quoting from M. Cochut: JSM does not indicate this quotation.

776.30 l'eau. . . . C'est] l'eau; il fallait ainsi volontairement se faire une condition de vie très-inférieure à celle qu'on aurait pu se procurer comme simple salarié, et que pis est, il fallait souvent faire partager ces souffrances à des femmes, à des enfants, qui semblaient avoir le droit de se plaindre d'être sacrifiés par leurs maris, par leurs pères! [*paragraph*] C'est à ce prix, c'est (112)

777.13 refusa* refusa* [*footnote:*] *Je dois reconnaître qu'au dernier moment les délégués finirent par consentir à une diminution; ils abaissèrent leur demande à 197,000 francs d'abord, et enfin à 140,000 francs. Mais ces concessions arrivèrent trop tard, quand la démission de plusieurs des membres de la commission avait enlevé à l'affaire toute chance de succès. (114)

777.17 fabrique] fabrication (114)

778.39 sociétaires. L'association] sociétaires. [*paragraph*] L'association (116)

778.n4 débuts: une] débuts. Une (116)

784.13 "les] Certes, les (37)

795.9 "La] Mais depuis, en y réfléchissant davantage, j'en suis venu à mieux comprendre que si la concurrence a beaucoup de puissance pour le mal, elle n'a pas moins de fécondité pour le bien, surtout en ce qui concerne le développement des facultés individuelles et le succès des innovations; et d'autre part, en étudiant plus profondément le problème de la misère, j'ai vu de plus en plus clairement que la (90)

795.12–15 Si . . . innovations."] [*see entry above; JSM has rearranged the text*]

FITZROY. Referred to: 766n, 1035

FOURIER. Referred to: 1028, 1031

FOX. Referred to: 1028

Fritob. Referred to: 248n

Fullarton, John. *On the Regulation of Currencies; being an Examination of the Principles, on which it is proposed to restrict, within certain fixed limits, the Future Issues on Credit of the Bank of England, and of the other Banking Establishments throughout the Country.* 2nd ed. London: Murray, 1845.

QUOTED: 516–17, 551–2, 662, 671–2, 674–7, 678ᵖ⁻ᵖ REFERRED TO: 661, 662–4, 670n, 684, 1071–2

516.9 "it rises] In August, the currency is found to be uniformly lowest; it rises (88)
516.12 taxes," and . . . loans. "Those] taxes.* These [*footnote:*] *See 'Report of the Commons' Committee of 1841,' pp. 5 and 59. (88)
516.16 payments have] payments which I have mentioned have (88)
516.16–17 superfluous" currency . . . million, "as] superfluous half-million as (88)
516.18 disappears."] disappears, and that on the mere cessation of the demand, without the slightest effort on the part of the banks. (89)
662.1 "the amount] I am not more disposed than most men to place implicit reliance on the testimony of parties who have personal interests depending on the question at issue; but it is impossible, I think, for any man, with the least pretensions to candour, to peruse the great mass of evidence furnished to the several Committees of the House of Commons by the intelligent body of country bankers, without attaching some faith to their unanimous and consistent assurances, sustained, too, as those assurances are, by all the collateral facts and probabilities of the case, that the amount (85)
662.4 their] those (86)
662.5 prescribes] prescribe (86)
662.8 source."] source.* [*JSM omits a long footnote of evidence*] (86)
671.17 "it] Then certainly, if the Bank complies with those applications, it (106)
671.35 market] markets (107)
671.39 exactly] precisely (107) [*see* 671ᵈ⁻ᵈ]
674.22 population.* [*JSM's footnote*] (72)
675.2 authorities,] authorities,* [*footnote:*] *See Sir William Clay's 'Remarks,' &c., p. 25. (72)
675.11 demands. That] demands. The purpose of banks, according to the excellent aphorism of Adam Smith, is not to supply the trader "with the whole or even any considerable part of the capital with which he trades, but that part of it only which he would otherwise be obliged to keep by him unemployed, and in ready money, for answering occasional demands."* That [*footnote:*] *See Mr. M'Culloch's edition of 'The Wealth of Nations,' vol. ii. p. 49, 50. (73)
675.16–17 derangements] derangement (73)
675.17 proofs:" among others, "the] proofs. Among the examples most frequently referred to is the circumstance remarked by Lord King, that the displacement and expulsion of the entire metallic circulation of France by the assignats had been accomplished without producing, as he affirms, any sensible effect on the state of prices in the neighbouring kingdoms. So much uncertainty, however, hangs over the facts connected with this extraordinary operation, and there are such strong grounds for supposing, that by far the larger portion of the specie, which disappeared during the reign of the assignats, was not exported, but buried and concealed on the spot, that the case, perhaps, is scarcely one on which we can build any very confident argument. A much more conclusive inference may be drawn from the (73–4)
675.24 currency. . . . There] currency. Lord Ashburton estimated, in 1819, that little less than a hundred millions sterling would be required, for the completion of

Valuation Commissioner," No. VII in "Papers referred to in this Report," *Parliamentary Papers*, 1845, XIX, 48–53 [Devon Report].
REFERRED TO: 997–8

GROTE, GEORGE. *History of Greece*. Vol. IV. London, 1862, 11–12 (i.e., Chap. xliv).
REFERRED TO: 1045

GUILHAUD DE LAVERGNE. *See* Lavergne.

HARDENBERG. Referred to: 329, 995

HARDINGE. Referred to: 1075

HARGREAVES. Referred to: 96

HARRISON. Referred to: 1029–30

HASSELQUIST. Referred to: 1023

HAZARD. Referred to: 1089–90, 1092

HEAD. Referred to: 272

HENRI IV (of France). Referred to: 275, 296n, 1004

HENRY II (of England). Referred to: 578

HILL. Referred to: 272

Historisch- geographisch- statistisches Gemälde der Schweiz. Erstes Heft. Knonau, Gerold Meyer von. "Der Kanton Zürich." St. Gallen: Huber, 1834.
QUOTED: 258n, 393   REFERRED TO: 690–1

———— Zwölftes Heft. Im-Thurn, Edward. "Der Kanton Schaffhausen." St. Gallen: Huber, 1840.
QUOTED: 278n   REFERRED TO: 258n

———— Siebenzehntes Heft. Pupikofer, J. A. "Der Kanton Thürgau." St. Gallen: Huber, 1837.
QUOTED: 259n   REFERRED TO: 258n

258.n   [*the expression is on 80, but the discussion continues onto 81*]
259.n2   mehrere] mehre (72)
278.n1   übermenschliche] übermenschichen (53)
393.12–15   It is . . . machinery.] [*the translated passage is introduced by von Knonau as follows:*]
  Die Lichtseite der zürcherischen Fabrikation schildert ein ebenso erfahrner als beredter Sprecher des zürcherischen Handelstandes, Herr Stiftsamtmann Ernst, so: [*the passage reads:*] "Der zürcherische Arbeiter ist heute Fabrikant, morgen wieder Landbauer und mit den Jahreszeiten wechselt in beständigem Kreislaufe seine Beschäftigung. Hand in Hand schreiten Industrie und Landwirthschaft in unzertrennlichem Bunde vorwärts, und in dieser Vereinigung der beiden nährenden Beschäftigungen mag wohl das Geheimniss zu finden seyn, wie der unscheinbare und ungelehrte schweizerische Fabrikant neben jenen ausgedehnten, mit grossen ökonomischen und den noch wichtigern intellektuellen Mitteln ausgestatteten Anstalten noch immer concurrirt [*sic*] und seinen Wohlstand mehrt. Auch in denjenigen Gegenden des Kantons, wo die Fabrikation am weitesten sich ausgedehnt hat, gehören nur ein Siebentheil aller Haushaltungen ihr allein an, vier Siebentheile aber verbinden Fabrikation und Landwirthschaft mit einander. Der Vorzug dieser häuslichen oder Familien-fabrikation besteht hauptsächlich darin, dass sie alle andere Beschäftigungen zulässt oder vielmehr, dass sie zum Theil nur als Nebenverdienst betrachtet werden kann. Im Winter ist in den Wohnungen der Fabrikarbeiter alles mit dem sogenannten Handverdienste beschäftigt, die Erwachsenen weben, die Kleinen und die Betagten spulen, sowie aber der Frühling erwacht, verlassen diejenigen, welchen die ersten Feldgeschäfte obliegen, die Stube, manches Weberschiffchen ruht und nach und nach folgt bei der vermehrten Feldarbeit eines dem andern, bis am Ende in der Ernte und den sogeheissenen grossen Werken alle Hände die landwirthschaftlichen Werkzeuge ergriffen haben, bei ungünstiger Witterung aber oder in jeder sonst freien Stunde wird die Arbeit in der Stube fortgesetzt, und wenn dann die unfreundliche Jahreszeit wieder heranrückt, kehren in gleicher Reihenfolge die Hausbewohner zu der innern Beschäftigung zurück, bis sich zuletzt alle wieder dabei versammelt haben." (105)
393.n2–3   The cotton . . . population;] [*derived by JSM from the following passage:*] Das Ergebnis dieser Angaben zeigt, dass sich mit der Verarbeitung der Baumwolle und mit dem Handeln derselben 23,000 Menschen im Kanton Zürich oder beinahe der zehnte Theil seiner ganzen Bevölkerung beschäftigen und dafür mit 1,600,000 Gulden jährlichen Einkommens belohnt werden. (108)
393.n3–5   and they . . . England.] [*derived by JSM from the following passage:*] Nach statistischen Angaben soll die Bevölkerung Frankreichs im Durchschnitte für jedes Individuum jährlich 1 Pfund 12 Loth Baumwolle consumiren, England 1 Pfund 20 Loth für jeden Bewohner. Die grosse Wohlfeilheit der Zeuge macht, dass jeder Einwohner des Kantons Zürich 1¼ Pfund (ungefähr 9 bis 10 Pariserstab) gebraucht. (109–10)

HOLYOAKE, GEORGE JACOB. *Self-help by the People. History of Co-operation in Rochdale.* London: Holyoake and Co., [1858].

QUOTED: 786–9, 788n, 794n   REFERRED TO: 790–1, 1032

787.11   1852] 1855 (33)
787.16   members] member (33)
787.26   been opened. In] have been lately opened. A members' meeting can no longer be held at the Store Rooms. 1,600 members make a public meeting, and the business meetings of the Society are held in the public hall of the town. In (35)
787.31–5   "Every . . . business. One . . . library.] One . . . library. Every . . . business. (37) [*i.e., JSM has reversed the order of the passages*]
787.36–8   club." . . . "The] club, and the (49)

787.36 "free] The quarterly meeting passed a resolution that the News-room should be free (49n)
788.2 free. From] free. In their News-room, conveniently and well fitted up, a member may read, if he has the time, twelve hours a day, also free. [*paragraph*] From (50)
788.5 mutual instruction] mutual and other instruction (50)
788.10 kind. The] kind. It is now spoken of as 'the Society's New Mill in Weir Street, near the Commissioners' Rooms.' The (37)
788.20 persons. . . . ."] [*ellipsis indicates 5-sentence omission*] (37)
788.25 hosiery] hosiery,* [*footnote:*] *In 1855 the drapery stock was ordered to be insured with the Globe for £ 1000. (37)
788.29 and cheerful] and crowds of cheerful (38)
788.n2 brilliancy] brilliance (38)
788.n6 other. . . . . These] other; and Toad Lane on Saturday night, while as gay as the Lowther Arcade in London, is ten times more moral. These (38)
789.n6–8 (Last . . . duty.)] [*in footnote, without parentheses*] (39)
789.n17 these.] these.* [*footnote:*] *The Arbitrators . . . *as in* 789.n25–6 . . . quarrels. The peaceableness of the Co-operators amounts to what elsewhere would be termed 'contempt of court.' (39) [*i.e., JSM transposes the sentence from Holyoake's footnote*]
789.n20–1 The . . . quarrels.] [*see* 789.n22 *above*] (39)
790.n14 *They . . . chicanery.* [*JSM's italics*] (39)

HOWITT, WILLIAM. *The Rural and Domestic Life of Germany: with characteristic sketches of its cities and scenery, collected in a general tour, and during a residence in the country in the years 1840, 41 and 42.* London: Longman, Brown, Green, and Longmans, 1842.

QUOTED: 263–4, 328–9

263.11 among] amongst (40.) [*see* 263[b]]
263.12 multitude. . . . . . The] multitude; and wherever you go, instead of the great halls, the vast parks, and the broad lands of the nobility and gentry, as in England, you see the perpetual evidences of an agrarian system. The exceptions to this, which I shall afterwards point out, are the exceptions, they are not the rule. The (40)
263.17 themselves. . . . . . The] [*ellipsis indicates 6-sentence omission*] (41)
263.19 trees, commonly] trees, as we have seen commonly (41)
263.19 heavy] hung (41)
263.25 greater. The] greater. [*paragraph*] The (41)
263.27 time. . . . . . They] time. You never witness that scene of stir and hurry that you often do in England; that shouting to one another and running, where the need of dispatch rouses all the life and energy of the English character. They (41–2)
262.32 purposeless. . . . . . The] purposeless, and at once the terror and the victim of the capitalists. The (42)
262.34 in the] in his (42)
262.35 neighbours; no man] neighbours; he is content with his black bread, because his labour has at once created it and sweetened it to his taste, and because no proud man (42)
264.2 one."] one; and he knows that when he dies, he shall not be buried between the vile boards of a pauper's coffin, threatening to fall asunder before they reach the grave, nor be consigned to the knife of the surgeon; but his children will lay him by his fathers, and plant the rose, the carnation, and the cross on his grave—*Zum Andenken des frommen Vaters*—to the memory of the good

father—and will live the same active and independent life, on his native soil, or seek it in America or Australia. (42)
264.4   of the] of that (44)
264.6   do. They] do. Of their in-door employments we shall speak elsewhere. They (44)
264.12   depths] depth (44) [*see* 264*c–c*]
264.13   you will] you (44) [*see* 264*d–d*]
264.26   buckwheat] [*3-sentence footnote omitted*] (50)
264.31   of] off (50) [*see* 264*e–e*]
264.33   anew: their] anew. Their (50)
264.35   after; their] after. Their (50)
264.36   when] where (51) [*see* 264*f–f*]

HUBBARD, JOHN C. "Report from the Select Committee on Income and Property Tax; together with the Proceedings of the Committee, Minutes of Evidence, and Appendix," *Parliamentary Papers*, 1861, VII, ix–xx.

QUOTED: 817n–818n

NOTE: Hubbard, Chairman of the Select Committee, prepared "a Draft of Report," or "proposed Report," which was amended. The passage JSM quotes is followed by this sentence: "This estimate of the relative savings of the two classes is avowedly an arbitrary one, but the concession which it involves agrees with the average result of the scientific computations of Dr. Farr, and receives the approval of Mr. John Stuart Mill." (xiv) JSM omits the Section No. ("44."), and the subsidiary letters ("*b*," "*c*," and "*d*").

817.n11–12   property are] property (or, as they are briefly called, *spontaneous incomes*) are (xiv)

HUBER, VICTOR AIMÉ. *Die gewerblichen und wirtschaftlichen Genossenschaften der arbeitenden Klassen in England, Frankreich und Deutschland.* Tübingen: Laupp, 1860.

REFERRED TO: 782n–783n (quoted by Cherbuliez)

HUME, DAVID. "Essay on Money," in *Essays, Moral, Political, and Literary*, II. Edinburgh, 1752.

REFERRED TO: 511, 564–5

HURLY, JOHN. "Evidence taken before the Commissioners Appointed to Inquire into the Occupation of Land in Ireland," *Parliamentary Papers*, 1845, XX, 850–4 [Devon Report].

QUOTED: 318

IM-THURN, EDWARD. See *Historisch- geographisch- statistisches Gemälde der Schweiz*.

INGLIS, HENRY DAVID. "CONWAY, DERWENT." *Switzerland, the South of France, and the Pyrenees, in 1830.* 2 vols. Edinburgh: Constable, 1831.

QUOTED: 256-7, 257-8   REFERRED TO: 273

256.23 vines. . . . It] vines. But there are other and better evidences of the industry of the Zurichers, than merely seeing them late and early at work. It (33)
257.6   two, or three] two and four (33)
257.12 not] nor (33) [*see* 257*c-c*]
257.15 powder; every] powder. Every (33)
257.18 thing] twig (33) [*see* 257*d-d*]
257.23 possessions. . . . Generally] possessions. If a peasant owns from eight to fifteen cows, and land sufficient for their support, as well as for growing what is consumed in his own family, he is esteemed in good circumstances. He consumes whatever part of the produce of his dairy is needed at home; and he sells the surplus, chiefly the cheese, which he keeps till the arrival of the travelling merchant, who buys it for exportation. Generally (110)
257.26 wine. Flax is] [*7-sentence omission*] In enumerating the articles which the Grison of the Engadine is supplied with from his own property, I omitted to mention flax, which is (111) [*see* 257*e*]
257.29 tailor. The] tailor: the latter vocation is invariably exercised by the females of the house. [*paragraph*] [*14-sentence omission*] The (111-13)
257.31 devise. There] [*33 pages omitted*] (113-46)
257.34 an ear of rye will ripen, there it is to be found] rye will succeed, there it is cultivated (146)
258.2   attempted. In] [*jump backwards of 37 pages*] (146-109)

"IRISH LANDLORD, AN," "Twenty-five Years' Work in Ireland," *The Gardener's Chronicle and Agricultural Gazette*, 3 Dec., 1864, 1162-4.

REFERRED TO: 1077, 1078n, 1081, 1088

ISABELLA (of Castille). Referred to: 955n

JACOB. Referred to: 248

JOHNSON, SAMUEL. Referred to: 889

NOTE: reference not located, but Louis Guilhaud de Lavergne says, in a work quoted by JSM (*Economie rurale*, p. 32): "L'avantage du droit d'aînesse, disait ironiquement en Angleterre le docteur Johnson, c'est qu'il ne fait qu'un sot par famille."

JONES, REV. RICHARD. *An Essay on the Distribution of Wealth, and on the Sources of Taxation.* London: Murray, 1831.

QUOTED: 247-8, 249, 283   REFERRED TO: 302, 305, 311

248.11 England.] England.* [*footnote:*] Schmalz, Vol. II, p. 103. (50)
248.20 of] for (51) [*see* 248*k-k*]
283.7   kind, are] kind, whatever may be the form of their rents, are (146)
283.9   restraint. The] restraint. The causes of this peculiarity we shall have hereafter to point out. The (146)
283.11 territory, very] territory, whatever be the form of their rents, very (146)

283.14–15   disposition] disposition* [*footnote:*]* The actual disposition of the population to increase with extreme rapidity shews that these apprehensions are far from fanciful. See Jacob's Second Report. (68)
283.17   or more] or of more (68) [*see* 283*b*]
283.17   people.] people, and if the too great subdivision of their allotments is not guarded against in time, they will probably, in the course of a very few generations, be more miserable than their ancestors were as serfs, and will certainly be more hopeless and helpless in their misery, since they will have no landlord to resort to. (68)

JONNÈS, MOREAU DE. Referred to: 288n

JOYCE, ARTHUR J. "The Progress of Mechanical Invention," *Edinburgh Review*, LXXXIX (Jan., 1849), 47–83.

QUOTED: 125n

JUSSERAUD. Referred to: 147n

KAY, JOSEPH. *The Social Condition of the People in England and Europe; Shewing the Results of the Primary Schools, and of the Division of Landed Property, in Foreign Countries.* Vol. I. London: Longman, Brown, Green, & Longmans, 1850.

QUOTED: 260n, 264–6, 266–7, 286, 286n, 348

260.n1   [*Kay does not "quote" from Reichensperger, but summarizes*] (I, 126)
260.n9   Germany, &c., in] Germany, and the district of Siegenshen, in (I, 126)
265.23   land, there] land, which they formerly held as the Irish hold their little leaseholds, viz., from and at the will of owners of great estates, there (I, 138)
265.38   seen. The] seen. The little plots of land belonging to the peasantry lie side by side, undivided by hedge or ditch or any other kind of separation. The (I, 139)
266.3   portions. All] portions; and this very rivalry tends to improve all the more the system of tillage and the value of the crops. [*paragraph*] All (I, 139)
266.20   gross] *gross* (I, 114)
266.23   net] *net* (I, 114)
266.23   latter. . . . He] [*ellipsis indicates 2-page omission*] (I, 114–16)
266.24   of the land] of land (I, 116)
266.31–2   *as . . . prosperous*] as . . . prosperous (I, 117)
266.34   gross] *gross* (I, 117)
266.35   net] *net* (I, 117)
266.37   a great proprietor] great proprietors (I, 117)
267.6–7   (Grundsatz . . . Landwirthschaft)] [*in footnote*] (I, 117)
267.9   tenants. . . . This] [*ellipsis indicates omission of 1 sentence quoted from Thaer*] (I, 117–18)
267.11   farms." . . . "The] farms. [*paragraph*] But whether the *net* produce of the land cultivated by peasant proprietors be greater than its *net* produce when cultivated by great proprietors, or not, all accounts agree in showing that the cultivation and productiveness of the land has very much improved, and is in a state [of] progressive improvement, wherever trade in land has been rendered free, and wherever the peasants have been able to acquire. [*paragraph*] The (I, 118)

286.4 thirty. . . . Nor] [*ellipsis indicates omission of 2 sentences quoted below,* 348.18–26, *q.v.*] (I, 68)
286.10 evening] evenings (I, 68)
286.25 "Wherever . . . population."] [*in Kay this passage appears between two quotations from this part of JSM's* Principles (*which appeared in earlier editions in the next section*)] (I, 90)
286.28 upon undue] upon the undue (I, 90)
286.n12–13 we . . . proprietors] [*in capitals in* Source] (I, 266)
348.18–26 [*see* 286.4 *above*]
348.18 "So] Indeed, so (I, 68)
348.26 years."] years; but I mention them rather as symptoms, than as causes of the prudence and self-denial of the peasantry. (I, 68)

KEMMETER. Referred to: 150n

KENNEDY, J. P. *Digest of Evidence taken before Her Majesty's Commissioners of Inquiry into the State of the Law and Practice in respect to the Occupation of Land In Ireland.* Part I, II. Dublin: Thorn, 1847–8.

NOTE: J. P. Kennedy was Secretary to Lord Devon's Commission. See also Devon, Lord.

QUOTED: 315n, 330*f*, 998n, 999

315.n1 "It] In the north of Ireland this system is pretty generally either authorized or connived at by the landlord; and it (I, 1)
315.n4–5 rent."—*Digest . . . adds,* "the] rent; and the (I, 1)
315.n8 is in] is, therefore, in (I, 2)
315.n10 "The present] They [the landlords] do not perceive that the present (I, 2)
315.n11 *copyhold.*"] *copyhold,* which must decline in value to the proprietor in proportion as the practice becomes confirmed, because the sum required by the outgoing tenant must regulate ultimately the balance of gross produce which will be left to meet the payment of rent. (I, 2–3)
315.n12 there, if] there, however, if (I, 319)
315.n12 ejected] evicted (I, 319)
315.n14—316.n1 "The disorganized] They [the landlords] do not perceive that the disorganized (I, 3)
316.n2 tenant-right."] tenant-right, or that an established practice not only may, but must, erect itself finally into law; and any one who will take the pains to analyze this growing practice will soon perceive how inevitable that consequence must be in the present case, unless the practice itself be superseded by a substitute that shall put the whole question on a sound, equitable, and invigorating basis. (I, 4)
330.n4 "The] [*paragraph*] The (I, 570)
330.n9–10 cottier." . . . "Here] [*the two passages are contiguous in* Source, *with no indication of where the compiler's remarks begin*]
998.n6 "There are] Taking this basis for our calculating, and referring to Appendix, No. 95[(2)] (see page 564), we find that there are (I, 399)
998.n10 them." It is shown by calculation, "that] them. [*paragraph*] In the same table, No. 95[(2)], page 564, the calculation is put forward, showing that (I, 399)
998.n19–20 "and that] And the evidence leads to the conviction, that this result can be obtained not only without any permanent loss, but with a very large permanent gain; as it appears that 3,755,000 acres of waste land, not now giving a gross produce exceeding, on the average, 4*s.* per acre, may be made to yield a gross

produce of £6. per acre, being a total increase from £751,000 to £22,530,000, and that (I, 565)

KINGSLEY. Referred to: 1032

KNONAU, GEROLD MEYER VON. See *Historisch- geographisch- statistisches Gemälde der Schweiz.*

LABRUYÈRE. Referred to: 442

LAING, SAMUEL (THE ELDER). *Journal of a Residence in Norway, during the Years 1834, 1835, and 1836; made with a view to inquire into the moral and political economy of that country, and the condition of its inhabitants.*

QUOTED: 260^d, 281^c, 285

260.n25–6 cultivators. . . . Good] [*ellipsis indicates 4-sentence omission*] (37)
260.n30–1 *It . . . condition*] [*no italics*] (37)
260.n36 have only] only have (37)
260.n38 the smallest] the very smallest (38)
281.n10 restraint] self-restraint (21)
285.30 of the] of (19) [*see* 285^{i-i}]
285.35 as another] as at another (19) [*see* 285^j]

———— *Notes of a Traveller, on the Social and Political State of France, Prussia, Switzerland, Italy, and other parts of Europe, during the Present Century.* London: Longman, Brown, Green and Longmans, 1842.

QUOTED: 105^{r-r}, 261–2, 261n–262n, 284, 364–5

261.16 Frith] Firth (299) [*see* 261^{e-e}]
261.29 than] as (299) [*see* 261^{f-f}]
261.36 terms] returns (300) [*see* 261^{g-g}]
262.n4–5 cheese. One] cheese; and if the man comes from Gruyere, all that he makes is called Gruyere cheese, although made far from Gruyere. One (352)
284.18 husbandry" under small properties. "The] husbandry under this social construction. The 46)
364.37 and maize] or maize (457)
365.3 or the inclination] or inclination (457)

———— *Observations on the Social and Political State of the European People in 1848 and 1849; being the Second Series of the Notes of a Traveller.* London: Longman, Brown, Green, and Longmans, 1850.

QUOTED: 294n

LAING, SAMUEL (THE YOUNGER). *Atlas Prize Essay. National Distress; its Causes and Remedies.* London: Longman, Brown, Green, and Longmans, 1844.

QUOTED: 769–70, 1007–8   REFERRED TO: 1089

NOTE: 1009–10 in Appendix D is the same as 769–70

770.11   Barham,] Barham,* [*footnote:*] *Report of Children's Employment Commission in Mines and Colleries [*sic*], Appendix, pp. 758, 759. (40) [*see* 770.n4–5]

770.17   terms.' . . . With] terms. The tributor, likewise, entertains a hope—often realised if he is a good miner—that some fortunate contracts will put him on a parity as to station with the wealthier individuals near him, who have for the most part, at no remote period, occupied some of the lower steps of the ladder on which he himself stands. [*paragraph*] With (40–1) [*in* Source, *the quotation which JSM ends at* terms *is not closed; in the British Museum copy a diagonal pencil line is drawn after* terms]

770.20   houses;'] houses,"* [*footnote:*] *Report of Children's Employment Commission in Mines and Collieries, Appendix, p. 753.

770.21   saving] savings' (41) [*cf.* 770^{c–c} *and* 1008 savings]

770.22   miners.' "] miners;"* [*footnote:*]* Ibid. p. 753. [*text:*] and, finally, that they are, as a class, "a religious people, leading habitually excellent and religious lives, and giving conclusive evidence of the real influence of the great doctrines of revelation on their hearts, by their equanimity under suffering and privation, and in calmness and resignation when death is known to be inevitable."* [*footnote:*] *Ibid. p. 760.

LANDI. Referred to: 307n

LAVERGNE, LOUIS GABRIEL LÉONCE GUILHAUD DE. Referred to: 262n, 289

———— "Dénombrement de la population de 1856," *Journal des Économistes*, 2ᵉ Série, XIII (Feb., 1857), 225–33.

REFERRED TO: 437

———— *Économie rurale de la France depuis 1789.* 2nd ed. Paris: Guillaumin, 1861.

QUOTED: 152, 290n–291n, 293, 436, 442   REFERRED TO: 435, 437

152.17–23   "We . . . attained."] [translated from:] Il ne nous a pas fallu moins de soixante-dix ans pour défricher deux millions d'hectares de landes, supprimer la moitié de nos jachères, doubler nos produits ruraux, accroître la population de 30 pour 100, le salaire de 100 pour 100, la rente de 150 pour 100. A ce compte, il nous faudrait encore trois quarts de siècle pour arriver au point où en est aujourd'hui l'Angleterre. (59)

291.n10   doublé . . . Cette] doublé. Ce genre de progrès marchait aussi vite avant 1789, car Arthur Young dit que, vingt-cinq ans seulement avant son voyage, le salaire moyen n'était que de *seize sols* par jour, et qu'il avait par conséquent monté de 20 pour 100 dans cet intervalle. [*paragraph*] Cette (57–8)

293.17–23   "In . . . best."] [*translated from:*] Sur quelques points, dans les environs de Paris, par exemple, où les avantages de la grande culture deviennent manifestes, l'étendue des fermes tend à s'accroître. On voit plusieurs fermes se réunir pour n'en former qu'une, et des fermiers s'arrondir en louant des parcelles à des propriétaires différents. Ailleurs les fermes trop grandes tendent à se diviser comme les trop grandes propriétés. La culture va d'elle-même à l'organisation qui lui convient le mieux. (455)

436.n1   pp. 23 and 51.] [*the figure of one-third is quoted on p. 23 from Arthur*

Young, and queried as being high for 1789. On p. 51 it is Lavergne's own figure, applied to the current situation]
436.11–14 "enjoy . . . wealth."] [*translated from:*] Ceux-là jouissent quelquefois d'une aisance véritable. Leurs biens se divisent par des héritages, mais beaucoup d'entre eux ne cessent d'acheter, et, en fin de compte, ils tendent plus à s'élever qu'à descendre dans l'échelle de la richesse. (451)
436.21 "car] Suivant toute apparence, ces évaluations sont aujourd'hui plutôt au-dessus qu'au-dessous de la vérité, car (454)
442.27—443.4 "Thanks . . . capital."] [*translated from:*] Grâce à cette meilleure division du sol, qui permet de consacrer 6 millions d'hectares de plus à la nourriture des animaux, et par conséquent à la production des fumiers; grâce à des marnages, des irrigations, des assainissements, des labours mieux faits, le rendement de toutes les cultures s'est élevé. Le froment, qui ne donnait en moyenne que 8 hectolitres à l'hectare, semence déduite, en a donné 12, et comme en même temps l'étendue semée s'est accrue, la production totale a plus que doublé. Le même fait s'est présenté pour le bétail, qui, recevant deux fois plus d'aliments, a grandi à la fois en nombre et en qualité, de manière à doubler ses produits; les cultures industrielles se sont développées, la soie et le colza ont quintuplé, le sucre indigène a pris naissance, la récolte en vin a doublé. Il n'y a pas jusqu'au bois qui, mieux défendu contre la dent des animaux, mieux exploité en vue des nouveaux débouchés, n'ait augmenté ses revenus annuels, mais trop souvent aux dépens du capital. (52–3)

———— *Essai sur l'économie rurale de l'Angleterre, de l'Écosse et de l'Irlande.* 3rd ed. Paris: Guillaumin, 1858.

QUOTED: 280   REFERRED TO: 448, 1075n

280.3–14 "In . . . Paris?" [*translated from:*] Transportons-nous, au contraire, dans les grasses plaines de la Flandre, sur les bords du Rhin, de la Garonne, de la Charente, du Rhône; nous y retrouvons la petite culture, mais bien autrement riche et productive. Toutes les pratiques qui peuvent féconder la terre et multiplier les effets du travail y sont connues des plus petits cultivateurs et employées par eux, quelles que soient les avances qu'elles supposent. Sous leurs mains, des engrais abondants, recueillis à grands frais, renouvellent et accroissent incessamment la fertilité du sol, malgré l'activité de la production; les races de bestiaux sont supérieures, les récoltes magnifiques. Ici c'est le tabac, le lin, le colza, la garance, la betterave, ailleurs la vigne, l'olivier, le prunier, le mûrier, qui demandent pour prodiguer leurs trésors, un peuple de travailleurs industrieux. N'est-ce pas aussi à la petite culture qu'on doit la plupart des produits maraîchers obtenus à force d'argent autour de Paris? (127)

LEATHAM. Referred to: 550n

LE BRUN. Referred to: 274

LECLAIRE, EDMÉ-JEAN. "M. Leclaire of Paris," *Chambers's Edinburgh Journal,* n.s. IV (Sept., 1845), 193–6.

QUOTED: 770–2, 1011–14   REFERRED TO: 773–4, 1010, 1016–17

NOTE: 1011–12 in Appendix D is the same as 771–2. In 771.9–18, JSM is quoting the reviewer in *Chambers's*; in 771.21–772.3, he is quoting Leclaire in translation from *Chambers's*. Leclaire's pamphlet is entitled: *Des améliorations qu'il serait possible d'apporter dans le sort des ouvriers peintres en bâtiments, suivies des règlements d'administration et de répartition des bénéfices que produit le travail.*

771.11   arrangement] arrangements (193) [*see* 771*e–e*]
771.17   in, his] in, then, he says, notwithstanding the stability which he had
         introduced into his establishment, and notwithstanding the attachment and zeal
         of many of his workmen, his (193)
771.21   "will] 'Under the present system,' says he, in his pamphlet of 1842, 'a
         master tradesman has to endure not only the disquiet arising from bad debts
         and the failure of persons he may be connected with in business—losses from
         these causes, especially from the latter, are always trifling when the tradesman
         is possessed of prudence—but what to him is an incessant cause of torment, is
         the losses which arise from the misconduct of the workmen in his service. We
         have no fear of being accused of exaggeration when we say that he will (193–4)
771.23   capable of] able for (194)
771.26   livelihood. If] [*4 sentences omitted; the next sentence begins:*] Accordingly,
         if (194)
771.32   anxiety. This] anxiety. [*paragraph*] This (194)
1011.20–1   arrangements] arrangements (193) [*see* 771.11 *above*]

LEGOYT, A. "Recensement de la population de la France en 1846 et du
     mouvement de la population en Europe," *Journal des Économistes*,
     2ᵉ Série, XVII (May, 1847), 169–94.

QUOTED: 288n, 289n

NOTE: the tables on 288n and 289n are translated by JSM.

289.n18   34.39] 34,49 (176) [*see* 289n]

LEROUX. Referred to: 1028

LONGFIELD, MOUNTIFORT. "Address by the President, Hon. Judge Long-
     field, at the Opening of the Eighteenth Session," *Journal of the
     Statistical and Social Inquiry Society of Ireland*, IV, Part 24 (January,
     1865), 129–46; "Appendix to the foregoing Address," *ibid.*, 146–54.

REFERRED TO: 333, 1040, 1042, 1057, 1073–4, 1079–80

LOUIS XI (of France). Referred to: 296n, 1004

LOUIS XII (of France). Referred to: 296n, 1004

LOUIS XIV (of France). Referred to: 441, 442n, 945

LOUIS-PHILIPPE (of France). Referred to: 445, 449

LOYD. *See* Overstone.

LYELL, CHARLES. *Travels in North America with Geological Observations
     on the United States, Canada and Nova Scotia.* 2 vols. London:
     Murray, 1845.

QUOTED: 226n   REFERRED TO: 175n

McCULLOCH, JOHN RAMSAY. Referred to: 45, 267, 283, 752, 818n, 838,
     890n

—————— *A Dictionary, Geographical, Statistical, and Historical, of the Various Countries, Places, and Principal Natural Objects in the World.* 2 vols. London: Longman, Orme, Brown, Green, and Longmans, 1841.

QUOTED: 267, 445–6

445.41   "France] The truth is that France (I, 855)

446.2   imported;" and in 1822 the duty "was] imported; and had the duty been allowed to continue at this reasonable rate it could not have been justly objected to. But in 1822 the duty of 3 fr. was (I,855–6)

446.3   francs,] fr.! (I, 856)

446.4   importation."] importation of cattle, and been productive of many mischievous results. (I,856)

—————— *The Principles of Political Economy: with some inquiries respecting their application, and a sketch of the rise and progress of the science.* 3rd ed. Edinburgh: Tait, 1843.

QUOTED: 302, 889–90

302.3   "Wherever] The practice of letting lands by proportional rents, or, as it is there termed, on the *métayer* principle, is very general on the continent; and wherever (471)

302.5   poverty."] [*3-sentence footnote omitted*] (471)

889.33   station] situation (264)

—————— *On the Succession to Property Vacant by Death.* London, 1848.

REFERRED TO: 890n

—————— *A Treatise on the Principles and Practical Influence of Taxation and the Funding System.* London: Longman, Brown, Green, and Longmans, 1845.

QUOTED: 859*f*–*f*

859.n12–13   increase. . . . In] [*ellipsis indicates omission of 3 paragraphs and a footnote*] (227–9)

859.n13   freehold, the duty is] freehold the stamp on the lease was the same as on the release, so that the duty was and still is (279)

859.n14   while on the] while in the (279)

859.n16   notice. It] notice [*paragraph*] It (279)

859.n17   this conveyance] this double (or doubly-stamped) conveyance (279)

859.n18   and the] and it is important to observe that the (279)

859.n21   "eighty times] The rate of the *ad valorem* duty, therefore, is 80 times (280)

859.n25   stamp duties in] stamp-duties, therefore, in (276)

860.n1   "it] And such being the case, it (281)

McDONNELL. Referred to: 1074

MACGREGOR. Referred to: 236n

MACMICKING, ROBERT. *Recollections of Manilla and the Philippines, during 1848, 1849, and 1850.* London: Bentley, 1851.

QUOTED: 774n

NOTE: JSM spells his name "McMicking".

MAINE, HENRY JAMES SUMNER. *Ancient Law: its Connection with the Early History of Society, and its Relation to Modern Ideas.* London: Murray, 1861.

REFERRED TO: 219n

MALTHUS, THOMAS ROBERT. Referred to: 67n, 154, 155n, 156n, 158, 162, 345, 346, 353, 359, 370, 570, 576, 581, 753

———— *An Inquiry into the Nature and Progress of Rent, and the Principles by which it is Regulated.* London: Murray, 1815.

REFERRED TO: 419

———— *Principles of Political Economy considered with a view to their Practical Application.* London: 1820.

QUOTED: 343n

343.n17 "a] And the result was, that, instead of an increase of population exclusively, a considerable portion of their increased real wages was expended in a (253–4)

MASON, WILLIAM SHAW. *A Statistical Account or Parochial Survey of Ireland.* Dublin: Cumming, 1814ff.

REFERRED TO: 1076

MAUPILLÉ, LÉON. See Bertin, Amédée.

MAZARIN. Referred to: 441n—442n

MEYER VON KNONAU, GEROLD. See *Historisch- geographisch- statistisches Gemälde der Schweiz.*

MICHELET, J. *Le peuple.* Paris: Hachette, Paulin, 1846.

QUOTED: 279n, 296n, 441n—442n, 1004

NOTE: 1004 in Appendix C is the same as 296.n5–24.

279.n21 apperçoit] aperçoit (2)
296.n5   Aux] [*paragraph*] Cette grande histoire, si peu connue, offre ce caractère singulier: aux (5)
296.n9   terre. Ces] [*3-sentence paragraph omitted*] (5–6)
296.n18 sol,] sol*, [*footnote:*] *Voir Froumenteau: Secret des finances de France (1581), Preuves, surtout p. 397–8.
296.n20 brulée] brûlée (6)
441.n8   journaliers. . . . Je] journaliers. Par quels incroyables efforts purent-ils, à

travers les guerres et les banqueroutes du grand roi, du régent, garder ou
reprendre les terres que nous avons vues plus haut se trouver dans leur mains
au dix-huitième siècle, c'est ce qu'on ne peut s'expliquer. [*paragraph*] Je (8)
442.n2–3 , réimprimé . . . Economistes] [*drawn from an omitted 4-sentence footnote to* Boisguillebert] (8)

MILL, HARRIET. Referred to: 1026–37

MILL, JAMES. *Commerce Defended. An Answer to the arguments by which
Mr. Spence, Mr. Cobbett, and others, have attempted to prove that
Commerce is not a Source of National Wealth.* London: Baldwin,
1808.

REFERRED TO: 576

———— *Elements of Political Economy.* 3rd ed. London: Baldwin,
Cradock, and Joy, 1826.

QUOTED: 589–90   REFERRED TO: 27^b, 28n, 818n

589.26   "It] If the cloth and the corn, each of which required 100 days' labour in
Poland, required each 150 days' labour in England, it (120)
590.15–16   "If," . . . "while] If, on the other hand, while (121)

———— *The History of British India.* Vol. III. London: Baldwin, Cradock,
and Joy, 1817.

QUOTED: 321–2

MILL, JOHN STUART. *Essays on Some Unsettled Questions of Political
Economy.* London: Parker, 1844.

QUOTED: 589–90, 596–9, 632n–634n, 851–4, 855–6   REFERRED TO: 49n, 701, 589n

NOTE: the full collation of these passages will be found in Vol. IV of this edition,
Essays on Economics and Society.

589.6   "it] It (2)
596.28   the other] another (7)
596.29   than the] than, it is self-evident, the (7)
596.32   "Suppose that] Suppose, for example, that (6)
597.7   of cloth] of broad cloth (7)
597.15   20. The] 20. [*paragraph*] The (8)
597.18   exchange] exchangeable (10)
597.21   at. Let] at. [*paragraph*] Let (10)
597.40   exchange] exchangeable (10)
598.6   suppositions] supposition (11)
598.7   has] had (11) [*see* 598^{b-b}]
598.15   this] that (11) [*see* 598^{c-c}]
598.16   would] could (11)
598.34   for one another] for another [*sic*] (12) [*altered to correct reading in 2nd
ed. (1874) of* Essays]
598.36   without further alteration] as they are (12)
598.38   exchange] exchangeable (12)
598.41   articles] article (12)

599.17   exchange] exchangeable (13)
599.33   that] one (13)
599.40   be a] be in a (14) [see 599ᵈ]
632.n7   yard.] yard.* [footnote:] *The figures used are of course arbitrary, having no reference to any existing prices. (14)
633.ₙ14   diminish. As] diminish. Although the increased exportation of cloth takes place at a lower price, and the diminished importation of linen at a higher, yet the total money value of the exportation would probably increase, that of the importation diminish. As (15)
634.n6   gainers. They] gainers. If they do not choose to increase their consumption of cloth, this does not prevent them from being gainers. They (17) [as in the previous entry, the omitted sentence ends with the same word as the previous sentence; both may be copying errors]
851.1   exports, we may, in] exports, for instance, we may, under (21)
851.9   "suppose] Suppose (21)
851.15   before. Or] before. It may diminish it in such a ratio, that the money value of the quantity consumed will be exactly the same as before. Or (22) [see note to 634.n6 above]
851.25   in some] under some (22)
851.35   total value] total money value (22)
851.35   would] will (22) [see 851ᵇ⁻ᵇ]
852.9   while] which [sic] (23) [altered in ink in JSM's own copy of the Essays (Somerville College, Oxford) to the reading of the Principles, which is reproduced in the 2nd ed. (1874) of the Essays]
852.10   the fall] consequent fall (23)
853.7   exports;] exports*: [7-sentence footnote omitted] (24–5)
853.15   "In any case, whatever] It is certain, however, that whatever (25)
853.18–19   exist." . . . "We] exist. Moreover, the imposition of such a tax frequently will, and always may, expose a country to lose this branch of its trade altogether, or to carry it on with diminished advantage, in consequence of the competition of untaxed exporters from other countries, or of the domestic producers in the country to which it exports. Even on the most selfish principles, therefore, the benefit of such a tax is always extremely precarious. [paragraph] 5. We
854.19   appropriate] be almost sure of appropriating (27)
855.9   "into] With a view to practical legislation, therefore, duties on importation may be divided into (27)
855.11   not. The] not. [paragraph] The (28)
855.33   means which] means of gain which (28)
855.38   linen] cloth (29)
855.39   cloth] linen (29)
855.40   linen] cloth (29)
856.5–6   when . . . commodities] so long as any other kind of taxes on commodities are retained, as a source of revenue (29)
856.6   little objectionable] unobjectionable (29)
856.6   too] moreover (29)
856.12   the revenue duties] the duties (29)
856.13–14   corresponding revenue duties] corresponding duties (29)
856.14   those] these (29)

——— "The Positive Philosophy of Auguste Comte," *Westminster Review*, LXXXIII (Apr., 1865), 339–405, and "Later Speculations of Auguste Comte," *ibid.*, LXXXIV (July, 1865), 1–42; republished together as *Auguste Comte and Positivism*. London: Trübner, 1865.

REFERRED TO: 1041

———— "Report from the Select Committee on Bank Acts; together with the Proceedings of the Committee, Minutes of Evidence, Appendix and Index," *Parliamentary Papers*, 1857 (Sess. 2), X.i, 177–206.

QUOTED: 680n

680.n1 "the double action of drains,"] Those who framed the Act [of 1844] do not seem to have adverted to what may be called the double action of drains. (179)

———— Unheaded articles on French agriculture. *Morning Chronicle*, 11, 13, and 16 Jan., 1847, pp. 4,4,4.

QUOTED: 434–51

NOTE: The MS of this Appendix consists of pasted-up extracts from the articles in the *Morning Chronicle*, with introductory matter and linking passages added in ink (all on rectos), and notes added in ink (on versos); occasionally alterations are made in ink on the columns. In most cases, therefore, the Source and MS readings are the same (and are so recorded in the variant notes to this Appendix, 431–51 above); consequently, when there is a variant between the Source and the 7th edition, there is usually a variant recorded in the variant notes: the cross-references between these variants and the list below are indicated below in square brackets after the Source reading. The page reference of the Source is omitted, as it is always the same (i.e., 4).

The arrangement of materials in the MS is as follows:[1] I: 433.1—434.5 In . . . France. *ink* (1v–2r); 434.6—438.7 The . . . increase of nearly [nearly *cancelled in ink*] *news* (2r–5r); 438.7–36 more than . . . diminished. *ink* (5r–6r); 438.37—439.17 It . . . subdivision. *news* (6r); 439.18–20 We . . . extraordinary *ink* [*clipping cut at hyphen division of* extra-/ordinary *so* ordinary *cancelled in ink*] (6r); 439.20–36 number . . . properties. *news* (6r); II: 439.37—442.11 We . . . favourable. *news* (7r–9r); 442.11–14 Compare . . . returns *ink* (9r); 442.14—444.24 of the rate . . . farming. *news* (9r–10r); III: 444.25—451.35 The . . . arrondisement." *news* (11r–15r); 451.36–9 We . . . France. *ink* (16r).

The passages at I: 439.18–20 and III: 451.36–9, although written in ink, are similar to the newspaper text (see variants below). Mill added footnote indicators in ink where necessary, and the appropriate notes (to the 1st edition) on the verso opposite, except for 446n, which appeared in the text of the newspaper article; 442.13, the MS has a note to "now.", which reads "Vide supra, p." (evidently a reference to the passage also noted at 448n), not reproduced in the 1st or any later edition. The MS corrections of a typographical error and two errors in French accents in the *Morning Chronicle* are here silently accepted.

434.22   collectors'] collector's
435.26   think as] think is as [*see* 435[b]]
435.29   acre. The] acre: the [*see* 435[c–c]]
435.39–40   acres—on that of] acres, of [*see* 435[d–d]]
436.1   only a third] much less than half [*see* 436[e–e]]
436.2   third] half [*see* 436[f–f]]
436.5–22   [*see* 436[g–g]]
436.26–7   that this] that it [*see* 436[h–h]]
437.17   increased] increases [*see* 437[i–i]]
438.1   had in 1846] has now [*see* 438[k–k]]

---

[1]The following abbreviations are used here: *ink* = material added in ink by JSM; *news* = pasted-in newspaper columns; I, II, III are JSM's headings for the separate articles from the *Morning Chronicle*; the page references are to the present edition; the folio references are to MS Vol. III.

438.7–8   of more . . . Let] of nearly 60,000. Let [Quarterly Review *also reads* 60,000]
438.8   600,000] 60,000
438.9   300,000] 30,000
438.12   consulted . . . on,] turned a few pages back
438.13   cause sufficient] cause amply sufficient
438.13   considerable portion of this] much larger
438.37   It] But it [But *cut off in* MS *clipping, and* i *altered to* I *in ink*]
439.12   among those] among these [*see* 439^{m-m}]
439.18   We . . . subject] Long as this article is, we cannot close it
439.25   against] *against* [*see* 439^{n-n}]
439.32   not] *not* [*see* 439^{o-o}]
439.33   poor] *poor* [*altered in* MS *clipping to roman*]
439.34   does] *does* [*see* 439^{p-p}]
439.35   which some] which, also, some [*altered in ink in* MS *clipping*]
439.36   properties. We] properties. [*paragraph*] We need not trouble our readers any further with the *Quarterly* reviewer; but the state of French agriculture, and the social condition of France, as connected with it, are subjects on which we have much more to say; and we shall take an early opportunity of attempting to show what is really amiss in these matters, and to what causes it is imputable. [*end of article*]
439.37   have shown] showed on Monday [*altered in ink in* MS *clipping*]
440.1   best authorities] best living authorities [*see* 440^q]
440.2   and from] and that from [*see* 440^r]
440.5   represent them to be] would represent them [*see* 440^{s-s}]
440.8–9   earth. [*paragraph*] We] [*3-sentence omission*] [*cut out of* MS *clipping*]
441.2–3   France. [*paragraph*] That] [*4-sentence omission*] [*see* 441^t]
441.21   the general] the food and general [*see* 441^u]
441n   [*not in* Source]
442.11–13   Compare . . . now.] While now, "the classes of the population who have only their wages, and who for that reason are the most exposed to indigence, are much better provided with the requisites of food, lodging, and clothing than they were at the beginning of the century. The fact may be established by the testimony of all who have a personal recollection of the earlier of the two epochs. If there could be a doubt on the subject, it might be dissipated by consulting aged cultivators and workpeople, as I have myself done in various localities, without meeting with a single opposing testimony: we may also refer to the facts collected on the subject by an exact observer, M. Villermé."—(From a recent work by an intelligent writer, "Recherches sur les Causes de l'Indigence, par A. Clément.") [*cf.* 290n]
442.13   M. Rubichon's] [*paragraph*] M. Rubichon's
443.26   millions are held only by] millions only are held by [*see* 443^{w-w}]
443.30–1   resident, a primitive relationship] resident; a sort of patriarchal relationship [*altered in ink in* MS *clipping*]
444.1   said by] said somewhere in these volumes, by [*see* 444^x]
444.6   frugality] prudence [*see* 444^{y-y}]
444.7–8   savings, . . . purpose, are] savings are [*see* 444^{z-z}]
444.21–2   the *grande*] *la grande* [*see* 444^{a-a}]
444.22   it. But] it. The thing would soon be done if the love of industrial progress should ever supplant in the French mind the love of national glory, or if the desire of national glorification should take that direction. But [*see* 444^b]
444.23   be little] be no [*see* 444^{c-c}]
444.24   farming.] farming. [*paragraph*] In one article more we hope to dispose of the remainder of the subject. [*end of article*]
445.10   (five ounces) "of meat per] (*quære* five ounces) per [*altered in ink in* MS *clipping*]

MIRABEAU. Referred to: 442

Moniteur. See De Persigny.

MONTESQUIEU, CHARLES DE SECONDAT, BARON DE. *De l'esprit des loix ou du rapport que les loix doivent avoir avec la constitution de chaque gouvernement, les moeurs, le climat, la religion, le commerce, &c. à quoi l'auteur a ajouté des recherches nouvelles sur les loix romaines touchant les successions, sur les loix françoises, & sur les loix féodales.* Geneva: Barillot, [1748].

QUOTED: 501   REFERRED TO: 503

NOTE: There is no indication which edition JSM used. Reference here is to the 1st edition.

501.19   "Il] Mais il (I,294)

MOOREHOUSE. Referred to: 787

MORAN. Referred to: 1086–8, 1090–1

MOUNIER, M. L. *De l'agriculture en France, d'après les documents officiels. Avec des remarques par M. Rubichon.* 2 vols. Paris: Guillaumin, 1846.

REFERRED TO: 433ff.

MUGGERIDGE, RICHARD M. "Hand-Loom Weavers. Report of the Commissioners," *Parliamentary Papers*, 1841, X.

QUOTED: 381–2

381.22   lead] leads (38)
381.24   recreation. There] recreation. Beyond the necessity imposed upon him of yielding a given quantity of labour to produce a given amount of earnings, he has little, if any, control. In the proportion he is willing to sacrifice the one, he can dispense with the other, and idleness carries with it no punishment, beyond the restrictions of enjoyment which arise from its being unremunerated. There (38)
381.26   mulcted of his] mulct his (38)

MUSHET, ROBERT. *A Series of Tables, Exhibiting the Gain and Loss to the Fundholder, Arising from the Fluctuations in the Value of the Currency, from 1800 to 1821.* 2nd ed., corrected. London: Baldwin, Cradock and Joy, 1821.

REFERRED TO: 568

NADAUD. Referred to: 1034

NAPOLEON. Referred to: 627n

NEWMARCH, WILLIAM. "Appendix, No. 39. Paper presented by Mr. Newmarch, 5 June 1857. Bills of Exchange (Inland Bills), England and Wales," in "Report from the Select Committee on Bank Acts; together with the proceedings of the Committee, minutes of evidence, appendix and index," *Parliamentary Papers*, 1857 (Sess. 2), X.ii, 324–7.

REFERRED TO: 550

———— *See also* Tooke, Thomas. *History of Prices*. Vols. V and VI.

NICHOLLS. Referred to: 996n

NIEBUHR, B. G. *The Life and Letters of Barthold George Niebuhr, with Essays on his Character and Influence, by the Chevalier Bunsen, and Professors Brandis and Loebell*. 2 vols. London: Chapman and Hall, 1852.

QUOTED: 271n

NORMAN. Referred to: 665

ŒDIPUS. Referred to: 445

ŒRSTED. Referred to: 42

OLMSTED. Referred to: 247

OVERSTONE (LOYD). Referred to: 665

OWEN. Referred to: 203, 775, 786

PAPINI. Referred to: 307n

PARENNIN. Referred to: 168

PARKER. Referred to: 1029–30, 1032–7

PASSY, HIPPOLYTE PHILBERT. "Des changements survenus dans la situation agricole du Département de l'Eure depuis l'année 1800," *Journal des Économistes*, I (Jan. [?], 1842), 44–66.

QUOTED: 292–3   REFERRED TO: 302n, 449, 450

293.1–16 "The . . . them."] [*translated from:*] [*paragraph*] L'exemple du département de l'Eure atteste, au surplus, qu'il n'existe pas, comme quelques écrivains l'ont supposé, entre les formes de la propriété et celles de la culture des liens qui tendent invinciblement à les assimiler. Nulle part les mutations foncières n'y ont influé sensiblement sur la distribution des exploitations. S'il est ordinaire dans les communes à petites cultures que des terres appartenant à la même personne soient affermées à de nombreux locataires, il n'est pas rare non plus, dans les lieux où règne la grande culture, qu'un fermier se charge des terres de plusieurs propriétaires. Dans les plaines du Vexin surtout, beaucoup de cultivateurs actifs et riches ne se contentent pas d'une seule ferme; d'autres, aux terres du faire-valoir principal réunissent toutes celles du voisinage qu'ils peuvent louer, et se composent ainsi des exploitations parmi lesquelles il en est qui atteignent ou dépassent 200 hectares. Plus les domaines se démembrent, plus ces sortes d'arrangements se propagent; et comme ils satisfont à toutes les convenances, il est vraisemblable que le temps ne fera que les confirmer. (63)

——— *Des systèmes de culture et de leur influence sur l'économie sociale.* Paris: Guillaumin, 1846.

QUOTED: 145n—147n, 151n   REFERRED TO: 437n

145.n27   contesté. En] contesté. [*paragraph*] En (116)
146.n6   35,] 35*, [*footnote:*] *D'après les documents statistiques publiés par le ministre de l'intérieur, troisième publication officielle. Il faut dans ces sortes d'évaluation s'en tenir à mesurer les quantités de bétail par les surfaces cultivées, puisque ce sont celles-là seules dont les animaux entretiennent la fertilité. (117) [*cf. next entry*]
146.n6–8   énorme. (D'après . . . officielle.) Il] énorme. Il (117) [*cf. previous entry*]
146.n24–25   (D'après . . . i.)] [*in footnote*] (118)
147.n5   terres. Dans] terres. [*paragraph*] Dans (119)
147.n24   s'appercevra] s'apercevra (120)

PEEL. Referred to: 567, 589n, 660, 857, 1031, 1069

PÉRIER, AUGUSTE VICTOR LAURENT CASIMIR. *Les sociétés de coopération: la consommation, la crédit, la production, l'amélioration morale et intellectuelle par l'association.* Paris: Dentu, 1864.

REFERRED TO: 785n

PHEIDIAS. Referred to: 16

PIM, JONATHAN. Referred to: 1074, 1079, 1088, 1092–3

——— *On the Connection between the Condition of Tenant Farmers and the Laws respecting the Ownership and Transfer of Land in Ireland.* Dublin, 1853.

REFERRED TO: 1074n

——— *The Land Question in Ireland.* Dublin: 1867.

REFERRED TO: 1074n

PITMAN. Referred to: 789n

PLATO. Referred to: 969

PLUMMER, JOHN. "Co-operation in Lancashire and Yorkshire," *Companion to the Almanac; or, Year-Book of General Information for 1862*, bound with *The British Almanac of the Society for the Diffusion of Useful Knowledge for the Year of Our Lord 1862*. London: Knight, [1863.]

QUOTED: 790   REFERRED TO: 785n–786n

POOR LAWS. "Foreign Communications: Appendix F to the Report from Her Majesty's Commissioners for inquiring into the Administration and Practical Operation of the Poor Laws," *Parliamentary Papers*, 1834, XXXIX.

QUOTED: 236n, 286, 286–7, 347–50, 347*b*

NOTE: Nassau Senior's "Preface," is on pp. iii–cii; also published separately, *Statement of the Provision for the Poor, and of the Condition of the Labouring Classes, in a Considerable Portion of America and Europe. Being the Preface to the Foreign Communications Contained in the Appendix to the Poor-Law Report.* London: Fellowes, 1835. In the following places JSM omits page or section references from his Source: 236.n2, 236.n7, 236.n13, 236.n15, 236.n18, 347.13 (reference to p. 697, where the Norwegian Report is given at length), 347.18, 347.22, 348.3.

287.6   horse and] horse or (268)
287.8   Denmark. Indeed] Denmark. He purchases cheap (all present charges on the land taken into consideration), and his way of living being very economical. Indeed (268)
347.10   Thus] [*paragraph*] Thus (xxxix)
347.20   words] word (xxxix)
347.30   "The] But the (xxxiii) [*the* minister *is Lord Erskine*]
347.31   The] [*paragraph*] The (xxxiii)

PRESCOTT, WILLIAM H. *History of the Conquest of Peru, with a Preliminary View of the Civilization of the Incas*. 2 vols. London: Bentley, 1847.

REFERRED TO: 975

PROUDHON. Referred to: 1027, 1031

PUPIKOFER, J. A. See *Historisch- geographisch- statistisches Gemälde der Schweiz.*

QUETELET, LAMBERT ADOLPHE JACQUES. *Sur l'homme et le développement de ses facultés, ou essai de physique sociale*. Vol. I. Paris: Bachelier, 1835.

QUOTED: 288n

NOTE: The table is translated by JSM, who omits the latter half of the table, drawn by Quetelet from Charles Dupin, *Forces productives*, which also includes figures for Prussia (as distinct from Rhenish Prussia) and Russia. (292)

RAE, JOHN. *Statement of Some New Principles on the Subject of Political Economy, Exposing the fallacies of the system of Free Trade, and of some other doctrines mentioned in the "Wealth of Nations."* Boston: Hilliard, Gray and Co., 1834.

QUOTED: 129, 162–3, 164–70, 869n–870n   REFERRED TO: 918

129.19   "If] But, as a man can only do one thing at once, if (164)
129.20   many different] these several (164)
129.21   be idle] lie idle (164)
129.25   employment. The] [*6-sentence omission*] (164–5) [*see* 129^i]
129.28   them.] them; being sooner exhausted they pass to a more quickly returning order. (165)
129.29–30   construction.] construction; the effective desire of accumulation carries them on to a class corresponding to its own strength. (165)
163.6   others, tend"] others, also tend (123)
163.17   train. For] train. [*paragraph*] For (123)
164.23—165.1   this state] it (131)
165.2   governed. . . . . . Besides] governed [*ellipsis indicates 4-page omission*] (131–5)
165.8   it." [*paragraph*] For instance: "Upon] it. [*paragraph*] These deficiencies in the motives to exertion, and in the habits of action of the Indian, serve to account for the condition of the remnants of the tribes scattered over the North American continent, in situations where they are in contact with the white man. There is a general similarity throughout, that will, I believe, render an example, taken from one part of the continent, sufficiently illustrative of the state of the whole. [*paragraph*] Upon (136)
165.16   it in] in it (136)
166.6   to more] to much more (137)
166.14   Indian, succeeding] Indian again, succeeding (137)
166.26   dyers," &c.] dyers, &c. (141)
166.37   hungry. . . .] [*ellipsis indicates 1-page omission*] (140–1)
166.38   These fathers, says Ulloa, have] "These fathers," says Ulloa, "have (141)
167.2   lost." "But] [*3 sentences from Charlevoix omitted*] (141)
167.3   superintendence," says Charlevoix, "and] superintendence, and (141)
167.5   embarrassed. It] embarrassed. This proceeds from three defects, of which the Indians have not yet been corrected, their improvidence, indolence* and want of economy, so that, it [*footnote:*] *Indolence and improvidence are, in our system, reduced to one defect. Indolence is, the not laying out present labor to secure future abundance. Improvidence, the squandering present abundance, in disregard of future coming want. They both proceed from the predominance of the present over the future, the low strength of the effective desire of accumulation. (141)
167.6   reserve to themselves] reserve themselves (141)
167.8   life."] life." (141) [i.e., *Rae's quotation also ends here*]
167.17   desire] strength (151)
167.22   fabrics.] fabrics.* [*footnote:*] *La Harp, Vol. 8. p. 289. Lettres édifiantes, Vol. X. p. 107.
167.23   year. A] year. [*paragraph*] A (152)
167.31   lands,] land, (152)
168.3   empire.] empire.* [*footnote:*] *Staunton, Vol. 2, p. 244. Ellis, p. 268 and 316; the best proof perhaps is in the premiums offered for their cultivation. See Lettres édifiantes, Vol. xi. p. 525. (152)

168.13–15   indeed, (who seems to have been one of the most intelligent of the Jesuits, and spent a long life among the Chinese of all classes,) asserts] [*JSM interpolates the parenthesis, summarizing from Rae's note to 153, the relevant part of which reads:*] The father Parennin seems to have been one of the most intelligent of the Jesuits, and had the very best opportunities for observation, having spent a long life among the Chinese of all classes. His testimony is much more to be depended on, concerning such a fact, than that of passing travellers, whose cursory observations extend only to what may be seen on the exterior of the habitations.
168.21   they were] they are (153)
168.27   soil of the] soil of a variety of the (154)
168.42   forced] found (154)
169.3   rivers,] waters (154)
169.19   content to] content, as we say, to
869.n1   "Were] Thus, were (369)
869.n7   some commodity] some other commodity (370)
869.n9–10   of legislators. . . . . it] of the legislators of the distant countries, it (370)
869.n17—870.n1   of society] of women in the society (371)
870.n3   If [*paragraph*] If (371)
870.n10–11   them." The net . . . "would] them. If we suppose the yearly expense of obtaining the pearls, and of collecting the duty on them, to amount to twenty thousand pounds, there would then remain to the legislator, a clear annual revenue from this source of eighty thousand pounds. This revenue would (371)

RAPP. Referred to: 202

RATHBONE. Referred to: 1091

RAU, KARL HEINRICH. *Traité d'économie nationale.* Trans. F. de Kemmeter, from the 3rd. ed. Brussels: Hauman, 1839.

QUOTED: 288n, 292   REFERRED TO: 150

292.21–7   "The . . . divided."] [*translated from:*] L'habitude de ne pas diviser les propriétés, et l'opinion que cela est avantageux se sont tellement conservées en Flandre, qu'aujourd'hui encore, lorsqu'un paysan vient à mourir laissant plusieurs enfants, ceux-ci ne songent pas à se partager son patrimoine, bien qu'il ne soit ni majoratisé ou donné en fidéicommis; et ils préfèrent le vendre en bloc, et s'en partager le prix, parce qu'ils le considèrent comme un joyau qui perd de sa valeur lorsqu'il est divisé. Voy. Schwertz, *Landwirthschaftliche Mittheilungen*, I, 185. (334n)

————— *Ueber die Landwirthschaft der Rheinpfalz und insbesondere in der Heidelberger Gegend.* Heidelberg: Winter, 1830.

QUOTED: 265, 291n   REFERRED TO: 266

NOTE: in George Grote's copy of this work (University of London Library) the three passages quoted by Mill have pencil marks drawn beside them in the margin; that on pp. 15–6 has "Good farming" written beside it in a hand that could be JSM's; that on p. 20 also has a penciled "X" beside it.
265.9–20   "The . . . harm."] [*translated from:*] Die Unverdrossenheit der Landleute, die man das ganze Jahr und den ganzen Tag in Thaetigkeit sieht, und die darum nicht muessig gehen, weil sie die Arbeiten gut eintheilen, und zu jeder

Zeit eine passende Beschaeftigung wissen, ist eben so anerkannt, als ihr Eifer in der Benutzung aller sich darbietenden Umstaende, in der Ergreifung des dargebotenen Neuen, woferne es sich nuetzlich erweisst, ja in der Ausspaehung neuer, vorteilhafterer Methoden gelobt werden muss. Leicht ueberzeugt man sich, dass der Bauer der hiesigen Gegend viel ueber sein Geschaeft nachgedacht hat, er weiss Gruende anzugeben fuer sein Verfahren, wenn sie auch nicht statthaft seyn sollten, er weiss die Zahlenverhaeltnisse so bestimmt mitzuteilen, als sie beim Mangel geordneter Aufzeichnung, im Gedaechtnis behalten werden koennen, er richtet sich in der Wahl der Fruechte nach den Preisen, er achtet auf allgemeine Zeiterscheinungen, von denen er Nutzen oder Schaden zu erkennen glaubt. (15–16)

291.n25   Sie] Die Kost kann auch auf 10 Kr. angeschlagen werden, da sie (20)
291.n25   heutigen] heutigens (20)
291.n27–30   "Such . . . increased.] [*translated from:*] Bekanntlich ist eine solche Erhoehung des Lohnes, die man nicht nach dem Geldbetrage, sondern nach der Menge von nothwendigen und nuetzlichen Guetern bemessen muss, welche der Arbeitsmann sich verschaffen kann, ein Zeichen, dass die vorhandene Capitalmasse sich vermehrt hat. (18)

RAUMER, VON. Referred to: 329, 995

REICHENSPERGER. Referred to: 260n, 266

REMQUET. Referred to: 779n

REVANS, JOHN. *Evils of the State of Ireland: their Causes and their Remedy—a Poor Law.* 2nd ed. London: Hatchard, 1837.

QUOTED: 317–18

317.17   fairly be] be fairly (10)
317.23   is most] is the most (10)
317.25   paying; and consequently] paying; consequently (10) [*see* 317[i–i]]
318.19   defer ejectment.] defer what must sooner or later happen—ejectment. (11)

———— *A Per Centage Tax on Domestic Expenditure, to Supply the Whole of the Public Revenue: the Customs, Excise, Stamp, Legacy, Assess, Income, and all other Government Taxes, and Tax Establishments; together with the Coast Guard and Revenue Cruisers to be Abolished.* London: Hatchard and Son, 1847.

REFERRED TO: 832–3

RHAM, REV. WILLIAM LEWIS. *Outlines of Flemish Husbandry.* In Burke, John L. (ed.) *British Husbandry.* Vol. III. Society for the Diffusion of Useful Knowledge: Library of Useful Knowledge. London: Baldwin and Cradock, 1840.

QUOTED: 145n, 267–70   REFERRED TO: 279

145.n7   greater. After] [*1-page omission*] (59–60)

145.n11–12   greater. It] greater; an ordinary cow fed on young clover will give at three milkings, for the first three months after calving, from fifteen to eighteen quarts per day, which will produce 1¼ lb. of butter, that is nearly 9 lbs. of butter per week. Where the number of cows is great, the average is much less, because when there are only two or three cows, a deficiency in one of them is immediately noticed; the cow is got rid of, and a better one purchased. In a great number, there are always a few inferior cows, and a lower average is the consequence. It (60)
267.28   sands] sand (11) [see 267^{b-b}]
267.29   sand] sands (11) [see 267^{c-c}]
268.3–4   itself:" . . . "and] itself: but there is a heap of dung and compost forming. The urine of the cow is collected in a small tank, or perhaps in a cask sunk in the earth; and (11)
268.5   around. . . . If] [1½-page omission] (11–12)
268.6   pure] poor (12) [see 268^{d-d}]
268.9   slight] certain (13) [see 268^{e-e}]
268.17   plants. . . . After] [ellipsis indicates ⅔-page omission] (13)
268.17   After] [paragraph] After (13)
268.30   The] Speaking with great impartiality, we may safely assert, that notwithstanding this [comparative conservatism of Flemish farmers], the (3)
268.31   or a moderate soil] on a moderate scale (3) [see 268^{g-g}]
269.1   peasant. But] peasant; but (3)
269.5   Flemings,"] Flemings; and a detailed account of the mode of cultivation, especially of light lands, in Flanders, cannot fail to be both interesting and instructive. (3)
269.10   "When] "Where (73)
269.14   family;" children soon beginning "to] family; and children, instead of being a burden, soon begin to (73)
269.21   Suppose] Supposing (73) [see 269^{i-i}]
269.22–3   manage;" . . . "if] [1 page summarized] (73–4)
269.23   "if] [paragraph] If (74)
269.37–9   Land." . . . "In] [½ page summarized] (75)
269.39   In] [paragraph] In (75)
270.1   ten] ten (75)
270.3   with] with a (75) [270^{j}]
270.4   fifteen] fifteen (75)
270.5   cultivated. . . . Thus] [ellipsis indicates 6-page omission] (75–81)
270.5   Thus] [paragraph] Thus, (81)
270.8   paying a good rent] paying a good rent (81)
270.16   the] The (81) [follows directly from previous quotation]
270.28   Accordingly] [follows directly from previous quotation]
270.28   they are gradually acquiring capital] they are gradually acquiring capital (81)
270.30   by] by the (81) [see 270^{m}]

RICARDO, DAVID. Referred to: 80, 341, 392, 413, 426–8, 457, 472, 479, 589, 648, 727, 823, 1052, 1055n, 1056, 1094

——— *Essay on the Influence of a Low Price of Corn on the Profits of Stock: shewing the Inexpediency of Restrictions on Importation; with Remarks on Mr. Malthus' Two Last Publications.* London: Murray, 1815.

REFERRED TO: 419

———— *On the Principles of Political Economy and Taxation.* 3rd ed. London: Murray, 1821.

QUOTED: 477–8, 636

477.28   "In] [*paragraph*] If we look to a state of society in which greater improvements have been made, and in which arts and commerce flourish, we shall still find that commodities vary in value conformably with this principle: in (19)
478.26   and command] and consequently command (19)

———— *Ibid.*, in *The Works of David Ricardo, Esq., M.P. with a Notice of the Life and Writings of the Author, by J. R. McCulloch.* London: Murray, 1846, 230–1.

REFERRED TO: 1052, 1055

RICHELIEU. Referred to: 296n, 1004

RIGBY. Referred to: 298n, 303n

ROBINSON, COLONEL. "Appendix No. 18.3. Report, by Colonel Robinson, to the Directors of the Irish Waste Land Improvement Society, 25th February, 1845," "in Appendix to Part II. of the Evidence taken before her Majesty's Commissioners of Inquiry into the State of the Law and Practice in Respect to the Occupation of Land in Ireland," *Parliamentary Papers*, 1845, XX, 84–8 [Devon Report].

QUOTED: 331n, 332n, 992–3

331.n11   industry] husbandry (84)
331.n16—332.n4   now . . . consist] [*in italics*] (84)
332.n1   tables] table (85) [*see* 332n]
332.n10   "occupants] Of the total number of tenants on the estates, nine-tenths have added greatly to the extent and value of their improvements and property since the publication of the tabular return in February last, the exceptions being some who are occupants (84)
332.n10–11   acres, a . . . improvements."] acres, (a . . . improvements,) a few who have persisted in the injurious practice of working off their farms, and the remainder are new tenants very recently come into possession. (84)
992.21   *thirty-one years lease*] [*not in italics*] (84)
992.26–34   [*as* 331.n16—332.n4]
993.3   "who are [*see* 332.n10]
993.4–6   [*as* 332.n10–11]

Rochdale Equitable Pioneers' Co-operative Society's Almanack for 1861. Rochdale: Lawton, [1862].

QUOTED: 789

789.*Titles of table.*   Amount of capital] Amount of Funds
Amount of cash sales in store (annual)] Business Done
Amount of profit (annual)] Profit Made

—— *An Outline of the Science of Political Economy* London: Clowes, 1836.

REFERRED TO: 843–4, 846, 1043

—— *Three Lectures on the Cost of Obtaining Money, and on some effects of Private and Government Paper Money; Delivered before the University of Oxford, in Trinity Term, 1829.* London: Murray, 1830.

REFERRED TO: 616

—— *Three Lectures on the Value of Money, Delivered before the University of Oxford, in 1829.* [Unpublished.] London: Fellowes, 1840.

QUOTED: 522

NOTE: the "Advertisement" says: "I have allowed a few copies to be printed for private distribution" (3)

522.31 will] in that case would (21)
522.33 production: and] production. It is obvious that twice as much money would be required to effect every exchange, if a day's labour could obtain from the washing places 34 grains of gold, as would be necessary if a day's labour could obtain only 17. And (21)
522.34 money would] money wanted would (21)

—— *See also* Poor Laws, "Preface to Foreign Communications."

SHELLEY. Referred to: 392, 1030

Siècle. See Anon., Unheaded article, *Le Siècle.*

SISMONDI, JEAN CHARLES LEONARDO SIMONDE DE. Referred to: 67n, 371, 570, 574, 576, 741, 869, 922

——*Études sur l'économie politique.* Paris: Treuttel et Würtz, 1837.

QUOTED: 227n–228n, 254–6, 298–300, 306–11, 311n–312n

227.n1 Ce qui] Alors l'homme dompta la nature et renouvela entièrement sa face; alors on put reconnaître la différence entre la richesse que la terre peut produire et la pauvreté de ses dons naturels; mais aussi on put reconnaître que ce qui (165–6)
227.n1–2 travaux, qui] travaux, que ce qui (166)
254.31 laboureur. On] laboureur. Soit qu'on parcoure le riant Emmethal, ou qu'on s'enfonce dans les vallées les plus reculées du canton de Berne, on (172)
254.31 admiration ces] admiration, sans attendrissement, ces (172)
255.6 santé.] santé, ils frappent par cette beauté de traits qui devient le caractère d'une race, lorsque pendant plusieurs générations elle n'a souffert ni du vice ni du besoin. (173)

255.10   retrouve les] retrouve des (170)
255.23   l'aquéduc] l'aqueduc (171)
255.25   sur les] sur ses (171)
255.35   enchère. [*paragraph*] Le] enchère! [*1½-page omission*] Le (171–3)
298.7–19   "This . . . another."] [*translated from:*] Cette convention est souvent
    l'objet d'un contrat, pour préciser certaines redevances et certains services aux-
    quels le métayer s'oblige; cependant les différences entre les obligations de
    l'un et celles de l'autre sont minimes; l'usage règle également tous ces contrats;
    il supplée aux stipulations qui n'ont pas été exprimées, et le maître qui voudrait
    s'écarter de l'usage, qui exigerait plus que son voisin, qui prendrait pour base
    autre chose que le partage égal des récoltes, se rendrait tellement odieux, il
    serait tellement sûr de ne pouvoir trouver de métayer honnête homme, que le
    contrat de tous les métayers peut être considéré comme identique tout au moins
    dans chaque province, et qu'il ne donne jamais lieu à aucune compétition entre
    les paysans qui cherchent à se placer, à aucune offre de travailler la terre à
    meilleur prix que l'autre. (290)
306.36   lit. . . . La] lit: les fenêtres n'ont que des volets, elles sont sans vitres, mais
    il faut se souvenir aussi que l'hiver est sans frimas. La (295)
307.14   Tout] [*paragraph*] Tout (296)
307.17   d'étoupe] d'étoupes (296) [*see* 307^{k–k}]
307.26–308.4 and 307n   [*JSM here rearranges Sismondi's text, transferring* "Cette
    épouse . . . 6 francs." *from Sismondi's footnote (where JSM indicates an
    ellipsis,* 307.n11), *and* "La dot . . . 600 francs." *from Sismondi's footnote
    (where it forms a paragraph between* "vie." *and* "Les hommes", 307.n13–4), *and
    omitting at* 308.2, *one sentence* ("francs. [*paragraph*] Toutes les épouses plus
    riches ont de plus *la verte di seta*, la grande robe de toilette, de soie, qu'elles ne
    portent que quatre ou cinq fois dans leur vie. [*paragraph*] La") (297n–298n)
308.18–20   But . . . mixture."] [*translated and summarized from Sismondi:*] Le
    paysan toscan est sobre, mais sa nourriture est saine et variée: sa base est
    un excellent pain de froment, brun, mais pur de son et de tout mélange. (305)
308.21   saison, il ne] saison, en effet, le laboureur a surtout besoin d'une nourriture
    chaude. Il ne (306)
308.21   fait que] fait alors que (306)
308.21   repas pour] repas par (306) [*silent correction in text*]
308.24   de feu] le feu (306)
308.36   nutritifs.] nutritifs*. [*footnote:*] *Les paysans de France, de Suisse et de
    Savoie, récoltent de même de l'huile de noix. S'il y avait de vrais paysans dans
    les îles Britanniques, ils cultiveraient les plantes oléagineuses pour en faire le
    même usage. (307)
308.37   et des] ou des (307)
309.3   cinquante] cinq cents (307)
309.22   "Le] Aussi le (292)
309.27–8   donner . . . Les] donner. Les collines du val de Nievole sont plantées
    d'oliviers, de vignes, de mûriers, de figuiers, d'arbres fruitiers de tout genre,
    et l'on cultive à leur pied le froment, plus encore pour entretenir la terre propre
    et meuble, que pour le profit que le blé peut rendre. Les (292)
309.36   une espace] un espace (292)
309.40   negliger] négliger (293)
310.6   couches de] couches du (293)

———— *Nouveaux principes d'économie politique, ou de la richesse dans
    ses rapports avec la population.* 2nd ed. 2 vols. Paris: Delaunay, 1827.

QUOTED: 256n, 284–5, 299n, 311n, 348n–349n, 369

256.n4–5   il n'est pas] n'est-il pas (I,168)

284.33–285.15 "In . . . population."] [*translated from:*] [*paragraph*] Dans les pays qui ont conservé l'exploitation patriarcale, la population s'accroît régulièrement et rapidement, jusqu'à ce qu'elle ait atteint ses limites naturelles: c'est-à-dire, que les héritages continuent à se diviser et à se subdiviser entre plusieurs fils, tant qu'avec une augmentation de travail, chaque famille peut tirer un égal revenu d'une moindre portion de terre. Le père qui possédait une vaste étendue de pâturages, les partage entre ses fils, pour que ceux-ci en fassent des champs et des prés; ces fils les partagent encore, pour exclure le système des jachères: chaque perfectionnement de la science rurale permet une nouvelle division de la propriété; mais il ne faut pas craindre que le propriétaire élève ses enfans pour en faire des mendians; il sait au juste l'héritage qu'il peut leur laisser; il sait que la loi le partagera également entre eux; il voit le terme où ce partage les ferait descendre du rang qu'il a occupé lui-même, et un juste orgueil de famille, qui se retrouve dans le paysan comme dans le gentilhomme, l'arrête avant qu'il appelle à la vie des enfans au sort desquels il ne pourrait pas pourvoir. S'ils naissent cependant, du moins ils ne se marient pas, ou ils choisissent eux-mêmes, entre plusieurs frères, celui qui continuera la famille. On ne voit point, dans les cantons suisses, les patrimoines des paysans se subdiviser jamais de manière à les faire descendre au-dessous d'une honnête aisance, quoique l'habitude du service étranger, en ouvrant aux enfans une carrière inconnue et incalculable, excite quelquefois une population surabondante. (I,170–1)

299.n4–8 "The . . . engagement."] [*translated from:*] Le même malheur serait probablement arrivé au peuple de Toscane, si l'opinion publique ne protégeait le cultivateur; mais un propriétaire n'oserait imposer des conditions inusitées dans le pays, et, en changeant un métayer contre un autre, il ne change rien au contrat primitif. (I, 199–200)

311.n7   lui-même] le premier (I, 190)

349.n11   jurande. On] jurande. [*paragraph*] On (I, 425)

349.n17   sustenter] substanter (I, 425)

349.n21   lucratives. L'apprenti] lucratives. [*paragraph*] L'apprenti (I, 426)

349.n28   *maître.* [*paragraph*] "Il] [*5-page omission*] (I, 426–31)

349.n31   surabondante. D'après] surabondante. Il est de même certain que cette population existe aujourd'hui, et qu'elle est le résultat nécessaire de l'ordre actuel. [*paragraph*] D'après (I, 431)

369.16   point] pas (II, 296)

369.21   aussi doit-il] aussi, lorsqu'il ne peut point augmenter son revenu, doit-il (II, 296)

SLANEY. Referred to: 786, 904n

SMITH, ADAM. Referred to: 4–5, 7, 29, 66, 116n, 127–8, 138–9, 162n, 349n, 405, 456, 465n, 472–3, 579–81, 592, 597, 642, 648, 733–4, 735, 753, 830, 833, 923, 1044

———— *An Inquiry into the Nature and Causes of the Wealth of Nations. With a Commentary by the Author of "England and America"* [E. G. Wakefield]. 4 vols. London: Knight, 1835–9.

QUOTED: 116–18, 122, 124–6, 300–1, 380–2, 383, 384, 385–92, 404, 733–4, 805–6, 924–5, 932   REFERRED TO: 349n, 1044

NOTE: this is the only edition specifically cited by JSM, and so has been used for comparison throughout.

116.14   is "of two] [*paragraph*] Co-operation appears to be of two (I, 26)
116.18–9   Co-operation. [*paragraph*] The] co-operation. It will be seen presently, that, until men help each other in simple operations, they cannot well help each other in operations which consist of several parts. [*paragraph*] The (I, 26)
122.26   paper . . . . . I] paper; and the important business of making a pin is, in this manner, divided into about eighteen distinct operations, which, in some manufactories, are all performed by distinct hands, though in others the same man will sometimes perform two or three of them. I (I, 8) [*JSM here has transposed part of the omitted passage; see* 122.20–2 *and* 122ᵃ]
122.26   manufactory where] manufactory of this kind where (I, 8)
122.35   pins in a day] pins a day (I, 8)
122.38   day."] day; that is, certainly, not the two hundred and fortieth, perhaps not the four thousand eight hundredth part of what they are at present capable of performing, in consequence of a proper division and combination of their different operations. (I, 8–9)
124.13   "First, the] first, to the (I, 12)
124.14   secondly, the] secondly, to the (I, 12)
124.15   lastly, the] lastly, to the (I, 12)
124.37   of certain] of those (I, 14)
125.19   "The advantage] Secondly, the advantage (I, 14)
300.15   "it could . . .] [*paragraph*] It could [*7 sentences and a footnote omitted*] (II, 21)
300.16   interest of] interest even of (II, 21)
300.16   this species] this last species (II, 21)
380.14   "from] partly from (I, 255)
380.17   others."] others; and partly from the policy of Europe, which no where leaves things at perfect liberty. (I, 256)
380.26–381.11, 381.12–7   [*JSM's comments are here interspersed amongst direct and consecutive sentences from* Source]
381.11   considered,"] considered, they are generally under-recompensed, as I shall endeavour to show by-and-by. (I, 257) [*see* 381ᵇ⁻ᵇ]
382.12   When the] Where the
382.16   wages. No] wages. Where common labourers earn four and five shillings a week, masons and bricklayers frequently earn seven and eight; where the former earn six, the latter often earn nine and ten, and where the former earn nine and ten, as in London, the latter commonly earn fifteen and eighteen No (I, 261)
382.16–17   learn than that] learn that that [*sic*] (I, 261)
382.17   bricklayers. The] bricklayers. Chairmen in London, during the summer season, are said sometimes to be employed as bricklayers. The (I, 262)
382.19–20   employment. [paragraph] "When] employment. [*7-sentence omission*] [paragraph] When (I, 262)
382.20   of the employment] of employment (I, 262)
382.22   most skilled] most skilful (I, 263) [*see* 382ᵉ⁻ᵉ]
382.30   the arrival] the arrivals (I, 263) [*see* 382ᶠ⁻ᶠ]
382.35–6   earn about four times the wages of common labour in London. How] earn from six to ten shillings a day. Six shillings are about four times the wages of common labour in London, and in every particular trade, the lowest earnings may always be considered as those of the far greater number. How (I, 263)
382.36   soever these] soever those (I, 263.) [*see* 382ᵍ⁻ᵍ]
384.27   a small] a very small (I, 265)
384.29   done."] done. The lottery of the law, therefore, is very far from being a perfectly fair lottery; and that, as well as many other liberal and honourable professions, is, in point of pecuniary gain, evidently under-recompensed. (I, 266) [*see* 384ʲ]

385.3   to sea . . . .] to sea, than in the eagerness of those of better fashion to enter into what are called the liberal professions. [*ellipsis indicates 2½-page omission*] (I, 270–3)

385.3   The dangers] [*paragraph*] The dangers (I, 273)

385.8   prospect] prospects (I, 273)

385.20   "The] Fourthly, the (I, 264)

385.21   The] [*paragraph*] The (I, 264)

385.25   We] [*paragraph*] We (I, 264)

385.29   in society] in the society (I, 264)

389.20   than what] than than what [*sic*] (I, 307)

389.22–3   or a chaplain] or chaplain (I, 308) [*see* 389*b–b*]

389.28   marks] merks [*sic*] (I, 308)

389.28   containing as] containing about as (I, 308)

390.6   year. This] year. There are journeyman shoe-makers in London who earn forty pounds a year, and there is scarce an industrious workman of any kind in that metropolis who does not earn more than twenty. This (I, 309)

390.6   sum does] sum indeed does (I, 309)

390.14   been either] either been (I, 309)

390.20–21   them." [*paragraph*] "In] [*1-paragraph omission*] (I, 309–10)

390.21   law (?) and] law and (I, 310)

390.29   recompense. [*paragraph*] That] recompense, to the entire degradation of the now respectable professions of law and physic. [*paragraph*] That (I, 310)

390.35   as to] as commonly to (I, 311)

391.5   teacher bears] teachers bears (I, 311) [*see* 391*d–d*]

404.39   cheapest. Thirty] cheapest. He must have all the knowledge, in short, that is necessary for a great merchant, which nothing hinders him from being but the want of a sufficient capital. Thirty (I, 276)

733.12   profits] profit (I, 210)

734.38   cultivators] cultivation (I, 217)

734.38   situation.] situation, and less interest can be afforded for the stock which is so employed. (I, 217)

805.6   contribute to] contribute towards (IV, 215)

805.9   state. In] state. The expense of government to the individuals of a great nation is like the expense of management to the joint tenants of a great estate, who are all obliged to contribute in proportion to their respective interests in the estate. In (IV, 215)

805.10   taxation. [*paragraph*] "2. The] taxation. Every tax, it must be observed once for all, which falls finally upon one only of the three sorts of revenue above mentioned, is necessarily unequal, in so far as it does not affect the other two. In the following examination of different taxes I shall seldom take much further notice of this sort of inequality, but shall, in most cases, confine my observations to that inequality which is occasioned by a particular tax falling unequally upon that particular sort of private revenue which is affected by it. [*paragraph*] II. The (IV, 216)

805.19   even when] even where (IV, 216)

805.27   at a] at the (IV, 217)

806.3   to him] for him (IV, 217)

806.6   inconvenience] inconveniency (IV, 217)

806.14–16   Secondly . . . employment,] [*JSM is summarizing the following:*] Secondly, it may obstruct the industry of the people, and discourage them from applying to certain branches of business which might give maintenance and employment to great multitudes. While it obliges the people to pay, it may thus diminish, or perhaps destroy, some of the funds which might enable them more easily to do so. (IV, 217–18)

806.19   derived] received (IV, 218)

806.20   smuggling. Fourthly] smuggling. But the penalties of smuggling must rise in proportion to the temptation. The law, contrary to all the ordinary principles of justice, first creates the temptation, and then punishes those who yield to it; and it commonly enhances the punishment too in proportion to the very circumstance which ought certainly to alleviate it, the temptation to commit the crime.* [*footnote:*] *See Sketches of the History of Man, page 474, et seq. [*text:*] Fourthly (IV, 218)

806.23   oppression:"] oppression; and though vexation is not, strictly speaking, expense, it is certainly equivalent to the expense at which every man would be willing to redeem himself from it. It is in some one or other of these four different ways that taxes are frequently so much more burdensome to the people than they are beneficial to the sovereign. (IV, 218)

924.39   "prodigals and projectors"] Where the legal rate of interest, on the contrary, is fixed but a very little above the lowest market rate, sober people are universally preferred, as borrowers, to prodigals and projectors. (I, 408–9)

932.20   "the higgling of the market"] . . . it is not easy to find any accurate measure either of hardship or ingenuity. In exchanging indeed the different productions of different sorts of labour [employment] for one another, some allowance is commonly made for both. It is adjusted, however, not by any accurate measure, but by the higgling and bargaining of the market, according to that sort of rough equality which, though not exact, is sufficient for carrying on the business of common life. (I, 102) [*Wakefield's square bracket*]

SMITH, GOLDWIN. Referred to: 1075n

SOPHOCLES. Referred to: 16

SPENCE. Referred to: 576

SPENSER. Referred to: 1075n

STEIN. Referred to: 329, 995

STEPHENSON. Referred to: 926

TAYLOR. Referred to: 1026n

THACKERAY. Referred to: 997n

THAER. Referred to: 267

THIERS, A. *De la propriété*. Paris: Paulin, L'Heureux et Cie, 1848.
REFERRED TO: 290n

THOM, ALEXANDER. *Thom's Irish Almanac and Official Directory of the United Kingdom of Great Britain and Ireland, for the year 1863*. Dublin: Thom, 1863.
REFERRED TO: 1074, 1084

THORNTON, HENRY. *An Enquiry into the Nature and Effects of the Paper Credit of Great Britain.* London: Hatchard, 1802.

QUOTED: 531–4

531.24   manufacturers] manufactures (25)
531.27   question, giving] question (for we may assume a sufficient quantity to be usually circulating in the place): giving (25)
531.30   manufacturers] shopkeepers (25)
531.32   saved. Letters] saved; and the traders in question would of course be, on the whole, enabled to sell their article at a price proportionably lower than that which they would otherwise require. Letters (25)
532.35–6   country, and] country (a topic which shall not be here anticipated), and (30)
533.3–7   "Real . . . real."] [*in this paragraph Thornton cites a supposed opponent's argument, and so uses quotation marks, which JSM ignores*] (30)
533.17   only one] one only (31)
533.17–18   property. [*paragraph*] "In] property [*paragraph*] In the next place it is obvious, that the number of those bills which are given in consequence of sales of goods, and which, nevertheless, do not represent property, is liable to be encreased through the extension of the length of credit given on the sale of goods. If, for instance, we had supposed the credit given to be a credit of twelve months instead of six, 1,200*l.* instead of 600*l.* would have been the amount of the bills drawn on the occasion of the sale of goods; and 1,100*l.* would have been the amount of that part of these which would represent no property. [*paragraph*] In (31)
533.41   forms] form (32)
534.27   "They] But they (40)
534.29–30   giving him] giving to him (40)
534.37   to a bearer] to bearer (40) [*see* 534[b–b]]
534.37   demand. A] demand. It will, however, have circulated in consequence chiefly of the confidence placed by each receiver of it in the last indorser, his own correspondent in trade; whereas, the circulation of a bank note is owing rather to the circumstance of the name of the issuer being so well known as to give to it an universal credit. A (40)
534.40   kingdom." [*5-sentence footnote omitted*] (40n–41n)

THORNTON, WILLIAM THOMAS. Referred to: 365, 608

———— *Over-Population and its Remedy; or, an Inquiry into the Extent and Causes of the Distress Prevailing among the Labouring Classes of the British Islands, and into the means of Remedying it.* London: Longman, Brown, Green, and Longmans, 1846.

QUOTED: 350, 997–1000

350.4   "are lodged] They are commonly hired by the half-year, for which period they are paid from 6*l.*10s. to 9*l.*10s., and are lodged (18)
350.7   farm. What . . . exist."] farm. "What . . . exist. Intersected in every direction by ranges of almost inaccessible and barren mountains, the population is thinly dotted over the intervening valleys," in due proportion to the facilities for cultivation and the opportunities for employment.* [*footnote:*] *Mr Voules' Report on Westmoreland and Cumberland, in Appendix to Second Annual Report of Poor Law Commissioners. Messrs. Bailey and Culley's Report on Northumberland, Cumberland, &c. (18–19)

———— A Plea for Peasant Proprietors; with the Outlines of a Plan for their Establishment in Ireland. London: Murray, 1848.

273.15   bushels. In] bushels, and, according to a statement resting on the same authority, the produce of the seed is "seldom less than twelve-fold, but if drilled, fourteen-fold, and if dibbled, sixteen, or even twenty-fold."* In [*footnote:*] *Speech of Mr. E. Chadwick, at a meeting of the Farmers' Club in the early part of 1847. (9–10)
273.16   Inglis] Inglis,* [*footnote:*] *Inglis's Channel Islands, vol. i. p. 186. (10)
273.18   1833.] 1833.* [*footnote:*] *Guernsey and Jersey Magazine, vol. iii. p. 106. (10)
273.19–20   is . . . crop."] "is . . . crop." (10) [*i.e., Thornton is quoting from Inglis*]
273.23   4*l*."] 4*l*., and in Switzerland the average rent seems to be 6*l*. per acre. (32)

Times. See Anon., "Australia"; and Anon., "Foreign Intelligence."

TOOKE, THOMAS. Referred to: 549, 567, 661–4, 673, 678, 714

———— *Considerations on the State of the Currency.* London: Murray, 1826.

REFERRED TO: 1061n, 1066, 1067n

———— *A History of Prices, and of the State of the Circulation, from 1793 to 1837.* 2 vols. London: Longman, Orme, Brown, Green, and Longmans, 1838.

QUOTED: 466n   REFERRED TO: 343n, 467n

———— *A History of Prices, and of the State of the Circulation, from 1838 to 1847.* 2 vols. [Vols. III and IV of the complete work.] London: Longman, Brown, Green, and Longmans, 1848.

QUOTED: 547   REFERRED TO: 1067

———— AND NEWMARCH, WILLIAM. *A History of Prices, and of the State of the Circulation, during the Nine Years 1848–1856.* 2 vols. [Vols. V and VI of the complete work.] London: Longman, Brown, Green, Longman, and Roberts, 1857.

REFERRED TO: 550n

466.n1   "The] It is perhaps superfluous to add, that no such strict rule [as Gregory King's] can be deduced; at the same time, there is some ground for supposing that the estimate is not very wide of the truth, from observation of the repeated occurrence of the fact, that the (I, 12–13)
466.n4   supplies. If] [*6-paragraph omission; see 466n*] (I, 13–15)
466.n5–7   If there should be a deficiency of the crops amounting to one-third, without any surplus from a former year, and without any chance of relief by importation, the price might rise five, six, or even tenfold."] But upon the principle here stated, the case would be widely different. In the event of a deficiency of one third of an average crop, a bushel of wheat might rise to 18*s*. and upwards.* [*footnote:*] *Considering the institutions of this country relative to the maintenance of the poor, if there should be a deficiency of the crops amounting to one-third, *without any surplus from a former year, and without*

any chance of relief by importation, the price might rise five, six, or even tenfold. (I, 15)

547.3   "Applications] The figures are correctly given; and, viewed in connection with the facts, the great increase of private securities serves to illustrate an observation which I have more than once had occasion to make in reference to this subject: namely, that applications (IV, 125)

547.11   on the spot] *on the spot* (IV, 125)

547.22   them. It] them. The term speculation, in its obnoxious sense, is not, in such cases, applied to the transaction; and the parties engaged have the credit of superior sagacity. [*paragraph*] It (IV, 126)

———— *An Inquiry into the Currency Principle; the Connection of the Currency with Prices, and the Expediency of a Separation of Issue from Banking.* London: Longman, Brown, Green, and Longmans, 1844.

QUOTED: 537, 547–50, 657–8

537.n4   "in] And some corroboration of the vastness of the amounts is afforded by a reference to the adjustments of the clearing house in London, which in (26–7)

547.33   "The] The truth is, that the (79)

547.36   of. . . .] of.* [*footnote:*] *See Appendix (B). (79) [*i.e., Tooke refers to his own Appendix B, from which JSM quotes his next sentence, and the following long passage*]

547.36   A] What I mean to say is, that a (136)

548.8   "Amongst] Among (137)

548.8   earlier] earliest (137) [*see* 548*a–a*]

548.22–3   Without . . . shape] [*in italics*] (137)

548.26   attention. In] attention. [*paragraph*] In (137)

548.32   realized, if] realised by sales, if (137)

657.40   or mining] or in mining (88)

658.3   subservient."] subservient, is unfortunately but too true. (88)

658.4   coin, is] coin, might it not be his business then, as now, in consideration of his care and trouble in keeping the cash and answering the depositors' drafts, to employ so much of the deposits as by experience he computes may not be immediately wanted by the depositors, in loans and discounts. How then can it be said that the issue of metallic money in ordinary circumstances yields no profit? And can it with truth be maintained that he cannot issue it in excess? Is (91)

658.9   depositors? In] depositors? Would not this be issuing metallic money in excess? In (91)

———— "Report from the Committee of Secrecy on the Bank of England Charter; with the Minutes of Evidence, Appendix and Index," *Parliamentary Papers,* 1831–2, VI, 269–304, 432–44.

QUOTED: 661–2

661.26–7   "In . . . in every] I have never called in question the principle, that, *cæteris paribus,* an increase or diminution of Bank of England notes, if they were to be taken as indicative of the whole amount of circulation, would produce a tendency to a rise or fall of prices; I have only observed, as far as my researches have gone, that in point of fact, and historically, in every (441)

661.27   rise or fall] rise of prices or a fall (441)

661.27   or fall] or the fall (441)

661.31   or contraction] or a contraction (441)

————— "Report from the Select Committee, to whom the Several Petitions Complaining of the Depressed State of the Agriculture of the United Kingdom, were Referred," *Parliamentary Papers*, 1821, IV, 224–40, 287–98, 344–55.

REFERRED TO: 467n

NOTE: Tooke is quoted with approval on this point, "Report," 8–9.

TORRENS, ROBERT. Referred to: 604n, 665, 1066

————— *The Economists Refuted; or, an Inquiry into the Nature and Extent of the Advantages derived from Trade.* London: Oddy, 1808.

REFERRED TO: 589n

NOTE: the reprint noted by JSM is in Torrens, Robert. *The Principles and Practical Operation of Sir Robert Peel's Act of 1844 Explained and Defended.* 2nd ed. London: Longman, Brown, Green, Longmans, and Roberts, 1857. Here Torrens claims his "right to be regarded as the original propounder of so much of the corrected theory of the nature and extent of the advantages derived from foreign trade as may be comprised in the view which [he] ventured to present to the public forty-nine years ago" (xvi). The work also includes "a critical examination of the chapter 'On the Regulation of a Convertible Paper Currency'" (III, xxiv) in JSM's *Principles*.

TURGOT. Referred to: 302

ULLOA. Referred to: 166

VAUBAN. Referred to: 442

VILLERMÉ, LOUIS-RENÉ. *Tableau de l'état physique et moral des ouvriers employés dans les manufactures de coton, de laine et de soie.* 2 vols. Paris: Renouard, 1840.

REFERRED TO: 290n

VILLIAUMÉ, NICOLAS. *Nouveau traité d'économie politique.* Vol. II. Paris: Guillaumin, 1857.

QUOTED: 772, 773n–774n, 779n–783n, 1015–20

NOTE: Appendix to Vol. II of JSM's *Principles* (4th ed. only; Appendix E in the present edition) is made up of quotations from this work, which were integrated into the text of the 5th edition. The following passages in the 7th ed. are the same as the passages in Appendix E which are given in parentheses: 773.n15—774.n13 (1015.9—1016.34), 772.19–25 (1017.8–14), 774.n14–19 (1017.15–20), 780.n10–781.n29 (1017.28—1019.16), 781.n31—782.n18 (1019.17—1020.15), 783.n4–10 (1020.16–22). Appendix E, 1016.35—1017.8, 1017.22–7 are not in the 7th ed.

772.19 "Quoiqu'il] Quant à M. Leclaire, quoiqu'il (82)
773.n34 recompense] récompense (80) [*see* 1016.12]

774.n13–14   semaines. . . . . [*paragraph*] M.] [*JSM moves from p. 81 to p. 271*]
780.n15   l'association] l'association* [*footnote:*] *En Octobre 1848. (88)
780.n33   réglement] règlement (88)
780.n34   en-deça] en deçà (89)
780.n37   désuetude] désuétude (89)
780.n41   Chavonne] Charonne (89)
781.n1   les] ses (89)
781.n2   resisté] résisté (89)
781.n3   suscités. Cette] suscités.

> Tout homme de courage est maître de son sort;
> Il range la fortune à son obéissance.

> Théophile, *Amours de Pyrame et Thisbé* (1826).

[*paragraph*] Cette (89)
781.n8   82,930] 82950 (89)
781.n15   169,831 55] 169851 55 (89)
781.n18   133] 135 (90)
781.n24   [*total omitted*]] 66752 65 (90)
781.n40–2   "Cette . . . capital.] [*transferred from footnote to* opérations. (781.n39)] (91)
782.n7   maladie. Chacun] maladie; chacun (92)
783.n4   l'habileté des] l'habileté du choix des (94)
783.n9   education] éducation (94)
1016.12   récompense] récompense [*cf.* 773.n34 *above*]
1018.4   l'election] l'élection (88)
1018.20   désuetude] désuétude (89)
1018.24   resisté] résisté (89)
1019.14   66,752 65] 66752 65 (90) [*cf.* 781.n24 *above*]
1020.16   l'habilité du choix des] [*ibid.*] (94) [*cf.* 783.n4 *above*]
1020.22   éducation] éducation (94) [*cf.* 783.n9 *above*]

WAKEFIELD, EDWARD GIBBON. Referred to: 116–18, 120, 130n, 143, 149, 150, 325, 376, 735–6, 742–3, 921, 958–9, 965–6, 1044n, 1046, 1072, 1087. *See also* Smith, Adam.

WALKER, GEORGE. "The Bank Charter Act. No. V.," *Aberdeen Herald*, 26 April, 1856, p. 6.

QUOTED: 682

NOTE: the series appeared in six issues, 15, 22, 29 March, 12, 26 April, and 3 May, 1856.

682.14   of eighteen] of the eighteen (6)
682.17   eighteen. . . . . . The] eighteen. The drain of six millions would, if unchecked, reduce the reserve to two millions; and along with that reduction there would be a convulsion. On the other hand, if attempts are made to check the drain, they are accompanied by evils, though much less intense than those of a panic, but still evils—a contraction of credit and a fall of prices, and that at a time when credit was not inflated nor prices high. In short, the (6)
682.18   is, that] is this (and the illustration which we have given may be multiplied indefinitely), (6)
682.18–20   the proceedings . . . department] [*in italics*] (6)
682.26   as it may fail] [*in italics*] (6)

WATT. Referred to: 42, 189, 344

WEST, EDWARD. *Essay on the Application of Capital to Land, with Observations shewing the Impolicy of any great restriction of the Importation of Corn, and that the Bounty of 1688 did not lower the Price of it.* London: Underwood, 1815.

REFERRED TO: 419

WESTBURY. Referred to: 885n

WHATELY, RICHARD. *Introductory Lectures on Political Economy.* London: Fellowes, 1831.

REFERRED TO: 317n, 1043

WORDSWORTH, WILLIAM. *A Description of the Scenery of the Lakes in the North of England.* 3rd ed. London: Longman, Hurst, Rees, Orme, and Brown, 1822.

QUOTED: 253n

253.n3 agriculturists, proprietors, for the most part, of the lands which they occupied and cultivated. The plough] Agriculturists, among whom the plough (63) [*see* 253n]

253.n6 neighbour.] [*4-sentence footnote omitted*] (64)

253.14 blood. . . . Corn] blood; —and venerable was the transition, when a curious traveller, descending from the heart of the mountains, had come to some ancient manorial residence in the more open parts of the Vales, which, through the rights attached to its proprietor, connected the almost visionary mountain Republic he had been contemplating with the substantial frame of society as existing in the laws and constitution of a mighty empire. [JSM *skips backward 14 pages*] Corn (65, 51)

253.15 vales sufficient] vales (through which no carriage-road had been made) sufficient (51)

253.15 family, no more. The] family, and no more: notwithstanding the union of several tenements, the possessions of each inhabitant still being small, in the same field was seen an intermixture of different crops; and the plough was interrupted by little rocks, mostly overgrown with wood, or by spongy places, which the tillers of the soil had neither leisure nor capital to convert into firm land. The (52)

YOUNG, ARTHUR. *Travels during the Years 1787, 1788, & 1789; undertaken more particularly with a view of ascertaining the cultivation, wealth, resources, and national prosperity of the Kingdom of France.* 2nd ed. 2 vols. London: Richardson, 1794.

QUOTED: 274, 275, 298n, 301-2, 303-4, 305 REFERRED TO: 273, 276, 278, 283, 291n

NOTE: JSM's italics usually indicate small capitals in Source.

274.14 Rossendal," (near Dunkirk) "where] Rossendal near the town, where (I, 88)

274.21 passed] pass (I, 51)

275.4-5 another. There] another. The men are all dressed with red caps, like the highlanders of Scotland. There (I, 56)

275.18   "are] The farms in the open country are generally large; but in the rich deep low vale of Flanders, they are (I, 322)

275.21   "is] I must, upon this, observe, that the whole Pays de Caux is (I, 325)

275.21   country, and farming] country; the properties usually small; and that farming (I, 325)

275.26   "Flanders] Maize is also an article of great consequence in the French husbandry; olives, silk, and lucerne are not to be forgotten; nor should we omit mentioning the fine pastures of Normandy, and every article of culture in the rich acquisitions of Flanders (I, 357)

275.27   Garonne, France] Garonne. In all this extent, and it is not small, France (I, 357)

275.27   own."] own; and it is from well seconding the fertility of nature in these districts, and from a proper attention to the plants adapted to the soil, that there has arisen any equality in the resources of the two kingdoms; for, without this, France, with all the ample advantages she otherwise derives from nature, would be but a petty power on comparison with Great Britain. (I, 357)

275.28   "are] Flanders, part of Artois, the rich plain of Alsace, the banks of the Garonne, and a considerable part of Quercy, are (I, 364)

275.30   properties."] properties; but this is not the place to examine that question, which is curious enough to demand a more particular discussion. (I, 364)

275.35   this is] this in (I, 364)

276.21   be well] well be (I, 412) [see 276^{g-g}]

298.n4   these. In] these. In Berry some are at half, some one-third, some one-fourth produce. In (I, 403)

298.n7   cattle. At] cattle. Near Falaise, in Normandy, I found metayers, where they should least of all be looked for, on the farms which gentlemen keep in their own hands; the consequence there is, that every gentleman's farm must be precisely the worst cultivated of all the neighbourhood:—this disgraceful circumstance needs no comment. At (I, 403)

298.n11   half. In] half. Produce sold for money divided. Butter and cheese used in the metayer's family, to any amount, compounded for at 5s. a cow. In (I, 403)

301.19   "There] This subject may be easily dispatched; for there (I, 404)

301.27   wicked. . . . In] wicked. Among some gentlemen I personally knew, I was acquainted with one at Bagnere de Luchon, who was obliged to sell his estate, because he was unable to restock it, the sheep having all died of epidemical distempers; proceeding, doubtless, from the execrable methods of the metayers cramming them into stables as hot as stoves, on reeking dunghills; and then in the common custom of the kingdom, shutting every hole and crack that could let in air.—In (I, 405)

301.28   land, the] land, after running the hazard of such losses, fatal in many instances, the (I, 405)

301.32   found . . . . Wherever] [ellipsis indicates 2-paragraph omission] (II, 151-2)

301.35   "their] All this proves the extreme poverty, and even misery, of these little farmers; and shews, that their (II, 153)

302.1   their] there (II, 217)

303.2   "in] In (I, 404)

303.4   landlords,"] landlords; it is commonly computed that half the tenantry are deeply in debt to the proprietor, so that he is often obliged to turn them off with the loss of these debts, in order to save his land from running waste. (I, 404)

305.21   live] be (I, 156)

305.23   money to] money to enable him to (II, 156)

305.23   half. . . . . The] half; but they hire farms with very little money, which is the old story of France, &c.; and indeed poverty and miserable agriculture are the sure attendants upon this way of letting land. The (II, 156)

Index

Page numbers in italic type refer to the Appendices.

ABSTINENCE: remuneration for, 34, 40, 400, 481, 736–7; and production, 37
Accumulation: effective desire of checked by future uncertainty, 163–4; desire of in North American Indians, 164–7, in Chinese, 167–70, in English, 170–2, in Asians, 172, 186–7, in Dutch, 172, in Australians and Americans, 191–2, in Russians and Poles, 192; minimum of profits depends on, 402, 736. *See also* Capital, Production, Profit
Africa: productiveness in, 100
Agriculture: as state of society, 11–12, 15–17; and continuous production, 33; as industry, 35–6, 43–4; and distribution of produce, 39, 235–8; dependent on town-population, 119–22; division of labour in, 142–3; method of production in, 184; improvements in, 190, 227–30, 342, 488, 713–14, 767–8; value of produce of, 584–6, 711–13; and fertility of soil, *920*; *988–1002, 1003 5, 1075 86. See also* Farming, Land, Peasant Properties, Property
America. *See* United States
Arabia: nomadic tribes of, 20; deserts of, 101, 417
Asia: monarchies of, 13; economic condition of, 15, 112, 157, 172, 186–7; property in, 403
Athens: maritime situation of, 102
Australia: wool-growers in, 44; Swan River settlement in, 65, 966; strong desire of accumulation in, 191–2; colonization in, 194; capital and population in, 344; gold production of, 504, 682
Austria: slavery in, 248; taxation in, 863

BANKS: and the joint-stock principle, 136–9; issuing practices of, 660–2; drains on, 680n; reserves of, 681–2; mismanagement in, 684–5

Baltic: free cities of the, 102
Bedford Level: drained, 92, 179, 227, 424
Belgium: cattle in, 145n, peasant-proprietors in, 267, 291–2; Poor Colonies of, 417
Brazil: slavery in, 250; bullion from, 618

CALIFORNIA: gold mines of, 504, 682
Canada: Indians of, 164–6; emigration to, 197; timber trade of, 407; De Quincey on, 462–3
Capital: defined 33–4, 55–62, 153, 235; and Not-capital, 56–7; and time, 482–5; *1058–68, 1090*
    propositions respecting: 1st, industry limited by c., 63–8; 2nd, c. result of saving, 68–70; 3rd, c. consumed in production, 70–8; 4th, demand for commodities not demand for labour, 78–88; qualifications and corollaries: unemployed c., 65–6; no assignable limit to increase of c. (Malthus, Chalmers, and Sismondi refuted), 66–8; perpetual reproduction of c., 73–5, 747–8, and effect of government loans and taxes, 75–8; *1042–9*
    circulating and fixed: defined, 91–2; conversion of circulating into fixed c., 93–9, 134, 749–51; c. as demand for labour, 337–54; c. as advances to labour, 411–12
    increase of: law of, 160–72; result of saving, 160–1; profit as motive for saving, 161; other factors governing accumulation, 161–72; and excess supply, 570–6; effect on rents, profits, wages, relative to growth of population, 719–32; and stationary state, 752–7
    taxes on, 822–4
    See also Accumulation, Cost of production, Interest, Production, Profit
Chancery, Court of: 884, 904

Employment: and minimum wage, 356–7; created by government, 357–8

England: House of Commons of, 18; prosperity of during Continental War, 75n–76n; Poor Laws of, 84–5, 108, 158–9, 183, 258, 359, 362, 389–90, 960–2; speculation in during 1845, 97; compared with Russia, 100, France, 149–50, Holland, 172, Channel Islands, 272–3; coal-fields of, 102; pursuit of wealth in, 105, 170–2; farming in, 144–6, 178–9, 272–3; increase of population in, 159, 189–90, 288–9, 341, 346, 350–1, 713; competition in, 216, 410; landed property in, 228–9; division of produce in, 235; opinion of slavery in, 250–1; attitude to peasant proprietors in, 252–4; wages in, 341–2; London mortality rate in, 345; gambling instinct in, 409; rent in, 420–8; methods of coining in, 519n; gold and silver coinage in, 526; and dispute with China in 1839, 548–9; depreciation of currency of, 566–9; as example in equation of international demand, 596–619; as bullion importer, 619–22; cost of labour in, 688–9; rate of interest in, 738–42; decline of profits in, 745–6, 845–6; railway speculation of 1844 in, 750–1; Limited Liability Act in, 773–5; co-operative societies in, 786–91; land tax in, 820; direct taxation in, 863–4; government loans in, 874–5; legal peculiarities of, 884, 888–9, 893, 901, 916–17, 925–6; adherence to custom in, 935; *990–2, 996, 1001, 1003–4, 1007–10. See also* Government, Great Britain

Entails and primogeniture: 893

Equality: in property, 202–3; under Communism, 207; and natural superiorities, 213; labouring class ideas of, 767

Esquimaux: type of society of, 20; misery of, 101

Europe. *See* entries for individual countries

Exchange. *See* International trade, Money, Value

Exports and imports. *See* International trade

FARMING: small, 144–8; large, 148–52; careless f. in United States, 175–6;

large f. in England, 178–9, 272–3; small and large f. in France, 443–8. *See also* Agriculture, Land, Peasant properties, Property

Fisheries: as natural resource, 30; rent of, 492–4

Flanders: Pays de Waes, 227; peasant properties in, 279–80; control of population in, 287–8; free cities of, 881

Food: increased production of, 19, 118; and increase of population, 190–3

Foreign exchange. *See* International trade

Foreign trade. *See* International trade

Fourierism: system of common ownership, 203; and Communism, 210–12; advantages of, 213; *982–5, 1028, 1031*

France: Tiers-Etat of, 18; quality of agriculture before Revolution in, 113, 236–7, 273, 298n, 302, 882; agricultural improvement in, 149–50, 152, 183, 441–3, 447, 449–51, 714; increase of population in, 159, 287, 342–3, 437, 447, 714; subdivision of land in, 150, 433–40, 888, 891, 894–5; taxation, effects of in, 183, types of in, 822, 863; effect of 1789 Revolution on labourers in, 183, 365, of 1848 Revolution, 775; Socialism in, 203, 210; law of bequest in, 224; distribution of produce in, 251; peasant properties of, 273–6; metayer system in, 298n, 302; law of inheritance in, 440, 888, 891, 894–5; small and large farming in, 443–8; assignats issued in, 561–2; co-operative associations in, 775–85; law of partnership in, 897, 904, 912n; trade unionism in, 929; government restrictions in, 945–6; *1006–12, 1015–20*

Fur trade: and protection, 64n; Carey on, 178; not a restraint on population, 190–3

GERMANY: free towns of, 18; peasant proprietors of, 262–7; and international values, 596–617

Gold. *See* Circulating medium, Money

Government: early forms of, 6, 11, 13; effect of on industry, 64–6; war-time expenditure of, 75–8, 652–3, 873–5; as protector of persons and property, 112–15, 201, 228–32, 800–3, 880–1, 883–6, 950–3; mental indolence of

210–12; just claim of to being tried, 213; aims of, 294; and competition, 794–5; *979–80, 985–7*

Spain: slavery in, 250; effect of the Inquisition on, 935

Supply. *See* Demand and supply

Switzerland: distribution of produce in, 236; peasant properties in, 254–9; effect of peasant properties on population in, 286; restraints on marriage in, 348

TAXATION: imposed by government, 6, 66; caused poor agriculture in pre-Revolutionary France, 183; confused with rent, 416; should be assessed equally, 805–8, 815–19; graduated scale of, 808–10; on realized property, 811–13; on temporary and permanent incomes, 813–14; on rent, 819–22, 825–6; should fall on capital, 822–4; on profits, 826–8, 838–9; on wages, 828–34; on building rent, 832–3; on ground-rent, 834–6; on consumer, 839–40; on necessaries, 840–1; in form of tithes, 846–7; and discriminating duties, 847–8; and corn laws, 849–50; disturbs equation of international demand, 850–6; other forms of, 857–61; direct, 862–4, 867–8; indirect, 865–8; on luxuries, 869–70; on imports, 870–2; detrimental effect of, 882–3; *1042–3; 1050–5. See also* Government, Labour, Land, Wages

Trade Unions. restrictions imposed by, 374; benefits of, 929–34. *See also* Labouring class

Trade, international. *See* International trade

UNITED STATES: hunting communities in, 20; mineral deposits in, 52, 682; states of, 52; careless farming in, 175–6; strong desire of accumulation in, 191–2, 890; emigration to, 194, from Ireland, 325, 333; population of, 194, 344; competition in, 216; distribution in, 236, 426; slavery in, 245, 247; cotton production in, 408, 690; gambling instinct in, 409; condition of labourers in, 414; cost of labour in, 688–9; communications in, 426; unused land in, 738; progress in, 754; taxation in Southern States of, 865; laws of partnership

in, 905–6; protectionism in, 918, 921; *1055–6, 1091–4*

Usury Laws: origin of, 922; and interest rate, 923–4; in England, 925. *See also* Interest

Utilities: produced by labour, 46–8

VALUE: in use and exchange, 456–7; and general prices, 457–9; determined by competition, 460–2; utility and difficulty of attainment, 462–4; three kinds of difficulty of attainment, 464–5; when commodities absolutely limited in quantity, 465–70; and cost of production, 470–2, 471–87; when commodities capable of increase without increase in cost, 471–6; natural v., 472–3; scarcity v., 486–8; when commodities capable of increase but at increasing cost, 488–96; and rent, 488–96; recapitulation and qualification of theory of v., 497–501; money does not affect, 506–9; measure of v. defined, 577, ambiguity of, 578–81; peculiar cases of, 582–6; in international trade, 587–9, 596–609, 612–17; progress diminishes fluctuations in, 714–15

Venice: convenient maritime situation of, 102; as trading community, 684

WAGES: depend on ratio between capital and population, 58–9, 337–8, 343, 412, 695, 719–23; and restraint on increase of population, 344–54, 376–9; regulated by competition, 337, 356, 385; effect of prices on, 339–41, 479, 691–3, 699; vary in different employments, 380–99, because of attractiveness, 380–5, natural monopolies, 385–8, subsidization, 388–91, independent means, 391–4, sex, 394–6, restrictive regulations, 396–9; profits depend on, 413–14, 696–701; influence of on value, 477–81; effect of low w. in international trade, 688–93; effect of improvements on, 719–32; effect of taxation on, 828–30, 840; combinations to raise, 930

artificial regulation of: by law, 355–6; minimum guaranteed wage and necessary legal conditions, 356–9; Allowance System, 360–2; Allotment System, 362–6